5

77-85

EXAM 1

#1 (D) ANSWER CORRECT

#13 (B) " "

5, 6, 20

1/2

LXXX

3|95

24039 16765

.35
40 /14.0
.120/
200
200

Labor and the Economy

Second Edition

Labor and the Economy

Second Edition

Howard M. Wachtel
The American University

Harcourt Brace Jovanovich, Publishers
and its subsidiary, Academic Press

San Diego   New York   Chicago   Austin   Washington, D.C.
London   Sydney   Tokyo   Toronto

To Marie

Cover Design: Rogondino & Associates

ISBN: 0-15-548886-4
Library of Congress Catalog Card Number: 87-81892
Printed in the United States of America

Preface to the Second Edition

The response to the first edition of *Labor and the Economy* confirmed the need for a comprehensive text in labor economics that integrated theory, policy, and institutions. In this second edition I have built on those strengths by updating the debates in labor economics through the mid-1980s. The emergence of supply-side economic ideas as it affects the labor market is given enhanced treatment here. Juxtaposed to the supply-side explanation of labor problems is an explanation based on labor displacement caused by foreign competition and structural change in the economy. This debate, however, is merely an extension of the central theme of the first edition: the debate between micro and structural explanations of problems in the labor market. The first edition, therefore, was quite applicable to the emergence in the 1980s of supply-side and labor displacement arguments, and this theme is developed further in the second edition.

The integration of theory, policy, and institutions, organized around controversies in labor economics, means that the traditional organization of labor textbooks has been amended in both editions of this book. While there are core chapters on the micro foundations of labor economics (Chapters 3, 4, and 5), many micro applications and extensions of the basic model are scattered throughout the book and are introduced where applicable. Material that in other texts is normally segregated into micro chapters is here placed in the chapters in which the concepts are used. This makes the learning of the micro foundations easier for students and pedagogically preferable for instructors.

For example, the core micro model of the labor market is extended and applied in Chapter 9, on the functional distribution of income; in Chapter 10, on human capital; in Chapter 12, on the economics of discrimination; in Chapter 14, on unemployment; in Chapter 17, on stagflation and the natural rate of unemployment; and in Chapter 23, on minimum wages. I find this method more suitable for instruction and learning than simply placing all the micro material in chapters labeled as such and neglecting to use the micro foundations where they are pertinent.

In addition to the increased attention of policymakers to the micro foundations of labor markets in the 1980s, the structural displacement school received confirmation by the weakening of the U.S. economy's manufacturing base through foreign competition and technological change. Deindustrialization and labor displacement are two new terms that have emerged in the 1980s to describe this phenomenon. The first edition highlighted these issues and placed the debate between micro and structural explanations in this context. Extending these ideas to the new supply-side and deindustrialization language, therefore, has been a natural evolution in the second edition.

The chapter on the future of industrial relations has a new section about the dramatically altered role of trade unions in the American economy. The extensive treatment of labor unions in the first edition made it possible to develop these ideas in the second and bring them into the late 1980s.

Users of the first edition found the integration of theory, policy, and institutions, organized around conflicting points of view, to be a useful method for teaching labor economics. Such an approach to the subject is needed even more in the latter part of the decade as the very issues highlighted in the first edition came to dominate public debate in the first half of the 1980s. I am grateful to users of the first edition for their many helpful comments, and I hope that this new edition clarifies whatever was ambiguous in the first.

The data have been updated to 1985 wherever possible, and I am grateful to David Demers for his assistance with this not inconsiderable task. I am grateful also to the following reviewers for their helpful comments: George Radakovic, Indiana University of Pennsylvania; Jane Lillydahl, University of Colorado, Boulder; Donald Coffin, Illinois State University; and George C. Archibald, University of British Columbia. The second edition of *Labor and the Economy* was guided to completion by Marguerite L. Egan, my editor at Harcourt Brace Jovanovich. On the production of the book, I had confident cross-continental contacts with Mary Miller of Miller/Scheier Associates and Michael A. Rogondino of Rogondino and Associates.

Howard M. Wachtel

From the Preface to the First Edition

For many years I have been dissatisfied with the existing textbooks in labor economics. Students in my classes have had difficulty with the several books I have used through the years. Economic theory did not seem to be integrated directly with economic policy. The theories never seemed to be exposed to adequate empirical tests. Usually only one theory in economics was presented, and I would have to supplement this material in class with the rich and exciting debate among competing schools of thought in labor economics.

Students respond better to economic theory if they know the reason they are asked to study economic theory. They also are reassured if they know that the theory will not simply be left as a set of unverified hypotheses but will be subjected to careful and critical empirical scrutiny. And they want to know how theory relates to programs for making the economy function more efficiently and improving the lives of those who work in the economy.

So I decided to write a book that would integrate economic theory, empirical studies of the labor force, and public policies that flow from the theories and empirical studies. Moreover, I decided to pursue this objective by putting the debate among supporters of competing models into a format that would enable students to see several different approaches to each problem. For example, unemployment problems and the consequent debate about minimum wages are examined through the Keynesian, neoclassical, structural, and dual-labor-market theories. For each theory, empirical studies are presented, and the conclusions from these studies are the basis for evaluating a public policy proposal—for example, a youth subminimum wage to stimulate employment among young people in the labor force.

The book I have written is set in the 1980s—not an inconsiderable advantage, since two of the major textbooks in this field were originally written in the 1940s and 1960s. The legacy of labor economics from the 1950s, 1960s, and 1970s forms an important backdrop for a consideration of the problems of the labor force in the 1980s. Trade unions and their impact on the economy were of paramount interest in the 1950s, and material on those subjects is integrated into the discussion of wage determination in this text. In the 1960s such Great Society issues as poverty, income inequality, and discrimination came to the fore, and these questions are integrated into the debate over theoretical models in the discussion of "Labor and Individual Incomes" in Part I of the book. Interest in human capital models in the early part of the 1970s gave way by the end of the decade to concern over stagflation. The problems we face in the labor force in the 1980s must be understood in this historical context so that we can prepare to enter the 1990s with the appropriate labor market policies. My hope is that this book will contribute to an understanding of what public policies are needed to overcome our present difficulties in the labor force.

I start with the definition of a problem, and then I present theory, empirical studies, and policy application. In too many textbooks the authors jump right in to examine economic theory and do not prepare the student adequately for the use of the theory in policy. A topic is stated and then theory is developed. My approach is different. A foundation is prepared by a thorough discussion of the problem first. Then theory is developed and tested and applied to economic policy. For example, in Part II of the book, a chapter on measuring unemployment and the labor force is presented first, followed by a chapter on employment theory and public policy. This method helps students understand the context of theory better and provides them some motivation for grappling with difficult theoretical material.

Since 1969 I have been teaching labor economics at both the graduate level and the undergraduate level at The American University. Interaction with the students in those classes through the years has provided me with a pedagogical laboratory to experiment with my approach to the study of labor economics. It works for me. I hope I have translated my classroom method into this text effectively. If I have, I know students will appreciate its scope and approach. Teachers will delight in having students responsive to the material of the course.

Acknowledgments

In acknowledging colleagues who helped with the writing of this book, I add the usual caveat: They are in no way implicated, and I take full responsibility for the content of the book.

While I was studying at the University of Michigan in the late 1960s, two teachers were important models for me in approaching the study of labor economics: Harold Levinson of the Department of Economics and Lou Ferman of the Institute of Labor and Industrial Relations. Throughout the 1970s, I prospered from my association with Barry Bluestone (now of Boston College), Bennett Harrison (now of M.I.T.), and Michael Reich (now of the University of California, Berkeley). We were all writing in similar ways about similar subjects, and that work as a whole influenced my approach to the study of labor economics. My coauthor for several of the articles I wrote during that period was Charles Betsey, and to him goes an equal share of the credit for those articles.

In writing this text, I have benefited from a score of readers' comments. Since many of these were anonymous, I do not know whom to thank for all of them. Readers I do know who have contributed substantially to the manuscript are Charles Craypo, Jon Wisman, Deb Figart, Michael Reich, Carol O'Cleireacain, Arne Anderson, Billy Dickens, Charles Betsey, Neil Garston, Naomi Davidson, and Lafayette G. Harter, Jr. Billy Dickens prepared the study questions. Nancy Smith was my excellent typist.

Contents

1

Labor and the Economy

Toward the end of the 1970s and during the 1980s a new refrain has been heard from the American people: "Why doesn't the economy work the way it used to?" In one form or another, this is the question people are asking. The question is posed to politicians. It is asked of business people and union leaders. And it is also directed at economists. Do we have adequate answers? What are these answers? Can they be successfully translated into policies and programs?

Aims of the Book

This is what this book is about—trying to find answers to the most perplexing problems we face in our economy in the 1980s. Inflation, wages, unemployment, poverty, and robotization are but a few of the important issues we look at in this book. In one way, this book is about the issues that are the substance of political campaigns and the basis for newspaper headlines. But in another sense, this is also a comprehensive textbook in an important branch of economics. In this capacity *Labor and the Economy* takes you through economic theory, economic statistics, empirical methodology, institutional frameworks, and public policy debates—all for the purpose of helping you understand contemporary economic and policy matters.

The focus of this book is on economic issues and debates. Starting with a definition of the problem, we apply the tools of labor economics in our analysis. Economic theories are used, empirical studies are examined, and public policy conclusions are reached.

There are few, if any, settled questions in labor economics. This is particularly true today because the economic upheavals of the late 1970s caused a breach in what had previously been a consensus on some issues. For this reason several alternative theories and points of view are introduced in this book in connection with each economic problem.

The problems of our economy in the past ten years have created an explosion of new ideas, theories, and empirical studies. There has probably been as much new material produced in labor economics in the last 20 years as in the previous 50. These new approaches to the study of labor economics form the core of many of the sections and chapters of this book.

Labor is an integral part of the economy. What labor does affects the economy and what happens in the economy affects labor. These interactions form a theme that runs through this book. Trade union wage settlements influence prices, other wages, and the general standard of living. Fiscal and monetary policies, on the other hand, affect unemployment, which in turn influences the activities of labor. Labor and the economy form a whole, and they must be looked at together.

In another sense labor is something different from the abstractions that textbooks use. We say we "work for a living," but that phrase is deceptive. Work *is* a means toward the end of consumption, as "working for a living" implies. But work is also tied up with living itself and cannot easily be disentangled from the roots of our existence. Our identities as human beings are defined in a significant way by our work. This fact makes the study of labor economics more difficult and complex, and at the same time richer and more challenging.

Recent History of Labor Economics

Labor economics today is at a juncture in the evolution of economic ideas. The complacency of the 1960s, when it appeared that economic problems could be managed by Keynesian fine tuning, has given way to sharp debate over what to do with an economy that seems to be unresponsive to the policies of an earlier era. Students wonder what has gone wrong with the economy; where definitive solutions are not immediately available, they seek clear alternatives based on careful reasoning.

The economy no longer responds to the stimuli of an earlier era to which we had become accustomed. Living standards are not growing the way they used to. Inflation erodes purchasing power and denigrates thrift. Frequent unemployment and high job turnover appear to be the norm for a segment of the American labor force. International competition threatens to undermine the manufacturing base of the American economy, turning it into an administrative economy.

Faced with these challenges, economics cannot go through the 1990s in a complacent mood. It must instead grapple with the knotty problems that Americans themselves face every day. But economists cannot tackle current issues without learning the history of earlier periods, for to do so would be to commit a sin of ignorance which would only come back to haunt us later.

Labor Economics after World War II: The High Wage Economy

The end of World War II marked a watershed in public affairs—in politics as well as economics. Keynesianism, which was no more than a set of ideas before the war, came to dominate economic thought and policy after the war. Economists became convinced that the economy could be stabilized and full employment achieved through wise fiscal and monetary management, thereby eliminating the most perplexing problem of a modern industrial market economy. Moreover, this could be accomplished without injury to price stability. Inflation, setting aside "hyperinflation," could also be controlled by monetary and fiscal management. Postwar euphoria was a general phenomenon, and economists did not escape it. How sweet that innocence seems today as we ponder our current economic fate.

Labor economics has traditionally been concerned with the price attached to the exchange relationship between employer and worker. The wage should reflect conditions of supply and demand in the labor market so resources would then be allocated most efficiently. The Keynesian revolution in economic thought had its counterpart in labor economics. The changes wrought by Keynesian economics added to the traditional concerns of labor economics.

From the mid-1940s to the mid-1960s, labor economics grew around the framework of an economic philosophy that could loosely be called *the model of a high-wage economy*. Dissenters from this consensual philosophy existed, but in the mainstream the model of a high-wage economy prevailed. Labor unions were accepted not simply as a legal fact but as a cornerstone of the liberal Keynesian economic philosophy of full employment, which dominated the profession. Trade union pressure, according to this view, produced high wages and better working conditions, which had two salutary effects on the economy beyond the individual benefits for the workers receiving them. First, the high-wage economy improved overall efficiency in the economy by weeding out the least productive firms, leaving only the firms that were capable of paying the high wages and still making sufficient profits to stay in business. The productivity of the economy as a whole was consequently enhanced, an idea first suggested by two British economists, Sidney and Beatrice Webb, writing near the end of the last century.[1] This was an intellectual epoch in which social Darwinism was very influential. Labor economics heartily embraced its own form of social Darwinism—the belief that economic survival of the fittest bred the greatest efficiency.

---

[1] Sidney and Beatrice Webb, *Industrial Democracy* (London: Longmans, Green and Co., 1897).

Second, the high wages increased consumer purchasing power, stimulating aggregate demand in a Keynesian sense and acting as a buffer against the threat of another Great Depression. If consumption, which is such a large part of gross national product, could grow, then the possibilities of economic stagnation would be prevented, according to this line of reasoning. This idea was suggested first by Marx in the middle of the nineteenth century, and then elaborated by Keynes nearly a century later. Keynes added the concept of the marginal propensity to consume—the proportion of any increase in disposable income that would show up in additional consumer spending. Workers tended to spend higher proportions of their growing disposable income and save less, so Keynes thought a redistribution toward labor would stimulate the economy and prevent its collapse.

The high-wage economy attracted firm support from labor economists after World War II because it seemed to be replete with benefits for all (today it would be called a positive-sum game). Growth would be created by the high rates of increase in labor productivity. Aggregate demand and high levels of employment would be sustained by consumer demand. The Employment Act of 1946 directed government to use fiscal and monetary policy to promote high levels of employment, as a complement to the private high-wage economy, thus ensuring optimal social welfare.

To be sure, there were rough edges around this core consensus. Discrimination against black workers produced a fissure in the model when the civil rights movement of the early 1960s aroused America's conscience. General conditions of poverty in the society revealed that not all workers received high wages, and America's self-image as an affluent society was challenged. An income distribution that remained unaltered for 20 years conflicted with the American dream of social mobility. But these problems were merely chinks in the Keynesian model and could be contained within it, at least according to its proponents.

The 1960s

As the issues of the 1960s arose, the majority of labor economists adopted a modification of the model of the high-wage economy, conceding these rough edges existed but contending that public policy efforts aimed at specific problems could alleviate them. Thus were born the Great Society programs to reduce hard-core unemployment among the "unemployables," eliminate poverty, and redistribute income through tax policies and transfer programs that specifically benefited the poorest in the nation. The idea of fine-tuning an economy to produce economic stability—that is, high employment and stable prices—was extended by the Keynesians to specific social problems. The Great Society reflected this notion of *extended fine-tuning*. Fiscal and monetary policies were to provide the context in which specific policies would be aimed at those ignored by Keynesian economic stabilization policy.

While public policy was wedded to an extended fine-tuning approach, two groups of labor economists split from the consensus. One group, called *structuralists*, contended that there were specific problems with the structure of the American economy that produced discrimination, hard-core unemployment, poverty, and income inequality. And these problems were not susceptible to an extended fine-tuning of the economy without bolder efforts at restructuring it.

The second group, the *human capital* school, sought to extend the ideas of microeconomic theory to the problems of the 1960s. The philosophical premise of individualism, which was the underpinning of traditional neoclassical economics, had its revival in human capital theory. This theory contended that discrimination, poverty, unemployment, and inequality were the result of a confluence of forces that produced specific decisions by individuals in the economy.

The 1970s

A debate started in the 1960s and continued into the 1970s among these three schools of thought in labor economics: the Keynesian extended fine-tuners, the structuralists, and the human capitalists. This clash of ideas in thought and in public policy prescriptions forms one of the important themes for the material presented in this book.

In retrospect, the problems of the labor force have proved to be more intractable to social policy than was thought during the 1960s. The quartet of social issues (poverty, inequality, unemployment, and discrimination) became a quintet in the 1970s, as inflation was added to the list. The reality of *economic inequality* (one dollar/one vote in the market place) clashed with the idea of *political equality* (one person/one vote in the voting booth), leading to an erosion of confidence in the ability of government to solve economic and social problems. Many of the important yardsticks of economic health showed dramatic structural shifts in the 1970s in contrast with the two decades immediately after World War II. In the 1970s real rates of economic growth declined and inflation intensified, making it all the more difficult to find both the resources and the political consensus to address the pressing social issues that had arisen during the 1960s.

Instead of a perpetually increasing real wage in the manufacturing sector, there was a decline in the purchasing power of workers' take-home pay in the 1970s. Families were able to increase their real income only by moonlighting or by adding members of the household to the work force. This situation resulted in substantially increased labor force participation rates for women and youth. Productivity barely increased at all in the 1970s, staying well below its rate of increase for the two decades after World War II. Government intervention in the economy for the purpose of preventing discrimination, reducing poverty, and aiding social mobility was perceived by critics as costly in terms of both tax dollars spent and private economic efficiency. Inflation was a new ailment—or perhaps an old ailment with new characteristics—that economics was unable to explain successfully to a skeptical public, let alone to design policies to control.

The 1980s

Supply-side economic ideas dominated the 1980s, and they had their severest test in the labor market. On one side of the debate, the contention was that labor markets were inefficient because government programs and union-generated high wages prevented labor markets from clearing. The public policy thrust, therefore, involved a weakening of labor union influence and a reduction in the rate of growth of public programs that interfered with the efficient operation of labor markets. In this category were minimum wages, unemployment compensation, and public welfare.

The 1980s, however, was also a decade in which profound structural change affected the economy. Foreign competition and technological change produced a new group of displaced workers who were not the cyclically unemployed of previous decades—individuals laid off during slack times and rehired during good times. Instead these were workers in their mid-lives, with family obligations, who found themselves without jobs and without any hope of recreating their stable, high-paid, middle class life-style. What some economists called the "missing middle" characterized this phenomenon: the disappearance of stable, middle class, production work on which the American dream had been built.

The clash between these two diametrically opposing views of the labor market will be a focus of this book. Which economic view explains the increasingly higher floor on the minimum acceptable unemployment rate is central to the public policy disputes that will carry into the 1990s.

Labor Economics Today

In the midst of this breakdown in economic theory and policy, a series of important new ideas have arisen in the field of labor economics. The richness of these new ideas and theories and of more rigorous empirical work provides us with a foundation on which to construct public policies in the 1990s. The accumulation of new research in labor economics is highlighted in this book.

In *Labor and the Economy* we will look at new theories in the context of their previous incarnations. Empirical studies that grew out of those theories provide a basis for testing the validity of new ideas. Following and building on the theories and empirical studies are the new public policy prescriptions. The emphasis in the book is on the new and its relationship to the past. The goal is to understand the present and suggest policies for the future.

Plan of the Book

This book is divided into four parts: Labor and the Microeconomy, Labor and the Macroeconomy, Labor and Economic Institutions, and Labor and Public Policy.

The first part of the book establishes the microeconomic foundations of labor economics, following Chapter 2, which provides important background material on the labor force and the American economy. The starting point for the analysis is the theory of wage determination in neoclassical economics. This theory looks at the wage rate as an important resource-allocating instrument in the economy. When trade unions are introduced into our consideration of the wage determination process, the theory of wage determination has to be modified. After this is done, empirical studies on wage determination are examined in detail.

At the microeconomic level, wages are part of the process of resource allocation; this is the motivating theme behind Chapters 3 through 7. To the worker who supplies labor, however, wages are a means of attaining income toward the end of consumption. Wages, therefore, are the basis for individual welfare, income distribution, and living standards. These topics are discussed in Chapters 8 through 12, which make up section B of Part I, called "Labor Markets and Individual Incomes." To set the stage for an examination of labor and individual incomes, there is a chapter on poverty and inequality followed by one on the functional distribution of income. The next three chapters examine three different approaches to the study of labor and individual incomes; Chapter 10 looks at human capital theory, Chapter 11 at labor market structures, and Chapter 12 at the economics of discrimination.

Next comes Part II, "Labor and the Macroeconomy." The interaction between labor's effect on the macroeconomy and the macroeconomy's effect on labor is a theme that runs throughout Chapters 13 through 17, which cover unemployment, inflation, and stagflation. This section of the book concludes with a chapter on wage-price policies and the role that labor plays in these policy efforts to control stagflation.

Trade unions are introduced briefly in the first part of the book in connection with their impact on wages. In Part III, "Labor and Economic Institutions," trade unions are examined as economic institutions interrelating with other institutions in the economy. A chapter on the history of American unions is followed by one on the institutional process that governs industrial relations in the United States. Important public policies are embodied in labor law, and this topic is taken up in Chapter 21. The concluding chapter of this section looks at the provocative question of the future of industrial relations in the United States.

Throughout the book a healthy interaction is developed among theory, empirical studies, institutional analysis, and public policy considerations. Some topics in public policy, though touched on briefly in several chapters, warrant a more complete treatment, separate from the content of those other chapters. For this reason I have included a final section of the book that contains three chapters on controversial public policy issues that face the nation in the 1980s: minimum wages; income security (including social security); health and safety; and employment policy.

As a whole the book provides a comprehensive treatment of labor and the economy in its interactive forms—in theory, in policy, in empirical research, and in institutional processes. Labor economics today is an exciting field because of the vigorous debates that are carried on constantly. These debates are clearly identified and developed throughout the book. Studying labor economics through this book will enable you to see how work, wages, and living standards combine to form a set of problems that pose exciting and difficult challenges to economists and the nation.

2

The Labor Force and the Economy

The labor force in 1985 consisted of more than 115 million people. It crossed the 100 million plateau under President Carter in 1978, having doubled since 1931, when it crossed the 50 million threshold toward the end of President Hoover's term of office.

When the baby boom generation began to enter the labor force in the 1970s, the labor force grew by 2.2 million people per year. Employment would have had to grow by at least 2.2 million jobs per year in the 1970s just to employ these additional people. Even more rapid growth in employment would have been needed to employ those people who were already in the labor force but without jobs. In the 1960s the labor force had grown at a slower rate. Each year in that decade, about 1.3 million more people entered the labor force. The 1970s produced growth in the labor force of 26.6 percent, compared with 18.8 percent growth in the 1960s. In the 1980s, the labor force has returned to its pre-baby boom rate of growth of just 1.3 percent per year.

There are several reasons for the more rapid growth in the labor force in the last decade compared with previous trends. First, there are the simple demographics of the population and the coming of age of the "baby boom" generation born after World War II. Second, inflation eroded living standards in the 1970s, and the only way many families could keep pace with inflation was by adding a second household member to the labor force. Third, changes in society's attitudes toward women working produced more opportunities for women, and they entered the labor force in larger numbers than at any time since World War II.

Whatever the reasons, the growth in the labor force in the last decade put additional burdens on the employment-creating potential of the economy. To complicate the picture, these additional burdens were placed on the American economy at a time when it was least able to support them. The decade of the 1970s was one of economic instability, unprecedented inflation, economic stagnation, and sharply increasing prices for basic commodities such as energy. It is no wonder, then, that the decade ended with the abrupt abandonment of Keynesian economic philosophy and the introduction of a new philosophy, supply-side economics, which promised a more aggressive and effective system of job creation.

Aside from these macroeconomic issues of unemployment and aggregate growth in the labor force, there are also microeconomic, structural questions involving balance in the labor market. The economy is dynamic and constantly in motion. Technological change alters the demand for specific occupations and creates demand for entirely new ones, such as robot design engineers. Consumers' tastes change as their incomes grow, and this fashions a demand for particular kinds of labor that may not be readily available. Whether the skills and talents of those available for work in the labor force match the demand for labor will determine whether structural unemployment exists.

The character and structure of the labor force is altered in response to technological changes and to changes in the final demand for goods and services in the economy. As a factor of production, labor experiences more dramatic and more rapid changes than does either land or physical capital. As labor is influenced by the forces of demand and technical change, it also undergoes transformations of its own, which reverberate through the economy. For example, inflation and stagnation have made it necessary for more women to seek work in order to support households. The shift toward a service economy has created more jobs traditionally filled by women. Added to these factors are an increase in the number of women who view work as a career and a growth in the number of female-headed households. All these forces produced substantial increases in the proportion of women who participate in the labor force. As a result of these increases, the composition of the labor force itself has changed: the proportion that is composed of women is greater now than in the previous two decades.

Labor Markets and the Economy
■

In an earlier day, when most production was conducted in the household, there was not much need for complex arrangements to integrate disparate parts of the economy. Markets did exist in earlier times, but they served mainly the practical function of bringing buyers and sellers together in a geographical place to exchange goods and services. For a large, complex industrial economy, however, besides serving this practical function, markets also coordinate activities of buyers and sellers through a system of incentives.

The labor market plays a central role in any analysis of the economy. If operating smoothly, it will match demands for and supplies of particular types of labor. It will bring overall macro balance of aggregate supply of and demand for labor into the economy if there is sufficient demand for labor and if the structure of labor supply merges with the character of labor demand. When these conditions do not exist, unemployment will occur.

Labor markets are impersonal institutions, whereas work is a human activity. Individual workers find that they are isolated from each other in the work place and that they have insufficient influence over a crucial aspect of their personal welfare. To remedy these problems, workers band together into trade unions and similar organizations, which are only the most recent manifestation of workers' efforts to address collectively their personal stake in the nature of work.

In this chapter we will look at several statistical series that are essential for understanding the role of labor in the economy. This is but a brief introduction to these statistical concepts; they will be treated more completely in subsequent chapters where the topics are examined in detail. The statistics on the labor force parallel the discussion of labor markets and the economy. We will look at the growth of the labor force, the rate of unemployment, the changing character of demand for labor, and the size and structure of labor unions. When considering these sometimes dry numbers, we should not forget that they represent a critical aspect of life itself: work.

The Labor Force

In 1985 there were over 115 million persons in the labor force in the United States, excluding the military. Some 64 million were males and about 51 million were females. By way of contrast, 35 years earlier, in 1950, the civilian labor force was half as large, 62 million, and males made up nearly 45 million of that total. In 1985 females composed about 44 percent of the total labor force; in 1950 they made up only 27 percent.[1]

Unemployment

Not everyone in the labor force is working. Some people are unemployed. The official definition of unemployment is narrow and may not be what you think. To be unemployed, not only must you be out of work, but you must also be actively looking for

---

[1] Figures taken from Council of Economic Advisers, *Economic Report of the President, 1986* (Washington: Government Printing Office, 1986), pp. 288, 290.

work during the period in which the survey of the labor force is taken each month. In 1985 an average of 8.3 million people were unemployed throughout the year (7.1 percent of the labor force). In 1950 an average of 5.3 percent of the labor force was unemployed throughout the year—some 3.3 million workers. In the decades of the 1950s and 1960s, the average unemployment rates were 4.5 percent and 4.7 percent, respectively. In the 1970s, however, the average unemployment rate was 6.2 percent, substantially higher than it had been in the previous 20 years and between 1980 and 1985 it averaged 8 percent.

Clearly, unemployment is more widespread and persistent today than it was in the quarter century after World War II. This phenomenon has posed a serious challenge to labor economists. Is the higher unemployment of the 1980s due to insufficient jobs in the aggregate, a wage rate that is too high to equilibrate the market for labor, social policies that make it attractive not to work, the higher proportion of the labor force that is young or female, or a structural mismatch between demand for and supply of labor? This is the subject of Part II of the book when we take up Labor and the Macroeconomy.

Younger labor force → (1) BABY BOOM (2) EARLY RETIREMENT

Demographic Composition of the Labor Force

The labor force has undergone important demographic shifts since World War II. Today it is younger and made up of more women. Changes in the age distribution of the labor force have been caused in part by the baby boom immediately after World War II, when the birth rate in the United States increased precipitously. Families that had postponed having children during the Great Depression began to have them after World War II. During the war many more births were postponed as men went into battle and their survival was in doubt. "By 1985," according to the *Wall Street Journal,* "the tens of millions who make up the 'baby boom' generation will have been absorbed into the labor force: After that, a relatively smaller number of people will be looking for entry-level jobs.[2] Because of the slowdown in the rate of growth of the labor force, the Morgan Guaranty Trust Co. predicts that in the 1990s "employers will find themselves in the unaccustomed position of scrambling for workers."[3] Another factor influencing the age composition of the labor force is earlier retirement. This has been caused in large measure by the broadening of the social security system since World War II.

As a result of these two factors—the baby boom and earlier retirement—the age structure of the labor force has changed since the end of the war. Figures pertaining to this change are shown in Table 2-1. Half the labor force was under 34 in 1985, compared with 43 percent in 1948. This has increased the need for entry-level jobs in the economy and is part of the explanation for youth unemployment rates ranging

---

[2] "Joblessness to Fall in Decade as Fewer Enter Labor Force," *Wall Street Journal,* June 30, 1980, p. 17.

[3] "The 1990s Economy: Impact of 'Baby Bust,'" *Wall Street Journal* April 14, 1986, p. 1.

Table 2-1 Composition of the Civilian Labor Force by Age, 1948–1985, Selected Years

Year	Total[a] (%)	16–24 (%)	25–34 (%)	35–44 (%)	45–54 (%)	55–64 (%)	65 + (%)
1948	100	19.5	23.5	22.1	18.0	12.1	4.8
1950	100	18.5	23.5	22.4	18.4	12.3	4.9
1955	100	15.0	23.2	23.7	20.0	13.1	5.1
1960	100	16.6	20.7	23.4	21.3	13.5	4.5
1965	100	19.0	19.1	22.6	21.1	13.9	4.3
1970	100	21.6	20.6	19.9	20.5	13.6	3.9
1975	100	24.1	24.4	18.2	18.2	12.1	3.2
1980	100	23.7	27.3	19.1	15.8	11.2	2.9
1985	100	20.5	29.1	22.6	15.0	10.4	2.5

[a] Because of rounding, percentages for some years may not total 100.
Sources: U.S. Department of Labor, *Handbook of Labor Statistics* (Washington: Government Printing Office, 1985), p. 14; U.S. Department of Labor, *Employment and Earnings* (Washington: Government Printing Office, Jan. 1981), p. 154.

from 15 to 41 percent in 1985. At the other end of the age distribution, individuals over 65 made up only 2.5 percent of the labor force in 1985, compared with 4.8 percent in 1948.

This trend toward a younger labor force will be reversed in the next two decades. There will be fewer young people available to enter the labor force. Projections of two Presidential Commissions formed under President Carter concluded that by the year 2025 one out of every five citizens would be over 65, compared with one out of nine today. If the demographic projections of these commissions are correct, the ratio of those working to those retired will drop steadily throughout the remainder of the century.[4] These demographic trends underscore the nation's concern for the viability of the social security system as currently constituted.[5] As the working-age population shrinks, relative to the retired population, the burden placed on those working to support those not working is intensified.

The household plays an important role in making decisions about the supply of labor in the economy.[6] How time is divided in the household, who works, and how many hours each works are issues that lend themselves to an economic analysis. For now, it is sufficient to look at some of the results of those decisions made in the household. Immediately after World War II, men made up about 72 percent of the

---

[4] Robert J. Samuelson, "Quelling the Conflicts as Our Population Ages," *Washington Post,* March 24, 1981, p. D7.

[5] Discussed further in Chapter 24.

[6] This is discussed in Chapter 4.

Table 2-2 Composition of the Civilian Labor Force by Sex,
1948–1985, Selected Years

Year	Male (%)	Female (%)
1948	71.4	28.6
1950	70.4	29.6
1955	68.4	31.6
1960	66.6	33.4
1965	64.8	35.2
1970	61.9	38.1
1975	60.0	40.0
1980	57.5	42.5
1985	55.8	44.2

Sources: U.S. Department of Labor, *Handbook of Labor Statistics* (Washington: Government Printing Office, 1985), pp. 14–15; U.S. Department of Labor, *Employment and Earnings* (Washington: Government Printing Office, Jan. 1986), p. 154.

labor force and women 28 percent. By 1985 the proportion of women in the labor force had grown to 44 percent and the male share of the labor force had fallen to 56 percent (see Table 2-2).

Many factors are at work producing these dramatic changes. First, changing social attitudes made it acceptable for a larger proportion of women to seek careers than was the case after the war. Second, a stagnant economy in the 1970s, coupled with inflation, eroded real standards of living for one-income families. This pushed more women into the labor force to seek additional income for the family. Third, owing to the higher divorce rate, there are many more families headed by women today. Fourth, the demand for labor has shifted toward service and administrative jobs and away from blue-collar manufacturing jobs, which traditionally are more often held by men.[7]

As a result of these factors, more women participate in the labor force today than previously. In Table 2-3 another measure of this phenomenon is shown: the labor force participation rate. This measures the percentage of men and women who are either working or looking for work, compared with the eligible population. For example, in 1950 only 34 percent of all women were working or looking for work; in 1985 the percentage was 54. The male participation rate fell from 86 percent to 77 percent, reflecting earlier retirement.

---

[7] Discrimination in the economy, which types certain jobs as male or female, is one of the most important issues in the study of labor economics. The same can be said of racial discrimination. In Chapter 12 we look at this in detail.

Table 2-3   Civilian Labor Force Participation Rates by Sex

	1950 (%)	1985 (%)
Males	86.4	77.0
Females	33.9	54.1
Total	59.2	65.0

Source: Council of Economic Advisers, *Economic Report of the President, 1986* (Washington: Government Printing Office), p. 294; U.S. Department of Labor, *Handbook of Labor Statistics* (Washington: Government Printing Office, 1985), p. 18.

The Changing Structure of Employment in the American Economy

The composition of employment changes because of technological changes and because of changes in the demand for goods and services. As an economy matures and real standards of living increase, the demand for services increases relative to the demand for tangible products. A more complex economy requires more white-collar employees to manage such industrial institutions as the conglomerate and the multinational corporation. These factors combine to change the structure of employment in the economy.

Technological change has made agriculture so productive that now only a handful of farmers feed us; once nearly half the working population was engaged in agriculture. Economic growth and personal affluence have shifted consumer demand, and the service sector of the economy has grown faster than the goods production sector. White-collar employment, accordingly, has increased its share of occupational activity, while blue-collar production work has experienced a proportionate decline in employment. These trends are shown in a series of tables on the structure of employment in the American economy.

Statistics on the proportions of farm and nonfarm employment are presented in Table 2-4. Nearly half the working population was once engaged in agricultural work; in 1985 only 3 percent of the working population is employed in agriculture. In 1870, when the first post–Civil War decennial census was taken, close to half the American work force was employed in agriculture. These figures include self-employed farmer–owners as well as farm employees. By the end of World War I, about one-quarter of the work force was engaged in agricultural activities, and this proportion had fallen to 12 percent by the first decennial census after World War II.

As a proportion of the total population in the country, only 1.4 percent produces food. This 1.4 percent of the American population feeds not just the people in our country but many more people around the world through our substantial export of

Table 2-4 Farm and Nonfarm Employment, 1870–1985, Selected Years

Year	Farm[a] (thousands)	(%)	Nonfarm (thousands)	(%)	Total Employment (thousands)
1870	5,949	47.6	6,557	52.4	12,506
1880	7,714	44.3	9,678	55.7	17,392
1890	9,148	39.2	14,170	60.8	23,318
1900	11,050	41.0	15,906	59.0	26,956
1910	11,260	32.6	23,299	67.4	34,559
1920	10,440	26.6	28,768	73.4	39,208
1930	10,340	23.4	33,843	76.6	44,183
1940	9,540	20.0	37,980	80.0	47,520
1950	7,160	12.1	51,758	87.9	58,918
1960	5,458	8.3	60,318	91.7	65,776
1970	3,463	4.4	75,215	95.6	78,678
1980	3,364	3.4	95,938	96.6	99,302
1985	3,179	2.9	103,971	97.1	107,150

[a]Includes Farm owners and managers as well as farm laborers.
Sources: U.S. Bureau of the Census, *Historical Statistics of the United States, Colonial Times to 1970* (Washington: Government Printing Office, 1976), pt. 1, pp. 126–127; U.S. Department of Labor, *Handbook of Labor Statistics* (Washington: Government Printing Office, 1985), p. 6; U.S. Department of Labor, *Employment and Earnings* (Washington: Government Printing Office, Jan. 1986) p. 12.

agricultural products. Over the past century the American work force has shifted dramatically from agricultural to nonagricultural employment. This is one important trend of the past hundred years. A second important trend is the shift in employment from goods production to service provision. In Table 2-5, data are presented to demonstrate this phenomenon.

Goods-producing industries are manufacturing, mining, and construction—those sectors of the economy in which some *tangible* commodity is created. Service provision occurs in transportation, trade, finance, insurance, real estate, services, and government. In 1919, after World War I, the work force was split almost evenly between these two economic activities. At the end of World War II about 60 percent of the working population was employed in service-providing activities and 40 percent in goods production. In 1985, 74 percent of employment was in service-providing activities and only 26 percent in goods production. Our economy has become predominantly a service-providing one, at least where the structure of employment is concerned.

One final set of statistics bears on this question of the changing structure of employment in the American economy in this century. Table 2-6 shows the changing composition of employment in terms of broad occupational categories: managers, professional employees, blue-collar workers, and white-collar workers. In 1900, two-

Table 2-5 Structure of Employment, 1919–1985, Selected Years (Excluding Agriculture)

Year	Total Employment Excluding Agriculture (thousands)	Goods-producing Employment[a]		Service-providing Employment[b]	
		(thousands)	(%)	(thousands)	(%)
1919	27,078	12,828	47.4	14,250	52.6
1930	29,409	11,958	40.7	17,451	59.3
1940	32,361	13,221	40.9	19,140	59.1
1950	45,197	18,506	40.9	26,691	59.1
1960	54,189	20,434	37.7	33,755	62.3
1970	70,880	23,578	33.2	47,302	66.8
1980	90,406	25,658	28.4	64,748	71.6
1985	97,700	25,057	25.6	72,643	74.4

[a]Includes manufacturing, mining, and construction.
[b]Includes transportation, trade, finance, insurance, real estate, services, and government.
Sources: U.S. Department of Labor, *Handbook of Labor Statistics* (Washington: Government Printing Office, 1985), pp. 174, 175; U.S. Department of Labor, *Employment and Earnings* (Washington: Government Printing Office, March 1986), p. 43.

thirds of American workers were blue-collar, goods-producing, direct-production workers. The remaining one-third of the work force was divided among the other three classifications shown in Table 2-6. By 1950 blue-collar employment had fallen to about 50 percent of employment in the private, nonfarm sector of the American economy. By 1980 just under 32 percent of American workers were employed in goods production as blue-collar factory employees. The classifications in which the largest growth in employment has occurred during this century are lower-level white-collar jobs and professional employment. Both more than doubled from 1900 to 1980 as proportions of total employment, while the proportion of blue-collar employment was cut in half.

These trends in the structure of employment in the American economy have important implications for economic questions that will be taken up in other chapters: labor productivity, industrial relations, and the evolution of trade unions. They are also critical to the future of the American economy; it is important to know whether the trends will continue throughout the remainder of this century.

Union Membership

There are many reasons individual workers join together to form trade unions. The trends just described form one set of reasons—the need to respond to the evolving industrialization and maturation of the American economy. Workers join together to

Table 2-6 Composition of Employment in Private, Nonfarm
Sector of the Economy, 1900–1980, Selected Years

Year	Managers, Officials, and Proprietors (%)	Professional Employees (%)	Wage and Salary Earners	
			Blue-Collar (%)	White-Collar[a] (%)
1900	9.3	6.8	66.1	17.8
1910	9.5	6.8	62.6	21.1
1920	9.1	7.4	59.7	23.8
1930	9.4	8.6	55.5	26.5
1940	8.8	9.1	53.8	28.3
1950	9.8	9.7	50.5	30.0
1960	8.9	11.4	48.3	31.4
1970	8.4	14.9	39.4	37.3
1980	11.2	16.1	31.7	40.7

[a]Includes clerical workers, sales workers, service workers (excluding private household employees).
Sources: U.S. Bureau of the Census, *Historical Statistics of the United States, Colonial Times to 1970* (Washington: Government Printing Office, 1976), pt. 1, p. 139; U.S. Bureau of the Census, *Statistical Abstract of the United States, 1981* (Washington: Government Printing Office), p. 401.

try to improve their working conditions and attain higher wages. They also attempt to acquire some control over their working environment so that safety and health can be improved. Unions also enable workers to play some role in decision making in the work place, establishing what labor historians refer to as "industrial democracy."[8]

Whatever the motivation for forming a union, trade unions play a significant role in the economy once they are created. Throughout this book we will have occasion to examine trade unions—how they work, how they influence economic outcomes, and how they have evolved. For now, it is useful to gain some insight into their size and penetration in the economy. Approximately 18 percent of the labor force belonged to labor unions in 1985. This comes to about 17 million American workers.

The American Federation of Labor (AFL) was founded in 1886. It was the first national trade union federation to survive the ups and downs of the economy. In 1900 only 2.7 percent of the labor force belonged to trade unions—primarily craft or

---

[8] A sampling of the literature in this area includes Sidney and Beatrice Webb, *Industrial Democracy* (London: Longmans, Green and Co., 1897); Frank Tannenbaum, *A Philosophy of Labor* (New York: Alfred A. Knopf, 1951); and Selig Perlman, *A Theory of the Labor Movement* (New York: Augustus M. Kelley, 1949). See also Part III of this book.

Table 2-7 Union Membership as a Percentage of the Labor Force, 1900–1985, Selected Years

Year	Union Membership	Year	Union Membership
1900	2.7	1940	15.5
1905	5.9	1945	21.9
1910	5.7	1950	22.3
1915	6.4	1955	24.7
1920	12.1	1960	23.6
1925	7.8	1965	22.4
1930	7.4	1970	22.6
1935	6.7	1975	20.7
1937[a]	12.9	1980	20.9
		1985	18.0

[a]This is the year industrial unions formed the Congress of Industrial Organizations (CIO); the Wagner Act was passed in 1935.
Sources: U.S. Department of Commerce, *Historical Statistics of the United States: Colonial Times to 1970* (Washington: Government Printing Office, 1976), pt. 1, pp. 126, 127, 176–78; U.S. Department of Labor, *Handbook of Labor Statistics* (Washington: Government Printing Office, 1980), p. 412; U.S. Department of Labor, "Corrected Data on Labor Organization Membership—1980" (Sept. 18, 1981), p. 3; U.S. Department of Labor, *Employment and Earnings* (Washington: Government Printing Office, Jan. 1986), p. 213.

occupation-based unions (Table 2-7). Union membership grew during World War I to about 12 percent of the labor force, as American labor and its representatives were integrated into the war production effort. Union membership then fell to less than 7 percent by 1935. Two factors contributed to this decline: First, antiunion sentiment was very intense after the war; second, during that period economic activity shifted to mass production industries, for which the old AFL craft structure was not suited.

Union membership rose to about 13 percent of the labor force in 1937, almost doubling in two years. The Wagner Act granted legitimacy to unions in 1935, and a new form of union emerged under the umbrella of the Congress of Industrial Organizations (CIO) which went on to organize the mass production industries of autos, steel, rubber, and the like.

Union membership continued to increase after World War II, as production in the unionized sectors grew, and peaked in 1955 at about one-quarter of the labor force. After that date union membership steadily declined to less than one-fifth of the labor force. Again, the changing structure of the American economy—this time the shift from goods production to service provision—has left unionization behind.

Not all sectors of the American economy have the same extent of unionization. Table 2-8 bears on this. About 75 percent of all workers in transportation, construc-

Table 2-8 Extent of Unionization by Industry, 1979

Less than 25%	25–49%	50–74%	75% and over
Printing, publishing	Telephone and telegraph	Transportation equipment	Transportation
Chemicals	Petroleum refining	Primary metals	Construction
Nonmanufacturing	Food and kindred products	Apparel	Mining
Textile mill products	Stone, clay, and glass products	Tobacco manufactures	
Instruments		Federal government	
Services	Fabricated metals	Paper	
Finance	Electrical machinery	Manufacturing	
Agriculture and fishing	Rubber		
Trade	Machinery, except electrical		
	Lumber		
	Leather		
	Electric, gas utilities		
	Furniture		
	Government		
	Local government		
	State government		

Source: U.S. Department of Labor, *Directory of National Unions and Employee Associations, 1979* (Washington: Government Printing Office, 1980), p. 99.

tion, and mining belong to unions. At the other extreme, less than one-quarter of all employees in such industries as services, finance, and agriculture belong to unions. These less unionized sectors have been growing as a proportion of total output in the American economy. Over the past two decades the decline in union membership among blue-collar workers has been compensated by the rapid growth of union membership among government employees.

Public attitudes toward unions and the role they play in American life have remained strong in the face of these statistical trends. A poll conducted in 1982 found that 60 percent of the people surveyed thought unions were needed and 56 percent thought nonunion workers would be better off if they belonged to a union. However, 57 percent of the same group thought union leaders were out of touch with their membership.[9]

[9] Barry Sussman, "Americans Favor Labor Unions, But Hold Leaders in Disrepute," *Washington Post*, February 7, 1982, p. A2.

Summary

The labor force has undergone dramatic changes in the past three decades. It is younger, more female, and less unionized today than in the mid-1950s. Throughout this century there has been a shift away from agricultural employment, as tremendous technological change has made agricultural production so efficient that only about 3 percent of the work force is needed to feed the rest of the American population—and a good share of the world population. As our economy has matured, demand has shifted from tangible goods production to the provision of services, and this shows up in the proportions of the labor force engaged in these types of economic activity.

Demographic changes in the population and trends toward earlier retirement have combined to make the labor force younger today than it has ever been. These trends will change by the end of the century as members of the postwar baby boom mature and members of the next generation, smaller in size, reach their early twenties. Economic exigencies and problems with financing the social security system will probably push retirement ages upward to even out somewhat the age composition of the labor force.

Changing social attitudes, the rising number of female-headed households, and growing financial need have worked together to increase the number of women in the labor force, compared with the period before 1960.

For labor union membership, some of these trends have presented problems. The typical blue-collar production worker in manufacturing who belongs to a trade union still is a member of a union, but there are simply fewer of them. White-collar service jobs that do not have a union tradition have been growing in number while manufacturing jobs have been shrinking. As a consequence, the rate of union membership has declined from about 25 percent of the labor force in the mid-1950s to about 18 percent in 1985. The one counteractive trend has been the rapid growth in union membership among government employees. Had this growth not occurred, union membership as a percentage of the total labor force would have declined even further.

I

Labor and the Microeconomy

A. Theory of Wages

3

Wage Theory:
Labor Demand

Today the vast majority of citizens in the United States acquire income through employment. Each employee is paid a wage (if a blue-collar worker) or a salary (if a white-collar worker). No longer is a significant portion of the population sustained by self-sufficient farming or handicrafts, as it was in an earlier time, when people used cash primarily to supplement their in-kind income. Nor do many people receive income exclusively through the ownership of capital.

Labor economics seeks an understanding of wages[1]—how they are established and how they influence the economy. This chapter and the four that follow present several theoretical explanations and empirical studies of the way wages are determined. The determination of wages is the centerpiece of the study of labor economics, and the theory of wage determination is its core.

The modern theory of wages traces its intellectual roots to the latter part of the nineteenth century. Prior to that time the study and practice of economics were dominated by classical political economy. Such names as Adam Smith, Thomas Malthus, David Ricardo, and Karl Marx are identified with this school of economic

---

[1] Although by convention the term *wages* is used throughout this book, salaries are susceptible to the same analysis.

thought. These scholars took as their fundamental issue for exploration the large question of how an economic system functions and changes.

In the latter third of the nineteenth century, this school of thought lost pre-eminence to what is today called *neoclassical economics*. Neoclassical economists study prices—how they are formed in markets, how they influence an individual's behavior in the economic system, and how they affect the way resources are allocated. The basic tool of analysis used by neoclassical economists is *marginalism*, the study of the effect on human behavior of small changes in some economic parameter.

The *marginal calculation*, as it has been called, was developed first by a group of Austrian economists, then transported to Great Britain, where Alfred Marshall intro-duced *neoclassical economics* to the English-speaking world.[2] The essence of the marginal revolution was a shift of emphasis from the grand *macro* dynamics of the evolution of economic systems to the *micro* functioning of markets and the behavior of individuals in an economic system. Concepts of equilibrium and the stationary state replaced those of evolution and change. The marginal analysis lent itself to the mathematics of calculus and to a seeming precision of measurement of economic phenomena. The revolution in the natural sciences of this period influenced economics, which staked an early claim to being the most "scientific" of the social sciences. Economists became enamored with such concepts as *maximization* and with charting responses to minute changes in economic parameters.

Neoclassical Wage Theory: A First Glimpse

Applying their techniques to the analysis of wage determination, the marginalists developed the *neoclassical theory of wages*. The determination of wages in a labor market is treated as a specific instance in the general theory of exchange, in which the interaction in a competitive market of the supply of a commodity and the demand for it results in the determination of its price.

The labor market contains a supply and demand curve as shown in Figure 3-1.[3] The supply curve slopes upward, indicating that individuals can be induced to offer more labor time to the market at higher wages. The downward-sloping demand curve indicates that employers will hire more workers at lower wages.

Only at the wage rate $\overline{W}$ will there be an equilibrium in which the employers will have hired the optimal number of work units and individuals will be content to offer just enough labor time to satisfy employers' needs. No other wage will be sustainable, since forces exist that will thrust the wage rate back to $\overline{W}$. For example, if the wage rate is W_1, the number of hours workers are willing to offer is E_s. This exceeds the

---

[2] Alfred Marshall, *Principles of Economics,* 8th ed. (London: Macmillan and Co., 1920).

[3] On the vertical axis is money wages—the wage received by an individual worker in nominal terms, unadjusted for inflation. On the horizontal axis, employment is measured in terms of hours of work, the product of the number of people working and the average number of hours each works.

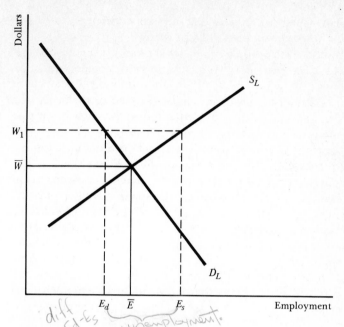

Figure 3-1 Wage Determination: Perfectly Competitive
Labor Market— *market Forces will push it back*

number of work units the employer is willing to pay for at that wage. The employer's
demand for labor at the wage W_1 is E_d, found by reading off the labor demand curve
the number of hours of employment that would be generated at that wage. Thus, the
quantity of labor supplied exceeds the amount of labor demanded at the relatively
high wage rate of W_1. The resulting unemployment (the difference between E_d and
E_s) will cause workers to bid the wage rate *down* as they compete with each other for
the limited employment opportunities available. The wage rate will fall until it reaches
$\overline{W}$ and is once again established at its equilibrium level, where there are no tendencies
to dislodge it.[4]

This process occurs in a *perfectly competitive labor market*. Economists use the term
labor market to refer to a process through which individuals learn about available jobs
and employers learn about potential employees. This can occur nationally or even
internationally. The professor who is teaching you this course was probably hired after
a nationwide search. The employee who serves you in your cafeteria was hired in the
local labor market after a search that did not extend beyond the confines of the city
in which your school is located.

---

[4] A market wage below the equilibrium will create an *excess demand* for labor, leading to a bidding war
among employers, which will force the wage rate back up to the equilibrium level. Go through the reasoning
for this, using a graph like Figure 3-1 to demonstrate the proposition.

Consider what happens when you return home for the summer and look for summer employment. Now you are a supplier of labor attempting to sell your labor services in a competitive labor market. If you try for a job at a fast food establishment, you encounter a market that begins to approximate the perfectly competitive labor market economists talk about.

The skills and talents you offer are probably similar to those of the dozens of other applicants for the jobs available. If there are many fast-food establishments in your hometown, no one employer will be so large that his or her employment decisions affect the wage rate paid. The wages paid by all employers will be roughly the same.

A perfectly competitive labor market, therefore, consists of many buyers and sellers and extends geographically as far as necessary to encompass the range of choices available to the buyers and sellers. In this labor market a common wage rate prevails. The suppliers of labor are essentially identical in skills and talents. The employers of labor are small enough that their employment decisions do not influence the wage.

Changes in Labor Supply and Demand: The Baby Boom and the Labor Force

The labor demand and supply curves shown in Figure 3-1 relate only two variables in the labor market: the wage rate and the amount of labor either supplied or demanded. In this chapter and the next we will examine in considerable detail what goes into deriving the slopes of these labor demand and supply curves. Other elements of the economy can affect labor demand and supply, however. They do so by shifting either the labor demand or supply curve. It is critically important, therefore, to distinguish between aspects of the economy that cause the curves to shift and those that produce movements along a labor demand or supply curve. Movements along the labor demand and supply curves are governed by behavioral responses to wage changes, summarized in the concept of elasticity which we will introduce in this chapter and extend in the next chapter.

Shifts in labor demand and supply occur when something happens that dislodges the curves from their existing position. To illustrate this process, let us look at what is called the baby boom and how it affects shifts in labor demand and supply. From the late 1940s until the early 1960s the birth rate increased substantially in the United States. This single demographic phenomenon produced some dramatic instabilities in labor markets, particularly in the markets for teachers.

In Figure 3-2 (panel A) the labor market for primary school teachers is shown before the impact of the baby boom made its presence felt in the labor market. As the higher stock of new babies aged, however, and began to enter primary school, suddenly the school systems in the United States experienced over-crowded classrooms and an increased demand for more teachers, as well as buildings and classrooms. This caused the demand for teachers to increase from D_{L1} to D_{L2}. At the old wage rate of W_1

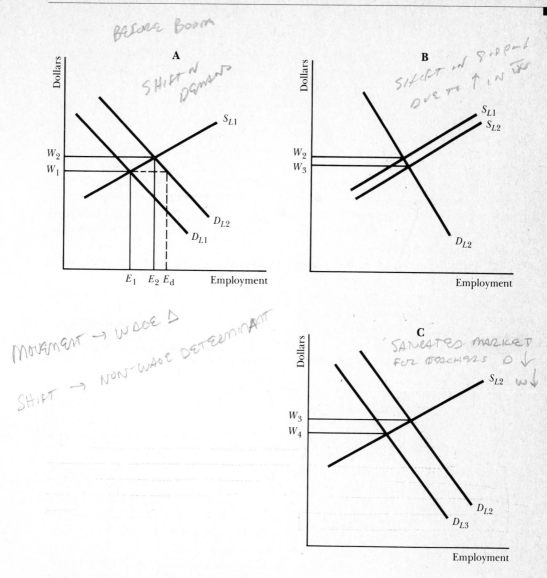

BEFORE BOOM

A

SHIFT N DEMAND

MOVEMENT → WAGE Δ

SHIFT → NON-WAGE DETERMINANT

B

SHIFT IN SUPPLY DUE TO ↑ IN W

C

SATURATED MARKET FOR TEACHERS D ↓

S_{L2} W ↓

Figure 3-2. Labor Market for Teachers

there is now an excess demand for teachers, the difference between E_1 and E_d. Any excess demand such as this will tend to bid the wage upward toward W_2.

The story does not end here, however. A higher wage for teachers will tend to influence individuals' choice of careers, and more will major in teaching. University enrollments in education majors grow and more teachers enter the labor market, causing the labor supply curve for teachers to increase. This is shown in the right-hand diagram on Figure 3-2, labelled B. There is no necessary increase in labor supply that can be specified because each individual is making his or her own decision about a future career and a college major. Labor supply could overshoot the demand of this labor market or undershoot it. As shown, simply for illustrative purposes, the supply of labor increases in response to the higher wage for teachers, from S_{L1} to S_{L2}, and the wage settles at W_3.

The demographics of the baby boom continue to have their impact felt as the natural consequence of aging unfolds. Most of you were probably born after the baby boom, and when you entered primary school, there was already an excess supply of teachers. The demand for teachers took a precipitous fall. With the existing supply of teachers plus those in the process of being trained in universities, the labor market for teachers was more than saturated. This is illustrated in Diagram C in Figure 3-2. The demand for teachers falls to D_{L3} and the wage to W_4. Students entering college no longer find teaching an attractive career as signalled by the lower wage rate emanating from the labor market.

The story about the impact of the baby boom generation and its affects on labor markets could be extended indefinitely. Suffice to say that it has had, and is still having, a significant impact on the demand for and supply of many categories of labor. Think for a moment about its implications as this population ages and begins to retire— what the effects in labor markets will be for those occupations in the health professions that service older people. And what will be its implications for funding the social security system from the wages and salaries you will be earning and paying into the system?

This phenomenon of the baby boom and the process of its maturation has been likened to a boa constrictor swallowing a mongoose. You can watch it pass through the snake, observing its bulges, much the same as the baby boom passing through the economy creates bulges in the labor market at different times and for different types of labor. This illustrates the important uses of the most elementary labor demand and supply analysis in which the distinction between movements along a labor demand or supply curve is separated from shifts in the curves caused by some change outside of the two-dimensional relationship between the wage rate and the quantities of labor that are either supplied or demanded. Although this point may appear to be elementary, policy makers continue to make serious mistakes because they fail to realize that the labor market produces its own responses to wage signals that may overshoot the adjustment required by some short-term and ephemeral shift in labor demand.

The General Nature of Labor Supply and Demand

In many ways, the market for labor is similar to the market for any other commodity. It has a supply curve and a demand curve; the interaction produces an equilibrium price. Competition governs the market and regulates its orderly functioning. To the extent these conditions hold true, the general theory of exchange can be applied to the labor market.

In some important ways, however, the market for labor is unique. The motivations to demand labor (on the part of employers) and to supply labor (on the part of individuals) are *derived* from other objectives. The employer who demands labor does so in order to employ it as a factor of production that will help create a product, which can then be sold on the market to make a profit. The individual who supplies labor sees work as a way of acquiring income to purchase goods and services.

The labor market by definition involves the buying and selling of a *human* resource—labor services. Compared with other, nonhuman commodities, the exchange of labor on a market presents unique problems. Once you buy an ice cream cone, the process of consuming it is relatively simple: You eat it. When a laborer's services are purchased on a labor market, however, problems arise in the use of those services. Conflicts over how the labor services are to be utilized are endemic to the environment in which labor is employed to produce a product.

Karl Polanyi, a social scientist from another era, described the uniqueness of labor among commodities as follows: "Labor is only another name for a human activity which goes with life itself, which in turn is not produced for sale but for entirely different reasons, nor can that activity be detached from the rest of life. . . ."[5]

What follows in this chapter is a discussion of the determinants of the demand for labor in the firm. Firms combine to make up the totality of the demand for labor in a market, but to understand the market we must first look at how a typical firm makes its decisions to employ labor.

Demand for Labor in the Firm: Initial Observations

The firm's demand for labor depends on two elements: the *technology* it uses to produce output and the *monetary value* that output acquires when it is sold on a product market. The technology used by the firm is summarized in its *production function*, which describes the way in which labor and capital are combined to produce output. In the neoclassical theory, the firm is presumed to use the most efficient technology available. The issue of choice of technology is not a problem to be analyzed in the initial development of the neoclassical theory of labor demand.

When examining the demand for labor, all other elements of the economy are held fixed. This condition, called *ceteris paribus*, is used to simplify the discussion of labor demand. For example, the prices of other factors of production (such as capital) are held fixed while we examine the demand for labor. Technology is held fixed. Toward the end of this chapter, some of these assumptions are relaxed, and the consideration of changes in these other elements is introduced into the analysis.

The *period* in which the firm makes its decisions about how much labor to employ is the *short run*. In the short run, the firm takes its capital stock as fixed, and the only

---

[5] Karl Polanyi, *The Great Transformation* (Boston: Beacon Press, 1944), p. 72.

[handwritten: LABOR — A VARIABLE RESOURCE IN THE SHORT RUN]

decision it has to make is how much of the *variable* factor of production, labor, it wishes to employ in order to *maximize its profits*.

The institutional environment in which the firm operates is *perfect competition* in labor and product markets.[6] This is a condition in which all the firms operating in a particular labor market are so small that their decisions concerning employment have no effect on the wage rate that is determined in the labor market. The firms have perfect information about the markets in which they operate, and no one firm is large enough to influence the price charged for its product. All the firms make roughly the same product. In other words, there is *product homogeneity.* Product differentiation, which would enable one firm to break out of the competitive pack and charge a different price from the one dictated by market conditions, does not exist. A uniform wage prevails in any specific labor market. In short, all the firms are *price and wage takers*. They passively receive information about prices and wages from the market in which they operate, and they make employment and production decisions within the constraints imposed by the labor and product markets.

[handwritten: HOMOGENITY → "SAME PRODUCT"]

Combining Labor with Capital: The Law of Diminishing Returns

[handwritten: SHORT RUN → VAR. LABOR + FIXED TECH.]

Operating with the most efficient technology available, the firm, in the short run, adds labor (a variable factor of production) to a fixed stock of capital. Adding increasing amounts of labor to a fixed stock of capital yields increased output in a particular way. In most cases each of the first few units of labor added to a fixed capital stock leads to increasing amounts of output that grow at an *increasing rate of change*. This is called the stage of *increasing returns*. Adding labor to a fixed capital stock typically increases output at an *increasing rate* if capital is underutilized. Once the fixed stock of capital is used more efficiently, however, a stage of *decreasing returns* begins, in which additional units of labor add to output but at a decreasing rate.

 For example, suppose that you manage to land a summer job in the fast-food establishment mentioned earlier. You are the fifth person hired. Before you were hired, there were two cooks to tend three grills, and there were two counter people. You are hired to tend the third grill. Probably in this set of circumstances the output of this establishment will grow at an increasing rate when you are hired. Not only do you contribute to output yourself but you also enable the other four employees to work more productively. Until you started work, the firm was underutilizing its fixed capital stock by having only two people tending three grills. This stage of increasing returns is typically short-lived, however, lasting only until the employer discovers the best way to use the capital stock.

---

[6] In subsequent chapters, imperfect competition in labor and product markets is analyzed.

POINT → WHEN CAPITAL IS UNDER UTILIZED.

As the sixth, seventh, eighth, and ninth workers are hired, output continues to grow, but the *rate* of increase in output starts to decline. The sixth employee might be used to tend the counter, the seventh to work on the grill, the eighth to tend the counter also, and the ninth to clean up. At some point, the number of employees create some congestion so that the rate of increase in output, though still positive, begins to decrease.

The law that governs this phenomenon is called the *law of diminishing returns.*[7] An important principle of production theory, it states that adding a variable factor of production to a fixed factor may yield increasing returns per unit of input initially—when capital is underutilized—but that diminishing returns set in as more of the variable factor of production is added to the fixed factor of production.

The reasoning behind this law is inherent in the everyday operations of a factory or a fast-food establishment. Once the optimal number of people are tending the machinery, additional workers tend to cause logjams, overloading the fixed number of machines and buildings with which they have to work.

This important law has an influence on the demand for labor by the firm. Because employing additional people yields additional output but only at a decreasing rate of growth, the firm's demand for labor is not insatiable. It butts up against the technological imperative that employing more individuals in the short run produces positive benefits for the employer in terms of additional output but only at a declining rate of growth.

The Marginal Product of Labor

As firms *add* labor to the production process, *additional* output occurs. The words *add* and *additional* are emphasized because in the neoclassical theory of the firm it is the *incremental changes* that are important for decision making, not average relationships. The part of neoclassical theory that applies to labor demand is called the *marginal productivity theory of labor demand* to indicate its reliance on the study of change at the margin. The firm is like the summer bather considering a dip in the ocean, testing the water with one toe to see if she wants to go further. The manager of the firm in neoclassical theory tests the waters by adding a little of some factor of production (in this case, labor) to see how profits are affected.

Basic to this theory is the concept of the *marginal product of labor.* The marginal product of labor measures the additional output produced by adding one more unit of labor. It is the ratio of the change in output to the change in labor input. Referring back to the discussion of the law of diminishing returns, we see that the marginal

---

[7] Also called the *law of variable proportions.*

MP_L = MEASURES THE ADDITIONAL OUTPUT PRODUCED BY ADDING 1 MORE UNIT OF LABOR.

Table 3-1 The Marginal Product of Labor

Labor Inputs (E)	Output (Q)	Change in Output (ΔQ)	Change in Labor Input (ΔE)	Marginal Product of Labor (ΔQ/ΔE)
(1)	(2)	(3)	(4)	(5)
0	0	0	0	0
1	20	20	1	20
2	45	25	1	25
3	95	50	1	50
4	143	48	1	48
5	183	40	1	40
6	215	32	1	32
7	237	22	1	22
8	247	10	1	10
9	252	5	1	5
10	240	− 12	1	− 12

$\dfrac{\Delta Q}{\Delta E}$

$MP_L \approx$

product of labor tells us whether an additional unit of labor will increase output at a higher or lower rate than the previous unit of labor added.

A numerical example will help explain the concept of the marginal product of labor. Table 3-1 shows how the level of production in a typical firm might be affected by the use of one factor of production, labor, holding capital constant. Column 1 shows the amount of labor employed and column 2 the resulting output. The third column indicates the change in output, and the fourth shows the change in the number of units of labor. Column 5 is the schedule of the marginal product of labor, showing the additional output from the use of each additional unit of labor. More precisely, it is the change in output divided by the change in labor input, or column 3 divided by column 4. The marginal product of labor increases up to the fourth unit of labor. Then it declines as more units of labor are used, because of the law of diminishing returns.

On a graph that relates change in output per additional labor inputs (on the vertical axis) to employment units (on the horizontal axis), the curve representing the marginal product of labor will first rise and then start to decline, as shown in Figure 3-3. The rational firm will always employ labor in the range of diminishing returns indicated by the segment *ab*. Beyond *b* the firm actually loses output by employing more units of labor. Up to *a* the firm could continue to do better by expanding employment, because higher levels of employment would yield proportionally greater increases in output. Employing more workers up to *a* makes the previously employed workers more productive.

The marginal product of labor and the law of diminishing returns give us an idea of why and how firms might employ labor. They employ labor in order to expand

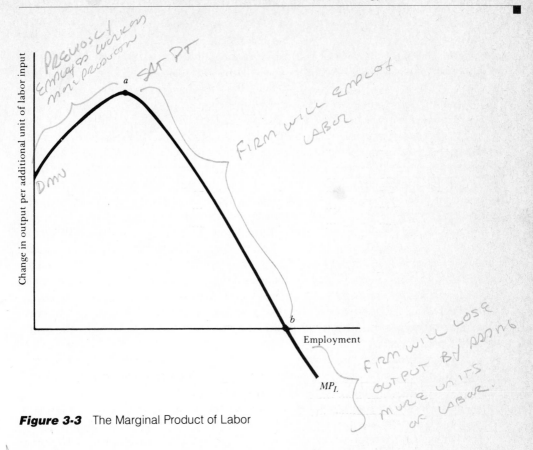

Handwritten annotations: PREVIOUSLY EMPLOYED WORKERS MORE PRODUCTIVE

SAT PT

Dmv

FIRM WILL EMPLOY LABOR

FIRM WILL LOSE OUTPUT BY ADDING MORE UNITS OF LABOR.

Figure 3-3   The Marginal Product of Labor

output. But their ability to expand output is limited by the conditions of technology, which are fixed, as is the firm's capital stock in the short run.

The Firm's Demand for Labor: Technology and Product Markets

In the analysis thus far, marginal productivity has been stated in *physical terms:* the additional output produced by the employment of an additional unit of labor. Dealing in a money economy, however, the firm is interested in the *monetary return* each additional unit of labor yields. Hence, it is concerned with the monetary *value* of the marginal product of labor. The *value of the marginal product of labor (VMP_L)* is found by multiplying the marginal product of labor by the price at which each unit of output is sold by the firm on the product market. The value of the marginal product of labor tells us the *average* amount of revenue the firm receives for the additional units of output produced by an additional unit of labor.

Returning to your summer employment in the fast-food establishment, suppose the addition of you as an employee enables this firm to produce 10 more hamburgers

Handwritten at bottom: VMP = MP × PRICE/UNIT → THE MONETARY VALUE OF THE MPL.

per hour than it could without you. Your marginal product is 10 hamburgers. If these hamburgers sell for $1.50 each, then the *value* of your marginal product to the owner is $15 per hour.

Although the average revenue received from your contribution of 10 hamburgers per hour is of interest to the owner of the fast-food establishment, the neoclassical model suggests that he should be even more interested in the *additional (or marginal) revenue* he receives for each additional hamburger produced and sold. If the fast-food establishment in which you are employed sells its hamburgers in a perfectly competitive market, the marginal revenue it receives for each hamburger will be $1.50, the same as the price of the hamburger. So the marginal revenue product you contribute will be the same as the value of your marginal product—$15 per hour.

Let us state this idea in a more formal way. In the neoclassical model of the economy, decisions are made "at the margin." Firms are more interested in the *additional revenue* the next unit of output will yield than they are in the average revenue. The additional revenue obtained from the last unit of labor hired is called the *marginal revenue product of labor (MRP$_L$)*, the revenue received from selling the additional output that is produced as a result of hiring an additional unit of labor. The marginal revenue product of labor is found by multiplying the marginal product of labor by the firm's marginal revenue.[8]

If there is perfect competition in the product market in which the firm operates, the market price *equals* the marginal revenue, so the value of the marginal product of labor equals the marginal revenue product of labor.[9] This occurs because each firm is so small, and sells such a minute fraction of the total sold in the market, that its decision concerning how much output to bring to the market has no effect on product price. The firm is a price taker—a passive recipient of price information provided to it by the market. Moreover, all the firms produce and sell identical products. There can be no price advantage obtained from product differentiation. Under these conditions of perfect competition, price equals marginal revenue, and as a result the MRP_L and the VMP_L are also equal.

Although perfect competition simplifies the analysis of the firm's demand for labor, it is important to understand the difference between the marginal revenue product of labor and the value of the marginal product of labor. In imperfect competition, which will be taken up in a later chapter, the two indicators of labor demand diverge, and confusing them can produce important differences in the outcome of the analysis.

[8] Note the difference between this concept and that of the value of the marginal product of labor. The VMP_L is the *product price* multiplied by the marginal product of labor, while the MRP_L is the *marginal revenue* multiplied by the marginal product of labor.

[9] The firm in perfect competition faces a perfectly elastic demand curve for its output—it can sell as many units as is profitable at the prevailing market price. In the following diagram, the firm's marginal cost of labor is shown (MC_L), assuming labor is the only variable factor of production, along with the product

PERFECT COMPETITION < MARKET PRICE = MR
So VMP$_L$ = MRP$_L$

A numerical example will help explain the concepts of the VMP_L and the MRP_L. Table 3-2 extends the example presented in Table 3-1, incorporating the influence of the market in which the firm sells its product. Since the firm's decisions start with the phase of diminishing returns, Table 3-2 begins with the fourth unit of labor employed.

The first five columns are identical to those in Table 3-1. Column 6 shows the price at which the firm sells its product. The price is the same ($1.25) for each unit of output, no matter how many products the firm brings to the market to sell because of perfect competition. The value of the marginal product of labor, found by multiplying the product price by the marginal product of labor, is shown in column 7. The additional revenues obtained by the firm by selling additional units of output are indicated in column 8, and column 9 shows the marginal revenue product of labor, found by multiplying the marginal revenue (column 8) by the marginal product of labor (column 5).

We are now ready to provide an answer to the question: What is the firm's demand for labor based on? The firm's demand for labor is described by the schedule of its *marginal revenue product of labor,* the monetary returns for each additional unit of labor employed. This is shown in column 9 of Table 3-2 and in Figure 3-4.

---

demand curve, D. At product price P, Average revenue (AR) equals marginal revenue (MR) across all levels of output, and the firm sets its output level at $\bar{Q}$, where $MC = MR$.

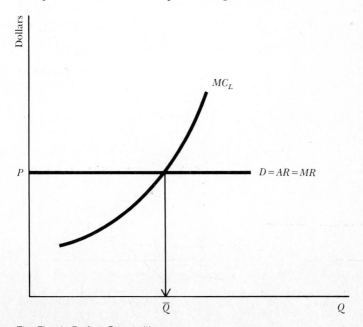

The Firm in Perfect Competition

Table 3-2 The Value of the Marginal Product of Labor and Marginal Revenue Product of Labor

Labor Inputs (E)	Output (Q)	Change in Output (ΔQ)	Cange in Labor Input (ΔE)	Marginal Product of Labor ($\Delta Q/\Delta E$)	Product Price (P)	Value of the Marginal Product of Labor (P)($\Delta Q/\Delta E$)	Marginal Revenue (ΔR)	Marginal Revenue Product of Labor (ΔR)($\Delta Q/\Delta E$)
(1)	(2)	(3)	(4)	(5)	(6)	(7)	(8)	(9)
4	143	48	1	48	$1.25	$60.00	$1.25	$60.00
5	183	40	1	40	1.25	50.00	1.25	50.00
6	215	32	1	32	1.25	40.00	1.25	40.00
7	237	22	1	22	1.25	27.50	1.25	27.50
8	247	10	1	10	1.25	12.50	1.25	12.50
9	252	5	1	5	1.25	6.25	1.25	6.25
10	240	− 12	1	− 12	1.25	− 15.00	1.25	− 15.00

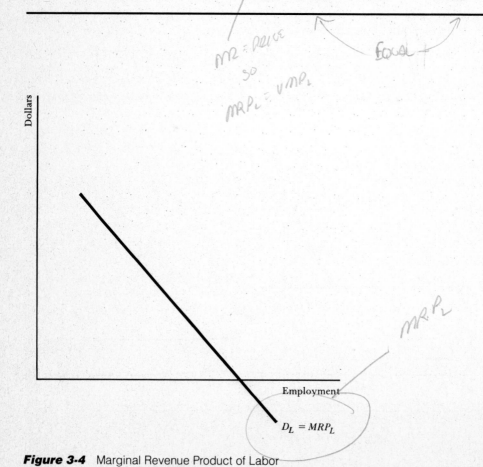

Figure 3-4 Marginal Revenue Product of Labor

The Level of Employment in the Firm

The problem confronting the firm is to find the level of employment that will maximize its profits. In making this determination, the firm must first take into account the marginal revenue brought in by the output of the workers it hires. This information defines the demand curve for labor, which we have just derived. In addition to revenues, the firm must also consider the *costs* of employing labor. These costs are represented by the *wage rate.*

In the fast-food restaurant in which you are working during the summer, you are paid the prevailing market wage for this type of work. Let us say this wage is $3.35 per hour, which is the present statutory minimum wage rate and the typical wage paid for entry-level jobs in the fast-food industry. Therefore, the marginal (or additional) cost of hiring you for an hour is $3.35, or the prevailing wage.

The question before the manager of this enterprise was whether to hire you at this wage. The answer hinged on the marginal revenues you would produce. As we hypothesized earlier in our development of this example, the marginal revenue product you create for this establishment is $15 per hour. You are paid only $3.35 per hour. Clearly, it is to the advantage of this manager to employ you, because you produce a net return at the margin (marginal profit) of $11.65 per hour. Marginal revenue exceeds marginal cost, so the employer should hire you.

This may appear to be an excessive profit on your labor, but recall that you were only the fifth person hired and that the establishment was not yet working efficiently. Therefore, *your* marginal product is very high, but marginal product starts to fall sharply, because of the law of diminishing returns, by the time the eighth or ninth worker is hired. Since each of you is paid the same wage, however, those employed first contribute most at the margin to the firm's revenues.

The firm in perfect competition has no influence on the wage rate which is determined in the labor market. Because the firm hires a very small proportion of the total amount of labor in the market, its decision about employing labor has no appreciable effect on the wage rate. The firm can hire as many workers as it wants at the prevailing wage; in effect, the supply of labor to the firm is infinite.

The firm reaches a conclusion about how much labor to employ in order to maximize profits once the wage rate and the marginal revenue product curve for labor are known. This is shown in Table 3-3, which continues the example of Table 3-2. The figures used in Table 3-2 have been extended, but only the labor input and marginal revenue product of labor columns have been repeated, because they are the only ones from Table 3-2 needed to illustrate the employment decision in the firm. If the wage rate is $5 per hour and each worker is employed for eight hours per day, the cost of hiring each worker for a day is $40. In column 3 these wage costs are shown. The firm can hire as many people as it likes at that wage, so each added unit of labor costs another $40 per day.

How many people should this firm employ? The answer is six. For the sixth employee the wage costs just equal the marginal revenue product. If the firm employed

Table 3-3 Employment Decisions in the Firm

Labor Inputs	Marginal Revenue Product of Labor	Wage Costs per Worker (per day)	Marginal Profit (2)−(3)
(1)	(2)	(3)	(4)
4	$60.00	$40.00	$20.00
5	50.00	40.00	10.00
6	40.00	40.00	0
7	27.50	40.00	− 12.50
8	12.50	40.00	− 27.50
9	6.25	40.00	− 33.75
10	− 15.00	40.00	− 55.00

only four units of labor, it would not be making as much profit as it could. The firm would be paying $40 for the fourth worker but receiving $60 in return for his or her labor. Thus, it would pay the employer to add another worker. With six workers the return received at the margin just equals the costs at the margin.[10] If the firm hired fewer than six workers, it would not be making as much profit as its cost constraint permits.

Hiring more than six workers, on the other hand, would lose money for the firm. The seventh worker would cost the employer $40 but return only $27.50. That worker would not be paying his or her way and would in fact reduce profits for the firm. Six workers is, therefore, the optimal level of employment for this firm, given wage costs, product price, and the technology.

By hiring six workers, the firm has followed the *profit-maximizing rule of equating marginal revenue and marginal cost*. Marginal revenue is represented by the marginal revenue product of labor and marginal cost by wage costs. The firm's decision process for the amount of labor to employ can be understood with the assistance of a graph, Figure 3-5, which shows how many units of labor the firm could employ at different wage rates. The function relating the employment level to the wage rate is the marginal revenue product of labor curve, which is also the labor demand curve. The firm operating in a perfectly competitive labor market will take the wage rate as given, since the firm is so small that its employment decisions do not affect the wage rate. In effect, the horizontal function indicated by the market wage ($\overline{W}$) in Figure 3-5 is

---

[10] This is shown in the fourth column, labeled "marginal profit." To be more precise, the employer will be indifferent between hiring five or six workers, since the sixth worker has a marginal profit of zero. This ambiguity arises in a real world example because an employer can hire only discrete units of labor. What the employer will do in this instance is use the sixth worker for something less than eight hours per day and maximize profits by using one worker on a part-time basis.

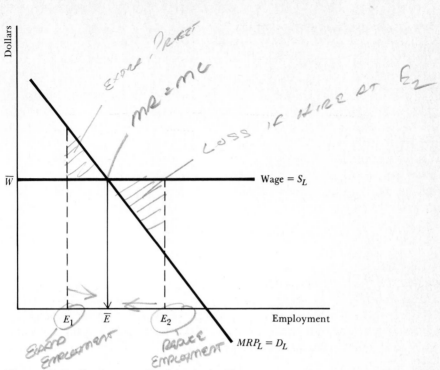

Figure 3-5 Employment Decision in the Firm

the firm's *labor supply curve*, since the firm is free to hire as many people as it needs at that wage.

For the given wage, $\overline{W}$, the firm will employ $\overline{E}$ units of labor in equilibrium. This is not only an equilibrium condition; it is also the level of employment that maximizes profits, because marginal revenue and marginal cost are equal only at that level of employment. To see why this is an equilibrium condition, consider what happens if the firm employs E_1 units of labor. In this instance profits would be *less* than they are at $\overline{E}$. The marginal revenue product of labor, the return provided by an additional unit of labor, exceeds the wage, the cost of an additional unit of labor. If labor returns more to the firm than it is costing, it is rational for the firm to expand employment until marginal revenue equals marginal cost, at point $\overline{E}$.

If E_2 units of labor were employed, the employment level would be sub-optimal because losses would be incurred on the production of all the workers beyond $\overline{E}$. Those workers would not be paying their way, since they would cost the firm more than they returned in additional revenue. As shown by the graph, the wage exceeds the marginal revenue product of labor at all levels of employment beyond $\overline{E}$. If the current level of employment is E_1, the profit-maximizing firm should expand employment; if the level is E_2, the firm should reduce employment to $\overline{E}$—the point of stable equilibrium.

The Marginal Revenue Products and Salaries of Professional Basketball Players

How can you compute the contribution to revenue made at the margin by the last individual hired, separate from all the other employees? This perplexing empirical problem has made it difficult, if not impossible, for economists to estimate directly the marginal revenue product of an individual employee. And if we do not know the marginal revenue product of a particular employee, it is not possible to say whether workers are paid more or less than their marginal revenue products.

Only when labor markets deviate from the perfectly competitive norm can we assign a marginal revenue product to a particular employee. Two areas where this is possible are professional sports and entertainment. Though not the perfectly competitive labor market of neoclassical theory, entertainment and professional sports are businesses that permit estimation of individual marginal revenue products.

Thomas P. Frazier, a student in my graduate seminar in labor economics, conducted a very interesting study of professional basketball.[11] He estimated the marginal revenue products of particular basketball players and compared those with the players' salaries. Adapting a model developed for baseball,[12] Frazier calculated first the relationship between a team's winning percentage and the revenues generated from attendance and radio and television broadcasts. He found that increasing a team's winning percentage from 50 percent to 60 percent produced marginal revenues for the team's owners of $514,800, based on figures for the 1978–79 and 1979–80 seasons.

Once he had estimated the marginal revenue associated with increasing the winning percentage, Frazier's next step was to estimate each player's contribution to an increase in the winning percentage, that is, the player's "marginal product." Once the "marginal product" had been estimated, it could be multiplied by the marginal revenue to find the player's marginal revenue product.

To estimate each player's "marginal product," Frazier considered the player's contributions to both offense and defense. For offense he used the average number of points scored per game, weighted by the number of minutes played.[13] For defense he used three variables: number of defensive rebounds, number of blocked shots, and number of steals.

Table 3-4 contains the results of this study for several players in the National Basketball Association in 1979–80. The marginal revenue products were computed by taking each player's contribution to his team's winning percentage and multiplying it by the marginal revenue from a one-percentage-point improvement in the team's

---

[11] Thomas P. Frazier, "Pay and Performance in the National Basketball Association," (April 1981).

[12] G. W. Scully, "Pay and Performance in Major League Baseball," *American Economic Review* 64, no. 6 (December 1974), pp. 915–30.

[13] This method is a bit flawed, as Frazier himself says in the paper, because it ignores "externalities," i.e., one player's contribution to another player's performance. *Marginal product* is placed in quotation marks to indicate that it only roughly corresponds to the pure theory of marginal productivity.

Table 3-4 Estimated Marginal Revenue Products and Salaries for Selected NBA Players

Player	Team	Estimated MRP	Salary[a]	Ratio: Salary/MRP
Larry Bird	Boston	$606,597	$600,000	0.99
Julius Erving	Philadelphia	673,338	600,000	0.89
Kareem Abdul-Jabbar	Los Angeles	788,820	725,000	0.92
Tom McMillen	Atlanta	106,446	120,000	1.13
Quinn Buckner	Milwaukee	207,861	175,000	0.84
Bill Lambert	Cleveland	51,362	100,000	1.94
Elvin Hayes	Washington	698,445	688,185	0.99

[a]These data are unofficial and are not in a common-year dollar base.

record. For all but one player there is a close association between estimated marginal revenue product and salary. Even though these salaries seem very high to the typical sports fan, in most instances the salary is justified by the player's contribution to the owner's marginal revenue product.[14]

$$E_d = \frac{\text{SENSATIVITY}}{d v} \text{ of EMPLOYMENT to } \Delta \text{ WAGES}$$

Wage Changes and Employment Changes: The Elasticity of Demand for Labor

When wages change in the labor market, whether because of trade union activity, government actions, or changes in labor market conditions, there are repercussions in the firm in terms of its employment decision. The extent to which the employment level in a firm is changed in response to wage changes is governed by the *elasticity of demand* for labor in the firm. The elasticity of demand reflects the sensitivity of employment to changes in wages.

The size of the elasticity of demand for labor is important for public policy purposes, and it is crucial for a trade union leader to know. For example, whether or not increases in the minimum wage will increase unemployment (a matter of frequent debate) depends on the elasticity of demand for those workers currently receiving the minimum wage. And the trade union leader, when told by management that the wage increase he wants will raise unemployment for his members, must know the size of the elasticity of demand for workers in his union in order to be able to respond intelligently.

---

[14] The last column of the table shows the ratio of salary to MRP. For Bill Lambert the ratio diverges substantially from 1. However, he is only an average player who never fulfilled his owner's performance expectations.

The elasticity of demand for labor is defined as the percentage change in labor employed in response to the percentage change in wages. The arithmetic formula for labor demand elasticity is:

$$\frac{\Delta E}{E} \bigg/ \frac{\Delta W}{W}$$

where E is employment, W is the wage, and the Greek letter Δ indicates "change."

Table 3-5 shows how this elasticity would be calculated for two different hypothetical cases. The elasticity of demand for labor is 0.6 in Case I and 2.0 in Case II.[15] The demand for labor in Case I is described as *inelastic* because the percentage reduction in labor employed is *less* than the percentage increase in wages, producing an elasticity of *less than 1*. In Case II, however, the percentage reduction in employment is *greater* than the percentage increase in wages. This is described as an *elastic* demand for labor, since the elasticity is *greater than 1*.

A situation in which the percentage increase in wages is exactly equal to the percentage reduction in employment would yield an elasticity *equal to 1*. This is called *unitary elasticity*.

What determines the size of the elasticity of demand for labor? An answer this question was provided by Alfred Marshall around the turn of the century and modified slightly by the British economist J. R. Hicks in the 1930s.[16] They identified four elements that affect the elasticity of demand for labor:

1. The easier it is to substitute capital for labor in response to a wage increase, the more elastic will be the demand for labor.[17] The ease of substitution is determined by the technology used by the firm. If labor can be replaced by capital, higher wages will lead to a proportionally greater decrease in labor employed; the demand for labor will be elastic.

2. If the demand for the firm's *product* is relatively elastic, the demand for labor will be elastic as well. This proposition follows from the fact that the demand for labor is a derived demand and depends in part on conditions in the product market. The more elastic are the conditions faced by the firm in the product market, the more elastic will be the labor demand curve, because higher labor costs will lead

---

[15] Demand for elasticities for labor are always *negative*, since *higher* wages lead to *reductions* in labor employed. By convention, however, the negative sign is not reproduced every time something is said about demand elasticity; the direction of change is understood. Elasticity calculations are always specific to the point of initial employment. Start from a different employment level, and the same absolute changes in employment will yield different elasticities. Using the numbers in Table 3-5, start from an initial employment level of 45 and compute the elasticities for the same absolute changes in employment: -3 in Case I and -10 in Case II.

[16] Marshall, *Principles of Economics*, bk. 5, chap. 6; J. R. Hicks, *The Theory of Wages*, 2nd ed. (New York: St. Martin's Press, 1963), chap. 1.

[17] The possibility of substituting capital for labor modifies the *ceteris paribus* condition, but it is necessary to do this in the discussion of elasticity of demand for labor.

Table 3-5   The Elasticity of Labor Demand

	Initial Employment	Employment after Increase in Wages	Change in Employment	Initial Wage per Hour	Higher Wage per Hour	Change in Wage per Hour
Case I	40	37	− 3	$4.00	$4.50	+ $0.50
Case II	40	30	− 10	4.00	4.50	+ 0.50

Elasticity of demand, Case I: $e = \dfrac{-3}{40} \bigg/ \dfrac{0.50}{4.00} = -0.6$

Elasticity of demand, Case II: $e = \dfrac{-10}{40} \bigg/ \dfrac{0.50}{4.00} = -2.00$

to a more than proportionate decline in sales. This decline will be reflected as a decrease in the demand for labor in the firm.

3. If labor costs are a high percentage of the firm's total costs, then, other things equal, the demand for labor will be elastic. When labor costs are a high percentage of total costs, the firm must raise its product price significantly in response to a wage increase. Depending upon the elasticity of demand for the firm's product, this will affect the elasticity of the firm's demand for labor.

4. The demand for labor will be elastic if the firm has an abundant supply of other inputs to call on. The existence of abundant substitutes means that the price of these factors of production will become relatively attractive and labor can be more readily replaced when wages increase.

In the past 25 years, a fifth factor has been identified—the *fixed cost* of labor.[18] The demand for labor will be more *inelastic* the greater the investment the employer has made in training that is specific to his firm. The amount of this *human capital* investment will depend on the skill levels needed by the workers to perform their tasks efficiently. The firm does not want to lose its investment by laying off employees. Consequently when wages increase, it will tend to hoard the labor in which it has a substantial investment, especially if it has not yet reaped all the returns from the investment. Other fixed costs associated with labor are recruitment costs, severance pay, and the higher unemployment insurance taxes that come with layoffs.[19]

In considering the dismissal of an employee in the face of higher wages, the firm must weigh the marginal returns of the dismissal against the marginal costs of

---

[18] Walter Y. Oi, "Labor as a Quasi-Fixed Factor," *Journal of Political Economy* 70 (December 1962), pp. 538–55.

[19] Consider what might happen to you if the minimum wage were increased from $3.35 per hour to $3.50 per hour and you were employed in the fast-food establishment. Under what circumstances would the demand for your labor and your fellow employees' labor be elastic enough to cause layoffs?

replacement should that necessity arise. The marginal returns are the savings on wages not paid, while the marginal costs are the search and training costs needed to bring a new employee up to the same level of efficiency as the one dismissed. Consequently, the demand for labor will be less elastic if there is a greater investment in human capital—relative to the wage—associated with the tasks performed by the workers.

Aside from the five factors already mentioned, the time period is also important. For all firms, no matter what the status of the five factors that affect elasticity, the *longer* the time period, the *more elastic* will be the demand for labor. In the short run, there are tighter limits on substituting other factors of production or making other adaptations than there are in the longer run.

Applications of the Elasticity of Labor Demand

The elasticity of labor demand can be applied to numerous situations. A failure to understand and apply the concept can lead to mistakes. For example, when a trade union attempts to negotiate higher wages, a subject we take up in detail later in this book, the public is always told that employment will fall drastically if the union gets its way. But will employment fall? That depends on the elasticity of demand for labor in the company with which the union is negotiating. If the elasticity is high, employment will be reduced substantially. If the demand for labor is inelastic, however, employment may not fall appreciably. In the short run, employment will fall less than it will in the long run.

Empirical estimates of the elasticity of demand for labor show great variation. A negotiator for a labor union should try to find out what the elasticity of demand for labor is in the particular industry in which he or she is negotiating. For example, empirical estimates of the elasticity of demand for labor in the nondurable goods sector of the American economy range from 0.3 in the printing industry to 1.5 in petroleum, with an average of 0.7 for all industries in that sector. In the durable goods sector, elasticities range from 0.1 in the furniture industry to 2.4 in fabricated metals, with an average of 1.5.[20] In a survey of a large number of studies on the elasticity of demand for labor, Daniel Hamermesh concluded that the short-run (one-year) elasticity of demand for labor was 0.15.[21]

Demand elasticity must also be considered in discussions of public policy. For example, debates on minimum wage laws suffer from a lack of attention to the elasticity of demand for labor. Opponents of the minimum wage law conjure up images of enormous reductions in employment as a result of increases in the minimum wage.

---

[20] Roger N. Waud, "Man-Hour Behavior in U.S. Manufacturing: A Neoclassical Interpretation," *Journal of Political Economy* 76 (May–June 1968), pp. 419–20.

[21] The short-run elasticity of demand for labor ranged from a high of 0.35 to a low of 0.05. Daniel Hamermesh, "Econometric Studies of Labor Demand and Their Application to Policy Analysis," *Journal of Human Resources* 11, no. 4 (Fall 1976), pp. 507–25.

However, they fail to produce estimates of the elasticity of demand for labor, and they do not differentiate between the short run and the long run. The proponents show an equal lack of interest in the elasticity of labor demand and instead base their support entirely on equity grounds. The minimum-wage question will be studied more thoroughly in a later chapter, but for now it is important to understand how the elasticity of demand for labor can be used as a critical tool in the debate.

Changes in the Demand for Labor

■

When economists speak of "changes in the demand for labor," they mean *shifts* in the entire marginal revenue product curve for labor. This is shown in Figure 3-6. Such shifts occur whenever the underlying parameters of the demand curve change. A change in the demand for labor, therefore, is caused by a change in the technology, in the conditions in the product market, or in the price of some other factor of production. For example, when the postwar baby boom generation started to attend school in large numbers in the 1960s, an enormous increase in the demand for teachers occurred which would shift the labor demand curve outward, as shown in Figure 3-6.

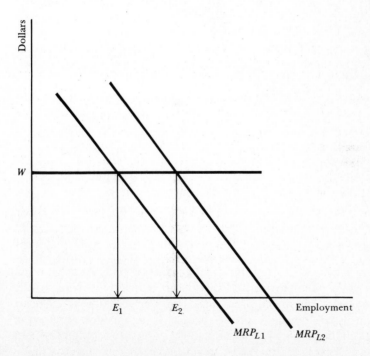

Figure 3-6 Changes in the Demand for Labor in the Firm

It is important to distinguish between *changes* in the demand for labor, which are shifts in the marginal revenue product curve, and *movements along* a labor demand curve. The concept of elasticity of demand for labor governs movements along the curve, which occur when wages change. Shifts in the labor demand curve occur when there are changes in the underlying parameters of the model.

Summary

The neoclassical marginal productivity theory of wages treats labor as a commodity whose price is determined by the interaction of a supply and demand curve. The determination of labor's supply and demand functions presents unusual problems, however, since both the demand for and supply of labor are *derived* from other economic purposes. Households supply labor in order to obtain income, an instrument for satisfying objective and subjective economic needs. Firms demand labor in order to produce a product that will enable them to maximize profits.

In this chapter we examined the derivation of the demand for labor; in the next chapter we will see how the supply of labor is determined. The derivation of the demand for labor starts with the theory of production in the firm. An entrepreneur faces known production technologies when he embarks on the activity of producing a product for sale in the market. The *production function* describes the various combinations of capital and labor that can be used to produce a commodity. In the neoclassical model, it is assumed that the production function embodies the most advanced techniques of production and that the firm's manager has complete knowledge of the most technologically efficient means of production.

From the production function, the firm's *marginal product of labor* can be determined. The marginal product of labor represents the increased output resulting from an increase in the use of labor. By itself, the marginal product of labor, which reflects the technological conditions in the firm, does not determine the demand for labor.

The reason the firm hires labor is to produce a commodity that can be sold in the market and make a profit for the entrepreneur. Logically, therefore, a link exists between the product price the firm receives for the commodity in the market and the demand for labor. The firm is not interested in the marginal product of labor stated in physical terms. It is concerned about the monetary value of the next unit of output produced by adding another unit of labor. This measure is called the *marginal revenue product of labor (MRP_L)* , which is the marginal revenue received by the firm for the sale of a unit of output, multiplied by the marginal product of labor. At the margin the firm establishes its level of employment so that the wage rate is just equal to the marginal revenue product of labor. The latter is the firm's demand-for-labor curve. By doing this, the firm also maximizes its profits, because there is a direct connection between the firm's output decision, which maximizes its profits, and its employment decision. Marginal revenue and marginal costs are equal when employment is set so that MRP_L equals the wage.

Changes in the demand for labor involve shifts in the entire MRP_L curve. Such changes occur if the technology changes, the product market conditions change, or the price of some other factor of production changes. Changes in the market wage do not change the demand curve, but they do affect employment in the firm. The extent to which employment is affected depends upon the elasticity of demand for labor in the firm. The more elastic the firm's demand for labor curve, the greater will be the reduction in employment in response to an increase in wages.

Study Questions

1. State precisely why the demand-for-labor curve slopes downward. Discuss the role of technology, and point out the economic assumptions made.

2. What is meant by the statement, "the demand for labor is a derived demand"? What are the premises about human behavior that are needed for an understanding of labor demand?

3. Under what economic conditions will the marginal revenue product of labor and the value of the marginal product of labor be equal? Explain!

4. Economic theory posits that entrepreneurs maximize short-run profits by hiring workers until the wage rate is equal to the marginal revenue product of the last worker hired. Apply this employment decision rule to an experience you have had.

5. Why are annual earnings extraordinarily high for some entertainers and professional athletes? How do decisions to hire them differ from the hiring decisions of McDonald's?

6. Critically evaluate the following statement: "If the consumer good is relatively price-inelastic, the demand for labor to produce the good will also be relatively inelastic."

7. Explain why an empirical investigation of the labor demand schedule can cause headaches for economists.

Further Reading

Hicks, J. R. *The Theory of Wages*. 2nd ed. New York: St. Martin's Press, 1963. Chap. 1.

Marshall, Alfred. *Principles of Economics*. 8th ed. London: Macmillan and Co., 1920. Bk. 6, chaps. 3–5.

Rothschild, K. W. *The Theory of Wages*. Oxford: Basil Blackwell, 1965. Chap. 2.

4

■
_____

Wage Theory:
Labor Supply

The household's decision to offer labor services to firms is part of its overall financial planning. Its objective is to obtain an income to sustain a target level of consumption. Members of the household do not offer their labor services for the sheer joy of it, according to the neoclassical philosophical basis for work. Rather, working is seen as an economic necessity for survival. If it did not offer labor services on a market, the household would have limited opportunities for obtaining an income by any other means.

Today, after centuries of socialization, this presumption concerning the motivation for work might need some revision. Work in the modern era provides certain important psychological benefits and is an item for consumption in and of itself, without reference to the income it generates. However, it can be argued that this independent psychological gratification from work is itself the product of a socialization process whereby modern industrial-market economies have stamped work with specific status and social psychological imperatives. The older neoclassical presumption about work—that it represents the "pain" that must be endured in order to enjoy the "pleasure" of consumption—can be observed from the behavior of young children. They typically do not eagerly take themselves away from the pursuit of play in order to offer their labor services inside or outside the household even if a monetary reward is available.

Labor supply involves three types of decisions made by households and individuals:

- how many hours of labor to offer to the labor market
- whether to seek work at all
- how much human capital (what level of skills and training) the individual will bring to the labor market

The original neoclassical theory of labor supply dealt primarily with the first issue—how many hours of work an individual will offer to the labor market. Interest in the question of whether an individual will seek work at all or will spend his or her time in nonmarket activities arose initially in the 1930s. This problem has taken on more importance in the past two decades as we have refined our measures of "labor force participation" and have developed models to explain why some individuals do not participate in the labor market. The human capital investment decision, which determines the level of training and skills an individual brings to the job, is the newest area of inquiry concerning labor supply.

Labor Supply: Hours of Work

The decision to supply a certain number of hours to the labor market is made by individuals living within a household, according to the institutional assumptions of the neoclassical theory of labor supply. The household is assumed to make its decision about labor supply independent of all other households making similar decisions. This institutional condition leads to the characterization of the household as an *atomized* decision-making unit, to reflect the fact that each household makes its decision in a vacuum, separate from other households. There is no "keeping-up-with-the-Joneses" effect in this model of the household. Decisions are made without imitating the behavior of other households. The household is said to have *independent* utility functions.[1] Moreover, each household is so small in proportion to the total amount of labor offered on the market that its decision about labor supply has no effect on the wage rate that will ultimately be determined.

The wage is determined in the labor market. Taking into consideration the wage set by conditions in the labor market, individuals decide how many hours of work they wish to supply to the labor market. In making this decision, the individual has two objectives: (1) to earn income by offering a certain number of hours to the labor

---

[1] A utility function compares two desirable and substitutable objectives. In this case, income- and non-income-producing activities are presumed to be trade-offs for each other. An independent utility function means the household makes its own unique decision about how to balance these two desirable objectives, without being influenced by how other households have responded to the same problem.

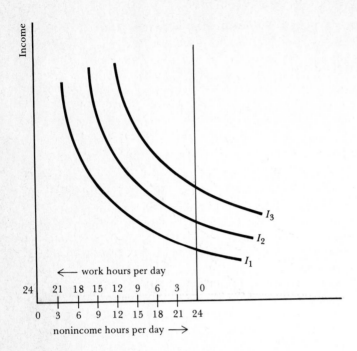

Figure 4-1   Household's Indifference Curves: Income-Producing and Non-Income-Producing Time

market; (2) to pursue non-income-producing activities—leisure, housework, child care, reading, and the like.[2]

The individual within the household faces a *trade-off* between these two desired outcomes—earning income and engaging in non-income-producing activities. This trade-off is assessed in light of the wage that is set in the labor market. Each individual and each household has a unique, independent trade-off between income-producing and non-income-producing activities. This is what is meant by the previously discussed independent utility function for the household.

The trade-off between time spent earning income and time used for non-income-producing activity can be represented on the household preference structure graph, adapted to the labor supply problem.[3] In Figure 4-1 income is measured on the vertical axis and "nonincome time" on the horizontal. The household is presumed to have some preference in ordering these two objectives, which yields an *indifference*

---

[2] Gary Becker, "A Theory of the Allocation of Time," *Economic Journal* 75 (September 1965), pp. 493–517.

[3] If a review of the theory of the household is needed, see Edwin Mansfield, *Micro-Economics: Theory and Applications,* 4th ed. (New York: W. W. Norton and Co., 1982), chap. 3.

curve as shown in Figure 4-1. The household is equally satisfied with every combination of income and nonincome time on any particular indifference curve. Work is represented on this graph as the difference between 24 hours (the total number of hours in a day) and the amount of time spent in non-income-producing activity. Therefore, work is measured, in effect, from right to left on this graph and nonincome time from left to right on the horizontal axis. This indicates that every additional hour offered for work is one hour less nonincome time.

In this analysis, the household faces the problem of how to divide the hours of the day between income-producing labor market activities and the non-income-producing activities it would like to pursue. For shorthand we will refer to this latter set of activities as "nonincome time" and trust that its larger meaning will be understood even though it will not be spelled out each time the term is used.

The indifference curve I_1 in Figure 4-1 indicates that the household will sacrifice nonincome time only if compensated by increasing amounts of income. Notice that an important assumption has been introduced into this analysis: the household, in the neoclassical model, is assumed to have the power to subdivide its waking hours into the hours it wants to work and the hours it does not want to work. Further, it is assumed that the household can do this over the full 24 hours in a day. Put differently, the neoclassical theory of labor supply does not impose any *institutional constraint*, such as the 40-hour work week, that would prevent the household from choosing, for example, to work 32 instead of 40 hours. The decision to supply labor is divisible at the margin, and the household has complete and ultimate authority to decide how it wants to divide its waking hours between work and nonwork, according to the model. No outside force, such as an employer, is presumed to meddle with this authority, except by offering wage incentives to induce the household to work the numbers of hours the employer would like. Obviously this assumption poses difficult analytical problems when we confront the institutional reality of the 40-hour work week.[4]

The household does, however, retain some flexibility in the labor market today, though not as much as the pure model suggests. The household is free to provide more or fewer individuals to the labor market. An individual can decide to moonlight (work a second job). Or an individual can decide to work overtime hours or to work part time.

The household will achieve greater satisfaction from its day if it can have more of both income and the fruits of nonincome activity, the best of both possible worlds. Therefore, indifference curve I_2 is preferred to I_1, and I_3 is preferred to both I_1 and I_2. However, since the world is not full of Al Capp's Schmoos, those adorable little creatures of the funnies that both multiply at will and supply whatever human need they are called upon to meet, the household cannot expand both its income and the fruits of nonincome activity without limit.

---

[4] In more complicated versions of the neoclassical model, the 40-hour work week can be incorporated.

The Wage and Hours of Work

By itself the household's desire to earn income and to spend time in non-income-producing pursuits, as summarized in its indifference curve, is insufficient to reach a determinate solution to the problem of how much labor will be supplied to the market. The household's preference function must be combined with some additional information that constrains its choice between income and nonincome time. This is a familiar problem in neoclassical economics: what combination of preferences and external constraints is used to arrive at an optimal solution for a decision-making unit.

The constraint imposed on the household, which enables it to choose among an infinite array of combinations of income and nonincome time, is the *wage rate*. The wage rate is determined in the labor market. It is outside the control of the household and is taken as given. In Figure 4-2 the wage rate is represented on the basic household decision-making graph, in which income is measured on the vertical axis and hours on the horizontal axis. The slope of the straight line *de* represents the hourly wage rate and shows how the household is compensated by the labor market for sacrificing hours of nonincome time. Note that *de* intersects the horizontal axis at 24 to indicate that there are only that many hours in the day.

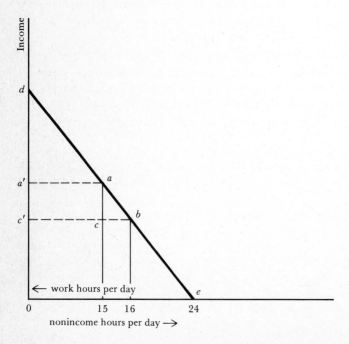

Figure 4-2   The Wage Rate

To see why this line represents the hourly wage rate, take any point on the horizontal axis—for example, 16 hours of nonincome time (or, what is the same, 8 hours of work). The income level associated with the consumption of 16 hours of nonincome time and 8 hours of work is represented by point c', which intersects the wage rate curve at b. Increase the number of hours of work by 1 hour, to 9 hours, leaving 15 hours of nonincome time. The income level associated with 9 hours of work and 15 hours of nonincome time is a', which intersects the wage curve at a. The wage rate, therefore, is simply the slope of the de curve—ac/cb. The distance ac represents the increase in income ($a'c'$), and cb represents an additional hour of work. Hence, the ratio ac/cb is the increase in income associated with an additional hour of work, which is the definition of a wage rate. The wage rate reflects the trade-off between income and nonincome time permitted by the labor market. Since the wage rate available to the household is the same no matter how many hours are worked, the slope of this line represents the same wage rate over the entire range of hours worked.[5]

Labor Time Supplied to the Market by the Household

The wage rate established in the labor market and taken by the household as a fixed piece of data becomes the constraining element in the household's quest for the maximization of income from labor market activity and the pursuit of non-income-producing activities. Figure 4-3 combines the household preference map for income and nonincome time with the wage constraint. The household maximizes its preferences for income and nonincome time at point a, which is on the highest indifference curve compatible with the wage rate. The household settles on its indifference curve I_2. A higher indifference curve, such as I_3, would be more desirable from the household's point of view, but it is unattainable in light of the market-determined wage rate. A lower indifference curve, such as I_1, is attainable by the household (say at point b), but this would not be rational, because the household could obtain a higher level of satisfaction by moving to the higher indifference curve, I_2. Only at point a is there agreement between the household's valuation of its time (the indifference curve) and the labor market's valuation of the household's time (the wage rate). This household maximizes its preference for income and nonincome time by consuming OL_1 hours of nonincome time, thereby working hours equal to L_1L_{24}, which yields it an income of OY_1.

---

[5] Wages that vary with the number of hours worked can be accommodated in more complicated models.

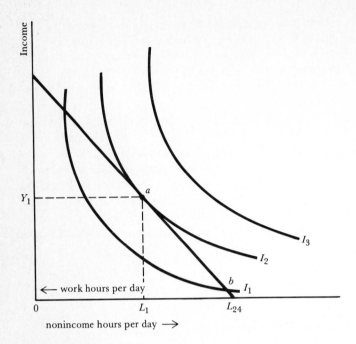

Figure 4-3 Labor Time Supplied for the Initial Wage Rate

The next question is: What happens to the number of hours of labor supplied to the market when the wage rate changes? The answer to this question is not as simple and straightforward as it might appear to be.

In Figure 4-4 the household is shown first maximizing its preference for income and leisure at point a, as derived previously, with the wage rate indicated by $L_{24}Y_x$. If the wage rate increases, the new wage is shown by the line $L_{24}Y_z$, which has a larger slope than the previous wage rate throughout. To verify this, continue the line aL_1 upward until it intersects the new higher wage rate line. Label that point a'. Note that more income, OY_2 (versus OY_1), is obtained for the same number of hours of work, L_1L_{24}. This is the definition of a higher wage rate. The slope L_1a'/L_1L_{24} is greater than L_1a/L_1L_{24}, indicating a higher wage rate.

In Figure 4-5 the household's equilibrium for the higher wage rate of $L_{24}Y_z$ is at point b. The household is on a higher indifference curve (I_3) and attains a greater level of satisfaction. More hours are now offered as labor supplied to the market, represented by the distance L_2L_{24}. Nonincome time has been reduced to OL_2, and income has increased from OY_1 to OY_2, due both to the higher wage rate per hour and to the increased number of hours offered for work.

The household, however, need not necessarily behave in this manner. Faced with a higher wage rate it might *reduce* the number of hours it offers to the labor market and simply consume more nonincome time. Figure 4-6 is a graphical depiction of this

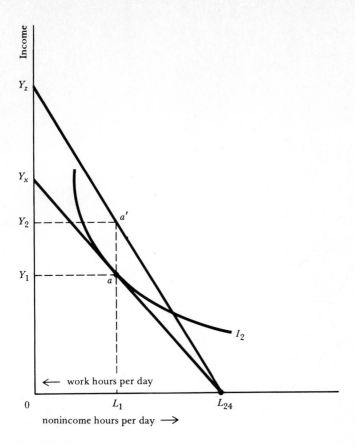

Figure 4-4 An Increase in the Wage Rate

case. The wage rate has increased to $L_{24}Y_w$, but now the household's new equilibrium at the higher wage is found at point c, where fewer hours are offered for work (L_3L_{24}) and more hours of nonincome time are consumed (OL_3). The household now receives a *higher* income than before $(OY_3$ compared to $OY_2)$ even though it works fewer hours. The higher wage rate per hour more than compensates for the reduced number of hours worked. The new equilibrium is represented by point c in Figure 4-6.

Figures 4-4 through 4-6 provide three data points that show specific numbers of hours offered for work associated with three different wage rates. These points (a, b, and c) are reproduced on Figure 4-7, the conventional labor supply graph, which relates wages paid, on the vertical axis, to employment, on the horizontal axis.[6] Notice

---

[6] Following standard practice, the horizontal axis in Figure 4-7 is labeled "Employment," defined in this instance as hours of work, to conform to the household's Income-Nonincome graph.

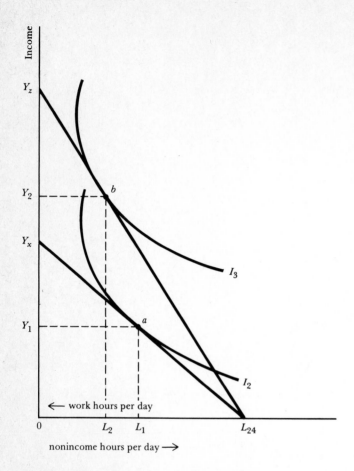

Figure 4-5 An Increase in the Wage Rate and an Increase in Hours Offered for Work

that the three data points produce a bow-like curve, which has a portion that is upward sloping (from *a* to *b*) and a segment that is *backward bending* (from *b* to *c*).

Income and Substitution Effects in the Household's Labor Supply Decision

To understand the reasons for a backward-bending supply segment, we must develop the household's response to a wage increase. This task involves separating the household's decision-making behavior into an *income effect* and a *substitution* effect, much

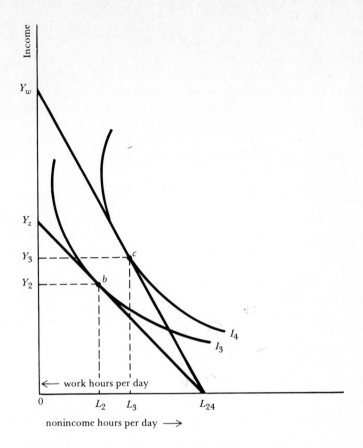

Figure 4-6   An Increase in the Wage Rate and a
Decrease in Hours Offered for Work

the same as is done with the household's consumption decisions in microeconomic theory.[7]

The substitution effect, which we will discuss first, always operates to increase the number of hours offered for work when wages increase. The substitution effect makes the "price" of non-income-producing time higher in that it becomes more "expensive" for the household not to work. Every hour of nonincome time is one not used for work that would yield more income. If the wage rate is higher, that hour consumed costs more in the sense of its *opportunity cost*. The opportunity cost of not working the additional hour has increased. Continuing to consume the same number

---

[7] The analytics of income and substitution effects are presented in the appendix to this chapter. If a review of these concepts is needed, see Mansfield, *Micro-Economics,* chap. 4.

of nonincome hours as before is, consequently, more "expensive" for the household. And if nonincome time is more expensive at the higher wage rate, the household should consume *less* of it, and offer more hours to the labor market. Hence, the substitution effect reflects a behavioral response that will always tend to make the household offer more hours for work in response to a higher wage rate.

Although the substitution effect will always cause more labor to be supplied at higher wages, the same cannot be said of the *income effect*, whose impact on labor supplied to the market contradicts the substitution effect. The income effect will lead to *less* labor being offered to the market at higher wages. The income effect in response to a higher wage rate enables the household to consume at its initial level of income by working fewer hours. If the wage rate per hour increases and if the household is satisfied with its initial income level, then it need not offer more hours of work to retain that income. In fact, it can offer fewer hours of work at the higher wage and have the same income as it had before at the lower wage rate. The income effect operates as a windfall gain; the household is presented with additional income without having to increase its work effort.[8]

The higher wage rate simply enables the household to obtain its *target level of income* without necessarily increasing the number of work hours it offers to the labor market. And if the household's target income level is not terribly ambitious, a higher wage rate will lead it to lower its work effort as it pursues the luxury of consuming additional non-income-producing hours. The troublesome anomaly of the backward-bending segment of the labor supply curve for an individual occurs if the income effect is large enough to overcompensate for the more normal substitution effect. In sum, if the income effect is large enough to offset the opposite impact of the substitution effect, then the household will supply fewer hours of work as wages increase.

Perspective on the Backward-Bending Supply Segment

Certain conditions can make it possible for a labor supply curve to have a backward-bending segment. First, countries at every low levels of economic development, with a comparatively immature "market mentality" among their workers, can have backward-bending supply segments in their labor supply curves. Workers in such countries tend to have low target levels of income, as they alternate between wage employment

---

[8] A popular television show of the 1950s, entitled "The Millionaire," provided a theatrical illustration of this economic concept. A man would knock on the door of an unsuspecting "victim" and announce that he was giving the family one million dollars. He was the agent for an eccentric multimillionaire named John Beresford Tipton. Tipton provided the money anonymously, on the condition that the family tell no one about the gift. The show then proceeded to trace the effect of this largesse on the family. The income effect works similarly in that it is considered a windfall gain to which the household can adjust its consumption of nonincome time and hours worked in order to attain a target level of income.

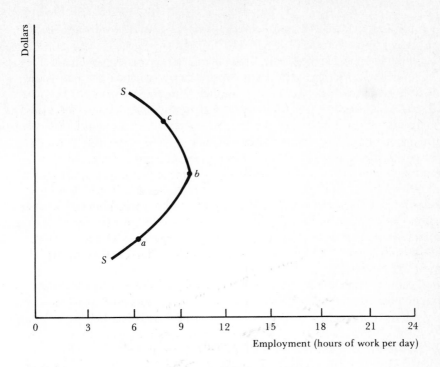

Figure 4-7 Hours Offered for Work at Three Different Wage Rates

and subsistence pursuits. Once their target levels of income are achieved, they tend to remove themselves from the labor force or work fewer hours at wage employment and more at their subsistence activities. Hence, higher wages may reduce work effort.[9] Hours of labor are offered in the wage sector to acquire sufficient income to support the minimal cash needs of the household. If wages are increased in this situation, hours of work will conceivably be reduced, because the individual can now obtain his or her target income level by offering fewer hours in the wage sector of the economy, thereby conserving more hours for self-sufficient, nonmarket economic activity.

Second, the backward-bending segment of the labor supply curve can prevail at very high wages in mature industrial economies. Employees in this situation have achieved their target income levels. Offers of higher wages may simply lead to the pursuit of more non-income-producing activities, once the target income level has been reached. For example, in a survey of 1,566 employees conducted by the National

---

[9] For a discussion of this phenomenon in less-developed countries, see Elliot J. Berg, "Backward-Sloping Labor Supply Functions in Dual Economies—The Africa Case," *Quarterly Journal of Economics* 75, no. 3 (August 1961), pp. 468–92.

Commission for Employment Policy, 65 percent said they would prefer more leisure time to a 2 percent wage increase.[10]

Although the theoretical possibility of a backward-bending supply segment does exist for an individual, the *aggregate* labor supply curve, which represents many individuals in a labor market, has less of a tendency toward a backward-bending segment. The number of individuals with a normal upward-sloping labor supply curve probably outweighs those with a backward-bending segment. When combined into an aggregate labor supply curve for the labor market, therefore, the possibility of a backward-bending segment is reduced.

Furthermore, even for the individual there are reasons for which the actual occurrence of a backward-bending labor supply segment is rare. The great drive for consumption, energized by advertising, constantly pushes the household's target income level upward as its wages increase. A household's target level of income is not static; it increases constantly and may even increase as a function of the wage rate. As a household's income rises due to higher wage rates, the household may take on more consumption obligations through debt and may then set its sights higher. The target income level can be expanding at a pace more rapid than that of the wage, thereby forestalling the point at which the labor supply curve begins to bend backward.

Hours of Work in the American Economy

The average workweek has *declined* in the United States during this century, while average hourly wages have *increased*. At first glance these two facts may seem to support the notion of a backward-bending segment of the labor supply curve. However, caution must be used in drawing that conclusion.

In Table 4-1, data are presented showing the average number of hours worked per week and the average hourly wage for blue-collar workers in the manufacturing sector of the American economy during this century. Since 1900 the average workweek has declined from 55 hours to about 40 hours. Most of this decline occurred between 1900 and 1930. The typical workweek has remained remarkably constant for the last 50 years. During this century, average hourly wages (unadjusted for inflation) have increased from $.16 per hour in 1900 to $9.52 per hour in 1985.

Wages have gone up more rapidly than hours have been reduced. However, some of the increase in wages must be discounted because of inflation. This is particularly true between 1970 and 1985 during which nominal wages have nearly tripled while real wages (nominal wages adjusted for inflation) have remained constant.

Use of these data to evaluate the theory of a backward-bending supply segment must be tempered by consideration of developments in the legislative arena that have

---

[10] "Labor Letter," *Wall Street Journal*, January 6, 1981, p. 1.

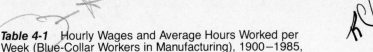

Table 4-1 Hourly Wages and Average Hours Worked per Week (Blue-Collar Workers in Manufacturing), 1900–1985, Selected Years

Year	Hours Worked Per Week	Hourly Wages
1900	55.0	$0.16
1909	51.0	0.19
1920	47.4	0.55
1930	42.1	0.55
1940	38.1	0.66
1950	40.5	1.44
1960	39.7	2.26
1970	39.8	3.35
1980	39.7	7.27
1985	40.5	9.52

Sources: U.S. Department of Commerce, Bureau of the Census, *Historical Statistics of the United States, Colonial Times to 1970*, Part 1 (Washington: Government Printing Office, 1975), pp. 168–170; Council of Economic Advisers, *Economic Report of the President, 1985* (Washington: Government Printing Office), p. 300; Ethel B. Jones, "New Estimates of Hours of Work per Week and Hourly Earnings, 1900–1957," *Review of Economics and Statistics* 45 (November 1963), p. 375.

affected hours of work. In 1938 the national Fair Labor Standards Act was passed, which stipulated that any hours worked beyond 44 per week would have to be paid at a higher, overtime rate. Two years later this was changed to 40 hours, thereby legislating the so-called 40-hour workweek in sectors covered by the law, although technically there is no limit on the number of hours someone may work. Rather, a worker must be paid at a higher rate if more than 40 hours are worked for the same employer in a given week. This legislation has affected the opportunities for working more than 40 hours per week for any *one* employer. Workers who wish to work more have moonlighted—obtained a second or third job. In 1979 there were 4.7 million American workers who held more than one job, out of a total labor force of 105 million.[11] The data in Table 4-1 do not take account of this phenomenon, and therefore they understate slightly the number of hours an individual works per week.

On the other hand, most jobs are by convention stated at 40 hours per week, and the employee accepts either 40 hours per week or nothing. Hence, decisions at the

---

[11] This amounts to 4.5 percent of the labor force. U.S. Department of Labor, *Handbook of Labor Statistics, 1980* (Washington: Government Printing Office), p. 106.

margin are precluded for most full-time workers for *less* than 40 hours per week. Decisions at the margin occur for some workers who have access to overtime hours.

Elasticity of Labor Supply

Implicit in the previous discussion of hours of work and wages in this century is the concept of the *elasticity of labor supply*. The elasticity of labor supply measures the sensitivity of hours worked to changes in the wage rate. It reflects the change in hours worked that occurs in response to a change in the wage rate. More specifically, the elasticity of labor supply is measured by the percentage change in hours worked in relation to the percentage change in wages.[12]

Whenever some percentage change in wages produces a *more than* equivalent percentage change in hours worked, the measured elasticity of labor supply will be greater than 1. In such circumstances the labor supply curve is said to be *elastic*. If some percentage change in wages leads to a *less* than proportional change in hours worked, the elasticity of labor supply will be less than 1. This is called an *inelastic* labor supply curve. When the percentage change in wages is followed by exactly the same percentage change in hours worked, the elasticity of labor supply is equal to 1 and is called *unitary elasticity*.

Many investigators have attempted to estimate the elasticity of labor supply. Because their studies differ in the time period investigated (long run or short run), the type of workers examined, and the methodology used, their estimates vary as to the elasticity of labor supply. A study that attempted to standardize all these estimates to produce a composite measure of the elasticity of labor supply reached the conclusion that it was +0.15.[13]

An elasticity of labor supply of +0.15 indicates that in the short run workers do offer more hours to the labor market when there is a wage increase, and devote fewer hours to non-income-producing pursuits. In the short run there is no evidence of a backward-bending *aggregate* labor supply curve, though one may exist for specific *individuals*. However, the labor supply curve is rather inelastic. Workers do not increase the number of hours offered to the labor market by the same percentage as the wage increase. This elasticity estimate indicates that a 10 percent increase in the wage would lead to only a 1.5 percent increase in the number of hours offered to the labor market.

Knowing the elasticity of labor supply is important for evaluating certain policy

---

[12] Elasticity of labor supply $= \dfrac{\Delta H}{H} \bigg/ \dfrac{\Delta w}{w}$

where H = hours worked and w = wages.

[13] Don Fullerton, "Can Tax Revenues Go Up When Tax Rates Go Down?" Department of Treasury, Office of Tax Analysis (September 1980), pp. 24–25.

proposals. For example, there is substantial interest today in the relationship between reductions in tax rates and increase in work effort. The proponents of such supply-side economic policies point to the added work effort that would be forthcoming from an *effective* increase in after-tax wages when taxes are reduced. A relatively inelastic labor supply curve of the type we find in the American economy means that the tax reduction would have to be substantial in order to call forth a significant increase in work effort.[14]

Income Maintenance Experiments and Labor Supply

In the 1970s economists were presented with an opportunity to study the labor supply effects associated with giving certain low-income individuals cash income grants while they were working. These programs, called *income maintenance* experiments, were introduced in several cities throughout the United States in the 1970s. Income maintenance programs were seen by some policymakers as alternatives to other forms of transfer payments for the poor, such as welfare. Although each experiment was slightly different, there were some common features. In each experiment, individuals within poverty households were provided cash grants. When they worked, these income transfers were taxed away at varying rates. The point at which the tax took effect also varied among the experiments.[15]

These experiments introduced a windfall income, similar to that in "The Millionaire," the television show in which an unsuspecting family was provided with a million dollars. The only difference, although it is an important one, is that the payment levels were much smaller. Nevertheless, a pure income effect was introduced into the household's decision about how much labor to supply to the market and how much time to set aside for non-income-producing activities.[16]

By observing the behavior of the household in such experiments, we can obtain an insight into its labor supply responses. We would expect the household to offer less labor to the market, according to the theory of household behavior, because of the income effect. This could take the form of fewer members of the household participating in the labor force or of fewer hours being offered for work by those members that do participate.

Let us look at the results of the income maintenance experiments on the question of the number of hours offered for work. The first surveys from the income

---

[14] Ibid.

[15] Christopher Green and Robert J. Lampman, "Schemes for Transferring Income to the Poor," *Industrial Relations* 6, no. 2 (February 1967), pp. 121–37; and Congressional Research Service, "New Approaches to Income Maintenance" (Washington: Library of Congress, 1970).

[16] Alfred Tella, Dorothy Tella, and Christopher Green, *The Hours of Work and Family Income Response to Negative Income Tax Plans: The Impact on the Working Poor* (Washington: The W. E. Upjohn Institute for Employment Research, 1971).

maintenance experiments in New Jersey did not provide strong support for the hypotheses derived from the model of household labor supply behavior. In some types of families, hours of labor supplied were reduced, as would be expected from the theory. However, in other instances hours of labor supplied increased slightly or did not change.[17] Typically, black families *increased* their labor force activity after receipt of income through an income maintenance program. This increase appeared both in more family members working and in more hours being offered to the labor market. While this behavior among black families was the opposite of that predicted by the theory of household behavior, the behavior of white families tended to conform to the theory. Hours of work and number of members of the household working were reduced among white families.

These ambiguous initial results from the first income maintenance experiments need not invalidate the model of household labor supply, for several reasons. First, the households may have viewed the income maintenance experiments as only temporary and therefore may not have sharply altered their labor supply behavior. Second, the families in the experiment were very poor. They were probably operating far below an income level that would satisfy their basic needs. Hence, more income might be seen simply as assisting them in trying to reach their target incomes; they were probably not at the point where a decision to reduce their work efforts would be rational.

Subsequent experiments in Seattle and Denver for a longer period of time showed more significant labor supply reductions in response to the income maintenance programs installed in those cities. Husbands reduced their work efforts by 6 percent and wives by 22 percent in response to a poverty-line income maintenance program and a 50 percent tax levied on earnings above the poverty line.[18] The general conclusion drawn from these income-maintenance experiments is that labor supply declines somewhat in response to the receipt of non-labor income when the program extends for a reasonable period of time.[19]

Labor Force Participation Rates

The household makes decisions not only about how many hours each individual in the labor market will supply, but also about how many people in the household will supply labor services in the first instance. This set of decisions is encompassed by the

---

[17] Albert Rees and Harold W. Watts, "An Overview of the Labor Supply Results," in Joseph A. Pechman and P. Michael Timpane, eds., *Work Incentives and Income Guarantees: The New Jersey Negative Income Tax Experiment* (Washington: The Brookings Institution, 1975), pp. 60–87.

[18] Robert J. Lampman, "Labor Supply and Social Welfare Benefits in the United States," in National Commission on Employment and Unemployment Statistics, *Concepts and Data Needs,* app. vol. 1 (Washington: NCEUS, 1980), p. 139.

[19] Mark R. Killingsworth, *Labor Supply* (Cambridge: Cambridge University Press, 1983), pp. 404–406.

Table 4-2 The Labor Force, Selected Years, 1950–1985

Year	Total Population[a] (thousands)	Total Labor Force (thousands)	Labor Force Participation Rate (%) (2)/(1)
	(1)	(2)	(3)
1950	106,164	63,377	59.7
1953	109,287	65,246	59.7
1956	112,919	68,517	60.7
1959	117,117	70,157	59.9
1962	122,214	72,675	59.5
1965	128,459	76,401	59.5
1968	134,281	80,990	60.3
1971	142,189	86,355	60.7
1974	151,841	93,670	61.7
1978	163,541	103,882	63.5
1982	173,939	111,872	64.3
1985	179,912	117,167	65.1

[a]Noninstitutional population, age 16 and over, including military personnel.
Sources: U.S. Department of Labor, *Handbook of Labor Statistics* (Washington: Government Printing Office, 1985), p. 6; U.S. Department of Labor, *Employment and Earnings* (Washington: Government Printing Office, Jan. 1986), p. 12.

concept of *labor force participation*. Labor force participation is influenced by education, demographics, legislation, cultural norms, and the economic needs of the household.

The relationship between those in the labor force and the total eligible population is called a *labor force participation rate* and is shown in column 3 of Table 4-2. Specifically, the labor force participation rate is the ratio of the number of labor force participants to the total eligible population.[20] The labor force participation rate has increased steadily since the end of World War II. In 1947 the labor force participation rate was 57 percent; by 1985 it had increased to 65 percent. Eight percentage points over a 39-year period may not seem like much of an increase. However, applied to a population base of nearly 180 million, the increased labor force participation rate means that the American economy must generate more jobs simply to accommodate the increased percentage of people who want to work.

Significant demographic shifts have occurred in the American economy since the

---

[20] A labor force participant is either employed or unemployed, but actively looking for work. The eligible population consists of persons over 16 who are not in a prison or mental hospital.

end of World War II, reflecting household decisions about the allocation of time. There are proportionally more women and more young workers in the labor force today than there were at the end of World War II. In the past 25 years the trend has accelerated toward higher proportions of the labor force being composed of women and young workers. For example, in 1958 women constituted 31.5 percent of the total labor force; in 1985 they made up 44 percent. Young workers, between the ages of 16 and 24, accounted for 17.2 percent of the total labor force in 1958 and 21 percent in 1984.[21]

Table 4-3 provides an insight into changes in female participation in the labor force, which are related to the postwar trend toward having proportionally more women in the labor force. Male participation rates have been steadily declining since the end of World War II, while female participation rates have been increasing. The male participation rate fell from 86 percent in 1950 to 77 percent in 1985. Taken by itself, this decline would have caused the overall labor force participation rate to decrease in the past 35 years. But it did not, as Table 4-3 reveals, and the reason is that women began entering the labor force in numbers more than sufficient to compensate for the declining labor force participation rate of men. Labor force participation rates for women have increased from 34 percent in 1950 to 54 percent in 1985.

No doubt this has occurred in part because of increased productivity in the home, which provides the technological base for women going to work. In addition, female participation rates have increased because of changing social mores, which make it more acceptable for women to work, more women who are career oriented, and the increased need for a second income in the household to offset the decline in real income caused by the inflation of the past decade. In 1985, among married-couple households, 49 percent had both husband and wife working, compared to 25 percent in 1960.[22] The traditional view of a husband working and a wife at home is no longer the norm for American households.

These observations are corroborated by a closer look at the statistics in Table 4-3. Most of the growth in the labor force participation rate for women has occurred since 1965, when the forces propelling women into the labor force took hold. During the period from that year through 1985, 15.2 percentage points were added to the participation rate for women; only 5.4 percentage points had been added in the previous 15 years. The overall participation rate for both men and women was constant from 1947 to 1965; then it began to increase, solely because of the growth of labor force participation rates among women. The steadily declining labor force participation rate for men, on the other hand, is due to earlier retirements and the phenomenon of stretching education over a longer time span.[23]

---

[21] U.S. Bureau of the Census, *Statistical Abstract of the United States, 1986* (Washington: Government Printing Office), p. 392; and Council of Economic Advisers, *Economic Report of the President, 1986* (Washington: Government Printing Office), p. 290.

[22] U.S. Bureau of the Census, *Statistical Abstract, 1986*, p. 399. Chapter 13 contains a more complete discussion of the reasons for these changes in labor force participation rates.

[23] Students are considered to be out of the labor force unless they evidence some specific job-seeking behavior or are employed.

Table 4-3 Labor Force Participation Rates by Sex,
Selected Years, 1950–1985

Year	Total (%)	Male (%)	Female (%)
1950	59.7	86.7	33.9
1953	59.7	86.6	34.5
1956	60.7	86.0	36.9
1959	59.9	84.3	37.2
1962	59.5	82.6	38.0
1965	59.5	81.3	39.3
1968	60.3	80.8	41.6
1971	60.7	79.7	43.4
1974	61.7	79.2	45.6
1978	63.5	78.3	50.0
1982	64.3	77.0	52.7
1985	65.1	76.7	54.5

Sources: U.S. Department of Labor, *Handbook of Labor Statistics* (Washington: Goverment Printing Office, 1985), pp. 6–17; U.S. Department of Labor, *Employment and Earnings* (Washington: Government Printing Office, Jan. 1986), pp. 12–13.

These figures on labor force participation reveal facts about some of the most important social phenomena in the United States in the past 15 years. Table 4-4 provides another, more-detailed examination of the changing participation rates for men and women. In this table the labor force participation rates for men and women are broken down into age groups and compared for the years 1950 and 1983. The labor force participation rate for men over 65 fell from over 45 percent in 1950 to 17 percent in 1983. This reflects more extensive retirement at age 65. The decline in male participation rates for the 55–64 age group, from 87 percent to 69 percent, is an indicator of the trend toward even earlier retirement. Whether this trend will continue into the future is problematic because of the impact of inflation, which erodes retirement nest eggs, and new federal legislation, which has increased the mandatory retirement age. Women of all age groups showed dramatic increases in their labor force participation rates. This was most pronounced in women under the age of 44— that group most affected by enhanced opportunities for women in the labor force.

Labor force participation rates vary by race and sex. In Table 4-5 labor force participation rates are shown for blacks and whites, men and women. The labor force participation rates for white and black men were virtually identical in 1956, but since that time they have diverged. By 1985 the black male labor force participation rate was 6 points below that for white men. Analysts speculate that this divergence is due to declining employment opportunities for black men compared with white men. The

Table 4-4   Civilian Labor Force Participation Rates by Age and Sex, 1950 and 1983

| | 1950 | | 1983 | |
Age Group	Male (%)	Female (%)	Male (%)	Female (%)
16 and 17	51.3	30.1	43.2	39.9
18 and 19	75.9	51.3	68.6	60.7
20–24	87.9	46.0	84.8	69.9
25–34	96.0	34.0	94.2	69.0
35–44	97.6	39.1	95.2	68.7
45–54	95.8	37.9	91.2	61.9
55–64	86.9	27.0	69.4	41.5
65 and over	45.8	9.7	17.4	7.8
Total	86.7	33.9	76.4	52.9

Source: U.S. Department of Labor, *Handbook of Labor Statistics* (Washington: Government Printing Office, 1985), pp. 18–19.

heavier weight of young people in the labor force is a major contributing factor to this divergence, since black male youth (ages 16–19) had a labor force participation rate of only 44.6 percent in 1985, compared with a participation rate of 60.0 percent among white male youth.[24]

The patterns of labor force participation rates for black and white women, as shown in Table 4-5, reveal some interesting social phenomena. In 1956 black women had a participation rate almost 12 points higher than that for white women. Both have grown since 1956, but by 1985 there was only a 2.4 percentage-point difference. While the labor force participation rates diverged for black and white men, they converged for women. This convergence reflects the very sharp increase in labor force participation rates for white women and the fact that black women have always had to participate more actively in the labor force in order to support their families. While employment opportunities for black men relative to white men have been weak, employment opportunities for black and white women have not been so dissimilar.

The data on labor force participation rates are presented here because they are a statistical manifestation of one aspect of labor supply—namely, the decision whether to enter the labor force at all and either work or look for a job. Men tend to participate in the labor force more than women, but in the past 15 years the rate of growth in labor force participation for women has been sharp, while for men the participation

---

[24] Council of Economic Advisers, *Economic Report of the President, 1986*, p. 294.

Robert Clark

Table 4-5   Civilian Labor Force Participation Rates by Race and Sex, Selected Years, 1956–1985

	Total (%)	Black		White	
		Male (%)	Female (%)	Male (%)	Female (%)
1956	60.0	85.1	47.3	85.6	35.7
1959	59.3	83.4	47.7	83.8	36.0
1962	58.8	80.8	48.0	82.1	36.7
1965	58.9	79.6	48.6	80.8	38.1
1968	59.6	77.6	49.3	80.4	40.7
1971	60.2	74.9	49.2	79.6	42.6
1974	61.3	72.9	49.0	79.4	45.2
1978	62.3	71.5	53.1	78.6	49.4
1982	64.0	70.1	53.7	77.4	52.4
1985	64.8	70.8	56.5	77.0	54.1

Source: Council of Economic Advisers, *Economic Report of the President, 1986* (Washington: Government Printing Office), p. 294.

rate has been declining. Participation rates for white and black men have diverged, while white female participation rates have just about caught up with the once-higher labor force participation rates for black women. Fewer older people are now participating in the labor force compared with 30 years ago. In sum, the labor force is younger and more female today than 30 years ago.

The Quality of Labor Supply: Human Capital

When an individual within a household supplies labor services, more than just time is offered. There is a certain *quality* of labor attached to that person. This quality is represented by the levels of education, training, and skills accumulated by a person. The sum total of investment made in education, training, and skill acquisition is called *human capital.*

Individuals accumulate human capital both through their own efforts and by acquiring skills while working on the job. Throughout a worker's life, whether in blue-collar production-line work or in high-level white-collar managerial work, human capital is constantly being accumulated. Initially investments in human capital occur in the classroom, as formal knowledge is acquired. Then investments in human capital take place on the job, as knowledge and skills are accumulated either through formal on-the-job training programs or through informal modes of skill acquistion. The body

Table 4-6   Years of Education by Occupation, March 1985

Occupation	School Completed
Professional, technical and kindred workers	16.8
Managers and administrators (except farm)	14.9
Sales workers	12.9
Clerical and kindred workers	12.9
Craft and kindred workers	12.5
Operatives, except transport	12.3
Transport equipment operatives	12.4
Laborers, except farm	12.2
Private household workers	11.6
Service workers (except private household)	12.3
Farm workers	12.3
All occupational groups	12.8

Source: Unpublished data from the March 1985 Current Population Survey, Bureau of the Census.

of theory relating to human capital is developed in detail in Chapter 10. However, for purposes of studying labor supply, we need to know something about the qualitative dimension of the labor force.

Investment in human capital through the education system is done by individuals and by the whole society. Individuals invest in themselves so long as the expected return from an investment at the margin exceeds the costs at the margin. Society invests in human capital up to the point where the returns (net of cost) at the margin are equal to net returns at the margin on alternative investments. Investments on the job in human capital are made primarily by firms. Firms invest in human capital so long as their expected returns at the margin exceed their costs at the margin.

The sum of all these investments in human capital made by individuals, the society, and firms produces a profile of the quality of the American labor force. One such profile is shown in Table 4-6, in which number of years of formal education is related to type of occupation.[25]

In March 1985 the average number of years of schooling completed for all occupation groups was only slightly above the high school level—12.8 years. The

---

[25] Reliable data on the more informal aspects of labor quality, such as skills and on-the-job training, are very difficult to find. Figures on formal education are available, but they are also misleading. First, formal schooling is only one dimension of labor quality. Second, the quality of schooling itself varies considerably from region to region and from school to school.

range of education went from slightly above a four-year college degree, for professional and technical employees, to slightly less than a high school education for household service workers.

There has been a slow but steady upward drift in median years of school completed in the United States. In 1940 it was 9.1 years, and in 1952 it was 11.1 years. Median years of school completed in this country reached the high school level (12 years) in 1959 and has remained above that level ever since.[26]

Today the demands of technology and the application of "credentialism" have produced educational requirements beyond high school for most jobs.[27] Whether the quality of the labor force has improved as a result of more education is a debatable point. The concern expressed about the decline in quality of the American worker is at odds with the increased formal education accumulated by America workers.

Labor Supply and Supply-Side Economics

In the 1980s, supply-side economics dominated economic policy. While not explicitly identified with issues surrounding labor supply, supply-side economics, nevertheless, found many of its applications to the economics of labor supply. Throughout this book, we will examine supply-side economic policies—as they affect poverty, minimum wages, and unemployment, for example. The central claim of supply-side economics is that the labor market, left to its own devices and unfettered by any government or institutional meddling, will produce the wage that best allocates labor. And if there are no options other than the wage for workers, then the labor market will also induce the maximum flexibility that is needed to allocate labor resources most efficiently.

To illustrate this concept, consider the issue of health and safety on the job. Since the early 1970s, the U. S. government has been committed to improving health and safety on the job through the Occupational Safety and Health Administration (OSHA) which attempts to identify and correct unsafe and unhealthy conditions of work. The supply-side approach has been critical of this direct form of government regulation of the workplace and proposes instead to permit the labor market to create sufficient wage differentials to compensate those workers who work in less safe and healthy environments. Such *compensating wage differentials*, as they are called, would

---

[26] U.S. Department of Labor, *Educational Attainment of Workers, March 1979* (Washington: Bureau of Labor Statistics, 1981), p. A-9.

[27] "Credentialism" refers to an employer's practice of imposing specific formal education requirements for entry to a job, even though in an earlier time that job was performed adequately by someone with much less formal education.

supposedly provide higher monetary rewards for workers taking more hazardous jobs.[28] The supply-side adherents, therefore, argue that direct government regulation, such as OSHA, preempts the labor market and prevents it from doing its job of creating the compensating wage differentials that would take care of the added health hazards associated with more dangerous work.

The defenders of traditional labor regulation point out that the labor market does not create accurate and accessible information about health hazards on the job and that medical science, for example, does not even know what the risks of low-level exposure to carcinogens might be. Moreover, individuals who are segmented into labor markets that have risky jobs are themselves prone to health risks in their lives outside of work, and the incremental effects of job-related risks may be so small as to render them insignificant when selecting from among available jobs. And finally, the supply-side model implicitly assumes full employment where the individual has a range of options and can choose that job based on the monetary rewards, tempered by risk. Absent full employment and the model breaks down—at least in its pure theoretical form.

Whether or not supply-side approaches to public policy will ever completely replace the past half century of labor regulation is doubtful. Nevertheless, the influence of supply-side economic thinking has had a profound impact on public policy as it relates to labor supply in just the first half of the decade of the 1980s. The debate over labor regulation has been permanently altered, and the supply-side ideas cannot be ignored.

Summary

Labor is supplied by individuals who are part of households. The supply of labor, therefore, is *derived* from the household's need to acquire income in order to purchase goods and services. In deciding how many hours in a day to offer as work, the household has to balance its desire to acquire income with its desire for non-income-producing time—the obverse of work. It attempts to obtain the optimal mixture of work and nonincome time in its day, balancing its quest for income with its desire for nonincome time. In so doing, the household is assumed, in the neoclassical model, to decide at the margin how many hours it wishes to consume as nonincome time and how many hours it is willing to offer as work.

As in other instances in the neoclassical system, the household's preferences for income and nonincome time are subject to an external constraint—in this instance, the wage rate established in the labor market and outside the control of the household.

---

[28] W. Kip Viscusi, *Employment Hazards. An Investigation of Market Performance* (Cambridge: Harvard University Press, 1979).

[29] Norman Waitzman, "Occupational Determinants of Health: A Labor Segmentation Analysis" (Washington, D.C.: American University, 1988).

Given a wage rate, the household will find its own unique optimal combination of income and nonincome time by attaining the highest level of satisfaction, represented by the trade-off between income and nonincome time. This is reflected in its *indifference curve*. As it makes this decision, it also decides how many hours to offer for work.

If the wage rate increases, the household then has to decide how to respond to this new condition. Typically, it will increase the number of hours it offers for work, receiving a higher level of income and consuming fewer hours of nonincome time. This is the most general and normal response; it leads to an increased supply of labor in response to the higher wage rate. As a consequence of this household behavior, the familiar labor supply curve will slope upward, reflecting the increased number of hours offered for work as wages increase.

There is an important exception to this general rule, however, that can cause *fewer* hours to be offered for work as wages increase. In this phenomenon, called the *backward-bending segment* of the labor supply curve, a higher wage rate results in reduced hours of work. The behavior dynamic that produces both the normal household response to wage increases and the paradox of a backward-bending supply segment can be understood through an analysis of the *income and substitution effects*.

The substitution effect will always work to produce a normal, upward-sloping supply segment. As the wage rate increases, the consumption of nonincome time becomes more "expensive." Time used outside of work has a price like all other items of consumption in the neoclassical model. And its price is the wage rate—the opportunity cost of not working. As the wage rate increases, the price of nonincome time goes up, since more income is forgone by not working. By consuming less nonincome time, the household offers more hours for work as wages increase.

The income effect, however, works in the opposite direction. If the household has a target income it wished to obtain, then a higher wage rate enables it to satisfy that target income by working fewer hours. As wages increase, the household tends to offer fewer hours for work, revealing the type of response that causes a backward-bending supply segment, because it can acquire its target income by working less and consuming more hours of nonincome time.

The substitution and income effects work at cross purposes: one leads to more hours being offered for work in response to a wage increase, the other to fewer hours being offered. Whether the supply curve has its normal upward slope or is backward bending depends on which of these two forces is greater. If the substitution effect prevails, the supply curve will slope upward; if the income effect prevails, it will bend backward. Although the possibility of a backward-bending supply curve exists, and there are examples of it operating in real economic situations, neoclassical economics proceeds by positing a normal upward-sloping supply curve over the range of wage rates being considered in the short term.

Aside from deciding upon how many hours each individual in the household will offer to the labor market, the household also decides how many individuals will seek work at all and what level of skills, education, and training each person will bring to the labor market. The labor force participation rate measures the number of individuals who participate in the labor market relative to an eligible population base. Human capital is the term given to the investments made by individuals, firms, and the society as a whole in the quality of the labor force.

In the past several decades there have been important changes in the demographics of labor force participation rates. Participation rates have fallen for men and risen for women. Older people of both sexes have reduced their participation in the labor force over the past 35 years, although the rate of decline is greater for men. Participation rates for black men have diverged from those for white men, leading to a wider gap in black and white male participation rates. On the other hand, rates have converged for black and white women, the white female rate growing to close the gap with what has always been a higher labor force participation rate for black women.

These demographic trends reflect the fact that more women are now in the labor force due to economic necessity, changes in social attitudes, and an increase in female-headed families. They also indicate that maturation of our social security system has led to earlier and more universal retirement. Differential employment opportunities for black men and women show up in labor force participation rate trends.

The quality of the labor force is a composite of formal education, on-the-job training, and experiential learning.

Study Questions

1. What specific assumptions must be made about how people evaluate their non-income-producing time in order to derive a normal, upward-sloping labor supply curve?

2. How would you integrate the "40-hour" workweek into the standard model of labor supply?

3. Economists look at wage rates as part of the general model of market exchange. Workers view the wage rate as providing income. Discuss and compare these two aspects of the wage rate.

4. What are the chief factors that produce a backward-bending labor supply curve? Discuss the policy implications for such a labor supply function in advanced industrial countries. In less-developed countries.

5. Black male teenage labor force participation rates have declined from 61 percent (1954) to 41 percent (1982). Provide an economic explanation for this labor market trend.

6. Discuss the implications of "supply-side" tax cuts if labor is stationed on the backward-bending section of the aggregate labor supply curve. How is this related, if at all, to the concept of elasticity of labor supply?

7. Why is it incorrect to use the concepts labor supply and labor force participation interchangeably?

8. Discuss the impact on labor supply of a more liberal immigration policy.

Further Reading

Fleisher, Belton M., and Thomas J. Kniesner. *Labor Economics, Theory, Evidence, and Policy.* 2nd ed. Englewood Cliffs, NJ: Prentice-Hall, 1980. Chap. 4.

Hicks, J. R. *The Theory of Wages.* 2nd ed. New York: St. Martin's Press, 1963. Chap. 5.

Rothschild, K. W. *The Theory of Wages.* Oxford: Basil Blackwell, 1965. Chap. 3.

APPENDIX

The Income and Substitution Effects and Household Labor Supply

The analytics of the household's income and substitution effects are presented in Figure 4-8, in which the household is shown to be initially maximizing its preferences for income and nonincome time at point *a* on indifference curve I_1. It is consuming OL_1 hours of nonincome time, working L_1L_{24} hours, and receiving an income of OY_1

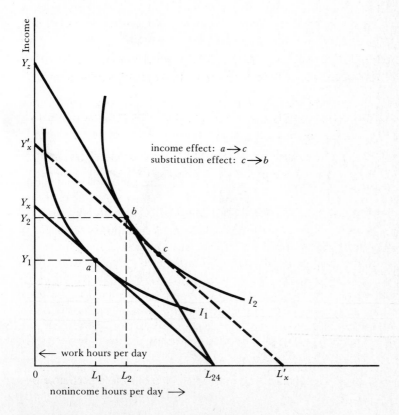

Figure 4-8 Income and Substitution Effects

for the given wage rate represented by the line $L_{24}Y_x$. Let the wage rate increase to $L_{24}Y_z$ and trace what happens to the household's decision to consume nonincome time and supply hours of labor.

The household obtains a new optimum at point b, which provides a higher level of satisfaction, represented by the indifference curve I_2. The household is now consuming more hours of nonincome time, OL_2, working fewer hours, L_2L_{24}, and receiving a higher income, OY_2. This is the backward-bending supply phenomenon in which a higher wage rate leads to fewer hours being offered for work. The behavior that produces this result can be shown through an analysis of the household's income and substitution effects.

To derive the income and substitution effects, construct a wage line, $L'_xY'_x$, that is parallel to the initial wage constraint, $L_{24}Y_x$. $L'_xY'_x$ represents the same wage rate as $L_{24}Y_x$ but at a higher base level of income in the household. This represents a pure windfall income gain for the household: a higher income received without a higher wage rate. The *income effect* is the movement represented by going from point a on indifference curve I_1 to point c on indifference curve I_2. The income effect answers the question, what will the household do in response to receiving a higher income for the same wage rate? Graphically this is depicted by holding the wage rate fixed—that is, by constructing a new wage rate line with the same slope as the initial one but at a higher level of income, as was done in Figure 4-8. A windfall income gain such as this results in more nonincome time being consumed and fewer hours being worked because now the household can obtain its target income level by offering fewer hours of work to the labor market.

The reduction in hours worked is offset, however, by the impact of the *substitution effect*, which always results in more hours being offered for work in response to a higher wage rate. This occurs because nonincome time becomes more expensive at the higher wage rate. As the opportunity cost of nonincome time increases, more hours are offered for work by the household in the labor market.

In Figure 4-8 the substitution effect is represented by the movement along indifference curve I_2 from c to b. Since the slope of the new, higher wage rate is greater than the slope of the old wage rate, the household will always reduce its consumption of nonincome time in favor of hours worked. Point b intersects indifference curve I_2 at a point of greater slope than point a. In this instance, however, the substitution effect, represented by the movement along indifference curve I_2 from c to b, is less than the income effect, represented by the movement from a to c. The net effect, or the movement from a to b, results in fewer hours of work being offered to the labor market and more hours of nonincome time being consumed, because the income effect outweighs the substitution effect.

5

Wage Determination and Market Structure

In perfect competition the wage is determined in the labor market. Firms and households respond to this wage and adapt their demand for and supply of labor accordingly. The factors that determine the wage in the labor market are derived from the behavior of individual firms and households. The labor market is an abstract concept; the real activities that take place in the labor market reflect the behavioral responses of firms and households to economic signals.

In the two previous chapters, the behavioral responses of households and firms to the market-determined wage were examined. In this chapter we investigate the labor market to see how wages are determined in different types of market structures.

Thus far the neoclassical theory of wage and employment determination has been developed within the context of a *perfectly competitive economy*. The most important of the conditions of a perfectly competitive economy are:

- Neither firms nor households are large enough to affect the wage rate when they decide how much labor to employ or how much labor to supply to the market.

- There is complete mobility of labor and capital, without any impediments to entry into any market.

- There is no institutional interference in the labor market by trade unions, government, or other groups.

■ Firms and households are homogeneous—that is, identical in the elements of their respective demand and supply curves.

■ Firms and households have complete and perfect information about the economic universe around them, including complete information about all the forces that influence their labor demand and supply decisions.

■ Firms take their product price as given and are not large enough to affect the price charged for their output.

Not all markets are perfectly competitive. In fact, the restrictive assumptions of a perfectly competitive market typically arouse skepticism about the model itself. According to its defenders, however, the model need not be discarded because of these restrictive assumptions. It is quite plausible for *predictions* based on the model to be useful even though the fundamental assumptions of the model are implausible.

Many markets are *imperfectly competitive*. In considering wage and employment determination under conditions of imperfect competition, some of the assumptions of perfect competition are relaxed. The most important assumption that is discarded is the one about firm size. In the models of imperfect competition the one common element is the proposition that firms have become large enough that their actions in the market affect the outcome of the market. No longer are they passive recipients of the forces emanating from the market; they can now intervene in the market and affect its outcome. For example, the first model of imperfect competition starts from the premise that firms have become large enough and the product market has become *concentrated* enough that the firms can set the price charged for their product rather than simply accept the price that is determined in an impersonal, self-regulating market.

The models of imperfect competition are important because they represent an alteration of the institutional context in which firms and households operate in markets. The system of perfect competition has difficulty perpetuating itself in an institutional setting. Firms in perfect competition have an incentive to control their economic environment and take steps to reduce competition. They accomplish this by monopolizing technological advances through the legal protection of patents and by acquiring competitive advantages through customer attachment. They attempt to prevent entry by increasing their scale of operations. As a consequence, the system of competition is institutionally unstable, in that it tends to create a powerful incentive among its participants to eliminate competition and substitute concentration. The legal system of property rights reinforces this tendency by protecting technological advantages through patent laws and by protecting customer attachment through copyright and trademark law.

Wage Determination in Perfectly Competitive Markets

The labor market is a composite of all the separate decisions made by firms and households. The labor demand curve in the labor market is an *aggregate* of all the separate labor demand curves derived from the employment decisions made by firms in their quests to maximize profits. The supply curve of labor in the labor market is an *aggregate* of all the separate decisions made by households to supply labor at different wage rates in order to achieve their highest levels of satisfaction as they pursue both the consumption of non-income-producing time and the acquisition of income.

To derive the labor market demand and supply curves, the individual firm demand curves and household supply curves must be *aggregated*—added together. The problem of aggregation over firms and households would be complicated were it not for one simplifying assumption. That is the assumption of *homogeneity*, which means that the separate units that are being added up are assumed to be *identical* in their crucial attributes. In the neoclassical model, the firms and households that compose a particular labor market are assumed to be homogeneous (or identical) with respect to all the relevant characteristics that make up the demand for and supply of labor.

The firms operating in a specific labor market will be identical along the following dimensions: type of product being produced, technology used to fabricate the product, and structure of the market in which the product is sold. The households that make up a particular labor market are identical with respect to skills, human capital, and occupation.

The process of aggregating to obtain a labor demand curve, for example, involves summing up individual firm decisions concerning how much labor to employ at different wages. For households, the process of aggregation of individual labor supply curves to obtain a supply curve for the labor market involves a similar adding-up procedure.

If the simplifying assumption of homogeneity were not used, the problem of aggregation would become substantially more complicated. The difficulty would arise in attempting to find a set of *weights* to apply to the different firms and households that make up a labor market. If disparate items are being added, say apples and oranges, a set of weights must be used to render each of the units into the same form for purposes of aggregation. This problem is sidestepped here by the assumption of homogeneity. But aggregation could be troublesome if homogeneity is not a good approximation of labor market conditions. We consider this problem in the next section.

The Cambridge Critique: Heterogeneity in the Labor Market

Cambridge, England, once the bastion of neoclassical orthodoxy, has recently given birth to a fundamental assault on marginal productivity theory. Alfred Marshall's home and place of work has spawned the *Cambridge critique* of neoclassical economic theory. In 1960 a relatively obscure Cambridge economist named Piero Sraffa pro-

Critique of M Productivity Theory

duced a brief volume, less than a hundred pages, that has caused a raging debate ever since in some circles in economic theory.[1]

The Sraffa model begins with the issue of how factors of production enter into a process that yields output. He pointed out what happens to be a major flaw in the inner logic of neoclassical economics in general and marginal productivity theory in particular. Sraffa initially identified this logical flaw in the marginal productivity theory as it applies to capital, but the same arguments can be used in analyzing labor as well.

Sraffa starts with the problem of how capital is to be measured in a complex industrial economy whenever there is a *heterogeneous* mixture of capital goods that make up the capital of a neoclassical production function. In order to aggregate these disparate units of capital, a set of *weights* must be found. How else can apples and oranges, or in this instance, lathes and sewing machines, be combined? Neoclassical economics solves this problem by using prices as weights so that lathes and sewing machines can be combined into one common form called capital, which then enters the neoclassical production function. But the price weight is the rate of return in equilibrium for each unit of disparate capital. Consequently, the rates of return have been used to derive the measure of capital, which then enters the production function that ultimately yields the rates of return on capital. However, we had to presume to know these rates of return in order to weight the disparate units of capital initially. If, by now, you feel dizzy from having gone around this carousel too quickly, do not be embarrassed.

There is a circularity in reasoning here that bares a significant flaw in the inner logic of neoclassical economics, according to the Cambridge critics. The rates of return on capital have to be known at the outset in order to create the capital that enters into the production function. But then that capital is used to find the aggregate rate of return on capital. Either the rates of return are known and taken as a given at the outset, being *exogenous* to the system of equations of the marginal productivity model, or they are not known and are a variable of the system to be derived through the analytics of the model.[2] They cannot be both unknowns and knowns at the same time, or so the Cambridge critics contend.

Put differently, the rates of return on capital have been asked to do double duty. The Cambridge critics claim a confusion exists in the neoclassical system. Capital is both a means of production and a fund of monetary value that represents a rate of return to a factor of production. And these are legitimate functions of capital. But the neoclassical model makes no such distinction, and in blurring this difference, they have confused the functions of capital. If the Cambridge critics are correct—and the jury of economists is still out on the issue—then the neoclassical model contains a

---

[1] Piero Sraffa, *Production of Commodities by Means of Commodities: Prelude to a Critique of Economic Theory* (Cambridge: Cambridge University Press, 1960).

[2] "Exogenous" means outside or separate from. In this case, the rates of return on capital either should be determined separate from the elements of the marginal productivity model or should not be the principal unknown in the model.

logical flaw that it is hard pressed to overcome. In effect, there are more variables in the model than there are equations, in a mathematical sense. Consequently, the system of equations implicit in the neoclassical model leads to an indeterminacy.

Though stated with respect to capital, the argument of the Cambridge critics applies with equal intensity to labor. If labor is *heterogeneous,* some means must be found of aggregating the disparate units of labor into the production function's labor input. In the neoclassical system this is accomplished by using the wage rates paid to different units of labor. But how can the wage rates be used as weights to aggregate the disparate units of labor if the purpose of the marginal productivity model is to find the wage rate in the first instance? Either the wage rate is known or it is not; one cannot have one's cake and eat it too. Hence we see the symmetry in argument between the problems of measuring capital and labor when heterogeneity is introduced into the analysis.

In the neoclassical model, how is the problem of heterogeneity handled? Firms and households that do not fit into a particular labor market are simply assigned to another labor market. Households and firms that are different in character from those that compose the specific labor market under investigation are assumed to belong to another labor market. By definition, therefore, a labor market in the neoclassical world is made up of *homogeneous* firms and households. There can be many labor markets in the short run, but each one consists of a grouping of homogeneous firms and households.[3]

It is important to know whether the economy is comprised of many heterogeneous labor markets or whether the heterogeneity among the labor markets of the economy is only a temporary manifestation. Separate labor markets that persist for a significant period of time imply a disequilibrium in the economy. If the economy has persistent disequilibria in its labor markets, a model is needed that starts with separate labor markets and embarks on the analysis from that point. Such a model of the economy is examined in Chapters 11 and 12.

Unfortunately, there is no consensus as to which condition prevails in the labor markets of the economy. This issue has framed an important theoretical debate that we will return to throughout this book. At this juncture, however, it is time to return to the development of the neoclassical model of wage determination and acquire a firmer foundation in its concepts before an alternative model is presented.

Wage Determination in a Perfectly Competitive Labor Market

The derivation of labor demand and supply curves is now complete for the firm operating in perfectly competitive product and labor markets made up of homoge-

---

[3] Over the longer run, the distinctions among separate labor and capital markets are supposed to atrophy as the mobility of labor and capital eliminate wage and profit differentials in the economy.

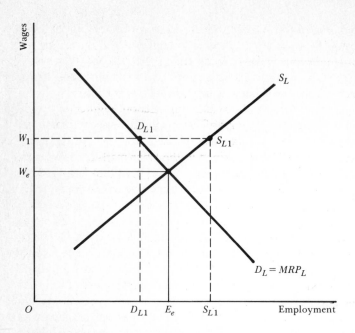

FIGURE 5-1   Effect of a Wage above Equilibrium in a Perfectly Competitive Labor Market

neous firms and households, as shown in Figure 5-1. The equilibrium wage rate determined in this market is W_e, and the equilibrium level of employment is E_e. Any wage rate other than W_e will not be sustainable by the underlying conditions that determine the supply of and demand for labor and the wage rate will tend to return to its equilibrium level. If, for instance, the wage rate were above the equilibrium, say W_1 in Figure 5-1, there would be an excess supply of labor at that point. Households would be offering more labor, OS_{L1}, than firms are prepared to employ (OD_{L1}). Facing this higher wage rate, firms cannot hire as many workers as they would at W_e and continue to maximize profits, so the number of people they are willing to hire declines. Households, on the other hand, see enhanced income opportunities while their nonincome time now "costs" more. Accordingly, they offer more hours of labor to the market. The excess supply of labor at wage rate W_1 is represented by the difference between OS_{L1} and OD_{L1}. This is *unemployment*, which forces workers to bid against each other for the relatively scarce jobs available. They begin to accept lower wages because of the competitive pressures engendered by unemployment, until the wage rate is pushed down toward W_e.

The process of equilibration for a wage rate below W_e is symmetric. In Figure 5-2 the wage rate is set at W_2, below the equilibrium wage rate of W_e. Firms now demand more labor in their pursuit of profit maximization than households are willing to supply. The excess demand for labor is the difference between OD_{L2} and OS_{L2}. This excess demand for labor forces firms to bid against each other for the relatively scarce labor supply. They do this by offering higher wages to induce workers into their firms and away from others. This process forces the wage rate upward toward W_e until that equilibrium position is reached. As the wage rate begins to creep upward, firms demand less labor while households begin to supply more labor, thereby thrusting the market on a trajectory toward a stable equilibrium. The same happens with a wage rate in excess of the equilibrium, as in the earlier illustration, Figure 5-1. In that case a falling wage rate reduces the amount of labor supplied to the market by households, while increasing the firms' demand for labor.

The equilibrium wage rate of W_e, determined in the labor market, becomes the datum taken as given by all the firms and households that make up this labor market, as each pursues its optimizing decision-making behavior. None of the firms or the households that participate in this labor market are large enough to have any influence whatever on the wage rate. They are passive recipients of wage information received from the labor market. Taking this wage rate as a given, the firm proceeds to make a decision about how much labor to employ, and the household makes a decision about how many hours of labor time to offer to the market.

In Figure 5-3 the relationship is shown between the determination of the equilibrium wage rate in the labor market and the employment decision in the firm. The left-hand side of this graph shows the process of wage determination in the labor market. Given this wage, the firm (shown on the right-hand side) sets its level of

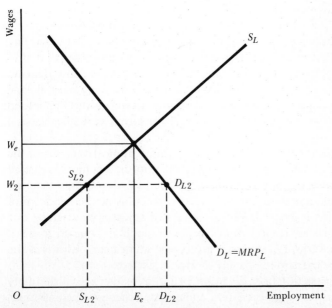

FIGURE 5-2   Effect of a Wage below Equilibrium in a Perfectly Competitive Labor Market

$MRP_L = MC_L$

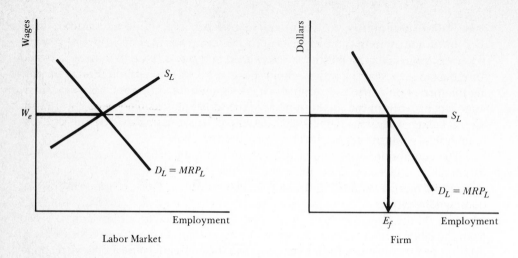

FIGURE 5-3 Relationship between the Determination of Wages in the Labor Market and the Determination of Employment in the Firm

employment at E_f. The firm can hire as many individuals as it likes at this wage. Therefore, the wage rate in the labor market becomes the labor supply curve to the firm. In the labor market the wage is determined. In the firm the level of employment is set, but the wage rate is *not* established by the firm in perfect competition.

However, there is a little sleight of hand being performed here. The wage rate can only be found *after* the firms' labor demand decision is consummated and after the household has made its labor supply decision. But to derive those labor demand and supply decisions in the firm and household, respectively, the wage must already be available. In sum, the wage must be known to derive the functions that are needed to derive the wage in the first instance. How is this puzzle solved in the neoclassical system?

Essentially, this perplexity in the model is circumvented in most versions of the neoclassical marginal productivity theory by making the implicit assumption that all decisions are made *simultaneously*, without time lags. The analytics of the model do not easily accommodate differential timing of decisions. There is neither a system of time lags nor any sense of the *dynamics* of the process of adjustment whereby one variable in the model adjusts after another changes. The model is assumed to work itself out in an instantaneous fashion in which everything immediately adjusts at the same time to shocks and changes in the parameters of the system.

Obviously this is an abstraction from the reality of a labor market, in which supply and demand conditions are changing all the time, and the attainment of an equilibrium wage is complicated further by the existence of a differential lagged response on the part of firms and households. If the time dimension were permitted to enter this model, things would become not only more complicated but perhaps indeterminate as well. Disequilibrium wages could trigger a time-lagged response from some other variable, for example, that would alter the underlying functions sufficiently to prevent the initial equilibrium from ever becoming reconstituted. This problem of time-lagged dynamics is important in understanding the actual operations of a labor market. But it does not nullify using the simplified neoclassical model without the dynamics of time-lagged adjustments. The analytics of the model and its tendencies, rather than the conclusions, are what counts—how firms and households make decisions and how they react to changes in wage rates.

Observation and Interpretation: Wage Determination in Perfect Competition
■

The complete neoclassical marginal productivity theory of wage determination contains an elegance unrivaled by any previous theory of wage and employment determination. This elegance does not mean that the neoclassical model is the best representation of the way in which wages and employment are actually determined in a complex, mature industrial-market economy, with labor unions, government, and large uncompetitive firms operating in an administered labor market—issues examined in this and other chapters in this book. Nevertheless, it represents a foundation for the study of labor economics and a major intellectual milestone in economics.

The wage determined in a market for labor feeds back into the decision-making process in both households and firms. The firm chooses an optimal level of employment that permits it to maximize profits, given conditions in the product market, the technology available, the wage rate determined in the labor market, and the rate of return on capital determined in the market for capital. When the firm chooses its optimal level of employment, it has by implication selected the level of output that maximizes its profits. The firm has also chosen the level of utilization of capital and labor in production that minimizes its cost of production by producing output using the most technically and economically efficient means of production.

Each of the households that make up a labor market has selected that combination of work and nonincome time that provides it with an optimal level of satisfaction, in light of its preferences and of the wage rate determined in the market in which it supplies its labor services.

Rarely has so little gone so far. The one piece of information about the wage rate determined in the labor market, interacting with the decision-making behavioral axioms in the households and firms that compose the labor market, is sufficient to yield a result in which firms have maximized profits while minimizing costs and households have maximized satisfaction from their lot in life.

In a more general welfare sense, individuals acting as entrepreneurs and as workers have each done the best they can with the constraints imposed upon them. For the society as a whole, the largest wealth has been created at minimum cost—again, under the constraints that have been imposed upon producers and suppliers of labor. Adam

Smith's hunch that the free market and laissez-faire government policy would create the greatest wealth of nations and the highest level of individual welfare has been reaffirmed in this model more than a century after he initially exposed the world to his thoughts on political economy.

To this point the neoclassical model has been based upon perfect competition in product and labor markets. It is now time to relax that set of institutional assumptions, starting first with a change in the institutional environment in the product market.

Imperfect Competition and Wage-Employment Determination

The 1930s produced a great deal of speculation among economists about the impact of economic concentration on the economy. Almost simultaneously two books were written that transformed this speculation into a formal economic model. One, by Joan Robinson from Great Britain, used the term *imperfect competition* to characterize twentieth century developments in the economy. The other, written by an American, E. Chamberlin, coined the term *monopolistic competition* to describe the same phenomenon.[4] Although the point of departure for these models is the product market, they do have relevance for the firm's decision concerning the optimal level of employment, because the demand for labor depends, in part, on the product market.

In the model of imperfect competition, the assumption of perfect competition in the product market is relaxed while the assumption of perfect competition in the labor market is retained. The essence of the altered institutional environment is that the firm is now a large enough supplier of output to the market in which it sells its product that it can set the price for its output rather than merely receiving the price from the market. It has become a *price setter* as opposed to its previous position in perfect competition, in which it was a passive price taker. In the labor market, on the other hand, the firm is still assumed to purchase a small enough proportion of the labor sold on that market that its employment decisions do not affect the wage rate. This is the same condition that prevailed in the perfectly competitive labor market encountered in earlier chapters.

The changed institutional context for the firm in the product market has implications for the wage rate and for the employment decision. The firm as a price setter in an imperfectly competitive product market faces a downward-sloping demand curve for its output, as depicted in Figure 5-4, in contrast to the horizontal, perfectly elastic product demand curve it faced in perfect competition. Associated with this downward-sloping product demand curve is a marginal revenue curve that also slopes downward and that lies below the demand curve at all levels of output. This configuration of

---

[4] Joan Robinson, *The Economics of Imperfect Competition,* 2nd ed. (London: Macmillan and Co., 1969); and E. Chamberlin, *The Theory of Monopolistic Competition* (Cambridge: Harvard University Press, 1933).

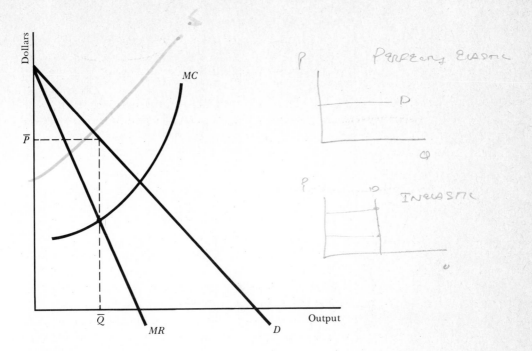

FIGURE 5-4 The Product Market for the Firm in Imperfect Condition

demand and marginal revenue contasts with the situation of perfect competition, in which the perfectly elastic demand curve is identical at all points to the firm's marginal revenue curve.[5]

This new product market condition affects the firm's decision to employ labor, because it alters the circumstances surrounding the profit-maximizing level of output. If the firm maximizes profits at the point at which marginal revenue equals marginal cost, it will now produce less than in perfect competition, since the marginal revenue curve now lies below the average revenue or demand curve at all levels of output. And if less output is produced, there will also be less employment. Since the demand-for-labor curve is influenced by the marginal revenue derived from the production and sale of the last unit of output, the fact that marginal revenue now behaves differently in imperfectly competitive product markets means that the marginal revenue product of labor curve will also be different.

---

[5] The demand curve in the neoclassical model is the same as the *average* curve—the revenue received per unit of sales. In imperfect competition the firm still produces where marginal revenue equals marginal cost, at point $\bar{Q}$ in Figure 5-4. However, since marginal revenue lies below average revenue (i.e., demand), the firm will produce less than it would have under conditions of perfect competition. For output level $\bar{Q}$, the firm charges its customers $\bar{P}$. This is the price the market will sustain.

Table 5-1 The Marginal Revenue Product of Labor Curve in Imperfect Competition

Labor Inputs (L)	Output (Q)	Changes in Output (ΔQ)	Changes in Labor Input (ΔL)	Marginal Product of Labor (ΔQ/ΔL)	Product Price (P)	Value of Marginal Product of Labor $(P)\left(\frac{\Delta Q}{\Delta L}\right)$	Wage per Unit of Labor (W)	Marginal Revenue (MR)	Marginal Revenue Product of Labor[a] $(MR)\left(\frac{\Delta Q}{\Delta L}\right)$
2	45	—	—	—	$1.24	—	$40.00	—	—
3	95	50	1	50	1.12	$56.00	40.00	$1.012	$50.60
4	143	48	1	48	1.00	48.00	40.00	.763	36.62
5	183	40	1	40	.89	35.60	40.00	.497	19.87
6	215	32	1	32	.79	25.28	40.00	.218	6.98
7	237	22	1	22	.70	15.40	40.00	-.79	-3.95
8	247	10	1	10	.63	6.30	40.00	-1.029	-10.29
9	252	5	1	5	.56	2.80	40.00	-2.898	-14.49

[a]Rounded to nearest cent.

This is shown formally in Table 5-1, which reproduces the arithmetic example introduced in Chapter 3. However, product price now declines, instead of being constant, to reflect the downward-sloping demand curve for the firm in imperfect competition. The value of the marginal product of labor curve is different from what it was in perfect competition, because of the declining price. Associated with this declining price is a falling marginal revenue curve. The marginal revenue product of labor curve is now less than the value of the marginal product of labor for every level of employment.[6]

The firm follows the same profit-maximizing decision rule as it did under perfect competition. It will employ labor at the point at which marginal revenue equals marginal cost. In this instance, slightly less than four full-time workers will be hired. The marginal cost of hiring the fourth worker is the wage cost, $40. The additional revenue produced by that fourth worker is $36.62—the marginal revenue product of labor.[7] Using the same decision rule as the firm followed in perfect competition, this imperfectly competitive firm now employs two workers less and maximizes its profits at a lower level of output.[8]

The same result can be demonstrated by using the familiar graph that shows the firm's decision-making process surrounding its employment of labor. This is done in Figure 5-5. The marginal revenue product of labor (MRP_L) lies below the value of the marginal product of labor curve (VMP_L) at all levels of employment. The firm still operates as a perfect competitor in the labor market in which it acquires labor. This is reflected by the familiar perfectly elastic, horizontal labor supply curve at the prevailing market-determined wage rate ($\overline{W}$). The firm can hire as many workers as it wishes at that wage.

Given a market-determined wage rate of $\overline{W}$, the firm sets its optimal level of employment at $\overline{E}$, the point at which the wage rate (marginal cost) just equals the marginal revenue product of labor. At this point the firm operating in an imperfectly competitive product market will maximize its profits and minimize its costs by choosing a level of employment at which marginal revenue equals marginal cost. If the firm were to employ E_p units of labor, as it would have done when it operated in a perfectly competitive product market, it would now earn less profit.[9] The wage rate, or the

---

[6] Compare this table with Table 3-2 in Chapter 3. Notice three important differences. First, price and marginal revenue are no longer equal to each other, and they decline as more employees are added to the firm. Second, the value of the marginal product of labor and the marginal revenue product of labor are no longer equal to each other. Third, the value of the marginal product of labor is different in imperfect competition compared with perfect competition in product markets, as is the marginal revenue product of labor.

[7] More precisely, slightly less than four units of labor will be employed. This is the difficulty of using discrete units of labor in an example when the pure model calls for exact decisions at the margin.

[8] With the same labor market conditions and the same wage costs, the firm in perfectly competitive product markets was previously employing six workers. See Chapter 3, page 36.

[9] In a perfectly competitive situation, $MRP_L = VMP_L$ and the firm sets its level of employment at E_p, where $\overline{W} = VMP_L = MRP_L$.

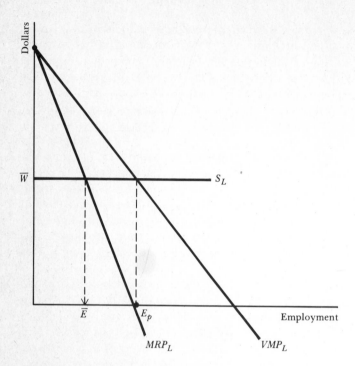

FIGURE 5-5 The Determination of Employment in a Firm Producing for an Imperfectly Competitive Product Market

marginal cost per unit of employment, would exceed the marginal revenue from all the units of labor hired above $\overline{E}$. Similarly, if the firm employed fewer than $\overline{E}$ units of labor, it would not be maximizing profits, since all units of labor employed below $\overline{E}$ would be yielding amounts of marginal revenue greater than their costs to the firm at the margin.

Under conditions of imperfect competition, therefore, employment and output in the firm are less, but profits are greater. The firm can set its price for the output it brings to the market and is a large enough supplier of products to the market that it can see the consequences of its pricing decisions. It now faces a downward-sloping product demand curve, which is more inelastic over the entire range than in perfect competition, where the firm faced a perfectly elastic, horizontal product demand curve over its entire range of operations. For the firm's employment decision, this means that the marginal revenue received from an additional unit of labor is less than the average revenue, and consequently fewer workers are needed to produce the lower level of output.

Oligopoly and Wage-Employment Determination

A specific form of imperfect competition in product markets is an *oligopoly*. This is a situation in which a few sellers dominate a product market that is characterized by a particular type of *reactive behavior* among the oligopolists. The auto, steel, and rubber industries, for example, are oligopolies, since in each of those sectors of the economy a few firms account for nearly all the output.

Many of these oligopolies were formed in the early part of this century, as large-scale industrial production replaced the smaller scale of operations that characterized the nineteenth century. As the scale of operations increased and a few firms came to dominate basic industries, perfect competition atrophied and was replaced by oligopolistic competition. In the 1930s the consensus about oligopoly pricing was that prices in those sectors were relatively stable in the face of changing market conditions. Many economists observed that in sectors of the economy that were controlled by oligopolies, prices were stable during the Great Depression, whereas the more competitive sectors of the economy showed evidence of declining prices during that downturn.[10] Today, of course, very few prices ever decline in an absolute sense, but they did during the Great Depression. Oligopolies and the way they form their prices are treated differently today by economists; this treatment will be examined in a later chapter (Chapter 17).

In the 1930s the static nature of oligopoly pricing led to the development of what is called the *kinked-demand-curve model*.[11] The kinked demand curve refers to the product market demand. But since the demand for labor is linked to the demand for the firm's product, it also has important implications for the firm's labor demand curve.

In the kinked-demand-curve model the assumption is retained that the firm is operating in a perfectly competitive market for labor while selling its product on an oligopolistic market. The firm operating in this market must consider how its rivals will react to price increases and decreases. The *reaction function,* as it is sometimes called, is the distinctive characteristic of an oligopolistic market. How a firm expects its rivals to respond to its moves, as in an industrial chess game, must be taken into account as the firm plots its pricing strategy. There can be many different presumptions about the reactions of rivals; so there are many different models of an oligopoly. But the kinked demand curve is one model that has interesting implications for pricing decisions and for the employment decision.

---

[10] Adolf A. Berle and Gardiner C. Means, *The Modern Corporation and Private Property,* rev. ed. (New York: Harcourt Brace Jovanovich, 1967).

[11] Paul M. Sweezy, "Demand Under Conditions of Oligopoly," *Journal of Political Economy* 47 (August 1939), pp. 568-73.

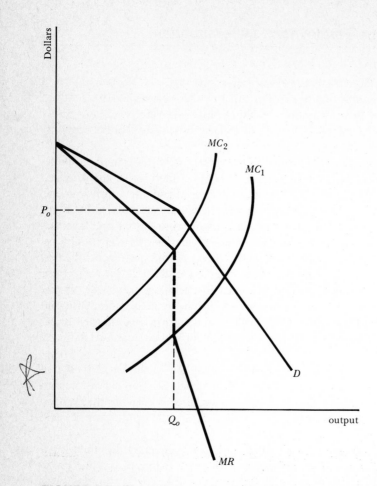

FIGURE 5-6 Kinked-Demand-Curve Model

In this model the reactions of rivals to price *increases* are presumed to be different from reactions to price *decreases*. If a firm *increases* its product price, the firm's rivals are assumed not to follow its lead. The rivals will keep their prices at the existing level and attempt to outcompete the firm by selling their output at a lower price than the firm that raised its price. Since price increases will not be emulated by the other oligopolistic rivals, the firm will lose substantial sales if it decides to go it alone with its price increase.

On the other hand, if the oligopolistic firm *lowers* its price, all the other firms will follow in order to protect themselves from being priced out of the market. Consequently, a price decrease by the firm will be met by other members of the oligopoly, and the firm will be able to increase its sales only slightly. As shown in Figure 5-6 the demand curve for the oligopolistic firm has two segments—an elastic portion above the prevailing price and an inelastic portion below it.[12]

Since none of the firms in this oligopolistic market can benefit from either price increases or price reductions, prices tend to remain fixed. They are "sticky" and do not change even in the face of cost changes. As a corollary to sticky prices, output will also tend to remain at a constant level, even in the face of cost changes.[13]

The consequence of this market structure is a peculiar sort of labor demand curve, illustrated by the marginal revenue product of labor curve in Figure 5-7. If we assume that the labor market is still operating in a perfectly competitive way, the firm takes the wage rate as given and decides on its optimal level of employment. If the wage were W_2 in Figure 5-7, the firm would employ $\overline{E}$ units of labor. If the wage rate fell to W_1, for example, it would still employ $\overline{E}$ units of labor. In fact, for any wage rate between W_1 and W_2, the level of employment does not change. This is consistent with the situation in the product market, where output and price do not change in response to changes in marginal costs.[14]

This model was quite controversial when it was first introduced. The implications run counter to those of standard neoclassical economics. In the neoclassical model, any reduction in wages will increase employment, holding other variables constant. During the Great Depression of the 1930s, policies of reducing wages in order to increase employment were frequently advocated by members of the economics profession. Not until Keynes came along in the late 1930s was there a serious intellectual competitor to the neoclassical policy prescription of lowering wages to increase employment. However, this kinked oligopoly demand curve model shows that if wages

---

[12] If the oligopolistic firm raises the price charged for its product, other firms in the market will not follow. Hence, this firm will lose substantial sales, so the demand curve above the prevailing price is *elastic*. However, for price cuts, other firms will follow, and the price-cutting firm will gain little in sales. Hence, the portion of the demand curve below the prevailing price is inelastic. In Figure 5-6 the oligopolistic firm faces a more elastic demand for its product above the prevailing price, P_o. Below the prevailing price, it faces a more inelastic demand. This shows up in the *kink* in the demand curve for the oligopolistic firm's product at the prevailing price. The marginal revenue curve associated with this kinked demand curve will have a discontinuity, shown by the dotted line that connects the upper and lower portions of the marginal revenue curve.

[13] The firm's product demand curve has a *kink* associated with it at the prevailing price. This kink reflects the fact that the elasticity of demand is different for price increases and price decreases. Consequently, the *marginal revenue* associated with this kinked demand curve has a discontinuity, which is reflected in the labor demand curve as well. In Figure 5-6 two marginal cost curves are shown—MC_1 and MC_2. Within that range of marginal costs, marginal revenue is, in effect, constant. Therefore, for marginal costs anywhere between MC_1 and MC_2, marginal revenue equals marginal cost at the same level of output, Q_o. Costs can change in the kinked-demand model, but output and prices will remain fixed at P_o and Q_o. In more intuitive terms, costs were falling during the Great Depression (say from MC_2 to MC_1), but in many concentrated sectors of the economy, prices did not fall and output did not increase. These results are consistent with the kinked-demand-curve model of an oligopoly.

[14] A fall in wages from W_2 to W_1 shows up in Figure 5-6 as the fall in marginal costs from MC_2 to MC_1. Prices do not fall as a consequence of the fall in wages and marginal costs, as they would in the perfectly competitive model. Because of this, output and employment do not increase when wages fall.

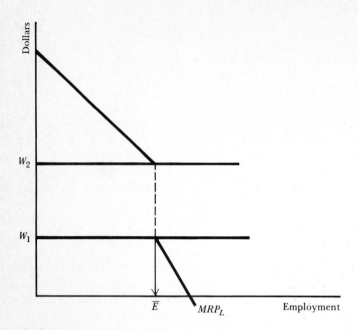

FIGURE 5-7 Employment Determination in the Kinked-Demand-Curve Model

are reduced within some range, employment will remain constant if the firm's pricing behavior operates according to the assumptions about oligopoly behavior. Rather than increasing employment, all a wage reduction does is produce more profits for the firm. So if the kinked-demand-curve model is an accurate depiction of oligopoly markets, wage reductions as a policy prescription to increase employment and reduce unemployment may not be successful.

Monopsony and Wage-Employment Determination

The previous discussion of imperfect and oligopolistic competition retained the assumption of perfect competition in the labor market while relaxing the assumption of perfect competition in the product market. *Monopsony* reverses this process: perfect competition is assumed to prevail in the product market, while the labor market is no longer perfectly competitive. Monopsony is a market situation in which there are only a few purchasers of labor. Consequently, any decisions made by the firm in this labor market affect the wage rate. No longer is the firm a passive recipient of wage information from the labor market. Instead of a wage-taker, under monopsony conditions the firm becomes a *wage-setter.* Unlike the institutional setting of atomistic competition, the firm in a monopsonistic situation is now a large enough employer of labor

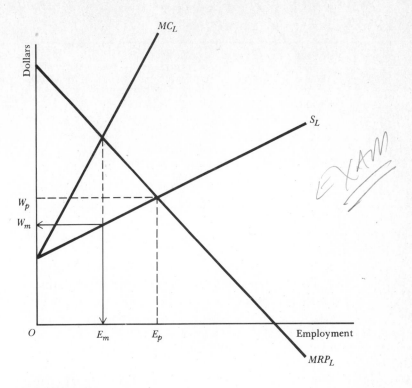

FIGURE 5-8 Monopsony

in a particular market that its decision to hire labor affects the wage rate it must pay to all the workers it employs. A company town is an example of a monopsony. Here, the firm is the only employer in town, and this provides it with substantial economic power vis-à-vis labor.

The impact of monopsony on the wage-employment decision is shown in Figure 5-8. The firm faces the familiar demand curve for labor of perfect competition—the marginal revenue product of labor curve. However, since the firm is a large enough employer of labor in this market, it now faces an upward-sloping labor supply curve rather than the perfectly elastic, horizontal labor supply curve of perfect competition. In effect, the monopsonistic firm has become the market for labor. In order to hire more labor, the firm must now pay a higher wage rate. It can no longer simply hire as much labor as it likes at a constant wage rate.

Since labor is homogeneous, whenever the monopsonistic firm hires an additional unit of labor at a higher wage rate it must also pay all the workers it had hired previously the same higher wage rate to attract the labor it needs to produce at a level that maximizes profits. This yields a *marginal cost of labor curve*, shown in Figure 5-8. The cost to the firm of hiring an additional worker is greater than the wage rate under conditions of perfect competition. The monopsonistic firm must now pay the higher

TABLE 5-2   Monopsony and the Marginal Cost of Labor

Labor Inputs (L)	Wage Rate per Hour (W)	Total Cost of Labor (W × L)	Marginal Cost of Labor
3	$1.00	$ 3.00	
4	1.50	6.00	$ 3.00
5	2.00	10.00	4.00
6	3.00	18.00	8.00
7	4.00	28.00	10.00
8	5.00	40.00	12.00
9	6.00	54.00	14.00
10	7.00	70.00	16.00

wage rate to all the previous workers it had employed, who are presumed to be homogeneous with respect to their human capital.[15] As a consequence, the marginal cost of labor curve (MC_L) lies above the labor supply curve at all levels of employment.

To understand why the marginal cost of labor curve lies above the labor supply curve, consider the circumstances shown in Table 5-2. A wage rate per hour that increases as more units of labor are hired is shown in the second column of that table. In the third column, there is the total cost for the firm of hiring the various units of labor at the rising wage rate per hour. The marginal cost of labor is the additional cost of hiring another unit of labor and is indicated in the fourth column. For example, the marginal cost to the firm of hiring a sixth unit of labor is $8, the difference between the total labor costs associated with the fifth unit ($10) and the sixth unit ($18). With a rising wage rate per unit of labor employed, the marginal cost of labor is greater than the wage rate for each unit of labor employed, as shown in Figure 5-7.

Under conditions of monopsony the *marginal cost* of hiring an additional worker is defined by the MC_L curve. In such a labor market, the firm will find its optimal level of employment by the familiar decision rule of equating marginal revenue and marginal cost. In Figure 5-8 this means that the firm's optimal employment level is E_m, found by equating the marginal revenue product of labor (MRP_L) with the marginal cost of labor (MC_L). To hire E_m units of labor, the firm pays a wage rate of W_m. This is found by reading the wage rate off the labor supply curve for employment level E_m. Note that the firm does *not* pay a wage rate corresponding to the point at which the marginal cost of labor curve intersects the demand for labor curve. The marginal cost of labor curve shows the marginal cost of hiring an additional worker. But it is the supply of labor curve that indicates the wage rate (W_m) the firm must

---

[15] If labor is not homogeneous, the monopsonistic firm can "discriminate" among its employees and pay the new, higher wage only to those workers who are the same as the new workers hired. This is called the case of a *discriminating monopsonist*. The idea behind this model is the same, although employment will vary from the level in the case being described.

pay to induce households to supply labor in sufficient quantities to meet the employment requirements of the firm (E_m).

The condition of monopsony in the labor market produces a lower level of employment than would be forthcoming under conditions of perfect competition, as well as a lower wage rate. In Figure 5-8, E_p and W_p reflect the higher level of employment and the higher wage rate, respectively, that would have prevailed if this market had been governed by conditions of perfect competition.

The firm, under conditions of monopsony, makes profits above those earned in perfect competition. Labor is paid a wage rate less than its marginal revenue product (see Figure 5-8). Therefore, the firm takes in revenue at the margin that *exceeds* its average cost for labor, and extra profits are earned. These additional profits accrue to the firm solely because it operates in a monopsonistic environment. Such extra earnings are called "monopsonistic profits."

Monopsony and the Minimum Wage

There is much controversy today surrounding minimum wage laws. These laws have been challenged on the grounds that they distort resource allocation and create unemployment by setting the wage above its competitive market-clearing level. In a later

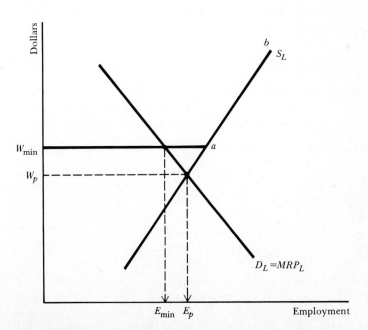

FIGURE 5-9 Minimum Wages and Perfectly Competitive Labor Markets

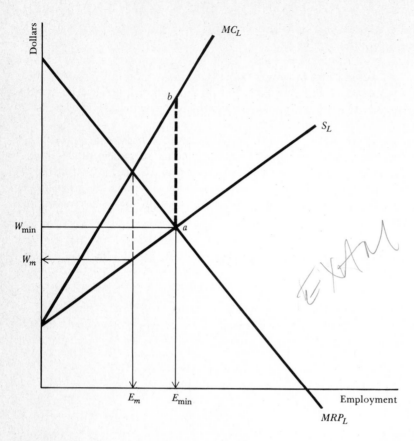

FIGURE 5-10   Minimum Wages and Monopsonistic Labor Markets

chapter of this book, minimum wage laws and the debate they have engendered will be examined in detail, along with empirical evidence pertaining to the impact of minimum wages on employment. In connection with this discussion of monopsony, however, minimum wage laws have some interesting and perhaps surprising implications.

In order to contrast the monopsony case, let us first look at the impact of minimum wage laws in perfect competition. If the minimum wage (W_{min}) is set above the market-clearing equilibrium wage of perfect competition (W_p), unemployment will result. This is shown in Figure 5-9. Employment after the introduction of a minimum wage has fallen to E_{min} from E_p. Firms in this labor market cannot hire anyone below the minimum wage. In effect, the supply curve for labor is now changed. It starts with the horizontal section that extends from the minimum wage to the upward-sloping supply curve of the market. This new supply curve is shown as $W_{min}ab$ in Figure 5-9. The firms in this labor market continue to follow the decision rule of equating marginal revenue and marginal cost to find their profit-maximizing levels of employment and output. Only now the marginal cost has risen to W_{min}, and without any compensating changes in marginal revenue, employment and output will have to be reduced.

Under conditions of monopsony in labor markets, a minimum wage law can, under certain circumstances, *increase* both employment and wages. Consider Figure 5-10: the monopsonist initially is employing E_m units of labor and paying a wage of W_m. Introduce a minimum wage law in which the wage is set at W_{min}. Now the marginal cost of labor is equal to the horizontal line $W_{min}a$, after which there is a discontinuity before the marginal cost of labor begins once again at bMC_L. In effect, for levels of employment up to E_{min}, the firm need not pay previously employed workers a higher wage, so its labor supply curve is horizontal up to the point at which the minimum wage intersects the upward-sloping labor supply curve.[16]

With the minimum wage at W_{min}, the firm employs E_{min} units of labor, following the decision rule of equating marginal revenue and marginal cost. Marginal revenue is the MRP_L curve, and marginal cost is the curve $W_{min}a$ and, after the discontinuity, bMC_L. Workers are paid more than they previously were (W_{min} versus W_m), and more are now employed (E_{min} compared with E_m). This level of employment and this wage rate are the ones that would have prevailed if perfect competition had existed in the labor market with a minimum wage equal to W_{min}. If the minimum wage were set above W_{min}, employment would be greater than under conditions of monopsony but less than it would be with the minimum wage established at the perfectly competitive level. The limit to increases in the minimum wage that would increase employment occurs at a wage rate at which the monopsonist's original MC_L and MRP_L are equal, at employment level E_m.[17]

A trade union that affects the wage established in a monopsonistic labor market can also produce a result that increases both employment and the wage for its members. If you substitute the trade union wage for the minimum wage under conditions of monopsony, all the same conclusions hold. A trade union that increases the wage above W_m can increase employment up to the limit at which the monopsonistic firm's original MC_L equals the MRP_L.

Market Structure and Wage-Employment Determination

■

The several different types of market structure discussed in this chapter have been summarized in Table 5-3, and the deviations in wage-employment determination from the perfectly competitive norm are indicated. Imperfect competition in product

---

[16] A horizontal labor supply segment reduces the monopsonistic firm to conditions of perfect competition over that segment in which $W = MC_L$.

[17] Many of these applications were first introduced in Gordon F. Bloom, "A Reconsideration of the Theory of Exploitation," *Quarterly Journal of Economics* (May 1941), pp. 413-42.

■

TABLE 5-3 Market Structure and Wage-Employment Determination

Type of Imperfect Competition	Compared to Perfect Competition	
	The Wage	Employment
Imperfect Competition in Product Markets	will be the same	will be lower
Oligopoly: Kinked Demand Curve in Product Market	will be the same	will be constant within a range of wage rates
Monopsony in Labor Market	will be lower	will be lower

markets and the kinked-demand oligopoly model produce the same wage rate as in perfect competition, but the employment outcome is different. Under conditions of imperfect competition, employment is lower, and with the kinked-demand-curve oligopoly model, employment is constant over some range of wage rates. Monopsony in the labor market produces both a lower wage rate and lower employment levels compared with the outcome under perfect competition.

Summary

■

Three models that relax the assumption of perfect competition have been presented in this chapter: imperfect (or monopolistic) competition, oligopolistic competition, and monopsonistic competition. The first two permit economic concentration to prevail in product markets, while monopsonistic competition refers to a condition that deviates from perfect competition in the labor market.

The model of *imperfect competition* yields a demand-for-labor curve that deviates from the demand curve of perfect competition. The marginal revenue product of labor curve lies below the value of the marginal product of labor at all levels of employment, because the firm's marginal revenue from the sales of its products lies below its average revenue per unit of sales. This produces a situation in which employment is less than it would have been for the same wage rate under perfect competition.

Oligopoly is a market situation in which a few firms dominate a product market. Market behavior is characterized by offensive and defensive moves, by thrust and counterthrust, and by response and counterresponse. Each member of the oligopolistic market makes its decision based on what it anticipates the response of its rivals will be. This is called a *reaction function*. One model of an oligopoly that has interesting implications for product prices and employment is the *kinked-demand-curve model*. Here the firm faces a demand curve for its product that is discontinuous; it has a relatively elastic portion above the prevailing price and an inelastic portion below the prevailing price. This produces a situation in which the accompanying marginal revenue product of labor curve has a segment in which the wage rate can fluctuate without changes in employment. And in the product market this means that marginal costs can vary within this range without affecting output or product price.

In the labor market condition of *monopsony,* the firm has become a large enough employer of labor that its decisions concerning how many workers to employ affect the wage rate. It has become a *wage-setter* in such a market condition, instead of a wage-taker, the role it assumes in perfect competition. The marginal cost to the firm of hiring the additional worker is no longer the wage rate; it lies above the existing supply curve at all levels of employment. The firm finds its optimal level of employment at the point at which marginal revenue (the demand for labor) equals marginal cost. This yields a situation in which wages and employment are lower than they would have been in perfect competition, while profits are higher. Laws that set minimum wages, or trade union activity that increases the wage, can have the effect of increasing employment and eliminating these "monopsonistic profits."

Study Questions

1. Discuss the importance of the aggregation problem in deriving labor market demand and supply curves. What set of assumptions is needed to construct such labor market functions?

2. What is the "Cambridge critique"? If you were defending the marginal productivity theory, how would you answer this critique?

3. Provide an analysis of wage determination in a perfectly competitive labor market by focusing on:
   a. how a disequilibrium is corrected;
   b. how a disequilibrium feeds on itself and becomes more of a disequilibrium.

4. Assume you are a member of the President's Council of Economic Advisers. Would you design an employment policy through wage reductions if product markets were predominantly imperfectly competitive? Explain!

5. What is meant by "exploitation" in the case of monopsony? What public policies can alleviate such exploitation?

6. What is the role of labor mobility in clearing labor markets? How does public policy aid or interfere with the clearing of labor markets?

Further Reading

Cartter, Allan M. *Theory of Wages and Employment.* Homewood, IL: Richard D. Irwin, 1959. Chaps. 3 and 6.

Chamberlin, E. *The Theory of Monopolistic Competition*. Cambridge: Harvard University Press, 1933.

Hicks, J. R. *The Theory of Wages*. 2nd ed. New York: St. Martin's Press, 1963. Chap. 1.

Robinson, Joan. *The Economics of Imperfect Competition*. 2nd ed. London: Macmillan and Co., 1969.

Rothschild, K. W. *The Theory of Wages*. Oxford: Basic Blackwell, 1965. Chaps. 7 and 8.

6

Trade Unions and Wage Determination

The "pure theory" of wage determination discussed in the previous chapters ignores the institution of trade unions and its role in the process of wage formation. In the marginal productivity model, the household is at the center of labor supply decisions. Its decisions cannot influence the wage rate. Instead, the individual supplier of labor is represented as a passive responder to wage information received from the labor market.

The institutional reality of a living economy is obviously quite different. In many sectors of the economy, large and powerful labor unions bargain over wages and other matters directly. In those sectors that are not unionized, the wage is influenced by agreements arrived at in the unionized sectors of the economy.

There is agreement among economists that the institutional assumptions of the pure theory do not conform to the reality of the existence of trade unions. However, here the consensus ends. Many economists who study wages and labor markets contend that trade unions have only a small effect on wages. Other economists argue that they have a substantial influence over wages.

Furthermore, there is a methodological dispute underlying the theoretical and empirical arguments about whether trade unions affect wages. *Institutional* economists contend that assumptions do matter. Models based on unreal assumptions are flawed, they argue, because these models can never accurately portray economic reality. On the other side of this methodological argument are the economists following a *positivist* methodology. Positivists claim that it does not matter what assumptions are made, so long as the model effectively predicts behavior that conforms with what happens in the economy. If firms and households behave *as if* they were following the course outlined for them by the assumptions and the marginal productivity model, then it does not matter whether the assumptions are realistic or not.[1]

The *as if* formulation is the foundation for the *positivist methodology,* on which the entire corpus of neoclassical theory is based. This methodology contends that what is important is the *predictability of events* based on the inner workings of the model. The underlying structural assumptions and parameters are of no consequence if the model is an accurate predictor of economic behavior. For example, if lower wages induce firms to hire more workers, as the model would predict, does it matter which structural

Table 6-1   Union Membership, Manufacturing Sector, 1975

Industry Group	Extent of Union Membership (%)
All manufacturing	49
Ordnance & accessories	64
Food and kindred products	52
Tobacco manufactures	42
Textile mill products	17
Apparel & other finished textile products	36
Lumber & wood products	30
Furniture & fixtures	29
Paper & allied products	67
Printing, publishing, & allied industries	38
Chemicals & allied products	46
Products of petroleum & coal	59
Rubber products	51
Leather & leather products	34
Stone, clay, & glass products	62
Primary metal industries	73
Fabricated metal industries	51
Machinery, except electrical	46
Electrical machinery	46
Transportation equipment	71
Instruments & related products	33
Miscellaneous manufacturing industries	34

Source: Richard B. Freeman and James L. Medoff, "New Estimates of Private Sector Unionism in the United States," *Industrial and Labor Relations Review* 32, no. 2 (January 1979), p. 173.

---

[1] This debate appears in Richard Lester, "Shortcomings of Marginal Analysis for Wage-Employment Problems," *American Economics Review* 36 (March 1946), pp. 63-82; Fritz Machlup, "Marginal Analysis and Empirical Research," *American Economic Review* 36 (September 1946), pp. 519-54; and George Stigler, "Professor Lester and the Marginalists," *American Economic Review* 37 (March 1947), pp. 154-57. Portions of these articles have been reprinted in: Richard Perlman, *Wage Determination: Market or Power Forces?* (Boston: D. C. Heath, 1964), pp. 9-54.

assumptions are used to construct a model that yields that outcome? The positivist methodology, on which the neoclassical marginal productivity theory is based, is like nail soup. How do you make nail soup? You start with some nails, then add water, chicken, carrots, potatoes, and celery, and cook for six hours. Then remove all the nails and you have a delicious nail soup!

This defense of marginal productivity theory is persuasive if there is no concern about the underlying structural assumptions and parameters of the model. Institutional theory starts from the point of attempting to define and establish a set of meaningful structural parameters so that the entire system can be better understood. For institutionalists the validity of the assumptions is crucial and cannot be ignored as in the cooking of nail soup. They are trying to describe an institutional reality in order to gain insight into the structure of an economic system.

In one sense this is an argument without a resolution. The methodology one chooses to use in examining an issue depends upon the question being asked and the answers sought. One need not line up on one side or the other in this debate. Eclecticism does not mean fuzziness. If the questions being asked require an institutionalist approach, then that methodology can be effectively employed. Other issues dictate the use of a positivist methodology.

In this chapter and in Part III of this book, institutional considerations are introduced into the body of economic theory as it pertains to the labor market.

Trade Union Membership in the United States

Between 18 and 19 percent of the labor force in the United States belonged to trade unions in 1985. This amounts to approximately 21 million wage and salary earners. Trade union membership peaked in the United States in the middle of the 1950s at about 25 percent of the labor force. Certain sectors of the American economy are more highly unionized than others. For example, about half of all workers in the manufacturing sector are members of trade unions. In services, trade, finance, and agriculture, less than 25 percent of the work force belongs to unions. Union membership among state and local government employees was the fastest-growing segment of organized labor in the 1970s. Between 1970 and 1978, for example, union membership in this sector of the economy grew from 948 thousand to slightly more than 2.2 million.[2]

Table 6-1 provides a detailed breakdown of the percentage of workers who are members of trade unions in various industries within the manufacturing sector of the American economy. There is a wide variation in union membership in this sector. In the middle of the 1970s, when these statistics were collected, the most-unionized

---

[2] U.S. Bureau of the Census, *Statistical Abstract of the United States, 1981* (Washington: Government Printing Office), p. 412.

industry was primary metals (73 percent).[3] At the other end, only 17 percent of the work force in textile mill products belonged to unions. This was the least-unionized industry in the manufacturing sector of the economy. It is not surprising, therefore, that trade union organizers have targeted the textile industry as a priority in their efforts to organize more workers. In 1980 a 20-year-long battle over unionization in the J. P. Stevens Company, the nation's second largest textile producer, ended with the union gaining recognition. For two decades the Amalgamated Clothing and Textile Workers sought union recognition in J. P. Stevens. After nearly two dozen court decisions that upheld the union, J. P. Stevens finally acceded to the granting of union recognition but not until an effective boycott campaign organized by the union had brought the company to the edge of bankruptcy.[4]

The Trade Union and Its Goals

The trade union as an organization will attempt to set objectives in its wage bargaining as it represents its members vis-à-vis an employer. While made up of the individual preferences and goals of its members, the trade union as an institution fashions those disparate individual objectives into a unified wage bargaining posture. Therefore, at a given time, the union's objectives may or may not coincide with the specific preferences of any one of its members. What those union objectives, goals, and ambitions are has been subject to substantial speculation by labor economists. There is no general consensus about the goals and objectives of a trade union when it represents the collective ambitions of its members. What follows is a discussion of the main ideas that have been advanced on this question and the debates these ideas have produced.

Economists have suggested several possible objectives for a trade union and its leadership.[5] A trade union might seek to obtain the highest possible wage without consideration of any other consequences within the market constraints it faces. Or the trade union might seek to maximize the size of its membership. Yet another possible goal for a trade union is to maximize its revenues by achieving the optimum combi-

---

[3] Reliable statistics on union membership by economic sector are difficult to find. The official data compiled by the Department of Labor, the department admits, "cannot be applied to industry employment with precision." (U.S. Department of Labor, *Director of National Unions and Employee Associations, 1979* [Washington: Government Printing Office], p. 70.) For this reason, the figures compiled from other sources and used here are deemed to be more reliable estimates of union membership by industry. Unfortunately, they are a bit dated. The Department of Labor's published estimates of union membership by sector are presented in Table 2-8 in this book. The Department of Labor stopped collecting statistics on union membership in 1981.

[4] James L. Rowe, Jr., "Stevens, Union Sign Pact; Boycott Ends," *Washington Post,* October 20, 1980, p. A6.

[5] John T. Dunlop, *Wage Determination under Trade Unions* (New York: Augustus M. Kelley, 1966; original edition, 1944), chap. 2.

nation of wages and employment. All of these objectives are plausible. The problem is to find the single objective that neatly defines trade union behavior. Such a pursuit has not, so far, found any one goal to be supreme over others.

If the trade union and its leadership seek to maximize the wage rate, they face several constraints. The first is a set of constraints imposed upon them by the conditions of the labor market. No union leadership will push wages so high that the union prices itself completely out of the market. This would be self-defeating because the wage rate would in effect become zero if the firm the union was dealing with went out of business.

The 1980s provided ample evidence that a trade union will not negotiate itself out of existence. Workers employed by the Chrysler Corporation, for example, who are members of the United Auto Workers (UAW), accepted a wage freeze for three years rather than see the corporation go bankrupt. The wage freeze, in total, cost the UAW members over one billion dollars in lost wages and benefits.[6] UAW-Chrysler workers voted to forgo this billion dollars in earnings, which had already been agreed to by Chrylser, in order to preserve their jobs.

The trade union that seeks to maximize its wage rate is paying more attention to existing members than to individuals who are not yet members of the union.[7] By seeking the highest possible wage, the union is sacrificing employment increases, which could potentially increase the size of its membership.

This consideration has led to a second possible union objective—namely, the maximization of its membership. When membership maximization is considered, the trade union and its leadership will take account of the employment effects of a higher wage. They will be prepared to make some concessions on wages in order to insure that their membership size does not suffer.

A close corollary of the membership maximization objective is the objective of maximization of total revenue for the trade union as an organization. The trade union collects dues from its members. The total of the dues collected depends on both the number of members in the union and the wages received by union members. The wage rate is an important factor in determining the size of the dues payment per union member, and the number of union members is another factor in establishing the revenue received by the union from its members.

If the trade union explicitly recognizes the trade-off between higher wages and employment, it will differentiate between situations in which demand is expanding in the firm with which it is negotiating and situations in which demand is falling. If we start from some existing wage, the trade union faces the problem of how to strike a negotiating posture when the demand for its labor is rising or falling.

---

[6] Warren Brown, "UAW Approves Chrysler Pay Cuts," *Washington Post,* February 3, 1981, p. E1.

[7] If the elasticity of demand for labor is high, a union-negotiated wage increase could also reduce existing employment (and union membership) in circumstances in which the demand for labor was not growing. Union leadership, however, tends to believe that it does not have any influence over employment or the demand for labor. We discuss this in more detail later in this chapter.

If demand is increasing, the trade union will be more interested in obtaining higher wages and will be prepared to trade those higher wages off against increased employment.[8] This, at least, is the consensus about this situation. However, when demand for its labor is declining, the trade union will seek to protect the existing wage. It does this by resisting wage reductions, which has the effect of reducing employment in the context of the wage-employment trade-off.

There are valid institutional reasons for a union's seeking to hold the line on wages even at the cost of a reduction in employment. The trade union never wants to give up previously negotiated gains. Its mind-set is one that places a high value on protecting and consolidating previous gains by establishing a floor on wages. This floor provides a foundation for future improvements in wages, according to a trade union leader's view of collective bargaining.

Declines in the demand for labor are seen typically as short-term adjustments occasioned by the downturn in the business cycle. If the decline in demand is more long-term and structural in character, then the generalization that trade unions will accept employment decreases for the sake of wage stability begins to lose its applicability. In the early 1980s many unions negotiated wage concessions—reductions in the wages and fringe benefits that had previously been negotiated into contracts. This occurred in the auto, trucking, and rubber industries, among others. Concession bargaining is an unusual situation caused by the steep declines in the demand for labor that were more than short-term adjustments to a business cycle.

A study of 45 instances of wage concessions in 1981 and 1982 concluded that only after the declines in employment were severe enough to reach the workers with the most seniority were union wage concessions negotiated. Daniel J. B. Mitchell, the author of this study, says that such a severe decline "has not happened in other postwar recessions."[9]

The differing trade-off a union would prefer to make for increases and reductions in demand for its labor is illustrated in Figure 6-1. The existing wage is $\overline{W}$. If demand were to increase, the union would prefer to move along the expansion path from $\overline{U}$ to U_1. Wages are increasing substantially and employment only a little. However, for cyclical reductions in the short-term demand for its labor, the union would prefer to move along the segment $\overline{U}U_2$ in Figure 6-1.[10] It is protecting the previously negotiated wage level and trading off employment. This version of the union's goals in a dynamic setting of increasing and declining demand implies that wages are a higher

---

[8] Allan M. Cartter, *Theory of Wages and Employment* (Homewood, IL: Richard D. Irwin, 1959), chaps. 7, 8.

[9] "Moderation's Chance to Survive," *Business Week,* April 19, 1982, p. 123.

[10] In the recent instances of wage concessions for long-term structural declines in demand, another segment of the curve of Figure 6-1 would start at around U_2 and take a more vertical drop. If the union has to accept unemployment in its trade-off for wage stability, it prefers to have its members put on *layoff,* waiting for recall, rather than discharged from the firm. This status gives the union member the right to recall when employment opportunities arise, and it does not jeopardize the benefits an employee accrues by virtue of seniority. See James L. Medoff, "Layoffs and Alternatives under Trade Unions in U.S. Manufacturing," *American Economic Review* 69, no. 3 (June 1979), pp. 380-95.

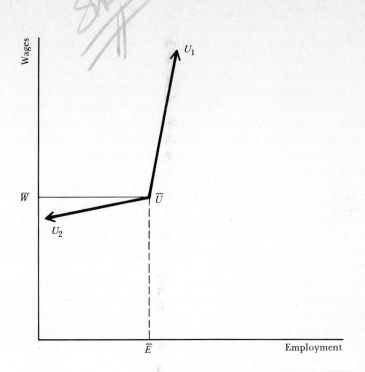

Figure 6-1 Union Wage-Employment Preferences

priority than employment for a trade union. Since the union can only *indirectly* affect employment, its preoccupation with wages is not unreasonable.

Figure 6-1 shows the union *preferences*. Whether it can obtain these objectives depends upon a set of factors which we will consider later in this chapter.

Institutional Theory and Wage Determination

Writing in the late 1940s, the labor economist Arthur Ross posed a fundamental challenge to virtually all of the formal models of wage determination, whether of the neoclassical marginal productivity variety or of the trade union sort discussed earlier in this chapter.[11] Ross contended that the trade union was such a distinctive institution that it could not be shoehorned into any formal model that yielded generalizations about wage determination. Ross's model of a trade union can be termed "pure institutionalism," a counterpart to the pure theory of neoclassical marginal productivity analysis.

---

[11] Arthur M. Ross, *Trade Union Wage Policy* (Berkeley: University of California Press, 1948).

Ross argued, first, that the trade union as an institution has behavior patterns of its own that are distinct from those of its individual members. He contended that a trade union can become larger than (or different from) the sum of its parts—taking on a life of its own, with its separate goals, responses to external stimuli, and behavior patterns. Ross argued further that trade union policy can be comprehended most effectively by examining the operational decisions made during the course of collective bargaining. The trade union is a social-political institution operating in an economic environment. And in this posture, it seeks, above all, *survival and growth.*

This is why unions threatened with extinction will mount long and costly strikes that can never have a purely objective payoff since the additional money gained from the strike, even if won, will never offset the income lost during the strike. Examples of this abound: the railroad unions that were threatened with extinction in the 1960s (and finally eliminated) and the various craft unions in the printing trades today that are slowly being forced out of existence by computer technology and aggressive newspaper management.

In terms of the union's wage goals, Ross made a major contribution when he introduced the notion that a trade union will *pattern* its wage-bargaining posture after unions operating in a similar industrial structure with which there has historically been some comparability of wages. For example, the United Auto Workers will pattern its wage demands after the United Steelworkers of America, or after the Rubber Workers, or vice-versa.

Ross characterized these wage patterns as "*orbits of coercive comparison.*" Union leaders will pattern their wage posture during *collective bargaining rounds* after other unions operating in similar industrial structures with some historical antecedent to the present bargaining situation. Part of the reason this is done is that trade union leaders are dependent on their members for reelection. If they stray too far from what is expected of them, they will not be reelected. One of the issues in the election process is how effective the existing trade union leadership has been in advancing the wage and working-condition demands of the membership. A union member's electoral decision will be influenced by how well the union leadership did in comparison with unions operating in similar situations.

Ross established the concept of *pattern bargaining,* and as we shall see in a later chapter, this was one of the most important empirical breakthroughs in the study of wage determination under trade unions. But as important as this contribution was, Ross also reminded us that the trade union is an institution of individual human beings, who are motivated not only by objective economic forces. They are also motivated by the subjective force of consciousness. And the subjective forces are the ones that energize and motivate individuals to endure great suffering and hardship. The trade union member has an enormous attachment to his or her union and will be prepared to absorb substantial costs whenever the union's integrity is challenged. For this reason, union members vote to strike, sometimes in opposition to their own leadership, when they feel abused by management, even though that strike has no objective basis—that is, no likelihood of ever returning enough financial rewards to offset the income lost during the strike. These social dynamics should not be lost in the maze of formal model-building, which has its place in labor economics but which is not the entire story of labor's role in the economy.

The Trade Union as an Economic Institution

A trade union can be conceived of as an institution that receives *inputs* from a variety of external sources, then filters those inputs through its own unique organizational *internal structures* and finally produces certain *outcomes*.

The inputs received by the trade union are:

- the unemployment rate, which is an indicator of general conditions of demand and supply in the labor market;

- the structure of the industry in which the union operates, including the degree of competition in the product market;

- the orbits of coercive comparison—that is, the other unions operating in similar industries to which the union in question has historically been compared;

- the state of public opinion about unions (is the public, in general, favorably or unfavorably disposed toward unions?);

- the legislative, executive, and judicial environments in which the unions have to operate (at different times, unions receive a more or less favorable hearing in the courts, the executive offices, and the legislatures in the nation).

These elements of the union's environment exist external to its own decision-making apparatus, yet they heavily influence the decisions a union makes. Unions also attempt to influence these external forces, where they can, to make them as favorable as possible to their own case. So, for example, unions attempt to influence public policy and the general climate of public opinion in order to loosen up the constraints on their actions.

Facing these same external factors, different unions will reach different decisions about collective bargaining objectives depending upon the *internal structure* of the union. This often-neglected aspect of union behavior is critial in understanding how a union sets priorities when it faces trade-offs between two equally desirable objectives. There are a number of aspects of the internal union structure that influence the character of the union's objectives.

- The age structure of the union will influence the union's decision to push for current wage increases as opposed to more fringe benefits in the form of health and pension programs. The younger the union members, the more likely the union will be to seek current wage increases; the older the union members, the more likely the union will be to press for pension and health benefits.

- The skill distribution of the union membership will influence how a union proceeds to establish a bargaining position on the wage structure for different skill groups in its union. The more diversified the skill levels in the union, the more likely it is that there will be a large wage differential. Furthermore, many industrial unions, which consist of a great array of skill levels and occupations, absorbed preexisting craft unions of skilled workers when they were organized in the 1930s. In some instances, the United Auto Workers being one prime example, the union will grant special voting privileges to the preexisting skilled worker group, thus giving them greater power over general union decisions.

- The size of the strike fund accumulated by the union will affect its militancy in negotiations and its ability to withstand a long strike.

- The degree of democracy in the union will affect wage structure decisions, the trade-off between benefits for young and old workers, and other decisions the union has to make during the course of its operational activities.

- The union's history and traditions represent an amorphous set of factors that exert an immense influence on the *consciousness* of the union member and the intensity of the member's support for the union's goals.

These are the more important *internal structures* of the union, which filter or mediate the *inputs* from the external environment in which the union operates. What results is a series of *outcomes,* the decisions the union makes when it is engaged in collective bargaining and when it proceeds with its normal day-to-day operations.

Table 6-2   Trade Union as an Economic Institution

Inputs	Internal Union Structures	Outcomes
1. Unemployment rate	1. Age structure of union members	1. Wage policy: a. wages vs. fringe benefits b. wage rates for different skills
2. Industry structure: degree of product market competition	2. Skill and occupational composition	2. Policy on working conditions
3. Orbits of coercive comparison	3. Size of strike fund	3. Allocation of union resources
4. State of public opinion	4. Degree of internal union democracy	
5. Legislative, executive, and judicial attitudes	5. Union history, traditions, and leadership	

These *outcomes* take the form of

- the wage policy of the union, including issues of wage structure among skill and occupation groups, the trade-off between current wage increases and fringe benefits, and the general level of wage increase the union will attempt to achieve during the collective bargaining process;

- the form of work rules the union will press for, including seniority rules, vacation time, and health and safety issues on the job;

- the allocation of the union's own resources, for example, the internal budgetary allocations within a union—the amount of resources set aside for new organizational campaigns, for education of the union members, for the strike fund, and so forth.

Table 6-2 summarizes the narrative just completed on the trade union as an economic institution. The trade union, viewed in this fashion, becomes a complex, large, modern institution that has to reach decisions based on a set of external and internal factors.

Bargaining Model of Wage Determination

Wages are determined through a process of collective bargaining for workers who belong to trade unions in the American economy. Many workers who are not members of unions receive wages that are influenced by the collective bargaining agreements established among unionized workers. Collective bargaining takes place within an atmosphere of conflict. Negotiations are influenced by conditions in the labor market, but the collective bargaining process filters those market influences through a negotiation process. Characteristic of all the conflict theories of wage determination is that they produce a range of indeterminacy between the wage rate that would prevail if employers had their way and the wage that would prevail if trade unions had their way.

Earlier in this chapter we examined one set of plausible trade union preferences as to what the union's bargaining posture would be when faced with the expectation of either expanding or contracting demand for labor (Figure 6-1, page 109). Faced with expanding labor demand, the trade union would place a greater weight on higher wages than on expanding employment. Faced with a declining demand for labor in the short run, the union would prefer employment reductions to large cuts in wages.[12]

---

[12] The UAW experience with Chrysler Corporation in 1980 is somewhat of an exception to this general proposition. But in this instance the union was faced with the alternative of a complete shutdown of all Chrysler operations or a wage freeze. This is an unusual situation and one that conforms more to Ross's argument that the union will avoid extinction at all costs.

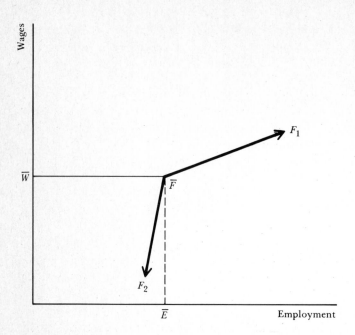

Figure 6-2   Employer Wage-Employment Preferences

The employer also faces a trade-off between wages and employment in the face of expected increases or decreases in the demand for labor. When there is an expectation of an increasing demand for labor, the employer would prefer to have substantial increases in employment and relatively smaller increases in wages. This is shown in Figure 6-2 as the path $\overline{F}F_1$. For an expected increase in the demand for labor, the employer would seek to employ more workers and hold the line on wages if it could.

For an expected decline in the demand for labor, the employer prefers to reduce wages while maintaining the previous level of employment as much as possible. The employer would prefer to move along $\overline{F}F_2$ in Figure 6-2. The employer will have invested in the human capital of his or her employees, and replacing them is costly. Labor is like a fixed factor of production to some extent, and an employer is reluctant to lay off employees who are accustomed to the routine of a particular work place.[13]

Both the union and the employer have a *wage-employment preference* for an expected decline or expansion in the demand for labor. These are shown in Figure 6-3, which combines Figures 6-1 and 6-2.[14] For both expected increases and expected decreases in the demand for labor, unions and employers disagree on what should happen to wages and employment. This creates a range of indeterminacy in the wage-employment

---

[13] Walter Y. Oi, "Labor as a Quasi-Fixed Factor," *Journal of Political Economy* 70 (December 1962), pp. 538-55.

[14] $\overline{W}$ is the existing wage, from which bargaining proceeds.

outcome, and the boundaries of the collective bargaining process are defined. For increases in the demand for labor, unions prefer higher wages to increases in employment. Employers, for the same increase in the demand for labor, prefer increases in employment, rather than the wage increases that unions seek. And for short-term decreases in the demand for labor, unions seek cuts in employment rather than in wages, while employers prefer reductions in wages and a maintenance of employment. This sets up a range of indeterminacy in wages, shown by the shaded areas of Figure 6-3, without any specific outcome for wages and employment readily definable.

A conflict is established by the differing preferences of unions and employers when faced with fluctuations in the demand for labor. In such circumstances, the relative bargaining strength of labor and management influences the outcome for wages and employment, a subject taken up in the next section of this chapter.

Collective Bargaining and Wage Determination

An exact resolution of the wage rate is impossible whenever a conflict model produces a range of indeterminacy. Wage disputes are resolved through the collective bargaining process, the outcome of which depends on the relative strength and negotiating talents

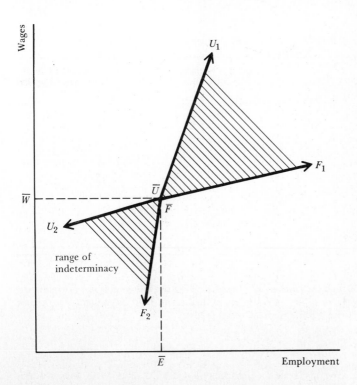

Figure 6-3 Conflict Model of Wage Determination

of labor and management. It is not possible to derive a precise wage rate from the range of possibilities presented in a conflict model. However, it is possible to state the conditions under which labor or management will be in a more advantageous bargaining position, which will tilt the wage bargains to one side or the other.[15]

Whenever an industrial dispute arises, there are costs for both sides. A union, its membership, and a firm all experience hardships if a collective bargaining process cannot be successfully concluded and a strike results. Of course, there are also benefits for both sides from refusing to agree to the terms of the other and going to the extreme of permitting the negotiations to break down and degenerate into a strike. This suggests that a union will not be prepared to settle an industrial dispute so long as the expected benefits from holding out for its own terms are greater than the costs of not agreeing to management's terms. The same is true for management. In brief, neither side will accept the other's wage offer unless the expected costs of holding out or disagreeing are greater than the "costs" of settling on the other side's terms.

This view of the collective bargaining process is taken through a purely objective and quantitative lens. The collective bargaining process is seen as being controlled by calculable parameters—costs and benefits. There is, however, another dimension to industrial disputes, which cannot be as easily circumscribed by a cost-and-benefit computation. Emotions, subjective forces, power struggles, and pure frustration also play a role in industrial disputes. Little can be said about these aspects of industrial

Table 6-3   Strikes in the United States, 1945-1981, Selected Years

Year	Number of Strikes	Average Number of Days on Strike	Percent of Total Employed Involved in Strikes
1945	4,750	9.9	8.2
1946	4,985	24.2	10.5
1950	4,843	19.2	5.1
1955	4,320	18.5	5.2
1960	3,333	23.4	2.4
1965	3,963	25.0	2.5
1970	5,716	25.0	4.7
1975	5,031	26.8	2.2
1977	5,600	29.3	2.8
1980	3,885	35.4	1.5
1981	2,568	n.a.[a]	1.2

[a]Not available.
Sources: U.S. Department of Labor, *Handbook of Labor Statistics, 1978 and 1980* (Washington: Government Printing Office, 1979 and 1981), pp. 508-9, 415; Bureau of the Census, *Statistical Abstract of the United States, 1982-83* (Washington: Government Printing Office), p. 410.

---

[15] A slightly different perspective on these same questions can be found in J. R. Hicks, *The Theory of Wages,* 2nd ed. (New York: St. Martin's Press, 1963) chap. 7.

disputes except to acknowledge that they exist and at times swamp the more objective parameters in importance.

In any particular year, about half of all the strikes are caused by disputes over wages and compensation issues. Statistics collected by the Department of Labor indicate that almost as many strikes are caused by nonwage as by wage issues.[16] In Table 6-3, data are presented showing the extent of strike activity in the United States for selected post-World War II years. Strike activity peaked in 1946, when about 10 percent of the work force was involved in work stoppages. During World War II there were virtually no strikes and wages were subject to national guidelines. The pressure cooker effect took hold immediately after the war and produced substantial demands for wage catch-ups, leading to the strike activity detailed in Table 6-3. Strike activity fell during the decades of the 1950s and the 1960s. During the 1950s typically about 5 percent of the work force was involved in work stoppages, and only 2.5 percent in the 1960s. During the 1970s strike activity remained about where it was in the previous two decades, and in the early 1980s it declined because of the severe recession.[17]

Empirical studies done on the causes of strikes indicate that strikes are more likely to occur if

- unemployment is low;

- real wages have not been increasing rapidly prior to the start of negotiations;

- the firm's profits have been high in recent periods.[18]

When unemployment is low, workers can earn income during a strike by finding alternative employment. They probably have been able to accumulate some savings prior to a strike and can draw on those financial resources during a strike. If real wages have been increasing rapidly prior to the end of a contract, workers will be *less* likely to strike because they have less to make up in earnings by going on strike. If profits have been high, strikes will be more likely to occur, as workers seek to acquire a share of the increasing profits.

In the economy today, these factors are mixed. Profits have been low in most industries, and unemployment is high. These forces would mitigate against strike activity. However, real wages have not been increasing in the past ten years, and this would tend to increase strike activity.

---

[16] U.S. Department of Labor, *Handbook of Labor Statistics, 1978* (Washington: Government Printing Office, 1979), pp. 514-26.

[17] There is substantial year-to-year variation in strike activity because of the timing of contract termination dates. After 1981, the statistics published by the Department of Labor are not compatible with earlier years.

[18] Orley Ashenfelter and George E. Johnson, "Bargaining Theory, Trade Unions, and Industrial Strike Activity," *American Economic Review* 59, no. 1 (March 1969), pp. 35-49; and Henry S. Farber, "Bargaining Theory, Wage Outcomes, and the Occurrence of Strikes: An Econometric Analysis," *American Economic Review* 68, no. 3 (June 1978), pp. 262-71.

Business Week has commented on this:

> In the past, such a long period of declining real income would almost certainly have produced a level of industrial conflict on the order of the incessant strikes of the immediate postwar years. But high unemployment has more recently damped workers' enthusiasm for striking.[19]

Strikes occur when the expected benefits at the margin exceed the expected costs at the margin from a work stoppage. Expectations play an important role in the decisions of both the union and management about whether to go ahead with a strike or accept the other side's offer. A union leadership must be aware of the patterns established in other collective bargaining agreements that have recently been completed. Except in unusual circumstances, it is difficult for a union leader to stand before the members and convince them to accept less than other workers have received, with historically similar wage patterns. The union leadership must take account of the elasticity of the demand for labor in the firm, and it cannot push so hard that employment is seriously jeopardized.

When a collective bargaining agreement expires and negotiations are about to commence, union and employer bargaining strengths come into play.

Union Bargaining Strength

Many of the factors that place a trade union in a relatively stronger bargaining position revolve around the tightness of the labor market. The *rate of unemployment* is a reliable indicator of this aspect of the labor market. During boom times, when the demand for labor is high, labor is in a relatively strong bargaining position.

First, the high levels of employment in the past have enabled the union to build up its strike fund, and union members are more likely to have private reserves they can fall back on during a strike.

Second, the employer, operating almost at full capacity during periods of full employment, has not been able to build up much of a stockpile that could be sold off while production was shut down during a strike.[20] The employer without an inventory is forced to depend on current production for sales and cannot do so if the plant is shut down. Most American unions bargain company-by-company, and if they shut down one company's operations, customers might take their business elsewhere. This is a substantial weapon in the hands of trade unions. Firms assiduously court customer attachment in imperfectly competitive markets, and they do not want to lose that customer attachment to other firms. Not only is there a loss of sales during the strike,

---

[19] "Why Labor Militancy Has Abated," *Business Week,* January 19, 1981, p. 22.

[20] The stockpiling factor pertains only to manufacturing, mining, and construction industries.

but repeat customers may be lost for good, so the company that is struck by its union experiences substantial costs by disagreeing with the union's terms.

Third, and perhaps the most important, conditions of full employment place the trade union in a strong position because its members have the opportunity to find other employment during a strike, and, therefore, the strike can last longer. It is common for workers to seek other employment while they are on strike, because union strike benefits are insufficient to sustain the membership at a livable rate for very long during a strike. If the demand for labor is strong in a local labor market, workers can find other employment during a strike and can hold out longer. If there are no other jobs available, then, other things equal, the strike will not last as long.[21]

A second element that affects union's strength in collective bargaining is the degree of trade union solidarity as a movement. If the strike gains the support of other unions, then the union out on strike will be in a stronger bargaining position. Recent strikes of California farm workers, southwestern textile workers, and others show the importance of this aspect of the labor movement in the United States.

All these factors increase labor's ability to sustain a strike, and they place labor in a relatively stronger bargaining position with respect to management than if the obverse of these conditions prevails.

If labor has such favorable conditions during collective bargaining, its costs of disagreeing with management seem low compared with the costs of agreeing to the terms offered them. The prognosis would be for a long strike unless the employer was prepared to concede quickly in order to avoid the costs it would absorb by virtue of disagreeing with the trade union.

The importance of the tightness of the labor market, reflected in the unemployment rate, explains why labor as a movement advocates strong full-employment policies in the national debate over economic policy. If one factor had to be selected that enhances labor's bargaining power, it is full employment. And that is why, aside from moral and philosophical reasons, labor pushes so aggressively for full-employment fiscal and monetary policies and makes economic growth the cornerstone of its economic policy posture in the national debate over economic objectives.

Employer Bargaining Strength

The employer is placed in a stronger bargaining position, in part, if labor is weaker. So, for example, periods of economic slack, when unemployment is high, favor the employer's bargaining position. Not only is labor comparatively weaker, but the employer is stronger because he or she has had the opportunity to stockpile production in anticipation of the strike by working the factory closer to full capacity before the bargaining process begins. Not all employers can do this, of course; it depends on the

---

[21] This explains why unions press in state legislatures for the payment of unemployment compensation to striking workers.

type of product being produced. A perishable commodity such as lettuce cannot easily be stockpiled, because it can only be harvested when nature says it is ready. And if labor strikes at a crucial time, it can do serious damage to the firm. Service, trade, and government employment are areas in which stockpiling cannot go on as readily as in steel or textiles. If garbage collectors go on strike, the garbage piles up, and there is no way the garbage can be collected in advance to forestall this happening. The same is true for supermarket checkout cashiers. Households can stockpile some food and, therefore, create their own type of inventory, which assists the company, but this is limited. If the employer can stockpile, however, he or she will be in an advantageous position with respect to the trade union. The employer can sustain a strike without a loss of sales and does not run the risk of losing customer attachment to other, nonstrike firms.

A second aspect of the employer's bargaining strength relates to the degree of competition in the product market in which the firm sells its output. Economic concentration in the product market influences the bargaining strength of labor and management—although the precise way in which it does is ambiguous and controversial.[22] On the one hand, the size of the firm and the degree of economic concentration in the industry strengthen the firm, because it has greater organizational slack— financial reserves—which provides it with the resources to withstand a strike. It can use its reserves to mount a propaganda campaign against the union through newspaper ads, community mobilization, and the like. If it operates in diversified sectors of the economy through a conglomerate structure, the company can shift production and resources to minimize the impact of a strike against it. If it is multinational, it can shift production to other countries and thereby limit its strike exposure.

On the other hand, a company operating in a concentrated industry can more easily pass on the higher wages that unions demand to consumers in the form of higher prices. Without competition as a regulator of behavior, the firm can more easily "escape" the union's wage pressure by simply passing the higher costs on to consumers. If it adopts this posture, its "will to resist" is limited, and the company will be prepared to accept, without much resistance, the union's wage demand.[23] In this situation, the union will be in a relatively stronger bargaining position than it would have been if the firm had been operating in a more competitive market structure.

Which of these forces will be operative? Does economic concentration weaken or strengthen labor's hand at the bargaining table? The answer is not clear; it depends on the individual case. It is more difficult for unions to organize initially in the concentrated, multinational, and conglomerate sectors of the economy. But once organized, the union is in a stronger position because of the limited will of the firm to

---

[22] Harold M. Levinson, "Unionism, Concentration, and Wage Change: Toward a Unified Theory," *Industrial and Labor Relations Review* 20 (January 1967), pp. 198-205.

[23] Clark Kerr, "Labor's Income Share and the Labor Movement," in George W. Taylor and Frank C. Pierson, eds., *New Concepts in Wage Determination* (New York: McGraw-Hill Book Co., 1957), pp. 260-98.

Table 6-4 Union and Employer Bargaining Strength

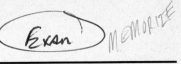

general condition of economy	Union	Employer
1. Low unemployment *(tight labor market)*	✓	
2. Ability to stockpile		✓
3. Large strike fund	✓	
4. Alternative employment opportunities during strike	✓	
5. Concentration in the product market[a]	✓ *(both)*	✓
6. Union solidarity *(togetherness of union)*	✓	

[a]Alongside "concentration in the product market" there are check marks in both the union and employer columns to convey the ambiguity of this factor.

resist. Recent discussions of so-called tax incentive plans (TIPs) to deal with inflation recognize this point and seek to place tax penalties on firms that do not abide by wage guidelines, in order to raise the cost to the firm of agreeing with union wage demands. This is designed to stiffen the resistance of firms operating in concentrated industries by using a tax penalty to increase their costs of agreeing to the union's wage demands.

Summing up, low rates of unemployment increase labor's bargaining power and reduce management's by providing alternative employment opportunities for workers while on strike and by limiting the ability of the firm to stockpile and sell off its inventories during a strike. The solidarity of the labor movement as a whole enhances labor's position. Economic concentration typically strengthens management's hand by providing it with more resources and tactical moves while reducing the cost of strikes to the firm by virtue of the company's ability to pass on the higher wage costs to consumers in the form of higher prices.

In Table 6-4 the elements that contribute to union and employer bargaining power are summarized, with a check mark in either the union or employer column signifying that the particular condition aids that side's negotiating power during the collective bargaining process.

Having said all this, we still cannot make any definitive statement on the outcome of a collective bargaining situation. Each strike, and each set of negotiations, must be studied for its own institutional uniqueness, recognizing all the time that there are general principles that apply to all collective bargaining situations.

A strike ends when the costs of disagreeing begin to outweigh the costs of agreeing to the other side's terms. *Time* is the most important element in this equation. As time goes on and the strike draws on, the costs of disagreeing begin to loom large for both sides. A mediator can enter the negotiations and, in effect, speed up this process. The early posturing gives way to more practical considerations, the strike ends, and a new wage agreement is consummated.

Summary

When trade unions are introduced into models of wage determination, a greater degree of uncertainty occurs in the outcome for wages and employment. Instead of independent atomized households making decisions in a vacuum about labor supply, the trade union attempts to influence the wage rate and thereby affects how many individuals will be employed.

One group of models posits conditions of conflict and collective bargaining that yield a range of possible wage rates but no one specific wage as an outcome. Various types of collective bargaining theories all have one result in common: a *range of indeterminacy* in wages is produced as an outcome of the conflict in which the union and the employer cannot agree on what the wage rate should be.

Although it is not possible to say definitively what the wage outcome will be of a collective bargaining situation, it is feasible to identify the economic conditions that will place either labor or management in a more strategic and powerful bargaining position. So long as the cost to one side of agreeing to the other's terms is greater than the costs associated with holding out for better terms, an industrial dispute in the form of a strike is likely to occur. Each side then tries to influence its economic environment so that it lowers the costs of disagreeing for itself while increasing the costs of recalcitrance for the other side.

A union will be in a stronger position if it has a larger strike fund, for example, because then its costs of holding out are reduced. It is also in a stronger bargaining position if the unemployment rate in the economy is low, since its members will be able to find alternative employment during a strike, thereby lowering its costs of disagreement. The degree of union solidarity among the membership will enhance the bargaining position of labor.

On the other side of the negotiating table, an employer will be in a stronger position if it has been able to stockpile inventories, which it can sell off during a strike, thus lessening the costs of the strike for itself.

Time is the most important factor in settling an industrial dispute. A mediator can influence the costs to both sides of agreement and disagreement, through adroit handling of the negotiating process. Eventually all strikes are settled because of the factor of time. As the industrial dispute drags on, both sides start to experience heavier costs for holding out. The union and its members face a drain on financial resources. The firm's inventories have been exhausted. At this point a settlement is imminent, although in the timing of a settlement and in its final terms, the art of the negotiator comes into play.

Aside from bargaining models of wage determination under trade unions, there are theories of the union that see it as a maximizer of revenues. The union seeks to maximize its revenues through the optimal combination of wages, which influence its level of dues, and membership, which is affected by the level of employment.

Institutional theory views the union as having complex goals, based on its history, its internal structure, and the economic environment in which it operates. Viewed in this light, the union has a variety of external forces that affect its decisions. These external forces are filtered through particular internal structures, such as the age and skill composition of the union membership, which affect the way in which the menu of union proposals is set forth at the bargaining table.

Study Questions

1. Discuss why the percentage of American workers who belong to trade unions has declined since World War II.

2. What specific changes would have to be made in the bargaining models of wage determination to accommodate wage concessions by unions in the face of declining demand for labor?

3. Some economists claim that trade union intervention in the labor market leads to a misallocation of resources. What is this argument? Evaluate its validity.

4. Some models of trade unions and wage determination are based more on economic variables than others, which use political and sociological explanations of union behavior. Contrast these views.

Further Reading

Cartter, Allen M. *Theory of Wages and Employment*. Homewood, IL: Richard D. Irwin, 1959. Chaps. 7 and 8.

Dunlop, John T. *Wage Determination under Trade Unions*. New York: Augustus M. Kelley, 1966; original edition, 1944. Chap. 2.

Hicks, J. R. *The Theory of Wages*. 2nd ed. New York: St. Martin's Press, 1963. Chap. 7.

Kerr, Clark. "Labor's Income Share and the Labor Movement." In *New Concepts in Wage Determination,* edited by George W. Taylor and Frank C. Pierson. New York: McGraw-Hill Book Co., 1957. Pp. 260-98.

Levinson, Harold M. "Unionism, Concentration, and Wage Change: Toward a Unified Theory." *Industrial and Labor Relations Review* 20 (January 1967), pp. 198-205.

Ross, Arthur M. *Trade Union Wage Policy*. Berkeley: University of California Press, 1948.

7

The Impact of Trade Unions on Wages

The title of this chapter betrays a hidden question: *Do* trade unions have an impact on wages? And if they do, what is the extent of their influence? Viewing it through the prism of conventional wisdom, one might wonder why the question of whether unions have an impact on wages is asked at all. "Certainly they do" would be the overwhelming answer from the public if a Gallup poll were taken on the issue.

The answer to this question is not as obvious as it first appears. Labor economists have been debating the issue for almost four decades as they have struggled with the problem of finding a methodology that can definitively resolve this controversy. Some labor economists content that trade unions cannot, over the long haul, extract higher wages through collective bargaining than the market forces would permit. Others argue that unions can obtain a higher wage through collective bargaining than workers would have received without the existence of a labor union.

Investigating the effect of trade unions on wages raises several problems. The first is one of defining the question. Is the question: Do workers who belong to unions receive wages higher than those who do not belong to unions? Or is the question stated thus: Do workers receive higher wages after joining a trade union than they received before they belonged to a union?[1] This latter formulation, though

---

[1] A slightly different way of stating this question is: Do workers in a particular factory receive higher wages after they unionize than they would have received if they had not been unionized?

very intriguing, is hardly ever examined, because it is difficult to find a body of data that would enable a researcher to construct an empirical study pertinent to that issue. Nearly all the empirical research looks at *wage differentials* between a grouping of workers who belong to trade unions and a grouping of workers who do not belong to trade unions.[2]

If the wage differential is the focus of analysis, the next problem to resolve is what type of wage differential. There can be wage differentials among individual workers, among occupations, among regions of the country, and among industries.

Methodological Problems

Conducting an empirical investigation of the impact of trade unions on wages raises certain problems that heretofore were avoided by staying with a strictly theoretical approach to wage determination. The real world economy of wage determination is a complex phenomenon. Each collective bargaining agreement is unique because each work situation has its own idiosyncrasies. However, a collective bargaining agreement cannot in its wage provisions ignore the market forces that affect labor. The question is, how much do unions alter the wage from what it would have been if market forces alone had been the determining force in establishing the wage?

Translating this problem into a manageable empirical study is fraught with problems. First, there is the problem of choosing a statistical universe to study. Most of the studies that have been done examine some type of wage differential. This involves identifying a particular wage differential and investigating the difference in wages between a group of workers that is heavily unionized and a group that is not as strongly unionized. This can be done for wage differentials between persons, as well as for differentials between regions, between occupations, or between industries. However, if a differential is found between a heavily unionized group and a less-unionized group, can one attribute this differential to the impact of unionization, when so many other forces that affect wages may also be operative? In brief, how can the influence of trade unionism be separated from the effect of all the other elements that influence the wage? If a differential in wages is found between a heavily unionized group of workers in one section of the nation and a less heavily unionized group in another section of the country, can we be sure that something else, other than trade unionism, is not causing this differential?

For example, the cost of living can be substantially different in various regions of the nation, and this can affect differentials in wages. The skill and education composition of the work force can vary and produce differences in wages. The marginal productivity of labor can be different in these regions because of different

---

[2] The wage differential can refer to some absolute difference in union and nonunion wages or to differentials in the rate of change of union and nonunion wages.

industrial composition and varying levels of technology. The age, sex, and race composition of the labor force might be different. All of these factors can affect the wage, independent of the trade union element. The problem is how to isolate the trade union impact on wages from all these other forces that can also cause wage differentials.

A second methodological problem that arises relates to the so-called *spillover effect* of unionization.[3] Many workers in the nonunion sector of the economy receive the benefits of unionization through the spillover effect. Some employers without unions in their plants will match or even exceed the union wage in order to prevent the unionization of their companies. The employer pays the same wage or a higher one so as not to give the workers an incentive to form a union. This is not an unusual phenomenon. Large firms, such as IBM and Xerox, do this as a matter of course so that they can claim the company pays better wages than would be the case with a union, in order to forestall unionization in the firm. The same is true of some medium-sized businesses hiring in a local labor market in which some of the firms are unionized. Paying the going union wage rate or above to prevent unionization is called the *threat effect.*[4]

Coal companies in Wyoming routinely match or better union contracts negotiated in eastern mines in order to prevent unionization. Wyoming coal executives believe "the costs of keeping their employees happy are worth the 'benefits' of keeping the unions out."[5] An official of the International Association of Machinists union (IAM), frustrated at trying to organize Delta Airlines, has said, "Every time IAM signs an agreement with one of Delta's competing carriers, . . . Delta supersedes our contract with a little more—5¢ or 10¢ an hour. The reason is to keep the unions off the property."[6]

Another aspect of the spillover of union wage rates into the nonunion sector is simply a market phenomenon. If unions in a particular labor market affect a substantial proportion of wage earners, an employer in the nonunion sector will have to meet the going wage in order to attract workers to his plant. He cannot pay substantially below the going union wage rate, even if he is nonunion, and expect to find workers willing to work for him.[7] The labor market will produce a spillover effect by transmitting the union wage scale to the nonunion sector.

Government laws codify the spillover effect and assure its impact. The most important of these laws is a national one, the Davis-Bacon Act, first passed in 1931.

---

[3] These methodological problems are discussed in C. Mulvey and J. M. Adowd, "Estimating the Union/Non-Union Wage Differential: A Statistical Issue," *Economica* 47, no. 185 (February 1980), pp. 73–79.

[4] Sherwin Rosen, "Trade Union Power, Threat Effects and the Extent of Organization," *Review of Economic Studies* 36 (April 1969), pp. 185–96.

[5] Warren Brown, "Powder River Basin Mines Try to Best Unions at Benefits Game," *Washington Post*, July 1, 1981, p. A2.

[6] Delta: The World's Most Profitable Airline," *Business Week*, August 31, 1981, p. 71.

[7] If there is substantial unemployment, it will be easier for the nonunion employer to hire workers below the going union wage rate.

This law provides that construction workers employed under federal government contracts must be paid the prevailing union wage rate for the construction trades even if they are not members of a union.

To the extent there is a spillover effect, the data will indicate less of a union impact on wages than might be the case. If a local labor market is being studied in which there is a large spillover effect, the data might reveal no wage differential between those workers that belong to trade unions and those that do not. However, this does not mean that unions have no impact on wages, since the nonunion wage has been patterned after the union wage.

Wage Differentials for Union and Nonunion Workers over Time

The first studies of the impact of trade unions on wages adopted a procedure that began by dividing the economy into a unionized sector and a nonunionized sector. Following this division of the economy, the wages of each group were tracked and compared to see which group did better in some time period.

 Paul Douglas, the late senator from Illinois, set the stage for future studies with the publication in 1930 of his trailblazing work on wages in the United States. He concluded that trade unions could obtain higher wages for their members under some circumstances. Their effectiveness in acquiring wage increases was greater at the initial stages of union organization and tended to atrophy as the union became settled in its relationships with management. Writing about the period from the formation of the AFL, in 1886, through the start of World War I, Douglas said,

> Unionism . . . very probably does give an appreciable increase in earnings during the early period of effective organization, but during the later and more mature years of union development, the relative rate of further progress seems . . . to be no more rapid on the whole for unionists than for non-unionists.[8]

Why might this be the case? First, during the formation of a union in a plant, militancy, consciousness, and solidarity tend to be strong. This strength provides the union leadership with a solid organizational base from which to launch an effective negotiation over wages. Second, relatively low wages in a plant will be one spur to union organization, and the catch-up effect of unionization will be reflected in a rapid increase in wages relative to nonunion wages at the initial stage of union organization. Over time, however, these forces propelling union wages ahead will weaken. The élan created in the first stages of union organization cannot be sustained. As the wage

---

[8] Paul H. Douglas, *Real Wages in the United States, 1890–1926* (Boston and New York: Houghton Mifflin Co., 1930), p. 564.

TIME SERIES DATA (Exam)

NOT RESPONSIBLE for Names of studies BUT for THE RESULTS

CROSS SECTION STUDIES

comes closer to its market level, further wage advances are less easily obtained, as the labor market becomes an effective constraint on wage increases.

Subsequent studies by Arthur Ross called into question some of Douglas's methodology. Ross pointed out that the *base wage* from which the comparison of increase in union and nonunion wages commences can affect the outcome.[10] He studied wages in 45 manufacturing and extractive industries between 1933 and 1945. In all of these industries there already existed a substantial degree of unionization. Ross's study sought for the first time to examine the impact of the *degree* of unionization on wages. He did this by dividing his sample, first, into wage categories, to control for the effect of a differential wage base on the outcome of the study, and second, into different degrees of unionization. His conclusion was that over this 12-year-period, which spanned the Great Depression and World War II, the wages of more highly unionized workers increased more rapidly than the wages of less-organized sectors of the economy.

A somewhat different approach to the problem of trade union impact on wages was used by Harold Levinson in a 1951 study.[11] He went back over much of the same period that Douglas and Ross had covered in their studies and divided the time period under investigation into more homogeneous segments.

BUSINESS CYCLE

Levinson found that during periods of economic expansion, when the economy was operating almost at full employment, unionization had no discernible effect on wage changes. In his sample, workers in the unionized sectors of the economy fared no better in terms of wage increases than workers in the nonunionized sectors. This was the case during both World War I and World War II, when full employment reigned. Full employment places the labor market at the forefront of wage determination, and union workers can do no better in wage increases than the market will allow. Nonunion workers now receive the benefits of a tight labor market, and their wages go up at the same rate as union workers.

Several case studies have corroborated these findings. Albert Rees, for example, examined wages in the steel industry during the period 1945–48, when the economy was operating at high levels of employment. He found that unions did not have an impact on wage increases and that "factors other than collective bargaining seem adequate to account for the wage increases which took place."[12] Rees went so far as to argue that "certain aspects of the union's presence and activity tended in themselves to restrain wage increases." The existence of the union prevented employers from making the necessary adaptation to a tight labor market by raising wages during the

---

[9] Arthur M. Ross, "The Influence of Unionism upon Earnings," *Quarterly Journal of Economics* 62, no. 2 (February 1948), pp. 263–86.

[10] This is a variant of the "index number problem," in which the base chosen influences the outcome of any series of data tracked over time.

[11] Harold M. Levinson, *Unionism, Wage Trends, and Income Distribution, 1914–1947* (Ann Arbor: University of Michigan Press, 1951), chap. 3.

[12] Albert Rees, "Postwar Wage Determination in the Basic Steel Industry," *American Economic Review* 41, no. 3 (June 1951), p. 402.

＋ LONGITUDINAL STUDIES

term of the contract. The fixed term of the contract precluded union members from taking advantage of the tight labor market during the life of the contract, according to Rees. These factors combined to place the union member at a *disadvantage* compared with the nonunion worker.

In periods of depression or recession, however, the situation is reversed. In these economic circumstances, trade unions can protect their members from wage cuts, and consequently, union workers fare better than nonunion workers in terms of wage changes. Levinson finds this to have been the case during the Great Depression of the 1930s, as well as during the recession of 1920–23. The "sympathetic pressure," as Levinson calls it, of the federal government toward unions during the Great Depression was also a factor, in his view, in strengthening union wage advances relative to nonunion wages during that period.

Levinson's study virtually completed the circuit for investigations of this type. To the question of whether trade unions can affect wages, the answer, based on these studies, is that it depends. It depends on whether there is full employment in the economy, in which case unions have little impact on wage changes above what nonunion workers receive in wage gains, or whether there is a recession. In the latter instance unions fare better, because they can protect their members from the vicissitudes of the recession. Unions tend to increase the wages of their members, compared with nonunion workers, when initially organized because they can take advantage of the consciousness, solidarity, and militancy workers possess in that early stage of union organization. Finally, a supportive political and governmental environment for unions will enhance their members' position relative to workers who do not belong to unions.

This general rule about the relationship between the business cycle and union impacts on wages has to be qualified somewhat for the period of the 1980s. The structural change taking place in the economy during this time has adversely affected the sectors of the economy that were highly unionized—steel, autos, machine tools, and other older, basic manufacturing industries. The rate of increase in wages in the nonunion sectors of the economy has increased at about twice the rate of the unionized sectors.

NON UNION WAGES TEND TO INCREASE 2x THE AMOUNT OF UNION WAGES !

The Impact of Trade Unions on Wages at a Fixed Point in Time

The previous studies of the trade union impact on wages dealt with movements in wages over some period. It is also possible to hold time fixed and look at the effect that trade unions have on absolute differentials in wages at a fixed point in time. This mode of analysis is called *cross-sectional* as opposed to the previously discussed *time series* form of empirical investigation.

In a 1960 study for the Joint Economic Committee of the U. S. Congress, Harold Levinson examined the impact of trade unions on wage differentials at a point in time.[13] He was seeking to establish the impact on wages of *different degrees of unionization,* as well as of such other factors as economic concentration, changes in the demand for labor, profits, and productivity.

Levinson arrayed some twenty manufacturing industries according to the percentage of workers in each industry that belonged to a trade union. All industries do not have the same degree of unionization, and Levinson sought to ferret out the way in which this variation affects wage differentials across industries in the manufacturing sector of the economy. After doing this, he correlated wage changes in each industry with degrees of unionization for two periods: 1947–53 and 1953–58. Levinson found very little evidence of a positive effect of degree of unionization on wage differentials. For the 1947–53 period, he found that the correlation between these two variables was close to zero, and for the later period, 1953–58, the correlation was only slightly positive.

Following up on this study, Martin Segal advanced a slightly modified hypothesis that turned out to be quite provocative.[14] He argued that a union does have an impact on wages but that it exercises its influence through the extent of the firm's product-market power. Specifically, he hypothesized that unions operating in more concentrated sectors of the economy will be able to extract higher wages. This occurs because the firm in concentrated product markets can more easily pass on the wage increases to consumers in the form of higher prices, and therefore, it has a weaker "will to resist" the union. In a more competitive situation, however, the market acts as a regulator of wage increases, and trade unions cannot do as well in those situations no matter what the degree of unionization is. Put differently, Segal contended that two industries with the same degree of unionization would exhibit different wage outcomes depending on the types of market structures in which the unions operated.

To test his hypothesis, Segal divided the economy into sectors by degree of economic concentration. He found that unions received higher wages in highly concentrated sectors of the economy, where competition in the product market was weak. They were able to extract wage increases beyond those of their nonunion counterparts. In the competitive sectors of the economy, on the other hand, unionized workers did not do appreciably better, in terms of wages, than nonunion workers.

Unionization and product market concentration interact with each other and affect the wage outcome. Leonard Weiss looked at how these two aspects of the economy interact and affect interindustry wage differentials.[15] Several possible market structures can interact with different degrees of unionization. Concentration in the product market can be high and union organization either high or low. The same is

---

[13] Harold M. Levinson, *Postwar Movements of Prices and Wages in Manufacturing Industries* (Study Paper No. 21), Joint Economic Committee, U. S. Congress (Washington: Government Printing Office, 1960).

[14] Martin Segal, "The Relation between Union Wage Impact and Market Structure," *Quarterly Journal of Economics* 78, no. 2 (February 1964), pp. 96–114.

[15] Leonard Weiss, "Concentration and Labor Earnings," *American Economic Review* 56, no. 1 (March 1966), p. 105. Economic concentration is measured by the percentage of sales in an industry accounted for by the four largest firms. This is called a *four-firm concentration ratio.*

true of circumstances where market concentration is low. Weiss found that a high degree of trade union organization can add about 9 percent to annual earnings where product market concentration is low. Where product market concentration is high, strong union organization adds only 4 percent to annual earnings. However, where unionization is weak, product market concentration adds 16 percent to annual earnings.

In summary, to the question of whether unions with a higher percentage of membership in a sector of the economy do more for their members than unions in another sector of the economy that is less unionized, the answer is, it depends. It depends, first, on the underlying economic conditions, as Levinson found. In his study the more highly unionized sectors of the economy did no better than the less-unionized sectors when there was full employment—immediately after World War II. But in a period of less buoyant economic conditions, in the 1950s, they did better. It depends, second, on the type of product market structure. The more concentrated the product market, the more power unions have in affecting wages, independent of their degree of unionization. A sector of the economy that is more highly unionized might fare worse in wage increases than another sector of less unionization if the firm operates in competitive markets. Textiles and food processing are examples of such situations. On the other hand, unions operating in concentrated markets can do quite well for their members in wage advances—witness the auto and steel industries, for example.

In connection with these studies, one additional methodological problem asserts itself. The authors of these studies implicitly assume that a higher percentage of unionization in some sector of the economy is directly connected with greater "union power." However, this need not be the case, since union power is a more comprehensive and subjective term that encompasses many other, qualitative elements beyond the mere quantitative measure of unionization. Economic conditions, worker solidarity, consciousness, and the trade union history will all influence union power. Because these *qualitative* factors are unquantifiable, the researcher is left with the "second best" measurement of union power, the degree of unionization.

The Magnitude of Trade Union Impacts on Wages

The studies analyzed in the previous sections of this chapter attempt to answer the question whether, and under what conditions, trade unions have an impact on wages. However, another issue is *how much* of an impact on wages unions have where they have been able to affect wages. The focus of this question is on the *magnitude* of union impacts on wages.

The first labor economist to tackle this problem systematically was H. Gregg Lewis in his classic study published in 1963.[16] In the early 1930s, during the Great

---

[16] H. Gregg Lewis, *Unionism and Relative Wages in the United States: An Empirical Inquiry.* (Chicago: University of Chicago Press, 1963).

Table 7-1 Estimates of Union Impact on Wages, 1920–1979

Time Period	Union Impact on Wages (%)[a]
1920–24	16
1925–29	23
1930–34 ⟩ DEPRESSION ——————→	38 ——→ HIGHEST IMPACT !
1935–39	20
1940–44 ⟩ DURING THE WAR ————→	6 ——→ LOW, HIGH EMP
1945–49	⟨2⟩
1950–54	11
1955–58	15
1967–70	12
1971–75	15
1976–79	18

[a]Reflects higher wages (in percent) for union workers than for nonunion workers.
Source: H. Gregg Lewis, *Unionism and Relative Wages in the United States: An Empirical Inquiry* (Chicago: University of Chicago Press, 1963), p. 222; and H. Gregg Lewis, *Union Relative Wage Effects. A Survey* (Chicago: University of Chicago Press, 1986), p. 9.

Depression, Lewis found that workers in trade unions received wages as much as 38 percent higher than workers who did not belong to trade unions. This is the kind of period in which trade unions have a substantial impact—a deep depression during which they can protect their members more effectively from wage cuts. At the other extreme, in the postwar period of 1945–49, when full employment prevailed, workers in trade unions received as little as 2 percent more than workers who did not belong to unions. And the in 1950s trade unions were able to obtain about 10–15 percent more for their members compared with workers who did not belong to unions. Between 1967 and 1979, unions added 15 percent to the wages of their members, while in the 1980s nonunion wages have risen faster than union wages.

Lewis's estimates of the extent to which unions affect wages are presented in Table 7-1. The figures in that table show the impact of unions on wages, measured by the percentage increase in wages associated with unionization.

Since Lewis's trailblazing study was completed, there have been many other investigations into the magnitude of trade union impacts on wages. These studies have employed newer statistical techniques with larger and different bodies of data than Lewis had to work with.

Using 1967 data, this author conducted a study of interpersonal wage differentials in which other factors that could affect wages were controlled so that the effect of unionization could be isolated.[17] Interpersonal wage differentials can be influenced by education, seniority on the job, race, age, sex, marital status, occupation or industry of employment, region of employment, and city size—as well as by unionization. After accounting for the effect of these other factors on wages, we found that unionization added another 8 percent to wages for an individual.

In the past decade there have been numerous studies on the impact of trade unions on wages of all types—interpersonal, interindustry, and interoccupational.[18] Differences in method, data used, and time period produce varying answers as to how much trade unions affect wages.

For example, one study of the impact of trade unions on occupational wage differentials found that in 1967 unionized laborers received nearly 25 percent more in wages than their nonunion counterparts, while unionized service workers received only 7 percent more than nonunion service workers.[19] In Table 7-2, estimates of the quantitative impact of unions on wages are presented for various occupational groups.

Unionization can affect wage differentials for black and white workers differently. In Table 7-3, statistics are presented showing the impact that unionization has on the wages for black and white workers for different occupational groups. For blue-collar workers, unionization affects both white and black wage differentials the same. As shown in Table 7-3, belonging to a union adds 44 percent to the wages of white craft workers and 46 percent to the wages of black craft workers. The percentage effect of

Table 7-2 Union Impact on Wages of Occupational Groups

Occupational Group	Union-Nonunion Wage Differential (%)
Professional and technical workers	19.0
Clerical workers	9.1
Sales workers	2.3
Craft workers	15.5
Operatives	15.2
Service workers	7.4
Laborers	24.7

Source: Michael J. Boskin, "Unions and Relative Real Wages," *American Economic Review* 62, no. 3 (June 1972), p. 469.

---

[17] Howard M. Wachtel and Charles Betsey, "Employment at Low Wages," *Review of Economics and Statistics* 54, no. 2 (May 1972), pp. 121–29.

[18] The results of these studies are summarized in C. J. Parsley, "Labor Union Effects on Wage Gains: A Survey of Recent Literature," *Journal of Economic Literature* 18, no. 1 (March 1980), pp. 1–31.

[19] Michael J. Boskin, "Unions and Relative Real Wages," *American Economic Review* 62, no. 3 (June 1972), pp. 466–72.

Table 7-3   Union Impact on Wages by Race and Occupation

	Union-Nonunion Wage Differential (%)	
Occupation	White Workers	Black Workers
Professional workers	11	16
Managerial workers	9	29
Clerical workers	23	36
Sales workers	7	39
Service workers	19	19
Craft workers[a]	44	46
Operatives[a]	48	45
Laborers[a]	31	32

(handwritten margin notes next to Black Workers column: +5, +20, +13, +32, —, +2, −3, +1)

(handwritten note below table: ✗ UNIONS RAISE BLACK WAGES MORE THAN WHITES)

[a] Employed outside the construction industry.
Source: Orley Ashenfelter, "Racial Discrimination and Trade Unionism," *Journal of Political Economy* 80, no. 3 (May–June 1972), p. 451.

unionization for the other two groups of blue-collar workers—operatives and laborers—is also similar for white and black workers. However, for white-collar workers unionization has a substantially greater impact on the wages of black workers than it does on the wages of white workers. For example, belonging to a union adds 39 percent to the wages of black sales workers, compared with their nonunion counterparts, but only 7 percent to the wages of unionized white sales workers, compared with nonunion white sales workers.

Unionization has a significant impact on matters of race and sex discrimination. A union contract typically mandates "equal pay for equal work" and thereby reduces whatever forms of wage discrimination may have previously existed. Occupational discrimination, however, may not be broken down as readily by unionization and may, in fact, become rigidified in some instances by the union contract.

The studies examined up to this point look at union and nonunion workers either at a point in time (cross-sectional analysis) or over a period of time (time series analysis). There is a third methodology that involves tracking the same sample of individuals over some period of time to see how becoming a member of a union, or changing from union to nonunion status, affects the same person. This is called a *panel* or *longitudinal* study. An individual is surveyed and resurveyed over a period of years, and various changes in the person's economic status are then studied.

(handwritten margin note: following one person)

A study that used this methodology analyzed samples of data drawn from the same population for a two-year period.[20] During the period studied, some individuals became union members, and other stopped being union members. The change in the

---

[20] Wesley Mellow, "Unionism and Wages: A Longitudinal Analysis," *Review of Economics and Statistics* 63, no. 1 (February 1981), pp. 43–52. The years used in this panel study were 1974–75 and 1977–78.

wage of these individuals who altered their union status could be tracked, after accounting for factors other than change in union status that might affect wages.

Individuals who became members of unions had an average wage increase of 7.5 percent, after accounting for other factors that might affect wage changes. Individuals who ceased being union members experienced a wage *decline* of 7 percent. Black workers who became members of unions experienced a larger wage increase than the average for all workers—13 percent. The impact of unionization in this longitudinal study was greater during periods of cyclical downturns, which confirms earlier research on the impact of unionization during the business cycle.

All the studies examined so far in this chapter have focused on the impact of trade unions on wages. Fringe benefits, such as health insurance, pensions, and vacation pay, can also be affected by unionization. Unionized workers tend to receive about 14 percent more in fringe benefits than nonunion workers. And the share of fringe benefits in total compensation (that is, wages plus fringe benefits) are higher for unionized workers. In the manufacturing sector of the economy, fringe benefits account for 25 percent of total compensation for union workers and 20 percent for nonunion workers. In the nonmanufacturing sector of the economy, fringe benefits are 23 percent of total compensation for unionized employees, compared with 17 percent for nonunionized workers.[21]

 To the question of the magnitude of a trade union's impact on wages, the answer is, it depends. It depends on economic conditions, as was discovered in previous studies. During periods of economic depression, the trade unions' impact on wages can be as much as 38 percent, whereas during boom times their impact can be as low as 2 percent. For a typical year one cannot go wrong in saying the impact of unions on wages is about 10–15 percent. Even this statement has to be qualified, however, because the union impact on wages can be different for various occupational groups and for different racial groups.

The Spillover Effect and Pattern Bargaining
■

The previous estimates of the magnitude of trade union impacts on wages are understated somewhat, because workers in the nonunion sector of the economy receive higher wages because of the existence of trade unions. This is called the *spillover effect*, in which union wage gains are transferred to the nonunion sector of the economy. Wages can be viewed as being established within an institutional context that takes account of both market forces and collective bargaining or power forces. There are "key wage rates" that establish the wages for a core group of pattern-setting sectors

---

[21] Richard B. Freeman and James L. Medoff, "The Two Faces of Unionism," *Public Interest* 57 (Fall 1979) p. 83; and Richard B. Freeman, "The Effects of Unionism on Fringe Benefits," *Industrial and Labor Relations Review* 34, no. 4 (July 1981), p. 496.

of the economy.[22] The key wage rates are the pacesetters; they establish the pattern of wage settlements both for the nonunion sectors of the economy and for the union sectors that are not in the key group. Typically, the wage settlement in the auto industry, for example, sets the pattern for unions in the rubber and electrical machinery industries, among others. Wages for workers in the nonunion sectors of the economy in similar industries will also be patterned after this settlement. Employers seek to forestall unionization in their unorganized plants and have to pay the going wage rate to attract labor.

The establishment of the key wage rate and the patterns that follow it are consummated within a *wage round*—a period of time in which the contracts in the organized sector are written and stay in force. Every three years, when the contracts in the key wage rate sectors are renegotiated, a new wage round ensues in which the key rates are established anew and the pattern-following wage rates are reestablished. These pattern rates need not be precisely equal to the key rate; in fact, they typically are not. However, they do bear some historical proportional relationship to the key wage rate and, consequently, can be said to be patterned after the key wage rates.

This complicated wage determination process was subjected to an empirical inquiry by Otto Eckstein and Thomas A. Wilson in the early 1960s.[23] Their study provided substantial evidence for the existence of a key wage concept and pattern settlement based on the key wages. They found that wages are initially established in wage rounds in the key wage group sector. Then those key wage rates are transferred to other sectors of the economy (both union and nonunion) in which wages are patterned after the key wage. The key rates are influenced by both market and power forces. Following the establishment of the key rate, the spillover effect takes hold through patterned wage settlements.[24]

A union can affect wages in many different ways. Beyond the spillover effect, the

---

[22] Many of the concepts used in this type of wage determination hypothesis were first introduced in John T. Dunlop, "The Task of Contemporary Wage Theory," in George W. Taylor and Frank C. Pierson, eds., *New Concepts in Wage Determination* (New York: McGraw-Hill Book Co., 1957), pp. 117–39.

[23] Otto Eckstein and Thomas A. Wilson, "The Determination of Money Wages in American Industry," *Quarterly Journal of Economics* 76, no. 3 (August 1962), pp. 379–414.

[24] Case studies of the pattern-bargaining process in specific industries lend additional corroboration to this wage-setting hypothesis. See, for example, Harold M. Levinson, "Pattern-Bargaining: A Case Study of the Automobile Workers," *Quarterly Journal of Economics* 74, no. 2 (May 1960), pp. 296–317. Some recent studies suggest either the absence of a spillover effect or a redirection of the spillover effect, in which the nonunion sector sets the pattern for the unionized sector (Robert J. Flanagan, "Wage Interdependence in Unionized Labor Markets," *Brookings Papers on Economic Activity*, no. 3 [1976], pp 635–73; and George E. Johnson, "The Determination of Wages in the Union and Non-Union Sectors," *British Journal of Industrial Relations* 15, no. 2 [July 1977], pp. 211–21). However, these statistical studies and their conclusions have been challenged and do not, at this time, represent a consensus view among labor economists (See Susan Vroman, "Union/Non-Union Spillovers," *British Journal of Industrial Relations* 18, no. 3 [November 1980], pp. 369–71; Daniel J. B. Mitchell, "Union/Non-Union Wage Spillovers: A Note," *British Journal of Industrial Relations* 18, no. 3 [November 1980], pp. 372–75; and Lawrence M. Kahn, "Union Strength and Wage Inflation," *Industrial Relations* 18, no. 2 [Spring 1979], pp. 144–55).

indirect impact of unions on wages can be important. Models have been developed that attempt to identify the direct as well as the indirect effects of unions on wages.[25]

In these models three effects of unionism on wages are examined: First, unions have a direct impact on wages through their bargaining power. Second, unions can have two types of indirect effects on wages. By raising wages, they make belonging to the union more attractive. This increases the size of union membership and can lead to further increases in wages because of the enhanced bargaining power that more union members have.[26] By raising wages, unions also induce adaptations in the work place that lead to further indirect effects on wages. Higher wages will stimulate firms to substitute capital for labor and skilled labor for unskilled labor, to tend the more sophisticated capital stock. On average, this will raise the marginal product of labor and the wage level in the firm. Average labor productivity tends to be higher in unionized sectors of the economy, a difference due, in part, to a greater capital intensity of production, induced by the higher union wages. This is one of the indirect impacts of trade unions in the economy. Complementing this factor, which would tend to increase average labor productivity, is the reduction in labor turnover associated with union contracts. One study estimates that labor turnover is reduced in unionized firms by 35–50 percent and that average labor productivity *is increased* in unionized firms by 20–25 percent.[27]

Union Influence: An Assessment

∎

In 1984 a book appeared with the title: *What Do Unions Do?*[28] By titling their book this way, the authors, Richard B. Freeman and James L. Medoff, were suggesting that perhaps non-wage issues were more important for union members in assessing what unions do. They propose two alternative views of the union as it impacts on economic outcomes: a pure economic view derived from marginal productivity theory and a new view which they call the "voice" aspect of unions.

In marginal productivity theory it is the last worker hired which identifies the locus of decision-making in the firm, while in the institutional setting of trade unions it is not the last worker hired that is central to the outcome but some weighted average of all workers' preferences. What Freeman and Medoff call "exit"—leaving the firm— is the way in which a worker expresses his or her dissatisfaction in traditional economic

---

[25] Lawrence M. Kahn, "Unionism and Relative Wages: Direct and Indirect Effects," *Industrial and Labor Relations Review* 32, no. 4 (July 1979), pp. 520–32.

[26] George E. Johnson, "Economic Analysis of Trade Unionism," *American Economic Review* 65, no. 2 (May 1975), pp. 23–28.

[27] Freeman and Medoff, "Two Faces of Unionism," pp. 79, 80.

[28] Richard B. Freeman and James L. Medoff, *What Do Unions Do?* (New York: Basic Books, 1984)

theory. Premised on full employment, this act presumably sends a signal to the firm that something is wrong and needs correcting if turnover and its resultant loss of productivity is to be avoided. The problem arises, however, in assessing how effective exit is as a tool in stating precisely what the problem is and how it may be corrected. For example, you, as a consumer of education in the college or university you attend, face the same dilemma. If you do not like the way your education is proceeding, you have two ways to express this disatisfaction: to exit the institution and hope the administration gets the message or to communicate directly and state the problem before you leave. The problem arises when only the exit option prevails. By the time the message gets through it may be too late, the institution may be irreparably damaged.

That is why Freeman and Medoff propose "voice" as a more effective instrument of communication between workers and their managers. Short of a large number leaving the firm, the discontent will probably not be taken seriously. Many reasons for exiting an institution may exist, and without effective voice, managers can speculate endlessly about why people are leaving their institution. A trade union, say Freeman and Medoff, provides a direct opportunity for collective voice to be heard. The union collects information, aggregates grievances, and expresses them directly to the plant managers. In this way it provides a critical function which is not acknowledged in marginal productivity theory—namely, a way in which the internal operations of a firm become central to its outcomes. Voice permits problems to become ventilated and by so doing improves the atmosphere in the firm.

This is the theoretical basis for the empirical outcome of higher labor productivity in unionized firms. By reducing turnover and substituting voice for exit, the trade union contributes significantly to the economic welfare of the firm and, when translated into higher wages, to the economic welfare of employees, as well. Freeman and Medoff, for example, estimate that the lower turnover of employees reduces costs in the unionized firm by 1–2 percent and increases labor productivity by anywhere from 15–25 percent.[29] Higher wages in the unionized sector of the economy, therefore, may not lead to economic distortions once the non-wage impacts of unions are factored into the equation.

Summary

Trade unions affect wages by obtaining higher wages for their members compared with the wages of workers who do not have a trade union behind them. However, this conclusion must be qualified. The empirical studies show that trade unions can affect wages when

---

[29] Ibid., pp. 109, 166–67.

- There is less than full employment in the economy. During periods of recession, trade unions protect wages from falling, and workers who belong to trade unions do better than workers who do not belong to trade unions. However, during periods of full employment, the trade union impact on wages is weaker.

- There is sympathetic government pressure behind unionism, as occurred during the Great Depression of the 1930s.

- The union has just been organized, and there is an intense esprit de corps among the union members.

- There is economic concentration in the product markets, which enables the firm to pass on the union-negotiated wage increases to consumers more readily.

Precise estimates of the difference a union makes in a worker's wages range from 38 percent at a maximum (during the Great Depression) to 2 percent at a minimum (immediately after World War II.) The best estimate in a typical year of the impact of trade unions on wages is around 10 percent.

The effect of unionization on wages is different for various occupations in the American economy. Lower-skilled blue-collar workers (laborers) receive about 25 percent more in wages than their nonunion counterparts, while more-skilled unionized blue-collar workers receive 15 percent more. Unionized black workers in most occupational groups show a relatively higher percentage difference in wages (compared with nonunion black workers) than do unionized white workers (compared with nonunion white workers).

These results must be qualified, however, because of certain methodological problems that are present in the research on trade union impacts on wages. A spillover effect, in which nonunion workers receive the benefits from the existence of unions, renders the estimates of trade union impacts lower than they should be. Measuring trade union power through degree of membership does not capture the qualitative dimension of the collective bargaining relationship and its relative power configurations. It is never possible to control completely for all the other forces that affect wages, and, therefore, unions may be attributed with influencing wages when some other variable may be at work.

These qualifications notwithstanding, trade unions do have an impact on wages, causing them to be higher than they would be in the absence of unions, but only under certain circumstances and to a much smaller degree than the general public would suppose. Higher wages for unionized workers are offset somewhat by higher labor productivity brought about by the reduced labor turnover in unionized sectors.

Study Questions

1. Discuss some of the methodological problems encountered when attempting to provide empirical estimates of the impact of trade unions on wages.

2. What are some of the important factors that help explain the existence of union-nonunion wage differentials over time?

3. What are some of the important factors that help explain the magnitude of union-nonunion wage differentials?

4. Why is the magnitude of union-nonunion wage differentials small for service-related occupational groups? Explain why the union-nonunion wage differential is larger for black white-collar workers than for white workers in the same occupational category.

5. Why is the spillover effect important in understanding the relationship between union and nonunion wage increases?

6. What is the concept of the key wage? How is it related to the wage determination process?

7. Recently many trade unions have forgone larger wage increases for greater job security. How can you explain these arrangements within the models of collective bargaining discussed in this chapter?

Further Reading

Freeman, Richard B. and James L. Medoff. *What Do Unions Do?* (New York: Basic Books, 1984).

Levinson, Harold M. *Unionism, Wage Trends, and Income Distribution, 1914–1947.* Ann Arbor, MI: University of Michigan Press, 1951.

Lewis, H. Gregg. *Unionism and Relative Wages in the United States: An Empirical Inquiry.* Chicago: University of Chicago Press, 1963.

Parsley, C. J. "Labor Union Effects on Wage Gains: A Survey of Recent Literature." *Journal of Economic Literature* 18, no. 1 (March 1980), pp. 1–31.

B. Labor Markets and Individual Incomes

8

■

Poverty and Inequality in the American Economy

In the early 1960s the problem of poverty in the American economy became a standard part of our political dialogue. The problem of poverty was not new; its recognition was. Several years later, by the middle of the 1960s, inequality became an issue hotly debated in the colleges and universities. Both poverty and inequality were part of the New Frontier that a youthful government under President John F. Kennedy sought to conquer. The goals of eliminating poverty and reducing inequality have shown themselves to be more elusive targets for conquest than were other parts of the New Frontier. Goals like the moon landing, based on scientific and technical knowledge, have been easier to realize than those that deal with people and the social fabric of the nation.

At rare times in our social history, books and their titles take on such importance that they define the dialogue of a decade. Toward the end of the 1950s, John Kenneth Galbraith's *Affluent Society* was one such book. The title captured the mood of the times. America was a society of vast private riches, Galbraith wrote. Alongside these private riches was public squalor—cities that were a disgrace, a public transportation system that was inadequate to the task of moving people around conveniently, a public housing stock that needed renewal, and so forth. The affluent society was a mixed blessing. It was also a society whose defects could be remedied by the federal government's spending more money on the public good. In this way the public sector could catch up with the private sector, matching its wealth and reducing public poverty.

The emergence of poverty as a national issue occurred as a reaction to this characterization of America as a privately affluent society. A young social worker, political activist, and social analyst, Michael Harrington, read Galbraith's book and wondered how Galbraith's view of the world could clash so much with the world of the streets of New York that Harrington knew. He wrote a book that defined a political dialogue for the 1960s. The book was called *The Other America*—the one not part of Galbraith's world view. Harrington's other America was the world of individual poverty and private squalor. His writing so piqued the conscience of President Kennedy and his advisors that they set about to fashion public programs to deal with pockets of poverty in the midst of affluence.

Following the assassination of Kennedy, President Lyndon Johnson took up the challenge and made the War on Poverty a centerpiece of his domestic policies. About the same time that Johnson was gearing up for his War on Poverty, economists began to look at the problem of poverty in relationship to economic inequality. Thus was born the realization that the twin problems of poverty and inequality were complements of each other so that one could not easily be managed without attention to the other.

Labor economics played a large role in the analysis and design of public policies to alleviate poverty and reduce economic inequality. It did this through its analysis of the causes of poverty and inequality, the measurement of poverty and inequality, and the design of public policies. The chapters in this section of the book trace this body of work and present alternative views on the issues of poverty and inequality. An important debate arose during the 1960s and 1970s concerning the causes of poverty and inequality and, by inference, the design of public policies to address the problems. This debate enriched the field of labor economics and provided it with new tools of analysis with which to examine the labor force.

The debate became structured around alternative theories and analyses of the determination of individual incomes. The determination of individual incomes is the starting point in any analysis of poverty and inequality because we are trying to understand why certain people have one income rather than another.

In Chapters 3 through 7 wage determination was examined in the context of the problem of resource allocation. This is of primary concern to economists and to neoclassical economic theory. However, wages are also the principal source of individual income for the vast majority of the population. In the next five chapters, this function of wages is the focus of analysis. Wages mean different things to different people. To the individuals receiving them, wages reflect a standard of living. To economists they are a critical aspect of efficient resource allocation. Keep this dichotomy in mind because it is at the root of many disputes in labor economics.

The detailed discussion of measures of poverty and income inequality sets the stage for an analysis of the determinants of individual incomes. Individual incomes were obscured in the early chapters behind larger wage categories. That analysis was appropriate for the task of understanding labor markets, wage rates, and resource allocation. However, for purposes of examining poverty and income inequality, additional tools have to be added that provide us with measures of these phenomena.

Poverty: Meaning and Measurement

Some Preliminary Problems

Defining and measuring poverty is not as simple an exercise as it might first appear. What is poverty and how should it be measured? Obviously, even the poorest American citizen is better off than most people in a very poor nation, one like Bangladesh. But are low-income Americans therefore not poor? American citizens today live better than their ancestors did. But does this mean that an individual today who is in obvious economic need is not poor?

These are some of the difficult conceptual problems that arose when economists first started to think about the problem of defining who is poor and how poverty should be measured. A century ago indoor plumbing was not available, nor were many other amenities we take for granted today. But simply having those amenities does not keep people from being poor, unless you compare them with their equivalents centuries ago or with citizens of Bangladesh. As intriguing as this comparison might be as an academic exercise, it misses the point of social analysis and public policy. People living today in a particular country must have their welfare assessed in relation to their experiences, not to those of another era or another part of the world.

Income is a concept that has a recognized standard of measurement on which the community has agreed. It is a measurement standard, as a foot or a mile is for length and distance. Poverty, however, requires a further leap. It reflects a *judgment* about someone's economic status. The problem of using an agreed-upon measure, like income, to define poverty can be seen through an analogy. Ask a friend how tall he or she is. The friend will tell you: so many feet and so many inches. If you question this word-of-mouth information, the two of you can refer to a ruler and find a definitive answer to the question of your friend's height. Now ask yourselves the question, is he or she short, tall, or just about average? This requires a further, subjective assessment, based on the objective information attained about height through an agreed-upon measure—feet and inches.

This is the same problem encountered in measuring poverty. Income can be objectively measured. Poverty requires an evaluation of whether that income renders one poor or not poor. Poverty is a *characterization* of social status based upon an objective measure of income. As such, it has the potential for evoking much controversy. And that potential has been realized in the debate over who is poor.

The stakes are high in this measurement game because important implications flow from it. Today many public programs permit access only if an individual is classified as poor. To expand or reduce such programs, therefore, all that need be done is to change the definition of poverty. For political reasons it may be useful to show that poverty has been reduced over a certain period of time. Change the definition and, presto, poverty has been reduced.

Is it possible to devise an "absolute" measure of poverty, or must the measure always be "subjective"? This is the way the problem became framed. Income is an absolute measure, just like feet and inches, because it is an acceptable standard of measurement. Poverty, shortness, and tallness are subjective qualities—*relative characterizations* based on some absolute standard of measurement. Poverty is a descriptive word applied to an individual's income.

The official definition of poverty and its measurement represents a compromise between the two extremes of a purely subjective and a purely objective measure of poverty.

The Official Definition of Poverty

The official definition and measurement of poverty was developed by Mollie Orshansky for the Social Security Administration in 1964.[1] In part, this activity of the Social Security Administration was initiated in preparation for a review of social security benefits. The issue the agency faced was, what was an adequate level of benefits for the social security system, based on some definition of need? There were few guideposts to follow in this search for a definition of need. Subsequently, many studies have been done that have provided much more information than was available to Orshansky in the early 1960s. But her basic definition and construction of the poverty measure remains in force to this day.

The official definition and measure of poverty is based primarily on a minimum food budget that will provide adequate nutrition. For this purpose, research done by the Department of Agriculture has been used. The Department of Agriculture conducted a study in 1961 in which it defined food plans that would have different costs and nutritional values depending on how ambitious was the food intake of the family. The department developed four food plans: economy, low-cost, moderate-cost, and liberal. Orshansky used as the basis for her poverty measure the 1961 estimate of the economy food plan—the lowest of the standards developed by the Department of Agriculture.[2]

Food expenditures were the cornerstone of the poverty measure constructed in the 1960s. In 1964 these were estimated to be about $1,000 per year for a nonfarm family of four by the nutritional standards of the Department of Agriculture's economy food plan. On a daily basis this came to 68 cents per person in 1964. A 1955 study of the composition of household budgets indicated that about one-third was spent on food. Using a multiplier of three, Orshansky devised a poverty standard of $3,000 per year for a four-person family, to conform to these two pieces of information—the economy food plan costs and the proportion of food expenditures in the total household budget.[3]

---

[1] The government's definition of poverty, the history of the definition, and the controversy surrounding it are contained in U.S. Department of Health, Education, and Welfare, *The Measure of Poverty* (Washington: Government Printing Office, 1976).

[2] U.S. Bureau of the Census, "Money Income and Poverty Status of Families and Persons in the United States: 1981," Series P-60, No. 134, Appendix A.

[3] Ibid.

3,000 = MIN INCOME A FAMILY of 4 shares need for nutrition

Table 8-1 Median Family Income and Official Poverty Level for a Four-Person Family, 1959–1985, Selected Years

Year	Median Income for a Four-Person Family	Poverty Level for a Four-Person Family	Poverty Level as a Percentage of Median Income
1959	$ 6,070	$ 2,973	49
1964	7,488	3,169	42
1969	10,623	3,743	35
1974	14,747	5,038	34
1977	18,723	6,191	33
1981	26,274	9,287	35
1985	27,735	10,989	40

Sources: U.S. Department of Health, Education, and Welfare, *The Measure of Poverty* (Washington: Government Printing Office, 1976), p. 72; U.S. Bureau of the Census, *Statistical Abstract of the United States* (Washington: Government Printing Office, 1979), pp. 454, 461; U.S. Bureau of the Census, "Money Income and Poverty Status of Families and Persons in the United States: 1985," Series P-60, No. 154, pp. 6, 33.

Annually, the poverty standard has been revised to reflect changes in the cost of the poor family's food budget, more current data on food plans, and more accurate information on the composition of family budgets. But the *market basket approach* to a measure of poverty, as it is called, has endured.

Table 8-1 presents the poverty standards used for selected years from 1959 to 1985 (column 2). In 1985 the poverty standard was set at $10,989 for a four-person, nonfarm family. About $2.50 per person, per day was allotted for food consumption in 1985. Notice that compared to the median family income for a four-person family, the poor lost ground in the 1970s and regained it in the 1980s. (Median family income is the midpoint of a distribution.) For example, the median family income for four people was $27,735 in 1985. This means that half the population lived in families with income higher than this, and half lower. The poverty standard relative to the median fell from 42 percent when first introduced in 1964 to 33 percent in 1977 and stood at 40 percent in 1985. This increase in the ratio of the poverty measure to median family income, however, was caused more by sluggish growth in median family income than by any revision of the poverty standard that would reflect a different concept of poverty in the American economy.

Some analysts have proposed measuring poverty at half the median—a standard that is more purely relative and one that drops any pretense of an absolute measure of poverty. Based on this standard, the poverty cutoffs would be higher than the official ones, but this does not mean that the same proportion of the population would always be living in poverty. For example, in 1985, at a standard of about $13,867, or half the median, the percentage of four-person families with incomes below that level could vary considerably.

The official Orshansky measure of poverty represents a combination of objective and subjective factors. It is decidedly a pure *physical subsistence* standard of living because the levels of income it embodies are so marginal. The problem of conceptualizing poverty hearkens back to the classical economists' difficulty of coming to terms with the idea of subsistence. Adam Smith, the father of classical economics, put the problem as follows: "By necessaries I understand, not only the commodities which are indispensably necessary for the support of life, but whatever the custom of the century renders it indecent for creditable people, even of the lowest order, to be without."[4] The poverty standard seeks to define minimal necessities of life in relation to what would be a decent standard of living for the poorest in America.

Counting the Poor

Subsequent to the original definition and measurement of poverty, the official statistics have been modified to take account of the fact that larger families need more income than smaller ones and farm families need less income than urban families. Hence, adjustments were made to the simple poverty index, based only on a four-person

Table 8-2 Poverty Levels, by Family Size, 1985[a]

Size of Family	Poverty Level
1 person under 65 years	$ 5,593
1 person 65 years and older	5,156
2 persons, head under 65 years	7,231
2 persons, head 65 years and older	6,503
3 persons	8,573
4 persons	10,989
5 persons	13,007
6 persons	14,696
7 persons	16,656
8 persons	18,512
9 persons or more	22,083

[a] Weighted average for farm and nonfarm families.
Source: U.S. Bureau of the Census, "Money Income and Poverty Status of Families and Persons in the United States: 1985," Series P-60, No. 154, p. 33

---

[4] Adam Smith, *The Wealth of Nations* (New York: Modern Library, 1937), p. 821.

Table 8-3 Persons below Poverty Level, 1959–1985, Selected Years

Year	Percentage of Total Population below Poverty Level
1959	22.4
1964	18.0
1969	12.1
1974	11.6
1977	11.6
1981	14.0
1985	14.0

Sources: U.S. Bureau of the Census, *Statistical Abstract of the United States* (Washington: Government Printing Office, 1979), p. 462; Council of Economic Advisers, *Economic Report of the President, 1966* (Washington: Government Printing Office), p. 111; U.S. Bureau of the Census, "Money Income and Poverty Status of Families and Persons in the United States: 1985," Series P-60, No. 154, p. 3.

family, to reflect these realities. In Table 8-2 the poverty cutoffs in 1985 are presented for families of different size. These represent a weighted average of farm and nonfarm families.

Two groups are presented for one- and two-person families—65 and over and under 65—to reflect the different income needs based on the life cycle of the family. For example, the official index of poverty allotted $7,231 in 1985 to a two-person family whose household head was under 65 and $6,503 to a family of the same size with the household head 65 or over. The standard four-person family had an income cutoff of $10,989.

Based on this more complex profile of poverty level cutoffs, the percentage of the population living in poverty is presented in Table 8-3 for certain years from 1959 to 1985. In 1964, the benchmark year in which the poverty statistics were first collected, 18 percent of the population were living in poverty. This is a remarkable statistic to contemplate for a moment. Based on a very parsimonious poverty cutoff level, which would leave a family barely at the physical subsistence level, nearly one in five were living in poverty in 1964. Indeed, there was and still is poverty amid affluence in the United States.

In 1977, and ever since 1969, about 12 percent of the population were living below the poverty line; since 1977 the percentage of the population living in poverty has increased to 14 percent. This is probably a minimal figure because it takes account only of changes in living costs and does not provide the poor any increase in their real standards of living, as the nonpoor have experienced. If this were taken into account and poverty were measured by some fixed relationship to median income, the percentage of people in poverty today would be unchanged from 1964.

Table 8-4 Incidence of Poverty by Age, Sex, and Race, 1985

Characteristic	Percentage of Persons below Poverty Level
Percentage of all persons below poverty level	14.0
Race:	
White	11.4
Black	31.3
Spanish origin	29.0
Sex of household head:	
Male	6.7
Female	34.0
Age 65 and over:	12.6
White	9.9
Black	30.5
Spanish origin	28.3

Source: U.S. Bureau of the Census, "Money Income and Poverty Status of Families and Persons in the United States: 1985," Series P-60, No. 154, pp. 21, 22.

Even the 14 percent figure in 1985 is striking in its importance. Look around you the next time you are in class. If the classroom were a precise random reflection of the society, one in seven would be living in poverty.

The Incidence of Poverty

Not all groups in the society experience poverty equally. The propensity of one demographic group to have a specific rate of poverty is called the *incidence of poverty*. Statistics on the incidence of poverty by race, sex, and age are presented in Table 8-4.

Blacks and women tend to have much higher rates of poverty than do whites and men. While the average poverty rate was 14 percent for everyone in the population in 1985, blacks had an incidence of poverty of 31 percent whereas whites had an incidence of 11 percent. Female-headed households had a poverty rate of nearly 34 percent, male-headed households less than 7 percent.

Older people over 65 tended to have a higher than average rate of poverty, but it was more severe for blacks and people of Spanish origin than it was for whites. The white incidence of poverty for people over 65 was below the national poverty average. Blacks over 65, however, had an incidence of poverty of 30 percent in 1985, and people of Spanish origin 28 percent.

Critics of the Official Poverty Measure

The poverty measure has been surrounded by substantial controversy. Some argue that the poverty measure *overstates* the problem; others have a contrary point of view. The issue of how poverty is measured excites passionate debate because the implications for the existence of poverty in the midst of American affluence are so difficult to accept.

The position that the official poverty index overstates the extent and severity of the problem revolves around two points: First, that the measure of poverty does not take into account "in-kind transfers" such as food stamps and medicaid payments, and second, that the index does not factor in personal wealth holdings of the poor. Home ownership, particulary for the poor over 65, is the primary point of reference for these arguments about personal wealth.

Cash and In-kind Transfers

Poor families are eligible to receive various types of assistance. These are called *transfer payments* because they represent a transfer of resources from some members of the society to others via government budgets. Some of these transfers are cash payments—social security, veteran's benefits, welfare, and so on. These cash transfers appear as family income and are counted toward a family's income when considering whether to classify the family as poor or not. These direct income transfer programs have become crucial in alleviating poverty for a sizable segment of the American population. For example, in 1976 some 21 percent of the population were living below the poverty line before income transfer payments were made. This is the same percentage that lived below the poverty line in 1965. After cash income transfers of social security, unemployment compensation, workers' compensation, and welfare, 12 percent of the population were living below the poverty line in 1976.[5] This is a reduction in poverty of nine percentage points. The reduction in poverty compared with 1965 was largely due to increased income transfer programs.

The same situation prevailed in 1980. According to a University of Wisconsin study, 20 percent of the population were below the poverty line before cash transfer programs. After the cash transfer programs were taken into account, 13 percent were below the poverty level.[6]

Other forms of transfers, however, do not involve a cash transfer. Instead, commodities or services are provided direct to the poor, and the cash payments never go

---

[5] Sheldon Danziger and Rober Plotnick, "Can Welfare Reform Eliminate Poverty?" *Social Service Review* (June 1979), p. 250.

[6] Institute for Research on Poverty, "Poverty in the United States: Where Do We Stand?" *Focus* 5, no. 2 (Winter 1981–82), p. 3.

through their hands. Food stamps, health assistance for the poor (medicaid), school lunch programs, and public housing are four of the most prominent forms of *in-kind transfers*. Since these in-kind transfers never show up as cash income for the poor but represent a form of income in kind, many contend they should be added to a family's income in order to determine whether the family is poor.

If the in-kind transfers of food stamps, child nutrition, housing assistance, medicare, and medicaid were included in family income, the count of the poor would have fallen by five percentage points in 1983—from 15 percent to 10 percent.[7] This is a substantial drop in the count of the poor, so the issue of whether to include in-kind transfers is not a trivial one.

In 1980 about three-fifths of all individuals in poverty received some form of in-kind transfer—medicaid, food stamps, free or reduced-price school lunches, or subsidized housing—according to a census study.[8] The controversy surrounds the issue of whether these in-kind benefits should be included along with the cash transfers. We will look at the arguments against inclusion of in-kind transfers shortly, after we look at the problem of excluding wealth from the measure of poverty.

Personal Wealth and the Count of the Poor

Many older people counted as poor own their own homes and have no mortgages left on them. Consequently, their need for a housing budget is minimized, although they still have to pay property taxes and utilities as well as provide for maintenance of their homes. These costs can be quite significant today as a result of inflation in the past decade. Notwithstanding this fact, many critics of the poverty measure contend that it overstates the count for older people by failing to take home ownership into account.

Including the imputed rental value of home ownership reduces the count of the poor by about 16 percent. When the official poverty index registers 12 percent, for example, including the imputed value of home ownership would reduce it to 10 percent.[9]

Are these legitimate qualifications of the official poverty index? The answer to that question is controversial. The level of income assigned to a poverty family is so meager that reducing its cash needs further by including in-kind transfers and imputed income from personal wealth can be seen as harsh. Obviously, if the family receives food or medical services without paying for them, its cash income can be stretched further. However, something like medical services is normally not consumed every

---

[7] U.S. Bureau of the Census, *Estimates of Poverty Including the Value of Noncash Benefits: 1983* (Washington: Government Printing Office, 1984), p. xiii.

[8] Reported in Spencer Rich, "Two-Fifths of U.S. Poor Get No In-Kind Benefits, Census Bureau Reports," *Washington Post*, July 7, 1982, p. A3.

[9] U.S. Department of Health, Education, and Welfare, *Measure of Poverty*, p. 98.

day, as food is, but only when it is needed. Distributing the total medical service transfer across the poor in some random fashion misses this point because it assumes all poor families have the same medical needs. Poverty could be reduced if the poor became ill and medicaid payments were made to them. But that is not the intended purpose of medicaid. Consider what would happen if the poor suddenly became more prone to illness. Medicaid and medicare payments would increase because these are entitlement programs, which expand when the need increases. These increased government expenditures would show up in government budgets as transfers to the poor. If the transfers were counted toward a poor person's income, conceivably many individuals previously classified as poor would no longer be officially counted as poor, even though their welfare was reduced by their illness.

Having your own home is an asset, but in today's inflationary times and with taxes as high as they are, many poor people who own their own homes cannot afford to keep them. They sell their homes, find cheaper housing, and use the proceeds of the sale to support themselves.

All this points to the *adequacy* of the poverty level income.[10] Barely at a level of physical subsistence, the poor have little margin for error in their family consumption standards. The adequacy of the poverty standard, or its inadequacy, is seen through the computation of family budgets by the Department of Labor.

Urban Family Budgets

Over the years, the Bureau of Labor Statistics (BLS) of the Department of Labor has provided estimates of family budget needs for typical urban families in the United States. What they previously called "minimum but adequate budgets" the BLS now calls *urban family budgets*. The budgets are constructed for three levels of living standards: lower, intermediate, and higher. In effect, they conform to what are conventionally called middle income, lower income, and upper income, all confined to the "middle class" of America.

The estimates of these budgets are very detailed. They contain over a hundred items of consumption. For 1981 a four-person urban family would have needed an annual income before taxes of $15,323 to be classified as lower middle income, $38,060 as upper middle income, and $25,407 as middle income.[11] In Table 8-5 these budget levels are presented, along with a relatively aggregated breakdown of what the budget pays for. The lowest of the three urban family budgets is about 65 percent higher than the poverty level. Even so, it does not provide for a terribly luxurious level of living, particularly in the face of today's inflation. For example, the food budget would have amounted to only $3.11 per person day in 1981. Little opportunity

---

[10] A critique of the adequacy of the poverty measure is contained in Center for Community Change, "Beyond the Numbers: The Failure of the Official Measure of Poverty" (December 1979).

[11] See Table 8-5. The Department of Labor stopped collecting these data after 1981.

Table 8-5   Annual Budgets for a Four-Person Family at Three Levels of Living, Urban United States, Autumn 1981

	Budget Level[a]		
	Lower	Intermediate	Higher
Total budget	$15,323	$25,407	$38,060
Total family consumption	12,069	18,240	25,008
Food	4,545	5,843	7,366
Housing	2,817	5,546	8,423
Transportation	1,311	2,372	3,075
Clothing	937	1,333	1,947
Personal care	379	508	719
Medical care	1,436	1,443	1,505
Other family consumption	644	1,196	1,972
Other items	621	1,021	1,718
Social security and disability	1,036	1,703	1,993
Personal income taxes	1,596	4,443	9,340

[a]Because of rounding, sums of individual items may not equal totals.
Source: U.S. Department of Labor, "Autumn 1981 Urban Family Budgets and Comparative Indexes for Selected Urban Area" (April 16, 1982).

for saving is afforded the lower-income family, from which to provide for education investments or precautions against unforeseen circumstances.

Dynamics of Poverty

Many of the stereotypes of the poor that existed in the 1960s and 1970s—who the poor are and how they became poor—have been reassessed in the 1980s because of an important study conducted by the Survey Research Center of the University of Michigan. Starting in 1968, and continuing for ten years, researchers at the Survey Research Center conducted repeated interviews with a panel of 5,000 families. These same families were continually surveyed over this ten-year period, creating what is called a longitudinal survey which permits us to understand how families move in and out of poverty. The results of this research have forced students of poverty to reconsider their earlier interpretations derived from a more static—or snapshot—view of poverty. The difference is between looking at a photograph and a moving picture.

In the Michigan study, only a little over half of the individuals who were poor in one year were poor in the next year.[12] The idea of a permanent poor, therefore, was not supported by the Michigan panel study. Only two percent of the population, for example, was dependent on welfare for an extended period of time in their study. One or two bad years pushed a family into poverty, typically caused by a change in family status: divorce, death, marriage, birth, or a child leaving home. Only 2.6 percent of the families were poor for eight or more years, while nearly a quarter were poor for only one year and then remained outside of poverty in the other nine years. Because poverty is such a fluid condition, however, it affects many more separate individuals than previously thought. Perhaps the most startling finding of the Michigan study was that about one-quarter of the U.S. families were poor some time during the decade between 1969 and 1978. If the classroom, therefore, was a random sample of the entire U.S. population, one in four of you would have experienced poverty between the late 1960s and the late 1970s.

Inequality in Income and Wealth

Poverty analysts quickly became aware of the fact that the problem of poverty in America could not be separated from the issue of inequality in wealth and income. The very phrase "poverty in the midst of affluence" connotes some sense of relative income status and, therefore, inequality. The poverty measure itself, although it purports to be as objectively based as possible, contains relative or subjective elements since it is based on living standards in the United States, not other countries, in the second half of the twentieth century. Comparing the poverty standard to median incomes makes the point that poverty cannot be divorced from the distribution of income. If you want to understand why someone is poor, you have to be able to explain why someone else is not poor; hence, the attention given to income distribution.

Income Distribution in the United States

Income distribution statistics are stated in terms of the proportions of the total personal income received by different percentiles in the population. Quintiles or fifths is the most common grouping for income distribution purposes. In Table 8-6 statistics on the distribution of income by quintiles are presented for selected years from 1929 to 1985. The figures can be interpreted as follows: In 1985 the lowest fifth of the

---

[12] Greg J. Duncan et al., *Years of Poverty. Years of Plenty.* (Ann Arbor, MI: Institute for Social Research, 1984). The page references to the information taken from this book are: 3,4,10,41, and 60. The survey was a representative random sample of all U.S. families.

Table 8-6 Income Distribution in the American Economy, 1929–1985, Selected Years (in Percent)

% of total family income

Family Income by Quintiles[a]	1929	1935–36	1941	1944	1950	1955	1960	1965	1970	1975	1981	1985
Lowest fifth		4	4	5	5	5	5	5	5	5	5	5
Second fifth	13[b]	9	10	11	12	12	12	12	12	12	12	11
Middle fifth	14	14	15	16	17	18	18	18	18	18	17	17
Fourth fifth	19	21	22	22	23	24	24	24	24	24	24	24
Highest fifth	54	52	49	46	43	41	41	41	41	41	42	43
Total, all families and unrelated individuals	100	100	100	100	100	100	100	100	100	100	100	100
Top 5 percent	30	27	24	21	17	16	16	16	16	16	15	16

increase in Reag. yr.

previously some[?]

[a]Family income represents pre-tax income and includes money transfer payments, such as social security. It excludes in-kind transfer payments.
[b]Lowest fifth and second fifth combined.
Sources: Herman Miller, *Income Distribution in the United States* (Washington: Government Printing Office, 1968), p. 3; U.S. Bureau of the Census, *Statistical Abstract of the United States* (Washington: Government Printing Office, 1985), p. 5; U.S. Bureau of the Census, "Money Income and Poverty Status of Families and Persons in the United States: 1985, "Series P-60, No. 152 (August 1986), p. 14.

income distribution received 5 percent of the total personal income in that year. The highest fifth of the income distribution received 43 percent of the total income in 1985. If income were equally distributed, each fifth of the population would have received 20 percent of the total income in 1985. Instead of the lowest fifth of the income distribution receiving only 5 percent of the total income, it would have received 20 percent. Therefore, a percentage *below* 20 percent in any cell in this table means that that income group received less than its "equal share."

The distribution of income in the United States has remained virtually unchanged since the end of World War II. There was a significant leveling of income distribution between 1929 and the end of World War II, but since the war, income distribution has not changed. The top 5 percent of the income ladder has received 16 percent of the total income since 1950. The lowest fifth of the income distribution has received 5 percent of the total income ever since 1950. Indeed, this remarkable stability in a complex phenomenon such as income distribution should make one stop and take notice. This is particularly important in the face of public policy that has sought to redistribute income through tax, transfers, and expenditure policies.[13]

---

[13] The income distribution figures include cash transfers, such as social security, unemployment compensation, and welfare. These are figures for personal income—that is, income before taxes have been paid.

INCOME OF INTEREST is: AFTER TAX INCOME.

The amount of income associated with each of these income quintiles is shown in Table 8-7. In 1985 the mean income for all families was $32,944. The lowest fifth of the income distribution had incomes of $13,192 and below. This is the meaning of that figure in Table 8-7. The middle fifth of the income distribution had a minimum income of $22,726 and a maximum income of $33,040. Compare your family's income in 1985 with these statistics to see where you stand in the income distribution of the United States.

Measuring Income Inequality: Lorenz Curves and Gini Coefficients

An array of income distribution figures such as appears in Table 8-6 is instructive, but it is rather difficult to interpret if the object is to compare changes in the distribution of income over time or the degree of income inequality between two countries. Two tools of analysis have been developed to facilitate comparisons and interpretations of income distribution statistics: the Lorenz Curve and the Gini Coefficient.

The *Lorenz Curve* is a graphical means of depicting an income distribution. Figure 8-1 presents the Lorenz Curve for the income distribution in 1981. Table 8-8 contains the data for 1985 that are used in the Lorenz Curve. For purposes of the Lorenz Curve, the *cumulative incomes* for the quintiles are used. Table 8-8 shows the lower 60 percent of the income distribution receiving 33 percent of total personal income in 1985, the lower 80 percent of income recipients receiving 57 percent of total personal income, and so forth. This is the meaning of the figures in the column labeled "cumulative percentages from lowest to highest quintiles," which are based on the raw statistics on income distribution in 1985 from Table 8-6.

Table 8-7   Income of Family Quintiles, 1985

	Current Dollars (1985)
Mean income, all families	$32,944
Upper limit of each quintile:	
Lowest fifth	13,192
Second fifth	22,725
Middle fifth	33,040
Fourth fifth	48,000
Highest 5 percent[a]	77,706

[a]Minimum income level that places a family in the top 5 percent of the income distribution.
Source: U.S. Bureau of the Census, "Money Income and Poverty Status of Families and Persons in the United States: 1985," Series P-60, No. 154, pp. 5, 11.

GINI COEFFICIENT for the U.S. have remained relatively stable.

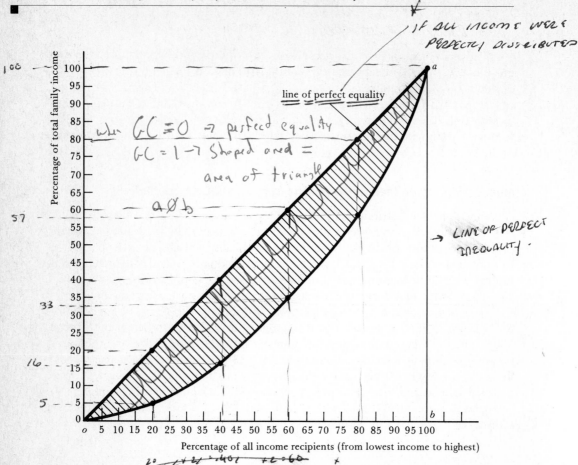

If all income were perfectly distributed

when $GC = 0 \rightarrow$ perfect equality
$GC = 1 \rightarrow$ sloped and $=$ area of triangle

$\rightarrow$ LINE OR PERFECT INEQUALITY.

Figure 8-1 Lorenz Curve for 1985

ACTUAL DISTRIBUTION $\rightarrow$ FALLS BETWEEN LINE OF PERFECT EQUALITY AND PERFECT INEQUALITY

If income had been distributed equally in that year, the lower 60 percent of all income recipients would have received 60 percent of personal income, the lower 80 percent of personal income and so on. In Figure 8-1 this is represented by the straight line through the axis, labeled "line of perfect equality." The actual cumulative distribution of income taken from Table 8-8 is the bowed segment, which shows the deviation of the distribution of income from perfect equality. The fact that the lowest 40 percent of income recipients received only 16 percent of personal income in 1985 is shown in Figure 8-1 by a point below the line of perfect equality.

Cumulative distributions of income can be presented for other years or for different countries, and in this way comparisons can be readily obtained. As an exercise, plot the cumulative income distribution figures for 1935–36 from Table 8-6. The Lorenz Curve for 1935–36 should lie outside the one for 1985, indicating greater income inequality in that earlier set of years. More-equal income distributions would lie inside the 1981 Lorenz Curve.

A summary statistic, called the *Gini Coefficient*, can be used to represent the degree of inequality for purposes of comparisons among different years and different countries. Referring to Figure 8-1, we compute the Gini Coefficient by taking the ratio of the bowed, shaded area to the total area of the triangle *oab*. The shaded area represents the "Lorenz bow"—the extent to which the actual distribution of income deviates from perfect equality. The larger the shaded area, the more unequal is income distribution. Therefore, at the limit, the Gini Coefficient would have the value 1.0. This means that the shaded area would begin to approximate the size of the triangle *oab*, and the ratio of the area of the shaded Lorenz bow to the triangle *oab* would approach 1.0. Perfect equality would indicate a Gini Coefficient of 0.0 because then there would be no shaded area and, consequently, the value of the ratio would approach 0.0. In short, the higher the Gini Coefficient, the more unequal is the income distribution, with limits of 0.0 and 1.0 for the size of the Gini Coefficient.

Since the end of World War II, the Gini Coefficient for the United States has ranged from 0.379 to 0.351, indicating that there has been virtually no change in income distribution since the end of the war. Some countries have more-equal income distributions than the United States, others more unequal. Denmark, for example, has a Gini Coefficient of 0.23, the Netherlands 0.28, and Japan 0.31. Australia has a Gini Coefficient roughly the same as that of the United States, while Great Britain and Italy have higher Gini Coefficients, indicating greater income inequality. For Italy the Gini Coefficient is 0.41, and for Great Britain it is 0.39.

Distribution of Personal Wealth

Personal wealth represents an asset of some sort—land, real estate, stocks, or bonds. Personal wealth is far more unequally distributed than is personal income. The two interact, however, since some personal income derives from the ownership of personal wealth. Dividends, rents, interest, and capital gains are all forms of income that derive from the ownership of personal wealth.

Table 8-8   Lorenz Curve for 1985

	Percentage of Total Family Income, 1981	Cumulative Percentages from Lowest to Highest Quintiles
Lowest fifth	5	5
Second fifth	11	16
Third fifth	17	33
Fourth fifth	24	57
Highest fifth	43	100

Source: Table 8-6.

Table 8-9 Share of Personal Wealth Owned by Top
1 Percent of Wealth Holders, 1922–1972, Selected Years

Year	Percentage of all personal wealth owned by top 1 percent of wealth holders
1922	31.6
1929	36.3
1933	28.3
1939	30.6
1945	23.3
1949	20.8
1953	24.3
1956	26.0
1958	23.8
1962	22.0
1965	23.4
1969	20.1
1972	20.7

Source: U.S. Bureau of the Census, *Statistical Abstract of the United States* (Washington: Government Printing Office, 1979), p. 470.

The distribution of personal wealth is presented in Table 8-9, which shows the percentage of total personal wealth owned by the top 1 percent of all wealth holders for selected years from 1922 to 1972, the last year wealth data of this type are available. This 1 percent of the population has owned over 20 percent of all the personal wealth of the nation throughout the entire century. In some years more than one-third of total personal wealth was concentrated in the hands of the top 1 pecent of wealth holders. A 1983 study, not directly comparable to these statistics, found that the top one percent of wealth holders owned 34 percent of all the wealth in the United States.[14]

The inequality in personal wealth feeds into the inequality in income, since political and economic power flow from the ownership of personal wealth. For example, important sources of income-producing wealth are more unequally distributed than is total personal wealth. In 1983 the top 0.5 percent of the income distribution owned 47 percent of all corporate stock and 44 percent of all bonds. Assets held in trusts were even more concentrated. The top 0.5 percent of income recipients owned 77 percent of all assests in trusts.[15] Only the distribution of real estate—primarily

---

[14] U.S. Congress, Joint Economic Committee, "The Concentration of Wealth in the United States" (July 1986), Table 4.

[15] Ibid., p. 24.

personal homes—made the overall distribution of personal wealth as equal as it appears in Table 8-9. *[handwritten: WHY? THE MORE WEALTH, THE GREATER CONCENTRATION IS]* *[handwritten: WHY? WEALTHY FAMILIES ARE smaller]*

[handwritten: THE DIST OF INCOME IS MORE EQUAL THAN DIST OF WEALTH!]

Some Observations on the Distribution of Wealth and Income

[handwritten: WHY? RICH MARRY RICH]

What is the optimal amount of income and wealth inequality? The answer to that question is a difficult one. Some amount of inequality is no doubt necessary to provide the economic incentives to stimulate people to work to their potential. But how much inequality is required for this incentive? Put differently, could we have more economic equality without the sacrifice of growth, productivity, and innovation? Other societies with more equality, such as Japan, certainly do not suffer from an absence of growth and productivity, while Great Britain has more inequality than we do, but its economy is stagnant.

Economic theory provides no signposts on the road to discovering how much inequality is optimal. Microeconomic theory starts with *any* distribution of income and proceeds to a conclusion that economic optimality can occur with any amount of economic inequality. Keynesian theory hints that more economic equality will provide greater economic stability because consumption is supported by greater equality. The higher reaches of the income distribution save more, and this will reduce aggregate demand if income is more heavily concentrated in the higher income strata of the distribution. But Keynes does not enable us to find out the extent to which income should be redistributed if this becomes a problem. Nor do Keynesians answer supply-side critics who claim that the savings rate is so low that investment and innovation have suffered, implying that income should be more unequally distributed than it is. On the other hand, some Keynesians have explicitly defended income redistribution policies on the grounds that these will help stabilize the economy at high levels of employment.

The relationship between equality and growth is an unknown entity that has engaged economists, philosophers, and social analysts through the ages. Today there is much speculation that the United States is experiencing slower growth because it has chosen the public policy path of more equity. But if income and wealth have become more equal in the United States, the statistics do not reveal it. In fact, income and wealth are no more equally distributed today than in the 1950s and 1960s, when our growth rates, productivity, unemployment, and inflation were more acceptable.

Public policy, which emphasized equality in the 1960s and 1970s, does not seem to have made any difference in the overall distribution of income. Without these policy efforts, however, income and wealth may have become more unequally distributed. Perhaps public policy played a finger-in-the-dike role. Without such public efforts, the forces tending toward inequality in the system might have outstripped the forces of equality.

Left to its own devices, our economic and social system would probably tend to intensify inequality from one generation to the next.[16] The real world does not operate like the game of Monopoly. Think of yourself playing a game of Monopoly with a friend. You distribute money *equally* at the start, something that society does not do. You play out the game; one person loses, the other wins. The loser says, "Let's play another game. Throw all your winnings into the pot, and we will distribute an equal amount of money again to start another game."

"Wait," says the winner. "I accumulated my wealth and income by the strength of my own wits. I will not relinquish either my property or my income. Now see if you can beat me in another game."

The outcome would be obvious. The winner of the first game would in all likelihood win the next game. The economy is like this. The forces that tend to perpetuate and intensify inequality from one generation to the next are stronger than the forces that tend to overcome inequalities in initial endowments. Public policy has played the role of refereeing the game of life so that its outcome does not become so unequal as to cause social unrest. In the process, critics would argue, initiative has been reduced in the society, and various distortions of the economy have occcurred, as government has pursued its policies directed toward more economic equality. The jury is not yet in on this conclusion, however, and economists know little about the relationship between a desired amount of inequality and its impact on the economy.

Summary

Poverty and inequality became important public issues in the 1960s. Initially, poverty was the great social problem, inspiring a "war" against it. Poverty is defined in terms of a family budget that would enable its members to live barely at the physical subsistence level. It is based primarily on the Department of Agriculture's economy food plan and augmented on the basis of studies that show the proportion of a household's budget spent on food.

In 1985 the poverty cutoff was set at $10,989 for a nonfarm family of four. This came to 40 percent of the median family income in 1985, a decline from 42 percent of the median family income in 1964, the year the measure was first introduced. This means that the poverty index was adjusted to take account of increases in the cost of the economy food plan but did not permit the poor to participate in the general growth in living standards that has taken place since 1964.

Based on the official poverty index, broken down by family size and farm versus nonfarm status, about 14 percent of the population in the United States were classified as poor in 1985. This amounts to 33.1 million individuals.

Not everyone accepts the poverty measure as adequate to the task of counting

---

[16] Lester C. Thurow, *Generating Inequality* (New York: Basic Books, 1975).

the poor. Some contend that the index is too parsimonious in what it enables a family to consume. They would prefer to use the lower of three family budgets that the Bureau of Labor Statistics identified in their urban family budget research. Based on that index, a standard of $15,323 would have been used in 1981 to indicate an individual's low-income status.

Other critics of the poverty index contend that it overstates the count of the poor because it does not take into account in-kind transfers and personal wealth. In the former category are items like food stamps and medicaid; in the latter category is home ownership. Including in-kind transfers would reduce the count of the poor by about five percentage points, and including home ownership, which affects primarily the aged poor, would reduce the count of the poor by about two percentage points.

Very quickly poverty analysts discovered that they could not study the poor without studying the nonpoor. The condition of poverty represented some standard with reference to the nonpoor, and analyses of why someone was poor had to take into account why someone else was not poor. Income distribution in the American economy became a corollary of poverty in the United States.

Studies of income distribution reveal that there was a reduction in inequality during World War II but that since the end of the war there has been no change in the distribution of income. This stability in the distribution of income occurs in the face of substantial public policy efforts to redistribute income through tax, transfer, and expenditure policies.

Personal wealth is far more unequally distributed than is income in the United States. This is particularly true for income-producing personal wealth, such as ownership of stocks, bonds, and trusts. The top 0.5 percent of all personal wealth holders own 47 percent of all corporate stock, 44 percent of all bonds, and 77 percent of all assets in trusts.

This inequality in income from wealth is a crucial factor in analyzing the overall distribution of income. A more extended discussion of the causes of inequality and poverty in the American economy has to start with an analysis of what are called *factor income shares*—income earned from capital ownership as opposed to labor services. This is the subject taken up in the next chapter.

Study Questions

1. What are the problems associated with an absolute measure of poverty? A relative measure of poverty? Which of these comes closest to describing the official measure of poverty?

2. Explain why some economists claim that the official measure of poverty overstates the severity of the problem. Explain why some economists make the opposite argument.

3. What are the factors that can be used to explain why there is a higher incidence of poverty among blacks, women, and the elderly?

4. What are the tools used by economists to measure inequality in income?

5. What are the economic costs and benefits associated with public policies designed to redistribute income? Have public policies in the United States had an effect on income distribution? If so, what is the effect?

6. Should government policy set a goal for income distribution? Would the free market reach the same distributional objectives? Compare these two points of view.

Further Reading

Miller, Herman. *Income Distribution in the United States*. Washington: Government Printing Office, 1968.

Thurow, Lester C. *Generating Inequality*. New York: Basic Books, 1975.

U.S. Department of Health, Education, and Welfare. *The Measure of Poverty*. Washington: Government Printing Office, 1976.

9

The Functional Distribution of Income

The functional distribution of income refers to the shares of the national income received by labor and capital as a result of their contributions to output and revenues. Labor and capital are the two principal factors of production. They are the basic inputs into all productive processes. Capital, as used in this context, is given its broadest meaning; it represents returns to the ownership of all forms of productive property. Included in returns to capital are rents, profits, interest, and dividends—all forms of income received from the ownership of productive assets.

The shares of the national income received by labor and capital provide the starting point for a discussion of the causes of inequality and poverty. The distribution of the fruits of production between the two principal factor inputs is the initial economic process that will ultimately determine a distribution of income. Some people receive income primarily from labor, others primarily from the ownership of capital. This fact alone affects the position of the individual in the overall distribution of income. It also affects the probability that an individual will be poor. Virtually no one who owns productive property that yields profits, rents, dividends, or interest is poor in the American economy, except for some small farmers. On the other hand, many wage and salary earners experience poverty, either while they are working or after they stop working and begin to receive income from social security.

The theory of the functional distribution of income is derived from the basic neoclassical marginal productivity theory of wage determination. This model was presented in Chapters 3 through 5 of this book; you may find it useful to review that material if the theoretical section of this chapter causes any problems.

Labor and Capital Shares of the National Income

The basic statistics on the functional distribution of income are presented in Table 9-1. Labor's and capital's shares of the national income are presented in that table for selected years from 1929 through 1985. Starting with the end of World War II, labor's share of the national income has increased gradually but steadily. From about 65 percent of the national income in 1948, labor's share had grown to 74 percent of the national income by 1985.

Part of this growth in labor's share of the national income is due to the structural changes that have occurred in the economy since the end of World War II.[1] Many self-employed farmers who received profits from their farming no longer own farms, and this, in and of itself, would reduce capital's share of the national income. If a self-employed farmer sells his or her land to a corporate enterprise, but continues to work the land as before, that farmer will no longer be receiving profits but will be paid a wage or salary. In terms of the statistics on the functional distribution of income, the farmer's profits will be transformed into the wage or salary. Thus, labor's share of the national income will rise because of this shift in ownership form. This same phenomenon has occurred in the small-retail-business sector of the economy, with similar consequences for the growth in labor's share of the national income.

These structural shifts in ownership patterns in the American economy show up as a statistical shift in the functional distribution of income, without indicating any shift in economic power toward labor and away from capital. At first glance it might appear that a shift in the functional distribution of income toward labor means that labor is more powerful in the economy and has prospered at the expense of capital. However, the statistics do not necessarily imply this, because, in part, they reflect a changing structure of ownership in the economy, which has no implication for growth or decline in labor's power in relation to the power of capital.

For another very important reason the statistics on labor and capital shares of the national income must be interpreted with great care. Not only have there been important changes in the structure of ownership in the American economy since World War II, but there have been equally significant alterations in the internal management of corporations, which affect the functional distribution of income. The problem arises because labor's share of the national income, as measured in the official statistics, includes the salaries of corporate executives along with the wages of blue-

---

[1] Allan M. Cartter, *Theory of Wages and Employment* (Homewood, IL: Richard D. Irwin, 1959), pp. 164–65.

Table 9-1 Labor and Capital Shares of the National Income, 1929–1985, Selected Years

Year	Shares of the National Income	
	Labor[a](%)	Capital[b](%)
1929 — *BEGINING OF DEPRESSION*	60.2 +	39.8 = 100
1933 — *DEPRESSION*	73.9	26.1
1939	67.5	32.5
1943	64.7	35.3
1948	64.5	35.5
1953	70.0	30.0
1958	70.9	29.1 *DECREASING TREND*
1963	71.0	29.0 *1. STRUCTURAL △ IN THE ECONOMY*
1968	72.8	27.2
1973	75.1	24.9
1979	75.8	24.2 *2.*
1982	76.2	23.8
1985	73.8	26.2

[a] Includes wages; salaries; and employers' contributions to social security, private pensions, health insurance, workers' compensation, and unemployment compensation.
[b] Includes rent, interest, corporate profits, and income of sole proprietors.
Source: Council of Economic Advisers, *Economic Report of the President, 1985* (Washington: Government Printing Office), pp. 278–79.

collar workers. Labor is given the widest possible definition in these statistics to include anyone who receives a wage or salary. It includes the million-dollar-plus salaries of the chief executive officers of the largest corporations alongside the wages of production workers.[2] The salary of the chief executive officer of General Motors is included in labor's share of the national income along with the wage paid to the janitor who cleans his executive suite.

Any data that have such a broad scope (such as data that include people of heterogeneous statuses) must be interpreted with great care. The most common error is to impute a growing power of labor from the statistics on labor's increasing share of the national income. The corollary is to infer a "profit squeeze" from capital's

[2] In 1985 Victor Posner, Chairman of DWG Corp., was the highest paid corporate executive, earning salary and bonus of $12.7 million, followed by T. Boone Pickens, Jr., of Mesa Petroleum, $4.2 million. ("Executive Pay: How the Boss Did In '85," *Business Week*, May 5, 1986, p. 49). Posner, however, was indicted for income tax evasion and convicted in July 1986 of evading $1.2 million in federal income taxes. (Gary Cohn, "Jury Convicts Victor Posner of Tax Evasion," *Wall Street Journal*, July 21, 1986, p. 4).

RECESSION → PROFITS FALL GREATLY COMPARED TO WAGES
RECOVERY → PROFITS RISE MORE THAN WAGES.

declining share of the national income.[3] Aside from the fact that the data on labor's share include the high salaries of corporate officials who manage capital, there is another reason why these data cannot be used to assess the relative power of capital and labor. Labor's share of the national income is a product of wage rates and number of people employed. A rising labor's share, therefore, could occur with falling wages if the number of people employed rose more rapidly to offset a fall in wages. Any price-quantity relationship must be analyzed carefully to disentangle, in this case, the wage from the employment aspect of a rising labor's share.

Since World War II there has been substantial growth in the managerial component of the corporation. Conglomerate and multinational corporate forms have hastened this process and helped cause the substantial growth in these segments of corporate employment. Persons in these managerial groups, particularly those in the executive categories, manage capital for absentee owners. Since they manage capital and since they receive their rewards on the basis of the profits received by the corporation, their salaries really should be counted as part of capital's share of the national income, rather than as part of labor's share.

For example, let us consider a situation in which a young entrepreneur opens a store that sells jeans. She becomes very successful and, after a few years, makes a profit of $100,000. In that year the $100,000 would be counted as part of the profit share of national income. In the next year, however, some large national chain decides to buy out the local businesswoman and retains the original entrepreneur by paying her a salary of $100,000, equal to last year's profits, for managing the store. In this year labor's share of the national income increases by $100,000. Simply by this one organizational change, the shares of national income have shifted, even though the original owner is performing the same function as before the buy-out. Now she manages capital for an owner whereas, before, she was the owner.

Unfortunately, there are no data that would permit us to track this phenomenon with any degree of precision.[4] This is a significant problem and represents a failure on the part of our statistics-gathering agencies in the government. Informed observation of the American society would lead one to conclude that managers, vice presidents, and corporate executives of all sorts have proliferated in the past decades as the American corporation has become larger, more complex, more diversified, and more international in its scope of operations. All this would point toward a growth of that segment of labor's share of the national income made up of those who manage capital for absentee owners. These groups receive their income from the profits of the corporation and perform a function that should reclassify their income as part of

---

[3] A typical article about the "squeeze" on profits, using unadjusted income-share data, is William D. Nordhaus, "The Falling Share of Profits," *Brookings Papers on Economic Activity* 1 (1974), pp. 169–208.

[4] I have made an attempt to identify the managerial component of labor's income share. Using the imprecise data available, I found that the managerial part of labor's income share rose from about 20 percent in the 1950s to around 30 percent in the 1970s. This shows the direction of change and the rough magnitude of the adjustment that would have to be made to labor's income share to compensate for this phenomenon.

capital's share of the national income. If this adjustment were made, the growth of labor's share of the national income would of necessity be smaller. Whether it would eliminate all of the growth of labor's share or whether it would show a growing share for capital is impossible to say without better statistics. For this reason the use and interpretation of national income shares should be undertaken carefully.

Income Inequality and the Functional Distribution of Income

A relationship exists between the income inequality encountered in the previous chapter and the functional distribution of income. The more an individual has access to income from the ownership of property, the higher is that person's income. Thus, wealth inequality feeds into income inequality. This is revealed through a further examination of the functional distribution of income.

In Table 9-2, data are presented showing the percentage of income received from labor and property sources by the size of income. Taxable income is the definition of income used for these purposes, because the statistics originate with personal income tax returns. In 1983 those with taxable income under $100,000 received between 82 and 90 percent of their income from wages and salaries; the remaining 10 to 18 percent came from the ownership of property and is labeled "property income" in Table 9-2. As incomes rise, the percentage of income received from property owner-

Table 9-2 Sources of Taxable Income by Income Size, 1983

Taxable Income Group	Percentage of Taxable Income Derived from:	
	Wages and Salaries	Property Income[a]
Under $10,000	84	16
$10,000–$20,000	83	17
$20,000–$30,000	88	12
$30,000–$50,000	90	10
$50,000–$100,000	82	18
$100,000–$200,000	67	33
$200,000–$500,000	54	46
$500,000–$1,000,000	37	63
$1,000,000 or more	21	79

[a]Includes income from business and professional self-employment, farm ownership, partnership, capital gains, dividends, rent, interest, royalties, estates.
Source: Department of the Treasury, *Statistics of Income—1983: Individual Income Tax Returns* (Washington: Government Printing Office, 1985), p. 12.

AS TAXABLE INCOME INCREASES, THE SHARE OF WAGES DECREASES AND THE SHARE OF PROPERTY INCOME RISES.

ship increases. For those with over $1,000,000 of taxable income, 79 percent originates with the ownership of property. Proportions of income originating in the forms of property income and labor income for other income groups can be found in Table 9-2. The moral of the story is clear: if you want to be rich and earn over $100,000 per year, you cannot do this solely through the receipt of wages and salaries. Income received through the ownership of property is absolutely essential at the upper reaches of the income distribution.

To the extent that wealth is unequally distributed, income inequality will be greater. The figures presented in the previous chapter on the inequality of the ownership of wealth show their connection to income inequality through the link of the functional distribution of income.

What determines the functional distribution of income? The remainder of this chapter addresses this question from the standpoint of several models economists have developed to explain changes in the functional distribution of income over the long run and during the course of the business cycle.

Neoclassical Theory of the Functional Distribution of Income

The neoclassical theory of the functional distribution of income starts from the premise that labor and capital are compensated according to their respective marginal productivities. If labor and capital are paid a return equal to the values of their marginal productivities, then markets are in equilibrium and are sufficiently competitive to conform to the requirements laid down by the general theory of neoclassical economics.

Labor will receive a monetary return equal to the wage paid per unit of labor employed by the firm, multiplied by the number of individuals employed by the enterprise. Represented symbolically,

$$L = wE,$$

where L = labor's return, w = wage rate, and E = number of individuals employed. The same will hold true for capital. Its return will be equal to

$$C = rK,$$

where C = returns to capital, r = rate of return per unit of capital used by the firm, and K = number of units of capital used by the firm. National income will be the sum of returns to labor and returns to capital. This is the functional distribution of income, which is equal to

$$Y = L + C$$

(1) A. SMITH

(2) MALTHUS

(3) RICARDO   ENGELS MARX

(4) MARSHALL

or

$$Y = wE + rK,$$

where Y = national income.

Labor's and capital's shares of the national income are a resultant of the decision of the firm to use labor and capital in the production process in combinations that depend on the relative prices of capital and labor. The *relative share* of capital to labor is another way of representing the functional distribution of income, which is essentially the same as showing each factor input's share of national income separately.[5] The relative share of capital to labor can be represented thus:

$$\frac{C}{L} = \frac{rK}{wE}$$

The relative shares of capital and labor show the comparative returns that each factor of production earns. Of more interest is the question of how these relative shares *change* over time. Specifically, the *percentage change* in the relative shares of capital and labor provides an important yardstick for gauging developments in the economy. The percentage change in the relative shares of the national income going to capital and labor is

$$\frac{\Delta \frac{C}{L}}{\frac{C}{L}} = \left(\frac{\Delta \frac{K}{E}}{\frac{K}{E}}\right) - \left(\frac{\Delta \frac{w}{r}}{\frac{w}{r}}\right)$$

where the symbol Δ indicates "change." This means that the percentage change in the relative shares of the national income earned by capital and labor depends on the relative percentage change in factor prices (r and w) and the relative percentage change in factor utilization in the firm (K and E).

There is a price and quantity relationship involved here that is similar to other price-quantity relationships in economics. They are governed by the principle of *elasticity*, which reflects the percentage change in some quantity in response to a percentage change in price. In this instance the change in relative factor shares depends on the respective demand elasticities for capital and labor when the relative prices of the factors of production change. If the price of one factor changes more rapidly than the price of the other, the change in each factor's share of the national income depends on how factor utilization changes. This is where the principle of elasticity enters the

---

[5] If labor's share of the national income = L/Y and capital's share of the national income = C/Y, then capital's share relative to labor's is

$$\frac{C/Y}{L/Y} = \frac{C}{Y} \cdot \frac{Y}{L} = \frac{C}{L}.$$

analysis. Depending on whether there is ample substitution between the factors of production, relative income shares could change to benefit either the factor of production whose price has risen more rapidly or the other factor of production, whose price did not rise as rapidly. The outcome depends on the demand elasticities in response to price changes for both the factors of production. In this instance what matters is a concept called the *elasticity of substitution* between capital and labor.

The Elasticity of Substitution

The elasticity of substitution between capital and labor measures the extent to which the firm can substitute the other factor of production for the factor whose price has risen more rapidly.[6] It reflects the ease of substitution between the two factors of production and depends on the nature of the technology that governs production. It is measured by the formula for the change in relative factor shares presented on page 171. Another way of looking at this formula is to view it as a representation of the relative demand elasticities between capital and labor.

As aggregate demand has risen for all goods and services over the years, demand has also risen for the two factors of production—labor and capital. Labor's supply is more fixed than is capital's supply, however, because labor is a human factor of production and can be expanded only at the pace and rhythm dictated by population growth and changes in the labor force participation rate. Capital, on the other hand, is an "artificial" creation of human labor and other capital. It can expand more rapidly in response to increased aggregate demand for goods and services. Consequently, the price of labor should, in general, rise more rapidly than the price of capital over the long run, because the supply response of labor to increased demand is more sluggish than is the supply response of capital. The price of labor will tend, other things equal, to rise more rapidly than the price of capital, which implies that the *relative price* structure that signals the use of factors of production will lead to capital being substituted for labor. The question is, however, can the firm substitute capital for labor easily enough to offset the higher price labor now extracts from the economy? This depends on the nature of the technology and on how quickly that technology can be altered through technological change.

If technology does not permit rapid substitution of capital for labor, labor's share relative to capital will increase, because labor will be able to benefit at the expense of capital from its more sharply rising price. On the other hand, if the technology permits rapid substitution, labor's share could fall compared with capital, because the firm has been able to adjust its factor utilization more than enough to compensate for any shift in relative factor prices.

---

[6] For a discussion of this concept see K. W. Rothschild, *The Theory of Wages* (Oxford: Basil Blackwell, 1965), chap. 5.

This is what the elasticity of substitution tells us. If the elasticity of substitution is *less than 1*, substitution is sluggish and labor's share of the national income will rise, compared with capital's share of the national income, in the face of a relative increase in wages.

If the elasticity of substitution is equal to 1, any proportional change in relative factor prices is exactly offset by the proportional change in the utilization of the factors of production. In this case the relative shares of labor and capital in the national income would not change.[7] If the elasticity of substitution is greater than 1, the factor of production whose price rises less rapidly will gain in its relative share of the national income. For example, if the price of labor rises more rapidly than the price of capital and the elasticity of substitution is greater than 1, the relative share of the national income accruing to capital will rise, because the substitution of capital for labor in production more than compensates for the increase in wages relative to the price of capital.

To summarize, the following possibilities exist:

If the elasticity of substitution is	If the price of labor rises more rapidly than the price of capital, labor's relative share of the national income will
less than one	increase
equal to one	remain the same
greater than one	decrease

There is no way to decide on the size of the elasticity of substitution a priori, solely through theoretical reasoning. The size of the elasticity of substitution is a purely empirical matter. Studies have shown that the elasticity of substitution in the American economy is about 0.65, which means that the factor of production whose price has risen more rapidly will gain in its share of the national income relative to the other factor of production.[8] Over the years labor's price has risen more rapidly than capital's, and firms have not been able to substitute sufficiently to offset this change. Consequently, labor's share of the national income has risen relative to capital's share.

The empirical studies suffer from the data specification problem explained at the outset of this chapter. To the extent that labor's share of the national income includes elements of salaried executives who manage capital, there is an overstatement of the change in some variables of the model, which will produce an elasticity less than one. The change in wages and in the price of capital will be distorted by this measurement

---

[7] Since the elasticity of substitution is related to the technology available, the firm's production function plays a role in the analysis. An elasticity of substitution equal to 1 is a condition embodied by one of the most commonly used production functions, the Cobb-Douglas production function.

[8] Irving Kravis, "Relative Income Shares in Fact and Theory," *American Economic Review* 49 (December 1959), pp. 917–49.

problem, and therefore, the empirical estimates of the elasticity of substitution must be qualified. The same is true for the overall statement that labor's relative share of the national income has increased.

How predictive is this theory of functional income distribution, setting aside the considerable data problems that exist? An interesting study conducted in the mid-1960s by the economist Lester Thurow revealed that over a long span of time, labor tended to receive a share of the national income less than would be predicted on the basis of the neoclassical theory of functional income distribution.[9] From 1929 to 1965, the period covered by his study, labor received about 60 percent of what it should have based on its marginal contributions to national income, and capital significantly more than its marginal contributions. He explains this in part as a result of imperfect competition, which skews the functional income distribution against labor. In the next section of this chapter, a conceptual framework is presented, based on monopoly power, that can be used to account for Thurow's empirical study of the functional distribution of income.

Monopoly Power and the Functional Distribution of Income

Concentrations of economic power can distort the functional income distribution from the norms of neoclassical economic theory. One of the more interesting and complete theories of the functional distribution of income under conditions of imperfect competition in product markets was produced by the Polish economist Michal Kalecki in the early 1930s. His model is quite elaborate, and the details do not warrant a full exposition here.[10] The conclusions he draws from his theory about the functional distribution of income are, however, quite important.

Kalecki starts with the premise that there is less than perfect competition in product markets. In each sector of the economy, he measures the degree of economic concentration (or degree of monopoly) by the extent to which product price exceeds marginal cost. Recall that under conditions of perfect competition product price equals the firm's marginal cost, whereas under conditions of imperfect competition product price exceeds marginal cost. Having established the degree of imperfect competition in each market, Kalecki then develops a weighted average measure of degree of monopoly by aggregating all sectors of the economy, weighted by the proportion of output each sector contributed to the total. *more here*.

This measure of imperfect competition is related to the issue of the functional distribution of income. In Kalecki's model labor's share of the national income is a

---

[9] Lester C. Thurow, "Disequilibrium and the Marginal Productivity of Capital and Labor," *Review of Economics and Statistics* 50, no. 1 (February 1968), pp. 23–31.

[10] Michal Kalecki, "The Distribution of the National Income," reprinted in *Selected Essays on the Dynamics of the Capitalist Economy* (Cambridge: Cambridge University Press, 1971), pp. 62–77.

residual—the reverse of the procedure normally followed. Marginal cost includes an amount that reflects the normal rate of return on capital—the opportunity cost of capital. Above-normal returns to capital occur either when there are disequilibria in markets or when there is monopoly power operating in markets. Disequilibria in markets are a transitory phenomenon, market power is permanent.

Capital's income share, above what would be received under perfect competition, occurs when product price exceeds marginal cost. This represents the price markup over costs. In Kalecki's model, therefore, the return to capital depends directly on the extent to which product price exceeds marginal cost. But this is nothing but the measure of monopoly power in markets. So capital's share of the national income, above what it would have received under conditions of perfect competition, depends directly on the degree of product market power exercised by firms over prices. Labor's share is a residual that is received after capital's share of the national income has been allocated through product markets and price markups.

Kalecki's model, though posited some 35 years earlier, provides corroboration for the work done by Lester Thurow and discussed in the previous section. Recall that Thurow found capital's share of the national income exceeding what it would have been under the neoclassical model based on perfect competition. Kalecki's theory accounts for this by developing a measure of monopoly power that reflects the existence of imperfect competition in product markets. To the extent there has been growing market power over time, capital's share of the national income should increase. Whether this shows up in the statistics on the functional distribution of income depends on how accurately the data measure the phenomenon under study. As indicated earlier, the statistics gathered on the functional distribution of income are not reliable because they bias changes over time toward showing a rising labor share of the national income when that may not be occurring at all.

IF THERE IS MONOPOLY IN THE PRODUCT MRKT, THEN THE SHARE OF MONOPOLIST WILL INCREASE THE SHARE OF PROFIT

The Functional Distribution of Income over the Business Cycle

The discussion thus far has focused on the trends in the movement of labor's and capital's shares of the national income over an extended period of time. A separate question relates to how the functional distribution of income fluctuates over the business cycle in the short run. There are regular and predictable movements in the shares of national income allocated to labor and capital over the business cycle.[11]

During periods of economic prosperity, but prior to the cycle's reaching its peak,

---

[11] The literature on this subject includes Charles L. Schultze, "Short-Run Movements of Income Shares," in National Bureau of Economic Research, *The Behavior of Income Shares* (Princeton, NJ: Princeton University Press, 1964), pp. 143–77; and Robin Hahnel and Howard J. Sherman, "Income Distribution and the Business Cycle: Three Conflicting Hypotheses," *Journal of Economic Issues* 16, no. 1 (March 1982), pp. 49–73.

MONOPOLIST % OF INCOME WITH HIS POWER WILL BE HIGHER, % OF WAGES ARE LOWER

capital's share of the national income tends to rise relative to labor's share. Labor productivity is increasing rapidly during the prosperity phase of the cycle. Wages lag behind the growth in labor productivity for a while, permitting profits per unit to rise, as unit labor costs do not place any pressures on the profit position of firms.

As the peak of the business cycle is approached, however, these forces start to change. Rates of increase in labor productivity slow down as full-capacity utilization is reached and less efficient workers are added to the labor force. Wages, which had lagged behind the general prosperity, start to catch up as unions demand higher wage increases. The combination of rising wages and sluggish productivity growth causes unit labor costs to rise and begins to cut into the profit posture of the firm. The familiar "profit squeeze" starts to appear. In terms of relative income shares, labor's begins to rise rapidly enough that at the peak of the cycle its share is rising faster than capital's. The tables have been turned. During the prosperity phase of the cycle, capital's relative share is rising. But at the peak of the cycle, at full employment, labor's share relative to capital's starts to increase. Indeed, this indicator signals the end of the boom and typically is a premonition that an economic downturn is likely to occur.

During the initial recession phase of the business cycle, but prior to the bottom's being reached, labor's share of the national income will continue to increase relative to capital's share. In the short term, capital will bear the brunt of a recession through a reduction in profits. This occurs because layoffs of workers tend to lag behind the pace of the economic downturn. Firms have invested heavily in the human capital of their employees and do not want to see this capital outlay squandered. Therefore, they *hoard* labor, hoping for the day when economic conditions will make it profitable to use that labor fully once again.

As a consequence of labor hoarding and declining output, labor productivity will show little increase and will perhaps even decline. With contracts that lock in wage increases, unit labor costs will rise. All of this makes for a bleak profit picture and a rising labor share of the national income.

As the recession proceeds, however, restorative forces are set in motion that tend to reverse these trends. Firms will eventually start to lay off larger numbers of workers, even though they suffer a loss in their human capital outlays by doing this. Times get so difficult that they can no longer justify labor hoarding. Once union contracts negotiated in the boom phase of the cycle have run their course, new ones with lower rates of wage increase are negotiated. These factors, taken together, tend to increase rates of increase in labor productivity once again and reduce unit labor costs. When this happens, conditions are ripe for a turning point in the cycle and a new prosperity phase.

The turning point that occurs at the trough of the cycle is signaled by a rising capital share of the national income, due to a reduction in unit labor costs through higher rates of increase in labor productivity and lower rates of wage increase. Hence, at the trough of the cycle, capital's share relative to labor's share starts to increase, setting in motion the incentive for firms to invest once again.

The regularity in the movement of labor's and capital's shares of the national income over the business cycle is very predictable and is one of the major factors that causes the business cycle to assume the characteristics it does. To summarize these fluctuations:

Prosperity phase of the cycle: Capital's share rises more rapidly than labor's.

Peak of the cycle: Labor's share rises more rapidly than capital's.

Recession phase of the cycle: Labor's share rises more rapidly than capital's.

Trough of the cycle: Capital's share rises more rapidly than labor's.

Of course, there is no precise dividing line for the phases of the business cycle. For example, capital's share will start to grow less rapidly than labor's before the peak of the cycle is reached. In fact, when this starts to occur you can expect the peak of the cycle to be reached very soon. Similarly, during a recession capital's share will start to rise relative to labor's before the absolute trough of the cycle is reached.

Summary

The *functional distribution of income* represents the shares of the national income accruing to capital and labor. These shares are of interest because they are the starting point for an empirical investigation of the distribution of income. Whether one has access to income from property or is relegated to receiving income solely from wages or salaries will set the outer boundaries on individual income. People who receive their income solely from wages and salaries rarely end up in the higher reaches of the income distribution. Individuals with income from capital, however, have the potential for being in the upper reaches of the income distribution, and they tend not to be in the lower segments of the income distribution.

Beyond this application to poverty and inequality, the functional distribution of income is of interest for what it tells us about movements in capital and labor shares of the national income over time as well as over the course of the business cycle. Since World War II, the statistics indicate labor's share of the national income has risen at the expense of capital's share, which has fallen. These data are misleading, however, because they count as part of labor's share of the national income executive and managerial salaries. Executives manage capital for absentee owners. Since World War II there has been a growth in such managerial activity in the firm because of the growth and expansion of the corporate form—including the growth of conglomerates and multinationals. The growth in labor's share of the national income has been overstated, because it includes salaried managers and executives whose incomes properly belong in the capital share category.

To explain changes in the functional distribution of income over time, two theories have been put forward. One, based on neoclassical economic analysis, locates changes in the functional distribution of income in the relative prices paid for labor and capital and the relative utilization of capital and labor induced by changes in their relative prices. The concept of the *elasticity of substitution* captures this phenomenon.

The elasticity of substitution measures the ease with which capital can be substituted for labor in response to some change in the relative prices of capital and labor. This is determined by the technology of the production function. If the technology does not permit easy substitution, a rise in the price of labor relative to capital will induce some substitution of capital for labor but not enough to compensate for the relative price shift. Consequently, under these circumstances, labor's share of the national income will rise, because labor is now receiving a relatively higher price, while its utilization has not fallen sufficiently to offset this change in relative factor prices.

Another theory of the evolution of the functional distribution of income focuses on the degree of economic concentration or monopoly power in product markets. Economic concentration is measured by the difference between price and marginal cost. The greater is this difference, the more monopoly power there is. Firms price by a markup system, which depends on market power, and capital's share of the national income is directly related to the degree of monopoly power in product markets.

Changes in the functional distribution occur with regularity over the business cycle. During periods of economic prosperity, but before the peak of the cycle is reached, capital's share of the national income will increase relative to labor's share. As the peak of the cycle is approached, labor's share will begin to rise more rapidly than capital's. This will continue throughout the early phases of the recessionary part of the cycle, but as the trough is reached, capital's share will once again begin to rise relative to labor's.

The analysis of the functional distribution of income has dealt with the broad categories of the *source* of income for individuals. The next step in a logical progression toward understanding poverty and inequality is the question of what determines individual wage and salary incomes in the American economy. This is taken up in the next several chapters.

Study Questions

1. What is the functional distribution of income?

2. Discuss some of the important factors that have led to a slight increase in labor's share of the national income over time.

3. What is the elasticity of substitution, and how does it affect the functional distribution of income?

4. How do factor shares fluctuate over the business cycle?

5. How does Kalecki's model of functional income distribution differ from the neoclassical marginal productivity model?

6. Discuss the relationship between the size distribution of income and the functional distribution of income. Which influences the other and how?

Further Reading

Kalecki, Michal. "The Distribution of the National Income." Reprinted in Michal Kalecki, *Selected Essays on the Dynamics of the Capitalist Economy*. Cambridge: Cambridge University Press, 1971, pp. 62–77.

Kravis, Irving. "Relative Income Shares in Fact and Theory." *American Economic Review* 49 (December 1959), pp. 917–49.

Rothschild, K. W. *The Theory of Wages*. Oxford: Basil Blackwell, 1965. Chap. 5.

Schultze, Charles L. "Short-Run Movements in Income Shares." In National Bureau of Economic Research. *The Behavior of Income Shares*. Princeton, NJ: Princeton University Press, 1964, pp. 143–77.

10

Theory of Human Capital

Poverty and inequality refer to differences in incomes among individuals. The functional distribution of income, examined in the previous chapter, provides an insight into why some individuals have higher incomes than others and why the members of one group (wage and salary earners) have a higher probability of becoming poor. The next step in the analysis of poverty and inequality is to ask the question, What explains the differences in income among individuals? To answer this question, several competing theories have been advanced, accompanied by supporting empirical studies. The issue of individual income differences engaged the imagination of labor economists starting in the 1960s and produced a body of work that was as innovative for the discipline as the earlier neoclassical marginal productivity theory had been.

The answer to the question of what determines differences in individual incomes has not been advanced without controversy, however. Several competing viewpoints have vied for the attention of labor economists. In this chapter, one body of thought is examined: the *human capital school*. In the next chapter, *structural* explanations for differences in individual incomes are discussed.

Human capital refers to those individual skills, talents, capacities, and elements of knowledge that improve one's contribution to the production of goods and services.[1] Human capital shows up in higher labor productivity for the individual worker

---

[1] Lester Thurow, *Investment in Human Captial* (Belmont, CA: Wadsworth Publishing Co., 1970).

180

and, if the worker is paid according to marginal revenue product, a higher wage or salary.

Human capital deals with the *qualitative* aspects of labor and is revealed in the extent to which the individual contributes to higher rates of labor productivity. Presumably, the more human capital one has, ceteris paribus, the more productive one is. These sentences contain important concepts which are worth a further elaboration.

Individual income differences imply that labor must be heterogeneous. These differences in the qualitative dimension of labor occur because of differences in human capital. In this context the analysis of *labor supply* has shifted from what it was in the standard neoclassical marginal productivity theory. Recall that labor was assumed to be identical or homogeneous in those aspects that yield a labor supply curve. Differences were ignored in the initial presentation of the marginal productivity theory of wage determination. What was assumed away becomes the centerpiece for the human capital analysis of individual income differences. Heterogeneity of the labor force, with differences in human capital, forms the core of the human capital analysis.

Human capital will contribute to higher rates of labor productivity only if certain other conditions are present. That is why the earlier statement that the more human capital one has, the higher will be labor productivity was qualified by the phrase *ceteris paribus*, which means "other things held fixed." The "other things" in this context are the *physical capital* the individual has to work with. The most skilled worker with the greatest quantity of human capital cannot produce much if he or she has unproductive tools and machines to work with. By the same token, the most productive machine will not produce up to its potential unless it has a worker with the requisite human capital to tend it. Productivity involves an interaction between the worker and the machine. True complementarity exists here because neither one will operate at its potential unless the other performs well.

Investment in Human Capital

To receive some return from deferring current consumption implies that an investment has been made. Economics traditionally thought of investments occurring only in plant and equipment—physical capital. But investment can also occur in human beings—human capital. The motivation to accumulate human capital is the prospect of a higher earning capacity. This is the financial *return* that justifies some investment in yourself. Investment in human capital is done by individuals, employers, and the society as a whole. Each invests in human capital in order to foster a more productive employee who can contribute more to productive activity. The recipient of such investment should receive a return in the form of higher earnings.

Economists view your decision to study at a college or university as a rational optimizing process in which you trade off current earnings, which you forgo while in school, to increase your future earning capacity. "Investment in oneself," according to an economist who has surveyed the human capital school of thought, "is the result of rational *optimizing* decisions (by individuals or their parents) made on the basis of estimates of the probable present value of alternative life-cycle income streams. . . ."[2]

Investment in human capital involves formal education, on-the-job training, and informal types of investment that augment human capital. An entire new field of economics—the economics of education and human resources—has arisen in the past two decades as a result of the concept of investment in human capital.[3]

Investment in human capital, however, raises certain issues that are not present with investment in physical capital. For example, consider the reasons you are attending college. They are complex, I am sure. One reason is to learn something so that you can develop a professional career. Another reason is just to study and learn. The proof of this is that you take many courses that are not required and that will contribute little, directly, to your career. This course, perhaps, falls into that category. Economists call this the "consumption" part of education, to distinguish it from the investment portion. These lines are fuzzy, however. You may not know today what will become very crucial to you later. For example, learning a foreign language may seem far removed from your career goals, but later in life you may have a job for which the knowledge of a foreign language is a great asset. This is the first note of caution about the formal models of investment in human capital: since the time period we are dealing with is so long, human capital investment decisions involve great uncertainty. That is why you take many courses today; you never know what will become indispensable later.

Individual Investment in Human Capital

Individuals invest in their own human capital by attending school beyond the statutory requirements. By so doing they abstain from current consumption and invest a sum of money toward the accumulation of human capital. The student may not do this solely through his or her own financial resources. Typically, this is not the case. Family contributions, loans, and scholarships are all forms of investment in an individual's human capital.

In making these investments, the individual is presumed to be following rules of rational decision making. This means he or she will invest so long as the *expected stream of returns* from the investment exceeds the costs incurred by making the investment. Let us consider the returns and the costs associated with investment in human capital separately.

---

[2] Gian S. Sahota, "Theories of Personal Income Distribution: A Survey," *Journal of Economic Literature* 16, no. 1 (March 1978), pp. 10–11. Emphasis in original.

[3] The literature about human capital is surveyed in Mark Blaug, "The Empirical Status of Human Capital Theory: A Slightly Jaundiced Survey," *Journal of Economic Literature* 14, no. 3 (September 1976), pp. 827–55.

The returns from an investment in human capital will accrue to the individual over an extended period of time—an entire lifetime, perhaps. Therefore, the stream of returns to the investment must be computed over time. Whenever time is introduced into an economic problem, the *discount rate*, or rate of return, on that investment has to be taken into account. For example, suppose you have $5,000 one year that you are contemplating investing. You have the choice of either going to school and investing that sum of money in your human capital or using the same amount for some other investment purpose. In short, there is an opportunity cost associated with your using the money for a human capital investment; that cost is the returns you could acquire from some other investment.

Suppose the going rate of return on a comparable investment is 10 percent. This becomes the opportunity cost to you of investing in your human capital. The $5,000 invested will produce for you in the first year $5,000 plus the 10 percent you can earn on the $5,000. This is written as follows:

$$\$5,000 + \$5,000\ (0.10) = \$5,000\ (1 + 0.10).$$

At the end of one year your alternative investment has produced earnings of $500, and your new resources at the end of the first year are $5,500.

Let us substitute some symbols for these numbers. If the original principal of $5,000 is designated as P_0, the rate of return is i, and the value of the investment at the end of one year as P_1, then

$$P_1 = P_0(1 + i).$$

If the principal plus interest is reinvested in the second year at the same rate of return, then

$$P_2 = P_1\ (1 + i) = P_0\ (1 + i)(1 + i) = P_0(1 + i)^2.$$

If the original investment and its returns are reinvested each year until the returns from the investment are fully earned in year t, then

$$P_t = P_0(1 + i)^t.$$

This formula is derived directly from the one above, except that now the time period has been extended to the year t. This says that the original principal of $5,000, invested at a rate of return of 10 percent that continues until the year t, will be worth so much in that final year. If the time period is ten years, for example, the investment will be worth

$$P_{10} = \$5,000(1 + 0.10)^{10}.$$

A simple calculator will aid in computation of this value.

Another way to look at this problem is to ask, What is the *present value* of the original principal ($5,000) invested over t years at a rate of return of 10 percent? From the general formula of $P_t = P_0(1 + i)^t$ this can readily be found, simply by solving for P_0. This yields

$$P_0 = \sum_{t=0}^{n} \frac{P_t}{(1 + i)^t}.$$

This equation can be read as "the present value of an original principal of $5,000 in t years invested at a rate of return of 10 percent (i)."

I have presented some detail on the general calculation of the present value of an investment because human capital investments are treated in the same way. A principal is invested in human capital, which will yield a rate of return over some period of time. The problem is to evaluate the worth of that sum of money, after taking into account its stream of returns. The procedure for making such a calculation is the same as the one that would be used if the money were put into an alternative investment that would yield the same rate of return.

The investor in human capital will seek to maximize the present value of the principal invested in human capital acquisition. The formula for doing this is

$$PV = \sum_{t=0}^{n} \frac{R_t}{(1 + i)^t}.$$

The goal will be to maximize the present value (PV) from some expected stream of returns (R), over t years, discounted by the interest rate (i).

Because this stream of returns on investment in human capital occurs over a long period of time, risk and uncertainty must be taken into account. *Risk* is defined as outcomes that occur with *known probabilities; uncertainty* is outcomes that occur with *unknown probabilities.* Both of these factors tend to *lower* the rate of return that is calculated without accounting for risk and uncertainty.[5] An investment is made today whose consequences must be lived with for a lifetime. People who became physicists in the 1950s found themselves out of work and not very marketable in the 1970s. Yet

---

[4] Thurow, *Investment in Human Capital*, p. 22.

[5] *Risk* is accommodated by introducing a statement about the probability *(P)* of some stream of returns being realized:

$$PV = \sum_{t=0}^{n} \frac{(P)(R_t)}{(1 + i)^t}.$$

Uncertainty (u) is added to the discount rate in the denominator:

$$PV = \sum_{t=0}^{n} \frac{(P)(R_t)}{(1 + i + u)^t}.$$

the substantial investment they made in their human capital did not provide sufficient flexibility for them to enter another occupation. Therefore, had they made a computation of their expected rates of return in the 1950s without taking into account risk and uncertainty, they would have miscalculated by overstating the potential rate of return from becoming a physicist.

Up to this point, the individual is attempting to maximize the present value from the stream of returns generated by an investment in human capital. However, there are also *costs* that must be taken into account in the individual's investment decision. These costs are of two types: First, there are direct costs—for example, tuition and books, associated with attending a college or university. Second, there are indirect costs, which include the income foregone by not working during the years attending school. These are the opportunity costs of deferring a current income-producing activity in order to acquire even greater income-earning capacity for the future. They are costs because, no matter what your future earnings might be, you can never replace the income foregone by not working during the years attending school.

The individual maximizes *net present value* of an investment in human capital by taking account of the costs as well as the returns. Formally, net present value is represented as the difference between returns and costs:

$$NPV = \sum_{t=0}^{n} \left(\frac{R_t}{(1 + i)^t} \right) - \sum_{t=0}^{n} \left(\frac{C_t}{(1 + i)^t} \right).$$

For purposes of simplicity the elements of risk and uncertainty have been excluded from this equation, although they should be included in a complete and accurate portrayal of the decision process. In fact, there are also risks and uncertainty associated with the cost side of the equation. These arise because it is not known with complete certainty what tuition and the costs of books will be over the time period of the investment. Nor is it known with certainty what the earning capacity of the individual will be during the period attending school. The treatment of risk and uncertainty on the cost side is completely analogous to that presented for the returns side.[6]

The individual deciding to invest in his or her human capital should follow the decision rule implied by the maximization of net present value. Investment should occur as long as the expected returns exceed the expected cost, discounted to take account of the future and adjusted for risk and uncertainty. If returns exceed costs, the individual has not invested enough in human capital. If the costs start to exceed expected returns, that is a signal to stop investing in human capital.

This decision to invest in human capital in order to maximize the net present value of the investment is a difficult one for the individual to execute. There is, first,

---

[6] Including risk and uncertainty on both the returns and cost sides yields

$$NPV = \sum_{t=0}^{n} \left[\frac{(P_r)(R_t)}{(1 + i + u_r)^t} \right] - \sum_{t=0}^{n} \left[\frac{(P_c)(C_t)}{(1 + i + u_c)^t} \right].$$

the problem of the extended time period over which the returns will be realized. This renders the elements of risk and uncertainty very crucial and also difficult to determine. Second, there is the all-or-nothing character of the investment in human capital. If a mistake is made that only becomes apparent 10 years later, it may be too late to alter the investment. The investment locks you into a particular trade or occupation, with limited flexibility. Third, there is the problem of uniqueness. Every individual is different and absorbs the human capital investment differently. Therefore, the experiences of others are only a limited guide to what will happen with your human capital investment. This is different from what happens with investment in physical capital, where the experience of others is a better guide. Fourth, part of the reason for attending school is the overall growth and maturity this activity provides. Separating the so-called consumption aspects of education from its investment aspects is difficult.

The problems associated with the human capital investment decision are more severe for lower-income families.[7] Risk and uncertainty are greater; the experiences of others are of little help in predicting what might happen to low-income persons' investments in their human capital. Moreover, access to the resources that enable one to invest adequately in human capital is more limited for lower-income individuals than for higher-income persons. Early educational opportunities will probably have been poorer for the low-income person. The need for the young person in a low-income family to earn current income is greater, and consequently, investment in human capital is discouraged. Having fewer financial assets limits access to the capital markets, which are an essential source of financing for higher education.

To the extent these factors exist, the human capital investment process will tend to magnify and exacerbate an existing structure of income inequality. Rather than being redistributive, the powerful forces of complementarity in the human capital investment process will tend to create more inequality in the system. This will not be true for everyone. Some individuals from lower-income families will be able to rise above their disadvantageous economic circumstances and succeed, while some persons from higher-income families will fail. On average, though, the opportunities afforded by family status will tend to influence what happens in the human capital investment process.

Recognizing this, makers of public policy have sought to provide the means to offset the financial advantages associated with family income status. They have done this by targeting specific financial aid programs toward those less able to afford investments in human capital solely by private financial means.

Human Capital Investment by the Firm

Individuals are not the only ones who make investments in human capital. Firms invest in human capital through on-the-job training, specialized formal training pro-

---

[7] Thurow, *Investment in Human Capital*, chap. 5.

grams, and informal training—"learning by doing."[8] The firm that invests in the human capital of its employees has no guarantee that it will be able to reap the benefits from the augmentation of the employee's human capital. This problem arises because the employer does not own the individual. Even where there is a legally binding contract that enables the employer to retain the employee's services for a specified period of time, the contract will expire before the returns on the investment in human capital have stopped.

The employer rents the services and human capital of an individual. An investment in human capital made by the firm is possessed by the individual recipient of the investment, not by the investor. In this way, investment in human capital is different from an investment in physical capital, which is legally owned by the investor, who receives a return on the investment as long as it is still producing one. The returns on investment in human capital, however, must be captured by the investor through the provision of sufficient incentives for the individual to remain in the employ of the investor.[9] This is why the firm will tend to hoard labor in which it has invested substantial human capital during the early stages of a recession and will dismiss such labor with great reluctance. By laying off workers in whom substantial human capital has been invested, the employer stands to lose the potential returns from his investment.

The returns from a firm's investment in human capital occur for two reasons. First, labor's marginal product should be increased by the investment in human capital. Second, the employer's physical capital should become more productive because of the complementarities that exist between investments in human and physical capital. A fancy new word-processing machine, for example, will not be utilized at its productive potential if the employee running the machine is not sufficiently trained to operate it efficiently. In this instance a secretary accustomed to working with an electric typewriter would have to be trained in new skills in order for the employer to receive the optimum return on its investment in this new piece of physical capital.

The firm, in deciding how much to invest in the human capital of its employees, will follow the familiar decision rule of investing as long as the expected returns from the investment exceed expected costs.[10] The returns take the form of increased productivity. Costs can be direct—training expenses—and indirect—the production forgone while the individual is receiving training. Both the costs and returns have risk and uncertainty attached to them, which must be taken into account when the firm is pondering whether to invest in an employee's human capital. This is particularly important on the returns side of the equation because of the probability that not all of the returns can be captured by the firm making the investment. And since the returns and costs must be spread over an extended time period, a discount factor must be added to the equation to reflect alternative uses to which the resources could be put. In sum, the firm will invest in an employee's human capital so long as the

---

[8] Gary S. Becker, *Human Capital,* 2nd ed. (New York: Columbia University Press, 1975), chap. 2.

[9] Control Data Corporation estimated that it cost $60,000 to hire, train, and move one computer programmer in 1980. "U.S. Job Security in the Japanese Style," *Business Week,* April 20, 1981, p. 36.

[10] Thurow, *Investment in Human Capital,* chap. 6.

discounted expected stream of returns exceeds the discounted expected costs, taking into account the risk and uncertainty associated with the investment.

Investments in human capital are always taking place, even when we are unaware of them. For example, virtually every new task requires some learning, even if the employee did the same job before in some other firm. This informal on-the-job training may not require a course, seminar, or training session. But if work time is lost by using one employee to instruct another, an investment in human capital has taken place. The firm, of course, will try to minimize these training requirements and structure the job so that the new employee can be put to work immediately. Have you ever worked at a fast-food establishment? Think about the time it took to prepare you for your first day at work, compared with what it would have taken to train you as a chef in a fancy restaurant.

Training can be specific or general. *Specific training* refers to an investment in human capital that is isolated to learning one task and the peculiarities of the firm's operations. *General training* is a broader skills-development program, which may not be focused on one task but may involve more general supervisory and technical skills. General training will more likely be useful to other employers, so the investor's potential for losing that investment to someone else is greater than in the case of specific training. The problem is that human capital investments are not protected by property law as are physical capital investments, which have patent, trademark, and copyright protections. The individual carries the human capital investment with him and can sell its services to whoever is willing to buy them.

Compare, for example, the training you would receive as a chef in a fancy restaurant with the minimal training you would be given at McDonald's. The chef's training can be taken with you if you leave one restaurant and go to another. You are worth more to the second restaurant after being trained by the first restaurant, and you can demand a higher salary. If you move from McDonald's to Roy Rogers, however, you are not necessarily worth more to the second employer, and you will probably be paid the same starting minimum wage at both places.

Firms tend to invest more in human capital that involves specific training, simply because the returns to such investment are more readily captured. This is particularly true for lower-skilled blue-collar and white-collar workers for whom there is substantial turnover. The higher up the skill and occupation ladder one moves, the more likely it is that there will be general training. For precisely this reason, governments have moved into the training and human capital formation process, because there are externalities to the education and training expenditure. This is the issue taken up in the next section.

/ Gov̄T.

Public Investment in Human Capital

By far the largest investor in human capital formation is the *public*, through government financing of education and training. From the earliest local government expenditures for public schools in the nineteenth century, to the land grant system of higher education in the middle of the nineteenth century, to more recent developments in public expenditures for training and for two-year community colleges, the government has played a pivotal role in shaping the scope and form of investment in human capital.

Not only does the government invest money in education at the high school level and below. It also expends great sums of money on higher education in four-year colleges and universities as well as two-year community colleges. Starting with its efforts in vocational education, the government now sponsors training programs outside the formal education system. Public policy in the area of training will be examined in a subsequent chapter. For now, it is sufficient to understand that these training programs, and more general support for education, represent investment in human capital undertaken through the public sector.

Society makes investments in human capital through public expenditures because the private market, left to its own devices, would not produce a sufficient level of investment. The private market does not produce sufficient investments in human capital for several reasons. First, there are *externalities* to investments in human capital. Not all of the returns and costs can be reflected in the formula for maximization of net present value. For example, how do you measure the returns to the education of someone like Jonas Salk, who found a way to prevent polio? Or Marie Curie, who won two Nobel prizes? Calculating investment in human capital solely on the basis of private costs and returns would neglect the *social returns* produced by human capital investment.

A second reason why governments invest in human capital is the imperfections in the private market for such undertakings. Young people may not be able to borrow sufficient amounts of money from private capital markets to finance their education because they have no collateral to offer except their future earning potential. Since future earning potential is so risky and uncertain, banks are not likely to accept it as collateral. Wealthy parents could secure such loans, but relying on this mechanism would distort an already unequal income distribution by favoring those from families with greater wealth.

Third, the high degree of risk and uncertainty associated with human capital investments means that there would be an underinvestment if investment were left solely to the private market. The individual contemplating an investment in his or her human capital would conceivably have such high risk and uncertainty factors that the investment would be scrapped because it did not generate a positive net present value. The government can lower the cost of such risk and uncertainty to some extent by paying for part of the human capital investment. Socializing risk and uncertainty removes these factors from the private market decision an individual would have to make.

The forms of investment in human capital undertaken by the government are an important issue because different segments of society have different interests. The most accepted human capital investment is that of universal primary and secondary education, up through high school. Presumably, every citizen in a democratic society needs that much education to function in a sufficiently informed way. Education beyond high school has been treated as a mixed private and public responsibility, at least since the middle of the nineteenth century, when the first land grant state universities were established. The proper mix for these forms of higher education has always been fluid and will continue to remain so.

Since the 1960s the government has begun to play a larger role in specialized vocational training through public training programs and two-year community colleges, all of which have supplemented the preexisting vocational education programs operated through the high schools. These expenditures represent a transfer of a portion of the human capital expenditures previously undertaken privately by individuals and firms. This transfer occurs because firms have not found a successful way to capture a sufficient amount of the returns from their human capital investments to induce a sufficient level of investment.

With billions of dollars spent on education by the public sector, it is still not obvious that the amount is sufficient in terms of the returns to education that accrue to the larger society. The Nobel prize–winning economist Theodore W. Schultz has summed up his years of study of this problem by saying that "underinvestment in knowledge and skill . . . would appear to be the rule and not the exception . . . even though we take pride . . . in the support we have given to education."[11]

Investment in Human Capital and Individual Incomes

The initial purpose of this exploration into the theory of human capital was to shed some light on how individual incomes are determined in the economy. Individuals, in conjunction with enterprises and the public, make investments in their human

Table 10-1 Income by Median Years of Schooling, 1980

Family Income Range	Median Years of Schooling, Family Head[a]	Family Income Range	Median Years of Schooling, Family Head[a]
Under $5,000	10.9	$20,000–24,999	12.6
$5,000–9,999	10.9	$25,000–34,999	12.8
$10,000–14,999	12.1	$35,000–49,999	13.6
$15,000–19,999	12.4	$50,000 and over	16.2

[a]Median years of schooling completed for all family heads in 1980 was 12.6.
Source: U.S. Bureau of the Census, *Statistical Abstract of the United States, 1982–1983* (Washington: Government Printing Office), p. 434.

As income ↑; the median ## year school rises also

[11] Theodore W. Schultz, "Investment in Human Capital," *American Economic Review* 51, no. 1 (March 1961), pp. 14–15.

Table 10-2   Distribution of Income and Education, 1968 and 1978[a]

(margin note: yrs of school)

	Percentage Share of Years of Education		Percentage Share of Income	
	1968	1978	1968	1978
Lowest fifth	10.6	12.4	7.4	7.5
Second fifth	17.9	18.7	14.1	13.6
Middle fifth	21.0	19.1	18.2	18.3
Fourth fifth	21.7	22.9	23.6	23.5
Highest fifth	28.7	26.8	36.7	37.0

(margin note: % of all income)

[a]For males, aged 25–64, who were year-round full-time wage and salary earners.
Source: Lester C. Thurow, "The Failure of Education as an Economic Strategy," *American Economic Review* 72, no. 2 (May 1982), p. 73

(margin note: THERE IS A GREATER DIST OF INCOMES THAN EDUCATION)

capital. Returns in the form of higher incomes are expected from these investments. The question is, To what extent does investment in human capital explain individual incomes? More specifically, do differences in investment in human capital among individuals explain income differences?

(margin note: SIMPLE) The most direct way to answer this question is by looking at average income levels for persons with different amounts of human capital investment, represented by years of education completed. This measure or proxy for human capital investment is fraught with pitfalls, which will be discussed later. For now, it can be presumed to be an adequate reflection of investment in human capital.

Table 10-1 contains statistics on the relationship between years of educational attainment and income for a typical year. There is a positive relationship between income and years of education. In 1980 individuals with less than a high school education (less than 12 years) could expect to earn only $10,000 or less; those with some college education, much more.

Although education explains some of the differences in income, the question is, how much of the difference does it explain? Another perspective on this question is provided by the data in Table 10-2, in which the income distribution for males aged 25–64 is compared with the distribution of education. The distribution of education is more equal than is the distribution of income. In 1978 the lower 60 percent of this income distribution received 50 percent of all education attained, whereas that same 60 percent received only 39 percent of income. The top 20 percent of this income distribution received 37 percent of all income but attained only 27 percent of all the educational years. Furthermore, the distribution of education narrowed between 1968 and 1978, while the distribution of income remained essentially unchanged.

Is there an inconsistency between Tables 10-1 and 10-2? One shows a relationship between years of education and income; the other shows differences in the distributions of income and education. The answer is no, there is no inconsistency. The problem arises because many other variables are active in explaining the distribution of income, besides simple years of educational attainment. To understand this, consider

Table 10-3 Hypothetical Example Relating Years of Education to Income

	Case A				Case B		
Individual	Years of Education	Income	Average Income	Individual	Years of Education	Income	Average Income
1	10	$6,000 ⎤		1	10	$ 2,000 ⎤	
2	10	6,000 ⎥		2	10	4,000 ⎥	
3	10	6,000 ⎬ $6,000		3	10	6,000 ⎬ $6,000	
4	10	6,000 ⎥		4	10	8,000 ⎥	
5	10	6,000 ⎦		5	10	10,000 ⎦	
6	12	8,000 ⎤		6	12	4,000 ⎤	
7	12	8,000 ⎥		7	12	6,000 ⎥	
8	12	8,000 ⎬ $8,000		8	12	8,000 ⎬ $8,000	
9	12	8,000 ⎥		9	12	10,000 ⎥	
10	12	8,000 ⎦		10	12	12,000 ⎦	

the following hypothetical example, shown in Table 10-3, which relates years of education to income.

In both Case A and Case B of Table 10-3 there are ten individuals; five have received 10 years of education; five, 12 years. In Case A the distribution of incomes associated with years of education would produce a result in which those individuals with 10 years of education had an average income of $6,000 while those with 12 years of income had an *average* income of $8,000.

In Case B, the same result occurs: those individuals with 10 years of education have an average income of $6,000, and those with 12 years of education have an average income of $8,000. But the distribution of income among these ten individuals in Case B is far different from the distribution in Case A. In Case B some individuals with only 10 years of education have incomes higher than individuals with 12 years of education.

Economists characterize these statistics by saying that in Case B the variance in incomes *within* each educational group is *greater* than the variance in income *between* the two educational groups. Whenever the within-group variance exceeds the between-group variance, a weak statistical relationship will emerge. This is the case with statistical and econometric studies that relate income differences to educational differences.

This weak statistical relationship does not mean that the theory of human capital as it pertains to individual income formation is inapplicable. Years of education may not be an adequate proxy measure for human capital. The *quality* of education varies widely, so the same number of years of education can mean very different things, depending upon the quality of the schools an individual has attended.[12]

---

[12] These issues are examined in Blaug, "Empirical Status," pp. 842–45.

Intelligence—what the individual brings to the educational experience—varies widely, and this also can affect human capital acquisition. The measure of human capital based simply on years of education cannot account for these factors, nor can it account for the accumulation of human capital acquired outside the formal education process. For example, on-the-job education and training, life experiences, and other such informal means of acquiring human capital contribute to an individual's earning capacity.

Studies that attempt to take these factors into account produce better statistical results, because human capital is being measured more effectively.[13] However, even a better specification of human capital does not explain a majority of the differences in incomes among individuals. Something else is going on that is not captured by even the best of human capital measures. What these other factors are that explain differences in incomes among individuals will be taken up in the next chapter.

Critics of the theory of human capital have seized on this empirical discrepancy to question the entire corpus of the human capital model of individual income determination. This criticism can be overdrawn. Differences in incomes among individuals represent a complex social and economic phenomenon. Normal standards of statistical accuracy may have to be lowered and adapted to this problem. Each individual is different, and this difference is reflected in the process by which income is attained. Certainly, human capital accounts for some of the difference in individual incomes. The fact that is does not account for more than is shown in the statistical studies has perplexed its advocates and has led to other investigations, which will be presented in the next chapter.

Beyond these technical problems with the empirical verification of the human capital theory, there are important conceptual difficulties with expecting a growth in the average level of human capital acquisition to redistribute income. If everyone's level of formal education increases by the same amount, the average level of educational attainment will increase, but its distribution will not. Everyone will simply move up together in lockstep, and the distribution will not change.

Education is what the social scientist Fred Hirsch calls a "positional goods."[14] By this he means a commodity whose acquisition can be enjoyed only if it is denied to others. As Hirsch puts it,

> The value to me of my education depends not only on how much I have but also on how much the man ahead of me in the job line has. . . . The utility of expenditure on a given

---

[13] Studies that use only years of education to explain income typically account for about 12–15 percent of the difference in individual incomes. This is quite low and is barely acceptable because it means that some 85–88 percent of the difference in incomes remains unexplained. Studies that measure human capital more effectively explain about 20 percent of the variation in individual incomes. See Howard M. Wachtel and Charles Betsey, "Employment at Low Wages," *Review of Economic and Statistics* 54, no. 2 (May 1972), pp. 121–29.

[14] Fred Hirsch, *Social Limits to Growth* (Cambridge: Harvard University Press, 1976), p. 11.

level of education as a means of access to the most sought after jobs will decline as more people attain that level of education.[15]

Education as a device for redistributing income, therefore, requires vastly unequal expenditures directed toward those at the lower reaches of the income distribution. This is not necessarily desirable, nor is it politically feasible. In fact, following such a path could conceivably reduce growth and efficiency as better-qualified individuals were denied access to the educational process solely because they came from families with higher incomes.

This brings us to the heart of the problem: Education is central to our social identity as a meritocracy. Denying anyone access to education because of income—whether it be too high or too low—conflicts with a meritocracy. For education to retain its central purpose in our society, we cannot lose sight of the importance it plays in our meritocratic social identity. For this reason, education is probably best seen as an opportunity for fulfillment that should not be denied to any individual because of income or family background. If we keep this in mind, our educational policy will be less contentious and more consistent with basic social values.

Summary

The theory of human capital and the empirical hypotheses this theory generates attempt to explain differences in individual incomes. Human capital deals with investments individuals make in themselves to improve the quality of their labor. The purpose for doing this is, in part, to enhance earning power. Individuals are not the only ones who invest in human capital, however. Business firms and the public, through government expenditures, also invest heavily in human capital. Each of these investors has a slightly different motivation for investing in human capital. Their decision rules are likewise different.

Individuals invest in human capital by deferring current consumption. The person reaping the benefits from an investment might not be the one doing the investing. For example, families typically invest heavily in their children in order to augment the earning capacity of those children. Individuals should invest in their human capital as long as the expected returns from the investments exceed the expected costs. Since the costs and returns are spread over a number of years, they must be *discounted*, using an appropriate discount rate that reflects the opportunity costs associated with alternative investments.

Investments by individuals in their human capital are also risky, and they involve substantial uncertainty. For this reason, factors for risk and uncertainty must be introduced into the calculation of the net present value, which is the difference between

---

[15] Ibid., p. 3.

discounted costs and returns, adjusted to take account of risk and uncertainty. The time dimension of the human capital investment and its riskiness and uncertainty render the decision on human capital investment different from decisions on physical capital investment. Private capital markets may not be adequate to the task of supplying sufficient resources to support the volume of investment warranted by society's needs. Hence, the public sector must provide a substantial amount of the resources for human capital investment. This public expenditure is justified on the grounds of *externalities*. The benefits from human capital investment accrue to society as much as to the individual, and therefore, society should bear some of the costs and socialize the risks associated with human capital investment.

Business firms invest in human capital through formal training programs, on-the-job training, and informal learning-by-doing that occurs while someone is working at a task. The firm, however, has no guarantee that its investment will remain within the enterprise. Individuals are free to move whenever they wish and can take their human capital with them. This poses a difficult problem for the firm: How can it capture its investment in human capital? In recent years a recognition of this fact has propelled the public sector into more support for training of all sorts—on-the-job training, formal training programs, and two-year community colleges that specialize in skill development. Such public programs tend to socialize the risk for the firm and have led to a substantial increase overall in investment in human capital.

The firm will invest in the human capital of its employees in order to increase their productivity—more specifically their marginal productivity. It will continue to invest as long as the expected returns exceed expected costs, discounted to take account of time and adjusted to account for risk and uncertainty.

The evidence relating human capital investment to individual income differences is suggestive and not as strong as the proponents of the human capital theory would have expected before they embarked on their empirical research. Higher incomes are associated with greater amounts of investment in human capital among individuals. But as much of the variation in individual incomes is left unexplained, after looking at the relationships with human capital, as is explained by human capital investments. Part of the problem relates to the difficulty of measuring some aspects of human capital, such as intelligence, quality of education, and the effort put forward by the individual. In addition, individual income differences involve so many variables that relying just on human capital misses the complexity of the process by which individual incomes are determined.

In the next chapter other theories and empirical studies of the causes of individual income differences are examined that explain some of the income differences not captured by the human capital model.

Study Questions

1. How do individuals invest in their human capital? Is this the same as or different from investment in fixed capital?

2. How do firms invest in human capital? What is the economic importance of the distinction between general and specific training?

3. What is the economic rationale for government investment in human capital formation?

4. Why is there generally a weak statistical relationship between individual incomes and years of schooling? How have labor economists explained this apparent paradox?

5. If you use a discount rate that is too low, how will this affect the human capital investment decision?

Further Reading

Becker, Gary S. *Human Capital*. 2nd ed. New York: Columbia University Press, 1975. Chapt. 2.

Sahota, Gian S. "Theories of Personal Income Distribution: A Survey." *Journal of Economic Literature* 16, no. 1 (March 1978), pp. 1–55.

Schultz, Theodore W. "Investment in Human Capital." *American Economic Review* 51, no. 1 (March 1961), pp. 1–17.

Thurow, Lester. *Investment in Human Capital*. Belmont, CA: Wadsworth Publishing Co., 1970.

11

Labor Market Structures

The human capital theory places the responsibility on the individual when his or her income is insufficient. Individual income determination and poverty are the result of inadequate or inefficient investments in human capital. The poor, therefore, are blamed for their own poverty. Theories of labor market structures, on the other hand, add another dimension to this question. Such investigations place the burden of individual income determination on the structure of the particular labor market in which the individual works. Poverty, low incomes, and income inequality are not simply the result of the individual's failure but derive from some larger institutional structure over which the individual has little control.

Aside from the technical issues raised by the debate between the structuralists and the human capitalists, there are intriguing philosophical questions behind this economic discourse.[1] The human capital theory descends from the philosophy of individualism which has been so influential throughout the history of the United States. Like a Horatio Alger hero, anyone can go from rags to riches, barring any physiological impediments to learning and the acquisition of human capital.

Labor market structure theorists contend that poverty, low incomes, and income

---

[1] See Howard M. Wachtel, "Looking at Poverty from a Radical Perspective," *Review of Radical Political Economics* 3, no. 3 (Summer 1971), pp. 1–2.

inequality are primarily a condition of society, instead of a consequence of individual characteristics. In this view labor market structure theorists have much in common with institutionalist economists. If poverty and inequality are conditions of the social system that manifest themselves most directly in the labor market, then policies must address those very institutions that lie at the heart of poverty and inequality. This is the proposition put forward by the labor market structure theorists.

Viewed from this vantage point, the characteristics of the poor and low-income populations provide only a demographic profile, which says little about the *causes* of poverty and inequality. In putting forward this hypothesis, the labor market structure theorists have had an enormous accumulation of intellectual and political history to offset in convincing policymakers on this point.

The industrial revolutions in the United States and Great Britain produced the ideology of individualism, which meant that the poor were blamed for their own poverty. The causes of poverty were assigned to the characteristics of the individual rather than to societal institutions. In nineteenth century America this was given a crude formulation within the industrializing ideology of individualism. The New Deal provided only a temporary break with this tradition. Public policy has mirrored these trends in social ideology, starting with the Elizabethan Poor Laws and continuing through their later American counterparts down to the present.

 Labor market structure theories of the causes of poverty and inequality fall into two categories: *dual-labor-market theory* and *labor market stratification theory*. These will be discussed in this chapter, and empirical evidence pertinent to the theories will be presented. Before proceeding to a discussion of those theories, however, a more general statement about the causes of poverty and inequality from a structuralist perspective will be offered to contrast with the human capital and individual-based explanations for poverty and inequality.

Structural Perspective on Poverty and Inequality

Poverty and inequality are viewed from a structural perspective as logical outcomes of the functioning of society's institutions. Structuralists reject the notion that poverty amid affluence is a *paradox*. Instead, poverty and inequality are seen to have a necessary relationship with the basic system defining institutions of capitalism.[2]

 What are these connecting links between capitalism as a system and poverty and inequality? First, wage and income inequality are necessary to induce labor to work at tasks that are at times dangerous, debilitating, and alienating. Second, the existence of poverty and a low-income underclass serves as a warning to the nonpoor that their fate could be much worse. This has a tendency to mitigate labor militancy by dividing

---

[2] For a more extended discussion of these ideas, consult Howard M. Wachtel, "Capitalism and Poverty in America: Paradox or Contradiction?" *American Economic Review* 62, no. 2 (May 1972), pp. 187–88.

workers along status lines. Middle-income workers see their progress and mobility blocked not by those above them but by the poor; witness the lack of support among middle-income workers for welfare policies. Third, to the extent that the poor form a "reserve army" of labor, wages are depressed, some unions are weakened, and labor's ability to obtain a greater share of the national income is diminished. Fourth, the nonpoor's real income is substantially increased by the existence of poverty, since commodities and services can be obtained at lower prices as long as wages are depressed by the existence of the poor. For example, your tuition would have to be higher if the cafeteria and maintenance workers at your school were paid more than a poverty wage. Many of these workers are probably being paid very low wages that place them close to or below the poverty level. As an exercise, check this out at your school, and compute what the rate of tuition increase would have to be, and what the price of a hamburger would be at your cafeteria, if these workers were paid substantially higher wages, set at the BLS moderate-but-adequate lower income standard (see Chapter 8). We all benefit from the existence of the poor, particularly the working poor.

This does not mean that the social system as we know it today could not survive without the precise amount of poverty and degree of inequality that presently exist. Poverty and inequality bear a *functional* relationship to the social system of capitalism. By functionalism we mean that things work better for the higher-income groups in society when there is a substantial degree of poverty and inequality. Poverty and inequality could, no doubt, be reduced somewhat without threatening the social system as a whole. Capitalism as a system can exist with varying degrees of poverty and inequality. This is apparent from any international comparison; different capitalist countries have different amounts of poverty and inequality.

The labor market—its structure and the way individual workers fit into it—is the key to understanding poverty and inequality from the structuralist perspective. Contrary to widely held beliefs, poverty can be traced to the position of the poor in the labor force. It is less a condition of the absence of work than of particular work at low pay.

The Relationship between Poverty and Work

In 1984, about one-half of all poverty families had some earnings from work.[3] If those retired from the active labor force were excluded from these figures, the percentage of the adult, working-age poor who worked some time during that year would have been near 55 percent. The structure of the labor market and the character of available jobs affect virtually every poor and low-income family.

There are the full-time working poor—those individuals who work full-time,

 # 1

---

[3] U.S. Bureau of the Census, "Money Income and Poverty Status of Families and Persons in the United States: 1984," Series P-60, No. 149 (March 1985), p. 28.

Table 11-1   The Relationship Between Poverty and Work, 1979, 1981, and 1984

	1979 (thousands)	1981 (thousands)	1984 (thousands)
Total persons below poverty level	25,300	31,822	33,700
(Less children, under 18)	(−9,700)	(−12,068)	(−12,900)
Adult poverty population (18 and over)	15,600	19,754	20,800
(Less persons 65 and over)	(−3,586)	(−3,853)	(−3,330)
Adult poverty population of working age (18–65)	12,014	15,901	17,470
(Less ill and disabled)	(−859)	(−2,933)	(−2,737)
Able-bodied poverty population of working age (18–65)	11,155	12,968	14,733
Working poor: Full-time year-round workers with incomes under the poverty level	2,590	2,724	3,022
Percent, working poor[a]	23.2%	21.0%	20.5%

[a]Working poor divided by able-bodied poverty population of working age, 18–65.
Sources: U.S. Bureau of the Census, *Statistical Abstract of the United States* (Washington: Government Printing Office, 1986), pp. 458, 459; U.S. Bureau of the Census, "Money Income and Poverty Status of Families in the United States: 1984," Series P-60, No. 149 (August 1985), p. 27.

year round but earn wages that are below the poverty standard. In 1984 there were 3 million such workers, which amounted to one-fifth of the able-bodied poverty population of working age. These figures are presented in Table 11-1. The working poor earn their poverty in arduous and difficult work environments. One in five of all poor adults who are not handicapped or disabled and are not over 65 fall into this category.

Next, there are the individuals over age 65 who are retired from the labor force and are classified as poor. There were about 3.3 million such individuals in 1984. These people also acquire their poverty from their position in the labor market. If they were not poor while employed, the likelihood is that they will be poor upon retirement. Poverty sets in at retirement if employment did not provide wages that would yield the maximum social security benefits, if the individual was not covered by social security, or if he or she had no private pension to supplement social security and did not earn enough income while working to acquire assets and to save for retirement. Many, if not all, of the aged poor can trace their poverty to the positions they had in the economy while they were working.

In 1984 there were 2.7 million individuals classified as poor because of a disabling work-related injury. The poverty status of these individuals can also be traced to the place of work and the resultant injuries suffered on the job.

#4

Finally, there are many poor who are sporadically employed throughout the year, suffering spells of unemployment between periods of employment. They are the part-time working poor. About 6 million in poverty worked less than full-time in 1984. Putting the three groups of work-related poverty together—full-time working poor, disabled, and retired—produces a figure of about 9 million in 1984. This amounts to 44 percent of all the adult poor. If the part-time working poor were added to this figure, 72 percent of the adult poor could trace their poverty directly or indirectly to their status in the labor force.[4]

The Structure of Labor Markets and the Working Poor

Since World War II there have been two separate schools of thought pertaining to the labor market and wage determination. One dominated during the 1950s, followed by a competing view of labor markets during the 1960s.

In the 1950s, with public attention directed toward the economic power of trade unions and concentrated industries, labor market analysis focused on the demand side of the market, in which characteristics of industries and labor markets were specified as determinants of wages among rather aggregated categories of labor markets. This view of the process of wage determination was presented in Chapters 3 through 7. Variables such as profits among industries, industrial concentration, labor union membership, and rates of change in productivity and employment were all used to uncover the determinants of wage differentials among industries.[5] The *structure* of an industry was analyzed for its impact on the wages of workers in that industry.

In the 1960s, with public attention diverted from problems of the interaction of unions and corporations and turned toward low-income concerns, labor market analysis became directed toward what can be construed as supply considerations—the "human capital" individuals bring to the labor market.[6] Of primary concern were the determinants of human capital, although some attention was directed toward the effect of human capital on an individual's opportunity in the labor market. The focus was on the inherent productivity of the individual.

A graphical depiction of this 1960s version of wage determination is presented in Figure 11-1. There is only one industry, homogeneous with respect to its structural chracteristics, which employs individuals with varying amounts of human capital. In

---

[4] U.S. Bureau of the Census, "Money Income and Poverty Status," p. 27.

[5] Important writings of this sort are Harold M. Levinson, *Postwar Movements of Wages and Prices in Manufacturing Industries* (Washington: Government Printing Office, 1960); A. M. Ross and W. Goldner, "Forces Affecting the Interindustry Wage Structure," *Quarterly Journal of Economics* 64 (May 1950), pp. 254–81; and M. Segal, "Unionism and Wage Movements," *Southern Economic Journal* 28 (October 1961), pp. 174–81.

[6] See Chapter 10.

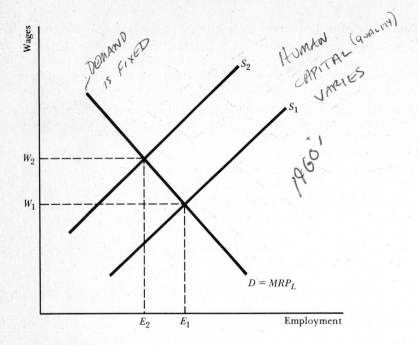

Figure 11-1 Wage Determination: Supply Side

this labor market two such groups of human capital exist. Given a homogeneous demand for labor, individuals earn different wages and are employed in different numbers as a unique function of variations in their human capital—formal education, on-the-job training, innate skills, and so forth.[7]

Individuals with more human capital are indicated by the supply curve S_2. The *reservation wage* is higher for this group than for the lower human capital segment of S_1.[8] Correspondingly higher wages are associated with greater amounts of human capital—W_2 compared with W_1.

The problem with this model of the labor market is that it ignores the potentially important effects on individual wages of differing industrial structures, identified in the research of the 1950s. Reversing the process, Figure 11-2 presents a model of the labor market in which the supply of labor is presumed to be homogeneous and the structures of different industries are permitted to vary.

Individuals employed in the industry represented by demand curve D_2 receive higher wages because of the higher marginal revenue product in that industry. This

---

[7] This discussion is based on Howard M. Wachtel and Charles Betsey, "Employment at Low Wages," *Review of Economics and Statistics* 54, no. 2 (May 1972), pp. 121–23.

[8] The reservation wage is the minimum wage that must be paid to induce an individual to accept a job offer.

can be related to higher physical marginal productivity of labor as well as to greater market concentration in the industry with demand curve D_2 compared with D_1.

In sum, there are two possible ways to analyze the labor market for its effects on wage determination in general and on the determination of wages for the poor in particular. The one view posits demand as fixed and examines variations in human capital among individual workers as the principal determinant of wages. The other posits supply as fixed and analyzes industrial structure for its effects on the determination of wages. It is a short theoretical step to a synthesis of these two models into a model of _labor market stratification_.

The model of labor market stratification is shown in Figure 11-3. The assumption of homogeneity is dropped, and stratification or heterogeneity is presumed to exist in both the demand and supply sides of the labor market.

The structure of different industries is indicated by I_1, I_2, and I_3. Variations in the human capital among individuals are represented by the curves H_1, H_2, and H_3, where H_3 indicates a larger stock of human capital than H_2 or H_1.[9] The curves attain their positions on the graph because of the higher reservation wage associated with

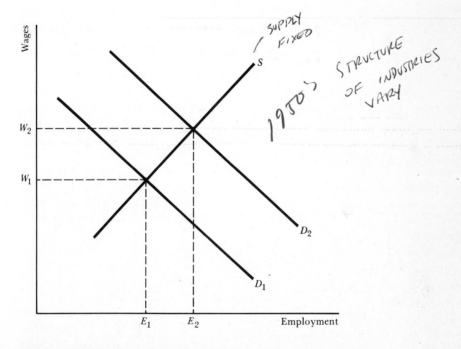

Figure 11-2   Wage Determination: Demand Side

---

[9] Wachtel and Betsey, "Employment at Low Wages"; and Barry Bluestone, "Low Wage Industries and the Working Poor," _Poverty and Human Resource Abstracts_ 3 (March–April 1968), pp. 1–4.

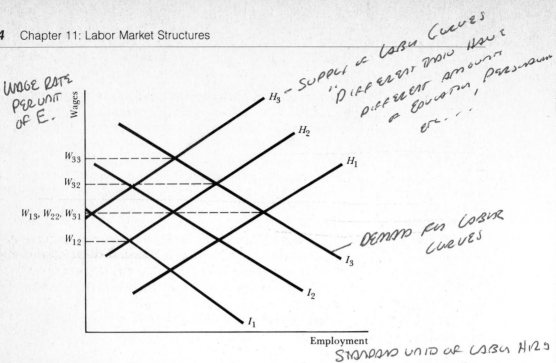

Handwritten annotations:

WAGE RATE PER UNIT OF E.

H_3 — SUPPLY OF LABOR CURVES "DIFFERENT INDIV HAVE DIFFERENT AMOUNTS OF EDUCATION, PERSERVERANCE ETC...."

DEMAND FOR LABOR CURVES

STANDARD UNIT OF LABOR HIRED

Figure 11-3 Wage Determination: Differing Human Capital and Industrial Structures

$I_1 =$ INDUSTRY # 1
$I_2 =$ INDUSTRY # 2 } — OFFER DIFFERENT WAGES BECAUSE MRP_L IS NOT IDENTICAL.

individuals possessing more human capital and because of the smaller numbers of individuals possessing the larger stocks of human capital. Now the problem of wage determination for the individual assumes more complexity but, we hope, greater realism. An individual with a substantial amount of human capital, represented by H_3, will be earning a wage of W_{13} working in industry I_1. The individual receives a maximum wage, in this example, of W_{33} if he or she works in industry I_3. Thus, wages vary across industries for individuals with identical human capital, depending on the structure of those industries. On the other hand, wages will vary within a given industry, depending on the differing amounts of human capital among the employees. Individuals employed in I_3 will earn anywhere from W_{33} to W_{31}, depending on their human capital.

A final implication is that individuals with low amounts of human capital will, under certain circumstances, earn the same as (or more than) individuals with larger amounts of human capital. In this example, an individual with human capital of H_3, working in industry I_1, will earn the same amount (W_{13}) as the individual with less human capital (H_1) working in industry I_3 (W_{31}). This occurs because of the stratification of labor markets and the important barriers to mobility that can persist in labor markets over long periods of time. These barriers can arise because of direct discrimination in the labor market (by sex and race), trade union barriers to entry, high financial cost and risk involved in geographical mobility, insufficient labor market information, artificial educational barriers to job entry, and so on.

These models of the labor market and wage determination set the stage for an empirical investigation of the determination of low-wage employment. If poverty is associated with low-wage employment, as the structural theory of poverty proposes, then the question is, What determines employment at low wages?

Employment at Low Wages

The model of labor market stratification introduced in the previous section led to several empirical investigations of the determinants of low-wage employment. One study used data from a 1967 survey that included information about 1,023 individuals, randomly selected from the entire population, who worked full-time, year round but earned only $6,223 on average.[10] This was a mean income level above the poverty cutoff at that time but approximately at the lower of the BLS budget standards.

Data were available from this survey on personal characteristics (such as age, race, and sex), human capital characteristics of the individuals in the survey, and the industries and occupations in which the individuals were employed. This set of data permitted a direct test of the human capital and industrial structure hypotheses of wage determination.

Using econometric techniques to sort out the complex interrelationships among the variables of the model, the statistical examination revealed that the industry-occupation variables were more important determinants of low-wage employment than were the human capital variables. About 14 percent of the 1,023 individuals in the study were working poor, so the results of this investigation bear directly on the question of what determines the relationship between poverty and the labor market.

To the extent that the occupation and industry of employment represent structural variables, the conclusion of this empirical study provided support for the proposition that low-wage employment was more closely associated with structural than with human capital variables.

The dispute between the proponents of a human capital model of wage determination and the proponents of a structural model is far from over. There is substantial support for each view, and the rigor with which empirical tests have been performed on both models is comparable. This debate framed the work in an important new area of labor economics throughout the 1970s. The jury is not yet in on which of these two competing propositions about individual wage determination will survive future examination.

Dual Labor Markets and Poverty

The theory of the dual labor market is another of the structural models of poverty and low incomes. The dual-labor-market theory posits the existence of two separate

---

[10] Wachtel and Betsey, "Employment at Low Wages," pp. 124–27.

1. *PRIMARY LABOR MARKET*

2. *SECONDARY LABOR MARKET*

labor markets; there is mobility *within* each market but no mobility *between* the two markets. The two labor markets in the "dual economy" are stratified along two general dimensions: the characteristics of jobs and the characteristics of individuals. These two forms of stratification interact to produce a cumulative portrait of the two markets.[11]

The primary sector contains the privileged members of the labor force. It is governed by an internal labor market in which there are relatively good working conditions, high pay, job security, administrative protection of job rights, and mobility along seniority tracks. These jobs require a particular type of worker with personality traits that are compatible with work in the primary sector. For example, the jobs require individuals who have a substantial degree of work discipline, reliability, trustworthiness, and receptivity to on-the-job training. The primary sector has evolved jobs with substantial skill specificity, which necessitate human capital investment through on-the-job training. An employer seeks a person who evidences a high probability of staying with the enterprise so that a return on the investment in the employee's human capital can be realized. Typically, the worker in the primary sector enters employment in a relatively low-skill job through a "port of entry" and, by virtue of seniority, progresses upward, receiving the necessary on-the-job training at each juncture.

The secondary sector consists of jobs that do not possess much skill specificity. The labor pool to fill these jobs is comparatively undifferentiated, approaching a homogeneous mass of raw labor power. There is little or no on-the-job training required to perform these jobs, and turnover is high. As a consequence of the absence of union protection, there is no codification of work rules and seniority privileges as is the case in the internal labor market of the primary sector. Moreover, the workers who fill these jobs manifest traits that are compatible with these jobs—poor work discipline, unstable work patterns, unreliability on the job, and the like. As a consequence, jobs in the secondary sector pay low wages, have poor working conditions, provide little job security, and have high turnover.

The dual-labor-market theory is not a new formulation, but rather a resurrection of older theoritical concepts that for many decades have been largely overlooked. John Stuart Mill, in his *Principles of Political Economy*, provides a quite contemporary formulation: "So complete, indeed, has hitherto been the separation, so strongly worked the line of demarcation, between the different grades of laborers, as to be almost equivalent to an hereditary distinction of caste."[12]

Mill also has a keen insight into why, in today's terminology, workers in the primary sector, working under relatively more pleasant conditions, would earn more than those in the secondary sector by virtue of their protection from competition: "The superiority of reward is not here the consequence of competition, but of its

---

[11] Peter B. Doeringer and Michael J. Piore, *Internal Labor Markets and Manpower Analysis* (Lexington, MA: D. C. Heath and Co., 1971).

[12] John Stuart Mill, *Principles of Political Economy* (London: Longmans, Green, and Co., 1929), p. 393.

absence: not a compensation for disadvantages inherent in employment but an extra advantage."[13]

With reference to the debate that arose in the 1970s between supporters of a structural interpretation of the labor market and defenders of a human capital perception, the dual-labor-market thesis has relevance in terms of its view of the stratification of the labor market between a primary and a secondary sector.[14] Employment in the secondary sector tends to be self-perpetuating; once employed in that sector, the laborer finds it hard to escape from it, because of the work habits and work history he or she acquires. Thus, by definition, low-wage employment and poverty are more closely associated with employment in the secondary sector of the economy than in the primary sector.[15]

The question is, what is the principal factor that assigns one to work in the secondary sector rather than the primary sector? Is it human capital that is the chief stratifying variable, or is it the structure of the labor market in which one is initially placed? Are low wages a consequence of human capital attributes that assign one to the secondary sector of the economy, or is it the character of the job in which the individual works that traps him or her into a "secondary" mode of work experience?

These are difficult questions to unravel because once an individual has been in the labor force for some period of time, there is a strong interaction and interrelationship between the human capital characteristics of the individual and the characteristics of jobs. Statistical techniques do not permit the types of subtle distinctions that would be required to offer a definitive answer to these questions.[16] Nor does economics have a laboratory where it can experiment in a controlled environment, which would enable researchers to find better answers to these difficult questions.

One piece of empirical research in the 1970s sought to untangle these questions. A statistical technique was used that could differentiate the most important stratifying variables. This technique permitted an identification of the factors that lead to work in either the primary or the secondary sector of the economy and, therefore,

---

[13] Ibid., p. 391

[14] For a response to the dual-labor-market and stratification models, from a neoclassical perspective, see Michael L. Wachter, "Primary and Secondary Labor Markets: A Critique of the Dual Approach," *Brookings Papers on Economic Activity* 3 (1974), pp. 637–80; and Glen G. Cain, "The Challenge of Segmented Labor Market Theories to Orthodox Theory: A Survey," *Journal of Economic Literature* 14, no. 4 (December 1976), pp. 1215–57.

[15] Subsequent refinements of the dual-labor-market model recognize the existence of "secondary" types of jobs within the primary economic sector. For example, the college or university you are studying at would be considered part of the primary sector of the economy. However, there are in your midst many jobs and employees with secondary-sector characteristics—for example, in maintenance and food service.

[16] The findings of the labor market dynamics literature that "unemployment, even in tight labor markets, is characterized by relatively few persons who are out of work a large part of the time," is consistent with the dual-labor-market view of the economy. See Kim B. Clark and Lawrence H. Summers, "Labor Market Dynamics and Unemployment: A Reconsideration," *Brookings Papers on Economic Activity* 1 (1979), pp. 13–60. (The quotation is from page 14 of this article.) The literature is surveyed in Chapters 13 and 14 of this book.

contributed to an understanding of what causes low-wage employment in the American economy.[17]

Comparing structural variables with human capital variables, this research indicated that structural variables, as captured by the industry and occupation of an individual's employment, were most important in stratifying the labor force between a primary and a secondary sector. Individuals employed in industries and occupations in the primary sector of the economy could expect to earn on average $7,634 annually in 1967, compared with annual earnings of $5,478 in the secondary sector.

The dual-labor-market theory and its supporting empirical research point toward an understanding of low-wage employment as a consequence of the structure of the economy. Human capital and other personal attributes do not have an independent life of their own, in this perception of the labor market, but instead interact with powerful structural factors to produce low-wage employment, poverty, and inequality.

This view found support in a study that attempted to integrate human capital and labor market theories. In this "vita" theory of the personal income distribution, one labor market is presumed to exist for each human capital category.[18] Human capital determines which labor market stratum the person can enter, and the qualifications for a labor market stratum depend on the vita. For example, your teacher has the requisite vita to teach this class, whereas the maintenance worker who cleans up after the class does not. Hence, the different jobs they hold—one primary, the other secondary.

The author of this study concluded that "inherent capabilities and family environment have important impacts upon life plans that culminate in occupational selection and personal incomes."[19] Once placed on the track, an individual proceeds to accumulate human capital, which prepares him or her for a particular stratum in the labor force. Consistent with the dual-labor-market theory, the individual cannot cross strata once the slotting takes place. Mobility exists within a particular stratum of the labor force but not between strata. Human capital determines the slotting process, but the wage and salary differentials are determined by the character of the different labor markets.

In this sense, both human capital and labor market structures are important for understanding income distribution. The character of labor markets sets the boundaries on incomes earned for individuals in a particular labor market, and human capital determines which labor market one can enter. By affecting the labor market strata

---

[17] The statistical technique is called *automatic interaction detection*, and the study was published in Howard M. Wachtel and Charles Betsey, "Low Wage Workers and the Dual Labor Market: An Empirical Investigation," *Review of Black Political Economy* 5, no. 3 (Spring 1975), pp. 288–301.

[18] A *vita* refers to the complete background of an individual—education, work experience, and so on. The study discussed here is E. Ray Canterbury, "A Vita Theory of the Personal Income Distribution," *Southern Economic Journal* 46, no. 1 (July 1979), pp. 12–48.

[19] Ibid., p. 44.

available, human capital influences income possibilities for an individual, while the labor market sets the context for earnings in the first instance.

Think of the economy as a series of niches or cubbyholes. Each one has a different earning potential associated with it. What you can earn depends on which niche you are qualified for. How do you qualify for the niche you want? You do this by human capital acquisition, which depends on your family circumstances, your cleverness with your human capital investment, and other factors. The niches represent the structures of labor markets, and your human capital investment predisposes you toward one niche or another.

The human capital and structuralist analyses of the labor market were major innovations of the 1970s. They arose because of the need to explain individual incomes in light of society's renewed interest in problems of poverty and inequality. The debate goes on into the 1980s, as labor economics seeks to come to terms with this important issue of individual welfare in our society.

Policy Implications of Labor Market Structure Theories

If poverty and low incomes are a consequence of both the structure of the economy and human capital, public policies that focus on the individual exclusively will not succeed. In 1984 it would have taken a transfer of only about $42 billion to bring everyone who was below poverty up to the poverty level.[20] This amount would have come to a little more than 1 percent of GNP and only 5 percent of total federal government expenditures in 1984. What accounts for the absence of a transfer program, through a family assistance plan or a negative income tax or an income maintenance program, that would accomplish the objective of eliminating poverty?

The answer is found in the structural analysis of the labor market. Any attempt to eliminate poverty through a direct transfer program would intrude on the functioning of the labor market. Since poverty is a result of the operations of the labor market, efforts to eliminate it through transfer programs seriously disrupt the structure of those labor markets. People will not work at jobs that pay low wages if they can acquire income in other ways.[21] This is apparent in the contemporary discussions of the disincentive for the unemployed to work when they can receive unemployment compensation in lieu of working. The same would be the case if poverty were eliminated through transfer programs. Low-wage work would cease to exist. Either the

---

[20] U.S. Bureau of the Census, "Money Income and Poverty Status of Families and Persons in the United States: 1984," Series P-60, No. 149 (August 1985), p. 30.

[21] According to *Business Week*, an AFDC recipient earning $100 per week at a job in 1980 would end up with only $14 more than if he or she had stayed on welfare. This takes account of direct welfare payments, food stamps, public housing subsidies, and taxes ("Why Income Transfers Are So Hard to Cut," *Business Week* 11 [September 29, 1980], p. 69).

jobs would begin to pay substantially higher wages, sufficient to induce people to take them, or they would be automated out of existence. If wages were increased, the prices paid by the nonpoor for vital goods and services would increase. This fact would produce substantial political opposition to any such transfer program that would reduce the welfare of the nonpoor, even though the welfare of the poor would be increased.

The structure of the labor market can be altered in a variety of ways, and alteration could occur gradually without abrupt disruptions. Public policy that made unionization of unorganized workers less difficult would tend to restructure jobs and the character of work. Such policy is a controversial issue today, involving reform of the labor laws, and will be taken up in a later chapter of this book (Chapter 21). Government spending itself has a dramatic effect on the structure of the economy.[22] Witness, for example, the economic growth and vitality of the South and Southwest, which is due in part to government expenditures in the high-technology space industry concentrated in that region of the country. As recently as two decades ago, the South was considered a depressed region; today it is looked on as raiding the North for jobs and capital.

The most important implication of the structural analysis of the labor market is that neither transfer programs nor human capital investment policies alone will do much to eliminate poverty, raise incomes of the lowest wage earners, or alter the income distribution. These outcomes are a consequence both of the structure of labor markets in the economy and of the process of human capital acquisition. Both must be addressed by public policy. The fundamental point, according to the structuralist view of the economy, is that transfer programs and human capital policies are illusory and cannot by themselves accomplish their objectives.

This is why poverty in the midst of affluence is a continuing reality even in the face of billions of dollars of expenditures, scores of scholars devoting their best efforts to the problem, and a huge bureaucracy whose task it is to eliminate poverty as a human condition.

Summary

Poverty, low incomes, and income inequality are due to the structure of labor markets and the positions individuals attain within these different labor market structures, according to a perspective on the economy developed by a group of labor economists in the 1970s. Their position contrasts with the human capital view in which individual incomes are seen as emanating from the particular characteristics of individuals. This

---

[22] Howard M. Wachtel and Larry B. Sawers, "Theory of the State, Government Purchasing Policy, and Income Distribution," *Review of Income and Wealth* 21, no. 1 (March 1975), pp. 111–24.

debate between an individual view of poverty and low incomes and a structural view consumed the attention of many labor economists in the last decade.

According to the structural view, poverty and low incomes are derived from the individual's position in the labor market. There are a substantial number of full-time working poor, as well as a large number of part-time working poor. A second large group of the poor is represented by those who are retired from active full-time participation in the labor force. Lacking sufficient retirement income and unable to acquire assets while of working age, these people fall into poverty because of their weak position in the labor force during the years they were working. Finally, there are those poor people who have suffered a disabling injury or occupational disease. Their poverty also derives from work.

Poverty is located in work, therefore, and an understanding of poverty must come from an analysis of what determines low-wage employment. Here there are two possible theses: One locates low-wage employment in the lack of sufficient human capital. The structural position, by way of contrast, looks at the structure of the labor market and the individual's place within it to determine low-wage status.

According to the structural view, the labor market is stratified into discrete segments; there is mobility within a particular segment but limited mobility among segments. Wages are primarily a function of industrial structures—productivity, unionization, and the degree of concentration in the product market. An individual's placement in one labor market structure or another depends on human capital and other factors. There is empirical support for this hypothesis, and some doubt is cast on the importance of human capital variables as a determinant of incomes when they are placed in the same model with industrial characteristics. Human capital plays a role of slotting individuals into particular labor market structures but does not determine earnings.

The dual-labor-market hypothesis is a more limited version of the general stratification thesis. In this model of the economy, there are two sectors, primary and secondary, and mobility is sluggish between the two. High wages are associated with the primary sector, along with certain elements of job security associated with the primary sector's internal labor market. Nothing of this sort exists in the secondary sector, which is characterized by low wages, high turnover, and frequent job changes by individuals.

Research indicates that the industry and occupation of employment is a more important determinant of the differentiation between these two sectors than are individual characteristics, including human capital attributes. This lends support to the structural hypothesis in that industrial and occupational variables are more important than personal characteristics in stratifying the labor force.

The policy implication of the structural thesis is that transfer programs and human capital investment strategies by themselves will not be successful, because they do not address the structural characteristics of the economy. That is why income maintenance schemes have never received sufficient support: if implemented, they would intrude on the labor market and cause resource allocation distortions in the economy.

This debate between competing theories and images of the labor market is far from settled. It is one of the most important and lively ongoing debates in labor economics. The outcome of this colloquy is crucial for public policy and individual welfare. Important decisions now being made can affect the success or failure of various programs either in place or being considered by policymakers.

Study Questions

1. What are the implications of basing explanations of poverty in the individual person rather than in the structure of the economy?

2. In what specific ways do dual-labor-market and labor market stratification models differ from human capital models in their explanation of the causes of poverty?

3. Discuss the internal dynamics of the dual-labor-market model. Why is intermarket mobility restricted in this model, and how does this compare with the traditional neoclassical view of the labor market?

4. Do you agree with the conclusion that the important determinants of poverty lie outside the individual's control? Explain.

Further Reading

Canterbury, E. Ray. "A Vita Theory of the Personal Income Distribution." *Southern Economic Journal* 46, no. 1 (July 1979), pp. 12–48.

Doeringer, Peter B., and Michael J. Piore. *Internal Labor Markets and Manpower Analysis*. Lexington, MA: D. C. Heath and Co., 1971.

Wachtel, Howard M. "Capitalism and Poverty in America: Paradox or Contradiction?" *American Economic Review* 62, no. 2 (May 1972), pp. 187–94.

Wachtel, Howard M., and Charles Betsey. "Employment at Low Wages." *Review of Economics and Statistics* 54, no. 2 (May 1972), pp. 121–29.

12

The Economics of Discrimination

If poverty and low incomes were randomly distributed among the citizens of the United States, there would not be any *systematic* differences in incomes among race and sex groups. However, as we all know, the incidence of poverty and low incomes is more frequent for women and for blacks in the population. This systematic concentration of poverty and low incomes among certain race and sex groups in the population requires an explanation. The economics of discrimination has been used in this context to study inequality between men and women, whites and blacks.

We observe inequality between blacks and whites and between men and women. The question is, what causes this inequality to exist and to persist over time? Once an understanding of the causes of racial and sexual inequality is arrived at, sensible policy measures can be designed to alleviate such inequalities, if society wants to pursue equality as a social objective.

On this point there has been confusion. Equality has different meanings in different contexts. First, equality is quite different from *equity*. Equity implies fairness of treatment, in which the individual is judged on his or her talents without undue subjectivity. A meritocracy is inherent in the concept of equity.

Equality can be similar to equity but can also be distinct from it. *Equality of opportunity* is one goal; it means that everyone should be given an equal chance in life to develop his or her talents to their full potential and to apply those fully developed talents as effectively as possible.

Equality of opportunity, however, is quite different from the way public policy has begun to approach the problem of discrimination in recent years. Too often equality of opportunity has been confused with the *equality of outcomes*. Guaranteeing the equality of outcomes is far different from providing either equity or equality of opportunity. Equality of outcomes is a utopian goal pursued without attention to any potentially serious negative consequences that might flow from such a social objective. For example, equality of outcome might reduce economic efficiency, undermine personal incentives, and promote the least productive members of society at the expense of the most productive ones. It is this point that has caused the most controversy in the area of antidiscrimination policy in the past years. The issue has arisen in the first instance because policymakers have not understood the differences among these concepts of equality: equity, equality of opportunity, and equality of outcomes. Policies designed to assure equality of opportunity are appropriate for the objective of attaining equitable outcomes, as distinct from policies designed to achieve equal outcomes.

Discrimination is a multifaceted phenomenon. Economics alone cannot explain the bases or causes of discrimination. History, psychology, sociology, and anthropology are at least as important as economics in unraveling the causes of discrimination. This is a book about economics, however, and consequently the main focus is on what economists bring to the study of discrimination.

Economists' interest in discrimination has stemmed from several sources. Some have considered the question, does discrimination reduce economic efficiency by distorting resource allocation? Other economists have been concerned with the broader philosophical questions of equity and equality of opportunity. Still others have pursued studies of the economics of discrimination out of a vague, ill-defined notion of what is right and wrong in society.

In this chapter, there will first be a discussion of the main economic indicators of discrimination, followed by sections on the theory of discrimination, evidence pertaining to the theories, and public policies to confront the economics of discrimination.[1]

Racial Inequalities

America is a society with profound racial attitudes that can be traced back to slavery. The specific manifestation today of differences in certain economic indicators must be viewed in that historical context. The most conclusive statistic that defines inequality

---

[1] The outcome of the economic game is different for blacks and whites, men and women. The roots of racial discrimination are different from those of sex discrimination. This important fact should be borne in mind throughout the remainder of this chapter, because for the most part, there will not be sufficient attention devoted to the differences in discrimination between race and sex groups. The constraint of space does not permit a thorough investigation of the differences in discrimination in society for racial versus sex groups.

Table 12-1   Ratio of Black Median Income to White Median
Income, 1945–1985, Selected Years

Year	Ratio of Black Median Income to White		
	Families	Males	Females
1945	0.56	n.a.[a]	n.a.[a]
1950	0.54	0.54	0.49
1955	0.55	0.53	0.54
1960	0.55	0.53	0.70
1965	0.55	0.57	0.73
1970	0.64	0.60	0.92
1975	0.65	0.63	0.92
1981	0.56	0.59	0.88
1985	0.57	0.63	0.85

[a]Not available.
Sources: Michael Reich, *Racial Inequality: A Political-Economic Analysis*
(Princeton, NJ: Princeton University Press, 1981), p. 32; U.S. Bureau
of the Census, "Money Income and Poverty Status of Families and
Persons in the United States: 1981," Series P-60, No. 134 (March
1982), pp. 7, 13, 14; U.S. Bureau of the Census, "Money Income and
Poverty Status of Families and Persons in the United States: 1985,"
Series P-60, No. 154 (August 1986), pp. 7, 13, 14.

among races is the ratio of black and white median incomes. These figures are presented
in Table 12-1 for all families in the economy and for male and female groups separately.
From 1945, at the end of World War II, until 1965 the ratio of black to white median
family income remained virtually unchanged. Typically, a black family's income would
be about 55 percent of a white family's income. After the civil rights movement of
the 1960s shook America's conscience and applied enormous political pressures, there
was some narrowing of the gap between black and white family incomes. In the 1970s
the ratio of black family income to white was in the range of 0.60 or more. It peaked
in 1975 at 0.65, implying that black family incomes were close to two-thirds of white
family incomes. However, by 1985 the ratio of black median family income to white
returned to its pre-1965 level (0.57).

These proportions are heavily influenced by the business cycle.[2] During periods
of prosperity, when employment levels are high, the black-to-white family income
ratio tends to narrow. During recessionary periods high rates of overall unemployment
tend to affect black workers more severely, and the ratio of black family income to

---

[2] Michael Reich, *Racial Inequality: A Political-Economic Analysis* (Princeton, NJ: Princeton University Press,
1981), chap. 2.

white family income typically falls. During the 1960s, when black-white differentials narrowed, the gains were most heavily concentrated among the most educated blacks and recent entrants to the labor force.[3] The authors of the study that reached this conclusion go on to say that the narrowing of black-white differentials was "exaggerated by . . . business cycle gains," corroborating the importance of full employment in reducing black-white income differentials.

Breaking these figures down between males and females yields some interesting statistical facts about inequality between whites and blacks. In Table 12-1 the ratio of black median income to white median income is shown separately for males and females. The male ratio behaved like the overall ratio. Between 1945 and 1965 it was relatively stable, and then it increased slightly in the 1970s, falling again in 1981. For females, however, the picture is quite different. Starting from a very low ratio in 1950 of 0.49, black female median incomes have been catching up with white female incomes. By the 1970s black females had incomes almost equal to white females.

Although black and white female median incomes are closer to each other than are black and white male median incomes, black females still have the lowest incomes of the four groups. In 1985, median income for white males was $17,111, compared

Table 12-2   Unemployment Rates by Race, 1948–1985, Selected Years

Year	Unemployment Rates (%)		Ratio of Unemployment Rates: Black and Other to White
	White	Black and Other	
1948	3.5	5.9	1.7
1950	4.9	9.0	1.8
1955	3.9	8.7	2.2
1960	4.9	10.2	2.1
1965	4.1	8.1	2.0
1970	4.5	8.2	1.8
1975	7.8	13.9	1.8
1979	5.1	11.3	2.2
1982	8.6	17.3	2.0
1985	6.2	13.7	2.2

Sources: Council of Economic Advisers, *Economic Report of the President, 1980* (Washington: Government Printing Office), p. 238; *Economic Report of the President, 1983*, p. 201; U.S. Department of Labor, *Employment and Earnings* (January 1986), pp. 155, 157.

---

[3] James P. Smith and Finis R. Welch, "Black-White Male Wage Ratios: 1960–70," *American Economic Review* 67, no. 3 (June 1977), p. 337.

Table 12-3 Ratio of Black Family Income to White, 1980,
Selected Occupations

Occupation of Household Head	Ratio of Black Mean Family Income to White
White-collar workers	0.67
Blue-collar workers	0.87
Farm workers	0.53
Service workers	0.75

[handwritten: → CLOSEST TO WHITES WHY? UNIONIZED JOBS OPEN TO EVERYONE, LESS DISCRIMINATION]

Source: U.S. Bureau of the Census, *Statistical Abstract of the United States, 1982–83* (Washington: Government Printing Office), p. 435.

with $10,768 for black males. Black females had a median income in that year of $6,277, compared with $7,357 for white females.[4] Both white and black females have lower incomes than their male counterparts, but black females carry the double burden of both their race and their sex.

A second important indicator of inequality between whites and blacks is the unemployment rate. Unemployment rates in the postwar period for whites and blacks are presented in Table 12-2. During periods of relatively full employment immediately after World War II, blacks had unemployment rates about 1.8 times those for whites. During the sluggish economic growth of the 1950s and early 1960s, this ratio increased to 2.0. In 1965, for example, the unemployment rate for blacks was 8.1, compared with 4.1 for whites.

The decade between 1965 and 1975 was a prosperous one for blacks, compared with the previous 15 years. Unemployment rates for blacks compared with whites fell to where they were immediately after World War II. Recently, however, this trend toward greater equality in unemployment rates has been reversed. In 1985 the black unemployment rate was more than twice as high as the white unemployment rate, standing at a ratio equal to what it was back in the mid-1950s.

In part, these unemployment rates represent cyclical phenomena. To what extent they are cyclical, however, rather than a new trend away from a commitment to equality of opportunity, is the concern of many social analysts and policymakers.

Inequality between black and white incomes can reflect either occupational differences between the races or unequal pay for equal work.[5] Of course, to some extent, occupational differences between the races may themselves be the result of discrimination. A more important question, however, is whether there are differences in incomes between blacks and whites for the same occupational groupings.

---

[4] Statistics taken from U.S. Bureau of the Census, "Money Income and Poverty Status of Families and Persons in the United States: 1985," Series P-60, No. 154 (August 1986), pp. 13–14.

[5] It is also possible that a combination of both "occupational" and "wage" discrimination prevails. This issue is examined later in this chapter.

Table 12-4 Income Distribution for Blacks and Whites, 1950 and 1985.

Percentage of Total Family Income	1950	1985
White	100.0	100.0
Lowest fifth	4.8	5.0
Second fifth	12.4	11.2
Middle fifth	17.4	16.9
Fourth fifth	23.2	23.9
Highest fifth	42.2	42.9
Highest 5 percent	17.2	16.5
Black and other races	100.0	100.0
Lowest fifth	3.5	3.7
Second fifth	10.3	9.1
Middle fifth	17.6	15.7
Fourth fifth	25.2	25.2
Highest fifth	43.4	46.3
Highest 5 percent	16.5	16.7

Sources: U.S. Bureau of the Census, *Statistical Abstract of the United States, 1979* (Washington: Government Printing Office), p. 452; U.S. Bureau of the Census, "Money Income and Poverty Status of Families and Persons in the United States: 1985," Series P-60, No. 154 (August 1986), p. 11.

Information pertinent to this question is presented in Table 12-3, in which the ratio of black mean income to white mean income in 1980 is presented for four different occupational categories. In each instance the ratio is less than 1, indicating that blacks receive less income in each occupational category than do whites. The greatest equality is found among blue-collar workers, the least among farm workers.

So far we have examined inequalities between whites and blacks along income and employment dimensions. Another interesting question to ask is, What is the extent of inequality in the income distribution for blacks as a group, compared with the income distribution for whites? In Table 12-4 statistics on the distribution of income are presented for whites and blacks as separate groups for the years 1950 and 1985.

Income is slightly more unequally distributed in the black population than it is in the white population, and this inequality has increased since 1950. The lowest 40 percent of the white population received 16 to 17 percent of the total income of whites. The lowest 40 percent of the black income distribution received just 13 to 14 percent of total black income in 1950 and 1985. The highest 20 percent of black income recipients received 46 percent of all black incomes in 1985; the equivalent figure for whites was 43 percent.

These statistics on income distribution reveal an important social aspect of economic life in the black population. There is a greater division between social classes in the black population than there is in the white population. The black population has a small but influential upper stratum, composed primarily of professional occupations and some small business owners, in which incomes are highly concentrated. Contrasted with this is a large and very poor lower-income grouping, which receives relatively small shares of the total income of the black population. In between is a middle class that, compared with its white counterpart, receives roughly the same proportion of the total income.

This does not mean that upper-income blacks receive higher incomes than do upper-income whites. In Table 12-5 statistics are presented that bear on this question. They show the income limits in 1985 associated with each income quintile and the average income for the top 5 percent of the income distribution for both whites and blacks. For the two lowest income quintiles, blacks have an upper limit less than 55 percent of whites; for the middle and next-to-highest quintiles, incomes begin to converge for blacks and whites, reaching a ratio of around two-thirds for the next-to-highest quintile and for the top 5 percent of the income distribution.

However, the spread of incomes is greater for blacks than it is for whites. Take the ratio of the income for the top 5 percent of the income distribution to the lowest 20 percent. For blacks this amounts to 8.0: the income of the top 5 percent of the black income distribution is 8 times higher than the income of the lowest 20 percent of the black income distribution. For whites the equivalent figure is 5.5: the income of the top 5 percent of the white income distribution is 5.5 times the income of the lowest quintile of the white income distribution.

Table 12-5 Family Income at Quintiles, 1985, by Race

	Upper Limit of Family Income		Ratio: Black to White
	White	Black	
Lowest fifth	$14,528	$ 6,750	.46
Second fifth	24,105	13,010	.54
Middle fifth	34,500	20,933	.61
Fourth fifth	49,401	33,613	.68
Top 5 percent	80,000	54,030	.67

Source: U.S. Bureau of the Census, "Money Income and Poverty Status of Families and Persons in the United States: 1985," Series P-60, No. 154 (August 1986), p. 11.

Sex Inequalities

Women have incomes that are about two-thirds of male incomes even though there is little difference in their respective unemployment rates. Tables 12-6 and 12-7 bear on this point. Incomes of females compared with males increased from 1970 to 1985, particularly in the age groups 20–44.

There are important differences in income inequalities between men and women for different age groups. There is far more equality between male and female incomes for those under 25 than there is for those over 25. This curious fact has stimulated various explanations: child-rearing duties, which interrupt a woman's labor force attachment, discrimination in career advancement after the entry level, or an intermittent pattern of labor force participation for women—although this is becoming less common with each passing year, as more women see themselves having a permanent career attachment to the labor force.

In Table 12-7, unemployment rates are presented for men and women. Unlike the statistical profile of unemployment rates by race, the unemployment rate differential is virtually non-existent for males and females. The evidence of income inequality for men and women is similar to that for blacks and whites, but their respective unemployment inequalities are quite different.

Table 12-6 Income of Male and Female Full-Time Workers, by Age, 1970 and 1985

| Age of Full-Time Workers | Median Annual Income | | | | Ratio of Median Income: Women to Men | |
| | Women | | Men | | | |
	1970	1985	1970	1985	1970	1985
14–19	$3,783	$ 8,372	$ 3,950	$ 9,050	0.96	0.92
20–24	4,928	11,757	6,655	13,827	0.74	0.85
25–34	5,923	16,740	9,126	22,321	0.65	0.75
35–44	5,531	18,032	10,258	28,966	0.54	0.62
45–54	5,588	17,009	9,931	29,880	0.56	0.57
55–64	5,468	16,761	9,071	28,387	0.60	0.59
65 and over	4,884	18,336	6,754	26,146	0.72	0.70
Total, all workers	5,440	16,252	9,184	24,999	0.59	0.65

Sources: U.S. Bureau of the Census, *Statistical Abstract of the United States* (Washington: Government Printing Office, 1979), p. 461; U.S. Bureau of the Census, "Money Income and Poverty Status of Families and Persons in the United States: 1985," Series P-60, No. 154 (August 1986), p. 16

Table 12-7 Unemployment Rates by Sex, 1948–1985, Selected Years

Year	Unemployment Rates[a] (%)		Ratio: Female to Male Unemployment Rates
	Male	Female	
1948	3.2	3.6	1.1
1950	4.7	5.1	1.1
1955	3.8	4.4	1.2
1960	4.7	5.1	1.1
1965	3.2	4.5	1.4
1970	3.5	4.8	1.4
1975	6.8	8.0	1.2
1981	6.3	6.8	1.1
1985	6.2	6.6	1.1

[a]Unemployment rates for persons 20 years of age and older.
Source: Council of Economic Advisers, *Economic Report of the President, 1986* (Washington: Government Printing Office), p. 293.

Income differentials by race or sex can be due to either occupational discrimination or wage discrimination (or a combination of both). Occupational discrimination refers to the clustering of blacks or women into lower-paid occupations. Wage discrimination involves unequal pay for equal work. One study that attempted to differentiate between these two aspects of income differentials concluded that women are exposed to both occupational and wage discrimination whereas blacks have lower incomes primarily because of occupational discrimination.[6]

Income Inequalities and Educational Inequalities

Differences in educational attainment by sex and race have narrowed dramatically during this century. Differences in income and labor market experience, therefore, cannot be ascribed to differences in years of educational attainment. Of course, there are differences in quality of education that are not accounted for in the statistics on educational attainment. That problem aside, inequalities for race and sex groups lie outside the area of human capital investments.

---

[6] Robert B. Strauss and Francis W. Horvath, "Wage Rate Differences by Race and Sex in the U.S. Labour Market: 1960–1970," *Economica* 43, no. 171 (August 1976), p. 297.

EDUCATION

Table 12-8 Median Years of School Completed, by Race and Sex, Selected Years, 1890–1984

| | Median Years of School Completed | | | |
| | Males | | Females | |
Year	White	Black	White	Black
1890	8.0	1.5	8.2	1.0
1900	8.2	3.7	8.3	3.8
1910	8.3	4.6	8.5	4.5
1920	8.5	5.1	8.6	5.6
1930	8.8	6.0	9.2	6.9
1940	10.7	7.4	11.2	8.1
1950	12.2	8.9	12.2	9.7
1960	12.4	10.5	12.3	11.1
1970	12.7	12.2	12.5	12.2
1980	12.5	12.0	12.6	12.0
1984	12.6	12.2	12.6	12.3

INEQUALITIES IN EDUCATION HAS DIMINISHED GREATLY.

Sources: Michael Reich, *Racial Inequality: A Political-Economic Analysis* (Princeton, NJ: Princeton University Press, 1981), p. 67; U.S. Bureau of the Census, *Statistical Abstract of the United States*, 1986 (Washington: Government Printing Office), p. 133.

Data pertinent to this proposition are presented in Table 12-8, in which median years of school completed are shown by race and sex for the years 1890 to 1984. In the early part of this century there were extraordinary differences in educational attainment for blacks and whites. In 1910, for example, the median number of years of education received by blacks, both males and females, was four and a half years, compared with over eight years for whites. Racial differences in educational attainment prevailed through 1960, when whites received from one to two years more education than blacks. By 1980 these differences had largely disappeared, and today blacks receive as many years of education as whites, setting aside the problem of quality differences in education.

Between sexes there has been much less inequality in educational attainment. In fact, where there has been inequality, females have received *more* years of education than males. Starting in the 1920s, black females received more years of education than black males, and these differences continued until 1960. In the 1930s and 1940s white females received more years of education than white males.

Incomes and employment experiences of blacks and women do not reflect this relative degree of equality in educational attainment by race and sex. This is one of the anomalies that the economics of discrimination has tried to explain.

One way of looking at the relationship between human capital formation and discrimination is to ask the question, what occupational outcomes would be predicted for some group based solely on the human capital of its members and on other situational variables? When this is done for men and women, the variables that form an occupational profile are predictive of the actual occupational profile for men but not for women. For example, one study selected a series of human capital variables (years of schooling, vocational training, labor market experience) and a series of situational variables (number of children, index of father's occupational status, and a psychological index designed to measure work adaptation). Based on these factors, the researchers predicted what occupations a sample of men and women would be most likely to enter and compared the results with the actual occupational structure of the same sample.[7]

The results are shown in Table 12-9, in which the predicted and actual occupational distributions are shown for men and women. The predicted and actual distributions are about the same for men, whereas for women the same variables predict an occupational distribution very different from the actual distribution. Women represent fewer positions in managerial and blue-collar craft occupations than would be predicted and are more heavily concentrated in clerical and service occupations than would be predicted by their human capital and situational variables.

Table 12-9 Predicted and Actual Occupational Distributions

	Men		Women	
Occupation	Predicted (%)	Actual (%)	Predicted (%)	Actual (%)
White-collar				
Professional and technical	9.6	9.1	8.6	12.1
Managerial	25.2	25.5	37.8	5.3
Clerical	5.3	5.1	6.9	40.0
Sales	5.0	4.7	3.4	7.5
Services	4.8	5.0	1.7	14.8
Blue-collar				
Craft	22.5	25.6	18.2	1.2
Operatives	18.6	18.5	19.5	16.4
Laborers	8.8	6.4	3.9	2.7

Source: Randall S. Brown, Marilyn Moon, and Barbara S. Zoloth, "Occupational Attainment and Segregation by Sex," *Industrial and Labor Relations Review* 33, no. 4 (July 1980), p. 512. © 1980 by Cornell University. All rights reserved. Adapted with permission.

---

[7] Randall S. Brown, Marilyn Moon, and Barbara S. Zoloth, "Occupational Attainment and Segregation by Sex," *Industrial and Labor Relations Review* 33, no. 4 (July 1980), pp. 506–17.

A somewhat different study conducted on black-white income differentials produced the same result. In this study the identical wage-estimating model was used on a sample of white workers and separately on black workers. The conclusion was that "in general: Blacks and whites with similar characteristics, other than race, will not experience the same results in the labor market."[8]

Aside from formal education, on-the-job training is an important source of human capital formation. In a study that examined the impact of on-the-job training by race and sex, the authors found that white males receive about twice as much training as members of other race and sex groups and that this training differential accounts for 20 percent of the wage gap between white and black men and 10 percent of the wage gap between white men and black or white women. What matters is the stock of on-the-job training, which varies with the amount of time one spends with a particular employer. The actual returns to training are about the same for any race or sex group, but the larger amount of training for white men accounts for their higher earnings.[9]

To explain these race and sex differences in economic experience in the labor market, economists have constructed economic theories of discrimination—a subject we now address.

Theories of Discrimination

There are several economic theories that purport to explain why discrimination exists in our society. The emphasis is on the *economic* in these theories. Other reasons for discrimination are best left to psychologists, sociologists, historians, or anthropologists.

Three economic theories of discrimination will be considered in this chapter: the neoclassical, the dual-labor-market, and the political-economic theories of discrimination.[10]

Neoclassical Theory of Discrimination

There are several variants of the neoclassical theory of discrimination. The first was put forward in the late 1950s by Gary Becker; his model has stimulated much contro-

---

[8] Glen C. Loury, "Black Economic Progress: The Reality and the Illusion," *Review of Black Political Economy* 10, no. 4 (Summer 1980), p. 372.

[9] Greg J. Duncan and Saul Hoffman, "On-the-Job Training and Earnings Differences by Race and Sex," *Review of Economics and Statistics* 61, no. 4 (November 1979), p. 597.

[10] For a review of the theories of discrimination, see Annette M. LaMond, "Economic Theories of Discrimination," in Phyllis A. Wallace and Annette M. LaMond, eds., *Women, Minorities, and Employment Discrimination* (Lexington, MA: Lexington Books, 1977), pp. 1–12; Kenneth J. Arrow, "Discrimination in the Labour Market," in J. E. King, ed., *Readings in Labour Economics* (Oxford: Oxford University Press, 1980), pp. 117–35; Reich, *Racial Inequality*, chap. 3; and Ray Marshall, "The Economcs of Racial Discrimination: A Survey," *Journal of Economic Literature* 12, no. 3 (September 1974), pp. 849–71.

Discrimination Roots from
1. *Employers*
2. *Employees*
3. *Customers*

versy ever since it was introduced.[11] Becker argues that discrimination reduces economic efficiency because it distorts resource allocation. His conclusion is that, over time, competition will reduce and eventually eliminate discrimination. To see how he reaches this somewhat paradoxical conclusion, we must work through some aspects of his model.

Becker argues that employers have a "taste" for discrimination, which is part of their general preference function. To support this taste, the employer pays something for the privilege of discriminating. What the employer pays is called a *discrimination coefficient* and reflects the higher wages he or she must pay to white workers as a cost for having a taste for discrimination. White workers receive higher wages in his model than they would receive without discrimination, because labor supply has been restricted. The profits, therefore, of white owners who discriminate are lower because they incur higher costs through the higher wages paid for white labor. Black workers receive lower wages, compared with some nondiscriminatory norm, because the supply of labor clustered in black occupations has increased. Everyone loses in this view of the world except white workers, whose wage is higher than it would be in the absence of discrimination.

Competition among employers should eliminate this discrimination if there is no interference in markets from outside forces. With competition in markets, one employer will discover that he can produce and market his product at a lower price if he does not pay a cost to support his taste for discrimination. He simply hires black workers at lower wages for what previously had been "white jobs" and undercuts his competitors through price competition. Other employers will have to follow or be forced out of business. The remaining firms are those that have not discriminated and, presto, discrimination has been eliminated through perfect competition.[12]

This representation may seem out of joint with your personal observation of the labor market, in which discrimination seems to have persisted over our entire history. Becker explains that historical fact in two ways: first, the intrusion into perfect competition occasioned by government activity in the economy, and second, the activity of labor unions in codifying discrimination and prohibiting the labor market from functioning freely enough to eliminate discrimination.

On this latter point there is some justification for pointing at least one guilty finger at trade unions and their discriminatory practices up to the 1960s.[13] Some unions have been discriminatory, particularly the craft unions. Other unions have fought hard against discrimination, however, and have been in the forefront of the movements for the removal of discriminatory practices. We cannot forget that trade

---

[11] Gary Becker, *The Economics of Discrimination*, 2nd ed. (Chicago: University of Chicago Press, 1971).

[12] Research has tended to support the proposition that there is more discrimination in firms operating in more-concentrated markets. See, for example, Walter Haessel and John Palmer, "Market Power and Employment Discrimination," *Journal of Human Resources* 13, no. 4 (Fall 1978), pp. 545–60.

[13] A sensitive and balanced treatment of this issue appears in Ray Marshall, *The Negro and Organized Labor* (New York: John Wiley and Sons, 1965).

Employers who do not have a taste for discrim. will have lower costs.

unions are a reflection of the social conditions in which we live and that their discriminatory practices are in some sense a mirror image of more profound social attitudes.

Becker's reliance on impediments to competition did not square with historical reality in the United States. Discrimination was probably greater in the late nineteenth and early twentieth centuries in the United States, when the economy was more competitive and less unionized and had fewer government regulations, than it has been since World War II, when there has been less competition in the economy.

Some writings of the early 1970s proposed a slightly altered model of discrimination, still within the neoclassical tradition. One such model was developed by Barbara Bergmann.[14] She also argued that the beneficiaries of discrimination were white workers, who received higher wages than they would have otherwise. Black workers were "crowded" into specific occupations, creating an oversupply of labor in those occupational groups to which blacks were relegated. Wages were therefore low for black workers because of excess supply over demand. White workers, on the other hand, received higher wages. In the occupations they controlled there was a relatively limited supply compared with the demand for their labor.

This result—high wages for white workers and low wages for black workers—can occur independent of the human capital or skill requirements associated with the occupations of blacks and whites. All that is necessary to produce this result is differences in supply relative to demand. Thus, wages can be different for equally skilled occupational groups in this model. Moreover, the emphasis is placed on occupational discrimination in this version of the neoclassical model, rather than on wage discrimination—unequal pay for equal work.

White workers' gains from employment discrimination were estimated to be about $15 billion in 1960, according to a study by Lester Thurow.[15] The crowding hypothesis also applies to sex discrimination. Figures for the early 1960s indicate that about half of all employed women worked in occupations that were 80 percent female.[16] This represented an increase from the occupational segregation that had existed in the early 1950s, according to a separate study of this problem, which concluded that occupational segregation decreased somewhat between 1960 and 1970.[17] By 1977, notwithstanding some limited progress in breaking down female occupational crowding, 79 percent of clerical workers were female, 62 percent of service workers, 83 percent of nurses, and 76 percent of textile workers.[18]

The neoclassical model of either the Becker or the Bergmann variant presumes

---

[14] Barbara Bergmann, "The Effect on White Incomes of Discrimination in Employment," *Journal of Political Economy* 2 (March–April 1971), pp. 294–313.

[15] Lester C. Thurow, *Poverty and Discrimination* (Washington: The Brookings Institution, 1969), p. 134.

[16] Alice H. Amsden, ed., *The Economics of Women and Work* (New York: St. Martins Press, 1980), p. 12.

[17] Francine D. Blau and Wallace E. Hendricks, "Occupational Segregation by Sex: Trends and Prospects," *Journal of Human Resources* 14, no. 2 (Spring 1979), p. 206.

[18] Nancy S. Barrett, "Women in the Job Market: Occupations, Earnings, and Career Opportunities," in Ralph E. Smith, ed., *The Subtle Revolution* (Washington: The Urban Institute, 1979), p. 47.

✗ Be fomiliar w/ diff.s in Becker, arrow, and Breimon.

both that there is some taste for discrimination and that there is some rational functional aspect of labor market discrimination that perpetuates the condition of racial inequality. Whites are presumed to prefer to be in proximity to other whites rather than blacks. In the work place this amounts to a taste for discrimination that produces occupational segregation.

Many critics of this behavioral proposition have pointed out that under slavery—an extreme form of occupational segregation—whites did associate in close proximity with blacks, particularly in the household, where one would have expected separation to be pervasive.[19] To amend this behavioral interpretation of occupational discrimination, Kenneth Arrow proposed an explanation based on "statistical discrimination." According to Arrow, a prospective employer incurs human capital investment costs whenever he or she hires someone. The employer does not know how to estimate future marginal productivities of the prospective workers with any precision, so he or she cannot estimate future returns to human capital investment with any degree of certainty. "The employer does know the race of the individual," according to Arrow, "and he holds some subjective beliefs about the respective probabilities that white and black workers are qualified."[20] And if the employer thinks that black workers have a lower probable rate of return to the human capital investment for specific occupations, he or she will hire fewer of them.

Taste for discrimination represents an irrational subjective aspect of behavior. The rational functional aspect of discrimination in these models is associated with the fact that one segment of society—white workers—prospers from the existence of discrimination at the expense of black workers and employers. This is the point at which the political-economic theory of discrimination challenges the neoclassical model.

Political-Economic Theory of Discrimination

conspiracy ic capitalist to divide people.

The political-economic theory of discrimination contends that both white and black workers lose from discrimination. The owners and employers are the ones who benefit from this condition in the labor market.[21] Segregation between the races is an institution that reduces the overall economic strength and bargaining power of workers—both white and black. White workers see their economic predicament as emanating from competition with black workers instead of seeing all workers in conflict with a common foe: white owners and employers. These divisions within labor, caused by discrimination, weaken labor as a movement.

Owners and employers are aware of this tactical advantage, which they can exploit. They follow a divide-and-conquer strategy in the labor market, playing one race off against the other to maximize their own bargaining strength against labor as a class.

---

[19] Arrow, "Discrimination in the Labour Market," p. 123.

[20] Ibid., p. 131.

[21] Reich, *Racial Inequality*, chap. 5.

There are barriers to full mobility in the market place.

According to this theory of discrimination, labor's share of the national income will be less than it would have been without discrimination, because labor as a movement is weakened by racism. Employers know this and play on those chords of discontent that optimize their position in the economy.

Two types of evidence are advanced in support of the political-economic theory of discrimination. First, historical evidence indicates that black workers have frequently been used as strikebreakers during periods of labor conflict.[22] Employers have always had racial categories into which workers were slotted. Stratifying the labor force by race reinforced racial animosities that were already present.

A second piece of evidence indicates that sections of the nation with less discrimination have higher labor shares of the national income that originates in those sections of the country.[23] This would be consistent with the political-economic theory of discrimination. Where there is less discrimination, labor's share of the national income is higher, implying that labor as a movement is stronger where there is less discrimination. The higher labor shares of the national income benefit both white and black workers. It cuts into capital's share and is consistent with the political-economic theory's hypothesis about who benefits from discrimination.

This intriguing proposition has also been used to explain why discrimination is so persistent and virulent in the face of massive efforts to eliminate it through public policy. Like poverty, discrimination has a distinct function in our society, enabling events to work out better for the dominant stratum in society. This does not mean that our economic system as we know it would cease to exist without discrimination. Rather, the functional aspects of discrimination (and one might add poverty) strengthen the hand of capital in its general conflict with labor, which is inherent in our economic system. That is the proposition put forward in the political-economic theory of discrimination.

Juxtaposing the neoclassical and political-economic theories of discrimination provides a clear distinction between the two in terms of who benefits from discrimination and what the motives are for discrimination. Yet a third theory of the economics of discrimination provides another explanation for discrimination, which is in the tradition of institutional models of the labor force. This is the dual-labor-market theory, to which we now turn.

Dual-Labor-Market Theory of Discrimination

The dual-labor-market theory provides an important description of how discrimination takes place in the labor market.[24] In the higher-paying primary sector of the economy, hiring is governed by personnel rules and personnel managers, who screen

---

[22] Marshal, *The Negro and Organized Labor*, pt. I.

[23] Reich, *Racial Inequality*, chap. 6.

[24] Peter B. Doeringer and Michael J. Piore, *Internal Labor Markets and Manpower Analysis* (Lexington, MA: D. C. Heath and Co., 1971), chap. 7.

potential applicants on the basis of certain criteria. These criteria are heavily influenced by the subjective judgment of the hiring officer and prevent blacks from breaching the "port of entry" into the primary sector of the economy. Recall that the primary sector is governed by a set of rules, which compose an internal labor market. This internal labor market has rules for promotion, seniority, layoffs, and other personnel decisions. Once hired, a person is presumed to have some minimal rights to the job.

Investments in human capital take place along the way as the individual proceeds up seniority ladders in the internal labor market. What is crucial for entry into this sector is the hiring officer's subjective impression of how well the prospective employee will perform in the internal labor market of the firm. Will he or she be a disciplined and conscientious worker? Will the worker develop an attachment to the firm that will make investments in human capital worthwhile? Such investments would be squandered if the individual did not stay with the firm.

In short, the hiring officer looks for possible points of future trouble. Decisions are being made that extend beyond the short term, as the prospective employee is evaluated in terms of how well he or she will fit into the firm's internal labor market. Discriminatory attitudes affect this hiring process, according to the dual-labor-market theory. Hiring officers practice what is called "statistical discrimination"—the barring from entry into the firm of certain workers based on the subjective impression of how one race or sex will fare in the internal labor market of the firm. Such subjective impressions may not hold up under empirical scrutiny. For example, black workers or women may do quite well if given an opportunity. But such objective facts are not an important enough part of the hiring process to transcend the subjective process of statistical discrimination that prevails.

The result of statistical discrimination is that black workers, for example, become concentrated in the secondary sector of the economy. There they develop traits associated with high job turnover, lack of work discipline, and limited opportunities for advancement. A self-fulfilling prophecy takes over. The black worker, having been barred initially from a job in the primary sector, has precisely the type of work history that will prevent him or her from gaining entry in the future into primary sector jobs.

The hiring officer, acting as the gatekeeper, looks over a record of work in the secondary sector that contains everything he or she is trying to avoid: high job turnover, poor work habits, and lack of mobility. The hiring officer concludes that such an individual will not do well in the internal labor market of the firm and rejects the application. Hence, the prophecy is fulfilled. Once having been barred from an entry-level job in the primary sector, the black worker finds it difficult to gain entry at a later date because of the work history accumulated in the secondary sector of the economy.

Public Policy and Economic Discrimination

Public policies designed to deal with economic discrimination have proceeded down a track that is not explicitly based on the economic theories we have just discussed.

Title VII of the Civil Rights Act of 1964 is the centerpiece for public policy efforts to eliminate economic discrimination. Under Title VII it is unlawful for any employer of 15 or more persons to discriminate on the basis of race, color, religion, sex, or national origin. To enforce the law Congress established the Equal Employment Opportunity Commission (EEOC), which has the power to hear complaints of discrimination and recommend resolutions of disputes under Title VII. If the individual or class of individuals seeking redress is not satisfied, a suit against the employer can be filed in federal district court, either as an individual or in a class action.[25]

After congressional enactment of the first federal statute in our history dealing with economic discrimination, the job was left to the courts to determine how economic discrimination would be established. Motive was an obvious candidate as a criterion, but in very few cases could overt discrimination be found. In virtually none of the cases involving economic discrimination was there a "smoking gun," to borrow a phrase. Instead of motive, the courts established the criterion of economic outcome. If a firm could be shown to have an employment profile by race, for example, that was inconsistent with the racial profile of the labor force in the local labor market, or in the industry as a whole, or in the occupation, then an inference of discrimination would be drawn, and the firm would be required to alter its employment practices or pay damages to the parties that had suffered discrimination or both.

In a famous case, *Griggs* v. *Duke Power Co.* (1971), the Supreme Court ruled that employment tests used by the company had the effect of discriminating against blacks and were not relevant to the job for which the individuals were being tested.[26] As a result of this ruling, an employer would be considered in violation of the Civil Rights Act if the criteria used in hiring could not be justified on the basis of the work involved and if the result of the hiring criteria was to exclude proportionally more members of one of the groups protected under Title VII. In effect, the court ruled in the Griggs case that attention should be focused on the outcomes of employment practices, not just their motivation.[27]

This ruling produced a test based on a type of "statistical discrimination," in which a case must be based on the statistical comparison of a company's employment outcome with that of some comparable group—the local labor market, the national market for the same occupation, or other firms in the industry.

Title VII provides a mechanism for redress of employment discrimination after it has occurred. In a companion area of activity the federal government seeks to reverse past discrimination and takes steps to ensure that it is not happening now. This is the area of the famous "affirmative action" rulings, which require all contractors with the

---

[25] A class action is a suit filed by a group of individuals on behalf of themselves and all others with the same complaint. For a discussion of Title VII of the Civil Rights Act of 1964, see Charles O. Gregory and Harold A. Katz, *Labor and the Law*, 3rd ed. (New York: W. W. Norton and Co., 1979), chap. 17.

[26] Ibid., pp. 550–54.

[27] Arthur B. Smith, Jr., "The Law and Equal Employment Opportunity: What's Past Should Not Be Prologue," *Industrial and Labor Relations Review* 33, no. 4 (July 1980), pp. 493–505.

federal government to devise plans by which groups covered under Title VII are actively sought to fill open positions, are considered for promotions once hired, and, in general, are afforded all the opportunities of workers not covered under Title VII.[28]

These affirmative action plans have been very controversial because there is a thin line between affirmative action and quota systems, the latter being specifically precluded from the intent of the federal contract compliance executive orders. The quota issue was confronted in the famous case of the *Regents of the University of California* v. *Bakke* (1978). In this case a white applicant (Bakke) was denied admission to the University of California (Davis campus) medical school. The university had set aside 16 places in the medical school entering class for blacks. Bakke scored higher on entrance exams than some of the 16 blacks who were admitted, yet was denied admission. He argued this constituted a quota system and was illegal under the federal contract compliance executive orders. The Supreme Court, in a 5–4 decision, upheld Bakke's complaint and ruled that the University of California system constituted an impermissible quota. At the same time, the majority of the Court held that race was an appropriate criterion for the university to use in admissions decisions. By leaving the door open for affirmative action criteria, the Court has left sufficient ambiguity that we can expect continuing litigation on these questions in the future.[29]

At this juncture, you might be wondering, what does this detour into public policy and economic discrimination have to do with economic theories of discrimination? "Not much" would be an appropriate answer. Public policy involving economic discrimination has become the purview of the law and lawyers. Law is directed at the practices of employers. Economic analysis of discrimination involves the labor market. Many of the approaches economists would suggest to alleviate economic discrimination fall under the umbrella of labor market policies—employment and training, human capital, labor market structures. In reading the later chapters of this book, in which some of these policies are examined, bear in mind that, aside from any other issues the policies are addressing, economic discrimination is also meant to be alleviated.

If we make the transition from economic theories of discrimination to economic policies, something can be said in connection with each of the theories of discrimination. The several theories of discrimination produce specific policy prescriptions.

In the initial version of the neoclassical theory, discrimination was considered the result of the absence of sufficient competition in labor and product markets. Policies to remove discrimination would, therefore, involve an elimination of those impediments to competition in markets. Such policies include the removal of government policies that affect competition in the product markets and an assault on trade unions, which supposedly codify discriminatory practices.

The political-economic theory of discrimination would place programmatic emphasis

---

[28] President Kennedy in 1961 issued the first executive order on these issues, and this was strengthened by President Johnson in his Executive Order 11246. See Gordon F. Bloom and Herbert R. Northrup, *Economics of Labor Relations*, 9th ed. (Homewood, IL: Richard D. Irwin, 1981), p. 793.

[29] For a discussion of the Bakke case, see Gregory and Katz, *Labor and the Law*, pp. 571–73.

on efforts to reduce intraclass rivalries among workers. Breaking down such barriers is the implied route to an effective assault on labor market discrimination in the political-economic perception. Support for efforts to alleviate discriminatory practices through government policy should be encouraged, but that support should be tempered by an understanding of the important functional character of discrimination. Strengthening trade union efforts to break down divisions between white and black workers is seen as essential to unify labor more effectively in its ongoing conflict with capital. The political-economic theory contends that labor's bargaining power will always be less than optimal as long as the labor movement does not come to terms with the divisions within itself caused by racial attitudes and discriminatory practices.

The dual-labor-market theory emphasizes the need to find ways that blacks can gain entrance into primary sector jobs. Efforts at training that simply augment human capital but do not confront the structure of labor markets and the attitudes that breed statistical discrimination will be found wanting. The key policy directives emanating from the dual-labor-market theory are to break down the barriers of entry into primary sector jobs and to foster the creation of more such jobs.

Whichever economic theory of discrimination is most appealing, they all fall short of an adequate explanation for the persistence of economic inequality by race and sex. Laws that have existed since 1964, though successful in their achievements, probably fall short of what was expected of them at the time they were enacted. Glenn Loury concludes that "equal opportunity laws cannot be relied on to eliminate economic differences between races, even over the long run," because inequality is a larger social process involving the intergenerational transmission of inequality.[30] Notwithstanding the difficulty of achieving the goal of eliminating economic discrimination, it is absolutely essential for the legitimacy of a democratic society that the goal be aggressively pursued.

Summary

In the late 1960s and early 1970s, the United States made a commitment to provide equality of opportunity and eliminate overt forms of racial and sexual discrimination in the labor market. A political movement of historical importance thrust such a commitment upon our society. In the decade since discrimination in employment was outlawed, the results have been mixed. There has been obvious improvement in the position of blacks and women in the economy. Yet the major statistical indicators stubbornly persist in reporting approximately the same level of inequality as existed before public policy was directed toward equality of opportunity.

[30] Glenn C. Loury, "A Dynamic Theory of Racial Income Differences," In Phyllis A. Wallace and Annette M. LaMond, eds., *Women, Minorities, and Employment Discrimination* (Lexington, MA: Lexington Books, 1977), p. 156.

To explain the economics of discrimination, economists have devised several models, which follow the paradigms of neoclassical economics, dual-labor-market theory, and political economy.

The neoclassical economic model places emphasis on the employer's taste for discrimination and the extra cost he bears to support this taste. White workers benefit from discrimination, according to this perspective, because their wages are elevated while black worker's are correspondingly lower than they would have been without discrimination. Labor supply in those occupations populated by white workers is reduced, while labor supply is increased among black workers because of their crowding into black occupations. This causes wages to be higher among white workers and lower among black workers than they would be without discrimination.

The political-economic theory challenges this presumption that the employer loses through discrimination. If the divisions among workers caused by racism reduce the overall bargaining power of labor, then capital as a class benefits at the expense of labor as a class. All workers, whether white or black, come out on the short end in this theory of discrimination. Racism is not irrational in this perception of the problem but is functional to capital in keeping the wage level lower than it would be otherwise.

The dual-labor-market theory contends that discrimination takes the form of barring the entry of blacks into jobs in the primary sector of the economy. Personnel directors, acting as gatekeepers, exercise statistical discrimination through their subjective opinion that blacks do not possess the type of work habits needed for successful participation in the internal labor market of the primary sector of the economy. Relegated to jobs in the secondary sector of the economy, black workers develop a work history and work attitude that effectively prevents them from gaining entry into the primary sector of the economy at some later date in their working lives. Public policy that fails to address itself to this aspect of the labor market will be doomed to failure.

For the most part, public policy efforts have been oriented toward direct regulation of discriminatory employment practices through statute and administrative procedures. Employers who work under federal contracts must file affirmative action plans in which they identify procedures they will follow in hiring. Any form of overt discrimination is illegal, and the employer can be fined heavily if found guilty of such practices. Complaints about discrimination in employment can be filed with the Equal Employment Opportunity Commission, whose task it is to monitor hiring practices in the economy.

The path toward equity, justice, and equality of opportunity is a treacherous one that has not been as easily traversed as some thought it would be in the late 1960s and early 1970s. As with so many other aspects of public policy, we have become impatient as a nation with achievements of public policy that do not live up to some set of very ambitious expectations. Toward the end of the 1970s, instead of going back to the drawing board and seeing how public policy could be improved, we began to doubt the wisdom of making public policy efforts at all. The election of Ronald Reagan in 1980 confirmed this national attitude and started a dismantling of some of the machinery for fighting employment discrimination. The United States has always come back to its commitment to equality of opportunity, however, whenever it has strayed from this objective before. I would anticipate the same return to first principles in the 1990s.

Study Questions

1. How have black-white income differentials changed over time (a) for families, (b) for men, and (c) for women?

2. How does the business cycle affect black-white income differentials?

3. In the past several decades, differentials in education between blacks and whites have narrowed, but income differentials have not. Provide an economic explanation for these apparent divergent trends.

4. What are the three basic models of racial and sexual discrimination in the labor market? Critically evaluate the public policy implications of each of these models. What has been the major thrust of public policy in the area of economic discrimination, and how does this relate (if at all) to economic theories of discrimination?

Further Reading

Arrow, Kenneth J. "Discrimination in the Labour Market." In *Readings in Labour Economics*, edited by J. E. King. Oxford: Oxford University Press, 1980. Pp. 117–35.

Becker, Gary. *The Economics of Discrimination*. 2nd ed. Chicago: University of Chicago Press, 1971.

Bergmann, Barbara. "The Effect on White Incomes of Discrimination in Employment" *Journal of Political Economy* 2 (March–April 1971), pp. 294–313.

Doeringer, Peter B., and Michael J. Piore. *Internal Labor Markets and Manpower Analysis*. Lexington, MA: D. C. Heath and Co., 1971. Chap. 7.

Reich, Michael. *Racial Inequality: A Political-Economic Analysis*. Princeton, NJ: Princeton University Press, 1981.

II

Labor and the Macroeconomy

13

Unemployment: Meaning and Measurement

Each month the press reports statistics on the unemployment rate. It has gone up or down by a fraction of a percentage point; the unemployment rate for blacks is at a certain level, the rate for whites is at a different level, and so on. We take for granted that these announcements about the unemployment rate have some meaning in terms of the way the economy is functioning, the strength or weakness of the economy, and the stage of the business cycle (whether the economy is entering a recession or recovering from one). The unemployment rate also connotes some sense of *individual welfare* in addition to its implications about the health of the economy. Economic distress is associated with a high level of unemployment. The Department of Labor's press releases on unemployment conjure up bleak images of bread lines from the Great Depression whenever the figures are adverse.

What does the unemployment rate measure and what does it mean? This is the issue examined in this chapter. And the answer is not what you might think. The measurement of unemployment is surrounded by controversy because different users of the statistic want it to convey different meanings. The announcement of an unemployment rate reverberates emotionally within us, since it conveys some sense of individual distress. At the same time, government statisticians want the unemployment rate to signify certain objective developments in the economy. Can one statistic tell us something about individual distress and also convey an objective measure of the state of the economy?

Many economists contend the answer to that question is no. A single statistic cannot do double duty, revealing the state of the economy and measuring individual welfare at the same time. The matter is complicated further by the fact that the unemployment rate is used in public policy as a triggering device for assistance to individuals and communities. So the debate about the need for a good measure of unemployment is not purely academic, although academic considerations are important for evaluating hypotheses about the causes of unemployment by comparing theories of unemployment with statistics. For administrators of government programs, the unemployment rate is a signal to initiate spending, and, therefore, the need for an accurate measure of unemployment is critical.

These problems with the measurement of unemployment have led to the creation of two national commissions in the past 25 years. The most recent one, the National Commission on Employment and Unemployment Statistics, issued its report in 1979. They concluded that, flawed though the unemployment measure may be, it is better than any alternative. The commission recommended no major changes in the way in which unemployment is measured or the way in which the statistics are gathered.

In this chapter we examine how unemployment is measured and what it means in the context of the federal government's statistical gathering procedures. Included in the chapter is a discussion of issues of labor force composition, labor force participation rates, and alternative measures of unemployment. In subsequent chapters the theoretical and policy issues raised by these statistics on unemployment will be examined.

The Labor Force in the American Economy

The labor force in the American economy provides the launching point for a discussion of unemployment—its meaning and measurement. The labor force is the most inclusive statistic on wage and salary earners in the economy. It includes those people working as well as those unemployed. Individuals of working age (16 years old and over), not presently housed in an institution (such as a prison or a mental institution), are considered in the labor force if they are either employed or unemployed.[1] Being employed or unemployed constitutes *participation* in the labor force and individuals in either of those two categories are called *labor force participants*. An individual who is neither employed nor unemployed yet is at least 16 years old and not housed in an institution is called a *nonparticipant* in the labor force. Such individuals show up in the statistics as *not in the labor force*. The labor force categories are shown schematically in Figure 13-1.

---

[1] Some concepts of the labor force include people in the military. A more narrow definition of a *civilian* labor force excludes military personnel. It is unclear which is better for measuring labor force behavior, particularly since the military is "all-volunteer" and competes in the labor market for its personnel like any other employer.

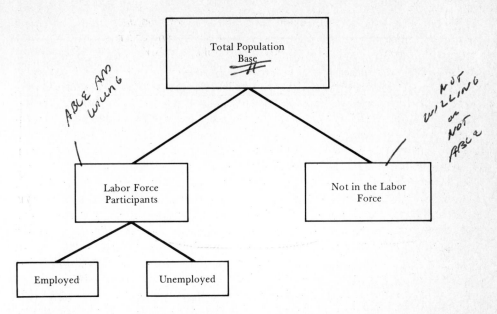

Handwritten annotations: "ABLE AND WILLING" (left), "NOT WILLING OR NOT ABLE" (right), crossed-out "H" under "Total Population Base"

Figure 13-1   The Labor Force Categories

At first glance such a tripartite classification—employed, unemployed, or not in the labor force—appears simple and straightforward. But looks are deceiving, and these three statistical concepts have occasioned as much controversy as any the government produces.

The basic data on the postwar labor force are contained in Table 13-1. The labor force concept used in this table includes all individuals (military and civilian), age 16 and over, who are not in an institution, such as a prison or a mental institution. In 1985, out of a total eligible population base of nearly 180 million, more than 117 million were counted as being in the labor force.

Handwritten: $1985 \rightarrow \frac{117}{180} = 65\%$ OF THE TOTAL ELIGIBLE POPULATION WERE IN THE LABOR FORCE!

Labor Force Participation Rates

The relationship between those in the labor force and the total eligible population is called a *labor force participation rate* and is shown in column 3 of Table 13-1. Specifically, the labor force participation rate is the ratio of labor force participants to the total eligible population. The labor force participation rate has steadily increased since the end of World War II. In 1947, the labor force participation rate was 59 percent and in 1985 it had increased to 65 percent. The six percentage point increase over a 29-year period may not seem like much of an increase. However, when applied to a large population base of nearly 180 million in 1985, the increased labor force participation rate means that the American economy must generate more jobs than it would have to otherwise simply to accommodate the increased percentage of people who want to work in the American economy.

Handwritten at bottom: LABOR FORCE PARTIC. RATE = THAT # IN THE LABOR FORCE / TOTAL ELIGIBLE POPULATION

Table 13-1 The Labor Force, Selected Years 1947–1985

Year	Total Population[a] (thousands)	Total Labor Force (thousands)	Labor Force Participation Rate (%) (2)/(1)
	(1)	(2)	(3)
1947	103,418	60,941	58.9
1950	106,645	63,858	59.9
1953	109,287	65,246	59.7
1956	112,919	68,517	60.7
1959	117,117	70,157	59.9
1962	122,214	72,675	59.5
1965	128,459	76,401	59.5
1968	134,281	80,990	60.3
1971	142,189	86,355	60.7
1974	151,841	93,670	61.7
1978	163,541	103,882	63.5
1980	169,349	108,544	64.1
1982	173,939	111,872	64.3
1985	179,912	117,167	65.1

INCREASING TREND (handwritten annotation)

[a]Noninstitutional population, age 16 years and over, including military personnel.
Source: U.S. Department of Labor, *Employment and Earnings*, (January, 1983), p. 11; and U.S. Department of Labor, *Employment and Earnings*, (January, 1986), p. 12.

Significant demographic shifts have occurred in the American economy since the end of World War II. There are today proportionally more women and young workers in the labor force than was the case at the end of World War II. In the past two decades the trend has accelerated toward higher proportions of the labor force concentrated among women and young workers. For example, in 1958 women constituted 31.5 percent of the total labor force; in 1985 they were over 47 percent. Young workers, between the ages of 16 and 24, accounted for 17.2 percent of the total labor force in 1958, and in 1984 they were 21 percent.[2] The changing age-sex demographics of the labor force is an important issue that will recur throughout the discussion of unemployment and inflation.

Table 13-2 provides an insight into what has been happening with female participation in the labor force and the postwar trend toward proportionally more women

[2] U.S. Bureau of the Census, *Statistical Abstract of the United States, 1986* (Washington: Government Printing Office), p. 392; Council of Economic Advisers, *Economic Report of the President, 1986* (Washington: Government Printing Office), p. 290.

U.S. labor force — ≈ 126,000,000

in the labor force. Male participation rates have been steadily declining since the end of World War II, while female participation rates have been increasing. The male participation rate fell from 86 percent in 1950 to 77 percent in 1985. Taken by itself, this would have meant that the overall labor force participation rate would have decreased during those 36 years. But it did not, as Table 13-2 reveals, and the reason is that women began entering the labor force in numbers more than sufficient to compensate for the declining labor force participation rate of men. Labor force participation rates for women increased from 34 percent in 1950 to 54 percent in 1985. The increase in female participation rates, as explained in Chapter 2, has been caused by the larger number of career-oriented women, an increased number of female-headed households, changing social attitudes about women working, and the need for a family to have two incomes to keep inflation from eroding the household's standard of living.

These observations are corroborated by a closer look at the statistics in Table 13-2. Most of the growth in the labor force participation rate for women has occurred since 1965, when the forces propelling women into the labor force took hold. From that year until 1985, 16 percentage points were added to the participation rate for

Table 13-2 Civilian Labor Force Participation Rates, by Sex, Selected Years, 1947–1985

Year	Labor Force Participation Rates (%)		
	Total	Male	Female
1947	57.4	n.a.[a]	n.a.[a]
1950	58.3	86.4	33.9
1953	57.0	86.0	34.4
1956	60.0	85.6	35.7
1959	59.3	83.8	36.0
1962	58.8	82.1	36.7
1965	58.9	80.8	38.1
1968	59.6	80.4	40.7
1971	60.2	79.6	42.6
1974	61.3	79.4	45.2
1978	63.2	78.6	49.4
1980	63.8	78.2	51.2
1982	64.0	77.4	52.4
1985	64.8	77.0	54.1

[a]Not available.

Source: U.S. Department of Labor, *Employment and Training Report of the President, 1979* (Washington: Government Printing Office), pp. 240, 241; *Employment and Training Report of the President, 1981*, pp. 126–27; Council of Economic Advisers, *Economic Report of the President, 1986* (Washington: Government Printing Office), p. 294.

Table 13-3 Civilian Labor Force Participation Rates by Age and Sex, 1950 and 1985.

(handwritten: MEN DECREASE IN ALL CATEGORIES)

(handwritten: OLDER MALES RETURN EARLIER)

(handwritten: WOMEN INCREASE IN ALL CATEGORIES)

	Labor Force Participation Rates (%)			
	1950		1985	
Age Group	Male	Female	Male	Female
16 and 17	51.3	30.1	45.1	42.1
18 and 19	75.8	51.3	68.9	61.7
20–24	87.9	46.0	85.0	71.8
25–34	96.0	34.0	94.7	70.9
35–44	97.6	39.1	95.0	71.8
45–54	95.8	37.9	91.0	64.4
55–64	86.9	27.0	67.9	42.0
65 and over	45.8	9.7	15.8	7.3
Total	86.4	33.9	76.3	54.5

(handwritten: LARGEST DECREASE)

(handwritten: SMALLEST INCREASE WOMEN)

Source: U.S. Department of Labor, *Handbook of Labor Statistics* (Washington: Government Printing Office, 1985), pp. 18–19; U.S. Department of Labor, *Employment and Earnings* (January, 1986), p. 154.

(handwritten: MORE YOUNG PEOPLE ARE STAYING IN SCHOOL)

women; only 4.2 percentage points had been added during the previous 15 years. The overall participation rate, for both men and women, was nearly constant from 1947 to 1965; then it began to increase, solely because of the growth of labor force participation rates among women.

The steadily declining labor force participation rate for men, on the other hand, is due to earlier retirements and the phenomenon of stretching education over a longer time span.[3]

These figures on labor force participation reveal facts about some of the most important social phenomena in the United States in the past 15 years. Table 13-3 provides another, more-detailed examination of the changing participation rates for men and women. In this table the labor force participation rates for men and women are broken down into age groups and are compared for the years 1950 and 1985. The labor force participation rate for men over 65 fell from more than 45 percent in 1950 to about 16 percent in 1985. This change reflects more extensive retirement at age 65. The decline in male participation rates for the 55–64 age group, from 87 percent to 68 percent, is an indicator of the trend toward even earlier retirement. Whether this trend will continue into the future is problematical because of the impact of inflation, which erodes retirement nest eggs, and because of new federal legislation,

---

[3] Students are *not* considered to be in the labor force unless they evidence some specific job-seeking behavior or are employed.

which has changed the mandatory retirement age. Women of all age groups showed dramatic increases in their labor force participation rates.

Measuring Unemployment

UNEMPLOYMENT = f (LAWS, SOCIOLOGICAL RACIAL, ECONMIC FORCES,) RATE

For a typical recent year, 1985, Table 13-4 provides a summary of the employment status of the civilian labor force broken down between racial groups—blacks and whites. In this table, military personnel have been subtracted from the noninstitutional population base to arrive at a *civilian* population base. A civilian individual 16 years or older, not housed in an institution, is assigned to one of three labor force categories: employed, unemployed, or not in the labor force. For whites, 35 percent were not in the labor force in 1985; the figure for blacks was 37 percent. Unemployment rates, however, vary substantially between blacks and whites. In 1985 the black unemployment rate was 15.1 percent, compared with 6.2 percent for whites. Since World War II, for all but a few years, the black unemployment rate has been about twice that of whites.

What distinguishes being counted as unemployed from being considered not in the labor force? There are thin lines in the official government statistics between the classifications of being employed, being unemployed, and not being in the labor force. Many times the divisions among these three categories are ambiguous.

The public at large also has some mistaken notions about how unemployment is measured in the American economy and what it represents. For example, it is widely believed that unemployment statistics indicate the number of persons receiving

Table 13-4 Employment Status of the Civilian Labor Force by Race, 1985[a]

	White	Black	Total
Civilian, noninstitutional population (thousands)	153,679	19,664[b]	178,206
Civilian labor force (thousands)	99,926	12,364	115,461
Percentage of civilian, noninstitutional population	65.0	62.9	64.8
Employed (thousands)	93,736	10,501	107,150
Percentage of civilian labor force	93.8	84.9	92.8
Unemployed (thousands)	6,191	1,864	8,312
Percentage of civilian labor force	6.2	15.1	7.2
Not in labor force (thousands)	53,753	7,299	62,744
Percentage of civilian, noninstitutional population	35.0	37.1	35.2

[a]Excludes military personnel   *EXCLUDES MILITARY PERSONELL*
[b]Black population only. Therefore, components do not add up to total.
Source: U.S. Department of Labor, *Employment and Earnings* (January, 1986), pp. 154–56.

unemployment compensation. This is not the case. Individuals who receive unemployment compensation are but a fraction of the total count of the unemployed. There are two reasons for this. First, not all individuals who are without work are eligible to collect unemployment compensation. Others have exhausted their benefits and are not collecting unemployment compensation although previously they had done so. Second, even among those eligible for unemployment compensation, there are individuals who do not register with the local employment office. Some may not be aware that they are eligible for unemployment compensation; others may not make the effort to register.

Beyond the manner in which the statistics are gathered, there are also misconceptions about how the government defines unemployment. The most widely held belief is that the official definition of unemployment—that statistic we hear so much about—includes all individuals who are not presently employed but would like to work. This is not the case. Not only must an individual be unemployed and desiring work, he or she must also be actively looking for work. The Bureau of Labor Statistics (BLS) of the Department of Labor, which collects and publishes the unemployment statistics, defines unemployment as including "those who did not work at all during the survey week, were looking for work, and were available for work."[4] The BLS goes on to specify what constitutes looking for work: registering at a public or private employment agency, applying for work directly, answering newspaper ads, and so forth. In short, in order for a person to be officially counted as being unemployed, he or she not only must be out of work but must be actively seeking a job, as evidenced by actions during the particular period of time for which the survey is taken.

 If you are unemployed but have not evidenced active job-seeking behavior as defined by the BLS, you are counted as neither employed nor unemployed but are considered to be *not in the labor force*. This is where the controversy begins. Those critics of the unemployment measure who claim it *understates* the problem point to the fact that many may be unemployed under a concept that stresses being out of work but interested in finding a job. Such people will not be counted as unemployed under the BLS definition, however, unless they have shown evidence of active job-seeking behavior during the period covered by the monthly survey.

The gray area between interest in finding a job and active job-seeking behavior becomes particularly acute during a recession or when the economy has been stagnant for some period of time. Many individuals will become discouraged under such economic circumstances and give up looking for work after months of unemployment. Instead of being counted as unemployed, the *discouraged unemployed worker* slides over into the not-in-the-labor-force category the moment he or she abandons active job seeking.

Such behavior might be quite understandable—even rational. Repeated failure at finding a job is a serious assault on one's identity. Avoidance of the psychological

---

[4] U.S. Department of Labor, *BLS Handbook of Methods* (Washington: Government Printing Office, 1976), p. 6.

disorientation repeated failures cause will take the form of not looking for work. When this occurs, an unemployed person begins to be counted as not in the labor force.

The problem becomes more complicated when we consider the concept of *job search*. There are costs and benefits to seeking a job. The costs arise in the form of bus fare, opportunity cost, and grooming and clothing expenses. The benefits are clear: a new job. For someone who has experienced repeated failures and is living on the margin of survival, however, spending the equivalent of a good meal to look for work might be economically irrational, particularly when the probability of success is perceived to be so low.

Economists have sought to measure this phenomenon of the discouraged worker. Some estimates place its impact at about half the measured unemployment rate. This means that when the rate of unemployment is 6 percent as measured by the BLS, counting all those who are out of work but interested in finding a job would increase the unemployment rate to 9 percent. This is the outer limit on such estimates. But whatever the magnitude of the discouraged worker effect, it does bias the measured unemployment rate toward an understatement of the magnitude of unemployment under an alternative definition that would not require active evidence of job-seeking behavior to qualify a person as unemployed.

Critics on the other side of this issue claim that the measured unemployment rate *overstates* the problem because it contains individuals whose attachment to the labor force is ephemeral. An individual will be counted as unemployed if he or she answered one newspaper ad during the survey month or went for one interview to tender an application. The *intensity* of the desire to work is missed by the rigid definition used by the BLS. Evidence in support of this proposition is offered by these critics by pointing to the large number of women who are now in the labor force. According to this view, many of these female workers are "secondary" because their earnings are not central to the household's survival but provide the margin for minimal luxury. Though counted as unemployed, these secondary workers have a low intensity of attachment to the labor force, and therefore, according to these critics, their inclusion overstates the unemployment problem.

In recent years, however, inflation has transferred more "secondary" workers into a primary earning necessity in the household. Without two income recipients in the household, many families would find their economic situations precarious and their decline in living standards unacceptable.

Whichever side of the debate will turn out to be more persuasive, on one point there is agreement: when the economy is growing and creating jobs, more people enter the labor force who were previously in the not-in-the-labor-force category, and as a consequence the unemployment rate responds more sluggishly than one might expect to increased economic activity. For example, in 1985 there were 8.3 million workers counted as unemployed by the BLS. Would it have taken 8.3 million additional jobs, over and above those that already existed, to employ everyone? No, it would have taken *more* than 8.3 million new jobs, because as the jobs were created, people would slide over from the not-in-the-labor-force category to either the employed or the unemployed category. They would either take jobs or begin to evidence the type

[handwritten annotation: (PT) — UNEMPLOYMENT RATES DO NOT TELL THE WHOLE STORY]

of job-seeking behavior that would place them in the count of the unemployed, although previously they had been considered not in the labor force.

[handwritten margin note: WOW]

Estimating the precise effect of additional labor force entrants absorbing the new jobs is difficult. A study done on this problem during the 1960s indicated that in the early part of that decade an increase of 1,000 new jobs would bring forth an additional 454 labor force participants.[5] This means that only 546 of the 1,000 new jobs would be taken by the preexisting measured unemployed. Two jobs would have to be created to reduce the measured unemployment by one unemployed person.

[handwritten margin note: ✗ Exam]

By the end of the 1960s, the same study indicated that new entrants were taking up proportionately more of the new jobs being created. In fact, the new entrants into the labor force in the late 1960s were taking up new jobs as fast as they were being created. There was nearly a one-to-one ratio; for every new job created, there would be one new entrant into the labor force. The aggregate demand policies to reduce unemployment had to work harder and harder just to stay even with the new entrants into the labor force in the late 1960s, as more women participated in the labor force compared with the 1940s or 1950s.[6]

[handwritten margin note: ✗]

The shift in measured labor force status from unemployed to not in the labor force is quite substantial. It is estimated that about half of all women who become unemployed drop out of the labor force for a time and one-third of men who are unemployed drift over into the not-in-the-labor-force category. About 40 percent of all measured unemployment originates from the not-in-the-labor-force category, as people change their status in the labor force and begin to search for jobs.[7]

The labor force is dynamic, and its measurements have a difficult time keeping up with this fluidity. "Unemployment is the most subjective statistic," says Glen Cain, "because respondents must give answers that depend on their beliefs about their ability to work and their sincerity in searching for work." However, "the usefulness of the labor force statistics for economic analysis depends mainly on the degree to which they measure changes in the 'objective' circumstances of the economy."[8]

The movements into and out of the labor force are so large that some researchers question whether the unemployment rate tells us anything about the business cycle. The BLS, which collects the statistics, reports that nearly 70 percent of those who become employed in a typical month were counted as being out of the labor force in

---

[5] Thomas F. Dernburg, "The Behavior of Unemployment, 1967–1969," in Harold L. Sheppard et al., *The Political Economy of Public Service Employment* (Lexington: D. C. Heath and Co., 1972), pp. 176–177.

[6] The shift from unemployed to not-in-the-labor-force status is examined for demographic groups in William G. Bowen and T. Aldrich Finegan, *The Economics of Labor Force Participation* (Princeton, NJ: Princeton University Press, 1969).

[7] George A. Akerlof and Brian G. M. Main, "Unemployment Spells and Unemployment Experience," *American Economic Review* 70, no. 5 (December 1980), p. 887.

[8] Glen G. Gain, "Labor Force Concepts and Definitions in View of Their Purposes," National Commission on Employment and Unemployment Statistics, *Concepts and Data Needs: Appendix Volume I* (Washington: National Commission on Employment and Unemployment Statistics, 1980), pp. 7–8.

the previous month.[9] In an average month between 1968 and 1976, 3.8 million people left the labor force and 4.0 million entered the labor force.[10] We return to this problem toward the end of this chapter when unemployment flows are considered more carefully. To understand the problem completely, we have to develop several more measures of employment and unemployment.

Alternative Measures of Unemployment

(PT) — BOTH ALTERNATIVE MEASURES CLAIM THAT BLS STATISTICS OVERSTATE unemploy!)

Dissatisfaction with the present way in which unemployment is measured has prompted experimentation with alternative conceptualizations and measures of unemployment. One focuses on an entirely different aspect to gauge the strength or weakness of the economy. This is the measure of the *employment rate*—an attempt to measure what proportion of the eligible population is actually employed. Another seeks to control for the changing composition of the labor force over time in order to obtain a better specification of the change in unemployment rates for different periods of time. This is called the *fixed weight unemployment measure*.

demographic

EXAM

The Employment Rate

The employment rate measures the proportion of the civilian noninstitutional population, age 16 and over, that is employed. It is an attempt to create some measure of the number of people in the American economy who are actually employed, in relation to the number of citizens who could potentially work. The employment rate is not simply the difference between the percentage of the labor force counted as unemployed and 100. The unemployment rate uses as its base the labor force; the employment rate uses as its base the total civilian population, excluding certain age groups and people in institutions. In this way the difficult distinction between being in the labor force and not being in the labor force need not be made.

Data on employment rates for selected years are presented in Table 13-5, along with the measured unemployment rates. Figure 13-2 represents a plot of these data. Notice first that the unemployment rate varies more widely from year to year than does the employment rate. This occurs because the unemployment rate is very sensitive to the measure of the labor force and shows the effect of people dropping out of and moving back into the labor force in response to changes in employment opportunities over the business cycle. The employment rate, on the other hand, does not suffer from

---

[9] Kim B. Clark and Lawrence H. Summers, "Labor Market Dynamics and Unemployment: A Reconsideration," *Brookings Papers on Economic Activity* 1 (1979), p. 25.

[10] Ibid.

Table 13-5 The Rates of Employment and Unemployment, Selected Years, 1947–1985

Year	Civilian Noninstitutional Population, 16 Years and Over (thousands)	Employment (thousands)	Employment Rate (%)	Unemployment Rate (%)
	(1)	(2)	(1)/(2)	(4)
1947	103,418	57,038	55.1	3.9
1950	106,645	58,918	55.2	5.3
1953	110,601	61,179	55.3	2.9
1956	113,811	63,779	56.0	4.1
1959	117,881	64,630	54.8	5.5
1962	122,981	66,702	54.2	5.5
1965	129,236	71,088	55.0	4.5
1968	135,562	75,920	56.0	3.6
1971	143,032	79,367	55.4	5.9
1974	152,349	86,794	57.0	5.6
1977	161,166	92,017	57.1	7.1
1982	174,451	99,526	57.1	9.7
1985	178,206	107,150	60.1	7.2

Source: Council of Economic Advisers, *Economic Report of the President, 1983* (Washington: Government Printing Office), p. 196; and U.S. Department of Labor, *Employment and Earnings* (January, 1986), p. 152.

that statistical problem. Second, the unemployment rate has increased since 1947, while the employment rate has remained constant over that same time period and, in fact, increased in the 1980s. How can both the unemployment rate and the employment rate increase at the same time? The answer is that more people are entering the labor force today and that people are doing so in greater proportions than ever before. As a consequence, the number of new jobs that have to be created each year must grow at an increasing rate to keep pace with the new entrants who want jobs and the unemployed who are seeking jobs. As pointed out earlier in this chapter, this is particularly true for women, who are entering the labor force in increasing proportions.

Those who criticize the use of the unemployment rate as a barometer of economic health point to this phenomenon of a steady, even rising, employment rate, which indicates that more Americans are working today, as a proportion of the eligible civilian population, than ever before—60 percent in 1985 compared to 55 percent in 1947. The traditional unemployment rate, in their eyes, overstates the weakness of the economy.

Which measure of economic health is legitimate—the employment rate or the unemployment rate? It is difficult to say, since the unemployment rate and the employ-

Employment Rate: ~~Eligible~~ Those Employed
––––––––––––––––––––––
Eligible Population

ment rate measure different aspects of the economy. The unemployment rate counts individuals who want to work and are prepared to actively seek work. For them, the economy has failed since it has not provided a job. On the other hand, the employment rate reflects the ability of our economy to accommodate the aspirations of a segment of society that heretofore did not seek employment at such a rate. This reflects a strength and buoyancy in the economy—an absorptive capacity of which we can be proud. However, this does not negate the despair that the unemployed face each day as they contemplate more time without work.

Fixed Weight Unemployment Rate

Unemployment affects different segments of the American population unevenly. Not every group in the American economy has the same unemployment rate. As long as the unemployment statistics have been gathered, the unemployment rates for youths, blacks, and women have been higher than they have been for prime-age white males. In 1985, for example, when the overall unemployment rate for the entire economy

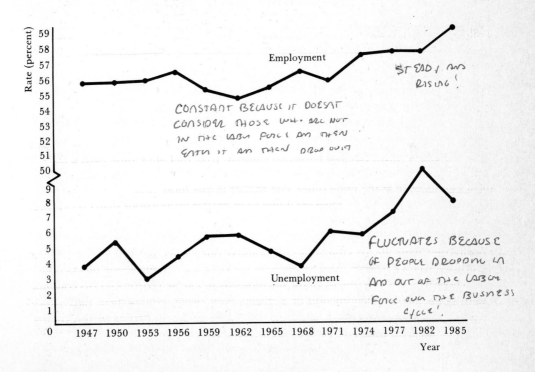

Figure 13-2 Employment and Unemployment Rates, Selected Years, 1947–1985

Table 13-6 Unemployment Rates by Age, Sex, and Race, (1985)   *1985*

	Unemployment Rates (%)				
	White		Black		
Age Group	Male	Female	Male	Female	All Workers
16–17	19.2	17.2	42.9	44.3	21.0
18–19	14.7	13.1	40.0	36.4	17.0
20–24	9.7	8.5	23.5	25.6	11.1
25–34	5.7	6.2	13.8	15.1	7.0
35–44	4.3	4.9	9.6	9.3	5.1
45–54	4.1	4.5	9.7	6.8	4.7
55–64	4.0	4.1	7.9	6.0	4.3
65 and over	2.7	3.1	8.9	5.2	3.2
Total, 16 years and over	6.1	6.4	15.3	14.9	7.2

HIGH %

MALES   FEMALE

Source: U.S. Department of Labor, *Employment and Earnings* (January, 1986), pp. 154–56.

was 7.2 percent, the rate for blacks was 15.1 percent. For young people, under 20 years of age, the unemployment rate in 1985 was 18.5 percent.[11]

In Table 13-6 data are presented for the year 1985, showing the unemployment rates for men and women, white and black, broken down by age categories. The unemployment rate for blacks is higher for every age group than it is for whites. The most stark unemployment figures are those for young workers. Blacks between the ages of 16 and 17 have unemployment rates in the 40 percent range. The rates improve slightly for the 18–19-year-olds and drop to the 20 percent range for 20–24-year-olds. For white youths, the picture is better.

The public policy problems posed by these statistics on youth unemployment will be considered in a later chapter. For the present, the implications of this phenomenon for the measurement of unemployment and the comparison of unemployment rates over time are important. The problem that arises in comparing unemployment rates over time is that although young workers and female workers have always had higher unemployment rates than prime-age white males, in recent years these two groups have made up larger proportions of the labor force. Statistics were presented on this phenomenon earlier in this chapter, but they are worth repeating here. In

---

[11] Council of Economic Advisers, *Economic Report of the President, 1986* (Washington: Government Printing Office), p. 290.

(PT) → Young people and women are predominately growing in the labor force. Fixed weight removes this effect.

1958 persons between the ages of 16 and 24 accounted for 17 percent of the labor force, and in 1984 they accounted for 21 percent. Women made up 31.5 percent of the labor force in 1958; they were 47 percent of the labor force in 1985. Since women and young people have always had higher unemployment rates, their increased share of the labor force would push the overall unemployment rate upward. The unemployment rate would increase because of the compositional shift in the labor force.

There has been an increased component of women in the labor force because of changing social attitudes toward work and the need for additional income earners in the household to keep pace with inflation. Young workers have increased their share of the labor force because of the sheer weight of the postwar demographics. In the 1970s the work force received a burst of new entrants, young workers who were born after World War II, when the baby boom distorted the demographics. Furthermore, increased retirements at earlier ages reduced the size of the labor force at the other end of the age structure.

(PT) → To the extent that young workers and female workers compose a larger proportion of the labor force, the average unemployment rate for the entire population will be higher. How much higher? In Table 13-7 calculations performed by the President's Council of Economic Advisers in 1978 are presented that bear on this issue. An adjusted unemployment rate is shown, which takes account of the shifting demographics of the labor force, along with the standard BLS measurement of unemployment. The adjusted unemployment rate was computed by using the demographic

Table 13-7 Fixed-Weight Unemployment Rate and Measured Unemployment Rate, Selected Years 1956–1977

Year	BLS Measured Unemployment Rate (%)	Fixed-Weight Unemployment Rate (%)[a]
1956	4.0	4.0
1965	4.4	4.1
1968	3.6	3.3
1970	4.9	4.4
1971	5.9	5.2
1972	5.6	4.8
1973	4.9	4.1
1974	5.6	4.8
1975	8.5	7.4
1976	7.7	6.7
1977 (4th quarter)	6.6	5.8

Lower than the actual statistics

Exam — Fixed weight stats are lower than the BLS statistics.

[a]Unemployment rate using labor force composition in 1956.
Source: Council of Economic Advisers, *Economic Report of the President, 1978* (Washington: Government Printing Office), p. 170.

composition of the labor force in 1956 in terms of age and sex and then applying those *fixed weights* to the unemployment rates for those demographic groups in other years. In essence, the adjusted unemployment rate provides an estimate of the unemployment rate for each year as if the composition of the labor force were the same as it was in 1956.[12] In this way, the effect of the addition of more young workers and more female workers to the labor force since 1956 has been removed.

The results show that the unemployment rate would have been lower in 1977 if there had been no demographic shifts in the composition of labor force since 1956. In 1977, for example, the average unemployment rate would have been 5.8 percent on a fixed weight basis, instead of the 6.6 percent reported by the BLS for the fourth quarter of that year.

Is this a legitimate adjustment? For the woman or young person without a job, the answer would be no. For the analyst of unemployment statistics the answer could be different. If the implicit presumption holds that unemployment for these groups is not as great a social problem as it is for prime-age males, then the conclusion would be that the BLS measured unemployment rate represents an overstatement of the unemployment problem. However, this requires a judgment that unemployment is of greater or lesser consequence depending on one's age and sex.

Analysts of the demographics of the labor force point out that the baby boom is over and that in the 1980s the labor force will tilt perceptibly toward a higher average age. In 1985 about 39 percent of the population was under 24 years of age. By 1990 this figure will drop to 36 percent. The population over 35 will increase from 42 percent to 46 percent by 1990.[13] This fact, in and of itself, will alleviate some of the problem with the average unemployment rate, if the rates for these different demographic groups remain as they are today, because fewer members of some high-risk unemployment groups will be in the population.

Measuring the Severity of Unemployment

Unemployment statistics show the cold, hard facts of economic life. They are both an average and an aggregate statistic. As such, the unemployment figures reported each month do not reveal the severity of the unemployment experience for an individual worker, nor do they tell us much about the incidence of unemployment in the economy. By incidence is meant the number of actual people afflicted by unemployment over a specific period of time. Something can be said about the severity of unemployment, but little is known about unemployment's incidence.

---

[12] See P. O. Flaim, "The Effect of Demographic Changes on the Nation's Unemployment Rate," *Monthly Labor Review* 102, no. 3 (March 1979), pp. 13–23.

[13] Alfred L. Malabre, "Sputtering '70's," *Wall Street Journal*, December 18, 1979, p. 1.

MEASUREMENT OF SEVERITY

One way to measure the severity of unemployment is through a measure of the *length of unemployment.* By convention, people who are unemployed for 15 consecutive weeks or longer are called the *long-term unemployed.* In 1985, for example, of the 8.3 million total unemployed, some 2.8 million had experienced unemployment that year of 15 weeks or more. Computing the ratio of long-term unemployed to total unemployed produces a *long-term unemployment rate.* These long-term unemployment rates are presented in Table 13-8, and they are plotted in Figure 13-3 along with the overall unemployment rate.

For some years the figures on long-term unemployment are quite high. In 1985 the rate was nearly 34 percent, a postwar peak. For other years it can fall as low as 13 percent, as it did in 1969. Normally it is in the 20 percent range. From Figure 13-3 it is clear that the long-term unemployment rate exhibits far more volatility than does the overall unemployment rate. The two rates move together somewhat, in that higher overall unemployment rates normally signify conditions that lead to higher long-term unemployment rates.

The fact that normally the long-term unemployed account for about one-fifth to one-quarter of the unemployed means that for a significant proportion of the unemployed the condition is not transitory. They are not the *frictionally unemployed*—people who have left one job and are awaiting the beginning of another job. For the long-term unemployed something more fundamental is going on that prevents them from finding a job quickly.

While there is some statistical information on the severity of unemployment, there is no direct measure of the incidence of unemployment. Incidence of unemployment refers to the number of people that actually experience some unemployment in a year. The problem arises from the way in which the unemployment statistics are gathered. Each month the BLS surveys a group of households and reports, for instance, that 6 percent of the labor force was unemployed in a particular month. The next month the BLS might again discover that 6 percent of the labor force was unemployed. In the second survey month, however, an entirely different 6 percent of the labor force could have become unemployed, while the 6 percent found unemployed in the first month could have begun working again. If this were the case, then over a two-month period 12 percent of the labor force would have experienced some unemployment, and for two months combined there would be a six percent *average* unemployment rate, which the BLS would report. The problem is that we know very little about the number of people who experience unemployment in a span of time.

When the BLS reports a 6 percent average unemployment rate for the year, this could mean that 72 percent of the labor force experienced some unemployment that year, if each month a different 6 percent of the population were unemployed. No doubt, the number of people who actually experience some unemployment during a year is nowhere near this rate. But there is also no doubt that more than 6 percent of the labor force have experienced unemployment during a year when the average unemployment rate is 6 percent.

The Bureau of Labor Statistics estimates that in 1985, when the average

Table 13-8 Long-Term Unemployment Rate and
Unemployment Rate, 1957–1985

Year	Long-Term Unemployment Rate (%)[a]	Unemployment Rate (%)
1957	19.1	4.2
1958	31.0	6.8
1959	27.2	5.5
1960	24.3	5.5
1961	31.9	6.7
1962	27.9	5.5
1963	26.1	5.7
1964	25.1	5.2
1965	21.8	4.5
1966	18.0	3.8
1967	15.1	3.8
1968	14.6	3.6
1969	13.2	3.5
1970	16.2	4.9
1971	23.6	5.9
1972	23.9	5.6
1973	18.9	4.9
1974	18.4	5.6
1975	31.7	8.5
1976	32.0	7.7
1977	27.9	7.0
1978	22.8	6.0
1979	20.2	5.8
1980	24.5	7.1
1981	27.6	7.6
1982	32.6	9.7
1985	33.8	7.2

[a]Number of people unemployed 15 weeks or more divided by total
unemployed.
Source: U.S. Department of Labor, *Handbook of Labor Statistics, 1978*
(Washington: Government Printing Office), p. 201; U.S. Department
of Labor, *Employment and Training Report of the President, 1979* (Washington: Government Printing Office), pp. 265, 279; Council of Economic Advisers, *Economic Report of the President, 1983* (Washington:
Government Printing Office), pp. 196, 202; U.S. Department of Labor,
Employment and Earnings (January, 1986), pp. 153, 167.

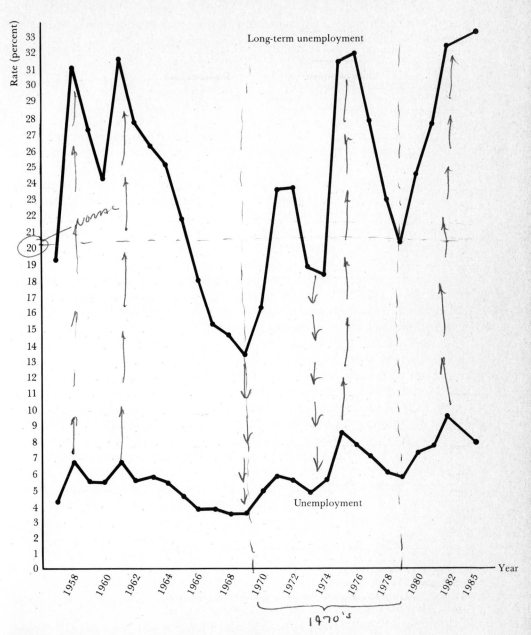

Figure 13-3 Long-Term Unemployment Rate and Unemployment Rate, 1957–1985

[handwritten: 1985 - UNEMPLOYMENT RATE = 7.2 → INCIDENCE = 18 % → ABOUT 2X]

unemployment rate was 7.2 percent, about 18 percent of the labor force experienced some unemployment during the year—some 21 million individuals.[14]

Unemployment Flows

The labor force is changing all the time. The shadings of meaning between being in the labor force and being out of the labor force do not reflect the real dynamics of an individual's activity in the economy. Whereas any one individual's activity in the economy is constantly changing, the measure of unemployment is static. The problem lies in trying to take an accurate snapshot of a fluid process that is constantly in motion.

To make some sense out of the dynamic character of the labor force, economists have devised the concept of *unemployment flows*. Each week some individuals enter the labor force to look for work; others stop looking for work and are no longer counted as being in the labor force. Some individuals who were previously unemployed find jobs; others lose their jobs and become unemployed. The probabilities associated with these changes in labor force status vary demographically and occupationally.[15] The dynamics of these unemployment flows are captured imperfectly by such a snapshot measure of unemployment as the one now defined by the BLS.

Associated with this problem with the measurement of unemployment is the distinction between the number of spells of unemployment an individual experiences in a particular period of time and the length of time of any one unemployment spell. Unemployment could be concentrated in a few spells of long duration or in a large number of spells of relatively short duration. Evidence accumulated during the 1970s showed that unemployment typically consists of roughly the same pool of individuals experiencing a large number of unemployment spells of relatively short duration.[16]

Whether this depiction of unemployment will be retained in the late 1980s, when the economy has been stagnant and unemployment levels high, remains to be seen. In the next chapter we will examine the causes of unemployment, including a view of the economy that could explain why unemployment consists of multiple spells for the same individuals.

---

[14] "Economic Diary," *Business Week*, December 1, 1986, p. 24.

[15] George L. Perry, "Unemployment Flows in the U.S. Labor Market," *Brookings Papers on Economic Activity* 2 (1972), p. 247.

[16] Kim B. Clark and Lawrence H. Summers, "Labor Market Dynamics and Unemployment: A Reconsideration," *Brookings Papers on Economic Activity* 1 (1979), pp. 13–60; G. K. Akerlof and B. G. M. Main, "Unemployment Spells and Unemployment Experience," *American Economic Review* 70, no. 5 (December 1980), pp. 885–93; and Robert H. Frank and Richard T. Freeman, "The Distribution of the Unemployment Burden: Do the Last Hired Leave First?" *Review of Economics and Statistics* 60, no. 3 (August 1978), pp. 380–91. There is some disagreement in the literature about the length of spells of unemployment, but there is no dispute that unemployment is a function of multiple spells rather than sustained duration.

Summary

The unemployment statistic reported each month by the Bureau of Labor Statistics (BLS) of the Department of Labor is one of the most widely used barometers of the health of the American economy. It is also one of the most misunderstood figures that come from the government. The unemployment rate as measured by the BLS reflects the percentage of individuals in the eligible population who are not working but evidence some form of *active job-seeking behavior* during the period covered by the survey. Many people who want to work do not get counted as unemployed but are placed in a category of "not in the labor force" if they have not sought work in the survey period.

This ambiguity between not being in the labor force and being unemployed has occasioned much of the controversy surrounding the measured unemployment rate. Some critics argue that the unemployment rate *understates* the phenomenon it seeks to measure because many able-bodied and willing workers do not get counted as unemployed if they have not met the BLS criteria for active job-seeking behavior. Others contend that the unemployment rate *overstates* the problem because it is not sensitive to the intensity of interest in finding work. Many people, according to this perspective, get counted as unemployed if they went for only one job interview in the survey period. Their interest in finding work is ephemeral at best, according to this viewpoint, and they should not be counted as unemployed.

The controversy surrounding the measurement of unemployment has intensified in the past decade because of the dramatic shifts in the composition of the labor force. Today there are far greater proportions of women and young people in the labor force than there have been before. The critics contend that since these two groups have a weaker attachment to the labor force, the unemployment rate has increased out of proportion to the increase in the unemployment problem.

The measure of this phenomenon is called the *labor force participation rate*, which indicates the ratio of people in the labor force, either working or unemployed, to the eligible population base. Labor force participation rates for women have increased dramatically in the past decade because of changing social attitudes, the need for second incomes in the household to keep pace with inflation, more female-headed households, and more career-oriented women. More young people are in the labor force today, as a proportion of the total, because of the baby boom after World War II and the tendency toward earlier retirements.

If the composition of the labor force were today what it was in 1956, the unemployment rate would be lower than it is by slightly less than one percentage point. On the other hand, if all those who want work were included in the measure of unemployment, not just those who seek work, the unemployment rate would be higher by at least one percentage point. The propensity toward an upward bias in the unemployment rate is offset by the tendency toward a downward bias in the measure of unemployment.

In this chapter a series of unemployment measures were introduced and applied to different age, sex, and racial groups in the labor force. Part of the controversy over employment policy relates to an understanding of how unemployment is measured and what it means. The labor force is constantly changing, while the measured unemployment rate is a static snapshot. Most unemployment is the result of a few individuals experiencing multiple spells of unemployment. A firm basis of understanding of these issues of measurement will aid comprehension of the later policy chapters.

Study Questions

1. How does the Bureau of Labor Statistics (BLS) define and measure unemployment? What are some of the shortcomings of its approach?

2. What are the trends in the age-sex composition of the labor force, and how have they affected the overall measured unemployment rate?

3. How does the BLS measure of unemployment underestimate the "true" unemployment rate? How does it overstate the "true" unemployment rate?

4. How do you explain the paradox of both an increasing rate of employment and an increasing rate of unemployment?

5. Compare the static nature of the measured unemployment rate with the dynamic process of labor market flows.

Further Reading

Statistical Publications

U.S. Department of Labor. *Employment and Training Report of the President*. Washington: Government Printing Office, annual.

U.S. Department of Labor. *Handbook of Labor Statistics*. Washington: Government Printing Office, annual.

General Reading

Clark, Kim B., and Lawrence H. Summers. "Labor Market Dynamics and Unemployment: A Reconsideration." *Brookings Papers on Economic Activity* 1 (1979), pp. 13–60.

National Commission on Employment and Unemployment Statistics. *Counting the Labor Force*. Washington: Government Printing Office, 1979.

14

Unemployment:
Causes and Policy Responses

The concern of economists with the causes of unemployment is a fairly recent phenomenon. The Great Depression of the 1930s fastened the attention of the economics profession on the problems of unemployment—its causes and consequences. Until that sobering decade economists had contended that sustained unemployment was not possible unless wages were too high to justify the employment of enough able-bodied workers on profitability criteria. The labor market was like any other; there was a market-clearing price in which the quantities of labor supplied and demanded were equal. Any disequilibrium in the labor market that resulted in unemployment would be self-correcting as long as wages fell to clear the market for labor. Business cycles could occur, of course, in which, during the downturn, there would be unemployment. But this was a temporary phenomenon, and the restorative power of a wage reduction would re-equilibrate the labor market at full employment.

The Great Depression changed the way economists viewed unemployment. While wages fell in real terms in many sectors of the economy during the Great Depression, unemployment continued. There seemed to be no way in which price and wage adjustments could restore equilibrium to markets. Economists wrestled with the question why their received doctrine was an insufficient guide to a solution of the massive unemployment problems that beset the market economies. Into the breach came John Maynard Keynes in the mid-1930s. With his *General Theory of Employment, Interest, and Money*, he was to revolutionize economic thought and action. Along the way he legitimated a new role for government in economic affairs whose end we have probably not yet seen.

Had this textbook been written in 1970, instead of now, the story could have ended there. Keynes did not solve all the problems of unemployment, but he did provide the economic policy context in which most of the unemployment could be resolved. Unemployed workers who were not susceptible to the Keynesian medicine could be treated with different potions. Demand management and Keynesian fine tuning were seen by a majority of economists as sufficient to deal with unemployment. The only challenge facing economists was to perfect their technical tools and computerized early warning systems through econometric forecasting so that the right policies could be introduced at the appropriate time.

This consensus evaporated during the late 1970s and 1980s as new issues came to the forefront in economics. Rather than being generalized, the unemployment problem seemed to be located in specific groups in the economy—for example, youths and blacks—which were not responsive to generalized demand management policies. Inflation reached proportions never before seen in the United States. Interacting with unemployment, a new problem—stagflation, the simultaneous occurrence of unemployment and inflation—moved to center stage.

In this chapter various theories that purport to explain why unemployment occurs will be investigated, along with proposed remedies. In the chapters that follow, inflation and stagflation will be examined. These chapters are sequenced to provide a development of the unemployment-inflation problem, and many of the ideas and themes developed in one chapter will reappear in a later chapter.

Neoclassical Theory of Unemployment (SHORT TERM PROBLEM)

The neoclassical theory of unemployment is derived from the marginal productivity analysis of wages set forth in Chapters 3 through 5. At root, the cause of unemployment in this model is a wage rate that is too high to clear the market for labor. This disequilibrium in the labor market arises because the wage rate being paid to labor exceeds the market-clearing equilibrium wage. Figure 14-1 illustrates this proposition.

If the wage being paid labor in this market is W_1, the number of individuals willing to work at this wage (E_s), exceeds the number of workers firms will be prepared to hire (E_d). The resulting level of unemployment is the difference $E_s - E_d$.[1] If wages

---

[1] More precisely, the condition shown in Figure 14-1 implies that the *quantity* of labor supplied exceeds the *quantity* of labor demanded at the wage W_1. These quantities of labor supplied and demanded are a combination of two factors: number of individuals and hours of work. Therefore, unemployment in this model requires an additional assumption—namely, that the number of hours of work is fixed and the factor isolated for investigation is the number of individuals who supply labor and are demanded by employers.

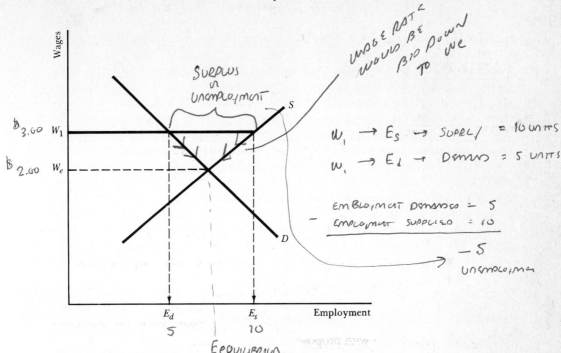

WAGE RATE WOULD BE BID DOWN TO W_e

SURPLUS or UNEMPLOYMENT

$$W_1 \rightarrow E_s \rightarrow SUPPLY = 10 \text{ UNITS}$$
$$W_1 \rightarrow E_d \rightarrow DEMAND = 5 \text{ UNITS}$$

EMPLOYMENT DEMANDED = 5
EMPLOYMENT SUPPLIED = 10

-5 UNEMPLOYMENT

3.00 W_1
2.00 W_e

E_d
5

E_s
10

Equilibrium

Figure 14-1 Unemployment in the Labor Market

are flexible, this level of unemployment will not be sustainable. Consequently, unemployment in the neoclassical model was seen as a short-term, temporary phenomenon that arose because the labor market was not in equilibrium. Those unemployed at the prevailing wage of W_1 would prefer to take a job at a lower wage rate than have none at all, particularly if there were no other means of financial support, such as unemployment compensation. The wage would be bid down until it reached a market-clearing level of W_e. In this sense the market for labor is like any other, in that some market-clearing price exists (in this case the wage) that will equilibrate supply and demand. Such an equilibrium wage leaves demand matched with supply and no idle resources in the form of unemployment.

If the cause of unemployment is a wage in excess of its market-clearing level, the policy response follows from this diagnosis. Public policy should ensure that there are no impediments to the market adjustment process. If there are forces preventing the wage from falling, they should be eliminated where possible. Trade unions that exact a wage in excess of the market-clearing level should be controlled if they create unemployment and prevent the market from accomplishing its equilibrating adjustment.

Unemployment compensation and other cushions that moderate the disciplining effects of the labor market should be challenged if unemployment is to be alleviated. Minimum wage laws, which prevent an employer from hiring someone below a certain

Policy

I. NEOCLASSICAL POLICY PRESCRIPTIONS for UNEMPLOYMENT
   A. Control
      1. Unions
      2. Compensation for Unemployment   } LAISSEZ FAIRE
      3. Min Wage Laws

[handwritten: UNEMPLOYMENT = MRP₂ < MC = WAGE]

wage, should be eliminated. In short, according to the strict neoclassical view, unemployment occurs because the market for labor is in disequilibrium. The marginal revenue product created by the last worker hired is less than the marginal costs—the wage—associated with hiring that individual. Therefore, it is irrational for the firm to hire workers above an equilibrium wage, because it will lose money. The only effective way to restore an equilibrium at full employment to this market is to let the wage adjust and the suppliers of labor respond without interference from public policy.

Seeing unemployment as merely the result of short-term disequilibrium in the labor market was challenged by the events of the Great Depression. Unemployment was high and remained high for an extended period of time. Undaunted, neoclassical economists stuck to the same prescription: to reduce wages in order to restore equilibrium in the labor market so that supply would once again equal demand. Even the British Labour party followed this formula when they achieved their first national political victory by gaining control of Parliament and choosing their first prime minister.

[handwritten: THE GREAT DEPRESSION CHALLENGES THE NEOCLASSICAL SHORT TERM PHENOMENA.]

Job-Search Theories of Unemployment

[handwritten: NEW NEOCLASSICAL THEORY BORN OUT OF THE DEPRESSION]

[handwritten: SOCIAL WAGE]

Keynes's work in the mid-1930s provided an alternative explanation for the causes of unemployment and a different set of policy prescriptions. For several decades the neoclassical theory of unemployment was therefore considered an insufficient explanation of the causes of unemployment. In the past decade, however, the neoclassical view of unemployment has reemerged in a slightly different form, called *job-search theory*.[3]

The wage level for the economy is now a more complex phenomenon. There is a "private" portion, which reflects the wages and fringe benefits received for work performed. There is also a "public" component, which represents various forms of transfer payments that one can receive either in lieu of a private wage or as a supplement to it. In this category are food stamps, welfare payments, unemployment compensation, medicaid, and workers' compensation. The sum of the private wage and public wage can be called a *social wage*.

The explanation of unemployment based on a wage in excess of its market-clearing level has been resurrected around the concept of the *social wage* and job-search theory.[4] The unemployed are said to have a high *reservation wage* because their ability to acquire income through unemployment compensation programs, food stamps, and welfare

[handwritten: EXAM]

---

[2] Minimum wages are discussed in Chapter 23. Unemployment compensation is examined in Chapter 24.

[3] The original job-search model was introduced in George J. Stigler, "The Economics of Information," *Journal of Political Economy* 69 (June 1961), pp. 213–25.

[4] Martin Feldstein, "The Economics of the New Unemployment," *Public Interest* (Fall 1973), pp. 3–42.

↑ UNEMPLOYMENT = SOCIAL WAGE > MRKT CLEARING WAGE .

EXAM
payments deters them from taking certain jobs. A reservation wage is the wage rate that will induce an individual to foresake unemployed status and accept a paying job. If the individual can acquire enough income through transfer payments without working, he or she will have little incentive to take a job when offered. Indeed, it is true that in many jurisdictions the public payments through transfers exceed the pay of many jobs in the private economy. It would be irrational for someone to devote eight hours to working for a wage that was less than could be received by not working.

The social wage level is a composite of the private wage level prevailing in the economy and the "public wage" of transfer payments. If the social wage is high enough, unemployment will result, because of a disequilibrium in the labor market. How large is this phenomenon? There is no accurate estimate of how many people are unemployed because of a social wage in excess of the market-clearing level. The proponents of this *↑* explanation of unemployment claim that most of the unemployment above the frictional level is due to this reason.[5] They point to the fact that the props to an individual's income stretch out the search period for a new job, thereby lengthening the duration of unemployment and increasing the number of people who are unemployed at any one time. Only when benefits expire or the individual finally lands a job that exceeds his or her reservation wage will the count of the unemployed drop.

B.   Job search refers to the process of rational calculation an individual goes through when looking for a job. If the jobs offered pay less than she or he is receiving by not working, the unemployed person will remain in that status. His or her reservation wage exceeds the wage that has been offered. Alternatively, an individual may entirely give up looking for work and become a "discouraged worker," dropping out of the labor force, if the costs of looking for work exceed the probability of finding a job that exceeds the reservation wage.

According to the job-search theory, most unemployment is voluntary and occurs because the returns to job search exceed the returns to remaining employed, accepting a new job, or dropping out of the labor force. When unemployed, individuals continue to engage in job search until they receive an employment offer whose compensation exceeds the returns to continued search.[6] Any cushions to the unemployment shock—unemployment compensation, food stamps, and the like—merely increase the returns to job search and, therefore, stretch it out longer. The prediction from this model is that the duration of unemployment will increase as the public part of the wage increases.

However the individual responds to the social wage, the public policy choice is

IF SOCIAL WAGE ↑ → JOB SEARCH ↑ → UNEMPLOY ↑
→ RES WAGE ↑

---

[5] Frictional unemployment consists of people changing jobs—those unemployed who have voluntarily left one job and are awaiting the start of another. Such unemployment will always exist in an economy but is of little consequence since it represents voluntary job changes, not a problem of involuntary unemployment.

[6] Kim B. Clark and Lawrence H. Summers, "Labor Market Dynamics and Unemployment: A Reconsideration," *Brookings Papers on Economic Activity* 1 (1979), pp. 51–52; Raymond P. H. Fishe, "Unemployment Insurance and the Reservation Wage of the Unemployed," *Review of Economics and Statistics* 64, 1 (February, 1982), pp. 12–17. For a survey of the job search literature, see Steven A. Lippman and John J. McCall, "The Economics of Job Search: A Survey," *Economic Inquiry* 14 (June 1976), pp. 155–89.

PUBLIC POLICY → REDUCE PUBLIC PORTION

clear: to reduce those elements of the social wage that contribute to an extended job search. In other words, the objective is to lower the individual's reservation wage by tightening up on access to programs that compose the "public wage" and by reducing financial benefits under the programs that produce a high reservation wage.

This is not terribly different from the general neoclassical proposition that unemployment results when the wage exceeds its market-clearing level. In the modern instance, however, public policy is to be directed at those elements of the social wage that are the creations of public policy: welfare, unemployment compensation, food stamps, medicaid, and workers' compensation. By making access more difficult and benefit levels lower, the reservation wage will be reduced. This will cause the unemployed to accept certain jobs sooner than would otherwise happen. The length of the job search will be reduced, and the unemployment rolls will be shorter.

The job-search theory of unemployment has been challenged empirically on two grounds. First, the duration of unemployment remained about the same from the 1960s to the 1970s, when more liberal transfer programs for the unemployed raised the public component of the wage. Presumably, if this increased the unemployed's reservation wage, job search would be stretched out and the duration of unemployment would increase. But this did not happen.[7] Second, "the majority of the unemployed search in ways that would be possible if they held a job," according to the results of a survey conducted on techniques of job search.[8] In this survey it was found that the unemployed devote only about 17 hours per month to job search, most jobs are found through networks that are readily accessible to an individual while employed, and most jobs can be sought while the individual is employed.[9]

III — The Natural Rate of Unemployment *THEORY* (*MONETARISM*) (*FRIEDMAN*)

The natural-rate theory of unemployment overlaps to some extent with the job-search theory. This model of unemployment takes as its foundation the microeconomics of neoclassical marginal productivity theory and proceeds to erect a macro model on these micro foundations. It is closely associated with monetarism and Milton Friedman.[10]

In the marginal productivity theory of the firm, individuals are hired if the monetary returns at the margin justify paying the going wage rate. If that wage rate is higher than the marginal returns, then individuals are not hired. Aggregated to a

IF W > MARGINAL RETURN, NOT HIRED!

---

[7] Clark and Summers, "Labor Market Dynamics," pp. 53–54.

[8] Ibid., p. 54.

[9] Carl Rosenfeld, "Job Search of the Unemployed, May 1976," *Monthly Labor Review* 100, no. 11 (November 1977), pp. 39–43.

[10] Milton Friedman, "The Role of Monetary Policy," *American Economic Review* 58, no. 1 (March 1968), pp. 1–17.

O → ZERO INFLATION.

macro level, the natural-rate theory argues that when labor markets are in equilibrium at some real wage rate, associated with that real wage rate is a unique level of unemployment called the *natural rate of unemployment*. Should the wage rate be higher than this equilibrium level and should the monetary authorities seek to reduce the unemployment that would result from a disequilibrium wage, the consequence would be inflation.[11]

Because of this connection among real wages, the rate of unemployment, and inflation, the natural rate of unemployment is sometimes defined as that rate of unemployment that is compatible with price stability.[12] A real wage rate that clears all labor markets implies price stability—*ceteris paribus*—and a rate of unemployment that has settled at its "natural" level. The deviation of an actual rate of unemployment from its natural level signifies a disequilibrium in the labor market, caused by real wages departing from their market-clearing level.[13]

The notion of a natural rate of unemployment is consistent with the postwar goal of reducing unemployment to its *frictional level*. Even at full employment there will always be some unemployment of the frictional variety. The rate of unemployment defined as full employment has changed over the years. Immediately after World War II, full employment was considered to be unemployment of about 2 percent of the labor force. This number was derived from the experience of wartime, when unemployment dipped below that rate for a time.

Each decade and each new presidential administration has brought with it an upward adjustment of the full-employment target. Eisenhower in the 1950s redefined the goal as 3 percent. When Kennedy assumed office in 1960, his Council of Economic Advisers revised the target to 4 percent. Then Nixon made it 5 percent, Carter 6 percent. In the 1980s the Reagan administration targeted 7 percent unemployment as its goal.

Although these are target rates of unemployment that fiscal and monetary policies seek to reach, they do have some implications for the concept of a natural rate of unemployment. The full employment rate of unemployment has informally begun to be defined as the rate that is compatible with price stability in the economy. What that rate is, is a debatable topic. The Humphrey-Hawkins Act, a 1970s congressional effort to commit public policy to specific employment targets, sets the goal at 4 percent. The natural-rate theorists would tend toward 7 percent or more. In view of our sluggish productivity growth in recent years and the inculcation of inflationary expectations into all sectors of the economy, a rate of unemployment of less than 7 percent may be incompatible with price stability.

A RATE LOWER THAN THE NATURAL RATE WILL BE INCOMPATIBLE W/ PRICE STABILITY.

---

[11] The trade-off between inflation and unemployment in the natural rate theory is discussed in Chapter 17.

[12] Robert J. Gordon, *Macroeconomics* (Boston: Little Brown and Co., 1978), pp. 212–15.

[13] Steven C. Salop, "A Model of the Natural Rate of Unemployment," *American Economic Review* 69, no. 1 (March 1979), p. 125.

CLASSICAL → PUBLIC POLICY → LOWER WAGE RATE

IV. *Keynesian Aggregate Demand Theories of Unemployment*

KEYNES → PUBLIC POLICY → MONETARY ; FISCAL POLICY ! } DEMAND MGMT.

The previous explanations of unemployment that revolve around a wage in excess of a market-clearing level make the implicit assumption that there are sufficient jobs available to employ everyone who wants to work. The only problem in the neoclassical, job-search, and natural-rate theories is that there are impediments to the labor market's doing its job of adjusting wages so that the market for labor will clear. There is no presumption that there may not be sufficient jobs to satisfy all the job seekers. In fact, this is not possible in the neoclassical framework. There will always be some wage rate that will clear the market for labor. That wage might be quite low but it does exist. The logic may be impeccable; its application is not.

A. This is where Keynes enters the picture. Keynes's *General Theory*, as it has come to be called, addressed the reality of high levels of unemployment that prevailed for a long period of time in the face of wages that were rigid downward.[14] He started with the assumption of rigid wages on the downward side. He did not agree, however, that the cause of unemployment was disequilibrium in the labor market, as the neoclassical economists contended. Rather, he departed from previous theories of unemployment by arguing that demand was insufficient to generate enough jobs in the economy to satisfy all those who would be seeking work, no matter what the wage level. Expectations of investors had become so depressed that whatever the rate of interest, they would not invest in productive assets but instead would hold their wealth in a monetary form. This is the famous *liquidity trap* of Keynes. Declines in the rate of interest could not restore investment, because of the deflated expectations of wealth holders about the future prospects for the economy.

Recovery in these circumstances was not possible through price, wage, and interest rate adjustments in private markets for goods, labor, and capital. Public policy could, however, restore employment opportunities to the economy through judicious use of tax, expenditure, and monetary policy. Thus was born the modern era of demand management to ensure high levels of employment. If expectations about the future were so depressed among wealth holders that no adjustment in prices, wages, and interest rates would induce investment and production to occur, government's role was to intervene in the economy through macro demand management policies. Economic stimulation would cause consumer spending to increase; investment and production would follow, thus stimulating employment.

Whether Keynes would have approved of the way his work has been interpreted and implemented is an open question. The vast array of government instruments to manage the economy have been legitimated by calling them "Keynesian." For example, many elements of the social wage, to which modern neoclassical theorists object, are

---

[14] John Maynard Keynes, *The General Theory of Employment, Interest and Money* (New York: Harcourt, Brace and Co., 1935).

KEYNES → UNEMPLOYMENT = INSUFFICIENT AD.

CLASSICALS → UNEMPLOYMENT = DISEQUILIBRIUM OF WAGES AND LABOR

justified on the basis of Keynes's work. Under-consumption was to be combated by welfare, unemployment compensation, food stamps, medicaid, and workers' compensation, and thereby the downturn of the business cycle would be cushioned against a major collapse. Deficit spending would stimulate the economy when there were idle resources. Legislation on employment committed the government to the objective of following policies that would promote high levels of employment, initially in the 1946 Employment Act and more recently with the 1978 Humphrey-Hawkins Act. These very employment policies are the ones contemporary neoclassical theorists point to as causing the high levels of unemployment through the government's promotion of a high reservation wage, which disequilibrates the labor market and produces a rate of unemployment above the natural rate. Keynes, if he were alive, might be saying, "Protect me from the Keynesians."

The issue dividing the neoclassical and Keynesian explanations of unemployment runs along two dimensions. First, is unemployment caused by disequilibrium prices, wages, and interest rates or by conditions in the investment and consumption sectors that do not generate enough aggregate demand to employ everyone seeking work? Second, what is the most efficient and propitious path toward a restoration of full employment? Keynes argued for demand stimulation policies through fiscal and monetary instruments; the neoclassical prescription calls for policies that lower the wage rate. Aside from the argument over how best to achieve full employment, there is a question of the welfare effects of both policies. Wage reductions reduce individual welfare and potentially distort income distribution, whereas fiscal and monetary policies have the potential for greater neutrality in their welfare and income distribution effects. This is what the Keynesians claim for their policies, although they would receive an argument about this from others.

The core of the debate centers around the question of whether unemployment is caused by wages in excess of a market-clearing level or by an insufficiency of aggregate demand. The several variants of the neoclassical explanation of unemployment contend that the cause is a disequilibrium price for labor. Keynesians contend the cause is a lack of aggregate demand—enough output to justify employment. Moreover, lowering wages will reduce aggregate demand further, thereby magnifying the problem, according to the Keynesians.

This is a debate without an easy resolution. There is, first, the problem of specifying the market-clearing wage in the neoclassical model to determine whether the actual wage exceeds its market-clearing level. However, it is not possible to say what the market-clearing wage should be, except by arguing that any unemployment implies a market wage above its market-clearing level. This method of argument is circular and cannot be used. The problem is that we have no way of determining what an equilibrium wage should be, separate from the prevailing wage levels in the economy.

In the Keynesian model there is much the same problem. Evidence of an insufficiency in aggregate demand is based on an actual unemployment rate above some target full-employment rate. Once again we encounter the problem of defining full employment through some variable outside the model. This having failed, circular

CLASSICAL PROBLEM → NO WAY TO DETERMINE EQUILIBRIUM WAGE

KEYNESIAN PROBLEM → NO " " " F.E.

reasoning intrudes on this model as well when the existing rate of unemployment is used to identify a situation of insufficient aggregate demand.

In both models there is an absence of an exogenous explanatory variable. In the neoclassical model there is no way, a priori, to specify an equilibrium market-clearing wage rate. In the Keynesian model there is no way to specify the full employment/unemployment rate. Lacking independent explanatory variables, the models produce circularity in reasoning.

Theory of Structural Unemployment

The unemployment problems that appeared in the 1970s and 1980s fit neither the Keynesian nor the neoclassical explanation for the causes of unemployment with precision. While overall unemployment rates were unexpectedly high, there were jobs available, as evidenced by ads in newspapers and the actual experiences of employers. Unemployment was more heavily concentrated among blacks than among whites and more heavily concentrated among younger workers. Some experienced unemployment for very long periods of time in the midst of apparently sufficient aggregate demand in the economy as a whole. Unemployment was higher in some regions than others, and labor mobility did not adapt to these circumstances. Job turnover was high for some workers, while employment was stable for others.

To explain these phenomena, the *theory of structural unemployment* arose. Unemployment is due to the shifting structure of the economy, according to this argument, and in the 1970s and 1980s the labor force was unable to adjust to technological change, plant relocation, or the need for new skills. People became unemployable because they did not have the requisite education to work with the new postwar technology, or they did not have sufficient information about where the jobs were to react to changing distributions of unemployment across the United States.

Structural unemployment resulted from a mismatch in the labor force; the unemployed did not have the skills desired by the employers, who themselves were frustrated in trying to meet their labor requirements. Unemployment in some skills existed side by side with labor scarcity in others. But the characteristics of those looking for work did not mesh with the needs of employers who had jobs available.

The most common explanation for this problem in the labor market is technology. And technology as a cause of structural unemployment was analyzed as early as the late 1950s. Automation was presumed to have taken hold in the American economy in the late 1950s, rendering people jobless. Employers with skilled labor needs could not find workers in the existing structure of the labor force.[15] The 1950s and 1960s

[15] The most persistent proponent of this view was Charles C. Killingsworth, "Structural Unemployment in the United States," in Jack Steiber, ed., *Employment Problems of Automation and Advanced Technology* (New York: St. Martin's Press, 1966), pp. 128–55.

TRAINING
IMPROVE INFO(

were decades in which technology took hold of the American psyche. We had the Russian sputnik scare, the introduction of computers, and the race for the moon. In the 1980s we may bemoan the fact that our technology is so obsolete that productivity is stagnant, but the problem was the polar opposite in the 1960s and 1970s, at least in terms of explaining unemployment.[16]

Critics of the structural-unemployment argument point to the fact that unemployment results from technological change only if the additional demand created through automation is insufficient to absorb those displaced by technology.[17] Structural-unemployment advocates counter by arguing that that is precisely the problem: although there was sufficient aggregate demand in the economy to employ more people, technological change had rendered those without jobs unemployable in light of the skill requirements of the new jobs.[18]

The policy proposals that flow from the structural-unemployment thesis depart from the Keynesian aggregate demand management view. Insufficient aggregate demand is less of a problem than structural imbalances in the labor market. To address the latter, policies that upgrade skills and foster more labor mobility are put forward. This was the basis for the large-scale employment training effort that was mounted in the United States starting in the early 1960s.[19] Although the reasons for employment training have shifted over the years, its original _raison d'être_ was to produce a better match of skills to job requirements. In addition to training programs, policies to improve labor market information about available jobs were created. Computerized job information banks, an upgrading of the capacity of the employment service to find jobs for the unemployed, and small experiments with job relocation policies were all tried in an effort to improve labor market mobility.

Was the unemployment of the 1950s due to structural factors or an insufficiency of aggregate demand? This was the issue that faced members of the Kennedy administration as they assumed office at the turn of the decade. Kennedy's Council of Economic Advisers supported an aggregate demand stimulation strategy to reduce unemployment, although it was prepared to acknowledge the problems of labor market imbalance that the structural theorists put forward as their explanation for unemployment. The council took the position that structural problems could most effectively be alleviated through aggregate demand stimulation. In its 1962 _Economic Report_, the council said, "A high level of over-all demand is a prerequisite for the efficient allocation of labor resources in a dynamic economy. It furnishes the most important single

---

[16] These issues are once again in the public consciousness as a result of the introduction of industrial robots into the auto industry. This development is examined in Chapter 22.

[17] Paul H. Douglas, _The Problem of Unemployment_ (New York: The Macmillan Co., 1931), pt. 3.

[18] Charles C. Killingsworth, "Automation, Jobs and Manpower," in Ray Marshall and Richard Perlman, eds., _An Anthology of Labor Economics: Readings and Commentary_ (New York: John Wiley and Sons, 1972), pp. 305–12.

[19] Employment training programs are discussed in Chapter 25.

incentive for economically desirable labor mobility—the magnetic attraction of available job openings."[20]

The structuralists countered by arguing that aggregate demand stimulation policies would only increase bottlenecks in the economy, which would be translated into inflation as the sectors of excess demand for labor received more demand while the labor force and the unemployed were not trained to meet the requirements of the high technology sectors.[21]

The choice between demand stimulation through Keynesian fiscal policy and employment training to relieve bottlenecks in the economy was the policy issue of the 1960s. In an important sense the debate was never resolved. Both demand stimulation and employment training were used during the 1960s, although more emphasis was put on the former. Unemployment did decline during that decade, but whether public policy caused this decline—and, if so, which public policy—remains an open question. Employment training programs have become a public policy fixture on the economic landscape, and their origins owe much to the proposition of structural unemployment advanced during the late 1950s and early 1960s.

Dual-Labor-Market Theory of Unemployment

SIMILAR TO STRUCTURALISTS

Is unemployment due to some trait of the individual, or is it caused by the economic environment in which the individual exists? This question reoccurs in many aspects of labor market policy. We have already examined this issue in the discussion of structures of the labor market in Chapter 11. It is important to identify where the different theories on the causes of unemployment stand on this question of interpretation of labor market imbalances.

The neoclassical proposition locates the problem of unemployment in the individual and consequently places the burden of its alleviation on some individual adjustment. If wages are too high and unemployment results, labor should absorb a wage cut. If job-search periods have been stretched out because of the social props to the wage, a reduction in access to and benefits from unemployment compensation will reduce unemployment. The same can be said of the minimum wage. If a person's human capital has become rusty and needs retooling, more education and training will adapt his or her skills to the requirements of the work force. Whichever of these views dominates a neoclassical discussion of the causes of unemployment, the burden of adjustment falls on the individual.

On the other hand, the Keynesian and structural theories of unemployment locate

---

[20] Council of Economic Advisers, *Economic Report of the President, 1962* (Washington: Government Printing Office), p. 93.

[21] This problem in the context of the Phillips curve trade-off is discussed in Chapter 17.

the causes of unemployment within the structure of the economy and the way that structure is changing. Unemployment results from some aspect of the economic environment, and the individual is an unwitting victim. For Keynes, unemployment results when the macroeconomy can no longer generate sufficient aggregate demand to employ everyone who would like to work. Nothing the individual can do by himself or herself will correct this deficiency in the economy. Similarly, structural analyses of unemployment point to the dynamic of technical and economic change as the force that displaces individuals, and nothing the individual can do can offset that force.

In the late 1960s and early 1970s a new theory of the labor market arose that extends this insight further: *the dual-labor-market theory*.[22] This theory of the labor market has many aspects that have relevance for different issues of labor market policy. For now, the discussion of the dual-labor-market theory will be confined to the issue of unemployment.

The unemployment problem that dual-labor-market analysis seeks to explain is similar to the one that structural theorists tackled. The labor market has unemployment rates that are persistently higher than warranted in the face of the level of aggregate demand. Among certain groups in the population unemployment has remained at Great Depression levels in the face of labor scarcity in other sectors. Into this breach comes the dual-labor-market analysis, as it seeks to explain these paradoxes.

The dual-labor-market theory posits the existence of two separate labor markets; there is mobility within each market but restricted mobility between the two markets. The two labor markets in the "dual economy" are stratified along two general dimensions: by the characteristics of jobs (and industries) and by the characteristics of individuals. These two principal forms of stratification interact, in the initial formulation of the theory, to produce a cumulative portrait of the two labor markets.

The *primary sector* contains the privileged members of the labor force. It is governed by an internal labor market in which there are relatively good working conditions, high pay, job security, administrative protection of jobs, mobility along seniority tracks, and so on. The primary sector has evolved jobs with substantial skill specificity, requiring on-the-job training as opposed to formal education. Typically, the worker enters at a relatively low-skill job in "ports of entry," and by virtue of seniority progresses upward to more-skilled jobs, receiving the necessary on-the-job training at each juncture.

The *secondary sector*, on the other hand, consists of jobs that do not possess much skill specificity. The labor pool to fill these jobs is comparatively undifferentiated, approaching a homogeneous mass of raw labor power. There is little or no on-the-job training required to perform these jobs, and turnover is high. Further, as a consequence of the absence of union protection, there is no codification of work rules and seniority privileges as is the case in the internal labor market of the primary sector.

---

[22] Peter B. Doeringer and Michael J. Piore, *Internal Labor Markets and Manpower Analysis* (Lexington, MA: D. C. Heath, 1971).

The workers who fill these jobs manifest traits that are compatible with these jobs: poor work discipline, high rates of turnover and instability, unreliability on the job, and the like. As a consequence, jobs in the secondary sector pay low wages, have poor working conditions, provide little job security, and have high turnover.

Unemployment results, in the dual-labor-market analysis, for different reasons depending upon whether the primary or secondary sector is being investigated. Within the primary sector, unemployment results from more traditional Keynesian considerations—insufficient aggregate demand, which may be localized, as, for example, when demand falls for automobiles. Unemployment in the secondary sector, however, is built into the structure of that market. Turnover is high as a matter of course, and workers begin to show a life-style that is compatible with high turnover rates. Unemployment in the secondary sector has a higher concentration among blacks, youth, and female workers. For these people, several jobs in the same year is not atypical. Work in fast-food outlets, car washes, restaurants, and similar establishments fits this profile of jobs in the secondary sector. Workers in the secondary sector acquire income through sporadic employment, unemployment compensation, welfare, and employment training programs. In fact, for many workers in the secondary sector, these are seen as substitutes, and the typical secondary sector worker will pass through all of these portals in a given year.[23]

Unemployment is built into the structure of these secondary labor markets. High turnover rates permit employers to pay relatively lower wages, and they develop their technology toward this end. Individuals trapped in this market develop a work history of unstable employment, which is an impediment to gaining access to jobs in the primary labor market. Their life-style, mode of personal deportment, and expectations become acclimated to a secondary labor market. As Michael Piore, one of the originators of the dual-labor-market thesis, says, "the basic explanation of the high relative unemployment of certain groups is that the jobs which they hold have relatively high rates of discharge and layoff, and the workers who hold these jobs have relatively high rates of entrance to and exit from the labor force."[24]

The policy responses that flow from this analysis of unemployment are two: first, manpower training that emphasizes work habits as well as work skills; second, policies that systematically seek to find jobs for the unemployed in the primary sector of the economy so that their secondary sector work habits can be interrupted. Once in the primary sector of the economy, the individual will be placed on a path of stable employment.

---

[23] This process has been studied by Bennett Harrison, "Public Employment and the Theory of the Dual Economy," in Harold I. Sheppard, Bennett Harrison, and William J. Springs, eds., *The Political Economy of Public Service Employment* (Lexington, MA: Lexington Books, 1972), pp. 41–76.

[24] Michael J. Piore, "Unemployment and Inflation: An Alternative View," *Challenge* (May–June 1978), p. 29.

Explanations of Unemployment: An Assessment

■

The several theories of unemployment examined in this chapter provide different explanations for the causes of unemployment and propose different policies to alleviate unemployment. The four theories of unemployment causes and policy prescriptions are summarized in Table 14-1.

It is tempting to say that unemployment is probably the result of all four of these explanations—a wage in excess of its market-clearing level (neoclassical), insufficient aggregate demand (Keynesian), a mismatch between the skills needed for available jobs and the human capital of the unemployed (structural), and the high turnover built into the nature of the jobs in the informal sector of the economy (dual labor markets). The problem is that the same facts and data can be used by protagonists of the different theories to support their points of view.

Methodologically, each theory has a shortcoming, in that it does not have an exogenous variable to establish independently a norm against which the economy and the labor market can be judged. In the neoclassical model we do not know what a market-clearing wage should be, independent of unemployment in the labor market. In the Keynesian model we do not know what full employment should be with aggregate demand in equilibrium with aggregate supply in a living economy. The structural argument depends on some exogenous formulation for measuring human capital requirements, and this has not yet been devised. The dual-labor-market model cannot identify high-risk workers except by the result of their experience in the labor market. In each instance we become trapped in a circular argument whenever the models are examined carefully.

To the extent that the "new unemployment" research of the 1970s points us in

Table 14-1 Unemployment: Causes and Policy Responses

Theory of Unemployment	Cause of Unemployment	Policy Response
1. Neoclassical (including job-search and natural-rate theories)	1. Wage in excess of market-clearing level	1. Elimination of barriers to market adjustment
2. Keynesian	2. Insufficient aggregate demand	2. Fiscal and monetary policies to stimulate aggregate demand
3. Structural	3. Imbalances in economy, caused by dynamics of economic change	3. Training, job information, and relocation policies
4. Dual-labor-market	4. Character of jobs in the secondary sector	4. Training policies and economic restructuring to change jobs in the secondary sector

one direction or another, it suggests that unemployment is concentrated among individuals who constantly move into and out of employed status.[25] These individuals experience employment of short duration followed by spells of unemployment of relatively short duration. This finding is consistent with the dual-labor-market explanation but can also reflect imperfect adjustment in the labor market in the neoclassical model.[26]

It will be interesting to see how these models of unemployment hold up in the future. With new forms of technological change beginning to enter the production process (e.g., mechanical robots)[27] and economic stagnation having persisted for a full decade—from the mid-1970s to the mid-1980s—I would expect the explanation for unemployment to take on more the coloration of the structural view. How public policy responds to these new features of unemployment should be watched carefully. Economists are like generals, always fighting the present war with the last war's tactics. Let us hope that economists can escape this trap in the 1990s.

Summary

The Employment Act of 1946 committed the federal government to follow policies that would lead to high levels of employment. Thirty-two years later, in 1978, Congress passed the Humphrey-Hawkins Full Employment and Balanced Growth Act, which required the president and his Council of Economic Advisers to follow policies that would reduce unemployment and inflation to specific rates. The goals were ambitious: a 4 percent unemployment rate for young workers, ages 16–19, and a 3 percent unemployment rate for all workers over 20. These goals were to be realized by 1983, along with a rate of inflation of 3 percent.[28] Very few economists think these goals can ever be reached within the structure of the present economy.

The problem of devising policies to reduce unemployment is that there are competing theories of what causes unemployment. Each theoretical conception of the cause of unemployment carries with it policy proposals for reducing unemployment. Most of these policy prescriptions are inconsistent with one another.

There are four groups of unemployment theories: neoclassical, Keynesian, structural, and dual-labor-market. Each of these theories has specific variations, but these four categories frame the discussion of unemployment theories.

---

[25] This research was summarized in the previous chapter. See Clark and Summers, "Labor Market Dynamics," for a review.

[26] For the latter explanation, see Feldstein, "The New Unemployment."

[27] Discussed in Chapter 22.

[28] Council of Economic Advisers, *Economic Report of the President, 1979* (Washington: Government Printing Office), pp. 106–12.

The neoclassical theory locates the cause of unemployment in market disequilibrium. The market wage prevailing is in excess of one that would clear the market for labor and leave no unemployment. This explanation of unemployment was put forward in the late nineteenth and early twentieth centuries. Economists used it during the Great Depression to advocate public policies that would reduce the wage and thereby restore full employment to the economy.

In the contemporary period, this view of unemployment has been adapted to confront the current problem of unemployment. Job-search theory is one modern application of the neoclassical theory of unemployment. Job-search theory contends that unemployment occurs because the props to the private wage are too high. Such props include unemployment compensation, workers' compensation, food stamps, medicaid, welfare, and the minimum wage. The combination of these programs has produced a "social" wage, which has increased the worker's reservation wage. The reservation wage is the wage that is necessary to induce someone to take a job. If the individual can acquire as much income or nearly as much income by not working, why accept a job? This is the question posed by the job-search theorists. Specifically, workers will stretch out their search for a new job once they become unemployed, or they will quit jobs more readily, because of the public props to the private wage. The result will be more unemployment than would have occurred without the public props. The public policy prescriptions that flow from this theory involve phasing out or reducing the public props that have increased the social wage and caused disequilibrium in the labor market.

All this has led to a debate over the natural rate of unemployment. The natural rate of unemployment is the rate that is consistent with general price stability. It occurs at the real wage that prevails in the labor market and equilibrates supply and demand for labor. Unemployment in excess of the natural rate can exist, but its cause is associated with a real wage that is in excess of a market-clearing wage. What this is in today's economy is debatable. Some argue that the natural rate of unemployment in the contemporary context is 7 percent or more, whereas 30 years ago economists envisioned an unemployment rate of about 3 percent as attainable within the context of price stability.

The first important challenge to the neoclassical theory of unemployment came from Keynes in the 1930s. He started with wages that were rigid on the downward side and then proceeded to show that no matter what the price adjustments were in capital, labor, and goods markets, the system was incapable of producing full employment. This was because the expectations of people in the economy were so depressed that they preferred to hold their wealth in nonproductive forms rather than to invest or to spend money on consumer goods. Consequently, price signals were inadequate to re-equilibrate markets. All price changes did was redistribute income away from consumers to wealth holders, and this redistribution in fact exacerbated the problem, according to Keynes.

The policy direction that flowed from Keynes's analysis is one that is now commonplace. The government should use its powers of taxation, spending, and money creation to create the conditions for full employment. Judicious management of fiscal and monetary policy could accomplish this in the face of an economic system that was responding perversely to price signals.

On this issue the two theories were divided: neoclassical theory says that an orderly adaptation to price signals will restore employment; Keynes showed that under certain expectational conditions this would not occur.

The experience of postwar unemployment in the United States posed a challenge to the Keynesian explanation of unemployment. Expectations were not depressed, as his model suggested, and aggregate demand seemed to be sufficient, yet unemployment rates were higher than appeared to be warranted. Moreover, unemployment was heavily concentrated among certain racial and age groups and in certain regions of the country.

This led to the structural-unemployment explanation, which contended that unemployment arose because of imbalances in markets. There was an excess demand for labor in certain parts of the country and for certain highly skilled jobs. Alongside this were pockets of unemployment. But the people unemployed did not have the skills to work with the new technology, and they were located in parts of the country far removed from where the jobs were. The policy proposal put forward was for employment training and job relocation.

During the 1960s a variant of the structural-unemployment thesis was put forward, called the dual-labor-market theory. In response to the civil rights upheavals of the 1960s, economists sought to explain why there was a permanent underclass in the United States—low paid, sporadically employed, and concentrated in certain sectors of the economy. The dual-labor-market theory explained this by arguing that the economy consisted of two sectors with little mobility between them. The primary sector had relatively high-paying jobs, stable employment, union protections, and good working conditions. The secondary sector had low pay, jobs with high turnover, and little job protection. Once a worker became trapped in the secondary sector, it would be hard for that worker to move to the primary sector, because previous work history would be counted against the secondary sector employee. As a result, a permanent underclass emerged, with high unemployment rates concentrated among blacks and young people.

Policy focused on a restructuring of the economy so that more jobs would be developed in the primary sector of the economy. Employment training was to prepare the unemployed for work in the primary sector. Dual-labor-market theorists advocated an orientation in public policy that looked at how people could be moved from the secondary to the primary sector of the economy. Existing employment training programs came under criticism in that they tended to place the trainees in the secondary sectors from which they came, and as a consequence little mobility was evident from the training programs.

There is a rich menu to choose from in confronting the problem of unemployment. But the problem persists in the face of this array of policy suggestions. Today the way out of the unemployment maze has been made more difficult by inflation, which frustrates many of the paths toward full employment.

Study Questions

1. What is meant by the "social wage," and how does it compare to the wage as construed in neoclassical economic theory?

2. What is the natural rate of unemployment, and how is this concept used in explaining the causes of unemployment?

3. What is the reservation wage, and what is its connection with the social wage and with job-search models?

4. Some analyses of unemployment start with the micro foundation of the labor market and work up toward the aggregate; others start with the aggregate and work down toward the micro level. Discuss and explain this difference in approaches.

5. What are the policy implications for the labor market of the various explanations of unemployment?

6. Is it correct to conclude that technological change always displaces labor and leads to higher unemployment rates? Give an illustration of the opposite effect.

Further Reading

Doeringer, Peter B., and Michael J. Piore. *Internal Labor Markets and Manpower Analysis*. Lexington, MA: D. C. Heath, 1971.

Feldstein, Martin. "The Economics of the New Unemployment." *Public Interest* (Fall 1973), pp. 3–42.

Friedman, Milton. "The Role of Monetary Policy," *American Economic Review* 58, no. 1 (March 1968), pp. 1–17.

Keynes, John Maynard. *The General Theory of Employment, Interest and Money*. New York: Harcourt, Brace and Co. 1935.

Killingsworth, Charles C. "Automation, Jobs and Manpower." In *An Anthology of Labor Economics: Readings and Commentary*, edited by Ray Marshall and Richard Perlman. New York: John Wiley and Sons, 1972. Pp. 305–12.

15

Inflation:
Meaning and Measurement

The 1970s can genuinely be called America's first inflationary decade. Never before in our history did we experience high levels of sustained inflation over such a long period of time. From 1970 through 1979 the consumer price index rose by slightly more than a hundred points. This was a first for the United States. The rate of inflation during that same period of time was 87 percent.[1] To put this in some perspective, the rate of inflation between 1913 and 1970 was only 74 percent. The consumer price index rose more in the 1970s than it had in the previous 58 years.[2]

Inflation is one of the most serious problems facing the American economy which jeopardizes social progress. Employment programs, income redistribution, poverty reduction, and improvements in the quality of life all depend on holding inflation at bay.

Inflation distorts the orderly functioning of an economy in many ways. Expectations become based on continued inflation, and this merely stokes the flames of inflation, causing it to become higher. Income distribution is affected by the distortion

---

[1] The difference between changes in the consumer price index and the rate of inflation will be explained later in this chapter.

[2] Even if we extend this period back into the nineteenth century, it is not possible to find a rate of inflation comparable to that of the 1970s.

in relative prices that accompanies inflation. Savings become eroded, and old people find their pensions and social security rendered less valuable. Thrift is denigrated, as people seek to protect themselves from the ravages of inflation, while speculation is rewarded.

Compounding the problem of inflation is the absence of clear policy responses. There is no Keynes available to solve this problem as he did for the massive unemployment of the Great Depression.

The next two chapters treat the problem of inflation. In this chapter the meaning and measurement of inflation will be discussed, and in the next chapter various theories that purport to explain the causes of inflation will be examined. Along with the various explanations for the causes of inflation, policy responses will also be presented in the next chapter.

Measuring Inflation

The *consumer price index* (*CPI*) is the most commonly used measure of inflation. Other price indexes exist—such as the producer price index and the implicit gross national product deflator—but the CPI is the most widely used measure of inflation. The CPI is based on tracking the prices of a fixed market basket of goods and services purchased by the typical household. The Bureau of Labor Statistics (BLS) establishes a base period against which subsequent and previous price changes are charted. In that base year the BLS identifies the purchase of goods and services by a typical urban family consisting of four people. It then holds that basket of goods and services fixed over time and computes the cost of the same market basket of goods and services in some subsequent time period. If the prices increase for the fixed basket of goods, the CPI will show an increase in the cost of living. Currently the year 1972–73 is used to establish a market basket against which price changes are measured. In that year the BLS did an extensive study of the buying habits of urban families. The 1967 prices of this market basket are used to establish a base year CPI.[3]

An illustration of the CPI computation will facilitate an understanding of this important statistic. In Table 15-1 a hypothetical CPI is computed for a student who is consuming only two products: hamburgers and records. In 1967 the student consumed 60 pounds of hamburgers and bought 50 records, at prices of $1.00 per pound of hamburger and $3.00 per record. Her total expenditures were $210.00 in 1967— $60.00 for hamburger and $150.00 for records. How much will the same amount of hamburger and the same number of records cost in 1980? We could look at each item separately, but that would be of limited value unless we can find a way to add up

---

[3] U.S. Department of Labor, *BLS Handbook of Methods* (Washington: Government Printing Office, 1976), pp. 87–108.

Table 15-1 Hypothetical Computation of Consumer Price Index

Goods and Services	Quantities Purchased 1967	Price 1967	Cost 1967	Price 1980	Cost of 1967 Market Basket at 1980 Prices
	(Q_{1967})	(P_{1967})	$(Q_{1967})\,(P_{1967})$	(P_{1980})	$(Q_{1967})\,(P_{1980})$
Hamburgers	60 pounds	$1.00/pound	$ 60.00	$2.25	$135.00
Records	50 records	3.00/record	150.00	6.00	300.00
Total			$210.00		$435.00

$$\text{CPI} = \frac{(Q_{1967})\,(P_{1980})}{(Q_{1967})\,(P_{1967})} \times 100 = \frac{\$435.00}{\$210.00} \times 100 = 207.1$$

records and hamburgers. The CPI enables us to do this; in effect, apples and oranges are combined to come up with a statistic that conveniently summarizes the relevant changes in the cost of living.

The student paid $2.25 per pound for hamburger and $6.00 per record in 1980. Holding the quantities of records and hamburgers consumed at their 1967 levels, we can compute a CPI. If the student consumed the same quantities of records and hamburgers in 1980 that she consumed in 1967, her expenditures were $135.00 for hamburgers and $300.00 for records. The total cost of the 1967 quantities of records and hamburgers at 1980 prices was $435.00. What was the percentage increase in cost of the fixed quantities between 1967 and 1980? The answer is found by dividing the total cost in 1980 by the original cost in 1967. This is shown in Table 15-1, and the answer is presented as an index—in this case, 207.1. This means that in 1980 the same quantities purchased in 1967 cost 207 percent more than they cost in 1967. The cost of living for this student more than doubled between 1967 and 1980.

Each consumer is different in terms of his or her individual market basket of goods and services, but the BLS does not compute a separate CPI for each person. Instead it seeks a norm, and it finds this in the typical four-person urban family. By identifying in substantial detail the purchases of such a family, the BLS establishes a fixed market basket in a base year. For subsequent years all it must do is find the price for each item in the market basket, add the costs up, and compute the CPI for that year as was done in Table 15-1 for our hypothetical student.

The Consumer Price Index since 1929

The Bureau of Labor Statistics has been compiling statistics on the cost of living since World War I. A summary of the movement in the CPI from 1929 through 1985 is presented in Table 15-2, using 1967 as the base year. In 1929 the 1972–73 market basket of goods and services of the typical urban family of four could have been purchased for roughly half of what it cost in 1967 and about 16 percent of what it cost in 1985. It took almost 40 years for prices to double between 1929 and 1968; it then took only 11 years for prices to double again between 1969 and 1979. This is an interpretation of the data in the first column of Table 15-2.

The *change* in the CPI from year to year is shown in the second column of that table. It indicates the number of percentage points of increase or decrease in the CPI, comparing one year with the previous year. Between 1929 and 1933, for example, the CPI declined by 12.5 points. Even in the post World War II period, there were occasional declines in prices—in 1949 and 1955. Actual declines in prices seem a relic of some ancient era, but they happened as recently as the mid-1950s.

The *rate of inflation* is something different from these year-to-year changes in the CPI. The rate of inflation is the percentage change in the CPI from one year to the next. It is found by taking the actual change in the CPI and dividing it by the previous year's CPI. So, for example, the rate of inflation in 1979 of 11.3 percent was found by dividing 22.0 by 195.4, the level of the CPI in 1978. Column 3 of Table 15-2 shows the rate of inflation. These data are reproduced graphically in Figure 15-1.

Figure 15-1 graphically illustrates the dramatic increase in the cost of living in the 1970s. During the 1950s inflation was in the range of 2 percent per year on average, except for 1951, a Korean War year. Through 1967 the rate of inflation remained in the 2 percent range and then started to creep up toward the end of the 1960s. The 1970s were an entirely different story. Inflation was in the 4 to 5 percent range from 1968 through 1972, before OPEC appeared on the scene to raise crude oil prices. After the watershed year of 1973, inflation reached dramatic proportions, ranging from 6 to 13 percent per year. Over the entire decade of the 1970s, the United States economy suffered more inflation than at any previous time in its history. During the first half of the decade of the 1980s inflation fell steadily.

The danger is that once the inflation genie escapes from the bottle, it is hard to stuff it back in. Like a science fiction amoeba, inflation begins to take on a life of its own, threatening everything in its path. The logic of inflationary behavior forces people to protect themselves from the devastating effects of inflation, but doing this only feeds inflation. For example, wage earners seek cost-of-living adjustment clauses in their union contracts, and this increases inflationary pressures in the economy. Corporations seek to protect their nominal profits from inflation and fashion a target rate of profits in real terms, which means they must raise their prices to keep up with inflation. This merely worsens an already bad inflationary situation. The attempt to index one's standard of living to the rate of inflation intensifies the underlying inflationary forces in the economy.

Once inflation gets started, a vicious circle keeps it going and makes it worse. Many nations have seen their societies torn apart by inflation. Austria, Hungary, and Germany after World War I and China in the 1930s and 1940s are powerful reminders of how quickly inflation can take over and destroy whatever lies in its path.

Table 15-2 Consumer Price Index, Selected Years, 1929–1985 (1967 = 100)

Year	Consumer Price Index	Change in Consumer Price Index	Rate of Inflation (%)[a]
	(1)	(2)	(3)
1929	51.3	—	—
1933	38.8	−12.5	−24.3
1939	41.6	2.8	7.2
1945	53.9	12.3	29.6
1948	72.1	18.2	33.7
1949	71.4	−0.7	−0.1
1950	72.1	0.7	0.1
1951	77.8	5.7	7.9
1952	79.5	1.7	2.2
1953	80.1	0.6	0.1
1954	80.5	0.4	negligible
1955	80.2	−0.3	negligible
1956	81.4	1.2	1.5
1957	84.3	2.9	3.6
1958	86.6	2.3	2.7
1959	87.3	0.7	0.8
1960	88.7	1.4	1.6
1961	89.6	0.9	1.0
1962	90.6	1.0	1.1
1963	91.7	1.1	1.2
1964	92.9	1.2	1.3
1965	94.5	1.6	1.7
1966	97.2	2.7	2.8
1967	100.0	2.8	2.9
1968	104.2	4.2	4.2
1969	109.8	5.6	5.3
1970	116.3	6.5	5.9
1971	121.3	5.0	4.3
1972	125.3	4.0	3.3
1973	133.1	7.8	6.2
1974	147.7	14.6	11.0
1975	161.2	13.5	9.1
1976	170.5	9.3	5.8
1977	181.5	11.0	6.5
1978	195.4	13.9	7.6
1979	217.4	22.0	11.3
1980	246.8	29.4	13.5

[Handwritten note alongside 1954–1967: "TOOK 40 YEARS FOR C.P.I. TO DOUBLE"]

[Handwritten note alongside 1971–1979: "TOOK ONLY 11 YEARS FOR C.P.I TO DOUBLE."]

Continued

Table 15-2 Continued

Year	Consumer Price Index	Change in Consumer Price Index	Rate of Inflation (%)[a]
1981	272.4	25.6	10.4
1982	289.1	16.7	6.1
1983	298.4	9.3	3.2
1984	311.1	12.7	4.3
1985	322.2	11.1	3.6

[a]Column 2 divided by the previous year in column 1. For example, the 1951 rate of inflation = 5.7/72.1.
Sources: Council of Economic Advisers, *Economic Report of the President, 1980* (Washington: Government Printing Office), p. 259; *Economic Report of the President, 1986*, p. 315.

Inflation and Income Distribution

Rapid inflation of the sort the economy experienced during the 1970s inevitably distorts prices. Some prices rise more rapidly during an inflationary period than others. Relative prices become distorted, and this has an impact on income distribution. If the price distortions affect one segment of the income distribution more seriously

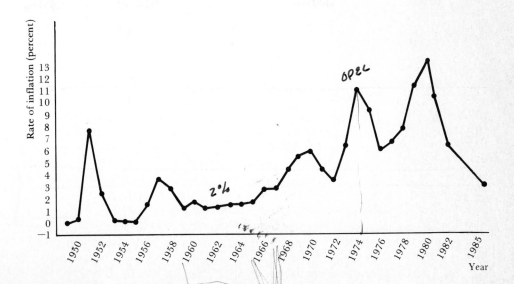

Figure 15-1 Rate of Inflation, 1949–1985

#1   #2   #3   #4

Table 15-3. Consumer Price Index, by Sector, 1967–1985 (1967 = 100)

Year	Total CPI	Food and Beverages	Housing[a]	Apparel and Upkeep	Transportation	Medical Care	Entertainment	Energy
1967	100.0	100.0	100.0	100.0	100.0	100.0	100.0	100.0
1968	104.2	103.6	104.0	105.4	103.2	106.1	105.7	101.5
1969	109.8	108.8	110.4	111.5	107.2	113.4	111.0	104.2
1970	116.3	114.7	118.2	116.1	112.7	120.6	116.7	107.0
1971	121.3	118.3	123.4	119.8	118.6	128.4	122.9	111.2
1972	125.3	123.2	128.1	122.3	119.9	132.5	126.5	114.3
1973	133.1	139.5	133.7	126.8	123.8	137.7	130.0	123.5
1974	147.7	158.7	148.8	136.2	137.7	150.5	139.8	159.7
1975	161.2	172.1	164.5	142.3	150.6	168.6	152.2	176.6
1976	170.5	177.4	174.6	147.6	165.5	184.7	159.8	189.3
1977	181.5	188.0	186.5	154.2	177.2	202.4	167.7	207.3
1978	195.4	206.3	202.8	159.6	185.5	219.4	176.6	220.4
1979	217.4	228.5	227.6	166.6	212.0	239.7	188.5	275.9
1980	246.8	248.0	263.3	178.4	249.7	265.9	205.3	361.1
1981	272.4	267.3	293.5	186.9	280.0	294.5	221.4	410.1
1982	289.1	278.2	314.7	191.8	291.5	328.7	235.8	416.1
1983	298.4	284.4	323.1	196.5	298.4	357.3	246.0	419.3
1984	311.1	295.1	336.5	200.2	311.7	379.5	255.1	423.6
1985	322.2	302.0	349.9	206.0	319.9	403.1	265.0	426.5

TOTAL   HOUSN   MEDICAL   ENERGY

[a]Includes rents on residential dwellings, purchase of homes, utilities, and fuel.
Source: Council of Economic Advisers, *Economic Report of the President, 1986* (Washington: Government Printing Office), p. 315.

than another, inflation can influence the distribution of income stated in "real terms." Households have different budgets depending on their incomes. We know that the lower a person's income, the more is spent, proportionally, on necessities—food, shelter, fuel, and the like. At the higher reaches of the income distribution, proportionally less is spent on necessities and more on luxury consumption.

The inflation of the 1970s was more severe for the necessities. This should not be surprising because these items tend to have lower demand elasticities than do luxury goods. Whenever something has to be cut from the budget of the household, luxuries go first. The household first must cover the cost of necessities. Therefore, necessities tend to have lower demand elasticities. An inflation that causes a fall in real incomes will tilt demand toward the necessities, and in the face of a low demand elasticity, their prices will rise more rapidly.

The statistics pertaining to this aspect of inflation are presented in Table 15-3. The CPI is broken down into its major component parts. Four items in the CPI accounted for about 70 percent of the expenditures for some three-quarters of American families in the years 1972 and 1973.[4] The four items were food and beverages, housing, medical care, and energy. For most Americans—the vast middle class—the inflation has been particularly vexing because the items they spend most of their money on have had more rapid price increases. For example, referring to Table 15-3, we see that housing had a CPI of 349.9 in 1985, compared with an overall CPI of 322.2. Energy had a CPI of 426.5, and medical care 403.1.

The general conclusion about the effects of inflation in the 1970s is that the burden has fallen more heavily on middle-to-low-income groups in the society. Their budgets have been most severely affected by inflation because inflation has been greater in the necessities. The result has been a distortion of the distribution of income, after taking into account price changes, from what it was in nominal terms.

Inflation and the Standard of Living of the American Worker

Rising standards of living have been synonymous with the American Dream. Although their lot in life might be difficult, the hope that it would improve has always motivated American workers to apply themselves, save, and work their way up the job ladder. The inflation of the 1970s and economic stagnation in the 1980s put a damper on this dream. The high standard of living of the American worker, which had been increasing steadily since World War II and was the envy of workers in other countries, was eroded by the inflationary 1970s and the recessionary 1980s.

Statistics pertaining to this are presented in Table 15-4. In the first column the average weekly earnings of the typical American worker are presented. Weekly earnings are used because they reflect a combination of hours worked per week and the wage rate per hour. Although the weekly earnings of American workers have been increasing in current-dollar or nominal terms, inflation has effectively eroded this increase. The constant-dollar figures for the average weekly earnings are shown in the second column of Table 15-4 and reproduced graphically in Figure 15-2. The slow, but steady, upward climb of real earnings reached a peak in 1972–73 and has declined since. Average real weekly earnings, adjusted for inflation, were lower in 1985 than they were in 1967 by more than eight dollars. From 1973 to 1985 real weekly earnings *declined* by 14.4 percent.

Inflation has made it more difficult for the American worker to improve his standard of living. One response to this problem has been for more members of the household to enter the labor force and seek work. As a consequence, labor force participation rates have increased dramatically for youth and women. These issues were discussed in Chapter 13. This has cushioned to some extent the impact of inflation

---

[4] The years 1972 and 1973 are used as a benchmark in specifying a market basket of commodities for the CPI. See Leslie Ellen Nulty, "How Inflation Hits the Majority," *Challenge* (January–February 1979), pp. 32–38.

Table 15-4 Average Weekly Earnings, Private Nonagricultural Sector, 1947–1985

Year	Current Dollars[a]	Constant Dollars[b] (1967 Dollars)	Index of Constant Earnings, 1967 = 100[c] (%)
1947	45.58	68.13	66.9
1948	49.00	67.96	66.7
1949	50.24	70.36	69.1
1950	53.13	73.69	72.3
1951	57.86	74.37	73.0
1952	60.65	76.29	74.9
1953	63.76	79.60	78.2
1954	64.52	80.15	78.7
1955	67.72	84.44	82.9
1956	70.74	86.90	85.3
1957	73.33	86.99	85.4
1958	75.08	86.70	85.1
1959	78.78	90.24	88.6
1960	80.67	90.95	89.3
1961	82.60	92.19	90.5
1962	85.91	94.82	93.1
1963	88.46	96.47	94.7
1964	91.33	98.31	96.5
1965	95.45	101.01	99.2
1966	98.82	101.67	99.8
1967	101.84	101.84	100.0
1968	107.73	103.39	101.5
1969	114.61	104.38	102.5
1970	119.83	103.04	101.2
1971	127.31	104.95	103.0
1972	136.90	109.26	107.3
1973	145.39	109.23	107.3
1974	154.76	104.78	102.9
1975	163.53	101.45	99.6
1976	175.45	102.90	101.0
1977	189.00	104.13	102.2
1978	203.70	104.30	102.4
1979	219.91	101.02	99.2
1980	235.10	95.25	93.5
1981	255.20	93.69	92.0
1982	266.92	92.32	90.7
1983	280.70	94.07	92.4

Continued

Table 15-4 Continued

Year	Current Dollars[a]	Constant Dollars[b] (1967 Dollars)	Index of Constant Earnings, 1967 = 100[c] (%)
1984	294.05	94.52	92.8
1985	301.16	93.47	91.8

[a]Average weekly earnings for production and nonsupervisory workers employed in the private nonagricultural sectors of the economy.
[b]Current dollar earnings divided by the consumer price index.
[c]This measures the change in real weekly earnings.
Sources: Council of Economic Advisers, *Economic Report of the President, 1980* (Washington: Government Printing Office), p. 245; *Economic Report of the President, 1983*, p. 207; *Economic Report of the President, 1986*, pp. 301, 315.

and recession on the family. While this was a successful ploy in the 1980s, it has its obvious limits. Once the spouse and teenagers in the household have gone to work, there are no additional members of the household to add to the labor force. About half of all wage-earning families had at least two members working in 1979.

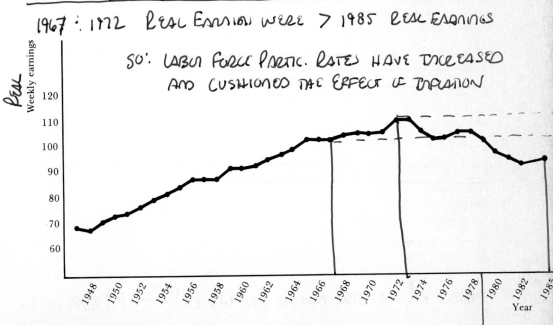

Figure 15-2 Average Real Weekly Earnings in Constant 1967 Dollars, Private Nonagricultural Sector, 1947–1985

Consequently, if rapid inflation reappears in the late 1980s, we can expect even more difficult adjustment problems in the household, as the last fail-safe option has already been used. Coping with inflation will place more severe strains on the household, the labor market, and the society.

↑ UNIT LABOR COSTS → ↑ PRICES

Inflation, Productivity, and Unit Labor Costs

Inflation is one reason the rate of growth in average real earnings for the American worker declined in the early 1980s. Another reason is the decline in the rate of growth of labor productivity. Labor productivity is the source of higher real earnings. As output per hour worked increases—the measure of labor productivity growth—wage increases become justified. Moreover, if wages are growing at the same rate as labor productivity, there is no increase in *unit labor costs*. Unit labor costs are a crucial ingredient in price changes: when they rise, prices rise; when they fall, prices tend to fall. Many firms structure their prices around unit labor costs. As a rule of thumb they use a price markup formula, which adds a percentage to unit labor costs, in order to derive the prices they will charge for their products.[5]

If wages increase by 3 percent per hour but the worker is producing 3 percent more output per hour, unit labor costs do not change. This is the condition for stable unit labor costs: a rate of increase of labor productivity in line with a rate of increase in wages. Inflation destroys the possibility of holding nominal wage increases equal to unit labor costs because workers add another factor to their wage posture—the cost of living. When prices are increasing, workers seek a wage increase that is not simply equal to the rate of increase in labor productivity but that takes account of the increased cost of living as well. They must do this to protect themselves from inflation. In most instances, labor cannot obtain a wage increase high enough to cover the increase in the cost of living and the increase in productivity when inflation gets out of control as it did in the second half of the 1970s. The result is the fall in real earnings we have just examined.

Compounding the difficulty of the high rates of inflation in the 1970s was the fall in the rate of growth of labor productivity. Data pertaining to this are presented in Table 15-5. The first column shows the rate of productivity change. The rates of productivity change vary substantially over the business cycle. During an upswing in the economy, labor productivity tends to grow rapidly, as output increases faster than the rate at which labor is added to production. Unused capacity is brought onto line, and some labor that was previously underutilized is used to its full potential. At the peak of the boom, however, the rate of productivity increase declines as full-capacity

WHEN P↑ → LABOR DEMANDS THAT WAGES↑ → P↑ EVEN MORE

---

[5] Markup pricing and its relationship to unit labor costs and inflation will be examined in detail in Chapter 17.

RESULT → ↓ REAL EARNINGS.

Table 15-5 Rates of Change in Labor Productivity, Unit Labor Costs, and Inflation, 1949–1985

Year	Rate of Productivity Change[a] (%)	Rate of Change in Unit Labor Costs (%)	Rate of Inflation (%)
1949	1.6	0.1	-0.1
1950	8.1	-0.7	0.1
1951	4.4	5.2	7.9
1952	3.0	3.1	2.2
1953	3.8	2.8	0.1
1954	1.7	1.6	negligible
1955	2.8	-0.3	negligible
1956	0.7	6.0	1.5
1957	2.7	3.7	3.6
1958	3.2	1.4	2.7
1959	3.3	1.0	0.8
1960	1.7	2.6	1.6
1961	3.5	0.3	1.0
1962	3.6	1.1	1.1
1963	4.0	-0.2	1.2
1964	4.3	0.8	1.3
1965	3.0	0.9	1.7
1966	2.8	4.1	2.8
1967	2.7	2.6	2.9
1968	2.7	5.0	4.2
1969	0.1	6.9	5.3
1970	0.7	6.5	5.9
1971	3.2	3.1	4.3
1972	3.2	3.3	3.3
1973	2.0	6.2	6.2
1974	-2.1	11.9	11.0
1975	2.0	7.6	9.1
1976	2.8	5.9	5.8
1977	1.7	6.0	6.5
1978	0.8	7.7	7.6
1979	-1.2	11.1	11.3
1980	-0.3	10.8	13.5
1981	1.5	7.7	10.4
1982	-0.4	8.2	6.1
1983	2.6	1.6	3.2
1984	2.1	1.8	4.3
1985	0.3	3.7	3.6

[a]Productivity is defined as output per hour in the private sector of the economy.

Source: Council of Economic Advisers, *Economic Report of the President, 1986* (Washington: Government Printing Office), p. 303.

utilization is reached and diminishing returns begin to appear. Less productive workers and machines are added to production, and this also causes the rate of labor productivity growth to decline at the peak of the boom.

The decline in the rate of growth of labor productivity is one of the reasons for the squeeze on profits at the peak of the boom that leads to a downswing in the economy. As the business cycle turns down, output falls more rapidly than the amount of labor employed, because firms tend to retain labor for a time. They do this because they have made some investment in workers' human capital, which they do not want to squander or deliver free to a competitor unless forced to. As the economic decline proceeds, however, labor is eventually let go, as the desire to achieve some short-term profits outweighs the tendency to hoard labor. At the trough of the business cycle, rates of labor productivity growth begin to increase once again, and this sets the stage for the economic recovery.

Because of this cyclical volatility in labor productivity change, the year-to-year movements in rates of labor productivity change are very erratic. To remove this cyclical volatility from the data and obtain a better insight into *trends* in labor productivity change, the figures in column 1 of Table 15-5 have been collapsed into discrete time periods that span the several business cycles that have occurred in the economy since World War II. These data are presented in Table 15-6.

Between 1948 and 1965 the trend rate of growth in labor productivity was around 2.5 percent per year for the private, nonfarm sector of the economy. Between 1965 and 1973 the rate of growth in labor productivity declined to 1.6 percent per year, and between 1973 and 1978 it averaged only 0.9 percent per year. In the first half of the 1980s, productivity growth "recovered" to a sluggish 1.9 percent per year. The manufacturing sector of the economy, by itself, shows a higher rate of growth in labor productivity than occurs in the overall economy, but its trend remains the same—downward. Up to the mid-1950s, labor productivity in manufacturing was growing at a rate of 3.2 percent per year; in the early 1980s it was growing at a rate of about 2.8 percent per year, up from 1.5 percent in the late 1970s.

Explanations abound for why the rate of labor productivity growth has fallen steadily since the immediate postwar period. A slower rate of economic growth contributes to a slower rate of growth in labor productivity. Government regulations on pollution control and other environmental matters is said to be partly responsible for the decline in rates of labor productivity growth in recent years. Capital formation has been sluggish, and investment in research and development has not produced sufficient technological breakthroughs to propel labor productivity growth upward. A shift in the composition of production in the economy also affects productivity growth, as more and more of our output is in the low-productivity-growth sectors: services, trade, and government. A reduction in worker morale because of the "blue-collar blues" has been identified as another reason for the decline in rates of growth in labor productivity. All this is happening at a time when our labor force is more educated than ever before and the stock of human capital has never been higher. According to the theory of human capital, this should promote high rates of growth in labor productivity, but it has not.

Why?

Table 15-6 Annual Growth Rates in Labor Productivity, Selected Periods, 1948–1984

	Percentage Change				
Private, Nonfarm Economy	1948–1955	1955–1965	1965–1973	1973–1978	1979–1984
Manufacturing	3.2	2.8	2.4	1.5	2.8
Nonmanufacturing	2.1	2.2	1.2	0.5	1.4
Total, nonfarm private sector	2.4	2.5	1.6	0.9	1.9

DECREASING   *INCREASE*

Source: Council of Economic Advisers, *Economic Report of the President, 1980* (Washington: Government Printing Office), p. 85; Bureau of the Census, *Statistical Abstract of the United States, 1986* (Washington: Government Printing Office), p. 416.

Decrease rate   *Increasing rate.*

There are as many explanations for the slower rate of growth in productivity as there are economists studying the problem. To provide just one illustration: In one study of productivity, the author locates the decline in the rate of growth in productivity in three factors—pollution control regulations, health and safety regulations at work, and dishonesty and crime.[6] In another study of the same problem the authors conclude that the slower rate of growth in labor productivity between 1973 and 1978 was due primarily to a reduction in the rate of capital formation and secondarily to changes in the composition of output.[7] Two vastly different explanations of the same phenomenon by respected economists should be ample evidence that we know little about the real forces affecting productivity in the American economy.

Whatever the reasons for the decline in rates of growth in labor productivity, the implication of this trend is important for understanding the power of inflationary pressures in the economy. To acquire some insight into this, return to Table 15-5. Column 2 in that table presents data on the rate of change in unit labor costs; these data are a composite of the rates of change in wages and labor productivity. The third column shows the rate of inflation.

Figure 15-3 contains the time series on rates of change in unit labor costs and inflation. Notice how closely the two series move together. Occasionally one leads or lags; overall, however, the two series move in synchronization. This does not mean that labor costs cause inflation—a common belief. What causes inflation is examined in the next two chapters. Wage increases that exceed rates of change in labor productivity, thereby causing unit labor costs to rise, can be as much a *symptom* of inflation as a cause. For example, when workers seek to offset the reductions in their real

[6] Edward F. Denison, "Effects of Selected Changes in the Institutional and Human Environment upon Output per Unit of Input," *Survey of Current Business* 58 (January 1978), pp. 21–44.

[7] J. R. Norsworthy, M. J. Harper, and K. Kunze, "The Slowdown in Productivity Growth: Analysis of Some Contributing Factors," *Brookings Papers on Economic Activity* 2 (1979), pp. 387–421.

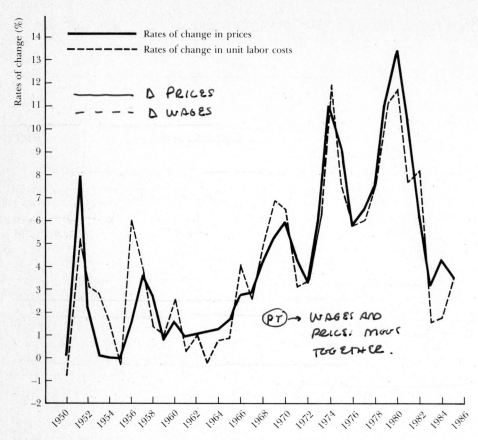

Figure 15-3   Rates of Change in Prices and Unit Labor Costs, 1950–1985

standards of living due to previous inflation, they cause unit labor costs to rise more rapidly. Is this a cause of the inflation or a symptomatic response to it?

Setting this controversial question aside, we can say that once inflation gets going, it tends to feed on itself, and the relationship between unit labor costs and inflation reveals this. As workers seek to catch up with inflation, higher unit labor costs lead to more inflation, as the higher costs are passed through to consumers in the form of higher prices. And the cycle begins anew. Public policy can attack the problem on the wage side of the unit labor cost problem by using wage-price policy or on the labor productivity side through "supply-side" policies. The latter approach tends to be more long-run than wage-price policy and has important welfare implications for the economy in terms of a redistribution of income toward the wealthy.[8]

---

[8] Wage-price policies are examined in Chapter 18.

Critique of the Way Inflation Is Measured

Is the inflation problem as serious as it is made out to be? Some analysts of the way inflation is measured say no. They point to the problems with the way in which the CPI purports to measure changes in the cost of living. First, there is the problem with the way in which some key items in the CPI are measured: housing and medical care. The change in the purchase price of homes enters the CPI, as does the change in the cost of medical care. In both instances the implicit assumption is made that the consumer buys a home every year (or every month in the case of the monthly CPI) and has major medical needs each period the CPI is announced. This is obviously not the case. The purchase of a home or the use of major medical services occurs only infrequently. The consumption of these items is not the same as the consumption of a hamburger or the purchase of a gallon of gasoline. However, the CPI treats both types of expenditures in the same way.

The problem is that some purchases by consumers occur only infrequently whereas others are happening all the time. The CPI does not make these distinctions. Rather, the CPI indicates what the increases in prices are for homes and medical care if you need to enter these markets. This defect in the CPI is compounded further by the specific reasons for the rapid price increases for homes and medical care.

In the case of housing, the most rapid increase has been the price of land. Land increased from 11 percent of the cost of a home in 1949 to 25 percent in 1978.[9] This, however, is due in part to inflation. Since land has been a traditional hedge against inflation in the United States, the demand for land has been increasing as people have sought to protect themselves from inflation. The increased demand for land has forced housing prices up however. Interest rates are also a major factor in housing prices and show up in mortgage payments.

The Bureau of Labor Statistics has initiated several "experimental" measures of the home ownership component of the CPI in order to take account of the problem with the way housing is evaluated in the existing CPI. They have used five different alternatives, and the impact of each on the CPI is significant. In 1978, for example, the CPI would have been reduced by 1.5 to 0.5 percentage points, depending on which alternative measure was used.[10]

In the case of medical care, the rising costs come from both the demand and the supply side. On the demand side, medicaid and medicare have made medical services available to people who would otherwise not have availed themselves of medical attention. The increase in the proportion of the population that is over 65 has placed

---

[9] James Carberry, "Land Plays Rising Role, Labor a Reduced One in the Long, Steep Climb in the Cost of New Homes," *Wall Street Journal*, October 11, 1978, p. 48.

[10] U.S. Department of Labor, "The Consumer Price Index—December 1979," news release, January 25, 1980. The alternative measures attempt to separate the cost of shelter from the investment aspects of home ownership and to distinguish changes in the cost of shelter from changes in the current housing market prices.

heavier demands on the existing supply of medical facilities. Treatment costs on the supply side have increased as modern technology has been applied to illness and disease in the past twenty years.

A second problem with the CPI relates to its reliance on a fixed market basket. The CPI measures the changes in prices of a given collection of goods and services. However, in response to changes in relative prices of goods and services, consumers alter their actual market basket of consumption items. This is what the theory of household consumption behavior is all about. If the price of steak goes up, fish and poultry are substituted. Consequently, the CPI is said by its critics to *overstate* the impact of inflation on the household, because people adapt to the altered circumstances caused by the rise in prices. Defenders of the CPI retort that although this adaptive behavior occurs, it does not negate using the CPI fixed-market-basket concept to measure what the cost would be if the household continued to consume as it did in the base period. If the household alters its consumption habits to offset inflationary impacts, it probably lowers its standard of living in terms of the quality of goods and services consumed.

On the other side of the fence are those interpreters of the CPI who contend that the measure *understates* the severity of the problem of inflation. The issue posed here is the *quality* of the goods and services purchased. Suppliers adjust to higher costs for their inputs into production by cutting corners on cost. This practice could lead to a lower-quality consumption item's being offered for sale. The CPI, on the other hand, assumes implicitly that the quality of the items in the fixed market basket has remained the same. If there has been quality deterioration, it does not appear in the CPI. To the extent this deterioration occurs, consumers are paying a higher price for a lower-quality item; they are getting less for more money.

These several criticisms of the CPI point to the need for more reliable and more current statistics on inflation than are now being provided by the BLS. The market basket should be revised more frequently during periods of rapid inflation. It makes little sense to continue to use a 1972–73 market basket of goods and services when the decade beginning in 1973 produced the most rapid inflation in our history. The quality of the products offered to the market should be monitored between periods of revision of the base-year market basket. A better specification of the measure of the cost of housing to the household should be devised, since a home is not purchased by every household during each period the CPI is measured.

This debate over the accuracy of the CPI's measure of inflation would be confined to academic economists and government statisticians were it not for the heavy impact of the CPI on the federal budget. Many government expenditures—such as social security and government workers' pensions—are indexed to inflation. Whenever the CPI increases, payments for these categorical programs increase along with it. Every 1 percent increase in the CPI automatically increases federal government expenditures by $2 billion.[11]

---

[11] "The Confounded Price Index," *Wall Street Journal*, May 13, 1981, p. 26.

In the private sector of the economy, many trade union contracts have partial or full adjustments to the CPI built into wage increases. Because the CPI triggers income adjustments, any suggestion of a change in the official measure of the CPI produces sharp political conflict.[12] In much the same way as the measure of unemployment, the CPI is made to do double duty. On one hand, it is used by economists and policymakers to track the rate of change in prices and take whatever policy measures are necessary to maintain a target rate of inflation. On the other hand, individual incomes are affected by the measure of the rate of inflation. At times, these two uses of the measure of inflation are in conflict.

Summary

Inflation is measured by the *consumer price index* (CPI), which tracks changes in the prices consumers pay for a fixed basket of goods and services. The rate of inflation in the 1970s was greater than in any comparable period of our history. Prices doubled between 1969 and 1979 as measured by the CPI. Prior to this period, it had taken forty years for the CPI to double.

Once inflation gets started, it is difficult to control, as the forces that propel inflation forward tend to take on a life of their own. Every segment of society attempts to protect itself from the ravages of inflation and in the process fuels the flames of inflation.

Inflation has an impact on several elements of personal welfare: income distribution, living standards, and economic growth. The inflation of the 1970s had a differential effect on prices of different goods and services. Prices of the necessities tended to increase faster because these items have a lower demand elasticity than do the prices of luxury goods and services. Consequently, lower-income groups suffered more in the inflation of the 1970s than did higher-income groups.

Wage increases for the average worker did not keep pace with inflation during the 1970s and 1980s. After adjusting for inflation, the weekly earnings of the average worker were less in 1985 than they were in 1967. To adapt to these circumstances, many households added a second member to the labor force. This cushioned the effects of inflation in the 1980s but will not be available to households in the 1990s because this card in the inflation game has already been played.

As workers sought to catch up with inflation, wages increased faster than labor productivity growth, driving up unit labor costs. These higher unit labor costs were

---

[12] Government estimates put the number of workers who have full or partial cost-of-living adjustments in their contracts at 9.5 million. This is in addition to the 34 million social security recipients whose payments are tied to inflation. See "Agency Defends Consumer Price Index But Will Study Other Inflation Measures," *Wall Street Journal*, January 22, 1980, p. 6.

translated into price increases and further inflation. This does not mean that labor and wages cause inflation—an issue that will be examined in the next chapter.

To make matters worse, the rate of increase in labor productivity slowed down in the 1970s. This added further pressures to unit labor costs, which became translated into more inflation.

Some critics of the CPI inflation measure contend that it overstates the problem. They point to the way in which price changes are measured for housing and medical care. These items are treated in the CPI as if they are consumed every time the CPI is measured. However, they are not the same as a movie or an ice cream cone; their consumption is a special event, not repeated very often. In addition, the use of a 1972–73 standard for a definition of the content of the typical household's market basket is said to be inadequate because consumers adjust to relative price changes by altering their market basket of consumption.

In defense of the CPI, its advocates claim that housing can be measured better and that the BLS is trying to do this. Using a fixed market basket is preferable, they say, because the CPI is a measure of the changing cost of a given bundle of goods and services, not of household adaptation to inflation.

There are some critics of the CPI who contend that it understates inflation by assuming quality is constant. Each item of the market basket is presumed to have a fixed quality over time. Firms, however, attempt to deal with their inflation problem by reducing quality in order to hold the line on costs. Thus, a given item may be costing more and providing less service because of quality reduction. This effect is not captured by the CPI measure.

Whatever the merits and demerits of the CPI measure, inflation remains an enormous problem that, if left unchecked, may devour us as it did other societies in this century. The forces that create more inflation are stronger than those that control it if the market is left to its own devices.

Study Questions

1. What is the consumer price index, and how does it attempt to measure inflation?

2. Discuss the relationship between inflation and unit labor costs. How do wages and productivity affect unit labor costs?

3. Does a decline in real wages represent a decrease in the economic welfare of households? Explain.

4. What is the relationship between inflation and income distribution? Who are typically the "winners" and the "losers" from inflation?

5. Under what circumstances would cost-of-living adjustments in union contracts *not* be inflationary?

6. Explain how the Consumer Price Index both overestimates and underestimates inflation.

Further Reading

Nulty, Leslie Ellen. "How Inflation Hits the Majority," *Challenge* (January–February 1979), pp. 32–38.

U.S. Department of Labor. *BLS Handbook of Methods*. Washington: Government Printing Office, 1976. Pp. 87–108.

16

Inflation: Causes and Policy Responses

No aspect of economics in recent years has produced as much controversy, confusion, and frustration as the problem of inflation. Just as unemployment posed an enigma for economics in the 1930s, inflation in the 1970s baffled everyone who sought to determine its cause and devise policies to alleviate it. It is truly "an awkward corner" for economics, as the British economist Joan Robinson characterized the problem some years ago.[1]

In the previous chapter the dimensions and anatomy of inflation were uncovered. In this chapter the focus shifts to several theories that purport to explain what causes inflation in a modern complex industrial economy. Along with these several explanations for the causes of inflation, specific policy prescriptions are presented where they exist.

Inflation has been studied from a Keynesian macro perspective and from a Friedman monetarist point of view. This text is about neither monetarism nor Keynesianism, per se. Rather, the focus in this chapter is on the role, if any, that labor plays in causing inflation, and on the way in which wage costs interact with the larger economic system to affect inflation.

---

[1] Joan Robinson, *Economics: An Awkward Corner* (New York: Pantheon Books, 1967), chap. 1.

I. Excess Demand Inflation
■

Inflation has been identified until recently as a problem of the macro economy. Keynes, the most influential macroeconomist of this century, provided an explanation for inflation that was a mirror image of his explanation for unemployment. If unemployment is caused by insufficient aggregate demand in relation to supply capacity, inflation is, consequently, a result of aggregate demand in excess of the capacity of the economy to supply goods and services. Too much money chasing too few goods is the aphorism used to describe this technical relationship in the economy.

If the aggregate price level and the economy's GNP are pictured graphically as in Figure 16-1, we can see that rapid inflation results from excess demand whenever the level of aggregate demand exceeds the full employment level of GNP. Aggregate supply is represented by the curve AS and aggregate demand by AD_0 and AD_1 in Figure 16-1. GNP cannot exceed GNP_0 in Figure 16-1 because that is the absolute capacity for the economy. As aggregate demand increases up to AD_0, prices rise slightly, but they take off into rapid inflation when aggregate demand exceeds AD_0— for example, at AD_1 in Figure 16-1. When aggregate demand increases to AD_1, prices increase from P_0 to P_1. The increase in aggregate demand above the full capacity utilization level of GNP_0 is reflected exclusively in higher prices, because the economy cannot expand its output and supply capabilities in the short run to absorb the increase in aggregate demand.

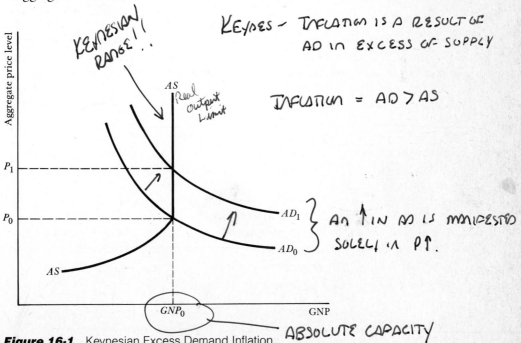

Figure 16-1 Keynesian Excess Demand Inflation

This is an extreme case, however. With mobility of factors of production limited in the short run, inflationary pressures can enter the economy before aggregate demand reaches absolute full capacity utilization. Bottlenecks arise before that point is reached, as some sectors of the economy reach their capacity utilization before others have reached theirs. If factors of production are not perfectly mobile in the short run, inflation will commence in the sectors in which bottlenecks have arisen, and the aggregate price level will begin to increase before the entire economy is at full capacity utilization.

The Keynesian version of excess demand inflation revolves around so-called real aggregates in the economy—demand for and supply of goods and services. On the demand side, Keynes is talking about consumption, investment, government spending, and foreign demand. On the supply side, he is referring to the actual physical capacity of an economy to produce the goods and services for those willing to purchase them.

In positing this theory of inflation, based on real phenomena, Keynes was striking out in a direction contrary to the received doctrine of aggregate economics in classical economics, which was based on the *quantity theory of money*.[2] In this view of the macroeconomy, inflation is a monetary phenomenon, not a "real" one. Inflation arises when the money supply increases at a rate that exceeds the rate of growth in the production of goods and services in the economy, assuming the velocity of money is held constant.

The distinction between these two theories of inflation is important because they point to different causes and, therefore, distinct policy approaches. The monetary theory of inflation locates the cause in the rate of growth in the money supply. Policy responses revolve around limiting the rate of growth in the money supply to that which would be warranted by the growth in the productive capacity of the economy. The Keynesian view holds that inflation is caused by an excess of real demand, evidenced by those with resources to make purchases in the economy, compared with the capacity of enterprises to meet this level of demand. The requisite policy response is to restrain this real demand by a mix of tax and expenditure policy rather than operating on the money supply. Keynesian fine tuning of an economy to bring aggregate demand and supply into balance is the approach of this brand of economics.

In the 1980s it has become fashionable to turn this policy reponse on its head by advocating programs that would expand supply rather than solely restraining demand. An imbalance in the macroeconomy between aggregate supply and aggregate demand can be corrected in one of two ways—by reducing demand or by increasing supply (or by a combination of the two). Increasing aggregate supply is called *supply-side economics* in today's parlance, to refer to policies that would stimulate enterprises

---

[2] For a review of these concepts, see Martin Bronfenbrenner and Franklyn D. Holzman, "Survey of Inflation Theory," *American Economic Review 53*, no. 4 (September 1963), pp 594–602.

to offer more goods and services in order to relieve conditions of excessive demand in markets.

These policy proposals have been put forward in the current context of economic affairs, which is different from that presented in the pure theory of excess-demand inflation. The economy is not at full capacity utilization and the inflation described in the previous chapter cannot easily be pigeonholed as having an excess-demand cause. Nevertheless, supply-side economic policies can be placed in this conceptual framework in terms of the reasons for their advocacy and their expected results. The next chapter on *stagflation* takes up these issues in more detail.

Cost-Push Inflation

Excess demand inflation results from aggregate demand increasing when the economy is at a level of full utilization of labor and capital. Prices rise, but the supply of goods and services does not, because there is no slack left in the economy. Prices under these circumstances are said to be *pulled along* by growing demand in the face of full utilization of existing capacity. This process is referred to as *demand-pull* inflation.

Starting after World War II, another explanation for inflation was offered—the so-called *cost-push* inflation. In this model prices are pushed upward by rising costs while the economy is operating at *less* than full capacity utilization. In part, this theory was propounded to explain why prices rose in the face of unemployed labor and of plants operating at less than full capacity utilization. The argument of this theory is that costs—usually labor costs—rise more rapidly than is warranted by the existing conditions of the labor market. These costs, in turn, are passed along to consumers in the form of rising prices. The rise in labor costs beyond that which would be justified by conditions in the labor market is said to be caused by strong trade unions.

As we saw in the previous chapter, wage increases in excess of labor productivity increases cause unit labor costs to rise. These higher unit labor costs are then passed on to consumers, and the result is rising prices, according to the cost-push theory of inflation. This can be depicted graphically as shown in Figure 16-2. With a level of demand of AD, which produces a less than full employment GNP (GNP_0), prices are initially at P_0. Aggregate supply is represented by the curve AS_0. Unit labor costs increase at the margin because wages rise in excess of the rate of increase in labor productivity, and the resulting increasing aggregate supply price is reflected by a shift in the aggregate supply curve to AS_1. Prices increase to P_1 in order to compensate the firm for the higher unit labor costs, while aggregate demand remains fixed at AD. All this transpires with the economy operating at less than the full employment of labor and capital of GNP_{fe}. The rise in prices due to the higher wages also reduces GNP, from GNP_0 to GNP_1.

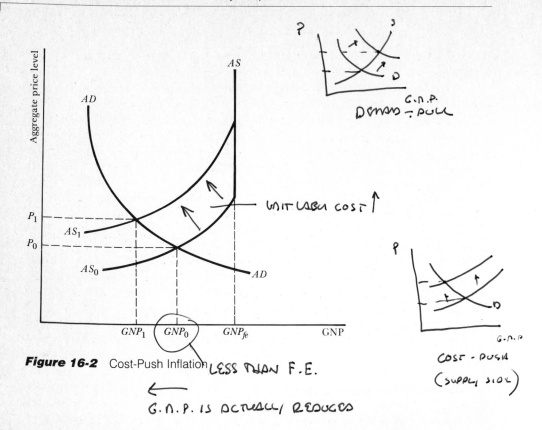

Figure 16-2   Cost-Push Inflation *LESS THAN F.E.*

← G.N.P. IS ACTUALLY REDUCED

The policy proposal implicit in this analysis is that wage increases must be restrained if inflation is to be brought under control. This can be accomplished in a variety of ways: wage controls, reductions in the power of trade unions, and reductions in the elements of the social wage (unemployment compensation, welfare, food stamps, and minimum wages).

Is this theory of inflation and its policy prescriptions valid? The answer to this question evokes perhaps more emotionally charged rhetoric than any other that will be encountered in this book. Cost-push, more specifically wage-push, inflation is widely regarded as the principal cause of inflation. Indeed, a casual glance at Figure 15-3, presented in the previous chapter, would seem to confirm the existence of wage-push inflation. The relationship between changes in unit labor costs and inflation is a close one. Labor unions are visible targets of the public media when it comes to the wage-setting process.

But casual impressions supporting this theory of inflation may turn out to be less convincing when subjected to a more careful scrutiny. First, when this question is studied empirically, it is unclear whether trade unions have the effect on wages they are purported to have. Recall the material presented in Chapter 7 that bears on this matter. Trade unions impose an 8–10 percent premium on wage rates over what the rates would be without a union. Translated into price increases, the effect of unions

COST PUSH = WAGE PUSH !!

is reduced further, because labor is only a portion of the firm's total costs, and labor productivity increases reduce further the effect of higher wages.[3]

Second, it is difficult if not impossible to unravel which comes first, the wage increases or the price increases that cause labor to seek higher wages. For example, in the 1970s, wage increases lagged behind price increases. If labor seeks to make up the ground it has lost because of inflation, is it the culprit in the drama, or are the causes located somewhere else? In 1979 the rate of inflation was 11 percent, and wages increased by 8 percent. If wages increased in 1980 in order to make up this shortfall in 1979, could one say that wage increases cause inflation? Stated differently, the problem of wages increasing in excess of labor productivity growth may be a *symptom* of a more fundamental problem in the economy rather than its cause.

A variant of the cost-push inflation thesis broadens the scope of the analysis to include groups other than labor. There are a wide variety of interest groups in the economy that compete for its resources. Labor is one such group. But there are others. Senior citizens seek higher social security benefits. Private firms constantly seek to make higher profits and will charge higher prices to do so unless the market is competitive enough to stop them. Veterans want more benefits from Congress. We all want more, and this places strains on the economy, particularly in a pluralistic democracy in which citizens have learned how to influence their legislators through lobbying and by organizing themselves as pressure groups during electoral campaigns. Indeed, this is what democracy is supposed to be about.

But the problem is that the aggregate of such claims on the economy's resources may exceed what it can deliver. There are "excess-demand" and "cost-push" pressures, but in a sense different from conventional usage. Here, the demands are public as well as private, and their manifestation in the economy takes the form of public budget deficits, wages rising in excess of labor productivity, and prices rising in excess of what would be justified by higher costs. The result is something that the economist Robert Heilbroner calls *inflationary capitalism*.[4] He refers by this term to the successful accomplishments of the modern welfare state in meeting the demands placed on it by its citizens. But the consequence of servicing these citizen claims is an inflationary trajectory in the economy, which has gone unchecked until now.

Inflationary capitalism infers that there is some more profound systemic character to inflation than can be described in a simple technical relationship between two variables. It represents an outcome of the success of our society in fashioning public programs and fostering private economic growth. As more people have received a hearing in Congress for their claims, and as the private economy has become more expansive, demands on resources have begun to exceed the ability of the economy to

---

[3] These issues are surveyed in Daniel J. B. Mitchell, *Unions, Wages, and Inflation* (Washington: The Brookings Institution, 1980).

[4] Robert Heilbroner, "Inflationary Capitalism," *New Yorker,* October 8, 1979, pp. 121–41.

meet them. Where the reductions in claims are to be made is a sticky political question; that is why inflation has become so difficult to eradicate.

The Phillips Curve: Inflation-Unemployment Trade-off

The Phillips curve represents an attempt to sort out demand-pull inflation from cost-push inflation. The empirical problems encountered in the earlier efforts to distinguish between cost-push and demand-pull inflation were substantial. In a dynamic economy many indicators move up at the same time. Costs rise, wage rates go up, and prices increase. Which comes first, and what is the cause versus the effect, is difficult if not impossible to ascertain.

Hypothetical Phillips Curve

Writing in 1958, A. W. Phillips provided an ingenious, yet simple, device for depicting the sources of inflation.[5] Perhaps no other analysis of inflation has better captured a neo-Keynesian approach to the problem. The Phillips curve, in its simplest version,

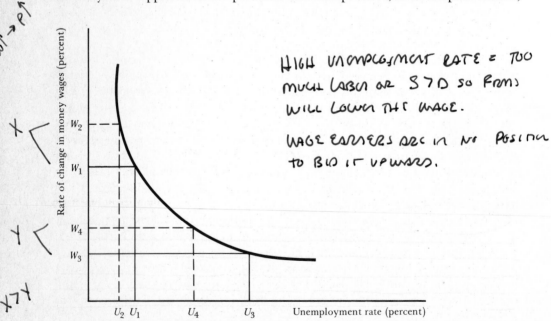

Figure 16-3   Hypothetical Phillips Curve

HIGH UNEMPLOYMENT RATE = TOO MUCH LABOR OR S > D SO FIRMS WILL LOWER THE WAGE.

WAGE EARNERS ARE IN NO POSITION TO BID IT UPWARDS.

---

[5] A. W. Phillips, "The Relation between Unemployment and the Rate of Change of Money Wage Rates in the United Kingdom, 1861–1957," *Economica* 25, no. 100 (November 1958), pp. 283–99.

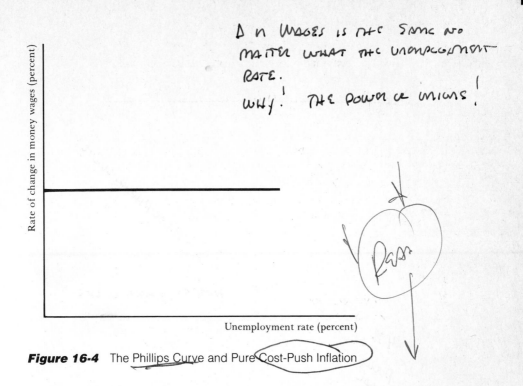

Handwritten annotations:
Δ in WAGES is the SAME no
MATTER WHAT THE UNEMPLOYMENT
RATE.
WHY! THE POWER of UNIONS!

Pass

Figure 16-4   The Phillips Curve and Pure Cost-Push Inflation

relates the rate of change in money wage rates to the rate of unemployment. A hypothetical Phillips curve is presented in Figure 16-3. This is the most common shape and form that the Phillips curve assumes. Notice first, that the curve is non-linear. This means that when unemployment rates are low, U_1 in Figure 16-3, a further small reduction in the unemployment rate will induce a sharp increase in wages. For example, when unemployment falls from U_1 to U_2, wages increase from W_1 to W_2. The increase in wage rates is far greater than the decline in unemployment rates. On the other hand, when unemployment is very high, for example at U_3, a relatively large reduction in unemployment rates (from U_3 to U_4) will have only a small effect on increases in the wage rate (W_3 to W_4). Nonlinearity, therefore, is the first aspect of the Phillips curve worth noting, since it has important economic implications, particularly for public policy.

Nonlinearity exists in the Phillips curve because the unemployment rate is a proxy measure of the extent to which demand pressures are occurring in the economy. If unemployment rates are low, the economy is approaching full capacity utilization of both labor and capital resources, and further reductions in unemployment produce relatively large wage increases. If unemployment rates are high, underutilized labor and capital resources exist. When unemployment rates are high, however, reductions in the unemployment rate will have a relatively smaller impact on wages.

How can the Phillips curve assist in unraveling the cost-push elements of inflation from demand-pull inflation? If inflation were solely a cost-push phenomenon, the Phillips curve would look like the the one shown in Figure 16-4. The horizontal line

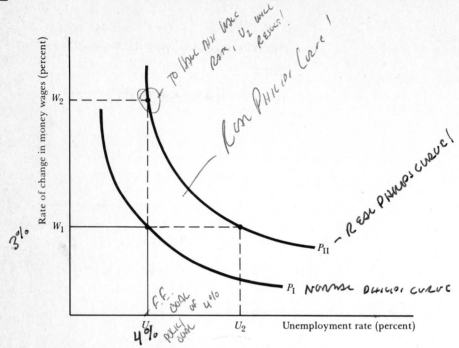

Figure 16-5   Two Phillips Curves and the Policy Dilemma

for the Phillips curve indicates that the rate of change in wages is the same no matter what the rate of unemployment. Wages are determined purely by "power" forces, and the influence of the market has been superseded by the importance of nonmarket actors in the wage-setting process, such as trade unions. This is an extreme case, and nowhere will we find an actual Phillips curve that is perfectly horizontal. But it is an important benchmark. The *flatter* the slope of the Phillips curve, the more important are cost-push factors in explaining the causes of inflation.

The shape of the Phillips curve is one important yardstick in determining whether inflation is demand induced or cost induced. Another use of the Phillips curve is for describing the *inflation propensity* of an economy. For example, consider the normal Phillips curve, P_1, shown in Figure 16-5. If the unemployment goal of policymakers is 4 percent, the Phillips curve can be used to infer how much inflation will be associated with that unemployment rate. In Figure 16-5, U_1 is the full-employment goal of 4 percent. Associated with that rate of unemployment is a rate of increase in wages of, say, 3 percent, represented by W_1 in Figure 16-5. If the rate of increase in labor productivity is also 3 percent, then the 4 percent unemployment goal will have no effect on prices, since unit labor costs will have remained constant. Recall that the key link between higher wages and higher prices is the rate of increase in labor productivity. If the two exactly offset each other, wages can rise without increasing unit labor costs and prices, as long as there is no monopoly pricing power in the markets for goods and services, which would result in higher price markups. The

3 percent rate of wage increase in Figure 16-5 would be a noninflationary one if labor productivity had increased by the same amount. That rate of wage increase is also compatible with an acceptable rate of unemployment of 4 percent.

NOTE The world just shown is a delight to policymakers, but unfortunately it is not one they encounter. The real Phillips curve normally lies to the right of the one indicated as P_I in Figure 16-5. A Phillips curve such as P_{II} highlights the unpleasant choice faced by policymakers. With the Phillips curve represented by P_{II}, full employment of 4 percent unemployed implies a rate of increase in wages of W_2—much higher than W_1. Combined with the same rate of increase in labor productivity as before, this would mean substantial increases in unit labor costs and prices. Alternatively, with a Phillips curve of P_{II}, a noninflationary rate of wage increase of W_1, implies a rate of unemployment of U_2. This is the dilemma policymakers face: either inflation can be reduced at the expense of unemployment or unemployment can be reduced at the expense of inflation.

The position of the Phillips curve is, consequently, important in identifying the extent of inflationary tendencies in an economy. The further to the northeast the curve is placed on a graph, the higher is the inflation propensity of an economy. If P_I and P_{II} represent different countries, the latter country is more inflation prone than the former. If the two Phillips curves represent the same country at different points in time, a movement from P_I to P_{II} means that the economy has increased its inflation propensity over time, rendering the trade-off between inflation and unemployment more difficult for policymakers to resolve.

A shifting Phillips curve that worsens the inflation-unemployment trade-off can be interpreted as support for the cost-push inflation hypothesis. Consider Figure 16-5 once again: if this is the same country, nonmarket forces are taking on increased importance. For instance, at the rate of unemployment represented by U_1, the rate of increase in wages was originally W_1, and then it rose to W_2 after the shift in the Phillips curve. This would indicate that for the same labor market conditions, the rate of increase in wages is greater. This could only happen, *ceteris paribus*, if labor exerted more power over wages and was able to escape labor market pressures.

Caution must be the watchword in rendering this interpretation, however, since the real dynamics of an economy might make it impossible to accept the *ceteris paribus* condition. Prices might have risen earlier, and labor might only be seeking to catch up with past real wage declines. Lags between unemployment and wage rate increases might exist, and the relation between these two variables, therefore, may be observable only over the entire business cycle. These are but a few of the problems in interpreting this hypothetical Phillips curve in relation to real world economic events.

Structural Imbalances and the Phillips Curve

What can account for the Phillips curve of one country being positioned farther to the right than that of another, or for the shift in the Phillips curve in a particular country over time? The answer is to be found in the notion of *structural imbalances* that occur in the economy—particularly those that exist in the labor market.

In the labor market there can be sectors with excess demand for labor, in which wages are rising rapidly, and other sectors with an excess supply of labor, which shows up in high unemployment rates. However, because of various institutional factors, wages in the sectors with an excess supply of labor may not fall sufficiently to offset the increase in wages that occurs in the sectors with excess demand for labor. The sum of these sectoral imbalances is that wages rise in the sectors with excess demand for labor and unemployment is high in the sectors of excess supply of labor. The Phillips curve will represent these conditions with a placement of the curve that depends on how large the wage increases are in the sectors with excess demand for labor and how high unemployment is in the sectors of excess supply of labor.[6]

Presumably the labor market should adjust through mobility and eliminate these structural imbalances. Unemployed workers should seek jobs in the sectors of the economy with an excess demand for labor. This should eliminate the unemployment in the excess-supply segment of the economy and reduce pressures on wages in the excess demand sector. But this may not occur if the skills needed in the sectors of excess demand for labor are not those possessed by the unemployed workers. This is *structural unemployment*, a concept discussed previously, in Chapter 14. The greater is the problem of structural unemployment in the economy, the worse is the inflation-unemployment trade-off. A shifting Phillips curve over time in the same country, or differences in Phillips curves among countries, can be explained by the different degrees of structural unemployment.

The policy implication, therefore, is to encourage labor mobility in order to remove the structural imbalances in the economy caused by a mismatch in skills between those seeking work and those wanting to hire workers. Employment training programs, improvements in the information about available jobs, and incentives to relocate are all labor market policies that flow from this analysis of the Phillips curve and the inflation-unemployment trade-off.

Phillips Curve for the United States

The data pertinent to the construction of a Phillips curve for the United States are presented in Table 16-1. The actual Phillips curve relationship between percentage changes in money wage rates and unemployment rates is shown in Figure 16-6. For the years 1948–1969 it is possible to construct a Phillips curve that best represents the observations of each year during that period of time. This is shown as the normal Phillips nonlinear curve in Figure 16-6. For the years 1970–1985, however, the Phillips curve relationship breaks down, and there is no way to construct a unique curve that would best represent the different observations for each year.

The Phillips curve for the years 1948–1969 shows a fairly regular relationship between unemployment and rates of change in money wages. The relationship is not

---

[6] Richard W. Lipsey, "The Relation between Unemployment and the Rate of Change of Money Wage Rates in the United Kingdom, 1862-1957: A Further Analysis," *Economica* 27, no. 105 (February 1960), pp. 1-31.

Table 16-1 Phillips Curve: Unemployment Rate, Rate of
Change in Money Wages, and Inflation Rate, 1948–1985

Year	Percentage Change in Money Wage Rates (%)	Inflation Rate (%)	Unemployment Rate (%)
1948	8.0	—	3.8
1949	4.8	−0.1	5.9
1950	3.7	0.1	5.3
1951	7.4	7.9	3.3
1952	5.0	2.2	3.0
1953	5.7	0.1	2.9
1954	3.5	negligible	5.5
1955	3.2	negligible	4.4
1956	5.2	1.5	4.1
1957	4.9	3.6	4.3
1958	4.1	2.7	6.8
1959	3.6	0.8	5.5
1960	3.4	1.6	5.5
1961	3.1	1.0	6.7
1962	3.3	1.1	5.5
1963	2.9	1.2	5.7
1964	2.7	1.3	5.2
1965	3.4	1.7	4.5
1966	4.5	2.8	3.8
1967	4.9	2.9	3.8
1968	6.2	4.2	3.6
1969	6.6	5.3	3.5
1970	6.6	5.9	4.9
1971	7.0	4.3	5.9
1972	6.4	3.3	5.6
1973	6.2	6.2	4.9
1974	7.9	11.0	5.6
1975	8.3	9.1	8.5
1976	7.3	5.8	7.7
1977	7.5	6.5	7.0
1978	8.2	7.6	6.0
1979	7.9	11.3	5.8
1980	9.0	13.5	7.1
1981	9.1	10.4	7.6
1982	6.8	6.1	9.7
1983	4.6	3.2	9.6
1984	3.4	4.3	7.5
1985	3.0	3.6	7.2

Source: Council of Economic Advisers, *Economic Report of the President,
1986* (Washington: Government Printing Office, 1986), pp. 293, 300,
318.

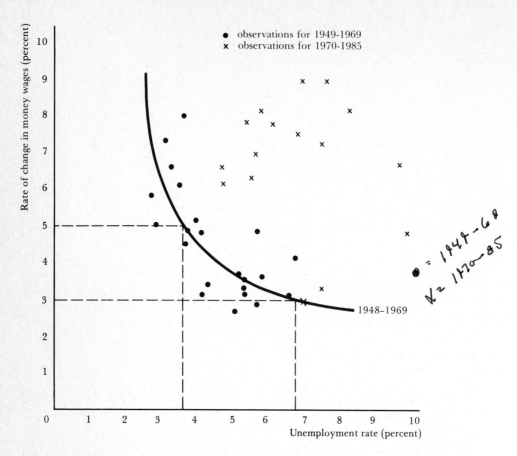

Figure 16-6 Phillips Curve for the United States, 1948–1985

a statistically strong one, however, although it does exist. During that 22-year period, the average rate of increase in labor productivity per year was 3.0 percent. If money wages were to increase at that same rate per year, leaving unit labor costs unchanged, unemployment would average slightly under 7 percent. This is implied in the Phillips curve for the 1948–1969 time period, shown in Figure 16-6. Allowing for the small increase in unit labor costs that would be implied by a 5 percent increase in money wages per year brings the unemployment rate down to a more acceptable level of about 3.8 percent. Therefore, until 1969 the goal of a 4 percent unemployment rate with only moderate increases in unit labor costs and inflation was attainable.

This changed in the 1970s, however. All the observations for the years 1970–1984 lie substantially to the right of the Phillips curve for the 1948–1969 period.[7]

---

[7] 1985 lies on the 1948–1969 Phillips curve.

The trade-off between unemployment and inflation has worsened considerably, leaving policymakers with the dilemma of inflating the economy or running up the unemployment rate. Furthermore, the inflationary propensity of the economy has been aggravated by a falloff in the rate of productivity increase as well. In the 1970s and early 1980s labor productivity increased, on average, only 1.3 percent per year in the manufacturing sector, compared with the earlier 3.0 percent rate. The economy has been blind-sided by two intersecting structural phenomena that have aggravated the inflation-unemployment trade-off: a worsening of the Phillips curve relationship between unemployment and changes in wage rates and a reduction in the rate of increase in labor productivity.

The worsening trade-off between unemployment and inflation is shown more directly in Figure 16-7, where the rate of *inflation* is plotted against the rate of unemployment for each year of the 1949–1985 period. The nonlinear curve for the

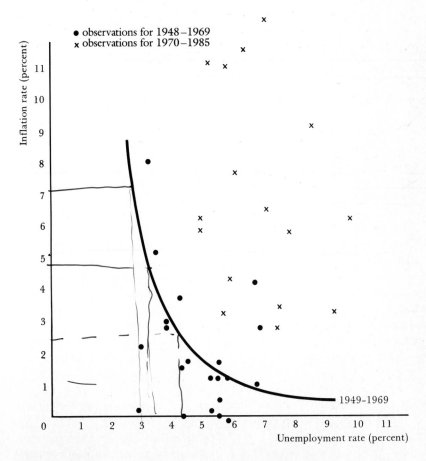

Figure 16-7 Rate of Inflation and Rate of Unemployment, 1949–1985

years 1949–1969 is a weaker statistical relationship than was the Phillips curve. This is to be expected, since the unemployment rate directly affects the rate of increase in wages but only indirectly affects inflation through the mediating influence of labor productivity changes. The observations for each year jump over the graph more erratically than do those for the normal Phillips curve relationship. Some years contain aberrant observations due to the instability in rates of change in labor productivity from year to year.

For the 1970–1985 period there is even less regularity in the relationship between inflation and unemployment, as shown by the observations for those years in Figure 16-7. All the points in the 1970s and early 1980s lie to the right of the 1949–1969 relationship between inflation and unemployment, confirming the worsening trade-off between those two macroeconomic policy objectives.

Inflation Policy and the 1970s Phillips Curve

There is no policy consensus about what to do about the problem of inflation, compared with what exists as a general policy approach to unemployment. Monetary restraint, balanced federal budgets, and wage-price controls are but a few of the ideas that emerge periodically in the assault against inflation. For our purposes, policies that deal with the role of the labor market in inflation are of singular interest. Several such policy proposals have been put forward to deal with the inflationary tendencies that emerge from the labor market. Some of these ideas will be discussed in more detail in the two succeeding chapters, on stagflation and wage-price policy, but it is worth mentioning them here as a prelude to that more complete discussion.

Incomes policies—the generic term for wage-price policy—is one approach to the inflationary pressures that emanate from the labor market. They deal with the symptom of the problem, however, rather than the cause.

To the extent the Phillips curve represents an increasing structural imbalance in the economy, the solution would be to construct policies that moderate these labor market problems. In this category are employment training, relocation, and the like.

Policies that deal with the problem of labor market immobilities are part of an emerging consensus forming around *supply-side* economic policies. Such programs seek to eliminate bottlenecks that occur in the economy because of supply rigidities. Another such effort would be policies to improve the rate of growth of labor productivity, which would reduce pressures on unit labor costs in the economy.

All these ideas are feeble, however, in the face of rapid inflation that has built-in tendencies toward its acceleration. Each segment of society seeks to protect its position and, in the process of doing so, exacerbates inflation. Expectations about continued inflation lead to behavior that is rational for the individual but merely worsens the problem for the entire economy. This is a vicious circle that must be interrupted or inflation will rapidly get out of control and take off into the hyper variety, which has eroded other apparently stable societies in the past. Inflationary psychology and expectations play a large role in producing a hyperinflation, and these subjective elements of the society must be discouraged before they take on a life of their own.

Summary

As with many other aspects of economics, events of the 1970s shattered the consensus among economists as to what causes inflation. Up to that time, ever since the Keynesian revolution took hold in economics, economists viewed inflation either as the mirror image of unemployment or as being caused by institutional conditions in the labor market that pushed wages up too rapidly. The former was called *excess-demand* inflation and the latter *cost-push* inflation.

Excess-demand inflation results from aggregate demand in the private and public sectors exceeding the supply capacities of the economy. When this occurs, the proper policy posture for the government is to restrain aggregate demand by a mixture of tax, expenditure, and monetary policies.

Cost-push inflation is supposed to result when wages rise in excess of the rate of increase in labor productivity. This causes unit labor costs to increase—an increase that becomes translated into higher prices. The important difference between this theory of inflation and excess-demand theories is that wages rise even though the economy is operating at less than full employment of labor and capital resources. The resulting manifestation of cost-push inflation is a price rise along with relatively high rates of unemployment and unused plant and equipment. The policy response to this phenomenon is some form of wage-price policy that seeks to restrain wage increases and bring them into line with the growth of labor productivity.

In the late 1950s A. W. Phillips sought to study whether inflation in Great Britain was caused by excess demand or by cost-push factors. In the process of conducting his study, he conceived of a relationship that has come to be called the *Phillips curve*. The Phillips curve relates the rate of change in money wages to the rate of unemployment.

Rates of money wage increases become translated into inflation through changes in unit labor costs. Rates of change in unit labor costs are dependent on rates of change in labor productivity as well as on increases in the money wage rate. The Phillips curve contains a trade-off: lower rates of inflation can only be attained through lower rates of change in money wages, which occur when unemployment is high. The dilemma facing policymakers is that they can either have more unemployment and less inflation or unemployment at the cost of more inflation. The dismal science of economics once more points out that there are opportunity costs to whatever policy goal is sought.

This choice between inflation and unemployment can be within an acceptable range. If the society is willing to tolerate some inflation and some unemployment, then it is possible that the Phillips curve could show a trade-off range that is within the boundaries society has established for inflation and unemployment. In the United States the Phillips curve was within an acceptable range throughout the 1950s and 1960s. But in the 1970s and early 1980s, the Phillips curve relationship, to the extent it existed, was outside the bounds of an acceptable level of inflation and unemployment. This has imposed an even crueler choice on the policymaker, who has to decide between two evils—inflation and unemployment.

Study Questions

1. What are the conditions in the labor market that can lead to cost-push inflation?

2. What is the "Phillips curve," and what are its implications for inflation and unemployment?

3. Assume you are a member of the President's Task Force on Inflation. You are given the assignment to design public policies for the labor market to reduce inflation. What would your report say?

4. What explains the shift in the Phillips curve in the United States in the 1970s and early 1980s?

5. What is the relationship between wages and unit labor costs? Between unit labor costs and inflation?

Further Reading

Bronfenbrenner, Martin, and Franklyn D. Holzman. "Survey of Inflation Theory." *American Economic Review* 53, no.4 (September 1963), pp. 593–661.

Frisch, Helmut. "Inflation Theory 1963–1975: A 'Second Generation' Survey." *Journal of Economic Literature* 15, no.4 (December 1977), pp. 1289–1317.

Phillips, A. W. "The Relation between Unemployment and the Rate of Change in Money Wage Rates in the United Kingdom, 1861–1957." *Economica* 25, no. 100 (November 1958), pp. 283–99.

17

Stagflation

The supposed trade-off between inflation and unemployment disappeared in the 1970s. For most years during that decade there were persistently high unemployment rates and high rates of inflation. Traditional Keynesian macroeconomic theory cannot account for such a phenomenon except in unusual circumstances. But it did occur during the 1970s, and it called into question the existence of a Phillips curve trade-off between inflation and unemployment. Economists now conjecture whether there exists a Phillips curve at all and, if one does not exist, what the implications are for macroeconomic theory and policy pertaining to inflation.

A new term was coined in the 1970s to explain the coexistence of high rates of unemployment and inflation. That term is *stagflation*. Stagflation refers to the simultaneous occurrence of unemployment and inflation that exceed the normal rates defined by policy objectives. Stagflation is a word that takes its segments from *stag*nation, to capture unemployment, and in*flation*, to capture the phenomenon of rising prices.

Being a relatively new phenomenon, stagflation has just begun to engage the attention of economists. For that reason there is little consensus as to what causes stagflation and what are the appropriate policy responses to deal with the problem. The models and policy proposals put forward in this chapter are therefore more tentative than some of the materials presented in the previous chapters of this part of the book.

The 1970s were an unusual decade for the economy. Certain external shocks jolted the economy at its foundation. The international monetary system, organized around fixed exchange rates, was formally ended in 1971, just as the decade was beginning. A vacuum was created, which remains unfilled even today, as the Bretton Woods system, put in place in 1946, ended a 25-year stint. This produced monetary instability in the world economy, which has had repercussions for inflation in the United States.[1]

The second great event of the 1970s was the emergence of the Organization of Petroleum Exporting Countries (OPEC) as a price-setter for crude oil. This produced a massive transfer of wealth from the industrial countries to the oil-producing countries, along with an explosion of debt in other less-developed countries. The supply of dollars grew internationally to support the higher level of crude oil prices, which exacerbated the already unstable international monetary system. The high oil prices had a dramatic impact on inflation in the United States.

These two events—the erosion of the Bretton Woods international monetary system and the rise of OPEC—caused inflation to be more severe in the United States than it would have otherwise. These historical events cannot be ignored in any analysis of stagflation. But the question is, are there inherent tendencies toward stagflation in the American economy? If there are, what are they? This is the formulation of the problem that is the focus of this chapter. External shocks, in this perception of the economy, simply exacerbate tendencies that are structurally imbedded in the economy. Public policy can best address the structure of the American economy; it cannot directly affect the pricing policies of OPEC.

The Anatomy of Stagflation

Stagflation is defined as the simultaneous occurrence of unemployment and inflation. It is measured, accordingly, as the sum of the rates of unemployment and inflation. These data are presented for the years 1949–1985 in Table 17-1 and reproduced graphically in Figure 17-1. The data reveal what we all experienced in the economy during the 1970s: there was a dramatic growth in the rate of stagflation in that decade compared with the previous two postwar decades. From 1980 to 1985 the rate of stagflation declined, but it remained above 10 percent.

What is an acceptable level of stagflation for the economy? This question has a limited answer because public policy goals are still established with reference to a separate objective for unemployment and a separate objective for inflation. This presumes the two do not systematically occur together but are substitutes for each other. The stagflationist view of the economy hypothesizes that inflation and unemployment might not be trade-offs with each other, but may instead complement each other. If

---

[1] Howard M. Wachtel, *The Money Mandarins. The Making of a New Supranational Economic Order* (New York: Pantheon Books, 1986).

Table 17-1   Stagflation, 1949–1985.

Year	Rate of Inflation (%)	Rate of Unemployment (%)	Rate of Stagflation (%)[a]
1949	−0.1	5.9	5.8
1950	0.1	5.3	5.4
1951	7.9	3.3	11.2
1952	2.2	3.0	5.2
1953	0.1	2.9	3.0
1954	negligible	5.5	5.5
1955	negligible	4.4	4.4
1956	1.5	4.1	5.6
1957	3.6	4.3	7.9
1958	2.7	6.8	9.5
1959	0.8	5.5	6.3
1960	1.6	5.5	7.1
1961	1.0	6.7	7.7
1962	1.1	5.5	6.6
1963	1.2	5.7	6.9
1964	1.3	5.2	6.5
1965	1.7	4.5	6.2
1966	2.8	3.8	6.6
1967	2.9	3.8	6.7
1968	4.2	3.6	7.8
1969	5.3	3.5	8.8
1970	5.9	4.9	10.8
1971	4.3	5.9	10.2
1972	3.3	5.6	8.9
1973	6.2	4.9	11.1
1974	11.0	5.6	16.6
1975	9.1	8.5	17.6
1976	5.8	7.7	13.5
1977	6.5	7.0	13.5
1978	7.6	6.0	13.6
1979	11.3	5.8	17.1
1980	13.5	7.1	20.6
1981	10.4	7.6	18.0
1982	6.1	9.7	15.8
1983	3.2	9.6	12.8
1984	4.3	7.5	11.8
1985	3.6	7.2	10.8

[a]Rate of stagflation is the sum of the rates of inflation and unemployment.
Source: Tables 15-2 and 16-1.

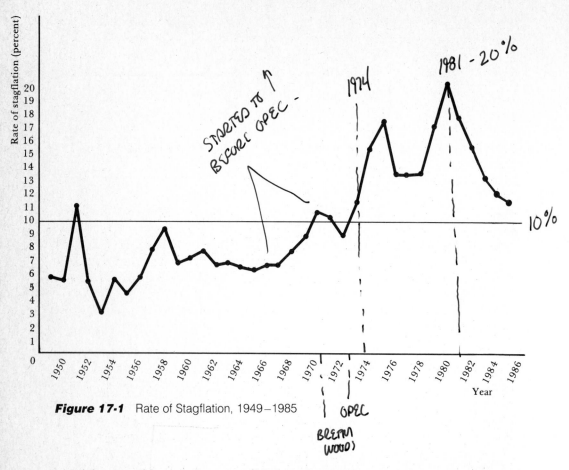

Figure 17-1   Rate of Stagflation, 1949–1985

true, it is reasonable, therefore, to establish a policy goal in terms of a rate of stagflation. Doing this means that policy goals for unemployment and inflation are no longer seen as independent objectives; rather they are "joint products."

Suppose a policy goal for the rate of stagflation were 10 percent—a combined rate of inflation and unemployment that did not exceed 10 percent. Based on that criterion, the economy did well in the 1950s and 1960s.[2] In only one year, 1951, did the rate of stagflation exceed 10 percent during the first two decades after World War II. The 11.2 percent stagflation in 1951, induced by the Korean War, was quickly reversed, however, and was more than halved by the next year.

The 1970s and early 1980s were a different story. The rate of stagflation went over 10 percent in 1970 and did not drop below that level except for one year, 1972. This amount of stagflation occurred before OPEC started its pricing policies in 1973,

---

[2] The solid line in the middle of Figure 17-1 represents the 10 percent stagflation policy objective.

so it is apparent that aspects of a stagflationary economy were evident before OPEC appeared on the scene. Since 1973 the situation has worsened, and events have merely exacerbated what was already becoming a serious stagflationary problem. Between 1973–1979, the rate of stagflation never dropped below 13.5 percent. In 1980, it reached a peak of more than 20 percent, to end a tumultuous decade for the economy.

Theory of Stagflation: Markup Pricing and Target Rates of Return

The previous chapter's discussion of the Phillips curve was incomplete in that the links between unemployment and prices failed to expose the intermediate steps. Unemployment rates affect wage rates, but wage rates affect prices only through the mediating influences of labor productivity, unit labor costs, and price markups. Stagflation is a resultant of the way in which prices are formed by enterprises in relation to the profit-seeking objectives of firms. One theory of stagflation combines the profit-seeking objectives of firms with their pricing policies during periods of economic stagnation.[3]

Theory of Markup Pricing and Target Rates of Return

The firm in traditional competitive theory is seen as taking the price it receives for its product as given; it is simply a passive recipient of price information generated by the market. Since it deals in a very competitive environment, according to this theory, it is fanciful and indeed self-destructive for the firm to try to influence in any meaningful way the price it charges for its product.

Once we depart from an assumption of perfect competition, the contours of the economic landscape change. The firm operating in concentrated markets is not a mere passive recipient of market prices but is an aggressive actor in the process of price formation. Instead of viewing the market in which it sells its products as competitive, the firm attempts to reduce the degree of competition in the market so that it may better control the price it charges for its product. In fact, even if there ever were a perfectly competitive system, it would not be self-sustaining, since the motivation of the dominant actors in such a system is to appropriate control over pricing decisions by beginning to control the markets for their products.

The price decision in the firm is based on its motivation to acquire profits. In traditional economic theory the firm maximizes profits within the constraints imposed

---

[3] Howard M. Wachtel and Peter D. Adelsheim, *The Inflationary Impact of Unemployment: Price Markups during the Post-war Recessions, 1947–1970*, U.S. Congress, Joint Economic Committee (Washington: Government Printing Office, 1976).

by the demand for its product, the technology available to produce its product, and the price it must pay to acquire the factors of production. All this information is summarized in the price the market sets for a product; therefore, the price seriously constrains the profits the firm can make. As a consequence, all the firm can do is set its level of production in such a way as to maximize its profits in light of the price it obtains for its output and the other constraints mentioned above, all of which lie outside of the firm's control. (The dynamic toward concentration and away from this form of competition is precisely to push against these constraints, forcing them further outward so that a modicum of control over the firm's activity is taken by the firm itself and not left to the "impersonal" decision of other in the market.)

The firm in concentrated markets has a different profit motivation and faces different forms of constraints. Rather than trying to maximize profits by adapting its level of output to a variety of parameters, the firm in economically concentrated industries attempts to attain a *target rate of profit* by adjusting both its price and (to a lesser extent) its level of output.[4] The target rate of profit is a result of a number of forces. First, the firm in a concentrated industry *patterns* its profit posture after firms whose structure—size, market power, type of product, and so forth—is similar. Executives of corporations in such concentrated industries are evaluated in terms of how effectively they keep up with the pattern set within the *orbit of firms* with which their firm can legitimately be compared.[5] The executives of such a firm will no doubt attempt to outstrip its patterned position by expanding profits beyond those normally indicated by its position within a particular orbit. But like the progress of a star circulating in its orbit, such movements are glacial and for the short term can be precluded from our consideration without doing violence to the propositions advanced here.

A second important consideration in the profit behavior we are describing is the profits attained by a firm in the recent past. Corporate executives will be evaluated by their stockholders according to how effectively they maintain a rate of profit to which the stockholders have become accustomed, as defined by profits in the most recent period of time. If you like, some sort of *profit "epoch"* is informally defined, placing strong expectations on corporate executives of what profits in their companies should be.[6]

Keep this type of profit behavior in mind as we consider the next question: How

---

[4] For a slightly different version of target profit behavior, see John M. Blair, "Inflation in the United States," in *The Roots of Inflation* (New York: Burt Franklin and Co., 1975), pp. 33–67.

[5] The similarity to pattern-determined wage targets among large trade unions should be noted. See Chapters 6 and 7.

[6] Putting these two considerations together and using more technical language, we may say that target profit rates depend on some weighted average of previous years' profit rates for the firm (with some weighted distributed lag function) and on the position of the firm in its profit orbit, as described by the patterned profit behavior of a particular firm in relation to other firms in its orbit.

is a target profit perspective translated into pricing behavior by the firm? The link in the argument is found in price markups. Whenever economists examine price behavior of firms in concrete situations, inevitably the words *price markup* appear.[7]

Markup pricing suggests that firms form their prices by first computing their labor and raw material costs, then adding a "markup" over raw material and labor costs in order to attain their profits. Theoretically, firms are constrained in their price markup primarily by the extent to which increases in the price markup will result in a loss of sales owing to the excessively high price charged for the product. This is the familiar concept of *demand elasticity* used in the theory of price formation. If the firm faces a *highly elastic demand* for its product—that is, if an increase in price will evoke a strong negative response by consumers, resulting in a more-than-proportionate loss in sales—then the ability of the firm to increase its price markup is severely limited. In competitive economic theory it is assumed that all firms face just such an elastic demand curve for their products. But any firm facing such a severe constraint, which cuts to the core of its profit-making ability, will undertake steps to offset or eliminate this obstacle as much as possible by gaining control over its market, thereby influencing the demand curve for its product. The most common ways in which the firm gains control over its market are acquisition of other firms, differentiation of its product (to obtain customer attachment), advertising, other forms of the sales effort, and the like. In short, it undertakes actions to concentrate market power within the firm rather than permitting this power to be dispersed in the anonymous market, where consumers have the upper hand. Thus, competition is unstable, and the dynamic is toward reductions in competition and the augmentation of economic concentration.

As the economy becomes more concentrated, induced by the normal motivation on the part of corporate executives to mitigate their competitive constraints, firms can set their price markups in order to attain their target profits. Here the two theoretical arguments intersect—the one about target profit rates and the one about markup pricing. Firms will establish a price in order to attain a target profit rate for any given level of sales. In a curious way the argument about what is taken is given by the firm

---

[7] The Polish economist Michal Kalecki developed an integrated micro and macro model, using a markup price system as his micro foundation, in the early 1930s, predating the work of Keynes. Kalecki's work appears in his *Theory of Economic Dynamics* (New York: Monthly Review Press, 1965) and *Selected Essays on the Dynamics of the Capitalist Economy* (Cambridge: Cambridge University Press, 1971). A most useful treatise on the work of Kalecki has been written by George R. Feiwel, *The Intellectual Capital of Michal Kalecki* (Knoxville: University of Tennessee Press, 1975). Additionally, the work done by R. L. Hall and Charles J. Hitch, "Price Theory and Business Behavior," *Oxford Economic Papers* (May 1939), pp. 12–45, initiated a debate surrounding markup pricing practices of concentrated firms, which is summarized in Frederic M. Sherer, *Industrial Market Structure and Economic Concentration* (Chicago: Rand McNally & Co., 1970), pp. 173–79. Gardiner C. Means, perhaps more than any economist, has persistently reminded us of the impact of concentration on price formation and economic instability. For example, see his essay, "Simultaneous Inflation and Unemployment," in *The Roots of Inflation* (New York: Burt Franklin & Co., 1975), pp. 1–31.

is reversed from traditional theory: with economic concentration the firm can adjust its price more readily than it can control its sales in the short term.[8]

Stagflation is the manifestation of rising prices during periods when there are unemployed labor and underutilized plant and equipment. The theory of markup pricing and profit-seeking behavior based on target rates of return can be used to explain this phenomenon. Consider a firm operating in a concentrated market environment and attaining its desired target profit rate. Then introduce a recession (from any cause). If the firm loses revenue through a sales reduction during the recession, it will try to recoup the lost revenue from those diminished sales by increasing the price markup for its remaining sales so that it can get closer to the target profit rate it started with. The motivation to do this is pressure from stockholders on the company executives, which takes the form of imposing some profit expectations on management as dictated by its previous profit posture and the profit position of others in the firm's orbit of comparison.

An arithmetic illustration is helpful in illuminating this theoretical point. For example, say a firm operating in a concentrated industry has direct costs (raw material and labor) of $200 per unit of output and sets its profit markup 20 percent above direct costs, therefore selling the product for $240 per unit and making a profit of $40 per unit. Let us say the firm has a target level of profits of $40,000 (derived from its target rate of profits); to realize this profit level it will have to sell 1,000 units at $240 per unit. Now we have unemployment and a recession, which cause the volume of sales to fall from 1,000 expected units to 950 units. But if the firm still has a target profit level of $40,000, which it wants to attain, it will have to raise its price to slightly over $242 per unit. It does this by raising its percentage markup over costs to 21 percent. Having increased its profit per unit, the firm now achieves its target profit

Table 17-2 Illustration of Price Markups and Target Rate of Return as a Cause of Stagflation

	Level of Sales	
	1000 units	950 units
Target profit level	$40,000	$40,000
Costs per unit (labor and raw materials)	200	200
Price markup per unit	40 (20%)	42 (21%)
Product price	240	242
Total profits	$40,000 = $40 × 1000 units	$39,900 = $42 × 950 units

---

[8] In traditional micro theory, full employment of resources is an assumption. Once this assumption is dropped, price adaptation, rather than output change, becomes the dominant active variable used to adjust to varying macro conditions.

level, but the consequence to the economy is the simultaneous occurrence of inflation and unemployment.[9] Table 17-2 illustrates this hypothetical case.

Stagflation and Markup Pricing

To examine the connection between markup pricing and stagflation, data were collected for over 100 manufacturing industries for the 1950s and 1960s. Five recessions were isolated during those decades to determine whether price mark-ups increased during periods of economic stagnation; such a pattern would be supportive of an explanation for the existence of stagflationary propensities in the economy. If economic concentration produced increased price markups in the short run during periods of economic stagnation, then an explanation for the existence of stagflation would be found in the pricing structure of the American economy.

The five recessions were 1948–49, 1953–54, 1957–58, 1960–61, and 1969–70. The 100 manufacturing industries were divided into three groups, based on the degree of economic concentration in each industry in 1967, as indicated by the *concentration ratio*. This is the standard measure of market concentration. It is found by computing the relationship between the value of shipments (sales) for the four largest firms in an industry and the value of shipments for the industry as a whole.

Markups and Level of Concentration

Table 17-3 presents the results of our first test of the perverse markup pricing hypothesis. In that table we have indicated the percentage of industries in the three concentration groups that show rising, declining, or stable markups during the five postwar recessions from 1948 to 1970. An industry was classified as having a rising markup from peak to trough of the cycle if it had more than a one-percentage-point increase in its markup, and as having a declining markup if the decrease was more than one percentage point.[10]

---

[9] This hypothetical example posits a very inelastic demand response. Such a restrictive case is presented for illustrative purposes, but even with a less inelastic demand response, the conclusion holds.

A query is in order here concerning the form of the demand curve posited. Before examining that issue, however, a caveat is warranted. Since we are dealing with *fluctuations* in the level of demand, we are encountering dynamic *shifts* in the demand curve for the firm's product, rather than static movements along a fixed demand curve.

If we start with a variant of the static kinked-demand-curve model, then *shifts* in that demand curve will yield a composite response in the market, which is initially inelastic but becomes elastic at low levels of output. The profits attained in this manner may or may not be optimal. The presumption is that such a profit-maximizing position is unknown whenever fluctuations in levels of demand exist. The search for optimal profits is conducted by varying the price markup, gauging consumer response to each alteration in the markup.

[10] Discussed further in Howard M. Wachtel and Peter D. Adelsheim, "How Recession Feeds Inflation: Price Markups in a Concentrated Economy," *Challenge*, September–October 1977, pp. 6–13.

100 INdustees!

Table 17-3 Percentage of Three-Digit Industries Showing Rising, Stable, or Declining Markups during Postwar Recessions, by Degree of Concentration

	Recession[a]				
	1969–70	1960–61	1957–58	1953–54	1948–49
High concentration[b]					
Number of industries	31	28	13	14	15
Markups:					
Percent declining	41.9	25.0	46.2	35.7	40.0
Percent stable	16.1	17.9	0.0	7.1	6.7
Percent rising	41.9	57.1	53.8	57.1	53.3
Medium concentration[b]					
Number of industries	66	61	20	17	16
Markups:					
Percent declining	27.3	27.9	45.0	29.4	62.5
Percent stable	30.0	36.1	15.0	11.8	12.5
Percent rising	42.4	36.1	40.0	58.8	25.0
Low concentration[b]					
Number of industries	43	38	20	17	14
Markups:					
Percent declining	23.2	18.4	50.0	35.3	64.3
Percent stable	25.5	36.8	20.0	23.5	0.0
Percent rising	51.2	44.7	30.0	41.2	35.7

[a]Markups measured from peak to trough.
[b]High concentration: four-firm concentration ratio 50 percent or more. Medium concentration: four-firm concentration ratio between 25 and 50 percent. Low concentration: four-firm concentration ratio less than 25 percent.

Source: Howard M. Wachtel and Peter D. Adelsheim, "How Recession Feeds Inflation: Price Markups in a Concentrated Economy," *Challenge*, September–October 1977, p. 9.

wht ?

Several interpretative points are worth noting about the data in this table:

1. In each recession, exclusive of 1969–70, a majority of the industries in the high-concentration sector exhibited perverse economic behavior. By way of contrast, less than 50 percent of the industries in the medium- and low-concentration sectors raised their markups during the postwar recessions, with but two exceptions—1953–54 in the medium-concentration sector, and 1969–70 in the low-concentration sector.

2. Although typically the low- and medium-concentration sectors exhibit less of a tendency toward perverse economic behavior than the sector of high concentration, the trend in these sectors over the postwar period has been to show increasing economic perversity.

3. These two sets of observations reveal how much more susceptible our economy is to the type of stagflation that occurred in the 1970s, because of the increasing similarity of the pricing behavior in the sectors of medium and low concentration to that of the high-concentration sector.

The precise amount of increase or decrease in the size of markups over the postwar business cycles is presented in Table 17-4, where the percentage change in the size of markups is shown for the three concentration groups. In this case the percentage change for both the expansion and recession phases of each postwar cycle is shown.

The data in Table 17-4 lend additional weight to the price-markup conclusions:

1. In each recession of the postwar period (excluding the 1969–70 recession), markups in the high-concentration sector increased in size. In the 1948–49 recession they increased by almost 11 percent; they reached a peak during the 1953–54 recession, when the increase was over 14 percent. By way of contrast, markups in the low- and medium-concentration sectors decreased during recessions, though this tendency weakened a bit in the 1960s.

2. While markups in the sector of high concentration were increasing during recessions, they typically decreased, or increased by less, during the expansion phase of the cycle. However, in the sectors of low and medium concentration, markups decreased during recessions and increased during periods of expansion, in some instances more than they did in the sector of high concentration.

3. As we discovered earlier, although the sectors of low and medium concentration exhibited more normal reactions to the business cycle, their behavior became more perverse in the 1960s. It took on more the characteristics of the sector of high concentration. Thus, even though the sector of high concentration had lower markup increases in the recessions of the late 1960s than it had had in the 1950s, the overall economy was more inflation-biased during recession. This is because

Table 17-4 Percentage Change in Size of Price Markup during Recessions and Expansions in Postwar Business Cycles, by Degree of Concentration

	High Concentration	Medium Concentration	Low Concentration
1948–52 cycle:[a]			
1948–49 recession _Increase_ +	10.78	_Decreas_ −8.52	_Decreas_ −8.16
1949–52 expansion	4.76	8.67	−4.54
1953–56 cycle:[b]			
1953–54 recession _Increase_ +	14.15	_Decreas_ −0.08	_Decreas_ −0.32
1954–56 expansion	6.97	14.42	3.60
1957–60 cycle:[c]			
1957–58 recession _Increase_ +	13.47	_Decreas_ −4.91	_Decreas_ −7.55
1958–60 expansion	−10.92	7.42	5.04
1960–69 cycle:[d]			
1960–61 recession _Increase_ +	5.29	_Decreas_ −1.86	_Increas_ + 1.34
1961–69 expansion	15.28	18.36	13.65
1969–70 cycle:[e]			
1969–70 recession _Decrease_	−1.05	_Increas_ 0.82	_Increas_ + 2.54
Excluding the auto industry[f]	1.75	—	—

[a]Base = 1947. [b]Base = 1952. [c]Base = 1956. [d]Base = 1960. [e]Base = 1969.
[f]The auto industry was removed from this calculation of the change in markups in the high-concentration sector.
Source: Howard M. Wachtel and Peter D. Adelsheim, "How Recession Feeds Inflation: Price Markups in a Concentrated Economy," *Challenge*, September–October 1977, p. 9.

the sectors of low and medium concentration were reinforcing the perverse behavior of markups in the sector of high concentration, instead of offsetting it.

In the three recessions between 1970 and 1982 (1973–75, 1979–80, and 1981–82) a similar pattern emerges. In each of those recessions, price markups increased in the high concentration sector while in two of the three recessions they declined in the medium concentration sector.[11] The empirical work supports the contention that stagflation is built into the structure of the American economy. As with any complex economic process, the model does not work perfectly, because other factors affect price markups. But, in general, the more concentrated the sector of the economy, the greater is the tendency for price markups to increase during periods of economic stagnation, leading to a stagflationary

[11] Robert G. Vivona, "Price Markups During Recessions" (xerox, March 13, 1986), p. 15.

outcome in the economy. Each decade after World War II produced an economy with intensified structural tendencies toward stagflation, as markup pricing and target profit gained a beachhead in more and more sectors of the American economy.

Stagflation and the Structure of the Labor Market

Another view of the causes of stagflation locates the problem in imbalances in the labor market. These ideas have been encountered in previous chapters in this part of the book, but they are worth a recapitulation here in the context of this issue of stagflation.

Labor market structure theories about stagflation assume several forms. There is, first, the proposition that the high levels of unemployment observed in the 1980s are in reality full-employment levels because those counted as unemployed have a weak attachment to the labor force and evidence substantial job turnover. One analyst summarizes this view of stagflation in terms of labor market structures as follows:

> The central problem seems to be that some groups in the labor force have rates of unemployment that are far in excess of the rates that would accord with the hypothesis that the unemployed are making a normal transition from one job to another . . . certain members of the labor force account for a disproportionate share of unemployment because they drift from one unsatisfactory job to another, spending the time between jobs either unemployed or out of the labor force.[12]

Coupled with this view of the labor market is a second proposition: that the length of job search has been extended and the number of spells of unemployment has increased because of the attractive benefits paid to those who are unemployed.[13] Elements of the social wage, such as unemployment compensation, food stamps, and welfare, have produced higher rates of unemployment because of both the stretch-out of job search and the increase in spells of unemployment.

The result of these aspects of the contemporary labor market has been a higher rate of unemployment than historically warranted. Policymakers, however, have not adapted to this new labor market reality and instead view these conditions as requiring expansion in aggregate demand. When this occurs, inflation is the result, along with high unemployment. The mistake is made by the policymakers who are operating on the basis of unemployment targets that are too low. When they pump up aggregate demand to employ more people, inflation is the result. Unemployment is only minimally reduced, however, because of structural imbalances in the labor market.

---

[12] Robert E. Hall, "Why Is the Unemployment Rate So High at Full Employment?" *Brookings Papers on Economic Activity* 3 (1970), p. 389.

[13] Martin Feldstein, "The Economics of the New Unemployment," *Public Interest*, Fall 1973, pp. 3–42.

A third view of the structure of the labor market is based on the institutionalist perception of trade unions and wage determination. Wages are established in key unionized sectors of the economy and then transmitted throughout by pattern-setting agreements. According to this perception, "the wage does not, and cannot, function to equate supply and demand. Instead, wages perform certain basic social and institutional functions. They define relationships between labor and management, between one group of workers and another."[14] Given this role of wages in society, inflation results when some external shock first triggers a price effect that tilts wages out of line with their traditional relationship to other parameters of the economy. As wage earners seek to catch up through cost-of-living adjustments in their wages, a second round of price increases is triggered, which now extends beyond the sector in which the initial price increase occurred.

Price increases due to some external shock start the process of inflation, and wages act as a transmitter of price increases throughout the economy. A price-wage-price spiral characterizes this process. Viewed this way, wages are established without reference to any rate of unemployment in the economy. If the price shocks are superimposed on a stagnant economy, subsequent wage and price increases will still occur, no matter what the rate of unemployment. Stagflation occurs, according to this view of the economy, when the initial external price shocks happen while unemployment rates are high. The transmittal of these price shocks throughout the economy via the wage-setting process extends the inflationary process set in motion by an initial price shock. The OPEC price shock in the early 1970s, and again in the late 1970s, was superimposed on an economy with high levels of unemployment. The pattern-wage-setting process then transmitted these price shocks throughout the economy.

Whatever form of structural argument is put forward, there is one common denominator: the wage rate does not clear the labor market. In one version this is because the wage rate is too high—the Feldstein argument. In the structuralist model, it is because of structural immobilities built into the skills needed for available jobs compared with the lower skills of the unemployed. Whatever the cause, the result is a labor market that does not clear at the prevailing wage.

Expectations and Stagflation

The 1970s produced a variant of the Phillips curve model that could explain stagflation and in the process produced a rejection of the existence of the normal type of Phillips curve. Variously called the *expectations* hypothesis, the *accelerationist* model of inflation, or the *natural-rate-of-unemployment* hypothesis, the model was based on the existence

---

[14] Michael J. Piore, "Unemployment and Inflation: An Alternative View," in Michael J. Piore, ed., *Unemployment and Inflation: Institutionalist and Structuralist Views* (White Plains, NY: M. E. Sharpe, Inc., 1979), p. 6.

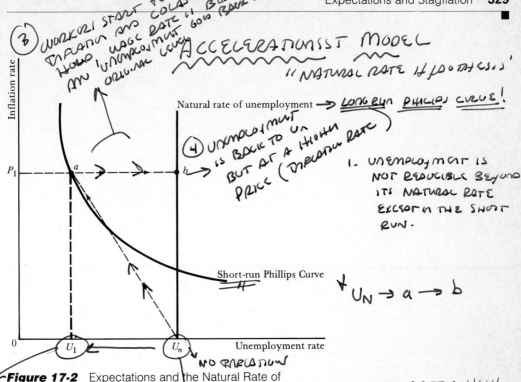

[handwritten annotations:]

③ WORKERS START TO PERCEIVE INFLATION AND COLAS MAKE HOLD WAGE RATE ↑ BID UP AN UNEMPLOYMENT GOES BACK TO ORIGINAL LEVEL

ACCELERATIONIST MODEL

"NATURAL RATE HYPOTHESIS"

Natural rate of unemployment → LONG RUN PHILLIPS CURVE!

④ UNEMPLOYMENT IS BACK TO Un BUT AT A HIGHER PRICE (INFLATION RATE)

1. UNEMPLOYMENT IS NOT REDUCIBLE BEYOND ITS NATURAL RATE EXCEPT IN THE SHORT RUN.

Short-run Phillips Curve

Un → a → b

Unemployment rate

NO INFLATION

Figure 17-2 Expectations and the Natural Rate of Unemployment

① POLICY MAKERS VIEW THIS RATE AS TOO HIGH AND SET OUT TO ↑ AD TO REDUCE IT TO U₁.

② AS UN MOVE TO U₁ AND LOWER UNEMPLOY, PRICES RISE FASTER THEN WAGES BECAUSE UN LONG TERM CONTRACTS ↓ REAL WAGES FALL

[printed text:]

of a long-run Phillips curve that took the form of a vertical line. This implied that unemployment was not reducible below its natural rate except in the short run. Once the expectations of wage earners were adjusted to inflation, unemployment would settle at its initial level but at a higher overall rate of inflation.[15]

The expectations model starts with the concept of a natural rate of unemployment—that rate of unemployment consistent with a particular real wage rate in the economy and a steady-state rate of inflation in the economy. Such a steady-state rate of inflation produces a condition in which the actual rate of inflation has merged with the expected rate of inflation. In Figure 17-2 this is indicated by the rate of unemployment U_n. At this rate of unemployment there is initially a zero rate of inflation.

Policymakers, viewing this rate of unemployment as too high and noting the absence of inflation, set out to expand aggregate demand in order to reduce the rate of unemployment. With reference to what was said previously about the debate over what is full employment, the policymakers are making a mistake by perceiving the existing rate of unemployment as being above a full-employment level. Be that as it

---

[15] Two interesting discussions of this model are Milton Friedman, "Nobel Lecture: Inflation and Unemployment," *Journal of Political Economy* 85, no. 3 (1977), pp. 451–72; and Thomas J. Humphrey, "Changing Views of the Phillips Curve," in Thomas M. Havrilesky and John T. Boorman, eds., *Current Issues in Monetary Theory and Policy*, 2nd ed. (Arlington Heights, IL: AHM Publishing Corp., 1980), pp. 171–86.

may, the result of their policies to expand aggregate demand is to reduce temporarily the level of unemployment, to U_1 in Figure 17-2. The increase in aggregate demand immediately increases prices to P_1, which appears to be compatible with a short-run Phillips curve as shown in Figure 17-2. Prices rise faster than wages initially because wage earners are locked into longer-term contracts and cannot adjust their wage posture as quickly as producers can increase their prices. The result is that real wages fall because prices rise faster than money wages, and this fall in real wages supports the higher levels of employment and output in the economy.

But this short-run impact of expansionary aggregate demand policies cannot last. Wage earners start to perceive the inflation as more than transitory and adjust their expectations to the higher steady-state rate of inflation. Demands for higher wages in order to recoup lost purchasing power become more pervasive in the economy. Producers have difficulties in finding workers with the qualifications they need; therefore, they bid up the money or nominal wage. The consequence is that once workers adjust their expectations to a higher steady-state rate of inflation, wages begin to rise at a rate that equals the rate of inflation. When that occurs, real wages rise to their original level, employment is reduced, and the rate of unemployment settles once again at its natural rate of U_n.

The dynamics of this adjustment process appear in Figure 17-2 as the tracing line, with the arrows, $U_n \rightarrow a \rightarrow b$. After wages catch up with inflation, unemployment once again settles at its natural rate of U_n, but with an important difference. Now the steady-state rate of inflation is P_1, not zero, because a price-wage-price cycle has been unleashed. The manifestation of this dynamic in the economy is the same rate of unemployment as before, but at higher rates of inflation, which become embedded in the structure of the economy.

To recapitulate: Stagflation occurs in the expectations model initially because policymakers seek to reduce the rate of unemployment below its natural rate through aggregate demand policies. In the short run there is a Phillips curve that indicates how this expansion in aggregate demand will manifest itself in price increases that rise more rapidly than do wages. A fall in the real wage ensues, which supports the higher levels of employment and output. But this is short-lived: when wages catch up with inflation, the real wage starts to rise, and unemployment is restored to its natural rate; inflation has reached a new steady-state level above where it started.

The long-run Phillips curve is a vertical line in this model, indicated in Figure 17-2 as $U_n b$. The new inflation-unemployment levels are P_1 and U_n, respectively. Only in the short run does a Phillips curve trade-off exist between inflation and unemployment, and this relationship is considered to be a disequilibrium one that occurs when the expected rate of inflation deviates from the actual rate of inflation. The Phillips curve, according to this view, is a statistical mirage based on static relationships in the economy. Once dynamic adjustment processes are permitted to enter the model, the Phillips curve becomes a vertical line at the natural rate of unemployment. This implies that the economy can experience virtually any rate of inflation consistent with the same natural rate of unemployment.

This dynamic process in the economy is further complicated by the response of households to the new higher steady-state rate of inflation. Additional workers enter the labor market in order to stabilize household purchasing power. The prospect of an ever-expanding aggregate demand also induces additional household members to seek work. These factors can nudge the natural rate of unemployment upward, as the labor force is swelled with additional members and policymakers do not adjust their unemployment targets accordingly. If another round of expansionary aggregate demand measures is introduced into the economy in order to reduce unemployment, the process of pushing up the steady-state rate of inflation will occur once again as before.

The model just presented is sometimes called the *adaptive-expectations* hypothesis because wage earners *adapt* their bargaining posture to their expectations about inflation. Another variant views expectations as *rational*, in the sense that all individuals in the economy structure their behavior on the basis of what they expect to happen, and they take account of future developments in the economy by discounting for them in their current behavior. Such a *rational-expectations* hypothesis means that adaptive behavior is not necessary, because wage earners instantaneously make adjustments on the basis of what they expect future rates of inflation to be. They have learned from the past, as have other actors in the economy, and can effectively discount for the future. In a rational-expectations model, therefore, no short-run Phillips curve exists at all, except as a random phenomenon.

Stagflation Policy

Toward the end of the 1970s, two competing theories about stagflation emerged. One was based on price markup behavior of firms operating in concentrated industries; the other was erected around the adapting of wage earners' expectations to initial price increases, all leading to an increase in the higher steady-state rate of inflation at the natural rate of unemployment. There has not been sufficient history of stagflation to know which model will endure the test of time.

In fact, the two models are not that inconsistent with each other. Once the price-wage spiral sets in, the question is, how do firms react in terms of their price markup policies? If they have sufficient market power to do so, they will react by nudging the price markup upward, creating a new steady-state rate of price markup. To the extent this occurs, inflation will be pushed up even higher than would be predicted solely by a rational-expectations model of stagflation. Both models yield prices and wages that do not clear markets because of structural problems.

The policy implications of these two competing models of inflation diverge, however. The approach that focuses on concentration and price markup behavior argues for an aggressive anticoncentration policy on the part of the government. This includes antitrust policies, new approaches to conglomerate mergers, and other strategies to prevent further concentration in markets. Failing that, some form of *selective* price policy is suggested by this view of stagflation; the firms isolated for price monitoring or price controls would be those whose price markup policy contributed to stagflation. This would imply that sectors of the economy that have a limited impact on the overall rate of inflation would be excluded, as would firms that did not evidence stagflationary tendencies in their price markup policies. Doing this would reduce the price control efforts of the government to a manageable dimension and would zero in on those firms that need attention to their pricing policies.[16]

The expectations model would reject these approaches to stagflation policy because they would distort the allocation of resources in the economy. In the view of the proponents of this model, this would cause more problems than it would solve. They argue that the government cannot reduce unemployment below its natural rate without a reduction in real wages. Inflating the economy will only reduce unemployment if wage increases lag permanently behind price increases. This is unlikely to happen, because of the strength of trade unions and the nature of labor markets.

The natural rate of unemployment has crept upward since World War II because of structural unemployment and demographic shifts in the composition of the labor force. Policymakers, however, have not accepted this change, according to the expectationists, and have attempted to reduce unemployment to levels that are not attainable over the long haul. This effort simply increases the steady-state rate of inflation without reducing unemployment. The most important policy consequence of this model is for the government to stop attempting to reduce unemployment below its natural rate. Otherwise, the economy is condemned to a spate of stop-go policies in which aggregate demand is pumped up for a time, then reduced after inflation occurs. But all this effort at balancing the economy at full employment and price stability is for naught. In fact, stop-go policies exacerbate the problem by establishing expectations and creating ratchet effects in the economy. On the positive side of public policy, the monetary authorities should hold a steady rate of growth in the money supply so that expectations of price- and wage-setters become stabilized over time.

Those who see stagflation as imbedded in the structure of labor markets propose policies to improve mobility in the labor market, expand employment training, and provide the means for matching unemployed workers with available jobs. The focus is on the labor market and its rigidities rather than on pricing policies of firms or on efforts of policymakers to manage aggregate demand.

Summary

Stagflation is defined as the simultaneous occurrence of unemployment and inflation. Measuring stagflation as the sum of the inflation and unemployment rates permits some interesting observations about the American economy. In the 1950s and 1960s stagflation was kept within an acceptable range, defined as a rate of stagflation below

---

[16] Wage-price policies are discussed further in the next chapter.

10 percent, and it did not drop below that barrier through 1985, except in one year. Stagflation reached a peak of more than 20 percent in 1980.

What accounts for the existence of economy-wide stagflation in the 1970s and the 1980s? Several answers have been given to this question. One model is based on the price markup behavior of firms operating in concentrated markets. Another model is based on the price- and wage-setters in the economy adapting their expectations to inflationary tendencies that are initiated by fiscal policy.

The first of these two models starts with the proposition that firms seek a target rate of return on their fixed capital and pursue profits in the marketplace in order to meet this target rate of return. They establish prices on the basis of a price markup over direct costs, defined as unit labor and raw material costs. In the short run, if sales fall, a firm operating in a concentrated sector of the economy will increase its price markup to recapture lost revenues occasioned by the reduction in sales. The more price-inelastic is the demand for the firm's product, the more this option is open to the firm. Prices will be more inelastic the greater the degree of market concentration and the shorter the time period over which the increased price markup occurs. Consumers will attempt to prevent a reduction in their real standard of living and will either borrow or dip into past savings in order to maintain their consumption levels. This is the familiar relative-income hypothesis, applied to the individual's consumption function.

The consequence of these developments is rising prices in the short run during periods of declining sales—stagflation. This model and its hypotheses were subjected to empirical inquiry, and the results of that study supported the general thrust of the theory.

An alternative model was put forward in the 1970s to explain stagflation, based on the existence of a natural rate of unemployment and a particular adaptation of the Phillips curve analysis. A natural rate of unemployment exists and is viewed by policy-makers as too high, relative to their full-employment objectives. They proceed to increase aggregate demand through fiscal policy, which drives up prices. Wage increases in the short run lag behind price increases, causing the real wage to fall. This supports the higher levels of employment and output, while reducing the unemployment rate temporarily. But not for long. Wage earners quickly adapt their expectations to a continued high rate of inflation and then seek wage adjustments that enable them to catch up with inflation. When that happens, real wages fall back to their original level, employment and output are reduced, and the unemployment rate is once more restored to its natural rate.

In the price area, however, important changes occur. A new steady-state rate of inflation, higher than the original rate, sets in at the natural rate of unemployment. In short, a natural rate of unemployment is compatible with any steady-state rate of inflation. The long-run Phillips curve is a vertical line, indicating that the natural rate of unemployment is consistent with any rate of inflation.

The policy implications of these two models of stagflation are different. The concentration model argues for anticoncentration efforts, selective price policies, and efforts to restore competition to the economy. The expectations model argues for a more rational fiscal policy, which would accept as the natural rate of unemployment a higher rate than so-called full-employment objectives would dictate.

Study Questions

1. What is meant by the term *stagflation?* How is it measured, and what was the pattern of stagflation in the 1960s? In the 1970s?

2. Critically evaluate the price-markup model of stagflation. What are the economic implications of this model? What are its key policy implications?

3. Critically evaluate the rational-expectations model of stagflation. Explain its policy implications.

4. Compare the price-markup and rational-expectations models of stagflation. What are the similarities of the two models, and what are the differences between them?

Further Reading

Friedman, Milton. "Nobel Lecture: Inflation and Unemployment." *Journal of Political Economy* 85, no. 3 (1977), pp. 451–72.

Sherman, Howard J. *Stagflation.* New York: Harper and Row, 1976.

Wachtel, Howard M., and Peter D. Adelsheim. *The Inflationary Impact of Unemployment: Price Markups during Postwar Recessions, 1947–1970.* U.S. Congress, Joint Economic Committee. Washington: Government Printing Office, 1976.

18

■

Wage-Price Policy

How can the government aggressively pursue full-employment policies and avoid the inflationary pressures that would cause it to abort its pursuit of full employment? This is the basic economic policy dilemma that has plagued not just the United States but every other industrial country in the world in the postwar period. Can the alternatives of full employment *or* price stability be converted into a complementary set of objectives so that full employment can be attained without negative inflationary consequences?

This is the precise question that wage-price policy (sometimes called incomes policy) is designed to address. On paper, and in theory, the idea sounds plausible: while the government is pursuing full employment policies, institute some form of agreed-upon wage and price increases among labor and business so that inflation does not gain steam. Like so many ideas of economists and politicians, however, the problem is not with the design of wage-price policies but with the way in which human behavior in the economy subverts the sensible objectives of policymakers.

The generic form of wage-price policies involves either establishing some criteria upon which wages and prices will be based or actually setting a fixed rate of increase for wages and prices. This is done with the consultation and, it is hoped, the support of key labor and business leaders. Sometimes the government will provide an umbrella of incentives for both parties to accept the wage-price policy, by using the tax system or offering other public policies that both business and labor seek, either together or separately. When this occurs, a type of *industrial social accord* is formed, in which labor and business sacrifice some of their private economic demands in return for public policies they desire.

In the United States we have experimented with wage-price policy less than any other major industrial country. There are several reasons for this. First, we do not have as large a segment of organized labor with whom the government can negotiate its wage-price policy. In countries with a larger proportion of union workers, it is easier to establish a wage-price policy and enforce it, because the trade unions provide an institutional base and public organization that can be identified as participating in the wage-price policy. The same can be said for the formal organization of business that, in many nations such as Germany or Sweden, parallels labor organizations.

Second, our economy is larger and far more complex than most other industrial nations. Geographic boundaries that, if transplanted, would encompass the entire continent of Europe, eastward from Calais to the borders of the Soviet Union, make any standardization of wage-price policy problematic. We have large firms and small firms, union and nonunion workers, agriculture and manufacturing, services and mining. The more diversified the economy, the more difficult it is to implement a wage-price policy.

Third, the economic tradition and ideology of free markets is stronger in the United States than in most other industrial countries. Our country was formed with an antistate ideology, opposed to the intervention of government in the economy, and this carries over to our skepticism about wage-price policy. This is not true in central and northern Europe, where the role of the state in the economy has long been accepted to a greater extent than it is in the United States. Except in wartime, Americans do not willingly accept wage-price policies, and even the individuals selected to administer the program frequently do not believe in it.[1]

Notwithstanding all these negatives associated with wage-price policy, we have had two serious attempts to implant one in the United States in recent decades. President Kennedy launched the first peacetime wage-price policy in 1962 with his *guidepost policy*, and President Nixon followed in 1971 with first a *wage-price freeze* and then a series of "phases" in which different wage-price policies were tried. And today economists and policymakers talk about different types of wage-price policies— tax-based incomes policies (so-called TIPs) or real-wage protection plans.

Whatever economists may think about wage-price policies—and the majority think they do not work—the idea will not go away, because politicians need to do something whenever inflation gets out of control. In the early 1980s, with the Reagan administration in place, wage-price policies of the government were seen as a last

---

[1] C. Jackson Grayson, who was selected by President Nixon to head his wage-price commission, has written a book about his experiences, in which it is apparent that he does not believe the government should have a wage-price policy. C. Jackson Grayson, *Confessions of a Price Controller* (Homewood, IL: Dow Jones-Irwin, 1974). For a discussion of wage-price policies in other countries, see Joint Economic Committee, *Wage and Price Policies in Australia, Austria, Canada, Japan, the Netherlands, and West Germany* (Washington: Government Printing Office, 1982).

resort. However, things may have changed radically by the late-1980s; and once again the nation may be debating what form of wage-price policy it should adopt.

The Kennedy Guideposts

While vigorously pursuing full-employment policies, the Kennedy administration wanted to prevent an inflationary fallout that would force them to abort their full-employment fiscal policies. To achieve both full employment and price stability, the Kennedy administration in 1962 announced its "guideposts for noninflationary wage and price behavior." "There are important segments of the economy," the announcement said, "where firms are large or employees well-organized, or both. In these sectors, private parties may exercise considerable discretion over the terms of wage bargains and price decisions."[2]

The guideposts start with the premise that concentrations of economic power among labor and capital enable firms and workers to escape the disciplining force of the market. To replace this constraining force, the Kennedy administration sought to substitute a set of wage and price guideposts that would enable "the public to judge whether a particular wage-price decision is in the national interest."[3]

Wages were to increase in all sectors of the economy at the rate of national labor productivity growth. Though initially there was no fixed number established, by 1964 it was set at 3.2 percent. Prices were to increase depending on the relationship between the specific rate of productivity increase in the firm and the national rate of productivity growth. If the rate of productivity increase in the particular firm was *higher* than the national rate of productivity growth, then prices were to *fall* by the difference between the two rates of productivity increase. The reasoning behind this was as follows: if workers receive the national rate of labor productivity increase and the firm has a higher rate of productivity increase, then unit labor costs will fall in this firm. These reduced unit labor costs should be passed on to consumers in the form of lower prices.

And the obverse would occur where the firm's rate of productivity increase was lower than the national average. This would signal a rise in unit labor costs, and these could also be passed on in the form of higher prices. However, if everyone followed the guideposts to the letter, the price increases would be exactly offset by the price decreases, and there would be no inflation. Workers would receive a *real* wage increase

---

[2] Council of Economic Advisers, *Economic Report of the President, 1962* (Washington: Government Printing Office), p. 185. The decision to launch the guideposts was taken only after substantial internal debate within the Kennedy administration. For an excellent history of this period, based on unpublished documents contained in the Kennedy library, see William J. Barber, "The Kennedy Years," in Craufurd D. Goodwin, ed., *Exhortation and Controls: The Search for a Wage-Price Policy, 1945–1971* (Washington: The Brookings Institution, 1975), pp. 135–91.

[3] Council of Economic Advisers, *Report of the President*, p. 185.

based on the rate of increase in national productivity. At the same time, the capital and labor shares of the national income would remain fixed.[4]

Some flexibility in the guidepost system was built in through various exceptions. For example, wages could increase more rapidly than the national productivity norm in a particular sector of the economy if it was growing rapidly and could not attract the labor it needed if held to the national productivity guideline. Also catch-up wage increases above the national norm would be permitted where a particular segment of labor had been receiving wage increases that were far below average wage increases in the rest of the economy prior to the introduction of the guideposts. On the price side, exceptions would be made where firms needed to attract capital, where profits had been low, and where a temporary price increase would generate the profits needed to accumulate capital.

Although a few exceptions were to be granted, in general the guideposts were elegant in their simplicity, requiring only six pages to explain. This is a lesson to store in your memory, because subsequent wage-price policies have become a jungle of complexity.

How effective were the guideposts in limiting inflationary tendencies while the Kennedy administration pursued an aggressive full-employment fiscal policy? Most economic analysts have concluded that the guideposts were effective in the first few years of their implementation. For example, during the five-year period from 1961 to 1965, the CPI increased at an average annual rate of 1.3 percent, compared with 1.5 percent for the previous five years. Total compensation for workers (wages plus fringe benefits) went up an average of 3.6 percent per year from 1961 through 1965, compared with 3.9 percent for the previous five years. Most important, perhaps, are the unemployment figures, which declined from an average of 6.2 percent during the 1957–61 period to 5.3 percent during the 1961–65 period.[5]

Summarizing a variety of economic studies, a congressional report concluded that the rate of increase in wholesale prices was reduced by the guideposts anywhere from 0.6 to 1.5 percentage points.[6]

After 1965 the guideposts were less effective, primarily because the economy was close to full employment. With sufficient or excess demand in the economy, supply bottlenecks began to appear, and the consensus about the guideposts began to break down. "Guideposts may be useful," concluded the Congressional Budget Office in its study, "in preventing inflation from developing as an economy moves toward full employment but they cannot prevent inflation if there is general excess demand in the system."[7] In the 1965–66 period, the CPI increased at a rate of 2.9 percent per year,

---

[4] The guideposts are described in ibid., pp. 185–90.

[5] John Sheahan, *The Wage-Price Guideposts* (Washington: The Brookings Institution, 1967), p. 80.

[6] Congressional Budget Office, *Incomes Policies in the United States*, (May 1977), p. 23. Wholesale prices measure the prices paid for commodities exchanged among producers.

[7] Ibid., p. 24

[handwritten: GUIDEPOSTS HAD 2x AS LARGE AN IMPACT ON UNIONIZED SECTORS THAN ON NON-UNIONIZE SECTORS.]

more than double its average annual rate of increase in the 1961–65 period. And total worker compensation increased at a rate of 6.5 percent per year, well above the productivity-based guidepost.[8]

Of interest to the labor economist is the impact of the guidepost policy on the determination of wages through trade unions. Do the guideposts act more effectively on wages in the highly unionized sectors of the economy, as they were designed to do? The answer is yes. One study of this question concluded that the guideposts had approximately twice as large an impact on the highly unionized sectors of the economy as on the less unionized sectors of the economy.[9]

This is not surprising, because any wage-price policy works best in the sectors with highest visibility. These parts of the economy can be identified, isolated, and targeted for attention. Tailor-made for this public relations gambit by the government are the highly unionized sectors of the economy, whose collective bargaining is very visible and affects a large number of workers in the economy. Moreover, if you recall the discussion in Chapter 6, patterns for wage increases are established in these unionized sectors of the economy, and the wage gains then spill over into the rest of the economy. Therefore, an efficient targeting of government attention to those sectors of high unionization would have a large payoff.

This raises another important question, which pertains to the fairness or equity of wage-price policy. Trade unions claim that they are adversely affected by wage-price policy, whatever it is, compared with firms. Wage negotiations, being highly visible, can be more effectively contained within any wage-price policy than can price increases, which occur in a more dispersed, less visible form. Moreover, every employer becomes the government's wage policy enforcer. All an employer has to do is stand by the government wage policy and implement it for the government. In fact, wage policy is used by firms to legitimate their wage posture. Who polices price increases, though? There is no comparable decentralized mechanism automatically built into the enforcement of price policy as there is for wage policy. Subtle changes in the size, content, and quality of commodities are difficult to monitor in any price policy. Is the candy bar you buy today for 25 cents the same as the one you buy tomorrow for the same or a higher price? Quality and size changes, visibility, and dispersed decision making all tend to make prices more difficult to monitor than wages.

The critique of wage-price policy from the perspective of strict neoclassical economic theory is that prices and wages are not merely statistical indicators of inflation. More importantly, they are pieces of critical economic information, used as signals that lead to resource allocation decisions. Artificially suppress those signals and

---

[8] Sheahan, *Wage-Price Guideposts*, p. 80. The problem with any evaluation of the impact of guidepost policy is that we do not know precisely what wages and prices would have been without the guideposts. This is the same methodological problem encountered in Chapter 7 in connection with the assessment of the trade union's impact on wages.

[9] Gail Pierson, "The Effect of Union Strength on the U.S. 'Phillips Curve,' " *American Economic Review* 58, no. 3 (June 1968), pp. 456–65.

distortions will arise in the economy that will come back to haunt the system sooner if not later. "To whatever extent the price system is displaced," argues Milton Friedman, "some other system of organizing resources and rationing output must be adopted."[10]

The retort to this critique is that the economy is not competitive like the textbook ideal and that prices and wages act as true signals for resource allocation only in a perfectly competitive environment. Friedman, and other critics of wage-price policy like them, compare guidepost policies with a theoretical ideal that is not attainable. The best one can do with the world is a "second best" pragmatic solution to wage-price problems, according to the defenders of wage-price policy. Of course, that is what the guideposts were designed to address:

> Individual wage and price decisions assume national importance when they involve large numbers of workers and large amounts of output directly or when they are regarded by large segments of the economy as setting a pattern. Because such decisions affect the progress of the whole economy, there is a legitimate reason for public interest in their content and consequences.[11]

With President Kennedy's assassination in 1963, his administration's experiments with wage-price policy did not come to an end immediately, but eventually they became consumed by economic, political, and military events in the Johnson administration. President Johnson continued to use guidepost policy up through 1966; by 1967 events had overtaken the guideposts, and for practical purposes they were dead.

There are several reasons for this. First, Johnson, more than Kennedy, wanted to focus his administration on a full-employment economy as a cornerstone of his Great Society programs. He pursued and effectively attained passage of the Kennedy-initiated tax cut. He started the War on Poverty. He expanded already-existing social programs, such as social security. All this might have been possible without inflation had he not escalated a "second-front war" in Indochina. But our economy, strong as it was in the 1960s, could not support a large-scale two-front war without inflationary consequences.

Second, as the economy moved toward full employment, any limited consensus that had existed about wage-price policy broke down. Corporate profits were growing very rapidly, and labor sought a part of those profits in the form of higher wage increases. Inflation began to inch up, indicating a failure to implement price policy, and labor asserted its traditional bargaining stance of productivity plus cost-of-living increases.

In a memorandum from Walter Heller, chairman of the Council of Economic

---

[10] Milton Friedman, "What Price Guideposts?" in Ray Marshall and Richard Perlman, eds., *An Anthology of Labor Economics: Readings and Commentary* (New York: John Wiley and Sons, 1972), p. 383.

[11] Council of Economic Advisers, *Report of the President*, p. 185. A defense of the guideposts is contained in Robert M. Solow, "The Case against the Case against the Guideposts," in Marshall and Perlman, *Anthology*, pp. 387–91.

Notes

Advisers, to Johnson, he reported on a meeting he had with Walter Reuther, then president of the United Auto Workers. Heller said,

> Our arguments about socially responsible collective bargaining, the need for price stability . . . made no apparent dent. He claims rank-and-file pressures require a dramatic settlement; that the AFL-CIO have been good boys long enough; that labor's share of income has been slipping while the corporations have been racking up unwarranted price increases . . . He says they're going to "unburden" GM (whose after-tax profits in the 12 months ending in September [1963] were $1.6 billion) of the biggest chunk of profits any company ever parted with.[12]

Subsequent to this meeting, which was held in December 1963, other discussions occurred through the spring and summer of 1964. Reuther proposed holding back on wage increases if the auto companies would agree to lower prices.[13] In this setting he could justify wage restraint to his members as part of a larger social accord and would be relieved of the pressure placed on him by the very high profits that were rolling in to the auto companies. This strategy failed, however, and the auto worker pact provided for a wage increase of about 4.5 percent. This broke the line on the guideposts and weakened their subsequent application.

This narrative should not be interpreted as providing a villain in the story. Economic events as much as individual personalities overtook the guideposts. What is most important to learn from this brief attempt at wage-price policy is that wage increases are far easier to restrain than price increases, for all the reasons pointed out earlier in this chapter. Once price increases take off as the economy approaches full employment, equity concerns become unavoidable with their subsequent consequences for highly visible wage negotiations.

Summing up the entire guidepost period of wage-price policy, Gardner Ackley, chairman of President Johnson's Council of Economic Advisers, wrote a memo to Johnson in 1967 in the midst of very difficult negotiations and a strike of the commercial airlines by the International Association of Machinists:

> Every free industrialized country which tries to maintain full employment faces this problem: strong unions have the power to push wages up faster than productivity and, thereby, to inflate costs and prices; and semimonopolistic industries have the power to push up prices even if costs are stable. No country has really solved it. Sooner or later we will have to come to grips with it. Now may not be the time. But if not now, soon.[14]

---

[12] James L. Cochrane, "The Johnson Years," in Craufurd D. Goodwin, ed., *Exhortation and Controls: The Search for a Wage-Price Policy, 1945–1971* (Washington: The Brookings Institution, 1975), p. 199.

[13] A high-level interdepartmental administration committee recommended an average $60 price reduction on all GM cars (ibid., p. 208).

[14] Ibid., pp. 261–62.

Nixon's New Economic Policy

After insisting for many years that he would never use any form of direct government wage-price policy, President Nixon on August 15, 1971, introduced a freeze on wages and prices, and he followed the freeze with nearly three additional years of rather detailed wage-price policy. The irony of this event is that the Democratic party had provided Nixon with the statutory authority to impose such detailed policies—authority that neither Kennedy nor Johnson had. In the Byzantine twists of Washington politics, the Democrats wanted to box Nixon into a corner by providing him with anti-inflation legislation, thinking he would never use it and they would have a good campaign issue. But he outfoxed them.

In a more technical sense, the initial wage-price freeze had some economic content to it. The forces that drove Nixon to impose the wage-price freeze (for 90 days) came largely from outside the United States. This is not the place to develop a history of the international economy; suffice it to say that the international economic system that was created after World War II, known as the Bretton Woods system, had begun to unravel in the late 1960s. The United States had been running persistently larger and larger balance-of-payments deficits since the late 1950s. There was an excess of dollars circulating throughout the world—known as *Eurodollars*. The dollar was overvalued, and a devaluation was needed, but the old Bretton Woods system made this difficult if not impossible for the United States to pursue.[15]

As bold steps were taken to restructure the world economy and American's role in it, domestic moves were required to insure that the fallout in the United States economy was controlled. Nixon was also committed to a reasonably strong employment-generating fiscal policy, and he did not want the additional inflationary problems caused by his international policies to undermine his domestic employment policy.

So on August 15, 1971, Nixon announced a dramatic set of policies, which he called the New Economic Policy. Included was a 90-day freeze on all wages and prices, our first ever outside wartime, to be followed by specific wage-price standards for business and labor.

The 90-day wage and price freeze was replaced by what came to be called Phase II of the Nixon wage-price policy. This lasted from November 14, 1971, to January 11, 1973. This 14-month program established specific criteria for wage and price increases. Wage increases were tied primarily to productivity, as they had been under the guidepost policy. Price increases were based on changes in the firm's unit labor costs, with an allowance for a "normal" markup over unit labor costs to cover the firm's profit margin.[16]

---

[15] This background is developed in Neil De Marchi, "The First Nixon Administration: Prelude to Controls," in Craufurd D. Goodwin, ed., *Exhortation and Controls: The Search for a Wage-Price Policy, 1945–1971* (Washington: The Brookings Institution, 1975), pp. 295–352; and Howard M. Wachtel, *The Money Mandarins. The Making of a New Supranational Economic Order* (New York: Pantheon Books, 1986).

[16] Congressional Budget Office, *Incomes Policies*, pp. 34–37.

A specific target of 5.5 percent for wages was set, based on the goal of a 3 percent increase in productivity and a 2.5 percent cost-of-living adjustment. The usual exceptions were written into the administrative rules to allow wage catch-ups to compensate for previously lower-than-average wage increases and to allow increases needed for attraction and retention of critical employees.

For the firms a price rule was established, based on their increase in unit labor costs and a "normal" profit margin. The latter concept caused considerable controversy, for how was a normal profit margin to be defined? Operationally, this meant arriving at some standard price markup over unit labor costs.

The economy was divided into "tiers" based on sales. The largest firms in the economy (Tier I) had to receive prior approval before raising prices; Tier II firms could raise prices but had to notify the Price Commission, which administered the program; Tier III firms had to observe the same standards as Tier I and II firms but did not have to provide any notification. The prices of Tier III firms were spot-checked by the IRS for compliance with the price standards.[17] The standard for price increases permitted both a passing-on of increases in unit labor costs and a price markup that allowed the firm a profit margin based on the highest profit margin attained in two out of the three fiscal years prior to August 15, 1971.[18]

During Phase I (the wage-price freeze) the CPI increased by just 2.0 percent. During the life of Phase II wage-price policies, the CPI increased by 3.7 percent. Wage increases remained within the guidelines of 5.5 percent.[19] This was a creditable performance by any criteria, and therein lies one of the problems with the Nixon period of wage-price policies. Because inflation and wage increases were moderating, there was an immediate reaction to remove the wage-price policies and return to unregulated wages and prices. Americans do not like controls and at the slightest hint of success want to eliminate them. The problem with our experience with wage-price policies may lie less with the policies themselves than with our attitudes toward them and with the problems we encounter as we attempt to dismantle wage-price policies.

The *Report* of Nixon's Council of Economic Advisers put it this way:

> With excess capacity declining at the end of 1972, there was a clear possibility that continuation of the Phase II controls program would interfere increasingly with production, productivity, and investment decisions, and raise administrative costs. . . . Against this backdrop it was decided to modify the price and wage controls program to . . . move toward the Administration's goal of eventually ending the controls.[20]

Phase III of the controls was inaugurated on January 11, 1973, and was designed

---

[17] Ibid., p. 36.

[18] Robert F. Lanzillotti et al., *Phase II in Review: The Price Commission Experience* (Washington: The Brookings Institution, 1975), pp. 34–35.

[19] Congressional Budget Office, *Incomes Policies*, p. 31.

[20] Council of Economic Advisers, *Economic Report of the President, 1974* (Washington: Government Printing Office), p. 89.

to loosen previous policies as a transition to having no wage-price policy in the economy. Six months later, however, as inflation heated up again, a new wage-price freeze had to be installed.

Under the transitional Phase III, the profit margin standard was loosened so that firms could now choose the highest profit margin for any two years in the period starting August 15, 1968. The sales standard for Tier I and II firms was raised so that only firms with quarterly sales over $250 million (compared with $100 million under Phase II) would have to receive prior approval before raising prices. The wage standard was slightly relaxed by providing more special exemptions and a blanket exemption for all workers earning less than $3.50 per hour.[21]

While designed as a transition to the removal of controls, Phase III was overtaken by events that drove inflation up very rapidly. "By Spring," according to the Council of Economic Advisers, "it was clear that . . . specific assumptions underlying forecasts for 1973 had gone awry."[22] Retail food prices were increasing at an annual rate of 8.1 percent, more than twice the rate of increase before Phase III. Driven by the start of higher energy prices as well, the overall CPI was running at a rate of 8.1 percent, more than twice the rate of increase before Phase III. So it was back to the wage-price freeze again on June 13, 1973. Nixon announced a new freeze to last 60 days, to be followed by a Phase IV controls system that would be tighter than Phase II.

Under Phase IV, price increases were limited to the passing-on of increases in unit labor costs; no longer could firms add on higher markups to reach earlier profit margin targets.[23] Wage standards remained essentially as they had been, because there had not been a large spate of wage increases during the ill-fated Phase III transitional period.

Legislative authority for the Nixon wage-price policies expired in late April 1974, when the Economic Stabilization Act ran out. By this time business was opposed to the Nixon wage-price policies, and labor was opposed because it was not able to catch up with the inflation that had occurred during the short decontrol period of Phase III. Congress did not extend the Economic Stabilization Act, and since that time the president has had no authority to initiate formal and specific wage-price policies.

In late 1973 and early 1974, world events began to overtake domestic wage-price policies, specifically the nearly four-fold increase in crude petroleum prices engineered by the OPEC cartel. During the eight months of Phase IV, before the expiration of Nixon's statutory authority, the CPI increased by 11.5 percent, and in the eight months after the expiration of the authority, the CPI increased by 12.2 percent.[24] Thus, the

---

[21] Ibid., p. 91.

[22] Ibid., p. 92.

[23] Ibid., p. 98.

[24] Congressional Budget Office, *Incomes Policies*, p. 31.

country was moving full steam ahead to the largest and most sustained period of inflation in its history.

Were the Nixon wage-price policies, with all their phases, tiers, and rules, effective in achieving their objective of restraining inflation? The answer to this question is as controversial and complex as the wage-price policies themselves. It is generally conceded that only under Phases I and II was there any success. By the time the ill-fated transitional phase, Phase III, came into place, events had begun to dominate domestic wage-policy. Phase IV was doomed from the outset. A question for which there is no answer is whether moving toward decontrol in January of 1973 was a mistake and whether Phase III, by doing this, set the stage for the inflation of the mid-1970s. Studies of Phase II estimate that prices were reduced by as much as 1.4 percentage points and wages by as much as 1 percentage point from what they would have been without Phase II wage-price policies.[25]

However, one of the most widely respected analyses of the Nixon wage-price policies would reject any effort to measure the wage-price effects of the program. "The marginal effects of controls of inflation," writes Marvin Kosters, who was involved with the implementation of the Nixon policies, "cannot be measured with any precision, because little confidence can be placed in the accuracy of estimates of the course inflation might have taken if there had been no program of wage and price controls."[26]

The Carter Years

When President Carter took office in January of 1977, he had no legislative authority to initiate wage-price policies with enforcement powers behind them, and he sought no such authority during his four years in office. In fact, he made it clear on many occasions that he was opposed to the use of enforceable wage-price policies. As inflation began to heat up in the early years of his administration, however, Carter retreated on this position and attempted to implement a voluntary wage-price policy.

In the fall of 1978 he announced his scheme. Wages and salaries (including fringe benefits) were to increase by no more than 7 percent. Firms were asked to reduce their average price increase by one-half of one percentage point from the average annual rate of increase during 1976 and 1977.[27]

Since these standards were voluntary, President Carter faced the difficult problem

---

[25] John Kraft and Blaine Roberts, "Wage and Price Controls: Success or Failure?" in John Kraft and Blaine Roberts, eds., *Wage and Price Controls: The U.S. Experiment* (New York: Praeger Publishers, 1975), pp. 145–46.

[26] Marvin H. Kosters, *Controls and Inflation* (Washington: The American Enterprise Institute, 1975), p. 117.

[27] There were also the usual escape clauses, providing for exceptions. See Council of Economic Advisers, *Economic Report of the President, 1980* (Washington: Government Printing Office), pp. 32–33.

of how to obtain compliance. In a qualified way, he announced that he would consider using federal contracts as an instrument for compliance. He said, in the words of his Council of Economic Advisers, that "the Federal Government would avoid purchasing from noncomplaint firms where feasible.[28] Carter never backed up his implied threat with systematic action, and the wage-price policies of his administration were largely a paper tiger.

Wage-Price Policies in the 1980s

Lacking statutory authority and being generally opposed to wage-price policy, President Carter did little in the way of extending existing wage-price policies or innovating new ones. But the debate over their usefulness did not go away. New ideas about wage-price policy continued to be debated in academic circles. Most of the new ideas centered on using the tax system as a means to implement wage-price policies. Two variants of the use of the tax system to encourage compliance with wage-price policies are "tax-based incomes policies" and "real-wage protection policies"

Tax-based incomes policies (TIPs) start from the premise that firms do not resist labor's demands for wage increases with sufficient vigor. Supposedly this phenomenon occurs more frequently in highly concentrated sectors of the economy, where the firms can escape the discipline of the market by passing wage increases on to consumers in the form of higher prices no matter what level of capacity utilization exists in the firm. TIPs seek to use the tax system as either a carrot or a stick to substitute public policy disciplines or incentives for what had previously been taken care of by competitive markets.

Here is how TIPs work. Under one variant, if a particular firm permits wages to increase by more than some national standard, that firm would have to pay a tax surcharge as a penalty for breaking the wage guidelines.[29] For example, if the wage guidelines called for a standard 5.5 percent increase and a particular firm raised wages by 8 percent, a surtax would be imposed for all or part of the 2.5 percentage point difference between the wage guideline and the actual wage increase.

From the standpoint of labor economics and the collective bargaining process, these penalty-based TIP plans raise some problems. First, is it accurate to conclude that there is not tough collective bargaining even in firms operating in concentrated markets? The evidence from collective bargaining does not enable one to conclude that negotiations are easy and that the market exercises no restraint on the parties. In fact, the reverse is the case. The literature summarized in Chapter 7 of this book

---

[28] Ibid., p. 32.

[29] Henry C. Wallich and Sidney Weintraub, "A Tax-based Incomes Policy," in Arthur M. Okun and George L. Perry, eds., *Curing Chronic Inflation* (Washington: The Brookings Institution, 1978), pp. 65–112.

suggests that the market is more important than any other single factor in determining the outcome of wage negotiations in the collective bargaining process.

2 -   Second, the proposition that wage increases are passed on to consumers in the form of higher prices is too simplistic. What is passed on is the increase in unit labor costs, which is a result of wage increases and labor productivity increases. Conceivably an 8 percent wage increase could be justified in a particular firm by its labor productivity increase without necessitating any price increase. In penalizing that firm, policy would be in error. In short, a mistake is made in not considering labor productivity increases as well as wage increases and in going from a national norm to the firm without taking account of the micro foundations that would be required to implement such a wage-price policy.

3 .   Third, if wage increases can be passed on to consumers in the form of higher prices—the premise of this policy—why would the tax increase not be passed on also? Evidence suggests that economically powerful firms transfer tax increases to the public via higher prices. A tax penalty surcharge would be treated likewise.

TIP advocates spend more time discussing the wage side of the inflation equation than they devote to the price side. Where price policy is considered, it is made symmetric; a tax surcharge would be levied where prices increased above some norm. The price policy criterion is always more difficult to specify, however, because products are not standardized, and the absence of equal attention to price problems has made organized labor skeptical about the fairness of TIP plans.

An alternative variant of the TIP plan is to provide positive tax incentives rather than negative tax penalties.[30] If workers received a wage increase below some norm and if prices rose less rapidly than the norm, both employees and employer would receive a tax rebate. Arthur Okun proposed the following scheme for 1978: If firms pledged at the beginning of 1978 to hold the average rate of wage increase to 6 percent and the average price increase to 4 percent, the workers in the firm would receive a 1.5 percent tax rebate and the firm would receive a 5 percent rebate against corporate profits taxes.[31]

II .   Another way of using the tax system to induce wage-price behavior is through *wage protection* schemes. Here the tax system is used to reward workers directly if they

A .   accept a wage increase below the norm. For example, if a wage settlement came in under the national norm, the workers affected would receive a tax rebate equal to all or part of the difference between what they settled for and what the wage norm imposed.

1 .   Such positive tax rebate plans could also be used to protect the *real* wages of workers. For example, if inflation was running at 8 percent per year and the government wanted to ratchet the wage-price spiral downward, it could offer tax rebates to

[30] Variants of TIP policies are discussed in Laurence S. Seidman, "Tax-Based Incomes Policies," in Arthur M. Okun and George L. Perry, eds., *Curing Chronic Inflation* (Washington: The Brookings Institution, 1978), pp. 65–112.

[31] Arthur M. Okun, "The Great Stagflation Swamp," *Challenge*, November–December 1977, p. 13.

workers who settled for less than 8 percent. So if a particular individual received a 6 percent wage increase, he or she would take a tax rebate of two percentage points to make up the difference and protect his or her real purchasing power from erosion. This type of plan has merit in that it provides a genuine incentive for wage restraint and places that incentive where it belongs—with the individual worker and his union.[32]

The last report to the Congress by President Carter's Council of Economic Advisers tentatively endorsed a tax-based wage and price policy. On the wage side, the council opted for a form of positive tax incentive and wage protection plan. On the price side of the equation, it supported a tax penalty imposed only on very large firms.[33]

Lessons from Our Experience with Wage-Price Policies

"There are no costless ways to reduce inflation," said President Carter's Council of Economic Advisers in its final report to the Congress. "Using demand restraint alone imposes very large costs of forgone output and unemployment for modest reductions in inflation."[34] Although there clearly are costs in economic distortions associated with wage-price policies, other anti-inflationary policies also have their costs—for example, recessing the economy and using unemployment as anti-inflation policy. The question is which types of costs associated with which types of anti-inflationary policies are easier for the economic system to absorb.

The lessons from nearly two decades of wage-price policy experiments in the United States are as follows:

- If you try to control all prices and wages, you end up controlling none, because the administrative task is too great. Therefore, selectively must be employed.

- Wage-price policy politicizes key economic decisions. This has its benefits, in that it makes previously private decisions more visible, but it also places burdens on the political system that it may not be able to handle.

- Any wage-price policy must be equitable in its design and implementation in order for it to be effective.

- Wage-price policies must be integrated with larger fiscal and monetary policy so that all three prongs of economic policy are working toward the same goals.

---

[32] President Carter proposed a variant of this—"real-wage insurance"—during his administration, but it failed to pass the Congress.

[33] Council of Economic Advisers, *Economic Report of the President, 1981* (Washington: Government Printing Office, 1981), pp. 57–68.

[34] Ibid., p. 67.

■ A social accord that includes other aspects of public policy (economic, social, and tax policy) must be part of the larger anti-inflation plan in order for wage-price policies to be effective.

Although at present wage-price policies are out of vogue, they will not remain so for long. The costs associated with unemployment to reduce inflation are too large for our society to be able to sustain them for long. When wage-price policies do reappear, they will probably take the form of some type of wage protection plan integrated into the tax system, in addition to tax penalties for excessive price increases, all accompanied by a broader social accord.

Summary

The United States has been a reluctant experimenter with wage-price policy, compared with other industrial nations. Nevertheless, we now have more than two decades of experience with wage-price policy in the United States from which we can learn and assess the value of such policies.

President Kennedy in 1962 launched his wage-price guidepost policy. Lacking statutory authority for enforcement, his policies relied on voluntary compliance and public pressure. A relatively simple set of guideposts was proposed. Wages were to increase at the rate of national labor productivity growth. Prices would increase, decrease, or remain the same depending on the rate of labor productivity growth in the firm. If labor productivity in a firm rose more than the national average, the firm was expected to lower its price and pass the savings in unit labor costs on to consumers in the form of reduced prices. If labor productivity grew less than the national average, the higher unit labor costs could be passed on as price increases.

The purpose of the guideposts, and all wage-price policies, is to permit the government to pursue full-employment policies without having those programs jeopardized by inflation. One of the lessons learned from the Kennedy guidepost period is that wage-price policy works better on the way toward full employment than it does when the economy has reached full employment. Then distortions begin to appear, supply-side bottlenecks occur, and equity problems emerge. Hence, by 1967, when the war-induced boom in the economy brought us to full employment, the consensus surrounding the guideposts began to evaporate.

We were effectively without a wage-price policy from 1967 until President Nixon initiated his wage-price freeze in 1971, followed by three years of different phases of wage-price policy. His policies and standards were more complex, but he was also dealing with a more complicated economy, particularly in the international area. Nixon had the advantage of statutory authority, which had been granted by the Congress, and therefore he had enforcement power. That authority ended in 1974, and so did his wage-price policies. But the program was as much a victim of OPEC-imposed price increases as it was of congressional failure to extend his statutory authority.

At present there is no discussion of a reimposition of wage-price policy. But the idea is not dead, and new forms of policies are beginning to gain support. Using the tax system to impose penalties or provide rewards for certain wage-price behavior is the most frequently discussed type of wage-price policy. President Carter's Council of Economic Advisers signaled support for these ideas in its last report to the Congress.

Study Questions

1. Discuss the design, implementation, and effectiveness of wage-price policies in the Kennedy administration.

2. What is the economic rationale for wage-price policies? Do you agree with those premises of wage-price policies? Discuss.

3. How did Nixon's wage-price program differ from Kennedy's? Compare the effectiveness of the two sets of policies.

4. Evaluate the "tax-based incomes policies" being proposed by some economists.

5. How would you characterize the Carter wage-price policies? Were they effective in reaching their objectives?

Further Reading

Congressional Budget Office. *Incomes Policies in the United States: Historical Review and Some Issues*. Washington: Congressional Budget Office, 1977.

Goodwin, Craufurd D., ed. *Exhortation and Controls: The Search for a Wage-Price Policy, 1945–1971*. Washington: The Brookings Institution, 1975.

Kosters, Marvin H. *Controls and Inflation*. Washington: The American Enterprise Institute, 1975.

Sheahan, John. *The Wage-Price Guideposts*. Washington: The Brookings Institution, 1967.

Part

III

Labor and Economic Institutions

19

The Evolution of
American Unions

Almost from the first day that large groups of individuals were hired as employees, attempts have been made by workers to join together for collective protection and influence over the conditions of work. Trade unions are the institutional form of labor organization. As one historian of labor puts it, "In terms of the individual, the union returns to the worker his 'society.' It gives him a fellowship, a part in a drama that he can understand, and life takes on meaning once again because he shares a value system common to others."[1]

Labor unions are complex. Each has its own peculiar history and culture and its own way of conducting its affairs. Unions are distinctly national institutions; their character and structure vary across countries. Even within the same country, trade unions have to tailor their economic and political posture to the historical conditions in which they find themselves, and, therefore, they behave differently in different historical periods. The richness, complexity, and variety of labor institutions make trade unions fascinating institutions to study, but they also mean that generalizations about trade union activity are fraught with difficulties. Care must be exercised, therefore, in approaching the study of the trade union as an economic institution trying

---

[1] Frank Tannenbaum, *A Philosophy of Labor* (New York: Alfred A. Knopf, 1951), p. 10.

to affect the welfare of its members. Generalize we must, or the exercise will become futile. But in the process of creating ideas about trade unions, caution must be exercised so that the variety of trade union activity does not become lost in the deviation of general principles.

To understand labor unions in the contemporary context, a historical perspective is absolutely essential. Institutions like trade unions do not exist in a historical vacuum. For this reason, a brief excursion into the history of trade unions in the United States forms the point of departure for an institutional analysis of labor and the economy.

In this chapter the history of trade unionism is examined, followed by an analysis of the process of collective bargaining in the next chapter. The final two chapters in the section treat labor law and the future of industrial relations in the United States.

Institutional Premise of Neoclassical Marginal Productivity Theory

The neoclassical marginal productivity theory of wages envisions an economy without trade unions. The institutional datum of this "pure theory" of wage determination is the household, each household making its own decision about supplying labor at different wage rates, separate from the decisions of all the other households in a particular labor market. Since each household in the neoclassical system is such a tiny portion of the labor market, it sees itself as being unable to influence the wage rate it can receive for its labor. Consequently it forgoes any attempt to influence the wage rate. In contrast, the purpose of a trade union is to affect the wage rate paid for labor through an organization of wage earners. The labor union breaks down the barriers imposed by the atomized decision process of separate households and seeks influence in the labor market by organizing the largest number of laborers. Rather than seeing the relation between buyer and seller of labor as one of harmonious exchange, the institutional world of trade unions starts and ends with conflict.

What is a trade union? How do labor economists define a trade union? The definition most widely accepted among labor economists is one first offered by the two British economists Sidney and Beatrice Webb, writing near the end of the last century. In their classic study of the history of British trade unionism, they define a trade union as a "continuous association of wage-earners for the purpose of maintaining or improving the conditions of their working lives."[2] By that definition, trade unions did not come into being in the United States until well after the Civil War. The precursors, however, of trade unionism in the Webbs' sense can be found in the entire history of work in America, starting with the prerevolutionary period.

---

[2] Sidney and Beatrice Webb, *The History of Trade Unionism* (London: Longmans, Green & Co., 1894), p. 1.

Each historical epoch has its unique forms of worker organization, which arise in response to the conditions of work present in a particular period of time. The framework of analysis carried through this chapter traces the evolution of working conditions and the response of workers to those conditions. It is not possible, for example, for industrial unions to exist without mass production industries. Craft unions arise organically to mirror the structure of production in which work takes place. That is why the historical model used in this chapter tracks the evolution of unionism as a response to differing forms of the work process.

Prerevolutionary Conditions of Work

The most common way for a laborer to arrive in the United States during the sixteenth and seventeenth centuries was through the system of *indentured labor.* Under this system the worker contracted with an employer (or the employer's agent) in England to work in the American colonies for a specified period of time in return for the cost of transport to the colonies. The term of indenture normally did not exceed seven years.

Supplementing this system was one called *redemption,* which was applied mainly to the non-English: Scotch, Irish, German, and Swiss. Arising in the eighteenth century, the system of redemption came into being to augment what had become an insufficient flow of labor deriving from the system of indenture. Redemption provided that the laborer sign the contract on arrival in the colonies rather than at the point of embarkation in the British Isles. The length of time a worker would be tied to an employer depended on the amount of debt the worker had accumulated for passage to America. Since the system of redemption operated more informally than indenture and was applied to the non-English, the contractual terms imposed on the worker were typically harsher and longer. To work off one's redemption required more time than an indenture, and since the means of transport were controlled by the employers, the amount of debt accumulated for the worker's transport could be adjusted to suit whatever time period was called for in the redemption contract.

Once freed from either indenture or redemption, a laborer typically entered the traditional guild system for the organization of work, which had prevailed in England and Europe for centuries. Starting as an apprentice, the worker would progress to the status of journeyman after about seven years, and then possibly to master. The guilds were the system of organization that regulated this structure of work organization, although they never had as much power in America as in Europe, because of the higher degree of labor mobility that characterized America from the very earliest days. The guilds, when they were operative, established prices for the products produced by the guildsmen and for the labor services they offered. A carpenter, for example, was bound to charge the price established by the carpenter's guild for a piece of furniture he produced or for services he offered. The guilds also monitored and regulated the supply of labor by virtue of their control over the process by which someone became an apprentice and progressed toward master status. As price-setting institutions for labor, the guilds functioned in much the same way as the craft unions that arose later in the nineteenth century.

Complementing this system of guilds was a second form of organization of the work process: the *licensed trades*. As defined by the labor historian Henry Pelling, licensed trades were "occupations regarded as essential to the public welfare, whose members were licensed and regulated by the city corporations."[3] Whether organized through the guilds or in licensed trades, workers in the prerevolutionary period could not just set up shop and start selling labor services. Either they had to gain access to the guilds, if the work tasks came under the guilds' orbit of regulation, or they had to get permission from the public authorities, if the jobs were part of the public regulatory process of licensed trades.

Strikes—the withholding of labor services—rarely occurred. When they did, they took one of two forms: either they were strikes of journeymen against their masters, who controlled the guilds, or they were strikes of particular licensed tradesmen against the public authorities over the price controls that were imposed on them. Of the latter, the earliest recorded strike was initiated by bakers in New York in 1741.[4] The first recorded strike of journeymen against masters in the "private" sector happened in the construction industry in 1791.[5]

Prerevolutionary America contained many of the seeds that eventually flowered into a postrevolutionary society of enormous economic vitality. Several of the labor characteristics of prerevolutionary America are worth noting at this time: First, there were substantial disparities in the standards of living among different strata of workers in the colonies. There were slaves on the one hand and skilled artisans on the other; master craftsmen who controlled the guilds fared better than apprentices or journeymen. The British indentured laborer received a better contract than the non-English worker caught in the system of redemption. Second, agriculture dominated the economic landscape, and virtually all labor activity represented either a backward or forward linkage to the rural sector of the economy. Third, immigration played an enormous role both in stocking the labor force and in stratifying it. There was the indentured versus the redemptioner, African versus Caucasian, one ethnic group versus another. Fourth, America at this time was a relatively high-wage society, with wage rates for particular trades running anywhere from 30 to 200 percent higher in the American colonies than in England.[6]

---

[3] Henry Pelling, *American Labor* (Chicago: University of Chicago Press, 1960), p. 12.

[4] Ibid., p. 13

[5] U.S. Department of Labor, *The American Worker* (Washington: Government Printing Office, 1977), p. 61.

[6] Pelling, *American Labor*, pp. 14–16.

The Emerging Economy: Labor from the Revolution to the Civil War

■

Emerging from its successful revolution, the American economy remained dominated by agriculture, small-scale artisan production in the Northeast, and slavery as a system of production in the South. The fledgling United States had an abundance of land and natural resources previously unfathomable by European standards. The dominance of agriculture in the newly formed United States is revealed in the first collection of statistics on the labor force. In the 1800 census the total labor force consisted of 1.9 million people, of whom nearly 1.4 million were free and 0.5 million slave. Of the free members of the labor force, 1.3 million were classified in the agricultural sector.[7]

Two themes dominate this period of labor history: One is the embryonic forms of labor organization that emerged, along with the first strikes by labor and capital's response to those strikes. The other is an attempt by workers to escape the factory system by organizing various forms of agricultural utopian societies. Most of these utopian societies were initiated by small religious sects. Some were organized by social reformers. But whatever the source, these utopian experiments found a welcome band of recruits among the factory workers who were exposed to the first wave of large-scale manufacturing, which drastically altered the workers' living standards as well as their entire relationship to the work process.

The forerunners of the modern trade union are found in the period after the American revolution. Trade associations arose as early as the 1790s among printers, carpenters, shoemakers (called cordwainers at the time), and tailors. Historians date the first labor organization having the trappings of a trade union (using the Webbs' definition) as beginning among the Philadelphia shoemakers in 1792.[8] That trade association engaged in one of the earliest strikes, sparking a legal response from the new nation that set important precedents in the law concerning labor organization.[9]

The fortunes of these early labor organizations ebbed and flowed. Organizations arose, achieved some accomplishments, battled with the public authorities over their legal status, and frequently declined into oblivion—only to be created anew several years later.

One of the economic forces that exerted a significant impact on the fortunes of labor during the first half of the eighteenth century was the *business cycle*. When times were good, during the boom phase of the cycle, labor prospered. Labor organizations

---

[7] The source of these statistics is U.S. Department of Commerce, *Historical Statistics of the United States: Colonial Times to 1970* (Washington: Government Printing Office, 1975), pt. 1, p. 139.

[8] John R. Commons, "American Shoemakers, 1648–1895: A Sketch of Industrial Evolution," *Quarterly Journal of Economics* 24 (November 1909), pp. 39–84.

[9] Labor law is discussed in Chapter 21.

gained strength in times of economic prosperity, only to be virtually eliminated when the depression phase of the business cycle ensued. This happened after the War of 1812, when the depression—or panic, as depressions were called at that time—wiped out essentially all labor organizations. The same happened in 1857, when that panic weakened the labor organizations that had been created during the 1820–50 period. In 1853–54 there were an estimated four hundred strikes, marking the militancy of labor during those years. By 1857 labor organizations were almost nonexistent.[10]

How does the business cycle affect the fortunes of labor? During a depression, when there is substantial unemployment, employers have an easy time replacing workers who belong to labor organizations. Strikes in such an economic context are severely weakened because an employer can simply fire all the strikers and replace them with the large and eager supply of able-bodied workers who do not have jobs. During boom times, on the other hand, when labor markets are tight and unemployment is low, employers are comparatively weaker in relation to labor and cannot as easily withstand a strike or other forms of pressure. Replacements for strikers are not as readily available because, by definition, a low unemployment rate means that there will be fewer workers without jobs ready to replace striking workers. Boom times also mean that the treasuries of labor organizations are fatter, since members can afford to pay dues when they have jobs and cannot when they are unemployed. So the shifting balance of the economy from boom times to depression alters the economic power and viability of labor organization. Although the business cycle has a less important effect today on the relative strength of capital and labor, it still exercises an important influence over the fortunes of labor.[11]

The business cycle affects not only the organizational fortunes of labor, but also the economic and political posture that labor assumes toward the economic system of capitalism in which it resides. John R. Commons, the dean of American labor historians, was the first to identify the impact of the business cycle on labor.[12] His thesis was that labor would be concerned about economic questions of wages and working conditions during boom times of the cycle, when the economy was providing sufficient jobs for the work force. But come bad times, when there were not enough jobs to go around, labor would become more enamored with grand schemes of social reform and would turn its attention more toward radical political activity. In such circumstances the economy and the system of capitalism were not delivering the goods, and labor became interested in the social reform and radical political schemes that were afoot in the land.

One such category of radical social reform was the various types of utopian

---

[10] U.S. Department of Labor, *American Worker*, p. 78.

[11] These ideas were examined in Chapter 7.

[12] John R. Commons and Associates, *History of Labor in the United States,* vols. 1–4 (New York: Macmillan, 1918–1935). This work by Commons and his colleagues at the University of Wisconsin is the classic work on the history of American labor. Volumes 1 and 3 explain Commons's views about the impact of the business cycle on labor.

communal experiments that had a small but influential following during the nineteenth century. The labor organizations that grew in the urban centers can be viewed as ways in which workers sought to *defend* themselves from the first wave of factory organization. Besides organizing labor for defensive purposes, workers also sought out avenues for *escaping* the harshness of the working conditions that were wreaking such havoc on work relations and family life. The attempt to escape took the form of utopian experiments. Most were agricultural in character. Many were motivated by austere fringe religious sects.[13] Others found their benefactors in wealthy industrialists, like Robert Owen in New Harmony, Indiana, who themselves were horrified by what industrialization had done to people's lives.

The same phenomenon of utopian experimentation as an escape from industrialization occurred in England a bit earlier. In fact, many of the experiments are direct descendants of comparable British ones. Some of the utopian communities in this country flourished, for example, that of the Rappites, who founded Harmony, Indiana, before selling it to Robert Owen, who named the settlement *New* Harmony. Others— for example, the Amana community—went on to become successful in manufacturing. But, by and large, the utopian communities did not survive, although their spirit lives on today with contemporary communards. The period of escape, despite the sincerity and nobility of spirit of its participants, was doomed to fail in the face of the juggernaut of industrialization that marched through the country after the Civil War as relentlessly as Sherman's army ransacked the South.

The End of the Age of Innocence: Civil War to the American Federation of Labor

The end of the Civil War marked the beginning of America's massive industrialization drive, which was not to end until the United States became a great world power in the twentieth century. Jeffersonian idealism and Jacksonian populism gave way to a pragmatic commercialism in American politics that went successfully unchallenged until the Progressive and New Deal politics of the present century.

The cold statistics of the decennial censuses of the United States tell a story of shifting economic structures. In 1820, out of a total work force of 2.8 million, only 800 thousand were listed as nonfarm, engaged in some economic pursuit outside farming. Agriculture accounted for 72 percent of all employment in 1820 and other activities 28 percent. By 1850 these proportions had shifted to 63 percent agriculture, 37 percent nonfarm. And ten years later, in 1860, 58 percent were engaged in agriculture and 42 percent in other pursuits.[14]

---

[13] Charles Nordhoff, *The Communistic Societies of the United States* (New York: Harper and Brothers, 1875); and Joseph G. Rayback, *A History of American Labor* (New York: Macmillan, 1963), chap. 7.

[14] U.S. Department of Commerce, *Historical Statistics*, p. 134.

In the space of forty years, the American economy had begun to show a trend toward manufacturing that is still continuing today. Born as an agricultural nation with an abundance of rich land for the production of food, the country's economy has, nevertheless, been moving away from its rural traditions since 1820. In the first decennial census after the Civil War, in 1870, the number of people engaged in agriculture and the number outside agriculture were nearly equal; by 1880 more people were engaged in economic pursuits outside agriculture than were working on farms. The proportions of people engaged in agriculture and people not engaged in agriculture have not shifted since. Subsequent decennial censuses have merely recounted the same trend.

The period from the end of the Civil War up to 1886, when the American Federation of Labor was founded, is characterized by several trends that emerge over and over again in the history of American labor.

- This was a period of rapid industrialization, and toward the end of the nineteenth century the first great wave of economic concentration occurred.

- In response to this development, labor organized itself into craft unions that had more staying power than those organized before the Civil War. Two new forms of labor organization arose as well during this period: first, industrial unions that spanned an entire industry, irrespective of craft or occupation; and second, general workers' unions that spanned the entire economy, irrespective of craft, occupation, or industry.

- Early attempts at forming a national labor union with a federated structure immediately after the Civil War failed until finally the American Federation of Labor, founded in 1886, survived.

- Immense waves of immigrants came to the United States to provide the labor necessary for America's great burst of industrialization.

- Socialist trade unions and political parties began to exert substantial, though never dominant, influence over the American labor movement.

- The frontier closed; the last wave of continental settlement occurred, and America stretched from ocean to ocean with no more continent left to subdue.

Within two years after the Civil War ended, 10 national labor unions were founded. An initial attempt at the creation of a national labor federation, the National Labor Union, occurred in 1866, but it collapsed a few years later. A second attempt took place in 1881, the Federation of Organized Trades and Labor Unions of the United States and Canada. Although this organization existed only a few years, it is considered the precursor of the American Federation of Labor (AFL).

The main form of labor union organized during this period was the *craft union*, although industrial unions and general workers' unions cannot be neglected. A craft union embraces a particular trade, such as carpentry, plumbing, or printing. It is a lineal descendant of the older guilds. The craft union was the earliest form of labor union both in the United States and Great Britain, principally because the work place was organized along craft lines. Semiskilled and unskilled labor existed, but they either fit into some craft system or had such little power in the work process that organization among them was unthinkable. Invariably, the members of a craft looked with scorn on the unskilled and semiskilled and refused to lend them any support in their efforts to organize.

The exclusive jurisdiction of craft unionism over the American labor movement began to crack slightly during the second half of the nineteenth century. Industrial unions and general workers' unions emerged but did not survive the pressure of economic conditions and employer opposition. The time had not yet come for industrial unions, since only a small proportion of the labor force was working in large-scale manufacturing plants that used mostly semiskilled and unskilled labor. The general workers' unions have never been able to withstand their own internal factionalism, wrought by the breadth of the coalition and the absence of any unifying work-related characteristic that would naturally bind the members together.

Industrial unions take their jurisdictional base from the industry as a whole, not from any particular craft within an industry. In the second half of the nineteenth century, the best example of a successful industrial union was the American Railway Union, organized by the prominent socialist leader of that time Eugene V. Debs. This union embraced many of the specific trades within the railway industry and achieved enormous power and influence until defeated in a series of bitter and bloody battles with the owners of the railway industry. This type of industrial union permits all the workers employed in that industry to join the union, without reference to the particular trade or craft involved, in marked contrast to a craft union of the AFL sort, which is occupation- and craft-specific.

A more general form of unionization that appeared after the Civil War was a general workers' union for everyone, irrespective of craft or industry. The largest and most powerful general workers' union ever in the United States was the *Knights of Labor*, founded after the Civil War by a garment cutter from Philadelphia, Uriah Stephens. The Knights grew from about 19,000 members in 1881 to 110,000 in 1885, and to an astounding 700,000 in 1886, the year the AFL was founded.[15] Organized along the lines of a lodge, the Knights practiced secret initiation rituals, although their organization was open to anyone who would subscribe to its principles.

Embracing workers of all skills and even some farmers and small businessmen, the Knights were the largest national organization of labor in the United States until the AFL emerged as the preeminent labor organization in the twentieth century. The Knights were populist in their politics, favoring small farmers, small business persons, and workers against the big monopolies and trusts. In this stance, they laid the

---

[15] Pelling, *American Labor*, pp. 66 and 70.

foundation for all future populist movements. The Knights stood for easy money policies and government regulation of the railroad rates. They pioneered the use of the boycott as a weapon against their foes instead of the strike, which was under attack in the courts at that time.

The very breadth of the Knights was their source of strength, but it also became the cause of their eventual demise. The coalition was too broad; interests were too divergent among the various sections of the Knights' organization. Ultimately, factionalism developed in which farmers were pitted against workers, small business owners against farmers, one ethnic group against another. Stephens had hoped to rely on the various rituals of the Knights to bind the disparate membership together and overcome the tendencies toward factionalism. Even that failed as the public began to question the secretive character of the Knights and blamed the organization for labor violence that began to occur in the late 1880s and early 1890s. The lesson for American labor, learned from the experience of the Knights of Labor, was that a general workers' union gave the labor movement strength in numbers but also created frictions that eventually became unbreachable.

This lesson did not go unnoticed by a young English immigrant cigar maker, Samuel Gompers, who became the first president of the American Federation of Labor (AFL) at a meeting held in Columbus, Ohio. Gompers perfected the system of craft union organization. Many of the craft unions had a distinct ethnic identity to them. This was a source of strength for the AFL at that time, in contrast to the factional difficulties that beset industrial and general workers' unions. The decentralization and autonomy of the member unions of the AFL enabled them to prosper from the strength of ethnic identity, although it prevented the national AFL from becoming a strong unified labor movement of the European sort.

The AFL structure mirrored the federation of the United States. Each member union was autonomous. The national AFL had little formal power in this decentralized structure. Gompers saw this as a necessity in view of both the strong ethnic character of American labor and the independence of the American worker. The central federation, though without much formal power, became enormously important in union organizing drives and in cementing the legitimacy of a national labor movement through the simple existence of the AFL. Much of the credit for this belongs to Gompers, who was an adroit administrator. He was constantly on the road, settling disputes among feuding unions or lending his organizational and political skills to new union drives.

When the AFL was founded, Gompers had a strong and growing base of labor from which to recruit. Between 1870 and 1910 the industrial labor force grew from 3.5 million to over 14 million. Twelve million immigrants arrived in the United States between 1865 and 1900.[16] Many of these newly arrived immigrants brought with

---

[16] U.S. Department of Labor, *American Worker*, pp. 109–110.

them not only their skills and ethnic heritage, but a strong trade union commitment as well. Frequently, their trade union commitment overlapped with socialist politics, which added to the home-grown variety that had sprouted in the United States after the Civil War.

Socialists organized their own trade unions and political parties, the first being the Socialist Labor Party in 1877, which exists to this day in the United States. Socialists gained strength during this period through the industrial unions, rivaling the craft form of organization and the Knights of Labor for influence among American workers. Frequently, lines of division were not clear-cut; there were socialists in craft unions and in the Knights of Labor. And there were nonsocialists in these groups too. The socialists tended to gain strength during periods of economic depression, when the purely economic tactics of craft unions were not sufficient to protect their members from economic hardship. The workers' attention became directed at the entire social system as the source of their unemployment. Great socialist leaders such as Daniel de Leon and Eugene V. Debs contributed much to American politics during this period of time, and to the emergence of a permanent American labor union tradition.

The story of this period of American labor history cannot be told without mentioning the seamier side of capital-labor conflict. The late nineteenth century produced the sharpest and bloodiest conflicts in all of American labor history. Armed battles were commonplace, with workers pitted against the private armies of the employers: the dreaded Pinkertons. In 1885 there were 695 recorded work stoppages involving a quarter of a million workers. And in 1886, the year the AFL was founded, there were 1,572 work stoppages, with 610,000 workers involved.[17] These figures reveal the labor militancy and consciousness that explain part of the reason for the emergence of the AFL.

The strikes were met with resistance by employers. This was a period of economic transition; the old craft forms of doing work were breaking down and industrialists were taking the first steps toward the introduction of mass production in the basic manufacturing industries in the United States. These mass production techniques eliminated many skills, and entire crafts were jeopardized in the process. Workers resisted through their unions, and bitter battles ensued. Haymarket Square in Chicago, the Pullman strike, the Homestead strike—these are events that symbolize the pitched battles American labor had to fight to gain the right to organize. The issues were recognition, wages, conditions of work, and the eight-hour day. The means by which the issues were adjudicated were frequently guns and clubs. Labor wanted to organize against the great industrial giants of the day—in the railroad industry, the steel industry, and other basic industries. Management resisted, and this set the stage for America's second civil war—one that was not as widespread as the first but still pitted American against American.

---

[17] U.S. Department of Commerce, *Historical Statistics*, p. 179.

The Rise of Industrial Unionism: From 1900 to the Founding of the CIO

■

At the turn of the century, the AFL was the predominant national labor organization in the United States. Its only serious competition for the loyalties of American labor came from the socialist industrial trade unions and, later, from the Industrial Workers of the World (the IWW, or the Wobblies, as they were called). A great wave of immigration began the decade; in some years of the early twentieth century as many as one million immigrants per year came to the United States. These were a different breed of immigrants from the German, Scotch, and Irish who had come earlier. They came from Central, Northern, Southern, and Eastern Europe. Jews, Scandinavians, Italians, Slavs, and Russians were the dominant ethnic groups. In 1905, for example, for the first time in our history, over one million immigrants came to the United States. Over three hundred thousand immigrants came from Central Europe, and nearly two hundred thousand came from Russia and Eastern Europe. Another quarter million came from Italy in that year and sixty thousand from the Scandinavian countries.[18]

Table 19-1 Trade Union Membership, 1900–1934, Selected Years

Year	Total Union Membership (thousands)	Total Labor Force (thousands)	Union Membership as Percentage of Labor Force	AFL Members (thousands)	AFL Members as Percentage of Total Union Membership
1897	440	n.a.[a]	n.a.[a]	265	60.2%
1900	791	28,500	2.7%	548	69.2
1905	1,918	32,408	5.9	1,494	77.9
1910	2,116	36,850	5.7	1,562	73.8
1915	2,560	39,774	6.4	1,946	76.0
1920	5,034	41,720	12.1	4,079	81.0
1925	3,566	45,431	7.8	2,877	80.7
1930	3,632	48,783	7.4	2,961	81.5
1934	3,728	51,910	7.2	3,045	81.7

[a]Not available.
Source: U.S. Department of Commerce, *Historical Statistics of the United States: Colonial Times to 1970* (Washington: Government Printing Office, 1975), pt. 1, pp. 126 and 177.

---

[18] Ibid., p. 105. In the Chicago stock yards in 1918, only 25 percent of the workers were citizens. However, 90 percent belonged to unions. See David Montgomery, "To Study the People: The American Working Class," *Labor History* 21, no. 4 (Fall 1980), p. 505.

These immigrants brought with them their trade union commitments. Many had been active in socialist trade unions and political parties in their own countries, and this tradition followed them to the United States. Immigration was one aspect that influenced the fortunes of American labor in the early part of the twentieth century. The other was the continuing transformation that occurred in the American economy at this time. While this immigration was under way, the American economy was rapidly developing the largest and most powerful industrial base in the world. Mass production industries in the basic durable goods sector of the economy flourished, with steel leading the way. By the time World War I broke out in Europe, the United States' economy was one of the most powerful in the world. Its labor force had grown substantially, at a rate of about one million per year, establishing a larger base for potential trade union membership.

During the early years of the century, trade union membership grew rapidly, and the AFL was the principal beneficiary of this growth. Table 19-1 contains the basic data on the growth of American trade unions up to the founding of the Congress of Industrial Organizations (CIO) in the mid-1930s.

Between 1900 and 1905 trade union membership more than doubled. From less than 3 percent of the labor force in 1900, American trade unions grew until they could claim to represent almost 6 percent of the labor force in 1905, and the AFL share of total trade union membership grew from 69 percent in 1900 to just under 78 percent in 1905.

This growth of the AFL and the craft union basis of organization did not proceed without challenge from the socialist and radical elements of American labor. Many socialist trade unions remained affiliated with the AFL even though they did not subscribe to the basic tenets of the organization. In 1905 the Industrial Workers of the World was organized as a general workers' union embracing all employed *and unemployed* workers. Radical in philosophy, syndicalist in tactics, and romantic to the core, the Wobblies carved out a niche in American labor history that is uniquely theirs. They advocated "one big union" as the only way to break down intraclass rivalries among American workers. They borrowed heavily from the French syndicalists in their tactics: sabotage, the sit-down strike, and other tactics that were to be replicated throughout this century. They organized among the down-and-out, the underclass of American society: the unemployed, hoboes, derelicts, lumberjacks, western miners— all those segments of American society that had been largely ignored by the traditional craft unions of the AFL. By the end of the First World War the Wobblies had essentially ceased to exist as an organization because of their opposition to American participation in the war and because of the subsequent fierce repression imposed on them by the federal government. But they left behind them a legacy of song, tradition, and folklore that is unrivaled by any other labor group in our history. The British labor historian, Henry Pelling, aptly sums up their niche in American labor history:

> The Wobblies fit naturally into the mythology of the West, along with the cowboys and the miners . . . , and their songs of the tough life they led, especially those of Joe Hill,

who was executed after being convicted of murder in 1915, belong now to the tradition of American folklore.[19]

Although the Wobblies did not survive the war and its repressive aftermath, the questions they raised about the structure of the American labor movement were fundamental. What the Wobbly movement represented was, first, the growth of mass production industry and the shift of some basic production activities to the West and, second, the failure of American labor to meet the needs of the underclass: the unemployed and the marginal workers who went from one dead-end, low-paying job to another. Though thirty years would have to pass before these questions were recognized by the official formation of the Committee for Industrial Organization, the organization of the Wobblies was a forerunner of important institutional developments in the American labor movement.[20]

While the AFL was consolidating its power among American trade unions and gaining an official legitimacy within business and government communities, its reliance on the skilled-worker, craft form of unionism was becoming increasingly out-of-date. Mass production industries that used semiskilled and unskilled labor were permanent fixtures on the American economic scene. By 1929 the auto industry was the largest manufacturing industry in the United States, employing a half million workers directly and another three million indirectly. Auto registrations were 23 million by 1929. In 1930 two of every five American families had a radio—a product of another mass production industry using semiskilled labor.[21]

Although the economic rationale for craft unions was eroding around them, the AFL gained widespread acceptance in the councils of business and government during World War I. To meet the war effort, the government needed the cooperation and support of labor. The AFL provided this in return for its participation on various types of war production boards. In 1916 Gompers was appointed to a seven-member advisory committee of the important Council of National Defense; in 1917 a Labor Adjustment Committee was established to mediate disputes between labor and management. The acceptance of Gompers as the chief spokesman for American labor was all the more striking because the socialists remained neutral during the war and the Wobblies actively opposed America's participation in World War I.[22]

Union membership grew rapidly during this period, from 1905 through 1920, and the AFL was the chief beneficiary of this growth. Referring back to Table 19-1, we see that union membership reached a peak of more than five million in 1920, nearly two and one-half times as large as in 1905. In 1920, 12 percent of the labor

---

[19] Pelling, *American Labor*, p. 114.

[20] The *Committee* for Industrial Organization was part of the AFL and preceded the formation of the *Congress* of Industrial Organizations.

[21] Pelling, *American Labor*, p. 130.

[22] The further irony was that Gompers was a pacifist of sorts before World War I. After the war he became a fervent supporter of the League of Nations and then a founder of the World Federalist organization.

force belonged to unions, and about 80 percent of all union members belonged to AFL affiliates.

After 1920, however, union membership rapidly declined, even though the industrial sector of the American economy grew as a proportion of total employment. This reflects the anachronism of the craft structure adhered to by the AFL. As mass production reduced the skill component of work, many individual crafts became obsolete. The unskilled and semiskilled production line worker represented the growing component of the American labor force, but the AFL tended to ignore this group and retained its craft orientation. The AFL did try to organize within mass production industries but did so on a craft basis, permitting existing craft unions jurisdiction over their particular occupations. This meant that many different craft unions might exist within one plant. But this was clearly insufficient to stem the tide of the decline in union membership between 1920 and 1935. By 1925 union membership had declined by about 1.5 million, leaving only 7 percent of the labor force unionized—down from the peak of 12 percent in 1920.

The stage was set for a new and important actor among American trade unions: the *industrial union*, which organized on an industry-wide basis, embracing all the skills and occupations employed in a particular industry. Samuel Gompers did not live to see this challenge to the AFL supremacy. He died in 1924, after leading the federation for 37 years (in one year he was not reelected to office) and leaving an imprint on American society that few men in this century can rival.

The Emergence of the CIO: 1935–1955

The Great Depression and its accompanying New Deal policy response fostered dramatic changes in the labor scene that established the legal and institutional context for the contemporary labor movement in the United States. The New Deal for labor in this period was represented by changes in the legal status of trade unions, which had the effect of granting, for the first time, official legal sanction to labor unions. This, in turn, brought labor a new public esteem and acceptance that it never had previously and has not had since. For the twenty years spanning the Great Depression and World War II and its aftermath, it is difficult, if not impossible, to disentangle the evolution of American labor from the policy changes in the law governing labor relations. Although these matters will be examined in greater detail later in this book (Chapter 21), it is not possible to discuss labor in the 1930s and 1940s, the rise of industrial unions and the CIO, or any other labor issue without providing a background in the changes in labor law that occurred during the New Deal years.

The Great Depression and the New Deal permanently established government in the economy. And labor was no exception to this general historical change in the United States. Prior to the changes in labor law in the 1930s, legislation and judicial decisions governing labor relations were hostile to labor. At best, labor was able to neutralize the opposition it faced from the courts and legislatures of the land. Perhaps the only time that labor received a favorable hearing in the courts was during World War I, when support for the war effort was so critical that a temporary truce was declared on public assaults on labor's right to organize. But this pertained only to Gompers and the AFL unions; socialist industrial trial unions and the Wobblies came under merciless attack from the government.

In the nineteenth century labor had to fight for the right to exist at all. In the early part of the twentieth century, labor had to contend with government for the right to engage in those practices, such as the strike, that it deemed essential for its existence as a representative of workers. These experiences bred a skepticism toward government in the ranks of labor. Many members of the AFL ruling group wanted nothing to do with public policy in the New Deal, anticipating that nothing good would come of it. They recalled that the early antitrust legislation of the twentieth century—the Sherman and Clayton antitrust acts—had first been applied to labor unions, even though the well-meaning reformers who wrote the laws had intended that they be applied to corporations. Labor was split over such major pieces of social reform as the Social Security Act, whose enactment was opposed by some unions.

Nearly all this opposition to New Deal public policy was confined to the ranks of the AFL. The newly emerging industrial union leadership favored government intervention into the labor-management process, and they became champions of New Deal reforms. Changed public attitudes toward labor and its growing strength in the 1930s led to legislation that for the first time provided legal status to labor unions. The National Labor Relations Act (NLRA), authored by Senator Robert F. Wagner of New York, granted labor, for the first time in American history, the statutory right to organize and strike. When the Supreme Court finally upheld the act in 1937, a watershed was crossed. Labor unions were now recognized as legal entities with rights and responsibilities before a court of law.

The Wagner Act, as the NLRA is sometimes called, was but a culmination of previous steps taken during the New Deal period that pointed toward full recognition of labor unions. The 1932 Norris–La Guardia Act restricted the power of federal courts to grant injunctions against unions engaged in peaceful strikes. The National Industrial Recovery Act of 1933 contained language, in section 7(a), that granted labor the "right to organize and bargain collectively through representation of their own choosing."[23] This language was eventually embodied in the Wagner Act, after the National Industrial Recovery Act was declared unconstitutional by the Supreme Court.

Of the many important provisions contained in the Wagner Act, two are worth pointing out at this juncture: One granted legal status to unions through a provision that required employers to recognize a union and negotiate with it after an election had been held under the provisions of the Wagner Act. The other provided that the National Labor Relations Board (NLRB), established under the act, had the right to

---

[23] Pelling, *American Labor*, p. 160.

conduct representational elections among employees in a bargaining unit to determine the exclusive bargaining representative for those employees. Thus, the NLRB had the right to grant what is called exclusive jurisdiction (or representation) to a union, which provided that one and only one union could represent the workers in a particular bargaining unit. What the bargaining unit was—a craft or an industrial unit—became a hotly debated issue, as the AFL craft unions and the emerging militant industrial unions vied for recognition from the NLRB in places where there had previously been no unions.

The issue of jurisdiction defines labor's evolution during this period. As the mass production industries grew in importance, the craft structure of the AFL became increasingly obsolete. To deal with this problem, the AFL, as early as 1933, authorized organizing campaigns in the mass production industries, but nothing of substance ever came of these efforts. The challenge to the AFL was posed directly at its 1935 convention, when the newly organized industrial unions, who were members of the AFL, raised the thorny question of jurisdiction. Would the AFL abandon its historical craft orientation in the mass production industries in favor of industrial unions, or would the AFL continue to support craft unions for the different trades employed in the mass production industries? The AFL answered by rejecting the proposal of a minority at that convention that would have moved the federation toward support for industrial unionism. The minority responded by forming a committee, the Committee for Industrial Organization, under the leadership of John L. Lewis of the United Mine Workers. Within a year they were expelled from the AFL under the charge of "dual unionism." The Committee for Industrial Organization was reconstituted as the Congress of Industrial Organizations, and thus was born the CIO.

Undaunted, the CIO, with Lewis at the helm, pushed ahead with its two-pronged strategy of intervention into electoral politics and heavy funding for large organizational campaigns in the mass production industries. In 1936, for example, the CIO contributed $700,000 toward President Roosevelt's reelection, compared with a total expenditure of $95,000 in political campaigns by the AFL over the previous 30 years. The CIO thought nothing of investing a half million dollars in a major organizing campaign in a large industry, a staggering sum even by the standard of today's cheapened dollar.[24] Helped by the new tactic of the sit-down strike, in which workers simply refused to leave the plant, the CIO mounted successful organizing drives in autos, steel, textiles, rubber, electrical machinery, and other basic industries. Membership was extended to workers of all crafts, skills, and ethnic origins, in contradistinction to the highly stratified structure of the traditional AFL craft unions.

The extraordinarily rapid growth of union membership during these few years had never occurred previously and has not been duplicated since. From 3.7 million members in 1935, union membership leaped by 2 million in just two years. All this growth can be attributed to the CIO strength in the basic industries of the economy

---

[24] Ibid., p. 166.

Table 19-2 Trade Union Membership, 1935–1955, Selected Years

Year	AFL Membership (millions)	CIO Membership (millions)	Unaffiliated Membership (millions)	Total Union Membership (millions)	Union Membership as Percentage of Total Labor Force
1935	3.2	—	0.5	3.7	6.7%
1937[a]	3.2	2.0	0.6	5.8	12.9
1940	4.3	2.1	0.8	7.2	15.5
1945	6.9	3.9	1.7	12.5	21.9
1950	8.5	3.7	2.6	14.8	22.3
1955	10.6	4.6	1.8	17.0	24.7

[a]Year of formation of CIO.
Source: U.S. Department of Commerce, *Historical Statistics of the United States: Colonial Times to 1970* (Washington: Government Printing Office, 1975), pt. 1, pp. 176–78.

(see Table 19-2). As a percentage of the total labor force, trade union membership grew from less than 7 percent in 1935 to nearly 22 percent a decade later.

All was not peace and harmony during this period, however. Labor strife was almost as severe as in the 1890s. CIO organizing drives encountered violent resistance from management, which was answered in kind by labor. The battle of River Rouge in the late 1930s, for example, was a major event in the organizing drive of the United Auto Workers against the Ford Motor Company, which had a large plant near River Rouge outside Detroit. This followed the first large-scale sit-down strike against General Motors in 1937 and a violent conflict in the steel industry. Labor itself was a house divided between the older, more established AFL unions and the more militant CIO upstarts. John L. Lewis argued continually with President Roosevelt and with constituent unions of the CIO, finally resigning from the CIO presidency in 1940 over the issue of CIO endorsement of Roosevelt for the presidency of the United States.

In 1946 a wave of strikes occurred, reflecting demands for higher wages and better working conditions—demands that had been suppressed during World War II, when labor had offered unflinching support for the war effort. The number of days lost because of strikes that year—a combination of the number of persons on strike and the duration of the strike—was a staggering 116 million, representing nearly 1.5 percent of the total working time in that year and involving 4.6 million union members.[25] In no year before 1946 and in no year since have work stoppages reached such a degree of intensity.

The war years also marked the zenith of labor's strength in the American economy. Union membership grew slowly after the war, but unions could no longer exercise

---

[25] U.S. Department of Commerce, *Historical Statistics*, p. 179.

the sort of influence they had during the New Deal period and World War II. Shortly after the war the Taft-Hartley Act was passed, which restricted labor's ability to organize new sectors of the economy.[26] That act is still on the books today, and every effort of labor to reverse some of its harsh provisions has met with defeat.

The Taft-Hartley Act also symbolized a changed attitude of the public toward labor. Although never cherished in most households in the United States, labor had nevertheless managed to acquire a sympathetic following of far more people during the New Deal than it has ever been able to muster since that period. The Taft-Hartley Act, passed in 1947, indicated a transformation of that attitude. The act had enough support in Congress to be passed over President Truman's veto.

Important labor institutions were constructed during the New Deal that remain with us today and form the basic foundation of the modern period of labor relations. First, two great union structures consolidated their power during this period: the craft form of unionism and the industrial form. After the New Deal both remained in place, with a degree of membership stability. The craft union, with its organization based on the skill and occupation of the worker, and the industrial union, based on the company and industry of employment, are today still the primary forms of labor union organization. Second, the National Labor Relations Act established an administrative apparatus, through the National Labor Relations Board, that not only has functioned to grant exclusive representation to a particular union in each bargaining unit, but has also created an entire corpus of administrative law, which today forms the practice of labor law. This is an issue to which we shall return later, in the chapter on industrial relations law.

But labor as a house divided between two great national organizations—the AFL and the CIO—could not endure, particularly in light of the attacks on it after World War II. The stage was set for a reconciliation—or at least the formal merger—of the AFL and the CIO.

The Merged AFL-CIO: 1956 to the Present

American labor reached its zenith in both popular support and organizational strength during the New Deal and World War II years. After the war labor's fortunes declined. A reconstituted management opposition put labor on the defensive. The rise of the Cold War weakened labor's support among the population at large, since so many of its leaders had, at one time or another, been identified with socialist or communist activities. The shifting sands of American politics moved toward the right after the death of Roosevelt, and the passage of the Taft-Hartley Act in 1947, over President Truman's veto, symbolized labor's weakened position in the American society. The

---

[26] Discussed in Chapter 21.

Taft-Hartley Act was more than a symbol, however. It also represented real setbacks for labor in its ability to organize the unorganized workers and to confront management across the bargaining table with as much influence as it had during the New Deal and World War II periods.

All this may sound odd in view of the belief common today that labor is all-powerful and gets whatever it wants whenever it wants it. It is premature to attempt a thorough analysis of labor's strength in the American economy. That will have to await the further unfolding of the story of labor and the economy. But keep an open mind on the subject, and assess the attitudes and viewpoints you bring to this material. The issue is a complex one. In some ways labor is very strong in certain sectors of the economy. It has a powerful lobbying unit in Washington that until recently was able to obtain substantial legislative gains in the areas of social welfare, minimum wages, and unemployment relief. On the other side of this balance sheet, it has not been able to reverse the Taft-Hartley Act—a major legislative objective of labor ever since the passage of the act in 1947. Nor has it been able to expand its membership as a percentage of the total labor force. It is strong as a collective bargaining agent in the construction trades, but more and more construction now takes place with nonunion labor. The Teamsters are a powerful and formidable force to reckon with in the trucking industry, although less so today because of trucking deregulation. But labor's strength in other industries has been declining rather than increasing. At this stage of the development of the story of labor and the American economy, we can say that the degree of labor's power in the economy is mixed. There are sectors of strength and sectors of weakness.[27]

With hindsight it is possible to see why labor has been able to maintain some traditional areas of strength while losing ground in other ways. The attack on labor after World War II was clearly one of the elements that persuaded the AFL and CIO to consider merger, hoping that a reduction of internecine warfare would permit a more united stance against labor's opponents. With the deaths of William Green and Philip Murray, presidents, respectively, of the AFL and the CIO in 1952, the path was cleared for a reconciliation. Their replacements, George Meany of the AFL and Walter Reuther of the CIO, had the advantage of starting on the reconciliation process with little of the baggage of animosity that Green and Murray had accumulated during the 1930s and 1940s. In 1955 the two national labor federations merged into the AFL-CIO; they have remained together ever since, albeit with a few important defections and expulsions.

Membership in labor unions after the merger did not improve, however. As can be seen from Table 19-3, labor's percentage of the total labor force peaked in 1956 at 25.2 percent and has declined slightly ever since. In 1985 labor represented some 18 percent of the labor force and has a total membership of about 17 million. In

---

[27] The future of industrial relations is examined in detail in Chapter 22, including the growing sector of public employee unionism and the decline of unionization in the mass production industries, such as autos.

Table 19-3   Trade Union Membership, 1956–1985, Selected Years

Year	AFL-CIO Membership (millions)	Unaffiliated Membership (millions)	Total Union Membership (millions)	Union Membership as Percentage of Total Labor Force
1956	16.9	1.6	18.5	25.2%
1960	15.1	3.0	18.1	23.6
1965	15.6	2.9	18.5	22.2
1970	16.0	4.7	20.7	22.6
1974	16.9	4.7	21.6	21.8
1978	17.0	4.7	21.7	22.2
1980	n.a.[a]	n.a.[a]	22.4	20.9
1985	n.a.[a]	n.a.[a]	17.0	18.0

[a]Not available.
Sources: 1956–1974: U.S. Department of Labor, *Handbook of Labor Statistics, 1978* (Washington: Government Printing Office, 1979), pp. 506–7; 1978: U.S. Department of Labor, "Labor Union Membership and Employee Association Membership—1978," News Release, Sept. 3, 1979, pp. 1–2; 1980: U.S. Department of Labor, "Corrected Data on Labor Organization Membership—1980," News Release, Sept. 18, 1981, p. 3; U.S. Department of Labor, *Employment and Earnings* (January, 1986), p. 213.

1978, 17 million workers belonged to unions affiliated with the AFL-CIO and 5 million to unions that were not affiliated with the merged federation. Nearly all these unaffiliated workers belonged either to the Teamsters union, which was expelled from the AFL-CIO in the late 1950s, or to the United Auto Workers, which left the AFL-CIO in the late 1960s over policy disputes with George Meany, and then reaffiliated with the AFL-CIO in 1981.

This stagnation of the membership growth of trade unions has been caused in part by the shifting economic structure of the United States. Once again, as in the other periods examined in this chapter, the character and strength of the American labor movement depend on the forces that affect the workplace and on the underlying structure of the American economy. Since World War II the American economy has shifted from the production of goods to the provision of services. This is illustrated in Table 19-4, which shows the proportions of employment in the goods and service sectors of the economy. Goods production includes manufacturing, mining, and construction; service provision includes transportation, trade, finance, insurance, real estate, services, and all government. In 1947 about 42 percent of all employees on nonagricultural payrolls worked in the goods-producing sector of the economy; 58 percent worked in the service-provision sector. Unions have traditionally been stronger in the goods-producing sector than in the service-provision sector of the economy, excluding public employee unionism. Since 1947, however, the underlying structure of the American economy has shifted away from goods production toward service provision. By 1957, shortly after the merger of the AFL and CIO, goods

Table 19-4 Structure of Employment, Excluding Agriculture, 1947–1985, Selected Years

Year	Total Employment (Excluding Agriculture) (thousands)	Goods-producing Employment[a]		Service-providing Employment[b]	
		(thousands)	(%)	(thousands)	(%)
1947	43,881	18,482	42.1	25,399	57.9
1957	52,894	20,925	39.5	31,969	60.5
1967	65,857	23,268	35.3	42,589	64.7
1977	82,141	24,229	29.4	57,912	70.6
1980	90,656	25,857	28.5	64,799	71.5
1985	97,699	25,057	25.6	72,643	74.4

[a]Includes manufacturing, mining, and construction.
[b]Includes transportation, trade, finance, insurance, real estate, services, and government.
Sources: U.S. Department of Labor, *Handbook of Labor Statistics, 1978* (Washington: Government Printing Office, 1979), p. 134; U.S. Department of Labor, *Employment and Training Report of the President* (Washington: Government Printing Office, 1981), p. 211; U.S. Department of Labor, *Employment and Earnings* (March, 1986), p. 43.

production had fallen slightly, to 39 percent of employment. But 20 years later, in 1977, goods production had fallen to the point where it accounted for only 29 percent of total nonagricultural employment, and services accounted for nearly 71 percent of total employment. The traditional base of unionism in the goods-producing sector has eroded. In 1947 there were almost 18.5 million workers employed in the goods-producing sector; 38 years later, in 1985, there were 25 million—an increase of only 6.6 million workers. On the other hand, the service-provision sector of the economy employed over 72 million workers in 1985, nearly three times the number employed in goods provision and 47.2 million more workers than in 1947.

This dramatic shift in the underlying structure of the American economy affected labor in several ways. First, the expansion of trade union membership in the previously organized sectors of the economy was minimal because of the erosion of growth in those parts of the economy. Second, organization in the service-provision sector of the economy, though substantial by historical standards, was slow in relation to the rapid expansion of that sector of the economy. The service-provision sector of the economy poses unique problems for labor, which they have not yet overcome. Much of the growth in service provision has been in government; other growth has been in such quasi-professional types of employment as computer services, which typically are not constituents of labor union membership.

In spite of these problems, the fastest-growing unions in the United States are in the service-provision sector of the economy, in part because of the stagnant character of the goods-producing part of the economy. For example, the four unions that have grown most rapidly in the United States in the past decade are the American Federation of State, County and Municipal Employees, teachers' unions, unions of service employees, and the retail clerks union.[28]

Not only has union growth stagnated because of the structural shifts in the American economy, but labor has also had difficulty responding to the new forms of corporate organization represented by the conglomerate and the multinational corporation. Conglomerates, such as I.T.T. and TRW, that have no real industrial base in the American economy pose special organizational problems for American labor, which organizes itself along either craft or industrial lines. Which union has jurisdiction over I.T.T., for example, a company with activities in industries ranging from baking (Wonder bread and Hostess Twinkies) to missiles and telephone communications? How do you even start an organizing drive against such a behemoth? And the modern multinational corporation, with its ability to shut down operations in one country and move them to another, renders labor helpless in catching the runaway shop and the runaway jobs.

These are labor's contemporary problems. But organized labor has a solid footing in the American social fabric today that cannot be completely uprooted. Won by the hard-fought organizing battles and bitter strikes of an earlier era, American labor's place in the American experience is unique. Reviled by its opponents, idealized by its romantic followers, and cherished by its members, the American labor union survives with influence that at times waxes and wanes but, nevertheless, is always there.

The History of Work

A footnote to this chapter is in order, to identify a new orientation in labor history. This chapter has been about the history of trade unions—a legitimate historical orientation. In recent years, however, a "new" labor history has arisen that focuses on the history of work and the history of ordinary workers. The centerpiece of this historical orientation is a view of workers as attempting to "retain a degree of job satisfaction" and of managers as seeking to "subordinate them to a rationalized system of production."[29] Trade unions are seen in this context as one of the most important ways in which workers band together to seek influence over the part of their lives that

---

[28] U.S. Department of Labor, "Labor Union and Employee Association Membership—1978," News Release, Sept. 3, 1979, p. 6. Discussed further in Chapter 22.

[29] David Brody, "The Old Labor History and the New: In Search of an American Working Class," *Labor History*, 20, 1 (Winter 1979), p. 117. An important work on labor's efforts to retain control over the work process is: David Montgomery, *Workers' Control in America* (Cambridge: Cambridge University Press, 1979). Management's efforts to rationalize production in order to challenge workers' control over work is developed in: Harry Braverman, *Labor and Monopoly Capital* (New York: Monthly Review Press, 1974).

involves work. The cultural and ethnic backgrounds of workers add to this drama an ingredient that has produced the consciousness of American workers.

This historical orientation should not be forgotten as you begin to think about the role of labor in contemporary American society. The next several chapters are about the role of labor in the present and its prospects for the future.

Summary

The evolution of American labor is influenced by the structural changes that occur in the economy and the way production is organized in the work place. As the American economy evolves, the organization of work changes. The dominance of the craft structure of production gives way to the mass production assembly line. Manufacturing production fades, and service provision rises. Labor responds to these alterations in the structure of production in the economy by evolution of its internal organizational forms.

Trade unions as a "continuous association of wage-earners for the purpose of maintaining or improving the conditions of their working lives" did not take firm root in the American soil until after the Civil War. Before the Civil War trade unions existed, but their staying power was weak, and few could claim to be "continuous" associations of wage earners.

The first workers arrived on the American shore as either indentured labor or redemptioners. The indenture system applied mostly to British workers and provided for a set period of work in the new colonies, typically seven years, in return for the financing of passage to America. The system of redemption worked similarly except that the contractual obligation for working off transit to America was not determined before workers left their homeland but only after they arrived here. Typically the terms were harsher for the redemptioners, who were non-English—Scotch, Irish, German, and Swiss. Thus, the first wave of immigrants from abroad formed the work force of the new colonies—a phenomenon that was to be repeated in successive spurts until World War I.

In prerevolutionary America work was organized either through *guilds*, which were organizations of skilled artisans that controlled the prices for members' products and services, or through *licensed trades*, which were occupations considered critical to the public welfare and regulated by some public authority. The guilds organized the apprenticeship system, in which a worker would first begin to learn a trade as an apprentice and then work his way up to journeyman and master status. Such arrangements still prevail today in the craft unions.

After the Revolutionary War the American labor force grew, and the first labor unions began to emerge, although none achieved much permanence. Labor unions among skilled craftsmen tended to arise during good economic times and collapse in the depression phase of the business cycle. Along with these embryonic forms of the trade union occurred efforts to escape the beginnings of the factory system. Utopian experiments that sought a better life through collective self-reliance sprouted, mostly in rural settings but some in urban industrial areas as well.

After the Civil War, America went through a period of capital accumulation and industrialization that has not occurred since. New industries sprang up and old ones grew. On labor this had the effect of eroding skills and crafts while creating the basis for the organization of craft unions, which for the first time achieved the staying power to warrant calling them "continuous associations" of workers.

The American Federation of Labor (AFL) was formed in 1886, and it prevailed in the face of many obstacles where previous efforts had failed. As a federation of independent craft unions, the AFL, led by Samuel Gompers, placed its imprint on the American working scene. Competing with the AFL for the loyalties of labor were two other forms of organization: the Knights of Labor, a general workers' union that accepted all comers, and the industrial unions, many led by socialists, which attempted to organize all workers in an industry, irrespective of skill or craft. Neither of these forms of organization could compete with the AFL at that time, because economic conditions did not warrant such organization. Industrial unions became the backbone of labor in the 1930s, but a general workers' union of the type the Knights sought to organize has never been successful in the United States.

In the twentieth century labor gained wider acceptance and more membership. The dramatic shift from craft organization in the factories to semiskilled and unskilled assembly line production weakened the old craft-based unionism of the AFL and ultimately gave birth to a rival trade union federation, the Congress of Industrial Organizations (CIO), which organized workers in the basic industries along industrial rather than craft lines. Labor's membership peaked at about 25 percent of the labor force after World War II and has declined slightly since. After World War II the shift in the American economy from goods production to service provision decreased the potential constituency of labor and weakened the power of trade unions.

Study Questions

1. Discuss the formation of the labor force in the United States before the Revolutionary War, and describe the early forms of labor organization.

2. Compare and contrast the institutional forms of the Knights of Labor and the American Federation of Labor (AFL).

3. How does the institutional character of the Congress of Industrial Organizations (CIO) compare with that of the AFL?

4. What key factors explain the decline in trade union membership as a percentage of the total labor force in the United States?

Further Reading

Commons, John R., and Associates. *History of Labor in the United States*. 4 vols. New York: Macmillan, 1918–1935.

Pelling, Henry. *American labor*. Chicago: University of Chicago Press, 1960.

Rayback, Joseph G. *A History of American Labor*. New York: Macmillan, 1963.

U.S. Department of Labor. *The American Worker*. Washington: Government Printing Office, 1977.

20

Industrial Relations in the United States

In 1985 about 18 percent of all wage and salary earners in the American economy were represented by trade unions and worked under collective bargaining agreements. If government employees are excluded from this statistic, a much higher percentage emerges as working under collective bargaining agreements in the *private* sector of the economy. These 20 million wage and salary earners work under contracts negotiated by trade unions, which are formal collective bargaining agreements concluded between a recognized bargaining agent of the employees and management.

These agreements are enforceable in a court of law, particularly those made in sectors that fall under the jurisdiction of the National Labor Relations Board. Wages, working conditions, fringe benefits, grievance procedures, and union security are all issues that become codified in such agreements between labor and management. Without a collective bargaining arrangement with legal force, or a surrogate contract that exists outside this legal framework, individual employees are left to their own devices to bargain over wages and protect themselves from the arbitrariness of the employer. The "private government" embodied in industrial relations in the modern era is an important source of protection for the worker and enhances his or her welfare.

In an earlier day perhaps such bureaucratic mechanisms for adjudicating employment relations were not necessary. Moral codes had the force of law in societies dominated by religious teaching and community peer pressure. Self-sufficiency work processes, confined to the family, had their own system of norms and rewards, enforced by the codes of family behavior. As work arose outside the family, the guilds were created to organize a system for payment, access to work, and social mobility to protect craftsmen from the power of the merchant.

Today, these arrangements no longer prevail, although remnants of all these systems can be observed in daily life. The trade union and the collective bargaining agreement are the mechanisms by which relations in work are codified and administered in the modern industrial system, providing a modicum of industrial democracy in the work place. The collective bargaining instrument, for all its administrative and bureaucratic complexity, stands as a monument to human ingenuity. It is a marvel of social invention that deserves careful understanding by the student of labor economics.

The Nature of an Industrial Relations System

An *industrial relations system,* when applied to a modern complex market economy, means something more than just the way wages are established in the firm or work is organized to create a product and provide a service. The organization of work relations is a problem as old as work itself. From the first time humans went on a hunt for food to the automated production processes of today, work has been fashioned into a set of interdependent relationships among workers and between workers and their technology. This set of relationships is called a *labor process,* and it can assume different forms, depending on the historical epoch, form of technology, and type of economic system.

An industrial relations system is all this and more. It is composed of a *complex of rules* that *governs* the work place.[1] The rules can be *formal* or *informal.* Some may be incorporated in statutes and collective bargaining agreements with the force of law behind them. Other rules are based on a more informal tradition, which is as important as a formal rule but is not always enforceable in the eyes of the law. Looked at as a totality, the modern industrial relations system represents a form of "private government." It is a system that governs economic relationships between employer and employee and is arranged privately by the parties concerned without direct public government intervention.

The complex of rules that characterizes an industrial relations system contains provisions for

- *procedures* for establishing the rules;

---

[1] Writing in the mid-1950s, Clark Kerr and Abraham J. Siegel introduced the concept of a "web of rules" as a defining characteristic of an industrial relations system (Clark Kerr and Abraham J. Siegel, "The Structuring of the Labor Force in Industrial Societies: New Dimensions and New Questions," in Clark Kerr, ed., *Labor and Management in Industrial Society* [Garden City: Doubleday and Co., 1964], pp. 297–328).

- *substantive matters,* typically wages and fringe benefits, norms for work performance, and rights and responsibilities of the workers;
- *mechanisms* for the application of the substantive rules.[2]

In the United States the *collective bargaining agreement,* concluded between the employer and a recognized representative of the employees, is the most common manifestation of such a complex of rules. Collective bargaining agreements are signed between an authorized trade union and management, and those agreements are made within the framework of laws established under the National Labor Relations Act and other statutes applying to labor, such as the Taft-Hartley Act.

Even in the absence of a trade union and formal legal provisions governing labor relations, a complex of rules exists to monitor employment relations in nearly all instances. For example, a personnel manual will typically set forth many of the conditions of the labor contract that a collective bargaining agreement would contain. This fact should be borne in mind, even though the remaining sections of this chapter deal with the aspect of industrial relations that involves trade unions and their collective bargaining agreements with management.

How Trade Unions Gain Recognition

There are essentially two ways in which a trade union can come into being. A union and employer can themselves agree on recognition without the interposition of the National Labor Relations Board (NLRB). Or the NLRB can conduct a representational election in the bargaining unit after the receipt of a petition by the employees or from an organization claiming to represent the employees of that bargaining unit. Should a majority of the voting employees decide in favor of having a union represent them, the union is certified as an authorized bargaining agent for the employees, and collective bargaining ensues.

Union recognition battles are typically virulent and bitter. Rarely does an employer voluntarily recognize a union without intense pressure and sharp confrontation. The CIO efforts at union organization in the 1930s provide classic vignettes of American labor history. The efforts of the United Farm Workers to gain recognition in California and the Southwest and the Textile Workers Union organizing drive against J.P. Stevens are two recent examples of fierce competition between labor and management over the issue of recognition.

Not all certification elections are decided in the union's favor. In 1981, for example, the unions were successful in only 45 percent of the representation elections

---

[2] Max S. Wortman, Jr., and George C. Witteried, *Labor Relations and Collective Bargaining: Text and Cases* (Boston: Allyn and Bacon, 1969), pp. 1–8.

$\times$ = EXAM

held by the NLRB. This is down from a success rate of 59 percent in 1968 and a 75 percent success rate in 1950.[3]

The NLRB election process can drag on for months, even years, and become bogged down in expensive legal squabbles and delays. Most successful efforts at union recognition start with the NLRB machinery, but some recognition attempts succeed without an election ever occurring. Should a union reach the NLRB representational ballot stage, and should the vote be positive, the NLRB certifies the union as the *exclusive bargaining representative* for the employees in a specified bargaining unit. Under labor law, the certified union must then represent all the employees in the bargaining unit and cannot refuse membership to any qualified worker.

Toward the end of the 1970s, a new profession emerged, consisting of consultants who advise employers on defeating unions trying to gain recognition in the first instance and on decertifying unions if recognition already exists. The process of decertification involves an election to remove the union as a duly constituted bargaining agent after recognition by a vote of the union members. This has become a hotly contested issue, with unions claiming the consultants use questionable tactics of intimidation and other forms of coercion. Management claims that the practices are protected by the right of free speech and that workers vote against a union because of what the union stands for. Over $500 million was spent in 1980, according to a committee of the House of Representatives, on "union busting" consultants.[4] In 1981 856 decertification elections were held, and unions lost in 74 percent of the elections.[5]

Various types of institutional relationships between the union and the employer in a bargaining unit can exist. Before the Taft-Hartley Act of 1947, there was the *closed shop*, in which the worker had to be a member of the union to be hired by the employer. This arrangement was common in craft unions, particularly in the construction trades, before the Taft-Hartley Act made the closed shop illegal. The union in that situation played a much greater role in deciding who would work and for whom a union member would work. Additionally, the union could influence wage rates with the closed shop by controlling the supply of labor in a particular labor market, by virtue of its ability to control the number of people admitted to its union.

Although the closed shop is illegal today, the trade union and employer are still free to come to a *"hiring hall"* agreement, in which the employer contacts the union when the company needs someone to do a job, and the union assigns workers to fill such requests. In this way the formal closed shop prohibition is circumvented while the essence of a closed shop is retained. The construction trades, restaurant and hotel workers, and longshoremen are frequently organized this way.

---

[3] Thomas P. Frazier, *Consultants, Unions, and NLRB Elections* (Doctoral Dissertation, American University, 1984), p. 6.

[4] Joann S. Lublin, "Labor Strikes Back at Consultants That Help Firms Keep Unions Out," *Wall Street Journal*, April 2, 1981, p. 29.

[5] Frazier, *Consultants*, p. 6.

★ = EXAM

Most unions try to operate under what is called the *union shop,* and they achieve this objective in about half of all collective bargaining agreements. A union shop is a situation in which the employer is free to hire anyone, but once an individual is employed and passes through a probationary period, he or she must join the recognized union. This arrangement is typical of industrial unions. Unlike the closed shop, the worker need not be a member of the union before obtaining the job. In fact, in most instances the individual will not be a member of the union before starting work.

Under the Taft-Hartley Act each state has an option to pass its own law outlawing the union shop. Twenty-one states have such provisions, which are called, euphemistically, *"right-to-work"* laws. In these states, mostly in the South and West, other provisions have arisen to afford the union some protection, under arrangements that govern the relationships among a worker, the union, and the job.

In states with right-to-work laws, many unions have negotiated a contract with management that provides for an *agency shop.* Under the terms of an agency shop provision, the worker is not required to join the union, as in a union shop. However, if the worker chooses not to join the union, he or she must pay the union a service charge equal to union dues. This payment is for the union's services in negotiating and administering the collective bargaining agreement. In some states even the agency shop has been banned, and in those instances the most prevalent form of union-worker relationship is something called a *maintenance of membership* agreement, negotiated between the union and management. Under such provisions, the employer agrees that all union members (present and future) who belonged to the union at the time the contract was negotiated must remain in the union for the duration of the contract. At the expiration of the contract, there is an opportunity for the union member to leave the union without jeopardizing his or her employment with the company.[6]

The Collective Bargaining Process

Once a union has obtained recognition, it then proceeds to sit down with management and negotiate a contract. This is formally what is known as *collective bargaining.* It is the most visible of all union activities since it frequently attracts newspaper headlines as the parties stand their ground, anticipating a strike if they cannot agree on the terms of a new contract. A contract, once agreed on, has a limited life. Normally the term of a contract is three years, sometimes less, hardly ever longer. Sometimes the contract will provide for *reopening*—that is, for one or both parties to request that the existing contract be renegotiated before it has expired.

[6] For a discussion of these different provisions governing a worker's relationship to the union, see Gordon F. Bloom and Herbert R. Northrup, *Economics of Labor Relations,* 8th ed., (Homewood, IL: Richard D. Irwin, 1977), p. 175.

The obligation for labor and management to bargain collectively, once there is a duly certified union on the scene, has legal force behind it. The Taft-Hartley Act defines collective bargaining as the "performance of the mutual obligation of the employer and the representative of the employees to meet at reasonable times and confer in good faith with respect to wages, hours and other terms and conditions of employment. . . . " It goes on to state that union and management have a duty to execute a "written contract incorporating any agreement reached."[7]

Not only must the parties to a collective bargaining process agree to negotiate a contract without any compulsion that either side eventually agree to the other's terms, but they must also bargain "in good faith"; if they do not, one side can file a complaint with the NLRB. Such complaints fall under the provision for unfair union or employer practices. Obviously, the term "in good faith" is vague and general. It requires administrative interpretation by the NLRB. This is the meat of labor law, and it keeps a battery of labor lawyers employed by unions, employers, and the NLRB.

Legal problems intrude in virtually all areas of contemporary American life. Labor relations is no exception. In the past decade there has been a sharp growth in the number of legal disputes in industrial relations. What was once a system of private government between labor and management has become a battleground for high-paid lawyers. For example, the number of cases filed with the NLRB reached nearly 50,000 in 1983, up from slightly more than 31,00 in 1969.[8] The effect of this legal fetish has been to remove issues from the rank and file and even union leaders at times, placing them in the hands of outside lawyers.

The provisions of the collective bargaining agreement typically cover such issues as wages, hours of work, and conditions of work. In addition, the contract must contain, under the Taft-Hartley Act, sections on how the contract is to be administered, interpreted, and enforced during the term in which it is in force. This places an obligation on the trade union to police its own members during the life of a contract and to see that the provisions of the collective bargaining agreement are not violated by the membership of the trade union. For example, during the life of a contract, unions are normally not permitted to go on strike unless there is a clear-cut violation of the provisions of the contract that cannot be adjudicated within the terms of the contract. And if a strike move is contemplated by the union, it must follow a preannounced procedure for conducting a strike vote among its membership before calling the strike. The union must also be very certain that it has a good case, since the collective bargaining agreement is a legally enforceable contract. Should management take the union to court for breach of contract, the union must be confident that it can defend its position adequately.

Strikes do occur during the life of a contract. They are technically illegal in nearly all instances unless the union has negotiated in its contract a provision for such strikes.

---

[7] Sanford Cohen, *Labor Law* (Columbus, OH: Charles E. Merrill Books, 1964), p. 449.

[8] National Labor Relations Board, *Forty-Eighth Annual Report* (Washington: Government Printing Office, 1986), p. 164.

A strike called at the expiration of a contract is perfectly legal, however, since there is no longer any contract between the parties.

Unauthorized strikes during the life of a contract are called *wildcat strikes*. Wildcat strikes are technically illegal, since they violate the terms of a contract, and the union can be taken to court and assessed damages for such strikes. Typically, wildcat strikes are spur-of-the-moment actions by workers within one plant or in one part of a factory. They reflect frustrations with the work process and with the bureaucracy of union-management procedures for administering the existing contract.

[margin note: most strikes are illegal]

A collective bargaining agreement is very detailed. Normally, it will contain provisions for recognition of the union, union security provisions, wages, fringe benefits, hours of work and overtime compensation, paid vacations, grievance procedures, the suspension and discharge of workers, seniority provisions, union dues checkoff, and expiration of the contract.[9] The coverage is comprehensive and can be divided into several categories, which will be examined in more detail later in this chapter. There is a category for terms covering *wages and fringe benefits*. A second covers *hours and conditions of work*. Procedures for administering the contract while in force are handled through a *grievance procedure*, and that forms a third category. Fourth, there are provisions for *union security and management rights*.

[margin note: anything permitted by law is negotiable]

The actual collective bargaining situation is riddled with conflict. Here, all the submerged frustrations and animosities can bubble to the surface unless handled with sensitivity. It is a time for the union to show its muscle and for management to demonstrate its resolve. Frequently the parties can become deadlocked, at which point there are several options available. Union and management can agree to call in a mediator, a third party who acts as a lightning rod and attempts to deflect union and management hostility toward each other by channeling it through him or her. The mediator offers nonbinding suggestions for resolving the difficult issues, and often has substantial success. A less frequently used procedure is *binding arbitration*, in which the parties mutually agree to submit their dispute to a third party, who then makes a recommendation that is binding on both labor and management. Much has been written recently about the conflict aspect of collective bargaining, compared with some hypothetical ideal of a collaborative system of industrial relations. Conflict is part of the collective bargaining system because the labor process itself contains the conditions for a conflict between competing interests—management and labor. Nevertheless, the vast majority of collective bargaining situations—well over 90 percent—are resolved without a strike.

The Content of Collective Bargaining Agreements

[handwritten note: WHAT IT IS THAT IS NEGOTIATED . . .]

Collective bargaining agreements cover a number of aspects of the work situation. Some provisions of a union-management contract cover monetary issues; other

---

[9] Bloom and Northrup, *Economics of Labor Relations,* pp. 112-13.

provisions concern nonmonetary aspects of the work place—working conditions, health and safety, and union security.

As the cornerstone of the system of industrial relations in the United States, the collective bargaining agreement produces a set of rules that governs the work place. Of the many issues embraced by collective bargaining, several are of particular importance for the student of labor economics: wages, fringe benefits, working conditions, union security, and management rights.

Wages

The wage provisions of collective bargaining agreements address three problems. The first is the nature of the internal wage structure within the collective bargaining unit. Second, there is the problem of how this internal wage structure is arrived at. And third is the question of how workers are paid—by the hour, by the piece, by the day, or by some other measure.

The internal wage structure, taking that issue first, refers to the wage differentials for different workers. Workers receive different wage rates for different work, and the task of the collective bargaining agreement is to devise an internal wage structure to compensate the various categories of labor.

One system used to devise such an internal wage structure is *job evaluation.* Each job in the plant is analyzed and assigned a relative weight compared with all the other jobs in the plant. Once the average wage level has been established—which is typically based on such external factors as the average rate of labor productivity, comparable pay for workers doing a similar job in another company, and the cost of living—then the negotiators can turn their attention to the structure of wages that surrounds the average wage. The job evaluation process will normally take account of the intellectual and physical effort required to do the job, the level of education and experience needed to perform the task, the responsibility involved with the job, the danger and health conditions of a particular job, and so on. These job evaluations can vary with the character of the work process, since jobs will differ depending on the type of product being produced. In all instances, however, an effort is made to devise a system that, as far as possible, is based on objective criteria that are fair and equitable to all workers concerned. After the jobs are assigned weights, based on the criteria used in the evaluation, these ratings are then converted into rates of pay for different jobs.

The internal wage structure is part of the nuts and bolts of the collective bargaining system. This was dramatized in the 1982 strike of the National Football League's Players Association (NFLPA). Far removed from traditional blue-collar workers, the football players sought an internal wage structure that was not terribly different in form from those sought by unions in other sectors of the economy.

Traditionally, the NFL owners had negotiated contracts individually with each player—in fact, they had been doing this for 63 years. The new union contract contained salary provisions that accounted for about 60 percent of the total player compensation—up from 10 percent in an earlier contract. For a wage structure, the NFLPA negotiated minimum salaries for players depending on years in the league, with minimum pay starting in 1983 at $40,000 and increasing by $10,000 per year thereafter up to a maximum of $200,000.[10]

Players are awarded severance pay under the contract, starting at $60,000 for players with four years of experience and increasing by $10,000 for each additional year up to a maximum of $140,000. With such steep financial compensation, the players hoped to discourage arbitrary cuts by owners who replace experienced players with lower-paid rookies.

Whatever your personal views about the football players' strike in 1982, the specific issues taken up in that collective bargaining agreement dramatically illustrate the more general point that workers, no matter what their pay, seek control over their own destinies through the collective bargaining system.

Once the internal wage structure is established, the union and management negotiators proceed to bargain over the size of the wage increase. Several issues arise in this context, aside from the sensitive one of how large the increase will be. First, wages and fringe benefits are considered in a package. A union might trade off, for example, some of its demands for wage rate increases for higher fringe benefit increases. The various combinations and trade-offs that can be made between wages and fringe benefits within a general compensation package give both sides in the bargaining process some cards to play and some room in which to maneuver.

The second issue is how the average increase will be distributed. It could be done in an across-the-board cents-per-hour form, in which the same absolute amount of increase is paid to all workers. Or it could be done by an equal percentage increase for all workers. The first method, the equal cents per hour, would have the effect of reducing wage differentials in the plant, whereas the second would perpetuate an existing structure of wage differentials. Yet a third possibility is that there will be a differentiated percentage increase, which could be used either to level wage differentials or to increase them.

Having resolved these issues, the collective bargaining agreement will then address the matter of how wages are to be paid—either by the time a worker puts in on the job or by the amount he or she produces. If paid by the *time* the worker is on the job, an hourly rate is the most common form of pay for blue-collar production workers, while a weekly rate is common for salaried employees. *Piecework* is a system of pay in which the worker receives so much money per unit of output completed. There can also be a combination of the two systems of pay, in which the worker is provided a base pay by the hour and is also given a piece-rate bonus for exceeding an output quota.

Provision can be made in the collective bargaining agreement for adjustments in wage rates during the life of the contract. One way this is done is through a cost-of-living adjustment clause (COLA for short) which provides that wages will increase periodically during the life of the contract as the measured cost-of-living increases.

COLA — cost of living adjustment clause

---

[10] Salaries above $200,000 are, of course, possible. These figures are minima. See "The NFL Players Run Out of Time," *Business Week*, November 29, 1982, pp. 35–36.

For this purpose the Consumer Price Index (CPI) of the Bureau of Labor Statistics is used. The COLA can either be *full*, in which case wage rates will increase in direct proportion to the increase in the CPI, or be partial, in which case the wage rate will increase, for example, up to 60 percent of the increase in the CPI.

The first COLA was introduced in the 1948 UAW-GM collective bargaining agreement. After an initial interest in them, unions began to trade off the COLAs for other parts of the compensation package in the 1960s when inflation was of little consequence. In the 1970s many unions tried to reintroduce COLAs or establish them where they had not previously existed.

In the steel industry, for example, a COLA clause was first written into the contract with the United Steelworkers in 1956, but the union eliminated this provision three years later in 1959 as part of the settlement of a 116-day strike. In 1971 the steelworkers negotiated a new COLA provision in their contract. Between 1972 and 1982 fully two-thirds of the increase in the wages of steelworkers came from COLA payments.[11]

About half of all union contracts have some form of COLA. The majority of COLA agreements provide for only partial adjustment to inflation. Unions will trade off straight wage increases for COLA agreements. In 1980, for example, contracts negotiated without COLAs contained an average 11.7 percent wage increase in the first year of the contract. Agreements with COLAs averaged only an 8.0 percent wage increase in the first year of the contract. Over the life of the contracts, agreements without COLAs had an average negotiated wage increase of 7.3 percent per year, compared with 5.0 percent in contracts containing COLA provisions.[12]

Another way in which wage increases are built into the collective bargaining agreement is by stipulating increases to occur at the end of each year covered by the agreement. For example, a contract will call for a wage increase when the new contract takes effect and will provide for periodic increases during the life of the contract.

Just contemplating these wage issues provides an understanding of why collective bargaining is so time-consuming and can create such enormous tensions among the negotiators. Fortunately, not all of these issues have to be considered each time a contract is being negotiated. For example, once the wage structure has been set in place, it need be changed only if one side or the other wants to reopen the question. If there is no problem with the internal wage structure, the parties proceed directly to a discussion of the question of the percentage increase in wages and fringe benefits. The same can be said for the issue of time versus piece-rate payments. If these matters have already been resolved to everyone's satisfaction in previous contracts, the issues do not have to be renegotiated. New questions are always arising in this area, however—in contrast to the internal wage structure, which is more stable—because of

---

[13] This issue is examined in more detail in Chapter 22.

[14] "The Price of Peace at Chrysler," *Business Week,* November 12, 1979, p. 93.

[15] "The Pension Power Unions Might Wield," *Business Week,* September 17, 1979, p. 33.

the conflict that occurs over work norms or quotas. Management will be trying to push these norms higher, and the union will resist.

Fringe Benefits   ~non cash~

B. Nonwage compensation negotiated in the collective bargaining agreement falls into the category of fringe benefits. There are as many fringe benefit packages as there are collective bargaining agreements. Vacation and personal holidays, sick leave, and relief breaks on the job are but three specific types of fringe benefits that normally appear in union contracts. With space limited, I have chosen to look at three types of fringe benefits that are invariably found in collective bargaining agreements and that are illustrative of other types of fringe benefits:

- unemployment and job security

- retirement

- health and income security

C. ### Unemployment and Job Security

There are two principal types of provisions that cover unemployment and job security. The first is called *supplemental unemployment benefits (SUB)*. Under these provisions, the employer makes a financial contribution to a SUB fund, which is then activated whenever a union member covered by the contract is laid off by the firm. The worker will receive the normal unemployment compensation (discussed in Chapter 24) and will also receive a supplement from the SUB fund, which may be administered jointly by the union and the company.

The second type of economic security provision arises in response to the severe job losses in manufacturing in the 1980s. Unions have just begun to try to negotiate some form of job security. So far there have been only tentative experiments with the concept, including such ideas as prior notice of layoffs, provision for some amount of work-sharing, and skill retooling. More than just the union's desire to protect their members' jobs is at stake in these experiments, however. The hope is that productivity and product quality will be improved by such schemes, much as they are in Japan where job security is central to the Japanese productivity gains.

D. ### Retirement

A *private pension plan* to supplement the federal government's social security system is the basic retirement provision that most unions have negotiated into their collective bargaining agreements with management. The employer and employee agree to pay monies into the private pension fund, whose investments will be administered by the union, management, and an outside trustee. Besides the size of the employer payment and provisions concerning such issues as eligibility and vesting, the collective

EMPLOYEE STOCK OWNERSHIP.

bargaining agreement may also contain provisions for early retirement. In some instances the union-management contract will stipulate an age when the worker becomes eligible for early retirement—55, for example. In other instances the contract will contain a provision that permits the worker to take early retirement based on years of employment with the company—for example, a provision for "30 and out," which means that the worker can elect to retire after putting in 30 years of employment with the firm, no matter what his or her age. Under either of these types of provisions, the decision to retire is purely voluntary and is completely at the discretion of the individual worker.

Because of inflation, early retirement has become less of an advantage for workers, as they watch their fixed pensions dwindle in value because of the decline in the value of the dollar. Consequently, unions are now negotiating provisions in contracts that call for increasing the pension payments for those already retired so that they can better keep pace with inflation. The 1979 UAW contract with the auto industry broke new ground on this issue, although the union demand for complete COLA indexing of pensions was rejected by the auto companies.

As more unions have bargained for pension systems in their collective bargaining agreements and as the passage of time has led to the accumulation of larger and larger sums of money in the funds, union pension funds and what is done with them have become an important issue.[13] At the end of 1979 it was estimated that union pension funds had some $250 billion in assets. Of this $250 billion, about $60 billion fell under joint union and company trusteeship; the remainder was controlled by trustees appointed by management. In the 1979 UAW negotiations with Chrysler, the union was able to win a ground-breaking concession from management concerning the investments from the pension funds. The agreement stipulated that 10 percent of the new contributions to the pension fund would be used for "socially desirable projects," such as home mortgages, health maintenance centers, and other projects in communities with a concentration of Chrysler employees, in lieu of the traditional investments of pension funds in blue-chip stocks and corporate and government bonds.[14]

In recent years some union leaders and their members have raised important questions about the investment portfolios of these large union pension funds. For example, these funds are used to buy stocks in nonunion (and in some cases antiunion) companies. In 1979, 12 percent of the outstanding stock of Delta Airlines—a nonunion firm—was owned by union pension funds; 13 percent of Texas Instruments; and 13 percent of McDonald's.[15] We will encounter this issue again in Chapter 22, where the future of industrial relations will be discussed.

Health and Income Security

In the category of health and income security, collective bargaining agreements contain

---

[13] This issue is examined in more detail in Chapter 22.

[14] "The Price of Peace at Chrysler," *Business Week,* November 12, 1979, p. 93.

[15] "The Pension Power Unions Might Wield," *Business Week,* September 17, 1979, p. 33.

Is the worker eligible?

sections dealing with hospital-surgical plans, major medical, temporary disability, and supplemental workers' compensation.

Hospital-surgical plans are private health plans, such as Blue Cross-Blue Shield, that provide for payment to cover medical services. The coverage can vary depending on the type of plan, but the principle is the same: the employer pays monies into the plan, although typically the employer and the worker will share such payments in a ratio negotiated in the contract, as they will also do with pension contributions in most instances.

Major medical covers the problem of "catastrophic illness." Hospital-surgical plans typically have a cutoff in terms of the number of days of hospitalization covered. Should a major illness occur that requires hospitalization beyond that covered under the basic plan, major medical will pick up the additional days and costs associated with the illness. *Health care is fastest growing cost of component of COLAS*

Income security — If a worker is injured or otherwise incapacitated as a result of his or her work activity, provisions for *temporary or permanent disability* payments become activated. The worker will receive a payment, equal to a portion of earnings while employed, during the term of his or her disability. Associated with the payment for the disability is workers' compensation—a government program of payments for job-related injuries.[16] The union and management negotiate a supplemental plan, which adds to the basic state government payment for such disabilities.

This menu of fringe benefits conveys something of the richness and complexity of collective bargaining agreements. Health, safety, old age, and economic security— all need attention in a modern industrial society, either through public statute or private agreement. In the United States, as distinct from Europe, private collective bargaining agreements have become important instruments for protecting the economic welfare of workers.

The mixture of fringe benefits and direct wage payments, and the composition of fringe benefits in the overall compensation package, varies for each contract. It depends on the age structure of the bargaining unit, in part. For example, a union with a preponderance of older workers can be expected to bargain more closely over old age and retirement issues than one with more younger workers in it. A union that is dealing with difficult health and safety problems, such as the coal mines, can be expected to bargain more aggressively over the issues of health and safety than would a union in a work situation where the probability of injury and debilitating health problems was not as severe. An industry subjected to regular seasonal employment fluctuations, such as the garment industry, would call forth more provisions for economic security than another sector, such as the chemical industry, where work was not so seasonal in nature.

Overarching all these fringe benefits issues is the concept of seniority. Jealously protected by the union, seniority provisions in collective bargaining agreements give greater protection, more benefits, and higher-paying jobs to workers who have been

---

[16] This is discussed in detail in Chapter 24.

employed by the company longer. For example, a contract might contain a provision governing layoffs in which a last-hired-first-fired system is used. Here, the longer a worker has been employed, the smaller are his or her chances of being laid off. The same goes for promotions to higher-paying jobs. Contracts can contain provisions that the seniority principle will be used, or at least must be considered, by the company as it decides on a promotion. The longer a worker has been on the job, the greater his or her severance pay on dismissal. This provision will be part of the collective bargaining agreement, as will provisions for the vesting of pension payments, in which the worker will have more vested rights in the pension plan depending on the years in service with the company.

The seniority principle came up against civil rights pressures in the 1960s. Since white workers typically had more seniority than black workers, they fared better in an economic slowdown as well as in promotion. Is this discrimination? There have been many court cases on this subject, but in general the seniority principle has been upheld as nondiscriminatory since it, in fact, does not discriminate on the basis of race or sex but solely on the basis of years in service. However, seniority clauses in practice have been ruled illegal by the courts where they have led to the clustering of women and blacks in low-paying job classifications.

The Conditions of Work

Aside from wages and fringe benefits, trade unions bargain with management over the conditions of work on the job. For the worker, these issues at times take on more consequence than wage issues and lie at the very heart of the protection the union provides. For the employer, negotiations over the conditions of work intrude into management's prerogative to use labor as it likes.

Initially, management did have the right, enforced by judicial interpretation, to use labor as it saw fit during the time the worker was on the job. In essence, this was a form of property right. Although different from slavery, of course, in which the slave was actually owned by another individual, the wage system did contain an implicit contract between the employee and the employer that granted to the employer rights over the employee for the duration of employment. The right of property inhered in the time of employment. The employer was given the right to organize that time and to do what he or she wanted with the worker during the working day, without much restriction. Today the absolute right of an employer to do as he or she pleases with employees is restricted by union contracts and by state and federal law. However, such intrusions into management's prerogative happen slowly and are bitterly resisted by employers. Not so long ago, a top official of General Motors reiterated in the following way the concept of property rights during the time workers are employed by a company: "Within reason and without endangering their health, if we can occupy a man for 60 minutes we've got that right."[17]

---

[17] The quotation is from Joseph E. Godfrey, general manager of the General Motors Assembly Division. He made the statement in 1972. See Agis Salpukas, "GM's Toughest Division," *New York Times,* April 16, 1972, sec.3, pp. 1, 4.

[Handwritten annotations at top of page:]

$$E = mc^2$$
$$E - m = c(c)$$
$$-c^2 + E - m = 0$$
$$(c - E + m)(c + 2E - 2m)$$
$$c^2 + 2cE - 2mc - EC - 2E^2 + 2Em + c$$
$$c^2 + 2cE - 2mc - EC - 2E^2 + 2Em + cm - 2m = 2mcE$$
$$E - mc$$

There are two groups of working condition issues that are typically negotiated in trade union contracts: hours of work and health and safety conditions on the job.

G. Hours of Work

A collective bargaining agreement may contain provisions about hours of work that cover the length of the workweek (if wages are paid by the hour), provisions for overtime pay, rest periods, time for meals, paid holidays and vacations, personal time off and sick leave, and time for changing clothes before and after work.

Trade unions have been advocates of the shorter workweek ever since they became organized. Recently, however, unions have preferred to bargain over more paid holidays, vacations, and personal sick leave, while leaving the traditional 40-hour workweek intact. The issue of overtime hours has become one of the most contentious of all contemporary collective bargaining issues. The dispute arises not over increased pay for overtime hours but over the question of whether the overtime will be voluntary or involuntary. Voluntary overtime means that each individual worker can decide whether or not to work the overtime hours when asked to do so. Involuntary overtime removes this discretion from the employee and places it in the hands of the employer, who can assign overtime hours and require the worker to conform to those assignments.

As indicated in Chapter 4, the worker, by asserting rights in this area, is merely saying that he or she wants the freedom to choose between work and nonmarket time at the margin. The employer, on the other hand, wants the right to control overtime to be able to respond more adequately to seasonal and cyclical fluctuations in production and to reduce his fixed costs of hiring new employees. In general, overtime is still apportioned on an involuntary basis today, and the trade unions have not been able to effect much alteration in this management prerogative.

Break periods while on the job, time for preparation, and time for departure are issues that some unions have successfully negotiated into collective bargaining agreements in recent years. Where appropriate, they have put pressure on management to compensate the worker for the time it takes to change clothes by setting aside an allotted time segment to do this and, on the other end, when the workday is over, compensating the worker for the time it takes to change back into street clothes. These questions can be handled by direct compensation or, indirectly, by providing for paid time to prepare for work and the workday.

The final area of hours of work involves differential pay for different work shifts. Trade unions seek to obtain higher rates of pay for a night shift and for a split shift. The latter deals with the problem of peak loads in the production process. For example, restaurant workers or bus drivers could not be employed as profitably if they worked a straight shift that covered only one peak period of activity as they could if they went home after one peak load period and then returned for another peak load period. Unions have sought more compensation for such split shifts because of the added cost to the worker, not to mention the added inconvenience.

H. Health and Safety

Health and safety issues on the job are as old as work itself. In general, trade unions assert the right to negotiate over these conditions of work, while management argues that such matters as the environment in which the work is conducted fall into the category of management prerogatives. Over the years trade unions have whittled away at these management prerogatives, and they have been able to affect the health and safety conditions at work. Better lighting, more ventilation, a slower production line are but a few of the ways in which unions have had an impact in this area. A few years ago the United Mine Workers won an unprecedented clause that gave the individual worker the right to shut down an operation, pending verification, if he thought he was working in unsafe mining conditions. This clause has been softened since, but nevertheless the precedent was established. The Oil, Chemical, and Atomic Workers Union has been a leader in health and safety provisions because of the danger of the work in those industries.

Health and safety and hours of work receive less media and public attention in collective bargaining disputes than do wages. But for the member of a union, these issues are frequently of greater consequence than wage issues, which can be more easily resolved because of their relative simplicity. A worker who feels endangered at her place of work or subjected to arbitrary work hours and scheduling will become a dissatisfied worker, prone to militant strike activity when given the opportunity. Some of the most militant and lengthy strikes have occurred over these issues, and not over compensation matters.

Two parties face each other across the bargaining table—labor and management—and each views these questions of working conditions through a different prism. For management, any intrusion into their sovereignty over the work place is seen as an interruption of labor productivity—a make-work situation that costs money and produces no financial returns for them. To labor, these same matters are central to economic welfare and as important as the monetary aspects of collective bargaining, if not more so. In general, it has been easier to handle the monetary issues of collective bargaining than these knotty problems of welfare, which do not have so simple a monetary solution.

Grievance Procedures

Disputes that arise over the interpretation of an existing contract are channeled through a *grievance procedure*. Virtually every collective bargaining agreement contains elaborate machinery for administering a contract and adjudicating disputes over the contract's interpretation through a grievance procedure. Grievances can involve any aspect of the collective bargaining agreement. The procedure to settle them represents a fundamental right of the employee to "have his day in court" by filing a grievance when he feels the letter of the contract is not being upheld in his day-to-day work environment.[18]

---

[18] Unions retain the right to reject a grievance application, thereby screening grievance petitions before they reach the adjudication process.

There can be many different types of grievance procedures. Most contracts have provisions for standing grievance committees in different shops within a plant. Representatives of the union and management and the shop supervisor frequently sit on the grievance committee. A smoothly functioning and equitable grievance procedure can avoid costly production breakdowns.

The workers in a plant are not without ingenuity in sabotaging a production process if they feel the grievance procedure is not operating quickly, adequately, and equitably. As a last resort, they can engage in a wildcat strike—a strike unauthorized by the terms of the contract. Short of that, they can participate in a slowdown in production—a form of passive resistance—or they can create strategic bottlenecks in the flow of production by slowing down at one critical stage of the production process. A work-to-the-rule action may also be used to get the attention of management to worker dissatisfaction with the grievance machinery. Under such a job action, the absolute letter of the contract and work rules is followed by the workers. This invariably means that less work gets done and that what gets done is costlier and slower. Finally, the workers can flood the grievance machinery with every possible complaint they can legitimately file under the contract. All these forms of guerrilla warfare on the job are costly to everyone concerned and are most easily avoided through a fair grievance procedure that functions expeditiously.

Union Security

Having won a certification in a bargaining unit, the union is not without challenges to its security. There can be decertification elections, which are provided for in the National Labor Relations Act. A decertification procedure involves having a plebiscite in the bargaining unit to determine if the workers still want to be represented by their union. If the vote is in favor of decertification, that particular union no longer represents the workers, although another union can enter the scene and, after a subsequent certification election, can represent the employees if the vote is positive.

Within the framework of the collective bargaining agreement, the union will try to negotiate clauses that provide it with some security in the bargaining unit. There are four principal issues of union security that can become part of a collective bargaining agreement: the union shop, dues checkoff, control of subcontracting, and an orderly adaptation to technological change.

Union Shop

As discussed previously in this chapter, the union shop provides that the employer may hire whomever he or she wishes but that, after some minimal probationary period, the worker must join the union. An agreement to have a union shop is one that is negotiated in the collective bargaining agreement. It is one of the union's major demands and an issue that will not easily be bargained away by the union. In states where there are prohibitions against a union shop, the union will seek to negotiate an agency shop or the best possible situation it can obtain for itself. These questions of the union and agency shop are critical for a union's security, since they provide protection for the union against management's efforts to weaken its membership base.

Union Dues Checkoff

Another issue of union security is having union dues deducted at the source of payment—that is, from the worker's paycheck. This is called a *checkoff*. Under such provisions, the company will collect union dues by withholding them from the worker's paycheck and will turn over to the union whatever it has collected. The system of dues checkoff works the same way as the withholding of income taxes. Under the Taft-Hartley Act automatic checkoff is prohibited, and each worker must sign a card authorizing the employer to deduct dues from his or her paycheck. Peer pressure normally assures this happens where there is a strong union in the plant. The existence of a checkoff system, however, will be negotiated into the collective bargaining agreement within the confines of the Taft-Hartley Act. A checkoff system makes the union dues easier to collect, and this strengthens the union. Moreover, it removes the local union official from the unpleasant task of asking fellow workers for money all the time and thereby eliminates a source of friction between union officials and their members.

Subcontracting

Although dues checkoff and union or agency shop provisions have been negotiated into collective bargaining agreements, unions have been less effective on the issue of subcontracting, which management sees as its prerogative. The issue here is management's using nonunion subcontractors to produce output, thereby eliminating jobs from the union's area of jurisdiction. Unions try to negotiate into their contracts provisions that any subcontractor must also negotiate a collective bargaining agreement and recognize the union or, more frequently, that no work normally done or capable of being done in the bargaining unit may be subcontracted if it will lead to layoffs in the bargaining unit. These efforts are strongly resisted by management, who tend to see subcontracting as one area of their domain. One breakthrough occurred recently as the UAW sought to stem the tide of subcontracting by the automakers; though unable to negotiate such clauses in the collective bargaining agreement itself, the union obtained a letter of understanding from the companies about subcontracting.

Adaptation to Technological Change

At times technology renders an entire union obsolete, because the tasks performed by union members no longer need to be done. Firemen on railroads where steam power is no longer used, typesetting by hand where it is now done by word processing machines, and engineers on commercial aircraft where there is no longer engineering work to be done are but a few examples from recent years of entire occupations that have become technologically obsolete. A serious problem arises over what to do with these workers and with their union, which may be of the craft type and may contain only the craft that is becoming obsolete. When these issues arise, workers and their union will fight a rearguard action to preserve an institution that to them has been second in importance only to their families. Strikes of the longest duration occur in these circumstances because the workers feel they have nothing to lose, having already lost their occupation to technology. This is one of the great tragedies of industrialization. Along with the fruits of progress comes the dislocation of decay.

Enough of these situations have arisen in the past three decades that unions now have precedents for negotiating protection for their members, although the union is ultimately powerless to protect itself as an institution from obsolescence caused by technology.

A provision can be negotiated that no worker presently on the job can be laid off but that retirement and natural attrition must be the means by which the occupation is phased out of existence. Sometimes a monetary incentive is provided through an early retirement system in order to speed up the process of attrition. Another provision negotiated in some contracts is that the existing workers are guaranteed other jobs in the company and that retraining will be provided in order to facilitate this transition. Some unions have merged with others in the industry to provide continuity with the past and to construct an institutional means of protecting their members. In these cases a clause will be negotiated in a collective bargaining agreement that grants recognition to the new union into which the old one has merged.

8. *Management Rights*

The issue of *management rights* in the factory raises the most fundamental legal and philosophical questions about a modern industrial society. Indeed, the very fact that an employer must insist on having a clause in the collective bargaining agreement that stipulates management rights is an indication of how far unions have intruded into what heretofore have been management prerogatives.

Initially property law gave virtually an unfettered right to an owner of property to do what he or she wished with the property, without concern for public health and safety, the environment, or the economic and social condition of workers. An employer had a form of ownership over the time that workers spent in his or her employ, through an implicit contract that established a wage rate for work performed. Starting from this absolutist reign, the owner and the owner's managerial agents have had to concede management rights and prerogatives to unions through collective bargaining agreements and to the public through statutes. Companies are no longer free to pollute the air and water, place workers in unduly unsafe and unhealthy work environments, or produce products that threaten the safety of the consuming public. Statutes at the federal, state, and local levels pertain to these issues. And the collective bargaining agreement further intrudes on management prerogatives by determining the wage to be paid; by establishing seniority provisions, which restrict layoff and promotion decisions of management; and by setting up grievance procedures, which adjudicate work disputes—to mention but a few of the ways in which an absolutist interpretation of management rights has been eroded.

The differing interpretations of management rights and prerogatives in the factory came to a head at a conference called by President Harry S. Truman in 1945. As in an earlier conference convened by President Woodrow Wilson in 1919, labor and management representatives were unable to agree on a definition or even the legitimacy of management rights.[19] Management adopted the *residual thesis* of management rights. They argued that the laws of property provided that owners and their representatives had an absolute right over management issues. They could choose to delegate such rights to others—a union, for example—but they reserved the right to all residual matters not specifically ceded to unions through collective bargaining agreements.

At the 1945 conference management representatives declared that "labor must agree that certain specific functions and responsibilities of management are not subject to collective bargaining." Labor responded by saying that because of the "complexities" of labor-management relations, they thought it "unwise to specify and classify the functions and responsibilities of management."[20] Two fundamentally opposing positions still exist: labor's is that there are no inherent management rights, while management asserts its rights are inherent but alienable, in that they may be ceded in specific instances.

As a practical matter, most management rights clauses in collective bargaining agreements stipulate that the management of the enterprise lies in the hands of the employer and that all aspects of management that are not covered in the collective bargaining agreement inhere in the rights of management. Thus, in practice the residual theory normally applies, in which management asserts its rights to manage the company except where explicitly impeded by a provision of the collective bargaining agreement.

This discussion points up the creative role of the collective bargaining instrument in providing for a form of private government between employer and employee. This system has advantages. It is decentralized and tailored to specific employment conditions. Government regulations of the work place tend to be more clumsy in that they seek very general statutes that can be applied to all labor situations. But the work place is varied, and the private government of the collective bargaining agreement is better suited to adaptation to local conditions. Democracy is also enhanced by placing the point of influence closer to the worker and employer in the collective bargaining agreement.

As a nation we lost sight of the importance of systems of private government in the 1970s. In their place, laws were adopted at the national level for health and safety, environmental protection, and employee welfare, which may have been better handled through the collective bargaining system. Returning to a creative use of this flexible

---

[19] For an interesting discussion of management rights, see Edwin F. Beal, et al., *The Practice of Collective Bargaining,* 4th ed.(Homewood, IL: Richard D. Irwin, 1972), pp. 310–22.

[20] *President's National Labor Management Conference,* vol. III, doc. 125 II/13 (November 29, 1945), p. 47; and vol. III, doc. 120 II/11 (November 28, 1945), p. 45

instrument of decentralized private government has a place in resolving many fierce public disputes about the role of government regulation in the economy.

Summary

An industrial relations system is a set of rules that governs relations between workers and their employers at the work place. Both formal statutes enacted by the Congress and informal modes of interaction provide the context for a collective bargaining agreement, which establishes the rule of law in the work place.

In order for such rules to be established, workers must first organize themselves into a trade union and then seek recognition from their employers. There are essentially two ways in which labor gains recognition from management: One is direct pressure, in which the employer will accede to the existence of a trade union and thereby grant recognition. The other is for the workers seeking union recognition to petition the National Labor Relations Board for the holding of a certification election in the bargaining unit. If successful in its recognition contest, the trade union will be certified as the exclusive representative of the workers in the bargaining unit, and the employer will have to recognize the union.

One aspect of this recognition is the requirement imposed on both union and management to engage in collective bargaining for the purpose of concluding an agreement over wages and working conditions.

The collective bargaining agreement is a complex instrument, and it typically contains provisions that cover a wide variety of topics. Wages and fringe benefits, the monetary aspects of work relations, and a grievance procedure are of first importance for any agreement. Within each of these categories, there are several matters that must be resolved. The internal wage structure and the increase in rates of pay during the term of the contract are negotiated. Cost-of-living adjustments may be included. Fringe benefits include compensation for unemployment or for disability due to accidents on the job. Retirement income through a pension plan is a second major item of compensation through fringe benefits; a third is health benefits, covered by an insurance plan.

Aside from these pecuniary elements of the collective bargaining agreement, there are other provisions, which relate to security, grievances, and conditions of work. Unions will attempt to negotiate provisions that enhance their security with the workers they represent. They do this through the inclusion in the contract of provisions for dues checkoff and union shop (or agency shop where the union shop has been outlawed). The union will attempt to place controls on management's use of nonunion subcontracting shops and will seek protection for its members whose skills have been rendered technologically obsolete.

Under the category of conditions of work, the union will seek to influence hours of work as well as the speed of the production line and the health and safety conditions on the job.

For any disputes that may arise during the life of a contract, a grievance procedure will be established whereby any individual worker can challenge management through the union if he or she feels the letter of the contract has not been followed.

All these provisions place the union in a position of providing protection for the worker from the arbitrariness of the employer. This is the way the union perceives its role. On the other side, however, management typically looks at these provisions as intrusions into the prerogatives that are guaranteed by the rights of property. Consequently, employers seek clauses in collective bargaining agreements that reaffirm the right of management to manage. These are so-called management rights provisions. Obviously there is a sharp conflict here over what are management rights under property law and what are the rights of the unions to seek protection for their members.

The collective bargaining agreement is an instrument that provides the American worker with a degree of economic security and welfare he or she would not have without a union. Although workers in nonunion plants may also receive these protections, the existence of a trade union movement frequently is the reason for the benefits being extended to nonunion plants, as employers make these concessions to their employees in order to forestall unionization in their plants. The collective bargaining process is an important social institution in American life. It should not be seen only in its narrow context as a means by which unions extract concessions from management. In a profound sense the collective bargaining agreement is the cornerstone on which the entire edifice of economic welfare is built for the American worker.

Study Questions

1. What is the essence of a collective bargaining agreement, and what are the common elements that appear in virtually all collective bargaining agreements?

2. How does the age structure of union membership influence the contents of the collective bargaining agreements?

3. Does the collective bargaining agreement encroach on property rights? In your answer be sure to define what you mean by property rights.

4. What would the labor market look like without trade unions and the collective bargaining agreement?

5. Some economists and business persons argue that the economy would be better off without trade unions and collective bargaining. They have pursued the objective of an economy without unions through consultants who specialize in decertification of existing unions. What are your views on this issue?

Further Reading

Beal, Edwin F., Edward D. Wickersham, and Philip Kienast. *The Practice of Collective Bargaining*. 3rd ed. Homewood, IL: Richard D. Irwin, 1972.

Bloom, Gordon F., and Herbert R. Northrup. *Economics of Labor Relations.* 8th ed. Homewood, IL: Richard D. Irwin, 1977.

Davey, Harold W. *Contemporary Collective Bargaining.* 3rd ed. Englewood Cliffs, NJ: Prentice-Hall, 1972.

Wortman, Max S., Jr., and George C. Witteried. *Labor Relations and Collective Bargaining, Text and Cases.* Boston: Allyn and Bacon, 1969.

21
■

Industrial Relations Law

The history of industrial relations law goes back to the beginning of the nineteenth century. From the first time American workers tried to organize themselves into a group that could pressure their employers for higher wages and better working conditions, the law has been involved. In the nineteenth century this took the form of judicial action. Not until the third decade of the twentieth century did Congress pass laws governing industrial relations. Today there are mounds upon mounds of legal documents that cover industrial relations. The profession of "labor lawyer" has been created to deal with this mass of statutory and administrative law and with judicial interpretations of the law.

This book is not written for a course in the law and, therefore, cannot pretend to cover exhaustively the field of industrial relations law. Nevertheless, the student of labor economics should know something about industrial relations law in order to converse intelligently about the conditions under which labor can organize itself and the limitations imposed by the law on how labor and management can conduct themselves in the industrial relations system. These are the issues covered by industrial relations law, the subject of this chapter.

The organization of this chapter will be in part historical and in part thematic. We will trace the history of the law of industrial relations, more or less chronologically, and examine several important recurring issues in industrial relations—for example, the worker's right to strike and laws governing picketing and boycotts.

Four great overarching legal doctrines have dominated industrial relations law since the beginning of the nineteenth century. First, from 1806 until about 1880 the common law doctrine of conspiracy was applied to labor and effectively forbade trade union organization. Second, starting in 1880 and continuing through the early 1930s, the judicial device of injunction was used against labor. This effectively precluded trade unions from engaging in certain acts (such as striking) that would have enabled them to affect wages and conditions of work. While trade unions per se were not judged illegal after 1880, as they had been under the strict interpretation of the conspiracy doctrine, certain acts of unions were considered illegal by the courts. An injunction required a union to cease and desist whatever specific act was covered by the particular injunction.

The statutory, as opposed to judicial, part of industrial relations law started with the Sherman Antitrust Act of 1890, in which labor was defined as a combination in restraint of trade and, therefore, in violation of the act. This is the third important legal doctrine applied to industrial relations. Not until the New Deal was labor treated favorably in the law. Initially in the Norris–La Guardia Act of 1932 and finally in the National Labor Relations Act of 1935, trade unions were granted official legal status, and certain of their acts (such as picketing) were afforded protection under the law. This fourth legal doctrine governing industrial relations in the United States still prevails today.

In the postwar period two pieces of legislation amended and adapted industrial relations law to new circumstances: the Taft-Hartley Act of 1947 and the Landrum-Griffin Act of 1959. These two acts circumscribed labor activity somewhat and defined the rights of an individual worker with respect to the union. The late 1970s produced a heated debate about new labor legislation, but this attempt at labor law reform was never adopted by Congress.

Throughout this excursion into industrial relations law, many interesting questions emerge. For example, is picketing protected by the First Amendment guarantee of free speech in our Constitution, or does it interfere with interstate commerce—also protected by the Constitution? Do trade unions and their actions interfere with property rights under the common law doctrine that we inherited from the British? Where does coercion end and free speech begin? All these issues and others will be looked at in this chapter, which begins with a chronological history of industrial relations and proceeds to examine specific controversial issues.

 ## The Conspiracy Doctrine: 1806–1880

These are three types of law that govern industrial relations: common law, statutory law, and administrative law. Our common law is inherited from the British. It consists of the accumulated decisions of the judiciary, which have the force of law without specific statutes enacted by the legislature. This law dominated industrial relations in the United States until 1890. Statutory law consists of the laws passed by legislatures.

Since 1890 statutory law has been of preeminent importance in industrial relations law. Administrative law consists of the law established by agencies created by statute. For example, the National Labor Relations Board, created by an act of Congress, has made volumes of industrial relations law since the mid-1930s by virtue of the authority it received from Congress through the Wagner Act. In the modern period all three types of law coexist. Today we have statutory law, judicial law, and administrative law governing our industrial relations system.

Common law is all that existed until the late nineteenth century. And the common law doctrine that governed industrial relations in the early part of the nineteenth century was the *conspiracy doctrine*. If two or more people conspire to commit an illegal act, they need not actually commit the act to commit a crime under the conspiracy doctrine. All they must do is meet or engage in some other activity that constitutes an intent to commit an illegal act. As applied to trade unions, this meant that workers' organizations per se were considered illegal and a conspiracy since demanding higher pay and better working conditions was considered a violation of property rights. Under the common law conspiracy doctrine, every act of the illegal combination violates the law, and each member is held liable for the actions of the illegal conspiracy.[1]

Applied first in the famous Philadelphia cordwainer's case of 1806 (*Commonwealth v. Pullis*), the absolute interpretation of the conspiracy doctrine held until 1842, when it was modified somewhat. In the 1806 case a group of journeymen cordwainers (i.e., shoemakers) in Philadelphia met and decided to present to the master cordwainers a bill of particulars that included higher rates for the work they were doing and a statement that they would not work for anything below the rates listed. Moreover, they sought to prevent others from taking their place and substituting their work for that of the cordwainers' organization. In short, they banded together to demand higher pay and sought to prevent outsiders from undercutting their efforts. This is the classic trade union structure.

Their masters took them to court and won the case under the conspiracy doctrine of common law. The judge's charge to the jury in this case centered on the conspiracy doctrine, and the jury returned a verdict of guilty. The legal precedent was established that the very act of banding together to seek higher wages and better working conditions was on the face of it an illegal conspiracy under common law. Between 1806 and 1842 there were around 17 applications of this doctrine.[2] Needless to say, it put a chill on virtually any form of labor organization that went beyond a mere social club and sought to influence wages and conditions of work.

The conspiracy doctrine posed squarely the problem of two competing legal values: property rights and individual rights. Both are enshrined in our value system

---

[1] Sanford Cohen, *Labor Law* (Columbus, OH: Charles E. Merrill Books, 1964), pp. 98–99. This doctrine in the law was applied to many antiwar cases during the late 1960s and early 1970s, including the famous "Chicago 7" trial.

[2] Ibid., p. 99.

in the United States—although only individual rights are explicitly guaranteed in the Constitution, in the Bill of Rights. The Constitution contains no direct affirmation of property rights. Nevertheless, when these two forms of rights came into conflict, property rights prevailed in the early part of the nineteenth century.

The judge's charge to the jury in the Philadelphia cordwainer's case puts the matter bluntly:

> A combination of workmen to raise their wages may be considered in a two-fold point of view: one is to benefit themselves . . . the other is to injure those who do not join their society. The rule of law condemns both. . . . An act innocent in an individual, is rendered criminal by a confederacy to effect it.[3]

This charge to the jury both specifies the doctrine of conspiracy as applicable to labor organizations and poses the question of property versus individual rights in a form that favors property rights. Some legal scholars have even gone so far as to argue that the courts during this period sought to merge the legal doctrine of conspiracy with the economic doctrine of laissez-faire: "It is clear in retrospect that these economic views [laissez-faire] were really the law, while the doctrine of criminal conspiracy was merely the form in which it was presented for public consumption . . . a legal abracadabra in the name of which . . . judges made labor unionists conform to the principles of classical economics."[4] The courts in the early part of the nineteenth century accepted prevailing economic doctrine that a "laborer was worthy of his hire" and that this worth was determined by the labor market. Any organized effort to contravene the decision of the market was judged to be an intrusion into the employer's right of property.[5]

The absolute definition of property rights and its application to labor organizations was modified slightly in an important 1842 decision of the Massachusetts Supreme Court. In *Commonwealth v. Hunt* the court ruled that the simple act of combination by labor was not illegal per se. The test was whether the labor organization intended to commit an illegal act and whether the purpose of the organization was to engage in illegal acts. As Judge Shaw put it in his opinion, "In order to charge all those who become members of an association with the guilt of a criminal conspiracy, it must be averred and proved that the actual, if not the avowed object of the association was criminal. . . ."[6]

This modification of the conspiracy doctrine made the legal principle so fuzzy that its application began to wane. More and more challenges to the doctrine came before the courts, until—by the end of the Civil War—the application of the

---

[3] Quoted in ibid.

[4] Charles O. Gregory and Harold A. Katz, *Labor and the Law*, 3rd ed. (New York: W. W. Norton and Co., 1979), p. 30.

[5] Ibid., p. 19.

[6] Cohen, *Labor Law*, pp. 100–101.

conspiracy doctrine to labor organizations had just about run its course. The problem was determining intent to commit some illegal act at some unspecified future time when the organization of labor was first formed. This was the test applied in the *Commonwealth v. Hunt* case, and it made the conspiracy doctrine a cumbersome legal device to apply to labor organizations.[7]

The Injunction: 1880–1930

IRREPAIRABLE HARM

With the waning of the use of the conspiracy doctrine, which had outlawed trade unions per se, the courts began to distinguish among various tactics and activities of labor organizations. Some were considered within the law, others outside the law. The judicial remedy sought by employers to prevent unions from interfering with their activity was the *injunction*.   CEASE AND DESIST ORDER

An injunction is an order from a judge requiring a party to do or to cease doing whatever activities are specified in the injunction. The issuance of an injunction is a broad right of the court in civil suits. A judge can issue a temporary injunction (for a limited period of time) on the spot without a hearing and then schedule a hearing at which both parties to the dispute will have an opportunity to present their case. The judge can grant a permanent injunction after this hearing, or issue another temporary injunction, or withdraw the first injunction. If the enjoined parties violate the injunction, they are in contempt of court and can be fined or jailed.

First used against labor in 1880, the injunction became the standard judicial remedy for employers seeking to stop labor activity. The employer would go before the court and ask for an injunction against a trade union to force it to cease its activities. The most important case of the injunction was the Pullman strike of 1894, in which it effectively eliminated the American Railway Union.[8]

In using the injunction to restrain virtually all trade union activity that involved the pursuit of higher wages and better working conditions, the courts in effect assumed "that intangible business interests are also property."[9] If the right to do business is a property right and any outside interference a violation of this right, then virtually all trade union activities could be subject to the injunction. The injunction was a very effective device for restraining trade union tactics—such as strikes, picketing, and boycotts. It was widely used. One study places the number of injunctions used before 1931 at 1,872—probably an understatement because so many issued by lower courts are not readily traceable.[10]

---

[7] Gregory and Katz, *Labor and the Law*, p. 29.

[8] Cohen, *Labor Law*, pp. 103–106.

[9] Gregory and Katz, *Labor and the Law*, p. 98.

[10] Edwin E. Witte, *The Government in Labor Disputes* (New York: McGraw-Hill Book Co., 1932), p. 84.

Labor's legal challenge to the way the courts used the injunction involved separating legal from illegal acts. For example, the destruction of an employer's tangible property—breaking windows, destroying machines, and so forth—is illegal, and the use of an injunction to stop this was not challenged by labor. But what about activities of labor that did not involve an assault on the tangible property of business? Here the courts tended to apply the same principle; any interference with the ability of an entrepreneur to pursue profits—any interruption of output—was a violation of *intangible* property rights. Legal issues arose in the courts' use of the injunction that are still controversial today: the right to strike, the distinction between peaceful and violent picketing, and the use of primary versus secondary boycotts.[11]

Until 1890 all legal aspects of industrial relations were handled by the judicial system. Starting with the passage in 1890 of the Sherman Antitrust Act, attention shifted from the courts to Congress. With this shift came new legal doctrine, on which federal legislation was based. The new legal doctrine placed trade unions in the category of combinations in restraint of interstate commerce. It did not completely replace the use of court injunctions. Rather, the two co-existed, the Sherman Act constitutional principle providing a justification for the use of court injunctions to restrain trade unions from undertaking actions that would seek to raise their wages and improve working conditions.

Trade Unions and Congressional Antitrust Law

Ironically, although the Sherman Antitrust Act of 1890 was designed to curb industrial monopolies, its first use was against trade unions. In fact, during the first several decades of the twentieth century, the Sherman Antitrust Act was used more frequently against unions than against the corporations it had been intended to regulate. The congressional debate that led to the passage of the act included deliberations about an explicit union exemption from the law. The legislators ultimately rejected such an exception, however, because, according to one student of this issue, they could not see how the act could be construed so as to be used against trade unions.[12]

Section 1 of the Sherman Antitrust Act declares that "every combination in the form of trust or otherwise, or conspiracy, in restraint of trade or commerce among the several states, or with foreign nations, is hereby declared to be illegal."[13] The legal

---

[11] Public employee strikes, which are technically illegal in many states, frequently end up with injunctions being issued against the union. A primary boycott occurs when the parties directly affected refrain from using an employer's product. A secondary boycott is when a union seeks to apply third party pressure against an employer—for example, by refusing to work with materials from nonunion subcontractors or by picketing establishments that sell products produced in nonunion shops.

[12] Cohen, *Labor Law*, p. 117.

[13] Ibid.

doctrine on which this is based is the commerce clause of the Constitution, which grants Congress the power to make laws regulating interstate commerce.

In 1908 the use of the Sherman Antitrust Act against labor received its first Supreme Court review, in the Danbury Hatters case. After an unsuccessful organizational strike, the union of hatmakers (United Hatters of North America) instituted a secondary boycott against nonunion companies. One company, Loewe's of Danbury, Connecticut, took the union to court under the Sherman Act, and the Supreme Court upheld the lower court's decision in favor of the company, arguing that a secondary boycott fell in the category of a combination in restraint of trade and was therefore illegal under the Sherman Antitrust Act.[14] The court held that not only was the trade union as an organization financially liable for damages, but every member of the union was also financially liable.[15] This was a severe blow to the fortunes of labor; it added a new dimension to the limits on labor organization.

One source of the predicament in which labor found itself was the Populist reform movement of the late nineteenth century, which became the Progressive movement of the early twentieth century. The thrust of these reform movements was antimonopoly and antibigness; they sought to restore small-scale competition. The muckrakers' assaults against rising industrialization and against the great corporate combinations in steel, railroads, and minerals were the fuel that powered this reform movement. Labor unions were themselves combinations, but of a very different sort. That difference did not prevent them from being painted with the same brush of monopoly practices as were corporations. In fact, the position of Samuel Gompers, president of the AFL, was against any legislation governing economic affairs, save those laws which gave trade unions the right to organize and bargain for higher wages and better working conditions. It is not surprising that labor became the object of the application of these laws, because unions were far weaker politically than the great corporate trusts that had grown to dominate American political and social affairs in the late nineteenth century.

Because of the unexpected application of the Sherman Antitrust Act to trade unions, labor submitted a "Bill of Grievances" to the president and the Congress in 1906 in which it requested a specific exemption from the Sherman Act and relief from court-imposed injunctions. In 1914 labor thought it achieved these objectives through the enactment of the Clayton Act, which stipulated first that

> the labor of a human being is not a commodity or an article of commerce. Nothing contained in the anti-trust laws shall be construed to forbid the existence and operating

---

[14] Ibid., pp. 117–18. Through the membership network of the AFL, union members were urged not to buy hats made at Loewe's or deal with merchants who stocked Loewe's hats (Gregory and Katz, *Labor and the Law*, p. 209).

[15] The Sherman Act provides that, "every person who shall make any such combination or conspiracy, shall be deemed guilty of a misdemeanor . . ." (Gregory and Katz, *Labor and the Law*, p. 201). The judgment against the union was for over a half million dollars, a tidy sum of money in 1908 (Gregory and Katz, *Labor and the Law*, p. 207).

of labor ... organizations ... or to forbid or restrain individual members of such organizations from lawfully carrying out the legitimate objects thereof.[16]

The Clayton Act went on to declare that labor organizations could not be classified as "illegal combinations or conspiracies in restraint of trade under the antitrust laws."[17] As to injunctions, the Clayton Act said, "No restraining order or injunction shall be granted by any court of the United States ... unless necessary to prevent irreparable injury to property, or to a property right."[18]

Although on first reading one would have thought that the Clayton Act clarified the role of trade unions and gave labor what it wanted, it did not. In fact, nothing was changed by the Clayton Act. The courts continued to apply the Sherman Act to labor and to issue injunctions against labor. On closer reading of the Clayton Act, its loopholes become apparent. First, the provision supposedly exempting labor unions from the Sherman Act says that the act cannot be used to "forbid the existence" of trade unions. The Sherman Act had never been used for this purpose, however; it had been used only to find unions liable for damages in violation of the act. The provision on injunctions forbade them except when unions were engaged in "irreparable injury to property, or to a property right," which, of course, had been the basis for their use by the courts. In effect, the Clayton Act legitimated the use of the injunction as it had been employed by the courts and strengthened the judiciary's hand in using this legal device against labor by specifying its application in federal statute.

After the passage of the Clayton Act, the most frequent use of antitrust law against labor was in cases of secondary boycotts. Previously we saw how the Sherman Act was used in a case in which trade unions used their membership structure to impose a consumer boycott on merchants who stocked hats made in nonunion shops. Universal unionization in an industry was seen as crucial to union strategies in the 1920s because only in this way could unions achieve common wage standards and prevent work from going to nonunion shops. The tactic unions employed to achieve this objective and organize nonunion firms was the secondary boycott. In cases involving the Duplex Printing Company and the International Association of Machinists (1921) and the United Mine Workers of America and the Coronado Coal Company (1922), the Supreme Court upheld its prohibition against secondary boycotts and, in effect, reinstated the application of antitrust law to trade unions.[19]

There the matter of labor law remained until the ground-breaking legislation of the New Deal period radically changed the legal basis on which trade unions functioned in the United States. In a half century of legal battles, from 1880 to 1930, labor had won the right to have its own organizations, freeing itself from the conspiracy doctrine. However, the rights of labor organizations to engage in specific economic

Secondary Boycotts were seen as restraining the interests of others.

[16] Cohen, *Labor Law*, p. 119.

[17] Ibid.

[18] Ibid.

[19] Gregory and Katz, *Labor and the Law*, pp. 221–22; and Cohen, *Labor Law*, pp. 120–30.

actions were severely circumscribed. Establishing in the law the right of labor to organize and bargain collectively and freeing labor from the restrictive shackles of the courts and statutes were the political objectives of trade unions. These goals were, to some extent, realized during the New Deal period.

The New Deal Period

The landmark labor legislation of the New Deal period reached its zenith with the passage of the National Labor Relations Act (NLRA) in 1935. Prior to 1935, however, critically important labor law was enacted that paved the way for the comprehensive treatment of labor law in the NLRA.

Perhaps the most important of the precursors of the NLRA (or the Wagner Act, as it is commonly known) was the Norris–La Guardia Anti-Injunction Act of 1932, signed by Herbert Hoover as one of his last acts as president. As its name implies, the Norris–La Guardia Act sought to clarify the circumstances under which an injunction could be imposed against labor. Without prohibiting injunctions, the Norris–La Guardia Act limits their use to situations where there is no other legal remedy and where illegal acts either are being committed or will be committed unless restrained by injunction, where tangible property damage is or will be done, or where personal injury is probable.[20] Specifically prohibited is the use of federal court injunctions against strikes that do not have the characteristics just described. The burden of proof that an injunction is needed is now on the employer, who has to show evidence that a union's actions would lead to property damage or bodily injury.

The Norris–La Guardia Act also contained two other important provisions, which were later included in the NLRA. The first outlawed so-called yellow-dog contracts, which specified as a condition of employment that a worker agree not to join a trade union. The second was a public policy declaration that granted workers the right to organize into a trade union of their own choice and, through that organization, to bargain collectively over wages and conditions of work.

The Norris–La Guardia Act weakened some of the restrictions that had been imposed on labor's actions. It did not positively affirm labor's rights, however, nor did it establish machinery for enforcement of rights to organize trade unions and engage in collective bargaining. These positive rights of labor were contained in the landmark National Labor Relations Act of 1935.

In 1935 Congress passed the National Labor Relations Act—better known as the Wagner Act—which revolutionized labor law in the United States. It granted employees the right to have a trade union of their own choosing, and it established a procedure to implement this right. It outlawed yellow-dog contracts. It established

---

[20] Cohen, *Labor Law*, p. 143.

[handwritten annotations at top: "EXEMPTION OF WAGNER ACT   1. AGRICULTURAL WORKERS   2. GOVT. WORKERS"]

[handwritten marginal numbers: 3., 4., 5., A., 1., 2.]

employee rights, which included the right to engage in trade union activity, free of coercion or retribution; freedom from discharge or demotion as a result of trade union activities; and freedom from discrimination in hiring as a result of trade union sympathies. The Wagner Act specified certain employer activities as "unfair labor practices," which were now illegal under the law. If an employer sought to deny an employee rights guaranteed under the act, this was an unfair labor practice.

To enforce these provisions, the Wagner Act established the National Labor Relations Board (NLRB) and granted that board wide authority to enforce the statute. The NLRB has the authority to issue cease and desist orders when it finds a violation of the act. Over the years the NLRB has established volumes of administrative law, and the profession of labor lawyer exists largely because of legal work conducted by both employers and trade unions under the Wagner Act.

The Wagner Act is a long and complicated piece of legislation, and it has become even more complicated in the years since its passage as the courts and the NLRB have rendered interpretations of the provisions of the act. But two principles of the act stand out: first, the machinery created to enable a group of employees to gain recognition as a trade union and, second, the provisions identifying unfair labor practices by employers.

The NLRB has the authority to establish exclusive jurisdiction for one trade union in a bargaining unit. These issues were discussed in an earlier chapter (Chapter 19), but they are worth reiterating here briefly.

During the middle of the 1930s, two rival trade union structures competed for recognition. The older craft union form, in which trade unions were organized by specific occupational craft, dominated the American Federation of Labor (AFL). Starting with the revolution in production techniques that created the mass production industries, a new form of trade union structure emerged, based on the organization of an entire company. These industrial unions, as they were called, were organized through the Congress of Industrial Organizations (CIO). Now that the Wagner Act gave authority to the NLRB to define jurisdiction over a bargaining unit, the question was whether the bargaining unit would be defined as the craft-based occupation or as the entire company. For example, in an auto factory there are many different crafts used to produce a car. Would the bargaining unit specified by the NLRB be the occupation or the entire company?

From the beginning, the NLRB gave preference to the industrial form of unionization and defined the bargaining unit as the company, not the craft-based occupation. This catapulted the CIO-type union into the forefront of the American labor movement.[21]

Employees in a bargaining unit have the right to petition the NLRB to conduct

---

[21] John L. Lewis, president of the CIO, was a friend and political supporter of Roosevelt. This alliance, coupled with Roosevelt's new political coalition, no doubt contributed to the climate of opinion in which the NLRB made its early jurisdictional decisions. Added to this was the militancy of the CIO-led sit-down strikes in 1934 and the need to defuse social conflict. See Irving Bernstein, *Turbulent Years* (Boston: Houghton Mifflin Co., 1970).

an election to determine whether a specific trade union will represent them. The NLRB supervises the election, and employers are limited in what they may do and how they may conduct themselves during the preelection period. If a majority of the employees voting want to have the union, the NLRB certifies that trade union as the bargaining agent, and the employer must engage in good-faith collective bargaining with the union. The employer does not have to accept the union's bargaining position, but the employer must participate in good faith in the give and take that is part of negotiations.

The constitutionality of the Wagner Act was challenged. A case came before the Supreme Court in 1937—*National Labor Relations Board v. Jones and Laughlin Steel Corporation*. The Supreme Court, in a reversal of its earlier stand, now argued that the Wagner Act was constitutional under the interstate commerce clause of the Constitution. The Court said that "industrial strife would have a most serious effect upon interstate commerce" and that "the right of employees to self-organization and to have representatives of their own choosing for the purpose of collective bargaining is often an essential condition of industrial peace."[22]

With this interpretation the Supreme Court shifted its position 180 degrees. Earlier it had held that industrial strife interfered with the free flow of commerce and that, therefore, trade union activity should be controlled. Now, in 1937, it was arguing that industrial strife, which shut down production and interfered with interstate commerce, was caused not by the presence of trade unions but by their absence. Hence, the court supported the machinery established in the Wagner Act to create trade unions.

For the decade from 1935 to 1945 the legal system in the United States was supportive of trade unions for the first time in our history. This supportive legal environment produced the fastest growth in trade union membership that we have ever had.[23] The structure of the labor movement established during the first five years of the Wagner Act remains in place today and forms the backbone of the American labor movement. This legal environment was not to last long, however. Although they never had the support of the business community, the political forces behind the Wagner Act were able to prevail during the Great Depression. For many, organized labor was seen as a better option than more radical revolutionary movements, which were also vying for the loyalties of the American worker.

By the end of the Second World War, the political balance had tipped away from organized labor, and a reaction set in. Another great red scare, similar to the one after

---

[22] Cohen, *Labor Law*, pp. 157, 158.

[23] Union membership grew from just under 4 million (6.7 percent of the labor force) in 1935 to over 12 million (nearly 22 percent of the labor force) in 1945 (see Chapter 19). Two-thirds of the workers in the manufacturing sector of the economy were covered by union-negotiated collective bargaining agreements in 1947, and one-third of all employees in the nonmanufacturing sector of the economy (excluding agricultural and professional employees) were covered by union agreements (Archibald Cox, *Law and the National Labor Policy* [Berkeley, CA: Institute of Industrial Relations, 1960], p. 13).

World War I, quickly surfaced in American politics, and the labor movement was singled out for special attack as this wave of anti-Communism swept the country. Many strikes occurred in 1946 as labor sought to catch up with economic conditions after the war because wages had been frozen during the war. The political opposition to labor had time to regroup.

Adding to these political forces were the genuine problems that had emerged during the first ten years of application of the Wagner Act, inevitable for a piece of legislation so complicated. Many problems arose that had not been adequately treated in Congress's first attempt at a comprehensive industrial relations statute.

The political forces merged with the need to clean up some of the untidiness of the Wagner Act. This combination led in 1947 to the passage of the Taft-Hartley Act.

I. Taft-Hartley Act — *CHANGED THE GOVERNMENT POSITION TO BECOME A NEUTRAL UMPIRE.*

The Taft-Hartley Act is a much larger and more detailed statement about the law governing industrial relations than was the Wagner Act. By the time the Taft-Hartley Act was passed in 1947, many states had already passed laws limiting the Wagner Act. Sixteen states had laws either circumscribing or prohibiting the closed shop—a union contract with an employer in which an individual must be a member of a specific trade union before employment. Eleven states had laws regulating picketing, 12 had prohibitions on secondary boycotts, and 21 states had some laws dealing with strikes.[24]

The Taft-Hartley Act made federal law out of several of these provisions of state law. First, it outlawed the closed shop and gave states the power to outlaw the union shop as well—the so-called right-to-work provision.[25] Second, the act identified certain trade union practices as unfair labor practices.[26]

TAFT HARTLEY

- refusing to engage in collective bargaining
- coercion of union members
- engaging in jurisdictional strikes
- using the secondary boycott
- charging excessive or discriminatory initiation fees
- featherbedding—causing an employer to "pay for services not performed"

(1) OUTLAWED CLOSED SHOP
(2) GAVE STATES THE RIGHT TO PASS ITS OWN LEGISLATION (RIGHT TO WORK LAWS)
(3) IDENTIFIED AS UNFAIR LABOR PRACTICES ON THE PART OF THE UNIONS.

---

[24] Cohen, *Labor Law*, p. 169.

[25] A union shop agreement provides that membership in a specific trade union is not a condition of employment. But once an individual is employed, and passes beyond a probation period, membership in a specific trade union is mandatory.

[26] Cohen, *Labor Law*, p. 174.

(Third,) the Taft-Hartley Act established the "cooling-off period" in which the president has the authority to order union members back to work during a strike for as long as 80 days if the strike is deemed to "imperil the national health or safety."[27]

Much more could be said about the very detailed provisions of the Taft-Hartley Act, but these are the main outlines of its important provisions. More important, perhaps, is the altered social philosophy reflected by this statute compared with the philosophy behind the Wagner Act:

> The outright purpose of the Taft-Hartley Act was to correct certain flaws in the Wagner Act and to give workers, employers, and the general public some protection against an unrestrained exercise of union power. Implicitly, the purpose was to remove some of the legal shores supporting the growth of union power and the spread of collective bargaining.[28]

Although the principles of the Wagner Act that granted workers the right to choose a union and bargain collectively with their employers were reconfirmed in the Taft-Hartley Act, the tone of this statute was clearly different from the Wagner Act. The Wagner Act basically provided the legal structure for the recognition of trade unions and for their right to bargain collectively. It imposed on the employer the obligation to bargain collectively once a union was recognized and not to interfere improperly with the free exercise of choice by workers in selecting a trade union to represent them. Once that was accomplished, the two parties were left to their own devices to work out their problems, as long as they remained under the umbrella of the law.

The Taft-Hartley Act was more intrusive. It specified more precisely how the two parties were supposed to go about reaching a collective bargaining agreement—what they could not do and what they were supposed to do under the law.[29] This meant that more lawyers became involved with the industrial relations process, making the entire mechanism more cumbersome and legalistic.

For example, the NLRB has become intricately involved in deciding how far both the union and employer can go in attempting to influence the outcome of a recognition election in the firm. Where does freedom of speech end and freedom from coercion begin? Can workers use the employer's premises for solicitation? To show how hairs can be split on these issues, employers are free to use their premises for purposes of trying to convince their employees not to join the union, but the union is limited in when and how it can use the employer's premises. In the case of free speech and freedom from coercion under the Wagner Act, the NLRB looked at the total context in which the employer was seeking to prevent a union from gaining

---

[27] Ibid., p. 345.

[28] Ibid., p. 180.

[29] Cox, *National Labor Policy*, p. 16.

recognition. Under the Taft-Hartley Act, only the specific content of employer activity is deemed pertinent in determining whether coercion is present.

Another complicated issue is who has the right to vote during the representational election. If individual workers go on strike to try to influence an employer to recognize a union, do those strikers have the right to vote in a representational election? What if the employer dismisses a worker for cause (according to the employer's interpretation) and replaces that individual with someone who is unsympathetic to unionization? Who has the right to vote in the representational election?[30]

Picketing is another tricky issue. Some forms of picketing are informational, others clearly coercive. Where is the line drawn between freedom of speech and freedom from coercion? Once again these two important principles in the law may be in conflict, and where the line is drawn can heavily influence the outcome of an industrial dispute.

In all these areas, and many more, the lawyers have made our industrial relations system into a legal process and weakened its industrial democracy aspects. It is difficult for ordinary union members to become involved unless they want to devote a substantial part of their lives to a comprehension of the law. This is unfortunate because it has weakened union democracy and has permitted a bureaucratization of the American labor movement that hardly anyone connected with trade unions likes. But all unions have been trapped in this seemingly inevitable development.

The next and latest piece of industrial relations legislation passed by Congress sought to address the issue of union democracy and union corruption. The Landrum-Griffin Act, passed in 1959, came at a time of further union declines in public acceptance and the revelation through congressional hearings of instances of union corruption.

Landrum-Griffin Act   (LABOR/MGMT REPORTING ACT)

The Labor-Management Reporting Act of 1959, better known as the Landrum-Griffin Act (for its two authors), extended some of the restrictions imposed on labor by the Taft-Hartley Act. It also broke new ground, however, by codifying a set of rights that union members could exercise within their union. Rights associated with voting in elections, making nominations for union office, and running for union office

---

[30] The courts and the NLRB have gone back and forth on this question. At present, individual workers on strike who have been dismissed may vote in a representational election if the voting is held within 12 months of the beginning of the strike. The permanent replacements of the strikers are also entitled to vote. One of the problems for labor law reform, which we take up later in this chapter, is that employers can use legal delaying tactics and extend the process for more than 12 months. For a discussion of the rights of strikers to vote, see National Labor Relations Board, *A Guide to Basic Law and Procedures under the National Labor Relations Act*. (Washington: Government Printing Office, 1978), p. 17.

are all stipulated in the act. On the basis of this law, successful challenges against incumbent union officers have been mounted in many unions—most notably the defeat of Tony Boyle of the United Mine Workers by a reform slate headed by Arnold Miller in the early 1970s.

The act requires detailed reporting by union officers of their own activities. Detailed reports must also be filed by all unions concerning internal organizational matters. This provision was designed to prevent abuses of power, conflicts of interest, and union collusion with employers. It should be stressed that instances of union corruption are few in relation to the whole labor movement picture. When instances of abuse do occur, however, they tend to attract headlines because of the Hollywood-like drama that surrounds stories of union corruption.[31]

The Landrum-Griffin Act also stipulates certain general guidelines for union elections—for example, their frequency and the guarantee of secret ballot. When all is said and done, a trade union organization comes under tighter scrutiny than a corporation. It must report more about itself and its officers than a corporation. And the members of a trade union have more formal rights against their officers and organization than do corporate stockholders against those of the corporation.

Labor law has passed through several stages in this century. The Wagner Act sought to protect a union and its members from government obstruction and encouraged the system of trade union organization and collective bargaining. The Taft-Hartley Act sought to protect society from the very influence that unions had acquired in the decade under the Wagner Act. And the Landrum-Griffin Act was born in a climate in which legislators perceived the need to protect union members from their own organization and its officers.[32]

Summing up all this experience, one labor economist, who has studied the interaction between labor law and labor economics, says, "We have the ironical picture . . . of a union movement fostered in strength by the law, now being constrained by the law because it had become too strong."[33]

The labor movement has not been idle on the legislative front during the past decade. Starting in the mid-1970s, it began to launch a new attempt at labor law reform that would redress some of the imbalances it saw in industrial relations law since the passage of the Taft-Hartley and Landrum-Griffin acts. It sought to return industrial relations law to those first principles it had established during the Wagner Act era. The first role of industrial relations law, according to the trade union view, is to encourage collective bargaining by protecting the worker's rights to organize and bargain collectively without undue interference by the employer. And second, labor

---

[31] In a book-length study of the politics behind the passage of the Landrum-Griffin Act, the author concludes that "the most crucial factor in the total picture was the reaction of the public to the issue of labor corruption" (Alan K. McAdams, *Power and Politics in Labor Legislation* [New York: Columbia University Press, 1964], p. 273).

[32] Cohen, *Labor Law*, p. 188.

[33] Ibid., p. 197.

law should, by permitting the use of strikes, boycotts, and picketing, promote the freest exercise of the right to organize and bargain collectively.[34]

Labor Law Reform

Labor law reform legislation was introduced in the Ninety-fifth Congress in 1977. Although the bill passed the House by a substantial margin (257 in favor to 163 opposed), a filibuster in the Senate killed the legislation. That appeared to seal the fate of labor law reform, and no new legislation has since reached the floor of either house of Congress.

The bill called for

- speeding up the process of holding a representational election (under the act, elections had to be held anywhere from 25 to 75 days after the NLRB received an authorized petition for an election);

- "equal access" for the union to solicit members on company property during working hours if the employer had previously exercised its "captive audience" prerogative by using its property to promote opposition to the union;

- expanding the NLRB from five to seven members in order to accelerate the handling of complaints;

- the NLRB to award double back pay to an employee who was illegally fired for union activity;

- the NLRB to halt illegal firings of individuals for their union activity during an organizing drive;

- withholding government contracts for three years from companies with "frequent and flagrant" violations of labor law.[35]

Motivated by the legalisms and delays promoted by corporate lawyers, the labor movement saw this legislation as a means to streamline the process by which unions attain recognition. Union recognition is central to the philosophy of the Wagner Act, from which industrial relations law began. The legislative theory of that mid-1930s legislation was that inhibitions to fair and free election of union representatives caused undue industrial strife, which in turn contributed to interruptions of production. Such

---

[34] Cox, *National Labor Policy*, p. 10.

[35] Congressional Quarterly, *Almanac, 95th Congress*, vol. 33 (Washington: Congressional Quarterly, 1977), pp. 144–46.

interruptions of production caused unemployment and were permitted legislative attention by the interstate commerce clause of the Constitution.[36]

With the Taft-Hartley Act, industrial relations law shifted from the laissez-faire, self-regulation stance of the Wagner Act to a direct intrusion into the collective bargaining process. The legislative purpose of the Wagner Act was to promote the free election of union representatives and to protect that process through law. Once the election took place, however, its attitude was one of laissez-faire—letting the two parties bargain collectively as they saw fit within the broad context of the law. Taft-Hartley defined more closely how the collective bargaining was to occur and how the representational process was to unfold. The lawyers then took over and made industrial relations into a system of incessant legal maneuverings and delays.

This explains labor's rationale for promoting the labor law reform of the late 1970s. It was an effort to return to the legislative principles of the Wagner Act, which was supportive of the right of workers to organize into trade unions of their choice and promoted laissez-faire principles in the realm of collective bargaining.

The legislative effort failed, and labor law now stands on three main pillars: the Wagner, Taft-Hartley, and Landrum-Griffin acts. But structures do not stand well on three pillars, and it is labor's view that a fourth is needed to place industrial relations on a firm foundation.

In a bitter letter to the Business Roundtable after the defeat of labor law reform, Douglas Fraser, former president of the United Auto Workers, put it this way:

> Labor law reform itself would not have organized a single worker. Rather, it would have begun to limit the ability of certain rogue employers to keep workers from choosing democratically to be represented by unions through employer delay and outright violation of existing labor law.[37]

Summary

The history and evolution of industrial relations law mirror public attitudes toward the economic system. Starting with pure laissez-faire doctrine and an absolute definition of property rights, the law has evolved so that it now reflects our commitment to a mixed economy with a healthy tension between private incentives and the public good. No longer do we adhere to an absolute definition of property rights, and the law accepts intrusions into the right of owners to do as they see fit with their property. This intrusion extends to the employment contract and the role of collective organization in the representation of workers.

---

[36] Cox, *National Labor Policy*, chap. 1

[37] Douglas A. Fraser, "Letter to Labor-Management Group," in Aspen Institute for Humanistic Studies, *The Corporation and Society* (New York: Aspen Institute, 1979), p. 502.

Before 1880, however, the courts kept as close to a pure laissez-faire position as possible. Until 1842 unions that sought to influence wages and conditions of work were held to be illegal under the conspiracy doctrine. Between 1842 and 1880 unions per se were not illegal, but any economic actions they took were. After 1880 the courts used injunctions to order unions to cease such specific economic actions as strikes or boycotts.

The first federal legislative attention to trade unions occurred with the passage of the Sherman Antitrust Act. Though not originally intended as an instrument to control labor, the most frequent use of the act was precisely for this purpose. Union activities on the economic front were enjoined under the Sherman Act as a combination in restraint of trade. The Clayton Act of 1914, although intended to correct this application of the Sherman Act, in fact legitimated it.

Not until 1932, with the adoption of the Norris–La Guardia Act, did unions receive some relief from the judicial injunction. This was followed three years later by the adoption of the National Labor Relations Act (the Wagner Act), which turned national policy toward unions 180 degrees. Unions were afforded the right to exist and bargain collectively. A procedure was established whereby recognition of unions was acquired through a democratic voting process. Employers were restrained from interfering with this process except by exercising their right of free speech under the First Amendment. An administrative body with the power of law, the National Labor Relations Board, was created to enforce the act.

Under the Wagner Act labor prospered. But its prosperity was brief. By 1947 a reaction had set in against labor, and the result was adoption of the Taft-Hartley Act, which placed government more in the role of policing labor-management affairs. This act contained certain restrictions on labor's efforts to organize new union members. It relaxed some of the restrictions on employers' tactics in opposing unions. Most important, it made our private industrial relations system into a legal jungle, elevating lawyers and the government from "bit players" to important actors.

In 1959 the last piece of national labor law was adopted—the Landrum-Griffin Act, which defined the rights of union members against their union and gave government the power to police certain internal union practices.

Today neither unions nor employers are terribly pleased with the state of labor law. Unions claim that the democratic process has been so eroded by legalisms that the ordinary worker no longer can play a role in influencing his or her own working life. Employers claim that the law is still slanted toward unions. They tend to seek redress in the courts, which only makes the industrial relations system even more of a legal thicket. Over the next decade, we can expect this tension between the private and the public to erupt again into pressure for labor law reform.

Study Questions

1. What legal doctrine or doctrines were applied to labor organizations in the nineteenth century?

2. What were the first federal statutes that applied to trade unions, and how did these laws modify (if at all) existing common law treatment of labor organizations?

3. How did the National Labor Relations Act (the Wagner Act) reverse previous legal attitudes toward trade unions?

4. How did the Taft-Hartley Act modify (if at all) prevailing legal attitudes toward trade unions?

Further Reading

Cohen, Sanford. *Labor Law*. Columbus, OH: Charles E. Merrill Books, 1964.

Cox, Archibald. *Law and National Labor Policy*. Berkeley, CA: Institute of Industrial Relations, 1960.

Gregory, Charles O., and Harold A. Katz. *Labor and the Law*. 3rd ed. New York: W. W. Norton and Co., 1979.

① U.S (EXCLUSIVE JURISDICTION)
- ONE UNION FOR THAT PARTICULAR PLACE

ENGLAND
- SEVERAL UNIONS IN ONE PLACE

② U.S.
- CRAFT UNION IMPORTANCE

EUROPE
- NO EMPHASIS ON CRAFT UNIONS

③ U.S
- SINGLE COMPANY AGREEMENTS

EUROPE
- SEVERAL COMPANIES MAKE AGREEMENT

④ U.S
- LABOR CONTRACTS ARE COMPLEX AND HAVE DETAILED SPECIFICATIONS AND RESTRICT MGMT. (LEGALLY ENFORCEABLE CONTRACT)
  AUTHORH

- ENGLAND
  NOT A LEGALLY BOUND CONTRACT (GENTLEMAN AGREEMENT)

⑤ U.S
- LOCAL UNIONS ARE MORE COMMON AND DOMINANT AND LEADERS AT THE PLANT LEVEL HAVE MORE POWER

EUROPE
- NGTAS MUCH POWER AT PLANT LEVEL

⑥ U.S.
- OUR GRIEVANCE PROCEDURE IS FAR SUPERIOR

EUROPE
- GRIEVANCE PROCEDURE LACKS ESTABLISHMENT.

⑦ U.S.
- COLLECTIVE BARG. IS LESS POLITICAL

⑧ U.S.
- UNIONS DO NOT BELONG TO A PARTICULAR POLITICAL PARTY RIGID???
- JOIN UNION, JOIN POLITICAL PARTY

⑨ U.S. LIMITED GOVT INFLUENCE on WAGE RATES AND BENEFITS
EUROPE → MORE GOVT INFLUENCE

⑩ U.S. EXTENSIVE LEGAL REGULATION OF EMPLOYER AND UNION TACTICS

22 ■

The Future of Industrial Relations

Crystal ball gazing is a dangerous activity for economists. Someone once said that you should not compare economists to fortune tellers because they give fortune tellers a bad name. What appears to be a crisis today may not be tomorrow. But projecting institutional change into the future is important for the study of labor economics, no matter how chancy it may be.

There are significant changes happening right now in our system of industrial relations. Organized labor's share of the total labor force is declining, and labor is even having a difficult time maintaining its absolute numerical size. This fact fails to reveal some important trends within the segment that is organized, however. The proportion of trade union members who wear a blue collar is declining, and the percentage wearing a white collar is growing. Public employee unionism is the fastest-growing segment of organized labor, just as it is the fastest-growing segment of the labor force. This change in the composition of the unionized sector of the economy has not yet been reflected in the power relations within the national trade union federation, the AFL-CIO, but it will be by the end of this century.

Labor law is once again coming under careful review. The AFL-CIO will continue to press for labor law reform that, in its view, cleans up some of the problems created by the two major pieces of labor legislation of the postwar period—the Taft-Hartley

Act and the Landrum-Griffin Act.[1] On the other side, pressure is mounting for some change in the Davis-Bacon Act, legislation that regulates wages in the construction trades.

A new form of technological change—robotization—has been introduced into the basic manufacturing industries, and this is having a vast effect on unions in the basic industries. Coupled with robotization is a decline in America's international competitiveness in basic manufacturing industries, such as autos and steel. This decline has produced rates of unemployment in those sectors that rival the unemployment of the Great Depression. Collective bargaining has begun to respond to these developments with concession bargaining, more worker participation in decisions (through union participation in management decisions), and productivity agreements.

As unions have become less capable of protecting workers' wages, union members and their leaders have begun investigating how they might use the vast sums of monies in union pension funds for investments that more directly benefit the workers who contribute to the pension funds. More attention is also being given by unions to negotiating agreements that seek to improve the "quality of working life" on the job.

Many of these questions have arisen because the world economy, and the United States' position in it, is different today from the way it was between 1945 and 1970, when the basic postwar labor strategy was framed by unions. Multinational corporations and conglomerate mergers have changed the industrial landscape of the United States. The rise of industrial rivals to the United States has altered our position in the international division of labor. Immigration of labor is as high today as it has been at any time since the great wave of labor migration from Europe between 1870 and the start of World War I.

These issues and others will be examined in this chapter with caution because any attempt at firm predictions is hazardous. The signposts are there, however, and they cry out for interpretation.

Concession Bargaining

In the 1970s the term *"concession bargaining"* did not exist. In the early 1980s it became the centerpiece of major collective bargaining agreements in the basic manufacturing industries in the American economy. In concession bargaining trade unions give up previously negotiated elements of the collective bargaining contract. Wages and fringe benefits, as well as work rules, can be conceded by unions in new negotiations. Sometimes the existing contract is reopened and previously negotiated parts of the agreement are changed. In other instances, previously won gains by labor are omitted from a new contract that is negotiated when the existing contract expires.

---

[1] See Chapter 21.

1982 - Highest Unemploy Rate Since Depression
so Mgmt Has No Choice But to Ask
for Concessions from Workers.

Concession bargaining is occurring in order to save jobs. In the economic climate of the late 1970s and early 1980s, the loss of jobs in the heavily unionized basic manufacturing industries was staggering. To preserve some of these jobs and to promote the future competitiveness of basic industry in the American economy, unions have been willing to concede negotiated wage increases and relax work rules. In a 1982 survey of 400 executives from major companies in the United States, fully one-fourth—what *Business Week* called "a startlingly large proportion"—had negotiated some type of compensation or work rule concession.[2] A total of 50 percent of these executives who bargain with large trade unions had been involved in concession bargaining.

Economic conditions have also changed somewhat the pattern-setting wage process, which used to establish industry-wide wage scales structured around the pattern-setting agreements negotiated in key companies.[3] The *Wall Street Journal* has called this a "fundamental change in labor relations: the unravelling of the industry-wide national contract agreements that have set the pattern for bargaining throughout most of the past three decades. . . . Now, an increasing number of companies and unions . . .are modifying contracts to fit local situations, such as potential plant closings."[4]

A.   The pacesetter in this process of concession bargaining in the private sector was the first agreement negotiated between the United Auto Workers (UAW) and Chrysler Corporation in late 1979. After that agreement two more rounds of concession bargaining occurred between the UAW and Chrysler, the last one in early 1982. For the three sets of bargaining rounds combined, the union gave back slightly more than one billion dollars in previously negotiated wages and fringe benefits, along with changes in work rules that saved Chrysler additional money.[5] In effect, the union members provided Chrysler more than one billion dollars by turning back to the company contractual compensation for that amount. Of course, the reason UAW members agreed to this was to save the company and, more important, their jobs.[6]

The Chrysler concessions were replicated in the normal pattern-setting way at Ford and General Motors. In early 1982 General Motors walked away from the bargaining table with $2.5 billion in labor cost concessions covering the period 1982 through 1984. Ford Motor Company won labor cost savings of about one billion dollars for the same period.[7] Combined, the three giant auto companies received

---

[2] Harris Poll, "A Management Split over Labor Relations," *Business Week*, June 14, 1982, p. 19. The companies referred to in this sentence include those with unions and those without unions.

[3] See Chapter 7.

[4] Robert S. Greenberger, "Economic Gloom Cuts Labor-Union Demands for Big 1982 Contracts," *Wall Street Journal*, Sept. 30, 1981, p. 1.

[5] Warren Brown, "UAW Approves Chrysler Pay Cuts," *Washington Post*, February 3, 1981, p. E1.

[6] These give-backs are not completely free for the company; we will look at the quid pro quo for these arrangements later in this chapter.

[7] Warren Brown, "Nobody Lost When Union, GM Settled," *Washington Post*, March 23, 1982, p. C1. For a general discussion of concession bargaining, see Daniel J. B. Mitchell, "Recent Union Contract Concessions," *Brookings Papers on Economic Activity* 1 (1982), pp. 165–201.

UNIONS USUALLY GET SOMETHING IN RETURN FOR THEIR Concessions

compensation concessions amounting to four and one-half billion dollars for the five-year period from 1979 through 1984.

These dollar figures do not include future changes in work rules—the jealously guarded standards that the UAW has negotiated over the years for health, safety, and the quality of working life in the plant. *Business Week* quoted a GM official as saying these work rules were the "core of the contract." The UAW agreed to language in the contract that work-rule changes would be considered on a plant-by-plant basis to determine "which may be necessary to effectively utilize the services of employees."[8]

The list of other unions in other industries that have followed with concession bargaining of their own reads like a who's who in industrial relations in the United States. Steel, rubber, transport, airlines, meat processing, farm implements—these and other industries have been involved in concession bargaining. The names of the unions are equally impressive: Teamsters, United Rubber Workers, International Association of Machinists, United Steel Workers, and others—all have sat down at the bargaining table and agreed to concession packages. Not since the Great Depression of the 1930s has basic labor been subject to such substantial reductions in the rate of increase in their wages.

Labor leaders are, of course, not delighted with these developments. William Winpisinger, president of the International Association of Machinists, says, "This is the cure that's worse than the disease."[9] In return, the unions have sought concessions of their own that may reshape our entire industrial relations system.

The quid pro quo for wage and work-rule concessions by unions has been a greater say for workers in management decisions. These developments taken together might turn out to be a sideways entry into forms of worker participation in management that have been prevalent in central and northern Europe for several decades.

In return for concessions granted to General Motors, the UAW received commitments from GM for abandonment of decisions to close four plants; a prepaid legal services plan for union members; guaranteed income for workers who are laid off with 10 years or more of employment with the company; a profit-sharing plan; an experimental program in lifetime employment guarantees at four GM plants, patterned after the Japanese model of lifetime employment; and a two-year moratorium on all plant closings within GM.[10] At Chrysler, former UAW president Douglas Fraser became a member of the company's board of directors—a first in the history of industrial relations in the United States.[11] The UAW agreement with Ford contained similar types of provisions for job security, profit sharing, and participation in management decisions.

As in so many areas throughout the history of industrial relations in the postwar

---

[8] "The Work-Rule Changes GM Is Counting On," *Business Week*, April 5, 1982, p. 30.

[9] Robert S. Greenberger, "Economic Gloom," p. 22.

[10] Warren Brown, "Nobody Lost When Union, GM Settled," p. C1.

[11] Robert L. Simison, "Chrysler Lauds Strong Performance of UAW's Fraser as Board Member," *Wall Street Journal*, March 12, 1981, p. 33.

period, the UAW has once again become a trailblazer in using the collective bargaining system as a form of private government to adapt to new economic circumstances. But others have also begun to look at innovative ways to save jobs.[12]

With auto workers giving up pay increases, the UAW wanted to insure, first, that the company would not take the funds saved and invest them in plants outside the United States or in nonunion subcontracting firms. The GM-UAW agreement seeks to prevent these developments by giving the UAW some limited, indirect access to the books and records of GM. This has been a long-standing union goal—to "have a look at the books"—and for the first time this is happening, not just at GM but also at Pan Am, Chrysler, Uniroyal, United Airlines, and the New York Daily News.[13]

Second, UAW members wanted to insure that their wage concessions would result in lower car prices, not in higher profits. GM agreed to permit an independent auditor to look at confidential company data to determine whether the company was passing the cost savings on to consumers or using the compensation concessions to earn higher profits. While implementation was not as speedy and complete as the UAW had hoped, nevertheless the principle of quid-pro-quo bargaining remains important.

Step by step, unions are backing into more involvement in management decisions. Unions have become investors in the companies with whom they negotiate, by virtue of their wage concessions. Now they must behave as investors and seek to protect that investment by involving themselves more in what were previously management decisions.[14] The labor economist Jack Barbash has put the matter as follows:

> Now we're seeing primitive forms of codetermination [the West German system of labor representation on corporate boards], and employee ownership, which used to be only a fad, is being raised by companies that are hardly crackpots, such as in the steel industry.[15]

We should not lose sight of the fact that these developments occurred in the midst of terrible economic adversity; the unemployment rate in the auto industry was running at 25 percent, and similar rates prevailed in other basic manufacturing industries. Concession bargaining and the quid pro quo of more union involvement in the worker's investment may not survive in better economic conditions. Nor should we ignore the fact that many companies may seek to take advantage of the general public impression that concession bargaining is the way out of an economic dilemma. *Business Week* reported one such incident, in which a group of machinists, refusing to be

---

[12] For example, the supermarket chain A & P is experimenting with worker-ownership schemes in its Philadelphia stores (John Hoerr, "When Workers Share the Gains from Givebacks," *Business Week*, June 28, 1982, p. 45). The Rath Packing Company since 1979 has been kept alive through a worker-ownership and -management scheme ("An Acid Test for Worker-Owners," *Business Week*, August 2, 1982, pp. 67 and 70).

[13] "Tasting a New Kind of Power," *Business Week*, February 1, 1982, p. 16

[14] Ibid.

[15] "Moderation's Chance to Survive," *Business Week*, April 19, 1982, p. 126.

swayed by the threat of a plant shutdown if they did not agree to wage concessions, did their own investigation of what had been happening in the plant.

The case involved a plant owned by the multinational conglomerate Gulf and Western. The union found that Gulf and Western had invested only $800,000 in new equipment in this one plant between 1977 and 1981, compared with an investment of over $5 million in the previous five years. And, in 1981, out of total profits of $1.3 billion in this particular manufacturing segment of Gulf and Western, the company had invested only $6 million.[16] Disinvestment and the use of parts of its multinational-conglomerate structure as "cash cows" were the reasons for declining profitability, according to the union in this case, not high wages. Such disputes inevitably occur as more and more companies begin to seek wage and work-rule concessions from unions. Are such concessions justified? Will they restore employment or prevent it from falling further? Unions have been gambling that the answer to both questions is positive.

Company attitudes about concession bargaining have been studied, and we can discern certain trends. A Harris poll conducted in 1982 found that attitudes of cor-porate executives from 400 large companies differed depending on the degree of unionization in their enterprises. Executives of companies with over 70 percent union-ization were not keen on pressing unions for further concession bargaining unless they absolutely had to for the welfare of the company. These were executives dealing with what Harris refers to as "entrenched and sophisticated unions." However, exec-utives in companies with less unionization wanted to press unions for further conces-sions—some to the point of seeking to eliminate unions.[17] The majority of executives surveyed (57 percent) preferred work-rule concessions to wage concessions when pressing unions for relief.[18]

The major reason corporate executives are less enthusiastic about concession bargaining than one might expect is that they do not like the quid-pro-quo arrange-ments. Profit-sharing and stock-ownership plans were not received warmly by the executives surveyed. Only 2 percent favored granting "ironclad employment guaran-tees for the length of the contract," although 42 percent were willing to offer some job security concessions—a key union demand in concession bargaining.[19]

The UAW-Chrysler concession bargaining has established a pattern of sorts for the private sector. Some five years prior to this agreement, however, another precedent-setting agreement had been reached in the public sector between the city of New York and the local branch of the American Federation of State, County and Municipal Employees (AFSCME). The city of New York was facing financial ruin in the mid-1970s, and the commercial banks demanded extreme concessions from the city for a continuation of loans. AFSCME stepped in and used its pension funds to purchase

---

[16] Investment Becomes a Strike Issue," *Business Week*, July 5, 1982, p. 23.

[17] "A Management Split over Labor Relations," *Business Week*, June 14, 1982, p. 19.

[18] "Concessionary Bargaining: Will the New Cooperation Last?" *Business Week*, June 14, 1982, p. 66.

[19] "A Management Split over Labor Relations," p. 19.

[handwritten margin note: IF A BENEFIT COMES FREE OF COST, THEN IT IS VULNERABLE TO MISUSE. EX: MEDICAL BENEFITS THAT REQUIRE NO CONTRIBUTION ON THE PART OF THE EMPLOYEE.]

city bonds, which the commercial sector would not touch except under the tough conditions they wished to impose on the city.

In addition to this new use of union pension funds, which we take up later in this chapter, the union agreed to a series of concessions in return for job guarantees and an orderly reduction of the city work force. In late 1974 AFSCME agreed to various work-rule changes; in 1975 it agreed to defer all or part of a scheduled 6 percent wage increase. Other concessions were granted during the 1976–1978 period, relating to cost-of-living adjustments, minimum salaries for new employees, and reduced pension benefits. Total employment declined by nearly 25 percent over this period.[20]

Concession bargaining as a dominant aspect of labor relations in the early 1980s was imposed on collective bargaining by a steep recession and relatively long-term economic stagnation in the American economy. Moreover, American industry no longer enjoys the competitive position it once did in the world economy. Our economy's role in the world economy is changing dramatically, and this is adding to our internal economic problems. In the face of these trends, we can expect less aggressive bargaining postures on the part of labor for the foreseeable future, and the continuation of quid-pro-quo arrangements between labor and management as an attempt to adapt to these new economic circumstances.

Robotization

Declining demand in the basic manufacturing industries in the United States is on a collision course with another potential employment-reducing factor: robotization. Technological change has always caused a dilemma for industrial societies. On the one hand, technological change is the lifeblood of economic growth. On the other hand, it can displace workers and cause unemployment if the growth it causes in aggregate demand is not sufficient to absorb those workers displaced by it. Moreover, temporary structural problems can emerge, as the workers displaced by the new technology lack the requisite skills and abilities to staff the new jobs.

Three decades ago we were concerned about automation—the application of computer control techniques to manufacturing. That scare did not materialize, and the much-heralded automation of the American factory did not take hold. Today the concern is about a new technology: robots. Industrial robots are machines that can do jobs previously performed by humans. Aided by more sophisticated and cost-effective computer processes, these machines—with their mechanical arms—can be most effectively used in assembly work, taking parts previously fabricated and putting

---

[20] These developments are described in Carol O'Cleireacain, "The Unions' Economic Demands—the Case for Labor," *City Almanac* 16, no. 2 (August 1981), p. 2.

■ BENEFITS OF ROBOTS : DECREASED CHANCE OF DEFECTIONS
CAN WORK AROUND THE CLOCK
NO OPINIONS.

them together. They take the place of workers on an assembly line—the traditional system of mass production introduced in the early part of this century.

Just as the assembly line was first introduced in the manufacture of autos by Henry Ford, the most extensive use of robots today is also in the auto industry. Producing a car has been, up to the present, a labor-intensive production process. Parts are made either in the factories of the big companies or in subcontracting plants in the U.S. or in other countries. They are collected in large assembly plants and put together. Robots are now being introduced to do this assembly work.

Robotization is the term used to describe what is happening in assembly factories. It is difficult at this juncture to separate hard fact and concrete analysis from what might turn out to be social science fiction. *Business Week* has predicted that 45 percent of all jobs in the American economy might be affected by robots before the year 2000. The Japanese government took out a 28-page advertising supplement in *Business Week* to promote its production of robots and automated office equipment. "U.S. companies are on the verge of achieving a dream: manufacturing enterprises where push-button factories and executive suites, no matter how physically remote, become parts of the same integrated, computerized entity."[21] Will what *Business Week* called the "workerless factory" exist by the year 2000, or is this more science fiction than social science?

Trade union leaders do not have the luxury of speculating about this. They are placed under tremendous pressure by their members to respond. Plans are already afoot to provide funds for the training of displaced workers in auto factories, where robots are making their first impact. General Motors provided $120 million and Ford $25 million in the early 1980s for training programs under agreement with the UAW.[22]

Union leaders are trying to find ways to organize and include white-collar employees in their membership as more employees move from direct, blue-collar production work to indirect, white-collar production control work.[23] The UAW estimates that its auto industry membership will decline to about eight hundred thousand members from the present level of one million during the 1990s, assuming slight growth in auto output over this period.[24]

Major industrial unions are beginning to discuss possible mergers to counter this trend toward declining membership, to challenge more effectively the multinational-conglomerate structure of American industry, and to join forces in adapting to the introduction to robotization.[25]

U.S. → AUTO INDUSTRY LEADS ROBOTIZATION

[21] "The Speedup in Automation," *Business Week*, August 3, 1981, p. 58.

[22] "Retraining Displaced Workers: Too Little, Too Late?" *Business Week*, July 19, 1982, p. 178.

[23] NLRB rulings have tended to prohibit a manufacturing-based union from including white-collar workers in the same contract, although the union may organize such workers into a separate bargaining unit.

[24] "Speedup in Automation," p. 62.

[25] A merger of the United Auto Workers and the International Association of Machinists or the United Rubber Workers, or a merger of all three, is most frequently rumored. See "UAW May Discuss Combining with URW As It Also Explores Machinists Merger," *Wall Street Journal*, October 22, 1980, p. 5.

Robotization will become a major issue in collective bargaining and industrial relations over the next decade. Once again, strains will be placed on the innovative system of private government that took hold in this century. How it will adapt, through productivity agreements (which involve sharing the fruits of technology), retraining adaptations, and other structural changes, should be watched carefully as industrial relations responds to a new challenge.

 ## Unions and Investments of Pension Funds

Vast sums of money have been accumulated in trade union pension funds. Although workers contribute to these funds, they have little say over what investment will be made out of the funds, and in many instances investments are made that are antithetical to the workers' interests. For example, the investment houses or banks that manage the pension funds make loans to support investments by multinational corporations in foreign countries, which compete with employment in the United States. Or loans are made from union pension funds to companies that invest the money in new plants and equipment in the South, which has a history of strong opposition to unions. The irony of huge sums of money from union members' paychecks being used to make investments outside the United States, or in the anti-union Sunbelt, has not escaped some union leaders. And they have begun to press for changes in the law and changes in the way pension funds are managed so that this contradiction can be erased.

The sums of money involved in union pension funds are staggering. It is estimated that in 1982 there was over $650 billion in pension assets, up from $500 billion in 1978.[26] About 40 percent of this total came from the unionized sector. According to two authors who studied this problem in 1978,

> Over $200 billion in pension fund capital comes from combined deferred savings of 19 million union members and the public employee funds of the sixteen states that make up the northeast/midwest corridor. . . . The banks, in turn, have used these capital assets to shift jobs and production to the Sunbelt and overseas, thus crippling organized labor and the northern economies of the United States.[27]

The problem arises because of a conflict between the goals of the managers of the pension funds—typically large New York banks and investment houses—and the interests of the individuals who contribute to the pension funds. The pension fund manager insists on a conservative financial strategy, which best protects the principal of the contributors to the funds. This requires finding investments that have the

---

[26] "Targeting Pension Investments," *Business Week*, September 7, 1981, p. 87.

[27] Jeremy Rifkin and Randy Barber, *The North Will Rise Again: Pensions, Politics and Power in the 1980s* (Boston: Beacon Press, 1978), pp. 10–11.

■

CONFLICT OF GOALS BETWEEN PAYEES AND MANAGERS OF THE FUND

greatest probability of successful return and the least risk. Such investment strategies, however, may not be in the interest of the worker who contributes to the funds if they reduce the capital base of the industry in which he or she is employed and the money is invested either in nonunion domestic plants or in other countries. And in the decade of the 1970s, the typical rate of return on union pension funds was only around 4 percent.

Aside from the precedent of pension funds being managed by just a few banks and investments houses in the United States, unions face two specific legal obstacles. First, under the 1947 Taft-Hartley Act, no union may manage its pension fund by itself; at best, it can aspire to coadministration with management. According to an AFL-CIO study, in 1979 there was $228 billion held in pension funds in the private sector, of which about 40 percent was coadministered.[28] Second, the 1974 Employment Retirement Income Security Act (ERISA) stipulates that pension funds must be invested in a "prudent" manner. This has been interpreted to mean low-return, low-risk investments in blue-chip corporations, commercial bank paper, and government securities.

Outside the private sector, union members have contributed vast sums of money to public employee pension funds. Public employee pension funds of state and local employees more typically have union participation in their administration. The federal pension system does not. In 1984, there was $485 billion in public employee pension funds—$355 billion at the state and local level and $130 billion at the federal level.[29]

Unions have responded to the pension fund issue in a variety of ways. The agreement between the UAW and Chrysler provided for 10 percent of new pension fund contributions to be set aside for investments in the communities in which UAW members reside and for support of mortgages for UAW members. The New York City Retirement Systems bought bonds from the city when New York faced a financial crisis in the mid-1970s.[30] The AFL-CIO report recommended that pension funds be used to "increase employment through reindustrialization" and to promote housing and health care, that workers be given more influence over the investments of pension funds, and that pension funds be excluded from investment in companies "whose policies are hostile to workers' rights."[31]

Similar problems have been met in Europe with even greater ingenuity. In Sweden the so-called Meidner Plan called for the establishment of "wage-earner funds," which would become the largest single investment source in Sweden. This plan made use of Sweden's public retirement system—similar to our social security system—and man-

[28] See Carol O'Cleireacain, "Getting Serious about Pension Funds," *Working Papers*, July–August 1981, pp. 17 and 20; and AFL-CIO, *Investment of Union Pension Funds* (Washington: AFL-CIO, 1980), pp. 1–2.

[29] U.S. Department of Commerce, *Statistical Abstract of the United States, 1986* (Washington: Government Printing Office), p. 369.

[30] O'Cleireacain, "Getting Serious about Pension Funds," p. 20.

[31] AFL-CIO, *Investment of Union Pension Funds*, p. iii.

(1) *PENSION FUND INSURANCE FOR THE CASE OF BANKRUPTCY*

(2) *INFLATION ERODES PENSION POTENCY.*
  * *MOST PENSION PLAN DO NOT HAVE COLAS BUILT IN. (EMPLOYERS RESIST THESE COLAS)*

PUBLIC POLICY → REMEDY for INFLATIONARY DETERIORATION

dated the use of these funds for investments that would benefit the workers who directly contributed to the funds.[32] Not only would the investments be redirected, but they would also be used to move toward direct workers' ownership through the use of the wage-earner funds to buy stock in Swedish companies. Very controversial, the Meidner Plan has not been fully implemented in Sweden. But it remains the centerpiece of policy in the Swedish Social Democratic Party, and it is the major social reform goal of their trade union movement.

Any abrupt, dramatic, or immediate change in the management and use of union pension funds is probably not in the cards. But there is now a consciousness that will slowly cause changes in how union pension funds make investments. This evolutionary process, which should be noticeable in the remaining years of the century, will involve unions more intensively in financial decisions that, until now, have been made by union- and company-designated investment managers. This development will coincide with the one discussed earlier in this chapter, in connection with concession bargaining—the pushing of labor into more participation in work-place decisions and in investment policy.

At the root of the problem concerning pension funds is a discordance between labor and capital. Capital is international in its scope whereas labor tends to be confined within national boundaries. Capital can move around the world very quickly, today more quickly than ever through computers and other means of instantaneous communication. Labor is not as mobile.

Corporate forms have grown to reflect this phenomenon. The multinational corporation is a reflection of capital's international scope. The conglomerate form of corporate organization is a reflection of the increasing tendency for the modern corporation to be financially based and not rooted in the production of a particular product.

All these institutional changes place labor at a bargaining disadvantage. Labor is based in the nation and rooted in production.[33] The entire history of unionization and collective bargaining was founded on these premises. Now that labor is dealing with corporations that have no specific production base in an international economic setting, it finds itself lacking the institutional forms to confront the major new sources of corporate power. The issue over pension funds is symbolic of this deeper structural problem. Labor is groping for ways to come to terms with its new institutional environment, and this is an issue worthy of attention in the years to come.

The chief economist for District 37 (the New York City district) of the American Federation of State, County and Municipal Employees states the problem this way: "American workers already own, but do not control, a significant amount of capital:

---

[32] Rolf Eidem and Bernt Ohman, "Economic Democracy through Wage-Earner Funds," (Stockholm: Arbetslivscentrum, n.d.).

[33] These issues are examined in more detail in Howard M. Wachtel, *The Money Mandarins. The Making of a New Supranational Economic Order* (New York: Pantheon Books, 1986).

namely their pension funds."[34] Whether ownership and control of pension fund capital will begin to converge through the remainder of this century revolves around how unions begin to use the pension funds of their members.

[handwritten: ADVANTAGES OF PUBLIC UNIONIZATION FIRM]
[handwritten: 1. MORE STABLE JOBS]

Public Employee Unionization

[handwritten: DISADVANTAGE]
[handwritten: 1. WAGES LAG BEHIND PRIVATE SECTOR]

Albert Einstein, in joining the American Federation of Teachers, wrote, "I consider it important, indeed urgently necessary, for intellectual workers to get together, both to protect their own economic status and also, generally speaking, to secure their influence in the political field." The American Federation of Teachers is a public employee union, and Einstein, the great physicist of this century, was stating the case both for his joining the union and for public employee unionism. Since the end of World War II, public employee unionism has grown more rapidly than has unionism in any other sector of the economy. Not only are many teachers now unionized, but fire fighters, police, postal workers, sanitation workers, federal government employees, and employees of states, counties, and cities all have labor unions. *[handwritten: MANY AT LOCAL LEVEL]*

Unionization of public employees has grown in public acceptance. Laws now exist in most states and in the federal government to provide for public employee unionism. However, the right of public employees to strike is very controversial, and settlement of labor disputes is an issue in the public sector. President Franklin D. Roosevelt, himself a supporter of the right of workers to form unions, said of public employee strikes,

> A strike of public employees manifests nothing less than an intent . . . to prevent or obstruct the operations of government until their demands are satisfied. Such action looking towards the paralysis of government by those who have sworn to support it is unthinkable and intolerable.[35]

A statement such as this could have been made by President Ronald Reagan in 1981 when he fired striking air traffic controllers, an action that ultimately led to the demise of the Professional Air Traffic Controllers Organization (PATCO), the controllers' union.

Alongside the two issues of the right of public employees to form unions and the method of dispute settlement, we will also examine in this section some of the new problems confronted by public employees in an economic and political climate

---

[34] Carol O'Cleireacain, "Toward Democratic Control of Capital Formation in the United States: The Role of Pension Funds," in Nancy Leiber, ed., *Eurosocialism and America: Political Economy for the 1980s* (Philadelphia: Temple University Press, 1980), p. 47.

[35] Roosevelt made this statement in 1937. Quoted in Derek C. Bok and John T. Dunlop, *Labor and the American Community* (New York: Simon and Schuster, 1970), p. 331.

that is not as favorable as it was between 1945 and 1975. Public employees are blamed today for many of the ills of society. Employment in the public sector is not growing as rapidly as it once did. Government as a means toward solutions of our economic and social problems no longer is viewed the way it was in the 1960s. Tax revolts and spending limitations in states, counties, and municipalities have captured center stage. These strains on public employees are producing a form of concession bargaining in which public employees and government officials are under increasing pressure to produce results for the constituencies they serve. We will return to these issues, but first let us look at some of the facts and figures surrounding public employment and public employee unionism.

Between 1950 and 1984 public employment grew in the United States from just over 6 million to slightly over 16 million. During this 35-year period public employment increased from about 11 percent of all employment in the economy to nearly 16 percent. These figures are presented in Table 22-1. Contrary to popular belief, the fastest growth in public employment was in state and local government; federal government grew much more slowly. In 1950 federal government employment accounted for one-third of all public employment; by 1984 it had fallen to around 18 percent. From two-thirds of the public employment in 1950, state and local government employment increased to 82 percent of all public employment in 1984. In 1984 there were 2.9 million federal employees (up from 2.1 million in 1950) and 13.4 million state and local government employees (up from 4.2 million in 1950).[36] In sum, the vast growth in public employment occurred at the state and local levels in the period between 1950 and 1984, and that is where most of the new unionization has occurred.

The major public employee occupations and the unions they belong to are shown in Table 22-2. The three largest federal employee unions are the American Federation of Government Employees (AFGE) and the two postal unions. The largest of all public employee unions is the American Federation of State, County and Municipal Employees (AFSCME), whose membership was close to 1.1 million in 1980—larger than the three biggest federal employee unions combined. The growth of AFSCME has been tremendous—from 364,000 members in 1968 to 1.1 million in 1980, the last year for which reliable data is available. The other rapidly growing public employee union is the American Federation of Teachers (AFT), which went from 165,000 members in 1968 to 502,000 in 1980. The growth of these two public employee unions offset declines in membership in manufacturing unions during this period.[37]

In 1978 there were over 3 million government workers who belonged to unions

---

[36] U.S. Department of Commerce, *Statistical Abstract of the United States, 1981* (Washington: Government Printing Office), p. 306; and *Statistical Abstract of the United States, 1986*, p. 294.

[37] Excellent histories, along with contemporary problems, of the postal workers and teachers are contained in J. Joseph Loewenberg, "U.S. Postal Service," in Gerald G. Somers, ed., *Collective Bargaining: Contemporary American Experience* (Madison, WI: Industrial Relations Research Association, 1980), chap. 9; and Robert E. Doherty, "Public Education," ibid., chap. 10. For a history and analysis of AFSCME, see Michael H. Moskow et al., *Collective Bargaining in Public Employment* (New York: Random House, 1970), chap. 3.

Table 22-1 Public Employment, Selected Years, 1950–1984

	1950	1955	1960	1965	1970	1975	1980	1984
Total civilian employment[a]	58.9	62.2	65.8	71.1	78.6	84.8	97.3	105.0
Total government employment[a]	6.4	7.4	8.8	10.5	13.0	14.9	16.2	16.4
Government employment as percentage of total civilian employment	10.9%	11.9%	13.4%	14.8%	16.5%	17.6%	16.6%	15.6%
Percentage distribution of government employment:								
Federal	33.1%	32.0%	27.4%	24.4%	22.1%	18.9%	17.9%	17.9%
State	16.5	16.8	17.3	19.2	21.2	22.3	23.1	23.8
Local	50.4	51.2	55.3	56.4	56.7	58.8	59.0	58.4

[a]In millions.
Source: U.S. Department of Commerce, *Statistical Abstract of the United States, 1981* (Washington: Government Printing Office), pp. 306 and 379; and *Statistical Abstract of the United States, 1986*, pp. 294 and 390.

½ FEDERAL EMPLOYEES ARE UNIONIZED.

⅕ STATE → LOCAL

½

affiliated with the AFL-CIO.[38] About 48 percent of all federal government employees and 17.5 percent of all state and local government employees belonged to unions affiliated with the AFL-CIO. Federal government unionization remained roughly constant during the decade of the 1970s, but state and local unionization increased from 9.3 percent in 1970 to 17.5 percent in 1978.[39] As of 1978, there were close to

FEDERAL UNIONIZATION — CONSTANT   STATE → LOCAL — INCREASE

Table 22-2   Major Public Employee Unions, 1968–1980, Selected Years (in Thousands)[a]

Union	1964	1968	1972	1976	1980
Federal government employees:					
American Federation of Government Employees (AFGE)	200	295	293	260	255
American Postal Workers Union[b]	—	—	239	252	251
Letter Carriers	190	210	220	227	230
State and local government employees:					
American Federation of State, County and Municipal Employees (AFSCME)	281	364	529	750	1,098
Firefighters[c]	115	133	160	174	178
Transit workers[c]	135	134	130	150	162
American Federation of Teachers[d]	125	165	249	446	502

[a]Since 1980 the federal government has ceased collecting data on union membership. Although statistics exist for union membership since 1980, they are not comparable to previous years and are not reliable estimates of union membership.
[b]Formed in 1971 as a merger of postal clerks' union and four other postal workers' unions.
[c]Various local unions—no major national union.
[d]Many teachers belong to the National Education Association (NEA), which engages in collective bargaining as does a union. Technically, however, the NEA is a "bargaining association" and is not included in these data on labor unions. If the NEA were added to American Federation of Teachers members, the number of public school teachers covered by collective bargaining agreements would almost double.
Sources: U.S. Department of Commerce, *Statistical Abstract of the United States, 1981* (Washington: Government Printing Office), p. 411; *Statistical Abstract of the United States, 1969*, p. 237.

[38] Problems arise in any classification of public employee unions. First, there are unions affiliated with the AFL-CIO, and there are a few that are not affiliated. Second, there are employee professional associations that engage in collective bargaining but are not strictly trade unions. These associations—such as the National Education Association—are not affiliated with the AFL-CIO. (The statistics discussed here are taken from various editions of the *Statistical Abstract of the United States*.) There are about 3 million public employees who either belong to unions not affiliated with the AFL-CIO or are members of employee associations. In total in 1978, there were close to 6.1 million members of unions and associations that engaged in collective bargaining—about half affiliated with the AFL-CIO.

[39] In 1978 about 36 percent of all state and local government employees belonged to organizations that engaged in collective bargaining, including both unions and professional associations.

1.4 million federal government union members and 2.2 million state and local union members who belonged to unions, either affiliated with or independent of the AFL-CIO.

Statutes concerning the rights of public employees to belong to unions vary among the states. Federal government employees were granted the right to belong to unions under Executive Order 10988, issued by President Kennedy in January 1962. Federal employee unions may not strike and may not engage in bargaining over compensation. Eleven states have no statutes governing public employees. Three states explicitly prohibit public employees from belonging to unions. The remaining 36 states and the District of Columbia have laws that permit state and local government employees to belong to unions.[40]

The most controversial issue in public employee unionism is the right to strike. Nine states grant public employees a limited right to strike. Virtually all the states that have laws governing public employees provide for *impasse procedures*—the settling of disputes that cannot be resolved at the collective bargaining table.

Impasse procedures can involve fact finding by an outside consultant, mediation of disputes, and voluntary or compulsory arbitration. Some states that grant a limited right to strike limit such strikes to specific unions or to employees who do not perform essential tasks. In other states there are special provisions permitting strikes of teachers only. Some laws permit a strike only after the impasse procedures have been exhausted or if the union can show that the impasse procedure was not used in good faith by the employer. Some states permit strikes for nonessential employees at the local level while prohibiting them for state employees. The laws governing strikes are as varied as are the states themselves.[41]

While most states have laws prohibiting strikes of public employees, strikes do occur. Laws never successfully regulate behavior when individuals find no reason for following the laws. Even before the modern period there were strikes of public employees. The oldest on record occurred at the Philadelphia navy yard in 1836 over the issue of the 10-hour work day. In 1911 there was a strike at the Watertown Arsenal over the introduction of techniques of scientific management. In 1919 Calvin Coolidge, then governor of Massachusetts, started on a path toward the presidency by using the National Guard to suppress a strike among policemen in Boston.[42]

In the 1980s the growth of government appears to be slowing down. Public attitudes toward taxes and the public sector have shifted from what they were in the 1960s and 1970s. No doubt this will have an adverse impact on public employee unionism, and its rate of growth should be slower in the 1980s. On the other hand, with a more restricted public sector, the financial rewards of public employment will

---

[40] The various state laws governing public employee unionism are presented in U.S. Department of Labor, *Summary of Public Sector Labor Relations Policies* (Washington: Government Printing Office, 1979).

[41] Ibid.

[42] For a discussion of these strikes, see Bok and Dunlop, *Labor and the American Community*, p. 331.

become skimpier. This should produce greater militancy and may increase union organization in sectors that so far have not been highly unionized, for example, among teachers in state colleges and universities.

Past studies of the influence of public employee unions on wages have been mixed. Some have found a significant effect; others have not.[43] In the words of one researcher, who surveyed the existing literature on public employee union results, "There does not appear to be justification for the viewpoint that unionization must inevitably lead to a looted treasury."[44]

For the future, prospects are even dimmer that public employee unions will have a significant effect on wages. Although the elasticity of demand for public employees tends to be low, political forces now militate against rapid increases in public employee compensation.

The Davis-Bacon Act

So far in this chapter we have examined important industrial relations issues in the basic manufacturing industries and in the public sector. If we add to this the construction sector of the economy, the essential structure of employment in the postwar American economy is covered. The major public policy issue in industrial relations in the construction trades concerns the Davis-Bacon Act.

Under the Davis-Bacon Act, first passed in 1931, workers employed on federal construction projects valued at more than $2,000 must be paid "prevailing wages." Prevailing wages are determined by the Secretary of Labor; the term has come to mean the wages paid at the high end of construction union pay scales in a particular local labor market. Under Davis-Bacon all federal contractors, unionized or not, are required to pay these wage rates.[45]

Over the years the Davis-Bacon Act has taken a barrage of criticism, and virtually every president, whether Democrat or Republican, has vowed to change it when he first entered office. But the act remains in place a half century after it was passed by Congress. Somehow presidential administrations tend to retreat from a big fight over Davis-Bacon. During the Reagan administration's early days, Congress pushed to repeal Davis-Bacon and let the free market set wage rates for construction labor. The Reagan administration sought administrative changes in the operation of the act rather

---

[43] Daniel J. B. Mitchell, "The Impact of Collective Bargaining on Compensation in the Public Sector," in Benjamin Aaron et al., *Public Sector Bargaining* (Washington: Bureau of National Affairs, 1979), pp. 140–41.

[44] Ibid., p. 141.

[45] C. Arthur Williams, John G. Turnbull, and Earl F. Cheit, *Economic and Social Security*, 5th ed. (New York: John Wiley and Sons, 1982), p. 588.

than outright repeal.[46] These administrative changes revolved around the formula for computing "prevailing wages" in a local labor market. Instead of the so-called 30 percent rule—the Department of Labor previously used the pay for the highest 30 percent of construction workers—the Reagan administration used a weighted average of all wages for a particular trade in a local labor market.[47]

Paradoxically, if the Davis-Bacon Act were repealed, there would probably be a growth in unionization in the construction trades. If workers receive the benefits of union wage rates without belonging to a union, there is little incentive for them to form or join a union. The Davis-Bacon Act has had the effect of imposing higher wage rates in the nonunion construction trades than would have otherwise prevailed. Therefore, no incentive has existed to form unions in the South and Southwest, where unionization is sparse. If the act were repealed and wages were lower because they were not protected under Davis-Bacon, then the pressure for more unionization in construction would increase substantially. The opponents of Davis-Bacon from right-to-work states do not realize what the impact of its repeal would mean for the growth of unionization.

The Davis-Bacon Act remains controversial and over the next several years will probably undergo some administrative changes that will result in lower pay rates for nonunion construction labor. If this happens, look for growth in unionization in the construction trades, as nonunion workers begin to look toward unionization rather than the federal government for protection of their pay scales.

Industrial Relations in the 1980s

In no decade since the 1930s have industrial relations changed as dramatically as they did in the 1980s. Driven by structural changes in the U.S. economy and in the world economy, some of the largest unions in the country saw their membership base collapse. Membership in the United Steel Workers, for example stood at 220,000 in 1985, down from 700,000 a decade earlier; auto-worker membership fell by 18 percent from 1979 to 1985.[48] Placed on the defensive, unions have made concessions not only in the wage scales they have accepted—as pointed out previously in this chapter—but in the structure of the collective bargaining agreement itself. Two-tier wage systems, in which workers entering employment for the first time receive lower pay scales, and the breakdown of industry-wide bargaining in such industries as steel

---

[46] Robert S. Greenberger, "Davis-Bacon Pay Law May Face Big Changes despite Union Support," *Wall Street Journal*, May 12, 1981, p. 1.

[47] Al Kamen, "Reagan Changes in Davis-Bacon Upheld," *Washington Post*, July 6, 1983, p. C7.

[48] John Bussey, "Uncertainty on Strategy Confronts UAW," *Wall Street Journal*, May 30, 1986, p. 6; and "Industry Recasting: LTV's Filing for Bankruptcy May Lead Competitors to Consider Similar Action," *Wall Street Journal*, July 18, 1986, p. 9.

and truck transport are but two of the historical forms of collective bargaining that have been altered during the economic upheavals of the 1980s.

The AFL-CIO has attempted to respond to the challenges facing it by a re-thinking of the nature of work in the late twentieth century and the role of unions in that new character of work. The federation has inaugurated a new and bold program of affiliate membership where an individual employee outside of any collective bargaining situation can join the federation or one of its affiliates and receive some benefits which employees receive who are covered by collective bargaining agreements. Health care, consumer credit, and a retirement scheme are several of the benefits individual employees can receive as affiliate members. The AFL-CIO hopes that, by providing such services to workers not covered by collective bargaining agreements, their ability to organize these individuals during an organizing drive will be improved. Moreover, they also hope that the image of unionism can be dramatically changed by modernizing the approach unions take to unorganized workers.

Whether this effort will actually increase the AFL-CIO membership and the number of new sectors it can organize or whether this will just become another version of a financial services operation may determine the future of industrial relations in the United States.

Summary

Not since the Great Depression has the American labor movement been confronted with such challenges as those that are now reshaping its collective bargaining strategy, with ramifications for our system of industrial relations. The loss of jobs to foreign competition in the basic manufacturing industries has eroded further the employment base of the traditionally large industrial unions. Large-scale unemployment has forced these unions to engage in concession bargaining. The introduction of robots has produced a technological transformation of the workplace that has cost unions more jobs and forced them to examine productivity agreements through the collective bargaining process.

When granting concessions to companies, the industrial unions have sought concessions in return. These involve job security and more worker and union participation in what were previously managerial decisions. Forms of profit sharing and productivity sharing have been sought by unions as quid pro quo for their own concessions. More say over how pension monies will be invested is another issue that unions have been pursuing.

While the employment base in the basic manufacturing industries has been shrinking, the reverse has been occurring until recently in public employment. Government employment, particularly at the state and local levels, was the fastest growing segment of the labor force during the 1970s. And public employee unionism has grown more rapidly than any segment of the American labor movement. In fact, the growth in public employee unionism has nearly offset the decline in industrial union membership.

Our laws and traditions do not readily accommodate unionization among public employees or collective bargaining between public employees and the government. Particularly when impasses occur at the collective bargaining table, our institutions are not very adaptable to the possibility of a public employee strike. Laws have only begun to address these questions, and public attitudes probably lag behind the legal system in terms of acceptability of public employee unionism.

The old AFL construction trade unions face a challenge in coming to terms with the new political reality concerning the Davis-Bacon Act, which has been a principal source of protection of pay scales in the construction trades for the past half century. The unions do not realize that this act may be an impediment to further unionization in the construction trades and that its repeal or modification may unleash tremendous pressures for more unionization in the construction sector.

These issues and others will dominate the industrial relations landscape for the remainder of this century. How these problems are resolved will tell us whether our system of industrial relations is sufficiently adaptable to accommodate new challenges.

Study Questions

1. What economic factors have forced trade unions into concession bargaining? Define concession bargaining, and explain what labor hopes to achieve with concession bargaining.

2. Discuss the relationship between technological change and its impact on industrial relations.

3. "For any mature industrial economy, robotization is an absolute necessity and will increase, not decrease, employment possibilities." Do you agree with this statement? Explain.

4. Workers contribute substantial sums of money to union pension funds, but unions have only minority influence over the use of funds. What is the economic rationale (if any) for this?

5. With blue-collar employment declining and service-providing sectors of the economy growing, what is the future of organized labor in the United States?

Further Reading

Aaron, Benjamin, et al. *Public Sector Bargaining*. Washington: Bureau of National Affairs, 1979.

"Concessionary Bargaining: Will the New Cooperation Last?" *Business Week*. June 14, 1982, pp. 66–81.

Mitchell, Daniel J. B. "Recent Union Contract Concessions." *Brookings Papers on Economic Activity* 1 (1982), pp. 165–201.

"Robots Join the Labor Force." *Business Week*. June 9, 1980, pp. 62–84.

Part

IV

Labor and Public Policy

23
■

Minimum Wages

A national minimum wage that passed the constitutional test was first enacted by Congress in 1938 as part of the Fair Labor Standards Act. The law provides that employers covered by the act must pay at least a minimum wage to their employees. Today that minimum is set at $3.35 per hour.

Never immune from controversy, the minimum wage law today stands at the center of the debate over the high rates of unemployment for youth, particularly black youth. A full page ad in the September 13, 1979, *Wall Street Journal,* based on a study by Walter Williams, an economist and critic of the minimum wage law, was headlined "Minimum Wage, Maximum Folly." Williams is quoted in the ad as saying that the rise in black youth unemployment rates from 9.4 percent in 1948 to almost 40 percent in 1979 "lies in the limitation of the law itself." He goes on:

> By increasing the minimum wage, Congress has caused a significant loss in job opportunities for young blacks. When employers are required to pay a minimum labor *price* of $2.90 an hour, they have no economic incentive to hire workers whose labor *value,* in the production of goods or delivery of services, may be only $2.00 an hour. (Emphasis in original.)

On the other side of the argument, a labor-supported group called the National Committee for Full Employment responds by saying that "the minimum wage is not a major cause of youth unemployment. Other factors have caused high youth unemployment, including the maturation of the baby boom generation, and age and race discrimination." As for Williams's proposal for a lower youth minimum wage, the National Committee for Full Employment says, "Demographically, now is not the time for a youth subminimum. During the 1980s, there will be a significant decline in the youth population, which will result in a decline in youth unemployment." The trade union position, according to the newsletter of the National Committee for Full Employment, is that a youth subminimum would set a "dangerous precedent . . . because it violates the principle of equal pay for equal work."[1]

Which view is more accurate? Does the minimum wage increase rates of unemployment in the labor force generally and among youth particularly? These are two of the issues considered in this chapter, which begins with some background on how the minimum wage law operates and follows with analyses of the impact of minimum wage laws on the economy.

Minimum Wage Laws in the United States

The first minimum wage laws were enacted by individual states in 1912 and 1913 and applied exclusively to women and children. By 1923, 17 states had some type of law setting the minimum wage an employer had to pay his female and minor employees. In that year the Supreme Court ruled in a case involving the District of Columbia (*Adkins* v. *Children's Hospital*) that the minimum wage law was unconstitutional. No further legislative regulation of minimum wages was successfully enacted by the states until the Great Depression rekindled interest in a national minimum wage law.[2]

The National Industrial Recovery Act (NIRA), the centerpiece of the "first" New Deal, was enacted in 1933, and it contained a provision establishing a national minimum wage. In 1935 the Supreme Court struck down this law, thereby eliminating the national minimum wage. Legal arguments in support of a minimum wage were based on the government's right to enact legislation that protected the living standards and working conditions of labor. Opposed to this legal proposition was one that emphasized an employer's right under property law to employ labor without statutory interference. Up through 1937 the Supreme Court opposed legislation regulating work, arguing that it violated the commerce clause of the Constitution. After 1938 it reversed itself and upheld laws governing conditions of work and employment.[3]

---

[1] National Committee for Full Employment, "Jobs Impact," vol. 1,, no. 3 (March 27, 1981).

[2] John G. Turnbull, C. Arthur Williams, Jr., and Earl F. Cheit, *Economic and Social Security* (New York: The Ronald Press Co., 1973), pp. 634–35.

[3] *Report of the Minimum Wage Study Commission* (Washington: Government Printing Office, 1981), pp. 1–3.

After Roosevelt's unsuccessful attempts to increase the size of the Supreme Court, the attitudes and membership of the court changed enough that the members upheld a Washington state minimum wage law in 1937. In the next year (1938) the national Fair Labor Standards Act (FLSA) was passed, which established minimum wages and the maximum number of hours a worker could work per week without overtime payment. Both male and female workers were covered by the FLSA. Forty hours was the maximum an individual could be employed by any one employer in a week before overtime rates of one and one-half times the hourly rate had to be paid.

In the words of the Fair Labor Standards Act, its purpose was to

> correct and as rapidly as practicable eliminate . . . labor conditions detrimental to the maintenance of the minimum standard of living necessary for health, efficiency, and general well being of workers . . . without substantially curtailing employment or earning power.[4]

These purposes of the act were to be accomplished by setting standards for minimum wages, by determining the maximum number of hours an individual could be employed in a week before overtime pay was triggered, and by controlling child labor.

It is important to realize that the original purposes of the so-called minimum wage law were to improve the health and welfare of the working population by setting minimum regulatory standards for wages, hours, and child labor. The act encompassed much more than just minimum wages. Another goal was set by the FLSA, however: these welfare objectives were to be obtained without "substantially curtailing employment or earning power." Whether the welfare objectives of the FLSA can be obtained without sacrificing employment and earning power is a controversial issue that has exercised economists ever since the FLSA was enacted.

Not all workers were covered initially by the FLSA. The constitutional point of intervention on which the law was based was the interstate commerce clause. Therefore, only those enterprises engaged in interstate commerce came under the act. Moreover, various exemptions for size of operation, type of employment, or type of payment for work reduced coverage further. Initially, less than half of the private sector of the economy was covered by the minimum wage law.

The Fair Labor Standards Act has been amended six times since 1938. The first amendments were in 1950 and the most recent in 1977. The latter produced a schedule of increases in the minimum wage through 1981, where it stands as of 1986. The legislated national minimum wage since 1938 is shown in Table 23-1, along with the percentage of firms covered by the act. Not only has the minimum wage increased over time, but the percentage of firms covered has also grown. Today the minimum

---

[4] Turnbull, Williams, and Cheit, *Economic and Social Security*, p. 636.

Table 23-1 Statutory Minimum Wage Rates, 1938–1981

Month/Year of Statutory Change in Minimum Wage	Minimum Wage	Percentage of Companies Covered[a]
10/38	$0.25	43.4
10/39	0.30	47.1
10/45	0.40	55.4
1/50	0.75	53.4
3/56	1.00	53.1
9/61	1.15	62.1
9/63	1.25	62.1
2/67	1.40	75.3
2/68	1.60	72.6
5/74	2.00	83.7
1/75	2.10	83.3
1/76	2.30	83.0
1/78	2.65	83.8
1/79	2.90	83.8
1/80	3.10	83.8
1/81	3.35	83.8

[a]Private sector of the economy.
Source: Finis Welch, *Minimum Wages: Issues and Evidence* (Washington: American Enterprise Institute, 1978), p. 3.

wage is set at $3.35 per hour, and the percentage of firms covered has grown from 43 percent in 1938 to 84 percent.[5]

Starting from 25 cents per hour in 1938, the minimum wage increased to $3.35 by 1981, the last year the minimum wage was increased. During this same period of time, the average wage earned by the typical American worker has also grown. In 1985 the minimum wage represented about 35 percent of the average manufacturing wage. In 1938 the minimum wage was just under 42 percent of the average manufacturing wage. Between 1938 and 1985 there were changes in this ratio, and these are shown in Table 23-2. In 1968 the minimum wage as a percentage of the average

---

[5] The coverage of the minimum wage law is not as straightforward as it first appears. First, there is the question of what percentage of the firms in the private sector of the economy come under the act. These are the statistics presented in Table 23-1. Not all employees within covered firms come under the act, however, and some firms qualify for *exemptions* because of their size, the type of economic activity, or the number of employees hired. The Department of Labor estimates that about two-thirds of all eligible employees are covered by the minimum wage law. (U.S. Department of Labor, *Minimum Wage and Maximum Hours Standards under the Fair Labor Standards Act* [1979], pp. 63 and 74–76).

manufacturing wage peaked at 55.6 percent. The 1985 ratio of 35 percent of manu-facturing wages is some seven percentage points below the previous trough of 1945.

States can enact minimum wage laws, and today 40 states have such laws. Typically, the provisions carry the same minimum wage as the federal law, but their coverage is more inclusive. A few states and the District of Columbia have minimum wages that exceed the national. In this situation the employer is obligated to pay the higher of the two minimum wages.

While the minimum wage has declined in the 1980s, both in relation to the average manufacturing wage and in real terms—i.e., adjusted for inflation—youth unemployment has remained virtually constant. This presents a perplexing dilemma for those economists who thought a falling real minimum wage would increase employment among those most heavily affected by its policy consequences. Measured in constant 1981 dollars, for example, the minimum wage stood at $2.69 per hour in 1986 compared with its base of $3.35 in 1981. The teenage unemployment rate, however, had declined only a fraction from 19 percent to 18.4 percent over this same period of time. In fact, the fall in the real minimum wage has been so sharp that many

Table 23-2 Minimum Wage as a Percentage of Average Manufacturing Wage, 1938–1985, Selected Years

Year	Minimum Wage as Percentage of Average Manufacturing Wage
1938	41.7
1939	49.5
1945	42.1
1950	54.0
1956	52.9
1961	51.2
1963	52.7
1967	51.5
1968	55.6
1974	47.2
1975	45.1
1976	46.0
1978	42.9
1979	43.3
1980	42.6
1985	35.2

Source: 1938–76: Finis Welch, *Minimum Wages: Issues and Evidence* (Washington: American Enterprise Institute, 1978), p. 3; 1978–80: Council of Economic Advisers, *Economic Report of the President, 1981* (Washington: Goverment Printing Office), p. 274; U.S. Department of Labor, *Employment and Earnings* (January, 1986), p. 116.

Table 23-3 Employers at or below the Minimum Wage, by Age and Sex, 1980[a]

Age Group	Percentage of Employees at or below Minimum Wage		
	Males	Females	Both Sexes
16–19 years	38.2	50.9	44.2
20–24 years	11.4	17.4	14.2
25–64 years	3.6	12.9	7.7
65 years and over	27.4	40.2	38.0
Total, all employees	8.2	17.7	12.4

[a]Second quarter.
Source: *Report of the Minimum Wage Study Commission* (Washington: Government Printing Office, 1981), p. 9.

employers, such as fast food establishments, pay above the minimum wage in certain tight labor markets because otherwise they could not find individuals willing to work. Consequently, the number of individuals working at or below the minimum wage has fallen from about 12 percent of the total labor force in 1980 to around nine percent in 1985.

Characteristics of Minimum Wage Workers

Individuals earning at or below minimum wages tend to be young, old, black, Spanish, or female. They are concentrated in a handful of occupations and industries. The 1981 *Report of the Minimum Wage Study Commission* provided important information on the characteristics of the minimum-wage worker.

In Table 23-3, statistics are presented on the age and sex profile of the minimum-wage worker in 1980. About 18 percent of all female employees earned the minimum wage or less; 8 percent of male workers fell into this earnings category. For all employees combined, the figure was 12 percent. Younger and older workers have a higher incidence of minimum-wage employment. Half of all female teenagers and 38 percent of all male teenagers were earning at or below the minimum wage. Forty percent of all females over 65 and 27 percent of males over 65 earned at or below the minimum wage. For the prime-age working years, 25–64, the incidence of minimum-wage employment is much less.

More blacks and Spanish workers have earnings at or below the minimum wage than do whites. In 1980, 18 percent of all black workers, of whatever age, earned at or below the minimum wage, compared with 11 percent of all white workers. Twenty-three percent of black and Spanish *females* earned at or below the minimum wage, and 17 percent of white females earned at or below the minimum wage.[6]

Minimum-wage employment is most heavily concentrated in a few industries and occupations. Statistics pertaining to this issue are presented in Table 23-4. Farm workers, service workers, private household employees, sales workers, and laborers are the employees among whom minimum wage pay rates are heavily concentrated. The industries in which minimum-wage employment is heaviest are agriculture, retail trade, and services.

The fact that minimum-wage employment is concentrated in a handful of industries and occupations and is more prevalent for young and old workers does not diminish the controversy over this public policy issue. In the remainder of this chapter, we shall consider the policy disputes surrounding minimum-wage legislation.

Table 23-4   Occupations and Industries with Large Concentrations of Employees Earning at or below the Minimum Wage, 1980[a]

	Percentage of Employees Earning at or below the Minimum Wage
Occupation	
Sales workers	19.8
Nonfarm laborers	18.6
Private household	74.8
Other service workers	33.3
Farmers and farm managers	33.9
Farm laborers and foremen	47.4
Industry	
Agriculture	44.7
Agricultural Serivces	19.2
Retail trade	28.4
Private household services	71.5
Other services	19.9

[a]Second quarter. Occupations and industries with 15 percent or more employees earning at or below the minimum wage.
Source: *Report of the Minimum Wage Study Commission* (Washington: Government Printing Office, 1981), p. 20.

---

[6] *Minimum Wage Study Commission*, p. 12.

Wage Theory and Minimum Wages: Perfect Competition

The application of wage theory to minimum-wage policy appears very neat and tidy in perfect competition. A minimum wage in excess of the competitive market-clearing wage implies that the cost of hiring the next unit of labor exceeds its returns at the margin. Under such circumstances, the firm will reduce employment (and therefore output) until returns at the margin are once again equal to labor costs at the margin.

This competitive model is illustrated in Figure 23-1. In a perfectly competitive labor market, the market clearing wage is W_e and employment is E_e. Introduce a minimum wage of W_{min}, which is above W_e, and the demand for labor (E_d) is less than the supply of labor (E_s) at that wage. In effect, the firm is prohibited from employing anyone below the minimum wage, and the labor supply curve becomes abS_L. The problem is that for a level of employment of E_e and a wage of W_{min}, the returns at the margin are less than the costs at the margin, causing firms to reduce their demand for labor to E_d.

While this is occurring, units of labor supplied increase in response to the higher wage, because the labor supply curve slopes upward. This merely compounds the problem by adding more units of labor to a market that already has an excess supply

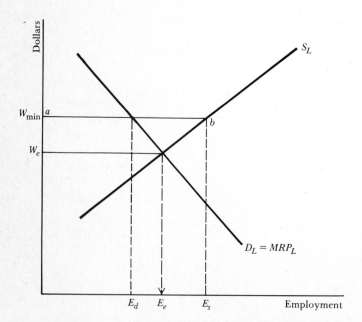

Figure 23-1   Minimum Wages and Perfectly Competitive Labor Markets

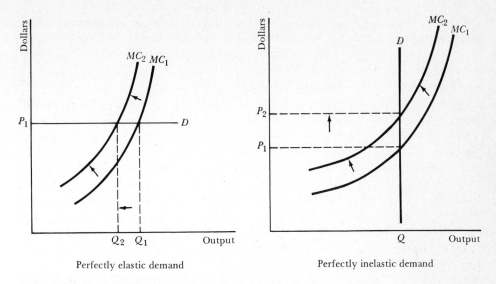

Figure 23-2 Elasticity of Product Demand and the Burden of Adjustments to Higher Minimum Wages

of labor in it. The result is unemployed labor, represented by the difference between E_s in Figure 23-1 and E_d—units of labor supplied and demanded, respectively.[7]

The extent to which employment will decline after the introduction of a minimum wage or after an increase in the minimum wage depends on the elasticity of demand for labor.[8] An increase in the minimum wage leads to an increase in the marginal cost of labor, because every unit of output produced at the margin now costs more per unit of labor employed at the margin. The increase in the marginal cost of labor will affect the supply price of the product being produced. The degree of elasticity of demand for the firm's product will then feed back into the labor market and affect the elasticity of demand for labor.[9]

This is illustrated for perfect competition in Figure 23-2, where two extreme

[7] Employment, as measured on the horizontal axis, is the combination of hours worked and individuals employed. One cannot make a strict conversion of the difference between E_s and E_d to unemployment as conventionally measured, therefore, without qualifying what makes up the horizontal axis. By convention, hours of work are held constant so that the horizontal axis can be translated into employment. The graphs in this chapter make this assumption.

[8] See Chapter 3 for a discussion of the elasticity of demand for labor.

[9] Other factors, besides the elasticity of demand for the firm's product, can also affect the elasticity of demand for labor. These include the extent to which capital can be substituted for labor, the proportion of total costs accounted for by labor costs, the time period, and the extent to which specific human capital skills are held by the firm's employees (see Chapter 3). For purposes of this discussion, we focus on product demand to show the trade-off between higher prices for consumers and higher wages for employees.

cases of the demand for the firm's product are shown—the case of a perfectly elastic product demand curve (the left panel) and the case of a perfectly inelastic product demand curve (the right panel). For the same increase in the minimum wage rate, marginal costs increase by the same amount in both instances (from MC_1 to MC_2). The only difference is in the elasticity of demand for the firm's product.

In the case of a perfectly elastic demand curve, prices do not rise at all, and the entire burden of adjustment is borne by reduced output (Q_1 to Q_2). In the labor market, this shows up as a sharp decline in employment. Ceteris paribus, the demand for labor will be very elastic, and employment will fall sharply in response to a higher minimum wage rate when the elasticity of product demand is high.

In the case of a perfectly inelastic demand for the firm's product (the right panel of Figure 23-2), the situation is reversed. Output does not change at all, and consumers bear the burden of a higher minimum wage through higher prices (from P_1 to P_2). In the labor market, employment will not fall by much, if at all, and the elasticity of demand for labor will be low or close to zero.

Depending on the elasticity of demand for the product being produced, either labor will bear the greater burden of adjustment through lower employment levels or consumers will pay higher prices.[10] In either case a welfare problem occurs, because some segments of society gain (those receiving higher wages) while others lose.

The elasticity of demand for a product in the market is the decisive factor in determining how much of the burden of adjustment to higher minimum wages is transmitted through price increases and how much through employment decreases. If demand for a particular product in the market is relatively inelastic, consumers bear the greater part of the adjustment through higher prices, other things held constant. If product demand at the level of the market is elastic, workers bear the greater part of the burden through employment decreases. We know that, in general, the product demand is less elastic in the short run than in the long run. Therefore, consumers will bear the greater part of the adjustment immediately after an increase in the minimum wage, and discharged workers will bear the burden over the longer haul.

A difficult set of welfare choices are implied by this analysis. Higher prices result in a welfare loss for consumers while higher wages result in a welfare gain for the workers who receive the higher compensation. When some people gain from public policy and others lose from the same public policy, economic theory has no means for evaluating whether the policy is appropriate, from a welfare economics standpoint, unless the winners are prepared to compensate the losers for the exact amount of their loss. The only welfare economic issues that have an unequivocal resolution in economic theory are those where everyone is made better off. Most policy questions in labor economics are not of this type. Instead, there are always some winners and some losers from public policy decisions that involve welfare. This presents economic theory with

---

[10] Most likely there will be a combination of lower employment levels and higher prices. The question in that case is whether employment changes or price changes will be greater. This depends on the elasticity of demand for labor.

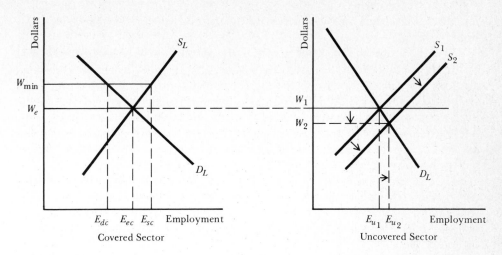

Figure 23-3 Covered and Uncovered Perfectly Competitive Labor Markets

the difficult problem of how to resolve "second best" welfare economic questions. In general, there are few accepted guidelines for proceeding with public policy when the best we can do is arrive at a second-best solution.

A good example of this problem in welfare economics and the minimum wage involves the distributional consequences of the introduction of a minimum wage, or an increase in the minimum wage, in a situation in which some workers are employed in a sector of the economy covered by minimum wages and other workers are employed in a sector not covered by minimum wages.[11]

Let us consider, for example, a situation in which there are two markets for labor—both perfectly competitive. Initially wages are the same in both markets—W_e. One market is covered by the minimum wage law, the other is not covered. This is illustrated in Figure 23-3. In the labor market covered by the minimum wage (the left panel), the demand for labor declines at W_{min}, and unemployed labor, represented by the difference between E_{sc} and E_{dc}, begins to seek some means of financial sustenance. In the absence of unemployment compensation, those unemployed workers will naturally seek employment wherever it can be found. This adds to labor supply in the *uncovered* sector of the economy, as shown in the right-hand panel of Figure 23-3. The labor supply curve shifts to the right, from S_1 to S_2, as the influx of those discharged from the covered sector enters this market. The wage rate falls from W_1 to W_2 in the uncovered sector because of the increase in labor supply. In response to

---

[11] For a discussion of this model, see Edward Gramlich, "Impact of Minimum Wages on Other Wages, Employment, and Family Incomes," *Brookings Papers on Economic Activity* 2 (1976), p. 412.

the lower wage rate, employment *increases* in the uncovered sector of the economy from E_{u_1} to E_{u_2}.

Will all the unemployed labor from the covered sector of the economy be absorbed by the uncovered sector? The answer to this question depends on the relative demand elasticities for labor in the two sectors. If the demand for labor is very elastic in the uncovered sector of the economy, compared with a less elastic demand for labor in the covered sector, it is conceivable that all the unemployed labor will be absorbed.

Even if this does occur and there is no *net* unemployment resulting from a higher minimum wage, the wage structure has been distorted. Wages are higher in the covered sector and lower in the uncovered sector than they otherwise would be. Workers employed in the covered sector have had an increase in their welfare while workers employed at lower wages in the uncovered sector have suffered a welfare loss. Is the condition of society better or worse according to a strict welfare economics criterion? Unfortunately, economics cannot provide a clear answer to this question.

Wage Theory and Minimum Wages: Monopsony

The discussion so far has looked at the impact of minimum wages in wage theory in the case of perfectly competitive labor markets. As we learned in Chapter 5, however, not all labor markets are perfectly competitive. Perfect competition is the starting place for all discussions of wage theory because it is the simplest case to explain and is the foundation for subsequent qualifications of the model of wage theory.

The perfectly competitive model and its conclusions are deceptively simple. Unfortunately, many policy discussions have been based on this very primitive model of a labor market. Many economists have continued to follow the lead of George Stigler, who said in a 1946 article,

> Each worker receives the value of his marginal product under competition. If a minimum wage is effective, it must therefore have one of two effects: first, workers whose services are worth less than the minimum wage are discharged . . . or, second, the productivity of low-efficiency workers is increased.[12]

This conclusion is not as clear-cut, from either a theoretical or an empirical standpoint, as might first be supposed. There is, first, the question of how a minimum wage can affect employment in a noncompetitive labor market, such as a monopsonistic labor market. Second, even within a competitive labor market, adjustments can occur in other labor markets, where the minimum wage has not been imposed, to absorb some of the disemployment effects of a minimum wage. Finally, there is the more difficult

---

[12] George Stigler, "The Economics of Minimum Wage Legislation," *American Economic Review* 36, no. 2 (June 1946), p. 358.

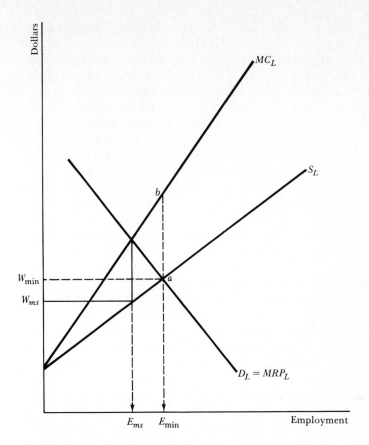

Figure 23-4   Minimum Wages and Monopsony in the Labor Market

problem of welfare economics when some segments of the society gain in welfare at the expense of other segments. When this occurs, how do we evaluate the gains and losses to see if society is better-off?

Under conditions of *monopsony* there may be no diminution in employment when minimum wages are increased. Recall from Chapter 5 that monopsony is a condition of imperfect competition in the labor market in which a few firms dominate employment. Firms face an upward-sloping supply curve under these circumstances, because they must offer a higher wage in order to employ more labor. The *marginal cost* of hiring the last worker is, therefore, no longer constant as it is under conditions of perfect competition. Instead, the marginal cost of hiring an additional unit of labor increases as more units of labor are employed.

A monopsonistic labor market is shown in Figure 23-4. Initially, without a minimum wage, the monopsonistic firm sets its level of employment where marginal revenue (MRP_L) equals marginal cost (MC_L). Employment is E_{ms} because that level of employment is compatible with the equality of the marginal revenue product of labor (demand) and the marginal cost of labor (MC_L). In order to employ that number of workers, the firm pays a wage of W_{ms}. That is the wage the firm has to pay in order to induce the requisite supply of labor (E_{ms}) to seek employment in its firm.

Introduce a minimum wage of W_{min}. Now the firm's marginal cost of labor is horizontal at W_{min} until it reaches the marginal revenue product of labor curve at point a, before it starts to slope upward from b to MC_L. The firm continues to follow the decision rule of setting its level of employment where the marginal revenue product of labor equals the marginal cost of labor. This occurs where the constant minimum wage intersects with the marginal revenue product of labor curve, producing a level of employment of E_{min}. The firm now makes lower profits than before, but employment has increased and wages have increased. Hence, a minimum wage, in the case of monopsony, can lead to higher wages and increased employment.

The monopsonistic firm before the introduction of a higher minimum wage had been extracting greater-than-normal profits, sometimes called monopsonistic profits. This provided the firm with a cushion and enabled it to absorb the higher labor costs in the short run through a reduction in profits. The Nobel Prize-winning economist Herbert Simon emphasized this aspect of the modern enterprise in his *organizational theory of the firm*. He called this cushion *organizational slack* and argued that all noncompetitive firms squirrel away some profits as a protection against unforeseen contingencies.[13] Such behavior is quite common for any organization—whether the organization exists for profit or not.

Organizational slack permits the firm to postpone any dramatic alterations in its operations in the short run while it plans for a smoother adjustment to its altered economic environment after the imposition of a higher minimum wage. This view of the firm does not posit such a restrictive degree of tautness as the conventional model would. Much as inventories on the production side, organizational slack is a financial device that provides an absorptive capacity for the firm so that it can weather short-term exogenous shocks and maintain a smooth production process over the longer term. The firm does not want to reduce its output and lose market shares unless forced to by circumstances it cannot avoid. Therefore, the restrictiveness of the competitive neoclassical model is something that the modern firm avoids through its organizational slack, according to the organizational theorists.

Even in the case of monopsony, where both employment and wages can conceivably increase in response to a higher minimum wage, there are still knotty welfare trade-offs to be made. Reductions in profits occur. In Figure 23-4, profits are where they would have been under perfect competition. If perfect competition is treated as

---

[13] The concept of organizational slack was introduced and used extensively in Richard M. Cyert and James G. March, *A Behavioral Theory of the Firm* (Englewood Cliffs, NJ: Prentice-Hall, 1963). chap. 2. Their work was inspired by Herbert Simon's earlier studies, for example, *Administrative Behavior* (New York: The Free Press, 1945).

some ideal, then the stockholders have simply been reduced to where they should be. In the real world of economic life, however, there have been some winners and some losers. Looked at this way, welfare choices have been introduced by public policy decisions, and this causes problems for economic analysis.

What we have learned so far in this chapter is that economic theory can only take us a limited distance in sorting out situations in which some people lose while others gain from a public policy. The problem is most acute when wages are involved. Wages mean different things to different people. To workers they are the sustenance of life— income that provides them with the means to buy goods and services. To employers wages are a basic and large cost of doing business. They are never low enough, and whenever wages are increased, dire consequences are predicted.

If you told an employer that energy costs would increase by 20 percent, the employer would probably shake his or her head, shrug, cuss a bit, and then say, "Well I will get by somehow. Maybe I will have to raise my prices, but if everyone else is feeling the pinch as much as I am, we will all raise prices together and I will not lose my customers." But tell the employer that minimum wages are going up by 20 percent and he or she will tell you, "I will just have to close up shop. I feel most sorry for the employees who have been loyal to me and now will be out of a job." The moral of this tale is that there is an extra psychological overlay to minimum wages that obstructs the objective rational thought process. Although energy costs went up faster than minimum wages in the 1970s, employers did not typically look on these increased costs in the same way they look on much smaller increases in the minimum wage.

To economists wages are a price for labor that is supposed to settle at a level that will clear the market for labor. Any intrusion into this market-clearing process by public policy is seen as producing resource allocation problems and distortions that prevent markets from clearing. A market that cannot clear is seen by neoclassical economic theory as detracting from efficiency and optimal economic welfare.

If economic theory can provide us with only partial guidelines for evaluating minimum wage policy, what of empirical studies that attempt to measure the quantitative effect of minimum-wage policy on the economy? If the negative effects of minimum wages are small, one conclusion might be reached. If they are substantial, another conclusion is warranted. We look at empirical studies of the effect of minimum wage policy on the economy in the next section of this chapter.

Minimum Wages and Youth Unemployment

The impact of minimum wage laws on unemployment has evoked controversy ever since the first law was passed in 1938. Today the question has heated up because of the very high rates of unemployment among youth, particularly among black youth. Before 1966 less than half of all black workers were employed in sectors of the economy covered by the minimum wage law. The 1966 and 1974 amendments extended

Table 23-5 Youth Unemployment Rates, 1954–1985, Selected Years

Year	Whites, 16–19 Years		Blacks, 16–19 Years	
	Male	Female	Male	Female
1954	13.4%	10.4%	14.4%	20.6%
1960	14.0	12.7	24.0	24.8
1965	12.9	14.0	23.3	31.7
1970	13.7	13.4	25.0	34.4
1975	18.3	17.4	35.4	38.5
1980	16.2	14.8	34.9	36.9
1985	16.5	14.8	41.0	39.2

Source: Council of Economic Advisers, *Economic Report of the President, 1981* (Washington: Government Printing Office), p. 269; *Economic Report of the President, 1986,* p. 296.

coverage of the law. After 1974, 88 percent of all black workers were employed in enterprises covered by the law.[14]

Youth unemployment rates are shown in Table 23-5. Unemployment rates for black males have risen from 14.4 percent in 1954 to 41 percent in 1985; for black females the unemployment rate has risen from 20.6 percent to 39.2 percent over the same period. The picture for white teenagers is not as bleak; their unemployment rates in 1985 were 16 percent for males and 15 percent for females.

Although unemployment rates are much higher for black youth than for white youth, their labor force participation rates are lower. In 1985 white males between the ages of 16 and 19 had a labor force participation rate of 59 percent; black males the same age had a labor force participation rate of only 45 percent, which had declined from 61 percent in 1954. White females had a labor force participation rate of 55 percent and black females 38 percent for the same age grouping.[15]

What inferences can one draw from these statistics placed alongside amendments to the Fair Labor Standards Act that have raised the minimum wage and extended its coverage? Economists have attempted to assess the impact of higher minimum wages on employment, but their conclusions do not produce a clear answer to the question of whether higher minimum wage laws cause higher unemployment rates. The reason for this is that many forces are buffeting the economy at any one point in time.

---

[14] Robert D. Mare and Christopher Winship, "Changes in the Relative Labor Force Status of Black and White Youths: A Review of the Literature," Institute for Research on Poverty (January 1980), p. 9.

[15] Council of Economic Advisers, *Economic Report of the President, 1986* (Washington: Government Printing Office), p. 294.

Minimum wage law changes are just one of these forces. Aggregate economic conditions are changing; the composition of the labor force is changing. Labor force participation rates for different cohorts in the population change. To draw a conclusion based simply on one factor is misleading. For example, the minimum wage was increased and its coverage expanded in 1966. Between 1965 and 1970, however, rates of unemployment for black youth increased no more rapidly than did the unemployment rates for the entire population. Aggregate economic conditions were strong during this period of time. During the decade of the 1970s, however, aggregate economic conditions deteriorated, and this deterioration, rather than the increase in the minimum wage, could have been the cause of higher youth unemployment.

The key analytical device in sorting out the effects of higher minimum wages on youth unemployment is the elasticity of labor demand. If the elasticity of demand for labor among young workers is high, we would expect the minimum wage to be a significant cause of the high and growing unemployment rates among teenagers. If the elasticity of demand for teenage workers is low, the opposite conclusion would be warranted.

The prevailing evidence suggests that the elasticity of demand for labor among teenagers is low. In a survey of several dozen econometric studies, the authors concluded that an increase of 10 percent in the minimum wage would increase teenage unemployment rates from zero to about three percentage points.[16] With an unemployment base of from 15 to 41 percent, this increase is insignificant. Teenagers are normally thought to be the group most adversely affected by increases in the minimum wage. But the evidence suggests a very inelastic demand for labor among teenagers and, therefore, an insignificant impact of minimum wages on their employment opportunities.

These estimates of labor demand elasticity are based on 34 econometric studies of labor markets conducted from 1970 through 1981. An earlier study by the Department of Labor used the case study method and reached similar conclusions. After the 1950 amendments to the Fair Labor Standards Act that increased the minimum wage, the Department of Labor pursued three avenues of investigation:

1. They conducted field studies in five low-wage manufacturing industries to see if the higher minimum wages had any effect on employment.

2. They looked into every plant shutdown, slowdown, or work force reduction in which the firm complained that it was reducing employment because of the higher minimum wage.

3. They compared employment and wage changes in both low-wage and high-wage industries to see if there was any distinction.[17]

---

[16] Charles Brown, Curtis Gilroy, and Andrew Kohen, "The Effect of the Minimum Wage on Employment and Unemployment," *Journal of Economic Literature* 20, no. 2 (June 1982), pp. 503–504.

[17] Reported in Turnbull, Williams, and Cheit, *Economic and Social Security,* pp. 656–58.

Based on this study, the Department of Labor concluded that the aggregate impact of higher minimum wages on employment was insignificant. They could not find any substantial evidence that higher minimum wages produced more plant closings or work force reductions.[18]

On the other side of this controversy, there are equally strong positions. Jacob Mincer has reached the conclusion, based on his empirical research, that "*disemployment* effects of minimum wage hikes are larger for teenagers . . . as one could expect."[19] (Emphasis in original.) This point is echoed by another researcher, James Ragan, who says, "Borne out by the data . . . are the hypotheses that minimum wage legislation reduces youth employment."[20] Finis Welch has said that "almost every serious scholar of minimum wages would argue on the basis of the available evidence that they have reduced employment of those, particularly teenagers, who would otherwise earn low wages."[21]

Why do such vastly different conclusions emerge from various studies of the minimum wage impact? One reason is the time period chosen for investigation. Studies based on the decade of the 1970s tend to reveal more of an effect than those based on previous years. Youth unemployment, as well as aggregate unemployment, increased more in that decade, and this shows up in the minimum wage impact studies. A second reason is the method of empirical inquiry. Those studies that try to account for a variety of causal factors end up concluding that the minimum wage is a minor reason for youth unemployment and that other forces are more important—such as the rate of growth in the economy and the rate of growth in employment. Ignoring these possible important causes of unemployment can be misleading because the minimum wage is saddled with the full burden of explaining unemployment among youth while other important factors are neglected.

Charles Betsey and Bruce Dunson concluded from their study that general economic conditions were more important than the minimum wage in explaining the rise in black teenage unemployment for the 1954–79 period. For the subperiod from 1970 to 1979, however, the minimum wage did show up as statistically significant in explaining black teenage unemployment, although the specific quantitative impact was still small.[22] This study supports the proposition that general economic conditions must be taken into account in identifying the causes of youth unemployment and that the time period chosen for investigation is important in explaining the differences in

---

[18] Ibid., p. 657

[19] Jacob Mincer, "Unemployment Effects of Minimum Wages," *Journal of Political Economy* 84, no. 4 (August 1976), p. S103.

[20] James Ragan, "Minimum Wages and the Youth Labor Market," *Review of Economics and Statistics* 59, no. 1 (May 1977), p. 136.

[21] Finis Welch, *Minimum Wages: Issues and Evidence* (Washington: American Enterprise Institute, 1978), p. 33.

[22] Charles L. Betsey and Bruce H. Dunson, "Federal Minimum Wage Laws and the Employment of Minority Youth," *American Economic Review* 71, no. 2 (May 1981), p. 379.

the conclusions reached by researchers studying the impact of the minimum wage on youth unemployment.

These differing conclusions drawn from the empirical studies motivated the Minimum Wage Study Commission to take a fresh look at the question of minimum wages and youth unemployment. Their econometric studies showed that minimum wage increases have very little effect on youth unemployment. Based on studies of the 1954–79 time period, an increase of 10 percent in the minimum wage would reduce teenage employment by about 1 percent—a very small effect. Teenage unemployment rates would go up in response to a 10 percent increase in the minimum wage, according to the commission's estimates, by less than one percentage point.[23] With unemployment rates in the 15 to 41 percent range for teenagers, adding less than one percentage point is a very small increase. What this suggests is that the demand for teenage employment is very *inelastic* and that an increase in the minimum wage has a barely perceptible impact on youth unemployment.

At the same time that the work of the Minimum Wage Study Commission was being conducted in the late 1970s and early 1980s, the American Enterprise Institute (AEI) pursued a set of parallel investigations. The AEI is generally of the persuasion that the minimum wage is an important cause of the rise in youth unemployment. Placing the results of the AEI studies alongside the investigations of the Minimum Wage Study Commission led two economists to conclude that "if one did not know which study had been funded by which group, one could not guess from the results. . . . [T]he vast bulk of the research studies funded by the two groups show modest/moderate impacts consistent with the professional consensus."[24]

Although both groups find that the demand for young workers is relatively inelastic and that the minimum wage has but a small impact on youth unemployment rates, the two groups diverge in their policy recommendations. The AEI supports changes in the minimum wage to increase employment; the commission rejects such recommendations.

Although there is a general consensus among economists about the empirical work on minimum wages, there the agreement ends. Two economists looking at the same results reach different conclusions about whether minimum wage policy contributes significantly to youth unemployment. As the saying goes, put two economists together and you come up with three different policy recommendations. President Harry Truman, when faced with economists who kept saying, "On the one hand, do this," and, "On the other hand, do that," was reputed to have asked his staff to find a one-armed economist!

The root of the problem is in the different economic theories of the cause of

---

[23] *Minimum Wage Study Commission,* p. 38. Estimates based on the 1970–79 period show a slightly greater effect on employment. The increase in teenage unemployment rates was estimated to range from 0.1 percentage points to 0.75 percentage points.

[24] Mary Eccles and Richard B. Freeman, "What! Another Minimum Wage Study?" *American Economic Review* 72, no. 2 (May 1982), p. 227.

unemployment.[25] According to the neoclassical view, unemployment is the result of a price distortion—specifically, a wage rate that is too high to clear the labor market. This proposition cannot be tested directly but is presumed to exist whenever there is unemployment. The existence of unemployment is sufficient to justify an argument that its cause is associated with a wage in excess of a market-clearing wage. Using this line of reasoning, neoclassical economists will argue that minimum wages contribute to unemployment of youth.

Keynesians believe that unemployment results when there is insufficient aggregate demand to support employment of everyone who is seeking work. The wage rate is not inconsequential in affecting unemployment but plays only a minor role, according to the Keynesian argument.

Hence, the two groups of economists might agree on the specific empirical results of the countless number of minimum wage studies but still disagree on what policy implications should be drawn from the empirical results. At root, the problem of what policies to follow concerning minimum wages is less a scientific question than a matter of political preference.

This point is illustrated by looking at two key contemporary issues in minimum wage policy: the youth subminimum wage and indexation.

Public Policy and the Minimum Wage: Youth Subminimum

In the past decade the debate over public policy and the minimum wage has become more heated because of the high rates of youth unemployment. A proposal has been put forward for a *youth subminimum wage*. A youth subminimum wage would set the minimum wage for teenagers (16–19 years old) at some reduced rate. Various senators and members of the House of Representatives have made different proposals, each slightly different from the others. Most would set the youth subminimum at 85 percent of the normal minimum wage. There would be a maximum length of time for which a young person could be employed at a youth subminimum wage—ranging from six months to one year. Employers would be penalized for noncompliance with these provisions.

The proponents of the youth subminimum base their arguments on the premise that a minimum wage in excess of a young person's marginal revenue product is the principal cause of the high rates of unemployment for teenagers. Teenagers have been blocked from obtaining a first job and, therefore, cannot get a foothold in the economy, which they need to function effectively in their adult years.[26] Denying young persons

---

[25] See Chapter 14.

[26] The debate over a youth subminimum wage is summarized in *Minimum Wage Study Commission*, chap. 2.

access to jobs in their teenage years keeps work habits from developing and prevents persons in their twenties from understanding how to go about finding and keeping a job. Skills are not acquired. A work record that would subsequently enable a young person to impress an employer is never accumulated.

Opponents of the youth subminimum point out that many factors other than the minimum wage cause youth unemployment. The evidence presented earlier in this chapter about the impact of the minimum wage on unemployment is often used to question the importance of the minimum wage in affecting unemployment. Moreover, the opponents contend that even if more young people were hired as a result of a youth subminimum, older workers would be displaced to make way for the younger employees. If there is a relatively fixed number of jobs at any one point in time, then changing the relative wages for teenagers and other age groups would merely reshuffle the age composition of those working and would not change the overall unemployment rate. The Minimum Wage Study Commission found "easy" substitution between teenage workers and older workers.[27]

The issue being argued here pierces to the heart of the debate in economics over what is the fundamental cause of unemployment. Neoclassical economic theory locates the cause of unemployment in a wage rate that exceeds the marginal revenue product of the worker. In such circumstances the supply of labor exceeds the demand for it in the firm, and unemployment results. Following this line of logic would lead one to conclude that the extraordinarily high rates of unemployment for teenagers are caused by a wage rate that is too high. Ergo, a youth subminimum is the way out of this trap.

The Keynesian theory of unemployment locates the cause of unemployment in an insufficiency of aggregate demand. No change in the relative structure of wages between different age groups will change this. Therefore, a youth subminimum would simply reallocate the existing fixed stock of jobs among different age groups and would not change the overall rate of unemployment. If a youth subminimum were enacted, Keynesians would predict that the overall unemployment rate would not change, ceteris paribus. Only the age composition of the unemployed would change.

The 1981 *Report of the Minimum Wage Study Commission* rejected the proposal for a youth subminimum, saying, "The record does not justify the establishment of a youth differential."[28] It offered four reasons for this conclusion:[29]

1. Estimates of labor demand elasticity are very low, so a lower youth minimum wage would not increase employment dramatically for teenagers.

2. Adult workers would be displaced by the lower youth minimum wage.

3. Teenage unemployment rates should come down over the next decade "as the large group of baby-boom teenagers passes into young adulthood."

---

[27] Ibid., p. 47.

[28] Ibid., p. 57.

[29] Ibid.

4. A youth subminimum departs from the public policy trend over the past several decades toward eliminating unequal pay for equal work.

Public Policy and the Minimum Wage: Indexation

Increases in the minimum wage since 1938 have come about through amendments to the original act. This has occurred six times since 1938, and some of the amendments have mandated several increases in the minimum wage spread over several years. Supporters of the minimum-wage approach to income maintenance have urged a process of *indexation,* whereby the minimum wage would automatically increase in response to some economic indicator. The consumer price index, the average manufacturing wage, or some other indicator could be used to index the minimum wage. The most frequent proposal is for the minimum wage to be set at 50 percent of average hourly manufacturing wages.

Opponents of minimum-wage indexation point to the inflation-feeding aspects of this proposal. Increasing the minimum wage automatically in response to the CPI or the average manufacturing wage would simply fuel inflationary fires, according to this argument.[30] Relative wages that emerge from the free functioning of the market would be distorted by a public policy that keys one wage rate to another. Distortions in the wage would lead to a misallocation of resources, according to this school of thought on indexation, because minimum wage rates would have ceased to respond to market-clearing forces.

As is pointed out in the 1981 *Report of the Minimum Wage Study Commission,* one's attitude toward indexation depends on the purpose of the minimum wage laws. Based on its examination, the commission concluded that

> indexation would have a small beneficial effect on the economy in the long run . . . regular and predictable increases in the minimum wage would be non-inflationary and would be easier for business to adjust to than the irregular increases of the present system.[31]

The commission recommended an annual change in the minimum wage, indexed to average hourly earnings in the private economy.

Many economists would disagree with the policy recommendations of the Minimum Wage Study Commission.[32] The space devoted to their recommendations and

---

[30] The debate over indexation is summarized in *Minimum Wage Study Commission,* chap. 4. Since 1938 the minimum wage has hovered around 48 percent of the average manufacturing wage (see Table 23-2 in this chapter).

[31] Ibid.

[32] For example, John M. Abowd and Mark R. Killingsworth, "The Minimum Wage Law's Winners and Losers," *Wall Street Journal,* September 10, 1981, p. 24.

conclusions in this chapter reflects the fact that this is the most recent (and probably not the last) congressional commission to be empowered to examine the minimum wage law. The commission and its staff assembled comprehensive empirical evidence on the effects of the minimum wage on different aspects of the economy. Their conclusions and recommendations have to be taken seriously simply because of the weight of authority behind their work.

Summary

Minimum wage laws evoke more controversy than perhaps any other aspect of public policy concerning labor. The empirical evidence suggests that minimum wages have little, if any, effect on unemployment rates, whether for adults or for teenagers. Yet analysts looking at the same empirical studies reach vastly different conclusions about public policy. The Minimum Wage Study Commission, authorized by Congress, concluded that there is no need to restrict the evolutionary growth of minimum wages, based on the evidence presented to them by staff economists and by economists who acted as outside consultants. Yet the *Wall Street Journal* editorializes:

> Anyone who has attempted to deal with the unemployment problem in an even halfway serious manner knows that there are hundreds of thousands of useful jobs that go unfilled because employers cannot afford to hire people at the artificial prices created by federal labor-support policies.[33]

Economics as a technical-scientific discipline can go only so far in resolving this controversy over minimum wages. At root, it is a political-economic question. There are two issues that cut across the question of minimum wages and color attitudes toward this public policy. First, neoclassical economists, Keynesians, and structuralists do not agree on what causes unemployment. Neoclassicists believe that unemployment is caused by the wage rate's being in excess of a market-clearing level. Keynesians believe there are not sufficient jobs in the aggregate that can be supported by the level of aggregate demand in the economy. Structuralists believe there is a mismatch between available jobs and available workers.

Second, wages are different things to different people. To workers wages represent income needed to purchase goods and services. To employers wages are a high cost of doing business. Wages are never too high for workers and are always too high for employers. Neoclassical economists see wages as a critical price in an exchange economy and believe they must be set at a level that clears the labor market.

First passed in 1938, minimum wage policy has probably pleased no one

---

[33] "Rhetoric and Reality," *Wall Street Journal*, August 14, 1980, p. 18.

completely. Attempts in recent years to change minimum wage policy have come from two directions. Opponents of the minimum wage have sought to introduce a lower rate for teenage workers, who have very high unemployment rates. Supporters of the minimum wage have sought an automatic indexing to the average manufacturing wage as a way to circumvent the lengthy and cumbersome process of periodic congressional amendment of the Fair Labor Standards Act. Neither side has been successful in changing the basic structure of the minimum wage law.

Study Questions

1. What legislation established the minimum wage, and what are the main features of the minimum wage law?

2. Discuss the demographic and industrial characteristics of minimum-wage employment. What are the principal factors that explain the incidence of minimum-wage employment?

3. Compare and contrast the employment outcomes of minimum-wage legislation in perfectly competitive and monopsonistic labor markets.

4. How does the firm's elasticity of demand for its product affect employment in the minimum-wage sector of the economy?

5. Empirical studies conclude that the employment effects of the minimum wage are small for teenage workers. How would you use these empirical results in evaluating public policy proposals concerning a youth subminimum wage?

6. The minimum-wage controversy appears to be locked in the conflict between distributional equity and economic efficiency. Explain.

Further Reading

Brown, Charles, Curtis Gilroy, and Andrew Kohen. "The Effect of the Minimum Wage on Employment and Unemployment." *Journal of Economic Literature* 20, no. 2 (June 1982), pp. 487–528.

Gramlich, Edward. "Impact of Minimum Wages on Other Wages, Employment and Family Incomes," *Brookings Papers on Economic Activity* 2 (1976), pp. 409–62.

Report of the Minimum Wage Study Commission. Washington: Government Printing Office, 1981.

Welch, Finis. *Minimum Wages, Issues and Evidence*. Washington: American Enterprise Institute, 1978.

24
■
Income Security,
Health, and Safety

Income security policies deal with instances in which the earning capacity of the
individual or family is ended or interrupted. For example, when unemployment causes
a temporary interruption in the income received by a family, *unemployment compen-*
sation payments are the public policy response to this unforeseen event. Or suppose
a worker receives a temporary or permanent injury on the job. Income is interrupted
in the case of a temporary injury and permanently ended in the case of a more serious
injury. *Workers' compensation* programs provide income to families and individuals
when such injuries occur.

The largest and most comprehensive of all income security programs is the *social*
security system. First enacted in the middle of the 1930s, the social security system has
become the centerpiece of income security policy. The best known of all the aspects
of this program is income for retirees.

Until the enactment of social security only about two generations ago, individuals
were cared for in old age by their families or by public institutions. When the nation
was more rural and more agriculture-based, family care was not an unsatisfactory way
to deal with old age. But as agriculture has waned and urban industrial life has become
the norm, taking care of old people in families has become more difficult for most
people. The literary critic Malcolm Cowley has observed that older tradition-rooted
agricultural societies valued the old and wanted them close because they were the
repositories of lore, custom, and knowledge and of ideas about how to cope with

unforeseen natural calamities. The urban industrial society is based on the present, with an eye on the future, and there is less room for older people, who represent the past in that vision of the world.[1]

The social security system has been our public response to the changing character of the way we live in the United States during this century. It has been a remarkable achievement. Older people have been provided with more opportunity, independence, and dignity through the social security system than they otherwise would have. In addition to the retirement provisions of the social security system, there are also provisions for medical care (enacted in 1965), which older people need more than younger people.

The social security system does not just take care of older people in their retirement years. It also provides for income payments to surviving spouses who are at least age 60—initially just widows but in more recent years widowers as well. It provides income payments to children of individuals who have died before reaching retirement age, up to the age of 18. Until 1982 such payments continued up to the age of 22 if the recipient was in school.

Amendments adopted in 1956 added provisions to the social security system for income payments to individuals who have become disabled as a result of some illness or accident.[2] Taken together, the social security system provides income in case of retirement, disability unrelated to work, or death of parent or spouse, and health care for the elderly. The actual name of the legislation that we conventionally call social security embodies all these aspects. It is called the Old Age, Survivors, Disability, and Health Insurance program.

In recent years, what was once a consensus about the value and effectiveness of these income security programs has been called into question. Controversy abounds concerning the fiscal soundness of these programs, their incentive effects on labor in the economy, and their macro impacts on savings and employment. These issues will be taken up in this chapter.

In this chapter we examine the social security system and such other income security programs as unemployment compensation, trade adjustment assistance, and workers' compensation. We will also look at a comparatively new aspect of public policy concerning labor: occupational safety and health. Taken together, these programs constitute the pillars of our public policy in the areas of income security, health, and safety.

Social Security

Legislation establishing the social security system was passed by Congress in 1935. Although few knew it at the time, the social security law would revolutionize the way

---

[1] Malcolm Cowley, *The View from 80* (New York: The Viking Press, 1980).

[2] Injuries that are work related are covered under workers' compensation laws while other injuries, not work related, are covered under social security.

Americans think about old age. The social security system is the centerpiece of our income security policy. It provides income for people whose earning capacity has been interrupted because of old age or disability. It also supports survivors of breadwinners who die. Since 1965 the social security system has provided health care for the elderly.

Initially the act establishing social security was called the Old Age, Survivors and Disability Insurance program (OASDI). It provided not only for retirement benefits, but also for survivors' benefits, disability benefits, and even unemployment compensation.[3] Amendments to the Social Security Act in 1965 contained provisions for medical care. Since that year, the act has been known as the Old Age, Survivors, Disability, and Health Insurance program (OASDHI).

Each aspect of the OASDHI covers a particular problem in social welfare. Retirement benefits support individuals when they are no longer working. Disability benefits provide income to individuals who have become disabled either temporarily or permanently.[4] Survivors' insurance provides income payments to individuals whose spouses have died and who are 60 years old or older. Under this program children of widows and widowers receive additional benefits, and even burial expenses are covered by this provision of the OASDHI. Medicare provides for hospital, doctor, and medical expenses for persons who have reached a retirement age specified in the act.

These programs add up to a complete and comprehensive social welfare system for particular segments of our society. They are costly, however, and in recent years they have become more controversial as the benefits have begun to burden the nation's capacity to finance them through taxes.

How Social Security Works

To be *eligible* for benefits under any OASDHI program, an individual must first be *covered* by the act. Today about 90 percent of wage and salary earners are covered by the OASDHI. Major exceptions are federal government employees hired prior to January 1, 1984, some state employees, and railroad employees. These groups are covered by other retirement systems.[5] To be eligible for benefits, an individual must have been employed and have paid into the social security system for a minimum number of years.

The amount of retirement, disability, or survivors' benefits received is related somewhat to how much the individual has paid into the system. The benefit formula provides slightly higher payouts to people who have paid more into the system.[6]

---

[3] The unemployment compensation system was always operated out of a separate tax, and after the passage of the 1935 OASDI, it was removed from that act and handled in separate legislation.

[4] Workers' compensation is a similar program that pays individuals for work-related injuries. Disability insurance, which is part of OASDHI, pays individuals for illnesses and injuries that are not connected with a job.

[5] John G. Turnbull, C. Arthur Williams, Jr., and Earl F. Cheit, *Economic and Social Security* (New York: Ronald Press Co., 1973), p. 66.

[6] Gordon F. Bloom and Herbert R. Northrup, *Economics of Labor Relations* (Homewood, IL: Richard D. Irwin, Inc., 1981), p. 579.

However, the benefit formula is not intended to equate directly amounts paid in and amounts paid out. The system as a whole can be said to favor lower-paid workers, who have paid less into the system. For this reason and others, the social security system does not operate as a private insurance or pension program, in which individual payouts would be more closely tied to amounts paid into the system by the same person. Taxes collected from those presently working are used to pay benefits to individuals who are no longer working. The amounts you pay in taxes into the social security system are not set aside for you to receive. Rather, you become eligible to collect benefits at a certain point in your life. Persons working at that time will have to pay enough in taxes to support your benefits, just as you will have done for beneficiaries through the taxes you paid while you were working.

The amendments to the act, made in 1977, set the benefit formula based on an *average indexed monthly earnings* calculation (AIME). Individuals who retire at age 65 receive the full monthly payments based on their AIME; those who retire between ages 62 and 65 receive less than the full amount—about 80 percent of full benefits. Disabled workers receive full benefits no matter when they become disabled. Survivors' benefits operate on specified fractions of the full benefit payment.

The 1972 amendments to the act provided for automatic cost-of-living increases in benefits, based on the consumer price index (CPI). This is called *indexation*. By indexing the benefits under all the categories of the OASDHI, Congress sought to protect beneficiaries from the vagaries of inflation. This they have done by providing for a twice-yearly automatic adjustment of the benefits, based on increases in the CPI. But the indexation system has been costly and is one of the more controversial aspects of the social security system. We will take up this issue in a later section of this chapter.

Benefit levels for an individual vary depending on previous earnings. In 1982 a low-wage worker who earned the minimum wage would receive social security retirement benefits that came to about 54 percent of 1982 earnings. An individual who

Table 24-1 Beneficiaries and Payments under OASDHI, 1982

	Number of Beneficiaries (millions)	Payments (billions of $)
Retirement	24.4	$104.9
Disability	4.0	17.3
Survivors	7.4	33.8
Medicare	a	50.8
Total	35.8	$206.8

[a] Retirees are eligible for medicare.
Source: U.S. Department of Commerce, Statistical Abstract of the United States, 1985 (Washington: Government Printing Office), pp. 365 and 371.

was earning just at the average would receive a higher absolute social security benefit payment but only about 41 percent of 1982 earnings. And an individual earning at the maximum taxable wage and salary base in 1982 would receive the highest allowable benefits, but these would amount to only 24 percent of 1982 earnings.[7]

Table 24-1 shows the total number of individuals who received benefits under the OASDHI in 1982 and the total cost of those payments to the federal government. Nearly $207 billion was paid out in 1982 to more than 35 million individuals in the United States. Aside from the defense budget, this is the largest single item in the federal government's budget. About two-thirds of the individuals who received benefits in 1982 came under the retirement provisions of the OASDHI. One hundred fifty-five billion dollars of the total of $207 billion was paid for retirement and medical care.[8]

Benefits paid out of the OASDHI are financed by a tax on wages and salaries. This "social security tax," as it is conventionally called, is divided equally between the employer and employee. There is a maximum level of wages and salaries that can be taxed. Beyond the "cap" on wages and salaries, additional earnings are not taxed. The total tax rate is divided among three trust funds that receive taxes and pay out benefits. The trust funds are associated with the types of benefits provided under OASDHI. They are retirement and survivors' benefits (OASI), disability benefits (DI), and health insurance (HI).

In Table 24-2 the social security tax for the years 1970 to 1990 is shown, divided between the health insurance (medicare) part and the retirement, disability, and survivors portion. The tax rates shown are levied both on the employee and the employer so the actual total tax bite in 1986, for example, is 14.30 percent, double the rates in the table. Social security taxes cease after an individual's earnings exceed the maximum taxable earnings base. In 1985 this occurred when income reached $39,600. In each year subsequent to 1985, the government sets the maximum taxable earnings base.

Social security taxes have risen rapidly in the past 35 years. In 1950, the combined employer and employee social security tax was 3.00 percent, and in 1970 it was 9.60 percent. The taxable wage base has also been increased, making the total increase in the social security tax even larger. In 1950 the ceiling on earnings subject to the tax was $3,000, and by 1970 it was $7,800. Between 1970 and 1980 the taxable earnings base tripled.

One reason for the increase in the aggregate social security tax burden was the addition of medicare to the system in 1965. Before that year there was no health insurance system for the elderly. Demands on the system for higher benefit payouts

---

[7] Congressional Budget Office, *Financing Social Security: Issues and Options for the Long Run*(Washington: Government Printing Office, 1982), p. 22.

[8] Medical care assistance has two components—medicare and medicaid. Medicare is paid for through social security taxes and covers hospital and nursing costs. Individuals can opt to pay a supplemental fee on their own to cover physicians' costs, at-home nursing care, and other medical costs. Medicaid is paid out of general tax revenues to low-income individuals who qualify on the basis of need.

Table 24-2 OASDHI Tax Rates, 1970–1990, Selected Years

Year	Retirement, Survivors, & Disability (OASDI)	Health (HI)	Total Tax[a] (OASDHI)	Maximum Taxable Earnings
1970	4.20%	.60%	4.80%	$7,800
1975	4.95	.90	5.85	14,100
1980	5.08	1.05	6.13	25,900
1981	5.35	1.30	6.65	29,700
1982	5.40	1.30	6.70	32,400
1983	5.40	1.30	6.70	35,700
1984	5.70	1.30	7.00	37,800
1985	5.70	1.35	7.05	39,600
1986	5.70	1.45	7.15	b
1987	5.70	1.45	7.15	b
1988	6.06	1.45	7.51	b
1989	6.06	1.45	7.51	b
1990	6.20	1.45	7.65	b

[a] Represents the tax rate for each employer and employee. Total tax rate, therefore, is double the one shown.
[b] Maximum taxable earnings base will be adjusted each year to reflect changes in personal income. Tax rates after 1986 are those enacted by Congress and scheduled to go into effect as of 1986.
Source: U.S. Department of Commerce, *Statistical Abstract of the United States, 1986* (Washington: Government Printing Office), p. 363.

and more liberal eligibility rules have also contributed to the rise in the social security tax. Whatever the reasons, the social security system is in trouble. At stake are both its financial solvency and its legitimacy in the eyes of voters, who once considered the social security system sacrosanct.

Is Social Security Solvent?

To prevent a threat to the financial solvency of the social security system, Congress in 1983 partially changed the benefit structure of the program and increased the social security tax.

The previous major overhaul of the social security system by Congress was a set of amendments adopted in 1977. According to a 1981 congressional study, "At the time of the amendment's passage, it was generally felt that the newly legislated tax increases would be sufficient to ensure the fiscal viability of the social security system for the ensuing 30 years."[9] By 1979 it had become clear that the social security system was rapidly approaching insolvency.

---

[9] Congressional Budget Office, *Paying for Social Security* (February 1981), p. 1.

In an earlier report to Congress, the Congressional Budget Office had reached a different conclusion. They declared in 1978 that the 1977 social security amendments "will . . . provide sufficient funds to keep the social security system solvent over the next four decades or so."[10]Something dramatic had occurred between August 1978, when the Congressional Budget Office had proclaimed the social security system in good health through the first two decades of the twenty-first century, and February 1981, when it reached the saddening conclusion that the system was going bankrupt.

During the decade of the 1970s, tax revenues increased less rapidly than anticipated, while benefit payments increased more rapidly than anticipated in the social security system. Slow economic growth, high levels of unemployment, slow growth in productivity, and falling real wages contributed to a reduction in tax receipts. On the benefit payout side, indexation of the payouts to inflation increased payments out of the OASI trust fund faster than anticipated because of the very high rates of inflation after 1973.

Every time the unemployment rate increases by 1 percent, the receipts through the social security payroll tax decline by $2 billion per year, because if people are not earning wages and salaries, they pay no social security tax. And every 1 percent increase in the CPI produces an automatic increase in benefit payments of $1.4 billion per year.[11] The unprecedented rates of inflation in the United States in the 1970s depleted the reserves of the social security trust funds, particularly OASI, which is indexed to the CPI. High unemployment rates in the 1980s reduced tax receipts below the expectations of social security administrators. On top of these developments, reduced employment opportunities led more people to take the early retirement option, placing additional payout burdens on the system while reducing the tax base. Finally, liberalized eligibility provisions for receiving disability benefits had been introduced in the late 1960s, increasing the taxes required for this aspect of the social security system. All these factors have contributed to the problems of the OASI trust fund.

Between 1970 and 1975 disability award rates rose by 50 percent. Disability award rates measure the relationship between the number of approved disability claims and the number of insured workers in the labor force. This rate rose from 4.84 per thousand covered workers in 1970 to 7.11 in 1975. Tighter eligibility standards arrested this growth, and by 1984 the rate per thousand had fallen once again to 4.0. Many of the individuals approved in prior years, however, when disability eligibility was more liberal, are still collecting benefits that are indexed to inflation, unless they have died or are no longer judged to be disabled.[12]

In addition to these problems with OASI, medical costs, rising at a rate faster

---

[10] Congressional Budget Office, *Aggregate Economic Effects of Changes in Social Security Taxes*(August 1978), p. ix.

[11] National Commission on Social Security, *Social Security in America's Future* (Washington: Government Printing Office, 1981), p. 12. Data are in constant 1980 dollars.

[12] Ibid., pp. 196–197; and U.S. Department of Commerce, *Statistical Abstract of the United States, 1986* (Washington: Government Printing Office), pp. 360, 364.

than the general rate of inflation, placed burdens on the medicare part of the social security system.

For all these reasons—indexation to inflation, more early retirement, easier eligibility for disability payments, and rising medical costs—the payouts from the system rose more rapidly than did the tax receipts.[13] Simply put, the factors that cause payments to increase grew much more rapidly than the factors that cause the revenues to increase. In the decade of the 1970s, wages grew less rapidly than the CPI, unemployment was higher than expected in the 1980s, and inflation was more severe. Therefore, when social security payments became indexed to inflation, the factor governing payments was growing more rapidly than were the elements that accounted for the growth in revenues. The result was a shortfall of revenues in relation to payout needs.

Benefit levels for the average social security recipient are not luxurious; people receiving the benefits are not getting rich from the system. In 1984 the average monthly benefit for a retired worker was $461, and for a two-person retired couple the average benefit level was around $769 per month. For the disabled worker the average benefit level was $471 per month.[14] The growth in retirement benefit levels in the United States was about average in comparison with the seven major industrial countries of Europe.[15] It is not necessarily the growth in average benefit levels that has caused our particular problems, since countries with the same rates of growth in benefit levels have not experienced the solvency problems we have.

The options available to correct the insolvency of the social security system are not pleasant. The system is organized on a current funding pay-in/pay-out basis. If funds are not available to meet all payment requirements, the managers of the Social Security Administration are obligated under law to hold up payments until there are sufficient funds to meet all the payment needs.

Solutions to this dilemma are divided between short-term remedies and longer-term adjustments. In the short run, options involve reducing benefits or finding ways to increase the financial resources of the OASI trust fund.[16]Schemes to reduce benefits include lowering payments for early retirement; changing the CPI formula used to index benefits;[17] using either a wage index or the CPI, whichever has a smaller increase; placing a cap on indexation; providing increases only at a fixed percentage of the CPI increase.

According to the 1981 Congressional Budget Office study, the most effective way to save money is by capping the indexation at two-thirds of the increase in the

---

[13] An excellent review of these issues is National Commission on Social Security, *Social Security in America's Future*, chap. 2.

[14] U.S. Department of Commerce, *Statistical Abstract of the United States, 1986* (Washington: Government Printing Office), p. 364.

[15] Ibid., p. 367.

[16] These proposals are discussed in Congressional Budget Office, *Paying for Social Security*.

[17] Such proposals typically involve changing housing costs in the CPI index.

CPI. This would have saved the OASI and DI trust funds more than $96 billion, cumulative, for the years 1981–86. Changing the formula for computing the CPI and the way in which housing costs are computed would have saved the system a little less than $11 billion from 1981 to 1986.[18]

The proposal for using the lower of a wage index or the CPI to increase benefits is based on the fact that OASI payments should be tied to increases in wages for the current working population. In the 1970s, when inflation outstripped the growth in wages, payments to retirees were increasing more rapidly than the taxable earnings base. In 1980, for example, wages rose by 9 percent while the social security benefits tied to the CPI went up 14 percent. By using a wage index, the system is assured that tax receipts will be linked to payments out of the system, since the tax is based on wages, not the CPI. The 1981 Congressional Budget Office study estimated that using a wage index would save $26 billion from 1981 through 1986.[19]

The general CPI may not be appropriate for older people, who have unique consumption patterns. Older people are not starting a household, so they do not need to purchase a home or stock it with furniture and appliances. Since home prices rose more rapidly than the overall CPI in the 1970s and 1980s, changing the shelter component of the CPI would reduce the index. On the other hand, older people spend more on medical care, which has also risen more rapidly than the average CPI. Giving this aspect of consumption a greater weight would raise the CPI for older people above the general CPI. These two factors would probably cancel each other out. The National Commission on Social Security calculated a special CPI for older people that took their consumption patterns into account. They found that for some years the special CPI for older people rose less rapidly than the general CPI. The average, however, for the 1969–79 period showed that the two indices rose at the same rate.[20]

There are other ways to reduce benefit levels—by phasing out entire categories of beneficiaries. One such proposal has been to eliminate student benefits. Under the Social Security Act, survivors' benefits are computed on the basis of the number of dependent children in the household. These benefits are normally paid until the children reach the age of 18, but after 1965 benefits could be received for a child until the age of 22 if the child was attending school. In effect, educational benefits had become a part of the social security system. Close to $9 billion would be saved between 1982 and 1986 if this category of benefits were eliminated, according to the 1981 Congressional Budget Office study.[21] The case for eliminating the benefits is based on the availability of other educational benefits for college. There is also no reason to conclude that the son or daughter of a deceased parent is more in need of educational financing than a student who has not lost either parent.

[18] Congressional Budget Office, *Paying for Social Security,* p. 31.

[19] Ibid.

[20] National Commission on Social Security, *Social Security in America's Future,* pp. 316–17.

[21] Congressional Budget Office, *Paying for Social Security,* p. 33. In the spring of 1982, these college educational benefits were eliminated for all new students who would have become eligible after that date.

Other benefit categories that have been proposed for elimination provide smaller savings. These include payments to survivors for burials, eliminating the "minimum benefit," and eliminating payments for children after the age of 15.[22] Savings of $4.5 billion would accrue for the years 1982–86.

Imbalances in the social security trust funds can be corrected by increasing revenue flows into the trust funds. The most obvious way is either to increase the tax rate on both employers and employees or to raise the maximum taxable base. One or the other of these steps could be taken by Congress, or a combination of both. Raising taxes during a period of general tax reduction is not a popular measure, however, particularly since the social security tax has been increasing faster than other taxes in our economy.

The Congress could authorize expenditures out of general income tax revenues for the social security trust funds. This proposal is criticized because any pay-as-you-go discipline would be undermined by dipping into general revenues. The Congress could authorize the administrators of the social security trust funds to borrow from the Treasury for short-term needs. This proposal has support, but opponents raise the same objection: that discipline would be removed from the system by disjoining expenditures from earmarked taxes.

An intermediate step has been proposed that would permit one trust fund within the OASDHI system to borrow from another that was in surplus. As presently constituted, each of the three trust funds, for OASI, DI, and HI, is separate, and funds cannot be transferred from one to the other. At most, two or three years of grace would be accomplished by this proposal before the trust funds presently in surplus would also develop deficits.[23]

Another approach is to tax all or some of the social security benefits and earmark those tax receipts for the trust funds. The motivation for this proposal is that some social security recipients are wealthy and have income from other sources. This program could exempt those with lower incomes before the tax was imposed so that low-income social security recipients would not have their living standards reduced. The objection to this proposal is that it penalizes those who have saved during their working years to supplement social security. Fears of a savings disincentive effect are raised by this proposal.

Another solution, which is more medium-term, is to make coverage of the Social Security Act more complete by adding federal government employees to the system. This would increase the taxable base quite significantly because salaries tend to be higher on the average in the federal government than they are in the private sector. The objection from federal government employees is that they are already covered by

---

[22] Ibid. The "minimum benefit" is used by many to acquire access to social security by working for a very short period of time before age 65 simply to become eligible for payments.

[23] In 1980 the Congress passed a stopgap measure that permitted funds to be borrowed by OASI from the DI trust fund for 1980 and 1981. See National Commission on Social Security, *Social Security in America's Future*, p. 57.

a more attractive pension plan and adding them to social security would lead to the ultimate demise of their retirement system. But many employees in the private sector, who have to supplement social security retirement benefits with an additional private pension to plan for a decent retirement income, face the same problems. If the social security system is so good for everyone else, why is it not just as good for federal government employees? Congress in 1983 decided that federal employees should be part of the social security system and provided that all new federal employees hired after December 31, 1983 would participate in social security. They left unanswered the question of what will happen to the existing separate federal employee pension program. In all likelihood, a merged social security and federal retirement system will go into effect for individuals hired after December 31, 1983. For federal employees hired before that date, the separate federal retirement system will provide pensions.

There are objections to every proposal to reduce benefits or increase revenues. The fact is that the short-term needs of the social security system are substantial. Some combination of many of these steps will have to be taken over the next five years to keep the system solvent. Over the longer term, special problems arise because of the shifting demographics of the American population.

Today the labor force has experienced a bulge due to the influx of the generation born during the "baby boom"—the period of relatively higher birth rates that occurred after World War II. By the late 1950s the birth rate had started to fall, and it reached a trough in the mid-1970s. In 1980 there were *five* active workers supporting every one retired person. By the year 2030, the Social Security Administration estimates, there will be only *two and a half* active workers supporting every one retired person.[24] Therefore, the burden on the wage and salary base to support the retired population will become more severe in the next century than it is today.

This rather pessimistic fact does not mean the social security system is doomed. There is plenty of time to forestall future problems. One change in the retirement policy in the United States that would alleviate much of the difficulty is to raise retirement age from the conventional 65, as it is today, to 70 or older. Many people who reach the age of 65 are still quite capable of doing a day's work, and they need not be sent out to pasture just because they have reached a particular chronological age. This does not mean that retirement at age 65 would not be possible; only that incentives could be structured to make it attractive to stay in the labor force, and *mandatory* retirement at age 65 might be eliminated. Today about 65 to 70 percent of all workers opt for early retirement at age 62, which provides them with 80 percent of the benefit level they would have received if they had waited until they were 65.

The Congress has already taken some steps in this direction and will probably adopt various policies that lead to this result. For some workers—those doing strenuous factory, farming, or mining work—retirement at age 65 or before is virtually a necessity, because their physical strength has deteriorated. For other types of labor

---

[24] Congressional Budget Office, *Financing Social Security: Issues and Options for the Long Run,* p. xiii.

this does not happen. Even for those who should retire at 62 or 65 for physical reasons, there may be other jobs in the economy that are less physically taxing.

Faced with these problems with social security, President Reagan and the Congress established a bipartisan commission under the direction of Alan Greenspan, former chairman of the Council of Economic Advisers. The commission proposed, and Congress adopted, a series of measures designed to make the social security system solvent. Tax increases scheduled to go into effect in later years were accelerated and took effect starting in 1983. The maximum taxable wage and salary base was increased. New federal employees hired after December 31, 1983, and all employees of private tax-exempt and nonprofit organizations were required to join the social security system. Early retirement benefits were reduced. These and other measures enacted by the Congress in April 1983 have bought some more time for the social security system. Its imminent problems have been postponed. The key to social security solvency, however, remains a strong economy—one that is growing rapidly and suffering little inflation. Without such economic conditions, the social security system will be in trouble again.

In addition, new problems emerge which call out for remedy through the social security system. In the 1980s the issue of so-called "catastrophic illness" insurance became an issue as the population continued to age and medical science contributed to people living longer. As a consequence, however, major illnesses, extended hospitalization, and nursing home care were medical needs not covered by either public insurance—medicare—or private insurance. Families saw their assets depleted for nuring home care, for example, that cost on average $22,000 per year in 1985. To provide insurance protection against catastrophic illness, proposals were introduced in 1986 to add this type of coverage to existing medicare insurance, with a cost-sharing formula divided between public taxation and personal contributions. The problem of catastrophic insurance and how to protect individuals from the financial disaster that accompanies serious illness or accident is the social security issue for the late 1980s, and its consequences extend beyond the aged to the general population as well.

The Economics of Social Security

Beyond the questions of the financial solvency of the social security system are several problems that have concerned economists in recent years. These involve the impact of the social security system on savings, tax incidence, and the substitution of capital for labor.

Several economists in recent years have argued that the existence of social security has reduced the individual's incentive to save for retirement and that thereby the savings rate for the entire economy has been reduced. Martin Feldstein of the National Bureau of Economic Research has been prominently identified with this conclusion.[25]

---

[25] Martin Feldstein, "Social Security, Induced Retirement and Aggregate Capital Accumulation," *Journal of Political Economy* 82, no. 5 (September–October 1974), pp. 905–26.

Feldstein's 1974 article made two points: First, incentives to save were reduced because individuals looked to the government-provided social security to support them during retirement, and they viewed their tax contributions as savings surrogates. Second, encouraging early retirement increased the number of years in which funds would be drawn during retirement, placing an additional burden on the economy. He found that personal savings were reduced by 50 percent because of social security. In one of the most curious events in the economics profession in recent years, Dean R. Leimer and Selig D. Lesnoy reproduced the Feldstein study and discovered a computer error in his work. After correcting this error, the two investigators from the Social Security Administration found that the social security system had no effect on savings. Feldstein has conceded the error existed in his earlier work.[26]

Concerns about the fiscal tax incidence and the impact of a payroll tax on the use of capital and labor are other questions that have been studied. In the early 1970s a study by John Brittain of the Brookings Institution led him to the conclusion that the social security payroll tax was shifted "backward" onto labor. That means that wage increases were reduced by the rate of increase of social security payroll taxes. Employers, in effect, traded off payroll tax increases for wage increases, and whenever the tax rates were increased, wage increases were negatively affected.[27] After a more recent study, the Congressional Budget Office concluded that only a portion of the payroll tax was shifted backward onto labor and the remainder was either absorbed in the short run as lower profits or shifted forward to consumers in the form of higher prices.[28]

In economic theory any tax on wages at the margin should result in a substitution of capital for labor in the production process. While economists have argued from pure theory that this "should" occur, there has never been any clear empirical evidence that the social security tax actually affects the choice of production technique. The theoretical speculation has never been confirmed because so many other factors affect the decision to use capital and labor in the production process. The social security tax rate is probably of minor consequence in the general set of variables a manager takes into account when he or she considers whether to substitute capital for labor.

It is hard to imagine a United States without the social security system—or even with a scaled-down version of it. Yet financial problems associated with the social security trust funds are serious and cannot be wished away. There is no lack of information about the problem or what to do about it. Nor will another study, presidential commission, or congressional hearing produce any breakthrough that we do not now know about. The problem is a political one in the first instance. Secondarily, the problems with the social security system are caused by stagflation. Unemployment reduces the taxable earnings base, and inflation increases payouts from the

---

[26] "Economic Diary," *Business Week*, September 22, 1980, p. 25; and Dean R. Leimer and Selig D. Lesnoy, "Social Security and Private Savings," Office of Research and Statistics, Social Security Administration (November 1980), pp. 30–31.

[27] John Brittain, *The Payroll Tax for Social Security* (Washington: The Brookings Institution, 1972).

[28] Congressional Budget Office, *Changes in Social Security Taxes*.

system. Until stagflation is arrested, the forces will continue to work against the financial solvency of the social security system. The key to a reasonably painless method of relieving the financial problems of the social security system rests with solving stagflation.

Unemployment Compensation

Unemployment compensation was first enacted at the federal level in the United States in the 1935 Social Security Act. Technically, it was an unemployment *insurance* program, and the terms unemployment compensation and unemployment insurance are used interchangeably. The first state unemployment compensation law was passed by Wisconsin in 1932, and four additional states had enacted such laws by the time Congress adopted a federal program in 1935.[29] The first bill introduced in a state legislature was in Massachusetts in 1916 and was modeled after the world's first unemployment compensation law, adopted by Great Britain in 1911.[30]

The unemployment compensation system is a unique blend of federal and state law. The original 1935 act provided that a tax of 3.0 percent would be levied on payrolls of firms that were covered by the law. Wages for each employee were subject to a tax, paid by the employer, up to a taxable wage limit of $3,000.[31] If a state adopted an approved unemployment compensation act, the employer would receive a tax credit on the federal tax equal to 2.7 percent, and the state would retain the 2.7 percent that it had levied. In effect, the employer would pay 2.7 percent on taxable wages to the state and 0.3 percent on taxable wages to the federal government. After the enactment of this federal law in 1935, every state quickly adopted an approved insurance law. Amendments to the original law have changed the tax rates only slightly since 1935. As of January, 1985, there was a 5.4 percent state tax on up to $7,000 of each covered employee's wages and a 0.8 percent federal tax. The total tax levied on employers is, therefore, 6.2 percent on the first $7,000 of wages per covered employee.[32]

The 6.2 percent tax is a *maximum* federal tax rate. Firms can pay a lower tax rate depending on the number of claims filed against them by their employees. If the firm has a good record of employment stability, it pays a lower tax rate. This process is

---

[29] Turnbull, Williams, and Cheit, *Economic and Social Security*, p. 207.

[30] National Commission on Unemployment Compensation, *Unemployment Compensation: Final Report* (Washington: Government Printing Office, 1980), p. 8.

[31] For a discussion of the formation of the unemployment compensation system, see Turnbull, Williams, and Cheit, *Economic and Social Security*, chap. 6; and National Commission on Unemployment Compensation, *Final Report*, chap. 2.

[32] Congressional Budget Office, *Promoting Employment and Maintaining Incomes With Unemployment Insurance* (Washington: Government Printing Office, 1985), p. 25. The $7,000 represents a federal minimum requirement, and states can use a higher taxable base limit. Thirty-four states have higher taxable base limits, ranging from $7,000 to $21,800.

called an "experience rating." Since World War II the average tax rate paid has been below the maximum. In the 1950s the effective tax rate was around 1.5 percent, because unemployment rates were low and the experience rating system lowered the tax rate for the average firm. In the 1960s the average tax rate was about 2.0 percent, and in the 1970s it was between 2.0 percent and 2.5 percent, significantly below the maximum. In 1980 the estimated average tax was 2.4 percent, and in 1985 it was around 3 percent.[33]

The mixture of state and federal law concerning unemployment compensation makes it one of the most confusing pieces of legislation in the entire catalog of social policy. For example, each state enacts its own tax, and it must enact the minimum tax called for in the federal legislation in order to receive the tax offset. Today that minimum tax stands at 5.4 percent. However, many states impose a higher maximum tax rate on firms operating within their jurisdiction. In 1985 the highest tax rate was in South Dakota—10.5 percent.[34]

If this is confusing, there is good reason. The states enact the tax rate and set the taxable wage limit. They must conform to a federal minimum but can set higher tax rates and a higher taxable wage base limit. Many states do this. But each employer is subject to an experience rating that can lower the tax rate. The overall impact of the experience rating system is to lower the average tax rate below the maximum tax rate.

Monies collected from the unemployment insurance tax are placed in a federal trust fund and drawn on by the states when needed. Until the mid-1970s the trust fund was in balance over the business cycle, drawing on reserves during recessions and building them up during prosperity. But a combination of sustained high levels of unemployment and extended benefit programs have rendered the unemployment insurance trust fund close to insolvency.

Unlike the OASDHI trust funds, the unemployment trust fund can borrow from the federal Treasury when it runs out of money. It has done this in recent years to sustain benefits payments. At the end of 1982, the trust fund had borrowed $15.3 billion.[35]

The countercyclical sensitivity of the unemployment compensation system has often been cited as an important automatic stabilizer in the macroeconomy. When economic conditions turn toward recession, tax receipts automatically begin to decline because fewer workers are employed. At the same time, payments to unemployed workers increase, supporting their consumption. Thus, from both the tax and expenditure sides, a degree of automatic stabilization occurs, and this operates without

[33] Turnbull, Williams, and Cheit, *Economic and Social Security,* p. 226; Congressional Budget Office, *Unemployment Compensation,* p. 8; National Commission on Unemployment Compensation, *Final Report,* p. 18; and Congressional Budget Office, *Promoting Employment,* p. 29.

[34] Congressional Budget Office, *Promoting Employment,* pp. 30–31.

[35] Congressional Budget Office, *Unemployment Insurance: Financial Condition and Options for Change* (June 1983), p. 29. Figures include both loans to the federal trust fund and loans to states to assist them in meeting unemployment insurance claims.

specific congressional legislation. The reverse occurs during the prosperity phase of the business cycle. Tax receipts rise and benefit payments fall, thereby dampening any excessive boom in the economy.

Benefits are distributed to unemployed workers who worked in enterprises covered by the unemployment compensation law. Today about 90 percent of all firms in the country are covered. The *eligibility* of an unemployed worker to collect unemployment compensation depends on several factors. First, the individual must have earned a specified amount of wages for a certain period of time. Second, the unemployed worker must be currently attached to the labor force and must demonstrate a willingness to look for and accept suitable employment if offered. Third, individuals are disqualified from unemployment compensation if they voluntarily quit instead of being laid off for economic reasons. Obviously, this distinction is difficult if not impossible to police. The individual cannot be discharged for cause and collect unemployment compensation. Finally, in most states individuals who are on strike are disqualified from collecting unemployment compensation.[36] Each state has its own eligibility criteria; this list reflects the most general principles. In 1983, 39 percent of the unemployed received unemployment compensation.[37]

The level of benefits received under unemployment compensation varies by state and reflects the previous level of pay the unemployed worker was receiving. In 1984 the average weekly benefit was $123 for the entire country. The range of maximum weekly benefits in 1984 went from $86 in Mississippi to $144 in Colorado. These benefit levels represent about 38 percent of previous earnings in 1984.[38] This figure is called the replacement rate, and it reflects the relationship between benefit levels and previous earnings. Proposals have been made to fix the replacement rate at 50 percent, but so far such a proposal has not been enacted into law.

Basic benefits are paid for 26 weeks. They can be extended to 39 weeks, however, if a "trigger level" of unemployment is reached in a state. Until 1982 many states qualified for extended benefits. Since 1982, however, the trigger unemployment rate has been so high that only a few are eligible to provide benefits for 39 weeks.[39]

During prolonged recessions many unemployed workers exhaust their unemployment benefits. In July of 1983, for example, 41 percent of the recipients of unemployment insurance had used up their benefits.[40]

Trade adjustment assistance is another program for the unemployed that supplements the regular unemployment compensation program. Under trade adjustment assistance, passed by Congress in 1974, a worker who becomes unemployed because

---

[36] For a discussion of eligibility criteria, see Turnbull, Williams, and Cheit, *Economic and Social Security,* pp. 218–21. Some states that do not pay benefits to those directly involved in strikes do pay benefits to individuals who are laid off as a result of a strike.

[37] Congressional Budget Office, *Promoting Employment,* p. 8.

[38] Ibid. pp. 16–17.

[39] Ibid. p. 5.

[40] Ibid. p. 18.

Table 24-3 Unemployment Benefits under Trade
Adjustment Assistance, Cumulative, 1975–81

Industry	Number of Workers[a]	Total Benefits Paid (millions of $)[a]
Auto	685,066	$2,155.1
Steel	136,176	347.5
Apparel	144,923	183.8
Footwear	75,565	90.6
Electronics	58,373	87.2
Fabricated metals	29,105	69.3
Textiles	25,827	43.1
Coal	4,605	17.7
Total	1,159,640	$2,994.3

[a] Cumulative totals, from April 1975 to May 31, 1981.
Source: "Labor Takes a Turn Away from Free Trade," *Business Week,*
July 27, 1981, p. 25.

of foreign trade competition is eligible to receive higher unemployment benefits for a longer period of time. The purpose of this program is to cushion the impacts of shifting trade patterns around the world that displace American workers. In Table 24-3, statistics are presented on the affected industries and the numbers of workers who have received trade adjustment assistance between 1975 and 1981, the last year this program was operative.

The dimensions of unemployment compensation programs are substantial. Payments for unemployment peaked in 1982 at $23.7 billion, averaging just over 4 million individuals per week. By 1984, unemployment compensation payments fell to $13.1 billion, and about 2.5 million individuals per week were collecting an average benefit check of $123.47.[41]

The unemployment compensation program provides an important source of income for the unemployed. First designed as a system of relief during the Great Depression, it has become a permanent fixture in our social welfare policy. After World War II the unemployment compensation program was conceived of as a countercyclical fiscal policy tool. In the decade of the 1980s, however, when our economy operated at higher levels of unemployment over a longer period of time, the unemployment compensation system began to show signs of financial weakness, and benefits were

---

[41] Council of Economic Advisers, *Economic Report of the President, 1986* (Washington: Government Printing Office), p. 297.

reduced from their peak 1970s level. Economists have also speculated about whether the program itself contributed to unemployment.

In recent years a controversy has arisen surrounding the work disincentive effect of the unemployment compensation system. If benefit payments are high and can be obtained for a substantial length of time, the unemployed will have less of an incentive to take a job. According to this argument, the time spent searching for a job increases because of the higher reservation wage induced by a generous system of unemployment compensation. The overall effect of longer job searches is a higher unemployment rate.

Estimates vary as to the effect of unemployment compensation payments on the unemployment rate. Summarizing the results of several studies, Daniel Hamermesh concluded that an increase of 10 percent in the replacement rate leads to an increase in the length of unemployment of from one-half week to one week when labor markets are tight.[42]

The regular 26-week unemployment compensation program has been estimated to increase the unemployment rate anywhere from 0.3 to 0.9 percentage points.[43] That means a normal unemployment rate, without the existence of unemployment compensation, of 6.0 percent would increase to 6.3 to 6.9 percent with the existence of the regular 26-week unemployment compensation program. It is estimated that extending the unemployment compensation program from 26 weeks to 65 weeks would increase the unemployment rate by an additional 0.2 percentage points.[44]

Workers' Compensation

An individual worker who becomes injured on the job or contracts an occupation-related disease is entitled to cash benefits, medical payments, and rehabilitation allowances under *workers' compensation* laws. This is the oldest of the social insurance programs in the United States and is solely a state-run program. The first workers' compensation law was passed in 1909 in the state of New York. By 1948 every state had enacted some form of workers' compensation.[45]

Workers' compensation covers primarily injury on the job whereas the disability insurance part of social security covers off-the-job illness and injury. Not all workers are covered under the various state laws. Some states exclude particular injuries or occupational diseases; others exclude specific occupations; still others exempt small businesses.

---

[42] Daniel Hamermesh, *Jobless Pay and the Economy* (Baltimore: Johns Hopkins University Press, 1977), p. 37.

[43] Congressional Budget Office, *Unemployment Compensation,* p. 43.

[44] Ibid., p. 40.

[45] Bloom and Northrup, *Economics of Labor Relations,* p. 601.

Benefits are paid in cash for living expenses, as well as in medical and rehabilitation services. The amount of benefits an individual receives depends on whether the injury is partially or totally disabling and whether the disability is temporary or permanent. Benefit levels vary by state, as well. Should an injury on the job result in death, survivors' benefits are paid. Some states limit the duration of payments for temporary disability; others permit payments for the entire period of the temporary disability.

There is limited federal involvement in the workers' compensation systems. States typically require all employers covered under their laws to have workers' compensation insurance. In some states the covered employer must purchase this insurance from a state agency. In other states there are both a state insurance plan and private insurance plans, which the employer can purchase at his or her discretion.

The injured worker files a claim against the employer with the insurance company, much as you would file a claim for damages suffered in an auto accident. The claim is then investigated, and a decision is made on the amount of disability benefits to which the worker is entitled, if any. If the individual worker does not agree with the decision, he or she may appeal it to a state-run board. As in any insurance situation, litigation and appeals can tie up the process for long periods of time.

In 1983 workers' compensation benefits of $17.5 billion were paid—about half by private insurance carriers.[46] Industrial injuries are more common than you would expect, unless you have firsthand experience with factory work. In 1984, the Department of Labor has estimated, 1 worker in every 12 in the private sector of the economy received some type of injury.[47] Workers' compensation now covers some 79 million workers in the United States—about 71 percent of all employees.

Not all disability payments are for permanent disabilities. The most common types of injuries on the job are loss of a limb, deafness or hearing impairment, back injury, and eye injury. The older the worker, the more likely that the years will have taken their toll, and the more likely a disabling injury. If you work in a factory your entire working life, there is little chance of escaping some form of disabling injury.

If a worker loses a limb or receives an eye injury as a result of a work-related accident, there is relatively little squabble over whether the disability was work-related—as long as the worker was not individually negligent. Increasingly, however, we are finding evidence of illness caused by exposure to low levels of carcinogens (cancer-causing substances) in the work place, or to chemicals that produce various nerve disorders. Are these illnesses work-related and therefore subject to workers' compensation laws, or are they not? The problem arises in the controversy surrounding standards of proof that some forms of cancer are caused by low-level exposure over a long period of time to carcinogens in the factory. Since medical science cannot be certain about cause and effect, the courts have found themselves in a quandary over whether to validate workers' compensation claims that are filed under these

---

[46] U.S. Department of Commerce, *Statistical Abstract of the United States, 1986*, p. 375.
[47] Ibid., p. 425.

circumstances. This will be the most hotly contested issue in workers' compensation over the next decade.

Black Lung Disease

In 1969 Congress enacted the Federal Coal Mine Health and Safety Act. In addition to calling for tougher health and safety standards in the mines, the act provided benefits for a particular disease of coal mining—pneumoconiosis, or black lung. Years of breathing coal dust cause lung deterioration. The result is a debilitating disease that cannot be reversed. It can strike at a very early age.

Coal miners who are certified as having black lung disease can collect benefits under the 1969 act. The survivors of those who die from the disease are eligible for survivors' benefits. In 1984 there were 314,000 persons collecting benefits from this program, broken down about equally among miners, widows, and dependents. Slightly more than $1.0 billion was paid out in benefits under the program. The average monthly benefits were about $458 to miners still living and $327 to widows.[48]

Occupational Safety and Health Act

Concern about low-level exposure to disease-producing elements in the work place and the absence of any preventive approach to health and safety on the job motivated Congress to enact the Occupational Safety and Health Act in 1970, which established the Occupational Safety and Health Administration (OSHA) in the Department of Labor. Workers' compensation laws were not able to deal with either prevention or low-level exposure to unhealthy working conditions. The costs to the economy were becoming staggering. Not only were there the direct costs of making workers' compensation and disability payments through the public treasury, but hours lost due to injury and reduced productivity due to a deterioration of human capital were enormous. They still are.

Concern for health and safety did not start with OSHA in 1970. Most unions place health and safety coequal with wages in collective bargaining. For some unions health and safety has at times been more important in collective bargaining than wages. Whether it is the United Mine Workers negotiating about mine disasters or the Teamsters about the safety of trucks, unions have long had a special interest in protecting the health of their members. As new forms of chemical products are introduced into our economy, health hazards in the work place take on new forms.

---

[48] U.S. Department of Commerce, *Statistical Abstract of the United States, 1986,* p. 374.

The Oil, Chemical and Atomic Workers International Union has pioneered research into chemical hazards, and their work is exemplary in the health and safety field.[49]

Injuries on the job are estimated to cost the economy one hundred thousand worker-years of production per year. Each year about 390,000 new cases of occupation-related diseases are reported to the medical authorities.[50] OSHA's twin goals were, first, to design some preventive measures in the work place—rather than to simply make compensation payments after an injury occurred—and, second, to identify occupation-related diseases and control their incidence through changes in the work environment. In pursuing these public health goals, OSHA has become embroiled in controversy. No one foresaw this controversy. The House of Representatives subcommittee that held hearings on the bill found not one witness to testify against it. OSHA passed by a vote of 383 to 5 in the House and 83 to 3 in the Senate.

The mechanism by which OSHA is to achieve its health and safety goals is the establishment of mandatory standards for conditions of work. It can take *corrective measures*—changes in operating procedures in the factory—or *preventive measures*—for example, medical screening and safety supervision.[51] The controversy arises over the way in which OSHA has attempted to design corrective and preventive measures.

There is the question of what is a safe working environment. It is inevitable that work will be hazardous, although it could be more or less hazardous. To eliminate all risk might be possible, but the costs would be astronomical. If not all risk is to be eliminated, how much should risk be reduced? The cost of reducing risk must be balanced against the value of a human life. The government has become involved with assigning cost values to human life, and this has not been an easy task.

Procedurally, OSHA conducts investigations into working conditions and sets standards for health and safety conditions. It goes beyond setting standards in some cases by actually specifying what changes have to be made in the work place to conform to its standards. If a firm fails to comply, it is subject to heavy fines. Originally, OSHA made unannounced inspections to see if firms were complying with its standards, but the Supreme Court ruled this violated search and seizure provisions of the Constitutions, and now OSHA inspectors must tell the firm when they are coming.

The most difficult area in which OSHA has sought to set standards is occupation-related diseases. Many of these diseases are caused by low-level exposure to waste produced in the factory, and their health effects may not show up for many years. Exposure to cotton dust, for example, is one of the more controversial issues that is still unresolved. It provides an important case study. Textile factories produce a cotton

---

[49] See Ray Davidson, *Peril on the Job* (Washington: Public Affairs Press, 1970). Many unions pioneered occupational safety and health provisions in their collective bargaining agreements. See Daniel M. Berman, *Death on the Job* (New York: Monthly Review Press, 1978), chap. 5.

[50] Robert Smith, *The Occupational Safety and Health Act of 1970: Its Goals and Achievements* (Washington: American Enterprise Institute, 1976), p. 5; and Bureau of National Affairs, *The Job Safety and Health Act of 1970* (Washington: Bureau of National Affairs, 1971), p. 13.

[51] Bloom and Northrup, *Economics of Labor Relations,* p. 611.

■

dust. When inhaled over long periods of time, this dust produces a disease that is technically called byssinosis. Brown lung is its more common name, and it produces lung deterioration similar to the black lung disease that coal miners suffer from. There is little controversy over the fact that exposure to cotton dust produces the disease. But what should be done about it?

OSHA proposed a standard that would require textile firms to blow the dust out of the factory and reduce the output of dust. These engineering changes would be very costly. The firms countered with a proposal to provide each worker with an oxygen-type mask—a piece of protective equipment. The option of using protective masks was rejected by the Department of Labor during the Carter administration, and, instead, engineering changes in the plants were mandated. The Department of Labor OSHA investigators claimed that the masks would not be as effective and that they would be very uncomfortable to wear inside factories whose temperatures normally exceed 100 degrees.[52]

The OSHA standards are presently being challenged in the courts and the outcome is unknown. So far, the courts have upheld the OSHA standard on brown lung control, but the final chapter has not yet been written on this issue.

Cotton dust control is by no means the only major health issue that OSHA has taken on. They have established standards for asbestos, vinyl chloride, 13 carcinogens, coke oven emissions, benzene, DECP, inorganic arsenic, and acrylonitrile.[53]

In a study conducted on the 1973–74 period, it was concluded that OSHA inspections *reduced* injury rates from what they otherwise would have been by 16 percent in 1973 and 5 percent in 1974.[54] The reduction in injury rates declined from 1973 to 1974 because OSHA started with the firms with the highest injury rates in 1973 and the firms inspected in 1974 had a safer work environment.

The Reagan administration disagreed sharply with the OSHA program and the aggressive way in which the Carter administration sought to establish and enforce standards. They proposed using cost-benefit criteria in establishing standards. This would mean that no standard could go into effect if the costs substantially outweighted the benefits. How such costs and benefits would be established is problematical. What is the monetary value that can be placed on a human life, for example, to measure the benefits of reducing illness? The Supreme Court ruled in 1981 that under the 1970 act cost-benefit standards are inappropriate and agreed with the way in which OSHA has proceeded to set absolute standards under the act. No doubt, this ambiguity in the act will be addressed by Congress when it reexamines OSHA.[55]

There are no easy answers to the problems that OSHA confronts. That our work

---

[52] "Making a Judgment on Human Health," *Washington Post,* November 11, 1980, pp. 1, 19, 20.

[53] Bloom and Northrup, *Economics of Labor Relations,* p. 614.

[54] R. S. Smith, "The Impact of OSHA Inspections on Manufacturing Injury Rates," *Journal of Human Resources* 14, no. 2 (Spring 1979), p. 168.

[55] "Restraining OSHA: It's Just a Matter of Time," *Business Week,* May 5, 1980, p. 110.

place is unhealthy and unsafe is difficult to deny. But it is healthier and safer today than it was a hundred years ago and probably better than factories in many other countries. Could it be safer and healthier? The answer to that question is certainly yes. But at what cost? Is the cost at the margin justified by the benefits at the margin? Our economy bears a heavy burden in compensation payments, disability benefits, and reduced productivity by not improving working conditions. And for the individual affected, the human tragedy is staggering. As Lacey Wright, a brown-lung victim puts it, "I've got two hands and two good feet, but I can't breathe. It feels like there's a thick rope tied tight around my chest and I can't get any air in there."[56] Whatever modifications are made in the future, OSHA is a permanent part of social policy in the United States and will continue to have a dramatic impact on labor in our country throughout the remainder of this century.

Summary

Income security programs, though only 50 years old, have come to play a central role in our economic lives in the United States. These "safety-net" programs, as the Reagan administration calls them, provide for income through various entitlement programs when earning capacity is interrupted. All the public policy programs examined in this chapter involve income transfer payments, except the occupational safety and health program and the Mine Safety Act. These latter programs attempt to take preventive and corrective steps in the work place to alleviate situations that would later result in expensive income transfer payments for individual workers who become ill or injured as a result of work.

The centerpiece of our income security structure is the social security system. First enacted in 1935, the social security program now provides cash transfer payments for retirement, disability, and survivors' benefits. It also provides for medical care payments for the elderly through amendments adopted by Congress in 1965. Taken together, social security spending is second in size to defense spending in the federal budget. In the past decade economic circumstances have overtaken the social security system, and what was once a healthy, solvent program now faces financial problems.

In 1972 amendments were adopted by Congress that provide for indexation of social security payments—a twice-yearly adjustment in the monthly payment to compensate for inflation as measured by the consumer price index. Congress could not foresee that immediately after 1972 we would experience the most rapid inflation during any peacetime decade in our history. This produced sharp increases in payouts from the social security system. Even though social security taxes were increased more rapidly than any other tax, revenue coming into the system could not keep pace with

---

[56] "Making a Judgment," p. 1.

outlays, largely because the economy was stagnant. With unemployment high, the tax base on which social security taxes were levied was depressed. The result was a financial problem that will imminently result in insufficient funds in the social security system to meet payment commitments.

Congress will no doubt take steps to alleviate this problem, but any move it makes will be controversial. It could reduce benefit payments or raise social security taxes (or the maximum tax base); neither of these options is popular in today's political environment. Congress could tax social security benefits above some minimum and earmark those income taxes for the social security funds. They could reduce the adjustment to inflation by changing the indexation formula. Congress could permit the social security funds to borrow from the Treasury or receive funds directly from general tax receipts.

Faced with the financial realities of the social security system, Congress adopted some short-term remedies in 1983 to buy some time. Tax increases scheduled to go into effect in later years were accelerated and levied starting in 1983. The maximum taxable wage and salary base was increased, and benefits for early retirement were reduced. Other changes in the complicated provisions of the social security system were made, and together these changes have postponed the day of reckoning for the social security system. Its long-term solvency, however, remains rooted in a strong economy—one that is growing and has little inflation.

In addition to the social security system, our income security structure also includes unemployment compensation, which provides for income payments to persons who lose their jobs through no fault of their own. Trade adjustment assistance provided up to 1981 an additional payment to persons who have lost their jobs through foreign competition. Workers' compensation pays individuals for permanent or temporary disabilities that occur through work-related injuries. Coal miners are eligible to receive income payments when they are certified as having black lung disease. All these programs are part of our income security structure in the United States. Each one has its own rules for eligibility. Some are administered by the states, others by the federal government, and still others by both the states and the federal government.

Finally, the newest pillar of our income security system pursues a different approach. The Occupational Safety and Health Administration (OSHA) was established in 1970 to prevent injuries and work-related health problems in the first instance through changes in the work place. This placed OSHA personnel in direct conflict with plant management over how work should be organized to promote safety in the work place and prevent debilitating illness. We have not heard the last of OSHA and the controversies it has spawned. It, too, is becoming a permanent fixture in labor policy in the United States.

Study Questions

1. What are the causes of the current financial difficulties of the social security system?

2. What short-term changes have been proposed for putting the social security system on a firmer financial foundation?

3. Why do economists refer to unemployment compensation as an "automatic stabilizer"?

4. Recently some economists have begun to claim that unemployment compensation contributes to our high rate of unemployment. Explain this proposition.

5. What are the arguments for and against requiring the Occupational Safety and Health Administration to use a cost-benefit analysis in writing regulations?

6. How does workers' compensation differ from disability insurance under social security? Do we need two separate programs?

Further Reading

Congressional Budget Office. *Paying for Social Security.* February, 1981.

Congressional Budget Office. *Promoting Employment and Maintaining Incomes with Unemployment Insurance.* March, 1985.

Hamermesh, Daniel S. *Jobless Pay and the Economy.* Baltimore: Johns Hopkins University Press, 1977.

National Commission on Social Security. *Social Security in America's Future.* Washington: Government Printing Office, 1981.

National Commission on Unemployment Compensation. *Unemployment Compensation: Final Report.* Washington: Government Printing Office, 1980.

Turnbull, John G., C. Arthur Williams, Jr., and Earl F. Cheit. *Economic and Social Security.* New York: The Ronald Press, 1982.

25
Employment Training Policy

The Manpower Development and Training Act of 1962 placed the federal government in the role of providing training programs for the unemployed. The United States as a nation was late in arriving at a training policy. Even today we have less in the way of a national training policy than do most of the countries of Europe.

Prior to 1962 the largest public training program was the system of vocational education administered through high schools and through apprenticeship training programs. The first piece of national legislation that contained training support was the Area Redevelopment Act of 1961, part of the New Frontier of the 1960s. This act provided resources to "depressed" areas of the nation, and some of the resources were for training the unemployed. The next year the Manpower Development and Training Act was passed. Training policy has gone through several stages, with new programs replacing old ones in response to changing needs.

When we stop and reflect for a moment on education and training, it is a curiosity that we organize our public education system the way we do. Formal education and training are bunched for the most part into the first 17–25 years of our lives. Yet we live in the midst of a dynamic and changing economy. Technological change is always occurring, and it is the source of real growth in the economy. Why should we assume that formal education and training acquired in the first two decades of our lives will serve us for the remaining four or five decades of our lives, when technology causes old skills to become obsolete and constantly requires new knowledge?

This is the problem we face in the labor market. Many individuals have skills and talents that have been rendered redundant by changing technology. How a society, through its public policy, addresses this problem is at the root of education and training issues.

Rationale for a Training Policy

Training policy has been justified by human capital theory, structural unemployment theory, and the Phillips curve.[1]

By providing training, public policy is directed toward augmenting and upgrading the human capital of the labor force. Presumably this will increase overall labor productivity in the economy, make the labor force more mobile, and increase the earning capacity of the individual receiving training. Making the trainee more employable will presumably reduce the costs associated with unemployment. This is the human capital rationale for a training policy.

Those who argue that unemployment is primarily structural make training policy a cornerstone of their assault on unemployment. Structural unemployment theorists contend that there is sufficient aggregate demand in the economy to reduce the overall unemployment rate but that there is a mismatch between the persons who are unemployed and the skills required for the jobs that are available. Those who are unemployed do not have the skills employers need to fill the jobs they have open. This explains the anomaly of high rates of unemployment in a city and pages of want ads in the newspaper advertising for individuals to fill jobs. Training policy is seen as the way out of this structural dilemma. If the unemployed are provided with the skills needed, the jobs that are advertised can be filled, according to the advocates of training policy.

At the macro level, Phillips curve analysts contend that the placement of the Phillips curve depends on the degree of structural imbalance in the labor force. To the extent there is structural unemployment, the Phillips curve trade-off between unemployment and inflation will be more severe. According to the structuralists, Keynesian demand management policies, which seek to reduce unemployment by stimulating aggregate demand, will merely worsen this trade-off by creating greater demand for highly skilled workers, who are not available to fill the jobs that are already available. Unemployment will not be measurably reduced, but inflation will increase because of the intensified bidding for a scarce commodity—skilled labor. Training can improve the Phillips curve trade-off by reducing structural unemployment.

---

[1] See Chapters 10, 11, 14, and 16 for more background on these topics.

Retraining the Technologically Unemployed

When the Manpower Development and Training Act (MDTA) was first passed in 1962, *technological unemployment* was seen as a serious problem. Automation and mechanization of work displaced many workers who had previously held jobs for substantial lengths of time. Heads of households were caught in a shift in technology in the 1950s that made their skills no longer useful in a new technological era.

This problem burst on the scene in the late 1950s, specifically in the deep recession of 1958. Many who had been employed before that recession were left redundant and could not find employment in the new technological environment. Detroit was a city hit by the recession of 1958, and the work force had a difficult time recovering from that shock. A study done on a sample of the long-term unemployment of the early 1960s in Detroit showed that more than half of the sample group had been born in the South. Fifty-nine percent of the long-term unemployed were black, and 80 percent of the black long-term unemployed in the sample had been born in the South.[2] The typical member of this group of long-term unemployed in 1962 had worked for a substantial period of time for the same employer before becoming unemployed. Forty percent of the long-term unemployed had worked in their last job for more than five years, almost one-third for more than ten years. They became displaced in the 1958 recession and never regained a toehold in the work force. More than half of all the respondents in this sample of long-term unemployed had been out of work for at least two of the six years between 1956 and 1962.

This was the group targeted by the MDTA. These people needed *re*training to get them back into employed status. They had good work habits, were accustomed to holding a job, and had shown the ability to work. What they lacked were skills appropriate to modern technologies. About half of this long-term unemployed group had never been to high school. They needed basic education as well as new skills.

The MDTA-established training programs were originally designed to deal with the technologically unemployed among heads of households. Two types of training programs were established. First, there was *on-the-job training,* which built on the foundation that already existed in firms and in trade union apprenticeship training programs. In these programs the individual is assigned to a potential job opening and then learns while at work. A second type of program became known as *institutional training*. This involved primarily study in the classroom, with practical demonstrations provided in a classroom setting. The earlier vocational education programs were a model for this type of training. Vocational education facilities in the high schools were used by the MDTA, causing a not-insignificant battle over bureaucratic turf.

---

[2] Howard M. Wachtel, "Hard-Core Unemployment in Detroit: Causes and Remedies," *Proceedings of the Industrial Relations Research Association* 18 (1965), pp. 2–5. When the survey was taken, in 1962, hard-core or long-term unemployment was defined as 26 weeks of continued unemployment. The sample consisted of 2,114 individuals.

By the end of 1963, the number of persons that had been enrolled in MDTA programs was 103,193. Almost all this training was in institutional programs—about 95 percent.[3] The first few years of MDTA were frantic ones. Congress had authorized the legislation for only three years, and there was a need for the MDTA administrators in the Department of Labor to demonstrate success. Programs were started as quickly as possible. Since there was no inventory of the skills needed in the economy, the occupations for which individuals were trained were decided on by hunch or instinct, not firm foundation in fact. This was inevitable in view of the massive nature of the undertaking, the paucity of experience and information, and the short time in which programs had to show results. As a consequence, the first results found in the evaluation of training programs were not promising.

When the employment experience of trainees was compared with the employment experience of a similar group of nontrainees, there was no statistical difference between the abilities of the two groups to find jobs during the first few years of the MDTA. Individuals were being trained for jobs that frequently did not exist. There was no evidence that trainees were finding jobs with any more ease than nontrainees.

There was one important finding from the first batch of trainees. Individuals who were enrolled in on-the-job training programs had superior employment records to those of persons who were enrolled in institutional training programs. On-the-job training programs were also less expensive to run per trainee. The cost per trainee in an institutional program was about $1,600, whereas the cost was only $420 per trainee in an on-the-job training program.[4] The reasons for this discrepancy were that some on-the-job costs were borne by the employer and that the time spent in training was shorter. Job prospects for on-the-job trainees were better because they were being trained in a firm for a slot that actually existed. Trainees did not have to be placed after receiving the training, as was the case with institutional training.

On the other hand, institutional training was viewed as more important because it provided the trainee with general educational skills that were transferable to a variety of occupational pursuits and were not limited to a specific job connected with a specific firm. A compromise of sorts was subsequently reached by providing "coupled training programs," which combined institutional and on-the-job training. Changes in the MDTA programs shifted emphasis from institutional to on-the-job training. By 1965 about 25 percent of all trainees were in on-the-job training programs. The total number of trainees that year reached 215,000.[5]

Evaluations of employment training programs have attempted to compare the benefits of training with the costs associated with the programs. If the benefit-cost

---

[3] U.S. Department of Labor, *Manpower Report of the President* (Washington: Government Printing Office, 1964), p. 252.

[4] Sar A. Levitan and Garth L. Mangum, *Federal Training and Work Program in the Sixties* (Ann Arbor, MI: Institute of Labor and Industrial Relations, 1969), p. 78.

[5] U.S. Department of Labor, *Manpower Report of the President* (Washington: Government Printing Office, 1966), p. 219.

ratio exceeds 1, the program is at least paying its way and is providing some positive benefit, net of costs, to the recipients of employment training.[6]

The benefits of training are of two types: First, there are income benefits—the *extra* income earned by an individual after training compared with what he or she was earning before training. Second, there are benefits associated with a more stable employment experience. If training reduces the amount of time the individual is unemployed, compared with the length of unemployment without training, society receives monetary benefits in the form of reduced welfare and unemployment compensation expenditures.

The costs associated with training are the direct costs of providing the training—including all the facilities and personnel costs—and the payments made to individuals while they are in training, normally set at the prevailing unemployment compensation rates for the local area.

Since the benefits from training occur over some period of time, a discount rate must be applied to the stream of benefits over time in order to arrive at a single number that accounts for all the benefits of training. There is no obvious discount rate that should be applied. The estimate of benefits from training is very sensitive to the discount rate used, and therefore the estimates of benefits from training can vary substantially.[7]

In order to control for the effects of training, a benefit-cost study of employment training must include a control group that has not received training. This provides a standard against which to measure the importance of training in assessing how an individual performs in the labor market after receiving training. Estimates from the early years of MDTA employment training programs placed the benefit-cost ratios in a range from a low just above 1.00 to a high of 3.28.[8] Benefit-cost ratios were substantially higher for on-the-job training programs than they were for institutional training programs. But the results may be biased in favor of on-the-job training because these studies do not track individuals over a longer period of time, in which, supposedly, institutional training provides the individual with more flexibility and mobility in the labor market.

Training for Youth and Blacks

The mid-1960s brought with them a change in orientation of employment training programs, toward youth and blacks with few skills. No longer was the emphasis on

---

[6] See Gerald G. Somers and Ernst Stormsdorfer, "A Benefit-Cost Analysis of Manpower Retraining," *Proceedings of the Industrial Relations Research Association* (December 1964).

[7] See Chapter 10 for a more complete discussion of this problem.

[8] Levitan and Mangum, *Federal Training and Work Programs,* pp. 85–86.

*re*training of the technologically unemployed head of household. Instead, training programs were designed and oriented to serve those who were then called the "disadvantaged"—individuals with few skills to bring to the labor market and limited employment experience. This was a more difficult constituency to serve because the trainees had less of an employment foundation on which to build. In many instances the task was to prepare a young person for his or her first real job.

There were several reasons for this change in orientation of training programs, which started around 1966. First, the overall rate of unemployment had declined from 1962, when MDTA was first introduced, and the more employable individuals had jobs. Second, the civil rights movement had pricked the conscience of a nation, and one response was to create a training program more geared to black needs. Third, President Johnson's War on Poverty found an application in a reorientation of training programs toward the poor. Fourth, the riots in the summer of 1967 induced a response that included the creation of several training programs for young blacks. All these factors combined to force a shift in the character of training programs between 1966 and 1968.

The changed orientation of training programs shows up in the characteristics of the trainees enrolled in various programs. In 1963, 64 percent of the trainees were in the prime working years, ages 22–44. By 1968 only half of the trainees were in this age group, with proportional growth occurring among trainees under the age of 21. Heads of households fell from 62 percent of all trainees in 1963 to 54 percent in 1968. The percentage of black trainees grew from 21 percent in 1963 to 51 percent in 1968. A trainee in 1968 was less likely to have a stable work history. In 1963, three-quarters of the trainees had worked for more than three years; in 1968 only 58 percent of the trainees had an equivalent work history.[9]

The two major new training programs directed toward youth were the *Job Corps* and the *Neighborhood Youth Corps*. The Job Corps program, which still exists today, was designed to remove young people from their neighborhood environments and place them in a residential center for at least six months. During this time they would receive employment training, basic education, and social skills needed to function in a work environment. In addition, the goal was to achieve a change in attitude by using peer pressure and by providing the young person with a "success" experience.[10]

By 1968 there were close to 33,000 young people enrolled in Jobs Corps centers. Some of the residential centers were rural, others were in urban areas. The costs per enrollee were high, about $8,000 in 1967. But enthusiasm about the concept of the Job Corps was equally high, and the costs did not deter its supporters. The Job Corps was a public policy response to the most serious domestic social forces of 1967 and 1968: the civil rights movement, poverty, urban decay, and summer riots on hot ghetto streets.

---

[9] U.S. Department of Labor, *Manpower Report of the President* (Washington: Government Printing Office, 1969), p. 239.

[10] Levitan and Mangum, *Federal Training and Work Program*, chap. 4.

■

The Job Corps has been one of the most successful of all employment training programs, even though its costs are high and the constituency it deals with is a difficult one. Studies done in the first few years showed a dramatic improvement in educational attainment (measured by test scores), good work histories after leaving the Job Corps, and a good rate of completion of the Job Corps program by enrollees.[11] Something important began to happen to the ghetto young people, when taken away from the negative reinforcing experience of the streets, that remained with them throughout their lives.

The second pillar of the youth employment training program was the Neighborhood Youth Corps, which does not exist today by this name but has been reborn under a new rubric. Today's summer jobs program for young people is descended from the Neighborhood Youth Corps. The goal of the Neighborhood Youth Corps, as articulated by its sponsor, Senator Hubert Humphrey, was "to put idle youth to work constructively and, in some cases, to help prevent high school dropouts by providing part-time work . . . in needed community jobs."[12] The idea was to provide localities with funds to provide part-time and summer jobs for high school students so that they would begin to acquire work habits that would stand them in good stead after they graduated from high school. The other objective was to reduce the rate of high school dropouts. In many instances young people drop out of high school because the family needs another income producer. The Neighborhood Youth Corps, by providing jobs for young people who remained in school, was designed to thwart this effect.

Enrollment in the Neighborhood Youth Corps peaked in 1972 at 863,000 enrollees. By 1974, enrollment had fallen to only 177,000. From its inception through 1974, the Neighborhood Youth Corps enrolled 5.3 million young people.[13]

From Welfare to Workfare

■

In the late 1960s and early 1970s, after the dust from the War on Poverty had settled, government attention was turned toward alleged abuses of the social programs started in the 1960s. The most frequent target of criticism was Aid to Families with Dependent Children (AFDC), which is known more generally as welfare. Though started decades earlier, the AFDC program is always subject to critical attention whenever society turns against social reform. Allegations of fraud and abuse are common among critics

---

[11] These results are summarized ibid., pp. 187–210.

[12] Quoted ibid., p. 211.

[13] U.S. Department of Labor, *Manpower Report of the President* (Washington: Government Printing Office, 1975), p. 317.

of the AFDC program. A typical response of such critics is to say, "Put these able-bodied people to work. I do not want to work and pay taxes to support others who can work but will not!"

Removing people from the welfare rolls and putting them on payrolls became a focus of the employment training machinery of the federal government in the late 1960s and early 1970s. The first such attempt to reduce welfare rolls was started in 1968—the Work Incentive Program (WIN). Until the enactment of the WIN program, people on relief had to sacrifice AFDC payments on a dollar-for-dollar basis whenever they worked. Every dollar earned at work meant that one dollar would be deducted from AFDC payments. There was, in effect, a 100 percent tax on earnings. With such a system, there was no incentive to work. The WIN program sought to change this, first, by permitting AFDC recipients to earn some income without losing their relief payments, and second, by creating public jobs and providing training to assist the entrance of AFDC recipients into the labor force. Though small in size, the WIN program was the first that involved job creation in the public sector as a companion to training.[14] Employment training programs of the 1970s gave this approach much more emphasis.

Between 1969 and 1973, 385,000 AFDC recipients participated in WIN programs, at a cost of $636 million.[15] As a part of the War on Poverty and employment training efforts by the government, this program was small. But, symbolically and politically, the welfare-workfare issue was extremely sensitive and remains so today. Every presidential administration since Johnson's has sought to convert most of welfare into workfare, but none has yet succeeded.

Public Sector Employment Training

Two changes dominated employment training programs in the 1970s. One was the consolidation of many scattered employment training programs into the Comprehensive Employment and Training Act (CETA), passed by Congress in 1973. The other was an emphasis on *job creation,* linked to training through public sector jobs programs.

By the end of the 1960s, an expanding alphabet of employment training programs and War on Poverty efforts resulted in a scattered assortment of agencies and programs that was becoming duplicative. In an effort to provide some coordination and consolidation, Congress enacted CETA in 1973. All the old MDTA programs, the youth training programs, and the new public sector jobs programs were consolidated under the Department of Labor. Several training programs, such as the WIN program for

---

[14] Levitan and Mangum, *Federal Training and Work Programs,* pp. 273–74.

[15] U.S. Department of Labor, *Manpower Report of the President* (Washington: Government Printing Office, 1974), p. 358.

AFDC recipients, were left outside the CETA umbrella, but most of the training programs started after 1962 were consolidated into CETA.

CETA also represented a shift in the philosophy of program management. One of the criticisms leveled at employment training programs in the 1960s was that the federal government in Washington did not know what the training needs were for a local community. With economies so diverse in different localities, it was virtually impossible for Washington to determine job needs and, based on those needs, the types of training communities should undertake. CETA attempted to rectify this anomaly. It established so-called *prime sponsors*. Most prime sponsors were local government entities, but private sector training enterprises could qualify as well. These prime sponsors submitted proposals to the CETA administrators in Washington, whose job it was to determine whether the prime sponsors' training proposals were in line with congressionally mandated federal guidelines.[16]

As with so many congressional enactments, the goals of the legislation were conflicting. Swept up by the rhetoric of a "New Federalism," CETA sought decentralization, local initiative, and dispersed administration. Yet CETA retained federal standards. This meant that a tension was built into CETA that has emerged whenever these two diametrically opposite goals—administrative decentralization and federal standards—have come into conflict.

The second new thrust that became an important part of CETA was the effort to link training with job creation in the public sector. In 1972, the first year for any major type of public sector employment program, enrollments were about 193,000. By 1979 all the public sector employment programs combined had reached a level

Table 25-1 Enrollments and Expenditures under CETA, 1979

	First-Time Enrollments (thousands)	Expenditures (millions)
Retraining	890.5	$ 1,942.9
Public-service employment	693.8	5,779.0
Youth programs	1,283.5	1,961.0
Other	175.7	445.4
Total	3,043.5	$10,128.3

Source: U.S. Department of Labor, *Employment and Training Report of the President* (Washington: Government Printing Office, 1980), p. 348.

---

[16] Sar A. Levitan, Garth L. Mangum, and Ray Marshall, *Human Resources and Labor Markets,* 3rd ed. (New York: Harper and Row, 1981), pp. 319–20.

just under 700,000. During the Carter administration, public sector employment under CETA was its major effort in the area of structural unemployment and job creation.

A breakdown of the types of training and expenditures under CETA is shown in Table 25-1. From a tentative beginning in 1962 with training programs under the MDTA, federal government training expenditures reached a peak above $10 billion in 1979. More than three million individuals were enrolled in some type of employment training program under CETA. The three sections of CETA that framed the Carter administration's concept of training were public sector employment training, youth programs, and retraining under the original MDTA-type system of institutional and on-the-job training.

CETA

The CETA program, first enacted in 1973, expired in 1982.[17] CETA encompassed a wide variety of employment training programs, which were contained in separate "titles" of the legislation creating CETA. The mainstays of employment training received a substantial part of CETA funds. These were the programs, developed under the original MDTA, that covered institutional, coupled, and on-the-job training. There were also a variety of youth employment training programs, which will be examined in a subsequent section of this chapter. Finally, there was a large component of CETA that attempted to break new ground in the 1970s—public-service employment.

Critics of the 1962 MDTA charged that the employment experience resulting from training did not justify the expense. People were being trained for jobs that did not exist. Therefore, public policy should address the problem of *job creation* along with the problem of structural unemployment. Job creation in CETA was addressed through funding of employment in state and local government for CETA trainees. "CETA workers" appeared everywhere, from the largest municipality to the smallest town in the United States. Participants in the CETA program were drawn from the "disadvantaged." About half were members of minorities, a third had less than a high school education, and a third were receiving AFDC; their median family income in 1980 was only $5,000.[18]

How effective were CETA programs in meeting their objectives of improved employment experience and higher wages for trainees? The results of the CETA program were mixed. They were very similar to the results of the 1962 MDTA program. In some instances results were positive; in others they were ambiguous. The Congressional Budget Office has estimated that the benefit-cost ratio was approximately 1. In other words, discounted benefits in the form of higher post-training

---

[17] The Reagan administration initially resisted the establishment of a new public training program to replace CETA. Congressional pressure, however, and growing unemployment in 1982 forced them to support training legislation in the form of the Job Training and Partnership Act, discussed later in this chapter.

[18] Congressional Budget Office, *CETA Training Programs—Do They Work for Adults?* (July 1982), p. 6.

earnings were estimated to have been about the same as costs, which were around $2,400 per trainee in 1980.[19]

This same study concluded that CETA participation did have a positive effect on involvement with the labor force. CETA participants tended to have higher post-training labor force participation rates and to work longer hours, even though their hourly wage rate was not improved by CETA training. This result was particularly apparent for women who were in CETA, although for men these results were less clear.[20] Only 22 percent of post-training additional earnings for women was due to hourly wage increases; 78 percent was accounted for by an increase in the number of hours worked.[21] Furthermore, the CETA employment training worked best for individuals with limited previous experience in the labor force. This was the case for all types of CETA training.

This conclusion reaffirms a benefit of employment training programs that has existed ever since the MDTA programs were introduced in 1962. Training provides confidence, hope, and the general skills associated with looking for and retaining a job. These more subtle results of employment training may, in fact, be more important than the specific cognitive training embodied in the particular skills being taught the trainee. In public policy these practical job skills and psychological elements of training have been neglected, and direct occupational skill training has been emphasized, even though many studies point to these more subtle, more subjective ingredients of training as more important in post-training experience.

Employment Training for Youth in CETA

In the early days of the CETA program, there was only one specific program for youth—the Job Corps, which was a holdover from the 1960s. Then in 1977 Congress passed the Youth Employment and Demonstration Projects Act (YEDPA), which became integrated into CETA. As we know from earlier chapters in this book, youth unemployment had reached staggering proportions in the 1970s, ranging by 1981 from 15 percent for white youth to 35 percent for black youth. In 1978, one out of every five employed black youths was working through CETA.[22]

As the name Youth Employment and Demonstration Projects Act implies, the CETA approach to youth unemployment was through a variety of programs, some experimental, others holdovers from the MDTA of the 1960s. In the latter category were summer employment, the Job Corps, and programs to encourage young people to stay in high school. Public-service employment, the cornerstone of CETA, was added to this menu. The results of these various programs, as measured by benefit-

---

[19] Ibid., pp. xxi and 8.

[20] Ibid., chap. 3.

[21] Ibid., p. 21.

[22] Congressional Budget Office, *Improving Youth Employment Prospects: Issues and Options* (February 1982), p. xiii.

cost ratios, are about the same as the results of MDTA in the 1960s.[23] All the benefit-cost ratios are positive, ranging from slightly over 2 for on-the-job training to just over 1 for classroom training. A comprehensive review by a National Academy of Sciences panel of experts found that the Job Corps was the most successful of all youth employment programs.[24]

An issue that arose from the public-service job component of CETA was its *displacement effect*. Displacement refers to the practice of state and local governments using CETA money to employ people for jobs that they would otherwise have funded out of their own revenues. If this was done, no new jobs were created through CETA. The local tax burden was simply shifted to the federal government to support local services that would have been funded by local revenues if CETA had not existed. This was not the purpose of public-service employment through CETA. New jobs and added local services were supposed to materialize as a result of CETA grants. Estimates of the displacement effect range all over the map. There have been estimates as low as 18 percent and as high as 80 percent.[25]

Job Training and Partnership Act

The expiration of CETA in 1982 created a vacuum in employment training programs until Congress, faced with constituent concerns about high unemployment, enacted the Job Training and Partnership Act (JTPA). The JTPA emphasizes the Reagan administration's reliance on the private sector for employment creation. The federal government has a more limited role than it did under CETA, and the governors of the states have more authority for the disbursement of JTPA funds. As the name of the act implies, emphasis will be placed on private sector training, subsidized through the JTPA.[26]

In 1984 and 1985, the first two full years of JTPA's operation, a total of $7.3 billion was spent on training for just under two million individuals.[27] Whether this

---

[23] The different programs under YEDPA are described and analyzed in Garth L. Mangum, "CETA as a 'Second Chance' System for Disadvantaged Youth," in Robert E. Taylor et al., eds., *Job Training for Youth* (Columbus: The National Center for Research in Vocational Education, 1982), chap. 7.

[24] Ibid., p. 126. As the commentator on this paper notes, however, this "represents a 'social' benefit-cost measure" in which estimates of savings on future transfer payments and savings through crime reduction are included in benefits. These estimates are speculative and render the benefit-cost measures less useful. See Marvin H. Kosters, "The CETA System of Job Training-Reactor Comments," in Taylor et al., *Job Training for Youth*, pp. 159–62; and National Academy of Sciences, *Youth Employment and Training Programs. The YEDPA Years* (Washington: National Academy Press, 1985), chap. 1.

[25] Mangum, " 'Second Chance' System," p. 116; and "The Impact of Government Jobs Programs," *Business Week,* September 8, 1980, p. 107.

[26] National Committee for Full Employment, *Jobs Impact,* vol. 2, no. 22 (November 19, 1982).

[27] U.S. Department of Labor, *Training and Employment Report of the Secretary of Labor, 1985* (Washington: Government Printing Office, 1986), pp. 7 and 9.

concept of training will produce a better result than the programs of the previous twenty years, which put more emphasis on the public sector, remains to be seen. The source of the problem is unemployment, and the best that training can aspire to is providing individuals with the skills needed when the jobs exist.

Employment Training Programs: An Assessment

We now have 25 years of experience with public employment training programs in the United States. Neither have these programs accomplished what their proponents hoped for 25 years ago, nor are they the waste of money that some conservative critics claim they are. Structural unemployment remains a serious problem, and in the early 1980s overall unemployment rates began to approach Great Depression levels. Obviously unemployment is a more serious problem today than it was when the first MDTA was introduced, but any suggestion that employment training programs have contributed to this problem is without foundation.

Perhaps the greatest disappointment of employment training is the post-training results for trainees. Benefit-cost ratios exceed 1 only when based on assumptions about savings in transfer payments and social costs. The original supporters of training, including this author, had expected much more from training results for the individuals who had conscientiously participated in the training programs. But what would unemployment and income levels be if we had not spent so much money on employment training in the past 25 years? Perhaps all employment training policy can aspire to is being a finger in the dike. Employment training programs cannot create jobs, except in the public sector, and cannot guarantee trainees jobs when they do not exist. Nor can they correct years and years of neglect that has its roots in the larger society.

The evolution over the past 25 years of public policy on employment training is about to change, with more emphasis placed on subsidizing private sector training. The supply-side economics of the Reagan administration interprets unemployment as arising from wages too high to justify employing those at the bottom of the economic heap. Government policy, according to the supply-siders, has interfered with the adjustment process in the labor market, which would have permitted it to clear if such programs as the minimum wage and employment training were not in existence.

The proof of this pudding will be in the eating. If supply-side economics is given its day in court in the 1980s and if unemployment rates decline, serious questions will have to be raised about the Keynesian and structural analyses of unemployment. If the new policies are found wanting, however, there will be a return to structural unemployment programs of the employment training sort. Then one can expect a resurrection in some new form, with new names, of the employment training apparatus that has been created over the past 25 years.

Summary

The Manpower Development and Training Act (MDTA) of 1962 marked our entry into national employment training policy. Before its passage the federal government's involvement in employment training had been through the vocational education system, which was heavily oriented toward agricultural occupations, and through apprenticeship training—largely in the construction trades. These two programs have continued to exist alongside other employment training programs.

The MDTA provided both classroom training and on-the-job training, initially to heads of households who had become technologically unemployed. The MDTA became a barometer for our shifting social policy in the 1960s. By the mid-1960s poverty had become a national issue, and the MDTA was changed to serve the disadvantaged. After the urban riots of 1967, the program shifted to aid young people with their employment problems through the creation of special youth training programs: the Job Corps and the Neighborhood Youth Corps.

The results of employment training under MDTA fell short of what its proponents had hoped for but were better than its critics were prepared to admit. Benefit-cost ratios, which seek to measure monetary returns for the trainee and society against costs, were only slightly positive. Post-training employment experience was frequently unrelated to the training. Additional earnings associated with training were less than had been hoped. Nevertheless, employment training did seem to impart more subtle job acquisition and retention skills and to provide the trainee with the confidence to participate effectively in the labor market.

By the early 1970s an alphabet of training programs had been created to serve different constituencies. To rationalize our training policy, which had grown like Topsy since the enactment of MDTA, Congress in 1973 adopted the Comprehensive Employment and Training Act (CETA). This act sought to consolidate most training programs that had been created since 1962 into one administrative home in the Department of Labor. It also attempted to decentralize training to the local community while it maintained general federal standards for employment training. Local prime sponsors conducted the training as they saw fit, but their projects had to receive federal approval and meet federal standards.

The backbone of CETA continued to be the classroom and on-the-job training used under the MDTA. It also continued some of the youth programs—particularly the Job Corps, which was considered to be an effective program. CETA broke new ground with a large, new public employment component to its private sector employment training. The criticism of MDTA was that it trained people for jobs that did not exist; therefore, public policy should find a way to create jobs as well as to provide the training for people to fill the jobs. Under CETA, grants were given to state and local governments to employ CETA workers.

Evaluations of the effectiveness of CETA are about the same as for MDTA. The benefit-cost ratios are slightly positive. The number of public-service jobs that were created was substantial, but the jobs came under criticism from the standpoint of their usefulness. An issue also arose whether these were new jobs or employment positions that state and local governments would have staffed with their own monies anyway.

CETA expired in 1982, and new employment training legislation was passed by Congress—the Job Training and Partnership Act (JTPA)—to start in 1983. The emphasis in this approach to training is on the private sector and on the subsidization of existing training in the private sector through programs administered by the governors of the states.

Although employment training strategies have changed in response to new challenges in the economy, the basic idea of a government program designed to develop and upgrade human capital is now a permanent part of social policy in the United States. We are still searching, however, for a policy design that achieves the ambitious objectives that proponents of employment training have sought.

Study Questions

1. What were the objectives of the Manpower Development and Training Act of 1962? What theory (or theories) of unemployment lay behind this legislation?

2. With scarce resources available for employment training programs, to which kind of program should more resources be allocated—institutional training or on-the-job training? What specific criteria did you use in arriving at this answer?

3. How might a benefit-cost criterion for evaluating employment training policy lead to an incorrect measure of program effectiveness?

4. What type of disincentive did the Work Incentive Program (WIN) attempt to correct? Has this program been successful in converting welfare to workfare? Explain.

5. From an economic point of view, why would it be advantageous for a private employer to undertake private sector training programs?

6. President Reagan eliminated the CETA program. What was his economic rationale for doing this?

Further Reading

Congressional Budget Office. *CETA Training Programs—Do They Work for Adults?* July 1982.

Levitan, Sar A., and Garth L. Mangum. *Federal Training and Work Programs in the Sixties.* Ann Arbor, MI: Institute of Labor and Industrial Relations, 1969.

Levitan, Sar A., Garth L. Mangum, and Ray Marshall. *Human Resources and Labor Markets.* 3rd ed. New York: Harper and Row, 1981.

U.S. Department of Labor. *Employment and Training Report of the President* (previous title: *Manpower Report of the President*). Washington: Government Printing Office, annual.

Index